H. G. Wells

a reference guide

A
Reference
Guide
to
Literature

H. G. Wells

a reference guide

WILLIAM J. SCHEICK and J. RANDOLPH COX

G.K.HALL &CO.
70 LINCOLN STREET, BOSTON, MASS.

Library of Congress Cataloging in Publication Data

Scheick, William J.
  H.G. Wells: a reference guide.

  (A Reference guide to literature)
  Includes index.
  1. Wells, H.G. (Herbert George), 1866–1946—
Bibliography. I. Cox, J. Randolph. II. Title.
III. Title: HG Wells. IV. Series.
Z8964.8.S34 1988 [PR5777]   016.823'912   88–5220
ISBN 0-8161-8946-3

This publication is printed on permanent/durable acid-free paper
MANUFACTURED IN THE UNITED STATES OF AMERICA

For

Hal Gerber and John C. Cox

and for

Catherine, Jessica, and Nathan

Contents

The Authors

William J. Scheick is J.R. Milliken Centennial Professor of
English and American Literature at the University of Texas at Austin,
where he also serves as editor of Texas Studies in Literature and
Language. His wide-ranging work has appeared in numerous journals and
his best-known books include: The Will and the Word: The Poetry of
Edward Taylor; The Writings of Jonathan Edwards: Theme, Motif, and
Style; The Slender Human Word: Emerson's Artistry in Prose; The Half-
Blood: A Cultural Symbol in Nineteenth-Century American Fiction; and
The Splintering Frame: The Later Fiction of H.G. Wells.

J. Randolph Cox is reference and government documents librarian,
with the rank of associate professor, at Saint Olaf College,
Northfield, Minnesota, where he also teaches special courses in
popular culture, especially detective fiction and Sherlock Holmes.
His publications have appeared in such diverse journals as English
Literature in Transition, The Armchair Detective, the Wilson Library
Bulletin, the Baker Street Journal, the Dime Novel Round-Up, Baker
Street Miscellanea, and Clues: A Journal of Detection. Editor of
Tad-Schrift: Twenty Years of Mystery Fandom in The Armchair
Detective.

Preface

From the outset this project, begun in 1970, seemed related to the
caterpillar's two-sided mushroom in Lewis Carroll's Alice's Adventures
in Wonderland (published a year before Wells's birth). On the one
hand, the book grew and grew until it threatened to become unmanage-
able. This expansive impulse toward comprehensiveness included critical books, biographies, reviews, general articles, chapters in books,
sundry references in articles and books, Ph.D. dissertations (cited
without abstracts), letters to editors, and introductions to editions
of Wells's works but excluded most solely descriptive or enumerative
items, reviews of secondary works, film reviews, undergraduate honor
and M.A. theses. The book was nonetheless predestined to remain
representative. Besides items in British newspapers and in foreign
journals to which the editors may have had a reference but which were
unlocated or unobtainable, there are, one can safely assume, many
reviews and comments on Wells's work that have not come to our attention. As a result this book is still growing, and users of the volume
are invited to bring to the editors' notice any omissions to be included in a possible subsequent new edition or, at least, in a supple-
mental listing to be published in English Literature in Transition.

On the other hand, like the caterpillar's mushroom, the project
has a diminishing or humbling side. This feature of the book not only
touches the editors' sense of smallness before the mass of the enter-
prise but also and more significantly underscores the precarious
vicissitudes of time regarding a man's work, in this instance that of
Wells and that of his critics. Not one of Wells's books, not even the
mild Story of a Great Schoolmaster or the juvenile Little Wars,
escaped the snarl of some contemporary critic; and, perhaps most
disheartening, as the years have passed, some critics have become
equally distempered in general over Wells's entire literary corpus.
Critics themselves, of course, are no less immune to the ravages of
time; for, as will become all too apparent to the reader of the
following abstracts, some of the most severe, self-aggrandizing remarks of the cocksure critic have not only paled with age but appear,
from our present perspective, downright stupid. One irony of a bibliography of this sort lies in the work's resuscitation of and, perhaps, bestowal of immortality upon the comments of certain critics

Preface

whose remarks, at least in this matter, would never and should never
have outlived their time. They manage to survive solely because the
coattails of their host are long enough to cloak them.

The primary purpose of this book is to make a broadly representative portion of the huge quantity of critical commentary written about
Wells from 1895 to 1986 more manageable and accessible to future
critics of his work. In a few instances we included items of dubious
value, such as Wells's award for his use of ellipsis during sexual
scenes and the mistaken attribution of George Meek, Bath Chairman to
him, because they contribute a glimmer of color to the overall portrait of his career. Although annotations of the sort included in
this bibliography do not always do complete justice to the articles or
books from which they derive, every effort has been made to make them
serve as an index to the primary focus of these articles or books. In
this way the critic of Wells's work is not only more informed generally but is alerted specifically to what he should certainly consult
while researching for his own work.

Entries are placed under the date of first publication, though in
the instance of books our use of an American edition sometimes results
in a somewhat later date. Dissertations listed in Dissertation
Abstracts or Dissertation Abstracts International appear under the
year of their abstraction in those journals. Data pertaining to
reprintings and revisions are included in the primary entry rather
than given a separate listing under other dates. The entries reflect
authorial voice, and the abstracter's critical remarks and cross-
references appear in square brackets at the end of an abstract.

Acknowledgments

We would like to express our gratitude to those individuals, librarians, and scholars who provided various abstracts, suggested items to be included, located the most obscure publications through the magic of Interlibrary Loan (especially MINITEX), and supplied valuable information. Without their help this bibliography would have been less than appears here: Robert E. Briney, Daniel Brink, Mary Ceibert, Carolyn A. Davis, Anna Marie Davisson, John T. Dizer, Jr., Glen Doolittle, Karl Fink, Mark Gregg, Katherine Hanson, Gretchen Hardgrove, John Harwood, JoAnne W. Hawkins, Elizabeth Larson, Edward S. Lauterbach, Melvin McCosh, David McMurray, Roberta Mancina, Bruce Morton, Joan Olson, Patrick Parrinder, Larry Richardson, Donald Rude, Steven Stilwell, David Welsh, and Michael Youngblood. We are also indebted to the University Research Institute of the University of Texas at Austin for financing the costly preparation of much of this manuscript. A special note of thanks goes to Catherine Rainwater for generous assistance during the time-consuming last phases of the production of this book. And our thanks extends, finally, to W. Eugene Davis, who served as editorial consultant in his capacity as the series editor of a number of annotated bibliographies on figures of the turn of the nineteenth century.

Introduction

The ninety-one years (1895-1986) of commentary on the writings of H.G. Wells do not condense into any simple generalizations or divide into convenient periods. The overall pattern of Wells's critical reception can, perhaps, be usefully graphed as four arcs similar to a chief structural principle--the "comet-like transit"--of his semi-autobiographical novel Tono-Bungay. Wells's rise to fame as an author of science fiction, of romances in a Dickensian manner, of novels reflecting contemporary society, and of prognostic works was in each instance rapid, its achievement of zenith brilliant, and its decline slow and disproportionate to the initial ascent. In none of these four genres was the upward trajectory of Wells's career entirely free from retarding gravitational or frictional forces causing occasional dips, as it were; but like certain birds that utilize wind currents to their advantage, the ascending stage of the four arcs of his writings actually gained momentum as a result of these influences.

Receiving more favorable than unfavorable notice, Select Conversations with an Uncle precariously launched the humorous and satiric phase of Wells's career in 1895. Endorsed by the Athenaeum and the Spectator (London) in the following year, The Wheels of Chance proved a runaway success, a critical fait-accompli. Although in later life Wells would refer to Love and Mr. Lewisham (1900) as a conscious work of art that never became "a very successful book" and in which "no critic discovered any sort of beauty or technical ability," in fact its decidedly positive, if serene, reception by reviewers advanced the achievement attained by the "bicycling romance" published four years earlier. With Kipps (1905) the Dickensian feature of Wells's rise to fame reached its apogee. Meriting rave reviews from the Academy, the Athenaeum, the Bookman (London), the Manchester Guardian, and the Sunday Times (London), among others, as well as hesitant acknowledgment from the Glasgow Herald and the Times Literary Supplement (London), Kipps was praised for its characterization, its portrait of the lower middle class, and its combination of satire and empathy. Heralded as a great work surpassing all his previous writings and as an extension of the frontier of the novel, Tono-Bungay (1909) allowed Wells to maintain this zenith; but vociferous complaints against the amorphous, subjective, leisurely, journalistic, and too inclusive

manner of the book also surfaced, signaling that this arc of his
career had begun to incline slightly downward. Although a year later
critics (e.g., in the Times Literary Supplement [London]) spoke kindly
of The History of Mr. Polly in the context of the novel's predeces-
sors, more than ever before they expressed dissatisfaction with the
intrusion of Wells's social views that mar the overall artistry of the
book. Thereafter, in spite of occasional flashes of intensity, the
curve of Wells's success as a Dickensian novelist declined, noticeably
dimming in such works as Boon and Bealby in 1915.

While enjoying the height of his popularity in this genre, Wells
had become increasingly self-conscious about his notions on the art of
fiction. In 1911 he wrote an essay entitled "The Contemporary Novel"
in which he explicitly defined his view of fiction as a "social media-
tor, the vehicle of understanding, the instrument of self-examination,
the parade of morals and the exchange of manners, the factory of
customs, the criticism of laws and institutions and of social dogmas
and ideas"; even as early as 1902, in a letter to Arnold Bennett, he
had observed that "there is something other than either story writing
or artistic merit which has emerged through the series of my books,
something one might regard as a new system of ideas." The publication
of Tono-Bungay, which in several respects contributed to the
Dickensian phase of Wells's career, actually initiated a new arc from
the zenith of the older one, which would begin to decline after the
appearance of Mr. Polly.

This new curve received major impetus from the critical reaction
to Ann Veronica (1909), a succès de scandale advancing the non-
Dickensian features of Tono-Bungay. Certain reviewers admired the
subject matter of Ann Veronica--what some judged as poor taste or as
pernicious, others assessed as innovation--and even favorably remarked
on the author's development of its central protagonist. More generally, however, critics deplored the book's alleged vulgarity, bad
logic, use of accident, and lack of form. Unlike the ascendancy of
the Dickensian phase of his work, but (as we shall see) like its
science fiction phase, the development of Wells's notoriety as a
novelist of contemporary society received its principal thrust from
the sensationalism of his subject matter, a factor equally evident in
critical reactions to The New Machiavelli (1911). The curve of this
phase of Wells's writing, however, was destined to be very brief, and
after The New Machiavelli it began to decline in conjunction with the
Dickensian arc that had fostered it. Wells's books in this mode
always received ample critical attention, most frequently more negative than positive; and following the publication of Ann Veronica
critics became increasingly certain that the artist had been sacrificed to the journalist in Wells.

At the start of Wells's career another arc initially paralleled
that of the Dickensian stage. Begun in 1895 by The Time Machine and
The Stolen Bacillus, Wells's science fiction emerged vividly, and the
publication of The Island of Dr. Moreau in 1896 guaranteed that his
writings in this genre would not be ignored. Although Dr. Moreau

received less praise for its artistry than condemnation for its grue-
someness, it dramatically demonstrated to many reviewers a laudable
accomplishment at the level of entertainment. The controversy over
the so-called materialism and the alleged bad taste of the book was
redressed by an energy, vitality, and spirit that, as with so many of
Wells's later works, made many disapproving critics equivocate their
censure. The sensationalism of the novel, similar to that of the
later Ann Veronica, actually augmented the rise and luminosity of this
phase of Wells's fame; but, again like the brevity of his later fame
as a novelist of contemporary society, the apogee of Wells's career as
a writer of science fiction, attained by The Invisible Man (1897) and
The War of the Worlds (1898), was brief. With the publication of When
the Sleeper Wakes in 1899, the curve of Wells's achievement in this
genre began to descend, and more than one reviewer of the book remarked on Wells's tendency toward journalistic forecast rather than
toward artistic expression. Although critical sensitivity to Wells's
science fiction endured for a long time and noticeably deepened in its
appreciation of his early work in this genre, its enthusiasm demon-
strably waned after the appearance of The First Men in the Moon
(1901), The Food of the Gods (1904), and In the Days of the Comet
(1906).

Wells in fact at times expressed impatience with embodying his
ideas artistically; and from the curve of his science fiction a second
arc, as it were, emerged with the publication of Anticipations in
1901. This work of prognostic journalism was very well received on
the whole, even by those critics expressing reservations. Mankind in
the Making added impetus the following year; but not until the appearance of A Modern Utopia (1905), cited as an original and ingenious
masterpiece, did this new arc attain its apogee (paralleling, inci-
dentally, the apex of the Dickensian curve achieved by Kipps in the
same year). The Future in America, printed in 1906, initiates the
decline of Wells's greatest fame among critics as a prophet, a much
more gradual declension than manifested by any of the other three
phases. As prognosticator, as commentator on contemporary matters,
and as historian Wells the journalist dominated Wells the artist, a
development sometimes all too blatant over the subsequent years when
Wells wrote in the other three genres; and it was in this capacity
that he most engaged his reviewers after 1911. In spite of the facts
that Wells's public image before the general populace had yet to
attain its zenith and that his subsequent works would frequently enjoy
the vogue of timeliness, after 1911, as far as his critics were concerned, all the curves of his four basic phases were declining.

Nevertheless, the prevalence of the journalistic elements of
Wells's work does not lend support to such generalizations as Alfred
Borrello's assertion that Wells's depreciation of his role as an
artist derived from a sensitivity to reviews of his books, that
"critics had far too consistently demonstrated greater interest in his
sociological ideas than the art he practiced." In fact, reviews of
Wells's early fiction time and again lauded or deplored specifically
literary features of his writings. The Manchester Guardian, for

instance, rarely ceased to address the issue of Wells's artistry, praising The Island of Dr. Moreau for its vigorous style, terse dialogue, and realistic detail; citing The War of the Worlds for its humor and standard of writing; acclaiming Love and Mr. Lewisham for its excellent description of the common things of life; noting the "jack-in-the-box" technique of The Food of the Gods; appreciating the humor and characterization of Kipps; remarking on the canvas technique of In the Days of the Comet; mentioning the successful narrative device of The War in the Air; observing the symbolism of Tono-Bungay; lamenting the loss of artistry in Ann Veronica; discussing the "knuckle-rapping" style, bold improvisations, imagery, "phrases of pouncing precision, and sudden epithets that leap like arrows to their mark" in Marriage; and so forth. If this bibliography puts to rest such generalizations as Borrello's, it will have performed an active critical function.

On the other hand, Wells's Dickensian and science fiction phases had decidedly metamorphosed into more realistic novels of social commentary and more journalistic works of prognostication, history, and contemporary assessment, a change disposing reviewers to be particularly alert to Wells's ideas. But it was not until he had passed the zenith of all four phases of his writing career in 1911 that critics focused more exclusively on Wells's ideas. Thus, blame, if indeed culpability is the issue, lies as much with Wells as it does with his reviewers. Although one may properly bemoan the general aesthetic insensitivity of critics commenting on, say, Apropos of Dolores (1938), they were, one must admit, partly conditioned by a major feature of Wells's conscious intent and so readily responded more and more to his ideas. The trouble has been and unfortunately remains, however, that Wells's later fiction is not only a vehicle for ideas; in fact it also frequently manifests aesthetic principles organic to the ideas he sought to express—a sophisticated combination of art and ideology providing a fertile area for future literary studies of his work.

As the latter part of this bibliography indicates, Wells remains almost as popular today as he was in his lifetime. In spite of the steady ebb of his literary reputation, certain of his novels, particularly Tono-Bungay, The History of Mr. Polly, and the early science fiction, have endured and continue to attract intelligent critical attention. During the last thirty years or so, in fact, something of a Wells revival has been in the offing; it has never quite arrived and perhaps never will. Clearly, however, more than ever before critical discussions of Wells's work have established a firm foundation for a careful literary as well as ideological analysis of his artistry. If ever a writer were suitable for revaluation, Wells is that person; and we, the editors, hope that this volume will serve as a stone in the foundation of this revival.

Abbreviations

After Democracy	After Democracy: Addresses and Papers on the Present World Situation
Anatomy	The Anatomy of Frustration: A Modern Synthesis
Ann Veronica	Ann Veronica: A Modern Love Story
Anticipations	Anticipations of the Reaction of Mechanical and Scientific Progress upon Human Life and Thought
Ararat	All Aboard for Ararat
Babes	Babes in the Darkling Wood
Bealby	Bealby: A Holiday
Belloc Objects	Mr. Belloc Objects to the Outline of History
Bishop	The Soul of a Bishop: A Novel (with Just a Little Love in It) about Conscience and Religion and The Real Troubles of Life
Boon	Boon, the Mind of the Race, the Wild Asses of the Devil, and the Last Trump, Being a First Selection from the Literary Remains of George Boon, Appropriate to the Times
Boots	This Misery of Boots
Britain at War	War and the Future: Italy, France, and Britain at War
Brothers	The Brothers: A Story
Brynhild	Brynhild, or the Show of Things
Bulpington	The Bulpington of Blup: Adventures, Poses, Stresses, Conflicts, and Disasters in a Contemporary Brain
Christina	Christina Alberta's Father
Clissold	The World of William Clissold: A Novel at a New Angle
Comet	In the Days of the Comet
Coming	What is Coming? A Forecast of Things after the War
Conspiracy	The Open Conspiracy: Blue Prints for a World Revolution
Conversations	Select Conversations with an Uncle, Now Extinct, and Two Other Reminiscences

Country	The Country of the Blind, and Other Stories
Country of the Blind	The Country of the Blind (rev. ed.)
Crux Ansata	Crux Ansata: An Indictment of the Roman Catholic Church
Democracy	Democracy under Revision: A Lecture Delivered at the Sorbonne
Discovery	The Discovery of the Future: A Discourse Delivered to the Royal Institution on January 24, 1902
Dr. Moreau	The Island of Dr. Moreau
Dolores	Apropos of Dolores
Dream	The Dream: A Novel
Englishman	An Englishman Looks at the World: Being a Series of Unrestrained Remarks upon Contemporary Matters
Experiment in Autobiography	Experiment in Autobiography: Discoveries and Conclusions of a Very Ordinary Brain since 1866
Famous Novels	Seven Famous Novels
Fate	The Fate of Homo Sapiens: An Unemotional Statement of the Things That Are Happening to Him Now and of the Immediate Possibilities Confronting Him
Faults	Faults of the Fabians
Fire	The Undying Fire: A Contemporary Novel
Food of the Gods	The Food of the Gods, and How It Came to Earth
'42-44	'42 to '44: A Contemporary Memoir upon Human Behaviour during the Crisis of the World Revolution
Fourth Year	In the Fourth Year: Anticipations of a World Peace
Friends	The Passionate Friends
Future in America	The Future in America; A Search for Realities
God	God the Invisible King
Going	The Way the World Is Going: Guesses and Forecasts of the Years Ahead
Hemispheres	Two Hemispheres or One World?
Idea	The Idea of a League of Nations
Imperialism	Imperialism and the Open Conspiracy
Invisible Man	The Invisible Man: A Grotesque Romance
Isaac Harman	The Wife of Sir Isaac Harman
Joan and Peter	Joan and Peter: The Story of an Education
King	The King Who Was a King: The Book of a Film
Kipps	Kipps: The Story of a Simple Soul
Last Things	First and Last Things: A Confession of Faith and Rule of Life
Little Wars	Little Wars: A Game for Boys of Twelve Years of Age to One Hundred and Fifty and for That More Intelligent Sort of Girls Who Like Boys' Games
Machiavelli	The New Machiavelli

Mankind	Mankind in the Making
Meanwhile	Meanwhile: The Picture of a Lady
Men in the Moon	The First Men in the Moon
Miracles	Man Who Could Work Miracles: A Film Story Based on the Material Contained in His Short Story
Mr. Blettsworthy	Mr. Blettsworthy on Rampole Island
Mr. Britling	Mr. Britling Sees It Through
Mr. Lewisham	Love and Mr. Lewisham
Mr. Parham	The Autocracy of Mr. Parham: His Remarkable Adventures in This Changing World
Mr. Polly	The History of Mr. Polly
New America	The New America: The New World
New Teaching	The New Teaching of History: With a Reply to Some Recent Criticism of the Outline of History
New World	Guide to the New World: A Handbook of Constructive World Revolution
New World Order	The New World Order, Whether It Is Obtainable, How It Can Be Attained, and What Sort of World a World at Peace Will Have to Be
New Worlds	New Worlds for Old
Our Lives	What Are We To Do with Our Lives?
Outline	The Outline of History, Being a Plain History of Life and Mankind
Outlook	The Outlook for Homo Sapiens: An Amalgamation and Modernization of Two Books
Personal Matters	Certain Personal Matters: A Collection of Material, Mainly Autobiographical
Phoenix	Phoenix: A Summary of the Inescapable Conditions of World Organization
Plattner Story	The Plattner Story, and Others
Player	The Croquet Player: A Story
Prophesying	A Year of Prophesying
Research	The Research Magnificent
Rights of Man	The Rights of Man, or What Are We Fighting For?
Russia	Russia in the Shadows
Salvaging	The Salvaging of Civilisation
Schoolmaster	The Story of a Great Schoolmaster: Being a Plain Account of the Life and Ideas of Sanderson of Oundle
Science of Life	The Science of Life: A Summary of Contemporary Knowledge about Life and Its Possibilities
Sea Lady	The Sea Lady: A Tissue of Moonshine
Secret Places	The Secret Places of the Heart
Shape of Things	The Shape of Things to Come: The Ultimate Revolution
Short History	A Short History of the World
Sleeper Wakes	When the Sleeper Wakes: A Story of the Years to Come

Social Forces	Social Forces in England and America
Socialism	Socialism and the Family
Star-Begotten	Star-Begotten: A Biological Fantasia
Stolen Bacillus	The Stolen Bacillus, and Other Incidents
Strange Stories	Thirty Strange Stories
Tales	Tales of Space and Time
Terror	The Holy Terror
Tether	Mind at the End of Its Tether
Things to Come	Things to Come: A Film Story Based on the Material Contained in His History of the Future, "The Shape of Things to Come"
Time Machine	The Time Machine: An Invention
Tommy	The Adventures of Tommy
Too Careful	You Can't Be Too Careful. A Sample of Life
Travels	Travels of a Republican Radical in Search of Hot Water
"Treasure"	"The Treasure in the Forest"
Turning	The Happy Turning: A Dream of Life
Twelve Stories	Twelve Stories and a Dream
Utopia	A Modern Utopia
War	The War That Will End War
War and Peace	The Common Sense of War and Peace: World Revolution or War Unending?
War in the Air	The War in the Air, and Particularly How Mr. Bert Smallways Fared while It Lasted
Washington	Washington and the Hope of Peace
Way	The Way to a League of Nations
Wheels of Chance	The Wheels of Chance: A Holiday Adventure
Wonderful Visit	The Wonderful Visit
Work	The Work, Wealth, and Happiness of Mankind
Works	The Works of H.G. Wells (Atlantic ed.)
World Encyclopaedia	The Idea of a World Encyclopaedia
World-Mind	Science and the World-Mind
World Peace	The Common Sense of World Peace: An Address Delivered to the Reichstag
World Set Free	The World Set Free: A Story of Mankind

SECONDARY WORKS

AAAP	Annals of the American Academy of Political and Social Science
ALA	American Library Association Booklist
AM	Atlantic Monthly
AM M	American Magazine
ARR	American Review of Reviews
BET	Boston Evening Transcript
Call	Call Magazine (New York Call)
CDT	Chicago Daily Tribune
CE	H.G. Wells: A Collection of Critical Essays (Englewood Cliffs, N.J.: Prentice-Hall, 1975).

CH	H.G. Wells: The Critical Heritage, ed. Patrick Parrinder (London and Boston: Routledge & Kegan Paul, 1972).
CL	Current Literature
CO	Current Opinion
CR	Contemporary Review
CSM	Christian Science Monitor
DC	Daily Chronicle (London)
DT	Daily Telegraph (London)
EFT	English Fiction in Transition
ELT	English Literature in Transition
EDR	Edinburgh Review
ER	English Review
FR	Fortnightly Review
GDN	Greensboro Daily News (North Carolina)
HJ	Hibbert Journal
HW	Harper's Weekly
JOL	John O'London's Weekly
LA	Living Age
LD	Literary Digest
LDI	Literary Digest International Book Review
LM	London Mercury
LR	Literary Review (New York Evening Post)
LW	Literary World (Boston)
MFS	Modern Fiction Studies
MG	Manchester Guardian
Modern SF	H.G. Wells and Modern Science Fiction, ed. Darko Suvin and Robert M. Philmus (Lewisburg, Pa.: Bucknell University Press, 1977).
NA	Nation and Athenaeum
NAR	North American Review
NCA	Nineteenth Century and After
NR	New Republic
NS	New Statesman
NSN	New Statesman and Nation
NWA	New Adelphi
NY	New Yorker
NYT	New York Times
NYTBM	New York Times Book Review and Magazine
NYTBR	New York Times Book Review
NYTRB	New York Times Review of Books
NYTSRB	New York Times Saturday Review of Books
NYTSRBA	New York Times Saturday Review of Books and Art
OS	Open Shelf (Cleveland)
PIFL	Pratt Institute Free Library Quarterly Booklist
PMLA	Publications of the Modern Language Society of America
PMM	Pall Mall Magazine
PW	Publisher's Weekly
QR	Quarterly Review

Abbreviations

RQ	Riverside Quarterly
RR	Review of Reviews
RRWW	Review of Reviews and World's Work
Scrapbook	The H.G. Wells Scrapbook, ed. Peter Haining (London: New English Library, 1978; New York: Clarkson N. Potter, 1979).
SDR	Springfield Daily Republican (Mass.)
SEP	Saturday Evening Post
SFC	San Francisco Chronicle
SFS	Science-Fiction Studies
SLI	Studies in the Literary Imagination
SLP	St. Louis Public Library Monthly Bulletin
SR	Saturday Review of Literature
SR (London)	Saturday Review (London)
SSR	Springfield Sunday Republican (Mass.)
SSUR	Springfield Sunday Union and Republican (Mass.)
TLS	Times Literary Supplement (London)
Trib	New York Tribune
TT	Time and Tide
UWR	University of Windsor Review
Wellsian	Wellsian: Journal of the H.G. Wells Society
WG	Westminster Gazette
WLB	Wilson Library Bulletin

Writings by H.G. Wells

Jilting of Jane," 1897; "In the Modern Vein," 1894; "A Catastrophe," 1895; "The Lost Inheritance," 1897; "The Sad Story of a Dramatic Critic," 1895; "A Slip Under the Microscope," 1893.

The Invisible Man: A Grotesque Romance. London and New York, 1897.

Thirty Strange Stories. New York, 1897.
   Contents: All seventeen stories from The Plattner Story, ten stories from The Stolen Bacillus, plus "The Reconciliation," "The Rajah's Treasure," and "Le Mari Terrible," previously unpublished.

The War of the Worlds. London and New York, 1898.

When the Sleeper Wakes: A Story of the Years to Come. London and New York, 1899. (Revised under title, The Sleeper Wakes. London, 1910.)

Tales of Space and Time. London and New York, 1899.
   Contents: "The Crystal Egg," 1897; "The Star," 1897; "A Story of the Stone Age," 1897; "A Story of the Days to Come," 1897; "The Man Who Could Work Miracles," 1898.

Love and Mr. Lewisham. London and New York, 1900.

The First Men in the Moon. London and Indianapolis, 1901.

The Sea Lady: A Tissue of Moonshine. London and New York (as The Sea Lady), 1902.

Twelve Stories and a Dream. London, 1903; New York, 1905.
   Contents: "Filmer," 1901; "The Magic Shop," 1903; "The Valley of Spiders," 1903; "The Truth About Pyecroft," 1903; "Mr. Skelmersdale in Fairyland," 1901; "The Inexperienced Ghost," 1902; "Jimmy Goggles the God," 1898; "The New Accelerator," 1901; "Mr. Ledbetter's Vacation," 1898; "The Stolen Body," 1898; "Mr. Brisher's Treasure," 1899; "Miss Winchelsea's Heart," 1898; "A Dream of Armageddon," 1901.

The Food of the Gods, and How It Came to Earth. London and New York, 1904.

A Modern Utopia. London and New York, 1905.

Kipps: The Story of a Simple Soul. London and New York, 1905.

In the Days of the Comet. London and New York, 1906.

The War in the Air, and Particularly How Mr. Bert Smallways Fared while It Lasted. London and New York, 1908.

Tono-Bungay. New York, 1908; London, 1909.

Ann Veronica: A Modern Love Story. London and New York, 1909.

Writings by H.G. Wells

The History of Mr. Polly. London and New York, 1910.

The New Machiavelli. New York, 1910; London, 1911.

The Country of the Blind, and Other Stories. London, 1911.
   Contents: Thirty-three stories, of which five are here first
   published in book form: "A Vision of Judgment," 1899; "The Empire
   of the Ants," 1905; "The Door in the Wall," 1906; "The Beautiful
   Suit," 1909; "The Country of the Blind," 1904.

Marriage. London and New York, 1912.

The Passionate Friends. London and New York, 1913.

The World Set Free: A Story of Mankind. London and New York, 1914.

The Wife of Sir Isaac Harman. London and New York, 1914.

Boon, the Mind of the Race, the Wild Asses of the Devil, and the Last
Trump, Being a First Selection from the Literary Remains of George
Boon, Appropriate to the Times. London and New York, 1915.

Bealby: A Holiday. London and New York, 1915.

The Research Magnificent. London and New York, 1915.

Mr. Britling Sees It Through. London and New York, 1916.

The Soul of a Bishop: A Novel (with Just a Little Love in It) about
Conscience and Religion and The Real Troubles of Life. London and New
York, 1917.

Joan and Peter: The Story of an Education. London and New York,
1918.

The Undying Fire: A Contemporary Novel. London and New York, 1919.

The Secret Places of the Heart. London and New York, 1922.

Men Like Gods. London and New York, 1923.

The Dream: A Novel. London and New York, 1924.

Cristina Alberta's Father. London and New York, 1925.

The World of William Clissold: A Novel at a New Angle. London and
New York, 1926,.

Meanwhile: The Picture of a Lady. London and New York, 1927.

Mr. Blettsworthy on Rampole Island. London and Garden City, N.Y.,
1928.

Writings by H.G. Wells

The King Who Was a King: The Book of a Film. London and Garden City, N.Y., 1929. (Also titled, The King Who Was King: An Unconventional Novel.)

The Adventures of Tommy. London, 1929; New York, 1967.

The Autocracy of Mr. Parham: His Remarkable Adventures in This Changing World. London and Garden City, N.Y., 1930.

The Bulpington of Blup: Adventures, Poses, Stresses, Conflicts, and Disasters in a Contemporary Brain. London, 1932; New York, 1933.

The Shape of Things to Come: The Ultimate Revolution. London and New York, 1933.

Things to Come: A Film Story Based on the Material Contained in His History of the Future, "The Shape of Things to Come." London and New York, 1935.

The Anatomy of Frustration: A Modern Synthesis. London and New York, 1936.

The Croquet Player: A Story. London, 1936; New York, 1937.

Man Who Could Work Miracles: A Film Story Based on the Material Contained in His Short Story. London and New York, 1936.

Star Begotten: A Biological Fantasia. London and New York, 1937.

Brynhild, or The Show of Things. London and New York, 1937.

The Camford Visitation. London, 1937.

The Brothers: A Story. London and New York, 1938.

Apropos of Dolores. London and New York, 1938.

The Country of the Blind. Revised and expanded. London, 1939.

The Holy Terror. London and New York, 1939.

Babes in the Darkling Wood. London and New York, 1940.

All Aboard for Ararat. London, 1940; New York, 1941.

You Can't Be Too Careful. A Sample of Life. London, 1941; New York, 1942.

The Desert Daisy. Urbana, Ill., 1957.

Hoopdriver's Holiday. Lafayette, Ind., 1964.

Writings by H.G. Wells

The Wealth of Mr. Waddy: A Novel. Carbondale, Ill., 1969.

Early Writings in Science and Science Fiction. Berkeley, Los Angeles, London, 1975.

B. Collected Editions

The Works of H.G. Wells. 28 vols. The Atlantic Edition. London, 1924.

The Works of H.G. Wells. 24 vols. The Essex Editioon. London, 1926-27.

The Short Stories. London, 1927; Garden City, N.Y., 1929. (Reprinted as The Complete Short Stories, London,. 1966.)

The Scientific Romances. London, 1933.
    Contents: Introduction by W; The Time Machine, The Island of Dr. Moreau, The Invisible Man, The War of the Worlds, The Men in the Moon, The Food of the Gods, In the Days of the Comet, Men Like Gods.

Seven Famous Novels. New York, 1934.
    Contents: Same as The Scientific Romances, but omits Men Like Gods.

The Collector's Book of Science Fiction by H.G. Wells. Seacaucus, N.J., 1978.
    Contents: "H.G. Wells: A Biographical Note"; The War of the Worlds, "The Country of the Blind," "The Flowering of the Strange Orchid," "Aepyornis Island," The First Men in the Moon, "The Diamond Maker," "The Story of the Inexperienced Ghost," "The Empire of the Ants," "Stories of the Stone Age," "The Stolen Bacillus," "In the Abyss," "The Valley of the Spiders," When the Sleeper Wakes, "The Man Who Could Work Miracles," "The Land Iron-clads." (Reprinted in facsimile of the original periodical appearances, with the original illustrations.)

The H.G. Wells Scrapbook. Edited by Peter Haining. London, 1978; New York, 1979.
    Contents (by W): Experiment (excerpts); "A Tale of the Twentieth Century," 1887 (previously uncollected); "The Man of the Year Million", and "The Queer Story of Brownlow's Newspaper," 1931 (previously uncollected).

The Man with a Nose and the Other Uncollected Short Stories of H.G. Wells. Edited by J.R. Hammond. London, 1984.
    Contents: "The Man with a Nose," "A Perfect Gentleman on Wheels," "Wayde's Essence," "The Queer Story of Brownlow's Newspaper," "Walcote," "The Devotee of Art," "A Misunderstood Artist," "Le Mari Terrible," "The Rajah's Treasure," "The Presence by the Fire," "Mr. Marshall's Doppelganger," "The Thing in No. 7," "The

Thumbmark," "A Family Elopement," "Our Little Neighbour," "The Loyalty of Esau Common," "The Wild Asses of the Devil," "Answer to Prayer," "The New Faust."

II. NONFICTION

A. Separate and Collected Works
(Pamphlets included in first book collection wherever possible.)

Textbook of Biology. London, 1893.

Honours Physiography. London, 1893.

Certain Personal Matters: A Collection of Material, Mainly Auto-biographical. London, 1897.

Anticipations of the Reaction of Mechanical and Scientific Progress upon Human Life and Thought. London, 1901, New York, 1902. [Reissued, with introduction by W, London, 1914.]

The Discovery of the Future: A Discourse Delivered to the Royal Institution on January 24, 1902. London, 1902; New York, 1913.

Mankind in the Making. London, 1903; New York, 1904. [Reissued with introduction by W, London, 1914.]

The Future in America; A Search after Realities. London and New York, 1906.

Faults of the Fabians. London, 1906.

Reconstruction of the Fabian Society. London, 1906.

Socialism and the Family. London, 1906.

This Misery of Boots. London, 1907.

New Worlds for Old. London and New York, 1908. [Includes "Will Socialism Destroy the Home?" London, 1907.]

First and Last Things: A Confession of Faith and Rule of Life. London and New York, 1908. [Revised, with new preface by W, London, 1917; def. ed. London, 1929.]

Floor Games. London, 1911; Boston, 1912.

The Great State: Essays in Construction. London and New York, 1912. [Essays; W's contribution: "The Past and the Great State."]

Liberalism and Its Party: What Are the Liberals to Do? London, 1913.

Writings by H.G. Wells

Little Wars: A Game for Boys of Twelve Years of Age to One Hundred and Fifty and for That More Intelligent Sort of Girls Who Like Boys' Games. London and New York, 1913. [Revised, London, 1931.]

An Englishman Looks at the World: Being a Series of Unrestrained Remarks upon Contemporary Matters. London, 1914; New York (as Social Forces in England and America), 1914.
    Contents include: "The So-called Science of Sociology," London, 1907; "The Labour Unrest," London, 1912; "The Common Sense of Warfare" [as "War and Common Sense," London, 1913.]

The War That Will End War. London and New York, 1914.

The Peace of the World. London, 1915.

What is Coming? A Forecast of Things after the War. London, 1916; New York [as What is Coming? A European Forecast], 1916.

The Elements of Reconstruction. London, 1916.

War and the Future: Italy, France, and Britain at War. London and New York, 1917.

God the Invisible King. London and New York, 1917.

In the Fourth Year: Anticipations of a World Peace. London and New York, 1918.
    Contents include: "A Reasonable Man's Peace," London, 1917.

British Nationalism and the League of Nations. London, 1918.

History Is One. New York, 1919.

The Idea of a League of Nations. London, 1919.

The Way to a League of Nations. London, 1919.

The Outline of History, Being a Plain History of Life and Mankind. London and New York, 1920. [Numerous revised editions.]

Russia in the Shadows. London, 1920; New York, 1921.

The Salvaging of Civilisation. London and New York, 1921.

The New Teaching of History: With a Reply to Some Recent Criticism of the Outline of History. London, 1921.

Washington and the Hope of Peace. London, 1922; New York [as Washington and the Riddle of Peace], 1922.

What H.G. Wells Thinks about "The Mind in the Making." New York, 1922; London [as introduction to James Harvey Robinson's The Mind in the Making], 1923.

University of London Election: An Electoral Letter. London, 1922.

The World, Its Debts, and the Rich Men. London, 1922.

A Short History of the World. London and New York, 1922. [Numerous revised editions.]

Socialism and the Scientific Motive. London, 1923.

To the Electors of London University, University General Election, 1923, from H.G. Wells, B.Sci, London. London, 1923.

The Labour Ideal of Education. London, 1923.

The Story of a Great Schoolmaster: Being a Plain Account of the Life and Ideas of Sanderson of Oundle. London and New York, 1924.

A Year of Prophesying. London, 1924; New York, 1925.
    Contents include: "The P.R. Parliament," London, 1924; "The Fantasies of Mr. Belloc and the Future of the World," "Winston," and "The Race Conflict: Is It Unavoidable?"

A Forecast of the World's Affairs. London, 1925.

Mr. Belloc Objects to the Outline of History. London and New York, 1926.

Democracy under Revision: A Lecture Delivered at the Sorbonne. London, 1927.

The Way the World Is Going: Guesses and Forecasts of the Years Ahead. London, 1928; Garden City, N.Y., 1929.
    Contents include: "Democracy Under Revision: A Lecture Delivered at the Sorbonne," London and New York, 1927; "Playing at Peace," London, 1927.

The Open Conspiracy: Blue Prints for a World Revolution. London and Garden City, N.Y., 1928. [Revised as What Are We to Do with Our Lives? London, 1931.]

The Common Sense of World Peace: An Address Delivered to the Reichstag. London, 1929.

Imperialism and the Open Conspiracy. London, 1929.

The Science of Life: A Summary of Contemporary Knowledge about Life and Its Possibilities. [In collaboration with Julian Huxley and G.P. Wells.] London and New York, 1929–30.

The Way to World Peace. London, 1930.

The Problem of the Troublesome Collaborators: An Account of Certain Difficulties in an Attempt to Produce a Work in Collaboration and of the Intervention of the Society of Authors Therein. Woking, 1930.

Settlement of the Trouble between Mr. Thring and Mr. Wells; A Footnote to the Problem of the Troublesome Collaborators. London, 1930.

The Work, Wealth, and Happiness of Mankind. Garden City, N.Y., 1931; London, 1932.

After Democracy: Addresses and Papers on the Present World Situation. London, 1932.
    Contents include: "The Common Sense of World Peace: An Address Delivered to the Reichstag," London, 1929.

Experiment in Autobiography: Discoveries and Conclusions of a Very Ordinary Brain since 1866. London and New York, 1934.

Stalin-Wells Talk: The Verbatim Record and a Discussion by G. Bernard Shaw, H.G. Wells, J.M. Keynes, Ernst Toller and Others. London, 1934; New York (as Marxism vs. Liberalism), 1947.

The New America: The New World. London and New York, 1935.

The Idea of a World Encyclopaedia. London, 1936.

The Informative Content of Education. London, 1937.

World Brain. London and Garden City, N.Y., 1938.
    Contents include: "The Idea of a World Encyclopaedia," London, 1936.

Travels of a Republican Radical in Search of Hot Water. Harmondsworth, 1939.

The Fate of Homo Sapiens: An Unemotional Statement of the Things That Are Happening to Him Now and of the Immediate Possibilities Confronting Him. London and New York, 1939.

The New World Order, Whether It Is Obtainable, How It Can Be Attained, and What Sort of World a World at Peace Will Have to Be. London and New York, 1940. [This work and the one preceding it were revised and reissued in one vol. as The Outlook for Homo Sapiens: An Amalgamation and Modernization of Two Books. London, 1942.]

The Rights of Man, or What Are We Fighting For? Harmondsworth, 1940.

The Common Sense of War and Peace: World Revolution or War Unending? Harmondsworth, 1940.

Two Hemispheres or One World? London, 1940.

Guide to the New World: A Handbook of Constructive World Revolution.
London, 1941.

Science and the World-Mind. London, 1942.

*Phoenix: A Summary of the Inescapable Conditions of World Organiza-
tion.* London, 1942.

The Conquest of Time. London, 1942. [Written to replace his *First
and Last Things*, 1908.]

The New Rights of Man. Girard, Kansas, 1942.

Crux Ansata: An Indictment of the Roman Catholic Church.
Harmondsworth, 1943.

The Mosley Outrage. London, 1943.

*'42 to '44: A Contemporary Memoir upon Human Behaviour during the
Crisis of the World Revolution.* London, 1944.
   Contents include: "A Thesis on the Quality of Illusion in the
   Continuity of Individual Life of the Higher Metazoa, with Particu-
   lar Reference to the Species Homo Sapiens, Submitted by H.G.
   Wells" [for the degree of Doctor of Science], London, 1942.

The Happy Turning: A Dream of Life. London, 1945.

Mind at the End of Its Tether. London and New York, 1945.

H.G. Wells in Love: Postscript to An Experiment in Autobiography.
Edited by G.P. Wells. London and Boston, 1984.

B. Collections and Selections

Wells's Social anticipations. Edited by H.W. Laidler. New York,
1927.

H.G. Wells, Journalism, and Prophecy, 1893-1946: An Anthology.
Edited by W.W. Wagar. Boston, 1964.

The Last Books of Wells. Edited by G.P. Wells. London, 1968.
   Contents: *The Happy Turning* and *Mind at the End of Its Tether.*

H.G. Wells's Literary Criticism. Edited by Patrick Parrinder and
Robert Philmus. Brighton, Eng.; Totowa, N.J., 1980.

III. LETTERS

Edel, L., and G.N. Ray, eds. *Henry James and H.G. Wells: A Record of
Their Friendship, Their Debate on the Art of Fiction and Their Quarrel.* Urbana, Ill., 1958.

Gerber, H.E., ed. "Some Letters of H.G. Wells from a Private Collection." English Fiction in Transition 3 (1960).

Wilson, H., ed. Arnold Bennett and H.G. Wells: A Record of a Personal and Literary Friendship. Urbana, Ill., 1960.

Getting, R.A., ed. Gissing and Wells: Their Friendship and Correspondence. Urbana, Ill., 1961.

Ray, G.N., ed. H.G. Wells and Rebecca West. New Haven and London, 1974.

Scheick, William J., ed. "Yours, H.G.: Some Missing Wells Letters to Arnold Bennett." English Literature in Transition 25 (1982).

Writings about H.G. Wells, 1895-1986

1   "The Book Mart." Bookman (New York) 2 (Dec.):355-56.
     [Remarks on the price of The Wonderful Visit.]

2   "Chronicle and Comment." Bookman (New York) 2 (Oct.):90.
     [Conversations and Wonderful Visit are favorably
recommended.]

3   COURTNEY, W.L. "Books of the Day." DT, 27 Sept., p. 8.
     Wonderful Visit, a charmingly unconventional and refresh-
ingly forceful romance, cannot be sufficiently praised for its
grace, delicacy, and humor. In the work are allegorical hints
pertaining to art and economics as well as touching on the ruinous
results of mixing the ideal sphere with the practical realm.

4   "Fiction." Critic (New York) 24 (14 Dec.):406.
     Successfully blending the fantastic, the comic, and the
matter-of-fact, Wonderful Visit is an effective satire on the
English rural community.

5   "Fiction." SR (London) 80 (20 July):86-87.
     The humor of Conversations bodes well for W's potentiality.
Time Machine reveals a writer of individual talent and
imagination.

6   "Fiction." SR (London) 80 (26 Oct.):554.
     Though not a novel, Wonderful Visit was well worth doing,
and W has done it better than perhaps any other living writer
could have.

7   "Fiction." SR (London) 80 (21 Dec.):843.
     Science and fiction are imaginatively blended in Stolen
Bacillus. W's method is more delicate, if not more forcible, than
that of Kipling.

1895

8   [HUTTON, RICHARD HOLD.] "In A.D. 802, 701." Spectator 75
     (13 July):41-43. Reprinted in CH, pp. 34-37; and in "The Time
     Machine," "The War of the Worlds," ed. Frank D. McConnell (New
     York: Oxford University Press, 1977), pp. 305-7.
        Time Machine fails to recognize that human nature requires
     hard work to keep it in order and that the competing energies of
     nature crush weak organizations. The clever book is worth reading
     if only because it draws attention to the moral and religious
     aspects of man that it seems to ignore.

9   "The Lounger." Critic (New York) 24 (9 Nov.):305.
        [Compares Wonderful Visit and Grant Allen's The British
     Barbarians.]

10   "The New Books: Notes from Our London Correspondent." ARR
     12:496.
        Time Machine deserves its current popularity because it
     exhibits unusual imagination.

11   "The New Books: Our London Letter About Books." ARR 12:
     628-29.
        Time Machine is exciting, powerful, and imaginative.

12   "New Novels." Athenaeum, no. 3548 (26 Oct.), p. 565.
        Although similar to stories by Andrew Lang and Nathaniel
     Hawthorne, Wonderful Visit provides amusing satire.

13   "The New Review." RR 11 (Jan.):56; (Feb.):154; (April):263;
     (May):416. April entry reprinted in CH, p. 33.
        [Notes that New Review is printing Time Machine and con-
     cludes that W's imaginative genius is as gruesome as that of Poe.]

14   "New Writers: Mr. H.G. Wells." Bookman (London) 8 (Aug.):
     134-35.
        [First biographical sketch of W.]

15   "Novel Notes." Bookman (London) 9 (Dec.):97-98.
        The stories in Stolen Bacillus are monstrous, humorous, or
     merely silly.

16   "Novel Notes." Bookman (New York) 2 (Oct.):145-46.
        [A favorable comment on Conversations.]

17   "Our Library Table." Athenaeum, no. 3532 (6 July), p. 32.
        Conversations is a dreary and foolish assemblage of common-
     place ideas expressed in stilted phraseology.

18   "Our Monthly Parcel of Books." RR 12 (Oct.):375-76.
      Wonderful Visit lacks the power of Time Machine. W should
take more time in writing his next book.

19   "A Pilgrim through Time." DC, 27 July, p. 3. Reprinted in CH,
      pp. 38-39; and in "The Time Machine," "The War of the Worlds,"
      ed. Frank D. McConnell (New York: Oxford University Press,
      1977), pp. 308-10.
      Although there are some dubious matters, particularly per-
taining to W's confusion of time with space, Time Machine is
strikingly original.

20   "Recent Novels." Times (London), 5 Nov., p. 11.
      Wonderful Visit would have been more humorous had W pos-
sessed a sense of humor. W lacks the qualities needed for this
sort of writing.

21   "Short Stories." Athenaeum, no. 3556 (21 Dec.), p. 868.
      Stolen Bacillus shows that W is more successful when being
humorous rather than when being harrowing.

22   "Speculative and Pessimistic." NYT 23 June, p. 27.
      Time Machine is ingenious in speculation but pessimistic in
message.

23   "The Time Machine." LW (Boston) 26:217.
      This work is uncommonly ingenious and interesting.

24   "An Uncle and His Talk." NYT, 24 Aug., p. 3.
      [Tongue-in-cheek review of Conversations, implying a negative
response.]

25   ZANGWILL, ISRAEL. "Without Prejudice." Pall Mall Magazine 8
      (Sept.):153-55. Reprinted in CH, pp. 40-42.
      In spite of the fact that its hero is more appropriate to
the sensational rather than to the scientific novel and that it
raises some dubious questions about time travel, Time Machine
provides an amusing fantasy.

                              1896

26   "Chronicle and Comment." Bookman (New York) 3 (June):293-94.
      [Brief comment on W's career and the forthcoming Dr. Moreau;
cf. Bookman (London) 8 (Aug.):134-35.]

27   "Coming and Going." SR (London) 82 (12 Dec.):630-31.
      Wheels of Chance is a good book, though it proves boring
initially and raises the question of whether or not W will ever
live up to his talent.

1896

28   COURTNEY, W.L. "Books of the Day." DT, 3 April, p. 6.
      Dr. Moreau may present W's doubts about vivisection or about
the limits of scientific experiment or about the central difficulties of the theory of evolution, but overall the purpose of the
book remains uncertain. Possibly W is unwittingly demonstrating
here his need for repression and discipline; for the imagination
can be diseased even as it can be healthy.

29   "Diary of a Bookseller." To-day 12 (19 Sept.):204;
      (10 Oct.):300; (17 Oct.):333, 339.
      [Reports, responds to, and prints letters concerning com-
plaints about the minute accuracy of W's portrait of a draper's
assistant in Wheels of Chance.]

30   "Fiction." Speaker 13 (18 April):429-30. Reprinted in CH,
      p. 50.
      Originality is achieved at the expense of decency in Dr.
Moreau. W has wasted his talent on degradation.

31   "Fiction Good and Bad." NYT, 16 Aug., p. 23.
      Although capable of stirring the reader deeply, Dr. Moreau
does not succeed as allegory because its meaning is too veiled.

32   [HUTTON, RICHARD HOLT.] "The Island of Dr. Moreau." Spectator
      76 (11 April):519-20. Reprinted in CH, pp. 46-48.
      Although this book is not for readers with sensitive nerves,
it nearly rivals Swift in the force and effect of its gruesome yet
salutary and impressive presentation.

33   ["The Island of Dr. Moreau."] Guardian, 3 June, p. 871.
      Reprinted in CH, pp. 52-53.
      The purpose of this unprofitable book is not clear, some-
times suggesting a satire on the presumptions of science while at
other times seeming a parody of God's act of and dealings with
creation. It must be admitted that the work displays W's clever,
original imagination.

34   ["The Island of Dr. Moreau."] LW 27:252.
      In this blood-curdling novel written with uncanny power, W's
vision exceeds the wildest horrors of Poe.

35   "Literature." Critic (New York) 26 (25 July):55-56.
      Of questionable scientific value, Dr. Moreau is saved from
grossness by the strong effect at the end of the story.

36   "Literature." Critic (New York) 26 (19 Dec.):401.
      Humorous incidents, a vivid portrait of human nature, and a
stress on the present are the assets of Wheels of Chance.

37   MITCHELL, P. CHALMERS. "The Island of Dr. Moreau." SR
      (London) 82 (7 Nov.):498.
           [A letter replying to one by W in the same issue discussing
      whether or not human and animal tissues can be grafted.]

38   _____. "Mr. Wells's Dr. Moreau." SR (London) 81
      (11 April):368-69. Reprinted in CH, pp. 43-46.
           Promising in idea, this book transgresses good taste in its
      horrific details.

39   "New Books and New Editions." Critic (New York) 25
      (11 April):253.
           [Superficial review of Conversations, favorable on the
      whole.]

40   "New Novels." Athenaeum, no. 3605 (28 Nov.), p. 752.
           Delightfully humorous, Wheels of Chance deserves a high
      place among current works of fanciful romance.

41   "Novels." MG, 14 April, p. 4. Reprinted in CH, pp. 48-49.
           Dr. Moreau evinces a vigorous narrative style, terse dia-
      logue, realistic detail; and although the subject of the work may
      not be a legitimate one for art, W has achieved an unquestionable
      and extraordinary success. W is too good to devote himself exclu-
      sively to fantastic themes.

42   "Novels." MG, 12 Nov., p. 7.
           In Wheels of Chance W displays a pleasant humanity.

43   "Our Monthly Parcel of Books." RR 14 (Nov.):470.
           Wheels of Chance, albeit entertaining, is not the sort of
      work W does best.

44   PICAROON. "Mr. H.G. Wells." Chap-book (Chicago) 5:366-74.
           The most notable of English writers, W will cleanse the
      English novel. When W eventually turns his attention away from
      the tour de force evident in his romances to date, he will cer-
      tainly write a great novel.

45   "Recent Novels." Spectator 77 (28 Nov.):770-71.
           A brilliant, entertaining book, Wheels of Chance presents a
      convincing protagonist who is at once diverting and pathetic.

46   "Recent Novels." Times (London), 17 June, p. 17.
           Dr. Moreau "is the strongest example we have met of
      the perverse quest after anything in any shape that is freshly
      sensational."

1896

47   "The Transformation of Living Tissues." Natural Science 13
      (May):291.
          Though gruesome and exciting, Dr. Moreau is scientifically
      dubious.

48   WAUGH, ARTHUR. "London Letter." Critic (New York) 25
      (21 March):203.
          [Reports a rumor that W will abandon short story writing for
      the novel.]

49   _____. "London Letter." Critic (New York) 26 (22 Aug.):121.
          Wheels of Chance is a spirited cycling idyll.

50   WEIL, MATHILDE. "A Modern Don Quixote." Bookman (New York) 4
      (Dec.):362-63.
          In Wheels of Chance W successfully blends idealism
      and humor, presenting a study of the prevalent spirit of social
      discontent.

51   [WILLIAMS, BASIL.] "New Novels." Athenaeum, no. 3576 (9 May),
      pp. 615-16. Reprinted in CH, pp. 51-52.
          The details of suffering presented in Dr. Moreau cannot be
      justified artistically and have a nauseating effect on the reader.

52   ["The Wonderful Visit."] LW 27:251.
          Unobtrusive in its satire, this novel delays its message
      until its conclusion when we discover that our grim little world
      can be transformed into something glorious by love and self-
      sacrifice.

53   ZANGWILL, I[SRAEL]. "Without Prejudice." PMM 8 (Jan.):168-69.
          Wonderful Visit is not original in concept nor completely
      successful with regard to W's efforts to explain the emotional
      effect of the angel's visit.

                              1897

54   "The Almost Incredible." DC, 20 May, p. 3.
          W adroitly avoids the pitfalls of too much and too little
      detail in The Plattner Story and Others. "The Sea Raiders," "The
      Red Room," and "The Cone" are especially noteworthy.

55   "Book Reviews Reviewed." Academy 52 (24 July):79.
          [A compilation of favorable comments on Plattner Story gar-
      nered from several newspapers.]

56   "Book Reviews Reviewed." Academy 52 (25 Sept.):247.
          [A survey of reviews of Invisible Man.]

57 "Books of the Week." <u>Times</u> (London), 29 Oct., p. 14.
     If not read too close together, the articles in <u>Personal</u>
<u>Matters</u> are amusing.

58 "Chronicle and Comment." <u>Bookman</u> (New York) 4 (Jan.):414-15.
     <u>Wheels of Chance</u> unites commonplace humanity and searching
satire. If W can develop this ability he will forge a permanent
place for himself in the field of fiction. [A note on W's attend-
ance at the Omar Khayyam Club.]

59 "Chronicle and Comment." <u>Bookman</u> (New York) 6 (Nov.):178-79.
     W's astounding tales reflect a strange verisimilitude. Al-
though he has done some very fine work, he has not been popular
until now. [Prints W's explanation of <u>Invisible Man</u> and disagrees
with W's evaluation of George Gissing's novels.]

60 CLEAR, CLAUDIUS. "The Fantastic Fiction; or, <u>The Invisible</u>
     <u>Man</u>." <u>Bookman</u> (New York) 6 (Nov.):250-51.
     Even if it is less well done than it should have been, this
work is an original and provocative book. W should write fewer
books and devote more time perfecting his art.

61 GOSSE, EDMUND. "The Abuse of the Supernatural in Fiction."
     <u>Bookman</u> (New York) 6 (Dec.):298-99.
     To a remarkable degree <u>Invisible Man</u> exemplifies the proper
use of the supernatural. The consistency and inevitability of
detail command belief even when the idea presented is absurd.

62 _____. "Ten Years of English Literature." <u>NAR</u> 165 (Aug.):145.
     Writers in scientific philosophy of the calibre of Tyndall
and Huxley no longer exist in England. W might have risen to it,
but "he prefers to tell little horrible stories about monsters."

63 ["<u>The Invisible Man</u>."] <u>LW</u> 28:479.
     W makes a fine "spook" out of nothing at all.

64 L., A.H. "Realism v. Romance." <u>To-day</u> 16 (11 Sept.):164-65.
     [An interesting interview with W in which he refutes the
absolute separation between romance and realism.]

65 MacARTHUR, JAMES. "A Bundle of Strange Tales." <u>Bookman</u> (New
     York) 6 (Sept.):69-70.
     <u>Strange Stories</u> is simple, ingenious entertainment. W could
be dubbed the Jules Verne of England.

66 "Mr. Wells's New Stories." <u>Academy</u> 51 (29 May):566.
     [Mentions <u>Plattner Story</u>.]

1897

67   "Mr. Wells's New Stories." SR (London) 84 (18 Sept.):321-22.
      [Review of Plattner Story and Invisible Man, stressing
   attention to detail as W's major asset.]

68   "Mr. Wells's New Story." DC, 17 Sept., p. 3.
      W manages the details of the invisible state in Invisible
   Man with great skill and fertility of imagination.

69   "New Novels." Athenaeum, no. 3648 (25 Sept.), p. 416.
      Invisible Man, albeit a successful tour de force, lacks
   interest. The depiction of the conduct of the villagers is particularly poor.

70   "New Novels." DT, 26 May, p. 9.
      Plattner Story reveals W's best fantastic tendencies as well
   as his realistic matter-of-fact narrative abilities. Vagueness of
   description, knowing just when to say no more, is one of W's chief
   powers. The stories treating simple people demonstrate an ability
   equivalent to W's scientific romances.

71   "New Novels." DT, 22 Sept., p. 9.
      Hurriedness in composition, inadequately joined parts, unes-
   sential improbabilities, lapses in dialect and faltering imagination weaken Invisible Man, making it less successful than Time
   Machine. Yet as ebullient farce with Swiftian overtones, it
   satisfies.

72   "Notes and News." Academy 52 (10 July):32-33.
      [Notes W's prophetic insight.]

73   "Novel Notes." Bookman (London) 11 (Jan.):124.
      Character development is the chief interest in Wheels of
   Chance.

74   "Novels and Short Stories of Varying Degrees of Merit."
      NYTSRBA, 15 May, pp. 4-5.
      Although it is questionable that true art can deal with the
   horrible, it is true that Strange Stories displays some genuine
   literary ability and imagination.

75   "Our Library Table." Athenaeum, no. 3655 (13 Nov.), p. 672.
      Sadly unconvincing, Personal Matters is wearisome and stale
   except for "Blades and Bladery."

76   PAYNE, WILLIAM MORTON. "Recent Fiction." Dial 22 (1 Jan.):21.
      Wheels of Chance is distinguished by its humor, unconven-
   tionality, scientific tinge, and mild satire.

77 _____. "Recent Fiction." Dial 23 (16 Dec.):390.
　　W's method in Invisible Man differs from that of his pred-
ecessors because he has not thought out the problem or faced
details squarely.

78 "Recent Literature." DT, 27 Oct., p. 6.
　　W's talent as a thinker and as a stylist is evident in
Personal Matters.

79 "Recent Novels." Spectator 79 (25 Sept.):408.
　　Although it lacks the charm of Wheels of Chance, Invisible
Man is amazingly clever and engrossing. W is another Swift, but
his method is more realistic. Griffin is really a tragic figure.

80 "Reviews of Recent Notable Publications: 'The Invisible Man.'"
　　SFC, 26 Dec., p. 4.
　　Like his earlier works, this book displays the breadth of
W's imagination and the strength of his narrative techniques.

81 SHORTER, CLEMENT. "The Invisible Man." Bookman (London) 13
　　(Oct.):19-20. Reprinted in CH, pp. 58-60.
　　Exemplifying a splendid mastery of detail, this amusing book
is not preachy.

82 "Sketches and Stories." Academy 52 (6 Nov.):371-72.
　　[Favorable comment on Personal Matters.]

83 "The Spinning of Two Wheels." NYTSRBA, 16 Jan., p. 2.
　　A pretty story, Wheels of Chance is amusingly and feelingly
related.

84 "Thirty Strange Stories." Critic (New York) 28 (31 July):59.
　　These stories are grotesque and frightful; but because they
are too unusual, they do not generally elicit a mysterious thrill
of horror. "The Lord of the Dynamos," a tale worthy of Kipling,
and "The Red Room," perhaps the only plausible ghost story ever
written, are the best works in the book.

85 "Two Volumes of Short Stories." Spectator 78 (19 June):871.
　　In Plattner Story W stands unrivalled in audacious imaginative insight into scientific possibilities. Certain qualities of
W's narrative suggest Swift. W is best when he keeps close to the
realm of the possible. His blend of whimsy and sympathy in portraying the middle class is a valuable supplement to George
Gissing's gloomy picture.

86 ["The Wheels of Chance."] LW 28:28.
　　This dull story may find followers among devotees of
bicycling.

1897

87   [WILLIAMS, BASIL.] "Short Stories." Athenaeum, no. 3635
     (26 June), p. 837. Reprinted in CH, p. 57.
          Precision in the inessential and vagueness in the essential
     provides the basis of W's art in Plattner Story.

88   "A Young Novelist Who Has 'Arrived.'" Sketch 19
     (15 Sept.):317.
          [An interview with W.]

1898

89   "Book Reviews Reviewed: The War of the Worlds." Academy 53
     (19 March):334.
          [Quotes from reviews appearing in SR (London) 85
     (29 Jan.):146-47; DC, 21 Jan., p. 3; Speaker; and the Scotsman.]

90   "The Book Table." Detroit Free Press, 28 March, p. 7.
          Evincing W's ingenious imagination, War of the Worlds capi-
     talizes on the current belief that Mars is inhabited. The Mar-
     tians are described very well, and the novel as a whole is saved
     from absurdity by W's sense and knowledge, which permit him to
     outstrip Jules Verne.

91   "Books." Spectator (London) 80 (29 Jan.):168-69.
          In War of the Worlds W's characters are more human and his
     details more concrete than are those of Poe, though the latter's
     art is probably greater. The book contains scenes of remarkable
     literary workmanship.

92   BOUTON, EMILY S. "'Cheerful Yesterdays.' 'As It Seems to
     Me.' 'Other Things.'" Toledo Blade, 30 April, p. 13.
          War of the Worlds contains much vivid realistic description
     but is marred by repulsive passages recounting the details of many
     abhorrent deaths.

93   BROOKS, SYDNEY. "The War of the Worlds." HW 42 (2 April):321.
          W is one of the most original, felicitous writers among
     younger English novelists. His new book not only relates a good
     story but also possesses the precision, reasonableness, sense of
     distance, and proportion that provide the foundation for imagina-
     tive literature.

94   FITCHE, GEORGE HAMLIN. "Reviews of Recent Books and Other
     Publications." SFC, 1 May, p. 4.
          In one of the best stories of the year and set apart from
     other science fiction by its ingenuity, War of the Worlds deftly
     interweaves science and fiction, making every part of the book
     interesting.

95   G[REGORY], R.A. "Science in Fiction." <u>Nature</u> 57
      (10 Feb.):339-40. Reprinted in <u>CH</u>, pp. <u>74-76.</u>
            Romances such as <u>War of the Worlds</u> further scientific inter-
      ests by attracting attention to a motivating sympathy for the work
      of scientists. W's imagination is properly grounded on scientific
      fact.

96   "Literature." <u>Critic</u> (New York) 29 (22 Jan.):56.
            Aside from a chronological error in the book, <u>Invisible Man</u>
      sucessfully provides suspense. Possibly W will benefit from the
      supernatural side of Poe's work in a manner similar to Arthur
      Conan Doyle's use of the analytic side.

97   "Literature." <u>Critic</u> (New York) 29 (23 April):282. Reprinted
      in <u>CH</u>, pp. 68-69.
            Quasi-scientific romances such as <u>War of the Worlds</u> suffer
      from a lack of artistic breadth and from a slipshod style. Yet
      W's work is daring as an imaginative piece.

98   "Mr. Wells' Confessions." <u>SR</u> (London) 85 (15 Jan.):87.
            Witty and humorous, <u>Personal Matters</u> lies lightly on the
      reader's mind.

99   "Mr. Wells' Latest Orgie." <u>Chicago Tribune</u>, 9 April, sec. 2,
      p. 10.
            However much fun W may have had in creating <u>War of the</u>
      <u>Worlds</u>, the book lacks human interest, deserts a possible stock
      romance midway in the narrative, appeals only to the pseudo-
      scientific imagination, and provides too many manufactured hor-
      rors, which pall before the tale concludes.

100   "More Fiction." <u>Nation</u> (New York) 66 (20 Jan.):54.
            Technical minuteness, a rare imagination, and a fortunate
      combination of clarity and lightness account for the excellent
      entertainment furnished by <u>Strange Stories</u>.

101   "More Novels." <u>Nation</u> (New York) 66 (9 June):447.
            Highly ingenious, <u>War of the Worlds</u> is convincing in its
      terror.

102   "New Books." <u>St. Paul</u> (Minn.) <u>Pioneer Press</u>, 17 April, p. 20.
            A success among works of its kind, <u>War of the Worlds</u> makes
      the reader wish that W would exercise his versatile talents on
      less sensational matter.

103   "New Books." <u>St. Paul</u> (Minn.) <u>Pioneer Press</u>, 26 June, p. 21.
            A blend of the grim and the humorous, <u>Strange Stories</u>
      evinces a graphic style and penetrating psychological insight in a
      manner not yet characteristic of W's longer works.

1898

104   "New Books: An Invasion from Mars." Brooklyn Eagle, 19 March,
       p.4.
           Good of its kind, War of the Worlds is an absorbing narra-
       tive because of the graphic description of the Martians, the
       narrator's well-conceived account of the Martians' personalities,
       and the ironic conclusion.

105   "New Publications." Baltimore Sun, 28 March, p. 10.
           War of the Worlds places W first among writers of the weird
       and uncanny. Especially noteworthy are the nonanthropomorphic
       Martians.

106   "Novels." MG, 25 Jan., p. 4.
           W's strength in War of the Worlds "lies in his grave wield-
       ing of the scientific manner, in what we may perhaps call his
       subcutaneous humour, and in the respectable standard of writing
       which he always maintains." Much of W's delicate fancy, however,
       is missing in this work.

107   "One of Well's [sic] Fancies." NYTSRBA, 16 July, p. 470.
           However an excellent example of its kind, Time Machine lacks
       artistic plausibility.

108   PAYNE, WILLIAM MORTON. "Recent Fiction." Dial 24
       (1 June):356.
           War of the Worlds is unconvincing even it it does follow the
       logical implications of its primary postulate. Although the imag-
       ination displayed is unusual in intensity, it is of a cheap sort.

109   "Portraits of Celebrities." Strand Magazine 16 (Dec.):675.
       [Brief biography with drawings.]

110   "Recent Literature." DT, 26 Jan., p. 6.
           In depicting details, in portraying the sombre and the
       terrible, W is excellently inventive in War of the Worlds, a work
       that one cannot leave unfinished. The novel contributes greatly
       to W's reputation "for this kind of work."

111   "Recent Novels." Times (London), 18 April, p. 7.
           Although the fantasy of War of the Worlds is ingenious, the
       book lacks human interest.

112   "Review: The War of the Worlds." Academy (Fiction
       Supplement) 53 (29 Jan.):121-22.
           In this novel, the crowning merit of which lies in the
       unobtrusiveness of its underlying moral idea, W combines his two
       gifts of scientific imagination and mundane observation.

113 "Reviews." Academy 53 (29 Jan.):121-22. Reprinted in CH,
     pp. 70-74.
       Scientific imagination and mundane observation are the chief
     assets of War of the Worlds.

114 SHORTER, CLEMENT. "Mr. Wells's War of the Worlds." Bookman
     (London) 13 (March):182-83. Reprinted Bookman (New York) 7
     (May):246-47.
       W's imagination is in fine form in this work, though he is
     not very optimistic about the future. In an age of scientific
     revival, W's pessimism is out of keeping in an otherwise socially
     relevant novel.

115 [STEAD, W.T.] "The Latest Apocalypse of the End of the World."
     RR 17 (April):389-96. Extract reprinted in CH, pp. 61-62.
     [Primarily plot summaries of several of W's works.]

116 [STRACHEY, JOHN ST. LOE.] "The War of the Worlds." Spectator
     (London) 80 (29 Jan.):168-69. Reprinted in CH, pp. 63-66.
       Replete with remarkable pieces of literary workmanship, this
     romance is one of the most exciting works of imagination ever
     written. There is not a dull page, though the inclusion of a
     weak-minded curate seems a flaw. [Some discussion comparing W
     favorably with Poe, Swift, and Defoe.]

117 "Thirty Strange Stories." LW 29:342-43.
       Concerned with the mysteries of life rather than the horrors
     of life, W's stories display imaginative power and ingenuity.

118 ["War of the Worlds."] Indianapolis News, 13 April, p. 5.
       W has done nothing better than this novel narrated so real-
     istically that the impossibilities of the story seem probable.

119 "War of the Worlds." LW 29:154.
       While W's nightmarish tale of the invasion of Earth cannot
     be recommended, it no doubt will appeal to readers who enjoy the
     macabre.

120 "The War of the Worlds." SR (London) 85 (29 Jan.):146-47.
       Unyielding to vulgar popular tastes for emotion, this book
     is vigorous, imaginative, and credible.

121 [WILLIAMS, BASIL.] "New Novels." Athenaeum, no. 3667
     (5 Feb.), p. 178. Reprinted in CH, p. 67.
       In imitating Jules Verne in War of the Worlds W has not
     learned that matter-of-fact details need not be vulgar. W writes
     too much, trusting solely to the effects of his ideas rather than
     giving them distinction.

1899

122 ALDEN, WILLIAM L. "London Literary Letter." <u>NYTSRBA</u>, 17 June, p. 388.
Errors of factual detail may not detract from interest in <u>War of the Worlds</u> and <u>Sleeper Wakes</u>, but they do indicate that W ought to take more time in writing.

123 "Fiction." <u>MG</u>, 20 June, p. 4.
Even the most obtuse of readers cannot fail to read the truths that underlie W's intentional extravagances in <u>Sleeper Wakes</u>.

124 "New Books." <u>Mirror</u> (St. Louis), 8 Nov., p. 12.
<u>Mr. Lewisham</u> will convince those who love W's romances that he can also write a charming love story.

125 "New Novels." <u>Athenaeum</u>, no. 3736 (3 June), p. 685.
The arid prophecy and incoherent protagonist of <u>Sleeper Wakes</u> are distinctly dull.

126 NICOLL, W. ROBERTSON. "Literary London." <u>Bookman</u> (New York) 8 (Jan.):489.
[A report on W's health.]

127 "Novel Notes." <u>Bookman</u> (New York) 9 (July):474.
A masterpiece of imaginative genius, <u>Sleeper Wakes</u> suffers from too much description.

128 "Novel Notes." <u>Bookman</u> (London) 17 (Dec.):90.
The focus on the future in <u>Tales</u> stimulates thought concerning the present-day world.

129 "Novels." <u>Outlook</u> (New York) 62 (24 June):445-46.
<u>Sleeper Wakes</u> may be thrilling at times but it actually lacks moral purpose.

130 "Novels." <u>SR</u> (London) 87 (27 May):663-64.
The future portrayed in <u>Sleeper Wakes</u> is too much like what one might imagine upon hasty reflection.

131 "Novels of the Week." <u>Spectator</u> (London) 82 (27 May):757-58.
Tricks of phrase and manner notwithstanding, <u>Sleeper Wakes</u> abounds in effective visualization. W alerts us to the potential dehumanization residing in future scientific control of men's lives.

1899

132   "Novels of the Week." Spectator (London) 83 (18 Nov.):754.
        Though interesting, suggestive, and disquieting, Tales lacks
the humor and humanity so evident in Wheels of Chance.

133   PAYNE, WILLIAM MORTON. "Recent Fiction." Dial 27
       (16 Sept.):176.
        Sleeper Wakes is disappointing. Despite its skillful elabo-
ration of details, it lacks "imaginative reach."

134   "Prophet v. Novelist." Academy 56 (10 June):624-25.
        In combining a story with his forecasts, labelling the
result as fiction, W has marred Sleeper Wakes.

135   "Recent Fiction." Critic (New York) 35 (Aug.):752-53.
        [Favorable mention of W's ingenious reworking of an old
motif in Sleeper Wakes.]

136   "Recent Novels." Nation (New York) 69 (3 Aug.):96.
        [Favorable descriptive review of Sleeper Wakes.]

137   "Recent Novels." Times (London), 22 July, p. 15.
        If Sleeper Wakes is intended as satire it fails because it
is too long a nightmare.

138   "Red Pottage" and Other Stories." SR (London) 88
       (11 Nov.):623.
        The good stories of Tales excellently join fiction and W's
personal philosophy.

139   "Short Stories." Athenaeum, no. 3762 (2 Dec.), p. 757.
        In general the conceptions presented in Tales are unutter-
ably dull. W's style must be a partial reason for his undeserved
success.

140   "The Star." Academy 57 (25 Nov.):597-98.
        Tales unveils W's strange gifts. Although not quite per-
fect, "The Star" is a masterpiece of dramatic progression.

141   "When the Sleeper Wakes." LW 30:236.
        Only W could succeed with this novel, which is less har-
rowing than one expects.

142   "When the Sleeper Wakes." NYTSRBA, 19 Aug., p. 547.
        In this book thought and feeling are fused through superb
literary execution. "Picture after picture rises . . . tinged
with bizarre imagery, painted with colors such as never were on
sea or sky or land, and yet everything somehow so matter of fact,
so astoundingly real, that the impossible and outrageous seem
sober, commonplace, and quite natural."

1899

143   W[ILLIAMS], J.E. H[ODDER]. "Mr. Wells' New Novel." <u>Bookman</u>
      (London) 16 (June):76-77.
          Although the theme of <u>Sleeper Wakes</u> is imaginative, too much
      description interferes with the story.

1900

144   "The Book-Buyer's Guide." <u>Critic</u> (New York) 36 (April):374-75.
      [Brief note citing W's imagination in <u>Tales</u>.

145   "Chronicle and Comment." <u>Bookman</u> (New York) 11 (March):4.
      W's talent seems on the decline in <u>Conversations</u>.

146   "Fiction." <u>Speaker</u>, n.s. 2 (16 June):312-13. Reprinted in <u>CH</u>,
      pp. 83-84.
          Weary disillusionment mars the artistic effect of <u>Mr.
      Lewisham</u> and other of W's books. Mr. Chaffery is a most original
      character, and the book as a whole is amusing and readable. "We
      only wish that Mr. Wells had not written it."

147   "Four Novels." <u>SR</u> (London) 89 (16 June):752-53. Reprinted in
      <u>CH</u>, p. 82.
          In <u>Mr. Lewisham</u> W has joined the "decadent school," to the
      novel's disadvantage.

148   ["Love and <u>Mr. Lewisham</u>."] <u>DT</u>, 6 June, p. 11. Reprinted in
      <u>CH</u>, pp. 78-80.
          Pathos and humor intermingle in this book, the method of
      which contrasts with the realistic spirit of modern literature.
      In the book W superbly combines his talent for the uncanny and for
      depicting the commonplace, to produce the most fascinating work he
      has yet published.

149   "Mr. Wells at His Best." <u>DC</u>, 14 June, p. 3. Reprinted in <u>CH</u>,
      pp. 80-81.
          <u>Mr. Lewisham</u>, marked by close observation of human nature,
      proves that the genre of <u>Wheels of Chance</u> is W's best. Whereas
      Anstey sees the poorer middle class as subjects for his wit and
      Gissing sees them in their sordid and sometimes sorrowful condi-
      tion, W treats them more genially. W's style is much improved,
      his dialogue quite real.

150   "The New Books: Fiction for Summer Reading." <u>ARR</u> 21:757-63.
          W's remarkable predictions in <u>Tales</u> will horrify contempo-
      rary readers.

151 "New Novels." <u>Athenaeum</u>, no. 3791 (23 June), p. 779.
      <u>Mr. Lewisham</u> indicates that the speculative semiscientific,
semiphilosophic romance is W's best area.

152 "New Novels." <u>MG</u>, 13 June, p. 3.
      <u>Mr. Lewisham</u> describes the sordid aspects of life without
losing sight of beauty and charm. This is W's first book that
reveals his ability to describe the common things of life.

153 "A Novelist of the Unknown." <u>Academy</u> 58 (23 June):535-36.
      Even though W's "stellar novels" are brilliantly conceived,
they have little to do with the art of the novel. In <u>Wheels of
Chance</u> and <u>Mr. Lewisham</u>, however, W is more than clever, having
possibly written two masterpieces but certainly having established
an atmosphere in which masterpieces are created.

154 "Novels of the Week." <u>Spectator</u> (London) 84 (9 June):813-14.
      In <u>Mr. Lewisham</u> "the characters without exception belong to
the category of the insignificant or the commonplace, but they are
not treated in a commonplace way, and inspire an interest and
compassion rarely excited by the 'dramatis personae' of the
middle-class novel."

155 "Recent Novels." <u>Times</u> (London), 23 Feb., p. 3.
      <u>Tales</u> reveals that W cannot transcend human conditions.

156 "Spiritualism Exposed." <u>NYTSRBA</u>, 10 Nov., p. 766.
      Written in a light vein, <u>Mr. Lewisham</u> offers much to think
about and, through W's artistic skill, makes the reader sympathize
with the hero.

157 W[ILLIAMS], J.E. H[ODDER]. "The New Mr. Wells." <u>Bookman</u>
      (London) 18 (Aug.):155.
      Totally different from his previous works, <u>Mr. Lewisham</u>
proves W to be a writer.

                          <u>1901</u>

158 "Books of the Month." <u>RR</u> 24 (Dec.):639-41.
      Although the predictions in <u>Anticipations</u> are excellent on
the whole, W depends too much on material considerations.

159 "By H.G. Wells." <u>NYTSRBA</u>, 16 Nov., p. 845.
      In <u>Men in the Moon</u>, as elsewhere, W lacks the ability to
balance the unearthly by the earthly. Unlike those of Jules
Verne, the imaginative ideas of W are not as exciting to the
reader uninformed about their plausibility.

1901

160   "Fiction." Academy 61 (7 Dec.):54.
      [Sketchy remarks on Men in the Moon.]

161   "The First Men in the Moon." Literary News 22 (Nov.):329.
          This curious, whimsical book benefits from sympathetic
      illustrations by Mr. Hering.

162   GHÉON, HENRI [pseud. of HENRI VANGEON]. ["The First Men in the
      Moon."] Ermitage 23 (Dec.):471-72. Translated in CH,
      pp. 99-100.
          W's works are richer and more mature than those of Jules
      Verne. His new romance parodies terrestrial reality even while it
      entertains.

163   "History, Adventure, and School Stories." SR (London) (Supple-
      ment) 92 (7 Dec.):x.
          The flights of imagination in Men in the Moon remind one
      more of the satire of Jonathan Swift than of the inventions of a
      Jules Verne.

164   "In A.D. 2000." Academy 61 (23 Nov.):476-78.
          Anticipations is a serious, important, and memorable criti-
      cism and forecast of society.

165   "Intelligent Anticipations." WG, 12 Nov., p. 1. Reprinted in
      CH, pp. 85-87.
          Although W fails to allow sufficiently for the romantic and
      mystical elements of human nature, the main theses of Anticipa-
      ions is more than worthy of careful attention.

166   JOHNSON, R. BRINLEY. "A Letter from England." Atlantic
      Monthly 87 (Jan.):62-63.
          Mr. Lewisham marks W's conversion to realism, auguring well
      for what we may expect from him in the future.

167   "Literature." Athenaeum, no. 3867 (7 Dec.), p. 767.
          In Anticipations W is successful in stimulating controversy.
      There is much to criticize in the book.

168   "The Lounger." Critic (New York) 29 (Aug.):109.
          [Notes the increasing popularity of W's work in French
      translation and anticipates rich entertainment in Sea Lady.]

169   "New Novels." Athenaeum, no. 3868 (14 Dec.), p. 807.
          An unexpected touch and a genuine pathos help make Men in
      the Moon the pleasantest of W's writings.

170   "New Novels." MG, 4 Dec., p. 3.
          At times Men in the Moon strains after a semblance of proba-
      bility, which is unnecessary because, from another perspective,

the book reads like a satire. The lunar civilization bears a dis-
quieting resemblance to our own. The work is at once a prophetic
glance into the future and a parody of utopias.

171   "Notes on Novels." Academy 61 (23 Nov.):484.
      [Introductory note to Men in the Moon.]

172   "Notes on Novels." Dial 31 (16 Nov.):373.
      [Brief comment relating W and Jules Verne.]

173   "Novels." Spectator (London) 87 (23 Nov.):805.
         In Men in the Moon, an interesting romance, W presents a
      sensational adventure with characters who are genial caricatures
      of stock types. It "is not so much an irresponsible exercise of
      the scientific imigination as a grim illustration of the Horatian
      saying, caelum ipsum petimus stultitia—with the emphasis on the
      last word."

174   "The Old Quest." Academy 61 (7 Dec.):565-66.
         [Criticizes W's reference to the purpose of God in the last
      chapter of Anticipations.]

175   "Recent Novels." Times (London), 27 Dec., p. 2.
         In light of the unconvincing incidents of Men in the Moon, W
      ought to neglect scientific fantasies for stories concerning men
      of this world.

176   "The Republic Beyond." SR (London) 92 (23 Nov.):652-53.
         Extraordinarily brilliant, Anticipations will shape current
      thought.

177   "Reviews of Books." Times (London), 18 Dec., p. 13.
         Certainly worth reading, Anticipations presumes too much on
      the permanency of present-day conditions and suffers too much from
      W's sesquipedalian verbiage.

178   WILLIAMS, J.E. HODDER. "Provocations by H.G. Wells." Bookman
      (London) 21 (Dec.):91-92.
         Although in Anticipations and Men in the Moon some of W's
      predictions are quite probable, many of his criticisms are unsub-
      stantiated and vulgar. W's man of the future is little more than
      a machine.

                              1902

179   ARCHER, WILLIAM. "Study and Stage." Morning Leader (London),
      8 March, p. 4.

1902

[Suggests that W should be publicly recognized for his prophetic role.]

180   BENNETT, E. ARNOLD. "Herbert George Wells and His Work." Cosmopolitan 33 (Aug.):465-71. Reprinted in Arnold Bennett and H.G. Wells, ed. Harris Wilson (Urbana: University of Illinois Press, 1960), pp. 260-76; and in The Author's Craft and Other Critical Writings of Arnold Bennett, ed. Samuel Hynes (Lincoln: University of Nebraska Press, 1968), pp. 186-97.
      It is mistaken to compare W to Jules Verne, who is usually scientifically inaccurate and merely entertaining. Under the guise of romance W presents serious criticisms of life. His imaginative artistry aids us to see life afresh even while he keeps man placed firmly in nature as a link in the chain of eternal evolution. W will become more and more concerned with the present, and he may become a prevalent political influence.

181   "A Book of Anticipations." LW, 1 Aug., p. 118. Reprinted in CH, p. 89.
      Anticipations, a narrow book and a travesty of possibilities, is generally ignorant of history, ethics, and the social sciences.

182   CHESTERTON, G.K. "Books to Read." PMM 26 (Jan.):133-35.
      Anticipations is a book to be read and disagreed with seriously. The weaknesses of this work are even more apparent in Men in the Moon and derive from W's skeptical attitude. As a human story the latter work is lifeless, finally failing "in spite of a wealth of world-wide fancy and gigantesque logic."

183   "Feeling Towards a New Religion." RR 25 (Sept.):280.
      [Announces in detail W's plans for and his ideas behind Mankind.]

184   "Fiction." Academy 63 (9 Aug.):155-56.
      In Sea Lady W takes an impossibility as a premise and follows the argument logically, "with just the same surprise at his own conclusion as the reader might be expected to feel."

185   FILON, AUGUSTIN. "L'avenir de Londres." Journal des débats, 19 March, p. 1. Translated in part in CH, pp. 100-101.
      [Contrasts W and Jules Verne.]

186   "H.G. Wells's Whims." NYTSRBA, 4 Oct., p. 666.
      In spite of its humor, Sea Lady lacks the imagination of Time Machine and the entertaining speculations of Anticipations.

187   "The Isolation of English Fiction." Academy 63 (8 Nov.):505.
       [W is the only Englishman whose novels are published simul-
taneously in two languages.]

188   LANKESTES, E. RAY. "The Present Judged by the future." Nature
       (supplement) 65 (13 March):iii-v.
       Anticipations provides a wide ranging survey of contemporary
problems. W's expressed hope in the future of mankind is thor-
oughly grounded on modern science.

189   "A Lunar Romance." Nature 65 (9 Jan.):218-19.
       Unlike the work of Jules Verne, Men in the Moon is most
careful with regard to scientific details and plausibility.

190   "More Fiction." Nation (New York) 75 (6 Nov.):369.
       Deep airy satire accents Sea Lady, a work revealing W's
humor and imagination even better than his previous writings.

191   "New Novels." Athenaeum, no. 3904 (23 Aug.), p. 249.
       Although satirically thin, Sea Lady benefits from W's
craftsmanship and will probably have its admirers.

192   "Notes on Novels." Academy 63 (2 Aug.):134.
       [Introductory note to Sea Lady.]

193   "Novels." SR (London) 94 (30 Aug.):271-72.
       An old rejected manuscript resurrected in the wake of W's
popularity, Sea Lady manifests almost every conceivable fault.

194   "Novels." Spectator (London) 89 (16 Aug):229-30.
       Besides the number of impossible situations, Sea Lady con-
tains an artistic blunder in the incongruity of its initial satire
and its concluding tragedy.

195   "The Sea Lady." TLS, 15 Aug., p. 244.
       The main character of this book is as disappointingly tame
as the entire work.

196   "The Seeds of Time and Mr. H.G. Wells." NYTSRBA, 22 March,
       p. 187.
       Anticipations is sane and robust in its argument.

197   "Twelve Months' Fiction." Academy 63 (8 Nov.):493-94.
       Men in the Moon fuses picturesque imagination, scientific
truth, and philosophic criticism; it must rank as W's best novel.
Sea Lady also deserves attention.

198   "What Mr. Wells Anticipates." Spectator (London) 88
       (18 Jan.):89-90.

1902

Although W's man of the future is too unemotional, Anticipa-
ions represents a remarkable work of social prophecy both in its
general conception and in its wealth of illustrative detail.

1903

199   "Babes of the Future." SR (London) 96 (10 Oct.):460-61.
        In Mankind, a socialist work, W "appears to plume himself
remarkably on his discovery of babies; as if nobody before him had
ever suspected their existence."

200   "Books." Spectator (London) 91 (3 Oct.):524-25.
        That W could so bitterly and unjustly denigrate the average
man in Mankind "is no doubt due to the defective system of education hitherto prevalent which he so frankly condemns." [A tongue-
in-cheek review.]

201   "Books and Their Writers." T.P.'s Weekly, 25 Sept., p. 521; 2
        Oct., p. 553; 9 Oct., p. 598.
        In Mankind, a sequel to the remarkable Anticipations, W
demonstrates his daring and thoughtfulness in forecasting man's
future. [Primarily excerpts.]

202   "Fiction." Academy 65 (21 Nov.):563.
        [Brief, favorable note on Twelve Stories.]

203   "Literature." Athenaeum, no. 3964 (17 Oct.), pp. 511-12.
        Based on premises that can be challenged and sometimes
wilfully obstinate, Mankind is nevertheless a courageous book.

204   MACALISTER, ALEX. "Mankind in the Making." Bookman (London)
        25 (Dec.):134-36.
        [Partially sympathetic with W's concerns, yet questions the
probability of ever realizing many of his utopian notions.]

205   "Mannikins in the Making." Monthly Review (London) 11
        (June):1-10.
        W's good intentions cannot be doubted, but his vocation as a
preacher is unconvincing. His reforms are contrary to the current
of English national life. Many of his propositions are not serious, only solemn, even when "the solemnity is sometimes intensi-
fied by italics."

206   "Novels." Spectator (London) 91 (19 Dec.):1085.
        The union of the extraordinary with the commonplace, as
exemplified in Twelve Stories, is nearly becoming a trite
convention.

207   [SHERARD, ROBERT H.] "Jules Verne Re-Visited." T.P.'s Weekly
      2 (9 Oct.):589. Reprinted in part in CH, pp. 101-2.
         [An interview with Jules Verne in which the French author
      claims that W's stories do not have scientific premises.]

208   "Short Stories." Athenaeum, no. 3969 (21 Nov.), p. 682.
         W is the first real literary man to turn his attention to
      the material accumulated by modern science. Twelve Stories makes
      good reading.

209   "Some Novels." T.P.'s Weekly, 13 Nov., p. 761.
         Twelve Stories is worth reading.

210   "Thought." Academy 65 (26 Sept.):285-86. Reprinted in CH,
      pp. 90-93.
         Mankind indicates that W is a serious thinker whose ideas
      are refreshing, if somewhat immature. W should have read Spencer.

211   "Twelve Stories and a Dream." TLS, 6 Nov., p. 320.
         The tales in this book represent "chips" from W's workshop.
      Humor, which is sometimes too extravagant or silly, distinguishes
      W's shorter work from his longer writings.

212   WATSON, H.B. MARRIOTT. "Fiction in 1902." PMM 29 (Jan.):134.
         [Defends W against the charge that his scientific novels
      required no imagination.]

                              1904

213   BETTANY, F.G. "The World of Books." Sunday Times (London), 9
      Oct., p. 6.
         More materialist than poet, W focuses on bigness in Food of
      the Gods. He misses the critical idea underlying his book and
      achieves at best a weak satiric effect.

214   BLUNT, FRANK. "M.H.G. Wells et le style." Nouvelle Revue 33
      (Sept.):186-92.
         W's style has been neglected in French critiques of his
      works, especially his use of unending repetitions of words and
      sounds. W's apparent failure to reread, correct, or perfect
      results in faults that French readers would find intolerable.
      There can be little doubt that translators have improved upon W's
      style, and these alterations may have contributed to W's popular-
      ity with the French.

215   CHESTERTON, G.K. "Mr. Wells and the Giants." Bookman (London)
      27 (Dec.):124.

1904

Retelling the story of Jack the Giant-Killer from the point
of view of the giant, Food of the Gods may undeservedly be taken
too lightly by its readers.

216 COOPER, FREDERIC TABER. "Trick of the Familiar Touch and Some
Recent Novels." Bookman (New York) 19 (July):495.
[Passing reference to W's use of the familiar touch in his
fantastic romances.]

217 "A Dealer in Magic and Spells." SR (London) 98 (22 Oct.):
520-21.
Food of the Gods demonstrates that W seeks popularity at any
price, whatever the sacrifice.

218 ELLIS, HAVELOCK. "Another Prophet: H.G. Wells." Weekly
Critical Review, 19 Feb. Reprinted in Views and Reviews: A
Selection of Uncollected Articles, 1884-1932, 1st ser.
(London: Harmsworth, 1932), pp. 204-12; and in CH, pp. 94-98.
Whereas in performing his prophetic functions Shaw shares in
the spirit of the banderillero, W is closer to the matador in
Mankind. [Offers some in-depth criticism of W's ideas, including
a detected sense of parochialism, but vigorously supports the
book.]

219 "Fiction." Academy 67 (15 Oct.):338.
Possessing humor and a moral Food of the Gods is not impervious to criticism. What the race really needs is food for the
moral sense.

220 FILON, AUGUSTIN. "Romancier, prophète et reformateur: H.G.
Wells." Revue des deux mondes 24 (1 Dec.):584-86. Translated
in CH, pp. 54-56.
Similar to the Calvinism of Defoe's Journal of the Plague
Year, the determinism of War of the Worlds is not without an
optimism concerning mankind. The tension between primitive instincts and artificial law in mankind is the theme of the work.

221 "The Food of the Gods." TLS 30 Sept., p. 296.
Although vulnerable to practical questions, this book is one
of the simplest, most ingenious creations W has written.

222 LEMONNIER, PIERRE. "Les livres." Nouvelle revue 27
(1 April):431.
Anticipations is a book that must be read by anyone who
wants to know the future.

223 "Mr. Wells's Ideas." NYTSRB, 21 May, p. 349.
Original and suggestive, Mankind is replete with vigorous
expression and clear vision.

224   "New Novels." Athenaeum, no. 4016 (15 Oct.), pp. 512-13.
        Less a novel than an inspired tract, Food of the Gods is a
flawed but imaginative effort pregnant with satire.

225   "New Novels." MG, 5 Oct., p. 3.
        Food of the Gods is a jack-in-the-box that "gives us a
series of very excellent springs, but when we have closed the box
we have nothing but a few questions to ask and an unsatisfying
sense of disappointment."

226   "Novel Notes." Bookman (London) 25 (Jan.):186-87.
        Frankly a book for an idle hour, Twelve Stories is various
and entertaining.

227   "Novels." Spectator (London) 93 (15 Oct.):561.
        Food of the Gods opens as an irresponsible and apparently
jocular expression of the scientific imagination but ends as a
sort of tragedy.

228   "On the Line." Monthly Review (London) 17 (Oct.):172-74.
        Though it might be dismissed by some as juvenile, Food of
the Gods has "power, brilliance, imagination, ingenuity, elo-
quence, and humour." W's satire is sometimes very cruel but never
savage.

229   PRATT, CORNELIA ATWOOD. "Notes of a Novel Reader." Critic
        (New York) 45 (Dec.):543-44.
        Although Food of the Gods demands at least grudging respect,
its author is a charming writer who misuses his talent.

230   "Reform and Mr. Kipling." SR (London) 98 (15 Oct.):494.
        [This review of Traffics and Discoveries opens with the
remark that French critics have recently been agitated over the
stylistic errors of Kipling and W, the two writers on the Conti-
nent as representative of the best in contemporary English literature. The imagination of both writers is praised.]

231   "Sociology." Critic (New York) 45 (Sept.):287-88.
        [Brief mention of Mankind.]

                            1905

232   ADCOCK, A. ST. JOHN. "The Perfect World." Bookman (London) 28
        (June):95.
        Highly imaginative, Utopia presents a more realistic utopia
than similar works preceding it.

1905

233   BETTANY, F.G. "The World of Books." Sunday Times (London),
       29 Oct., p. 4.
            W's tender genius for finding the pitiful and gracious in
       vulgar lives is evident in Kipps, a book resembling Carton's play
       entitled Mr. Hopkinson. Replete with comic zest, the book is
       kindly to its protagonist and ferocious toward Britain's class
       distinctions.

234   "Books." Spectator (London) 95 (21 Oct.):610-11.
            Utopia presents some clever analyses of modern-day problems,
       and the spirit of W's endeavor in this work deserves praise.

235   "Books of the Day: Mr. Wells as Sociologist." DC, 11 April,
       p. 3.
            Combining the best of today's individualism with the com-
       munism of his view of a world-state, in Utopia W creates a utopia
       that, however vague in its government and international commerce,
       contributes to his reputation as a thinker and reflects his high
       standard of literary excellence.

236   "Books of the Week." Outlook (New York) 79 (29 April):1062.
            Twelve Stories shows that W is at his best in forms of short
       fiction rather than in longer romances.

237   "Books of the Week." Outlook (New York) 80 (3 June):345.
            Whatever response one may have to several specifics of
       Utopia, it remains an interesting, thoughtful book.

238   "Books of the Week." Outlook (New York) 81 (14 Oct.):382-83.
            In substance Kipps is sordid and dull, failing in comparison
       to Wheels of Chance.

239   "British Authors and Subjects." RR 32 (Dec.):759.
            Kipps is a brilliant study of a character. One sympathizes
       with the hero even while smiling at him.

240   BROCK, L.G. "Kipps." Bookman (London) 29 (Dec.):134-35.
            A more than brilliant work, this novel marks W's more ma-
       ture, more sympathetic insight into human nature.

241   "Comedy and Sociology." Public Opinion 39 (11 Nov.):633.
            The broad humorous characterization in Kipps suggests
       Dickens, though W's serious substratum is more earnest than tender
       and more sociological than humane.

242   CROSLAND, T.W.H. The Suburbans. London: Long, 1905,
       pp. 203-8.
            From Utopia it is clear that if suburbia is a force to be
       defeated, then W must be considered an enemy to society.

243   CROZIER, JOHN BEATTIE. "Mr. Wells as a Sociologist." FR 84
      (1 Sept.):417-26.
      The future world portrayed in Utopia has details derived
from existing sociological, economic, and political facts and
offers no scheme of operation by which it might be realized.

244   "Fiction." Academy 69 (28 Oct.):1129-30.
      Kipps is the most amusing and tender book W has ever
written.

245   "Fiction." Critic (New York) 47 (Nov.):478.
      Kipps is a success, helped by W's understanding of the
details of life.

246   H., J.H. "A Paradise for the Bureaucrat." New Age 17
      (27 April):262.
      W is best with "the shadowy border world, where science is
being wrought into shapes of beauty and passed through the crucible of the imagination." Utopia is inspiring, but its plan is far
from perfect.

247   "Jules Verne." Nation (New York) 80 (30 March):242-43.
      [Remarks that W is a follower of Verne.]

248   "Kipps." TLS, 27 Oct., p. 358.
      Though the range of W's vision is limited, he does bring an
original and acute mind to bear on his concerns in this amusing
book.

249   "Kipps and Others." NYTSRB, 7 Oct., p. 649.
      Sociological interests remain subordinate to a refreshingly
humorous story with well-drawn characters.

250   "Literature." Athenaeum, no. 4044 (29 April), pp. 519-20.
      Although many of the ideas presented in Utopia are open to
question, that they are the product of a single mind is amazing.
This work is an astonishing book embodying imaginative science at
its highest and proving most suggestive where the reader most
differs from W's views.

251   M., A.N. "Mr. Wells's Kipps." MG, 1 Nov., p. 5.
      Entertaining as well as serious, this book provides an
excellent example of W's humor and sagacity. The protagonist is
very human and his story becomes intimate knowledge.

252   MASTERMAN, C[HARLES], F.G. ["Kipps."] Daily News (London), 25
      Oct., p. 4. Reprinted in CH, pp. 122-25.
      Although this work is the best story W has written, author-
ial intrusions mar its artistry. Told with an unqualified

27

1905

simplicity, the book presents a protagonist who never encounters reality.

253   MAYOR, R. "A Modern Utopia." Independent Review 7 (Oct.):235–40. Reprinted in CH, pp. 112–17.
      Plato is the primary source of this reasonable study of utopia. W has woven together apparently contradictory conceptions that neither he nor anyone else has ever before put together so well.

254   "Mr. Wells' Utopia." SR (London) 99 (15 April):492–93.
      The ideas in Utopia are well presented but not particularly original.

255   "Mr. Wells's Utopia." MG, 25 April, p. 5.
      A noble and worthy dream, Utopia makes a serious contribution to man's self-consciousness.

256   "Mr. Wells's Utopia." TLS, 5 May, p. 144.
      Utopia is the most interesting, creative, and probable of plans for utopias designed since science began to influence ideas of the future.

257   "A Modern Utopia." Academy 68 (15 April):414–15.
      This book demonstrates W's gift for making his speculations interesting to the general reader.

258   "A Modern Utopia." EDR 102 (July):56–78.
      W's outline for world reform is more credible than any other utopian history.

259   "A Modern Utopia." RR 31 (June):764.
      An admirable piece of literature, this book is replete with unlimited suggestiveness. As literature and as philosophy it is a masterpiece.

260   "New Novels." Athenaeum, no. 4073 (18 Nov.):681.
      An engrossing story of warm human life today, Kipps is the sort of work W should be doing. It fulfills the promise of Wheels of Chance.

261   "Notable Books of the Day." LD 31 (23 Sept.):427–28.
      [A negative response to Utopia, citing other reviews as well, concluding with the hope that this is W's last venture of the sort.]

262   "Novels." Spectator (London) 95 (4 Nov.):718–19.
      Too many reviewers have interpreted the aim of Kipps as satirical; on the contrary, in many ways the novel represents the most human and sympathetic of W's stories.

263   "Novels and Stories." Glasgow Herald, 9 Nov., p. 11.
       Although it presents its story somewhat mercilessly and
perhaps in too great detail, Kipps is ingeniously done and proves
generally diverting.

264   OLIVIER, SYDNEY. ["A Modern Utopia."] Fabian News 15
       (Aug.):38-39. Reprinted in CH, pp. 110-12.
       [Favorable review of the book.]

265   "A Review of the Season's Fiction." ARR 32:757-63.
       Making us sympathetic to him even as we smile at him, the
protagonist of Kipps is superbly presented.

266   ROOK, CLARENCE. "The Simple Draper." DC, 23 Oct., p. 3.
       Kipps is a satire on the English social system, which
triumphs over the protagonist in the novel. Tinged with underlying bitterness, W's humor is at its finest in this book.

267   S., F.C.S. "Sociological Speculations." Nature 72
       (10 Aug.):337-38.
       The spirit of Utopia is remarkably Platonic, excepting W's
stress on individual freedom. On the whole W is wiser than former
utopists in that he allows for progressive growth toward
perfection.

268   S[MALL], A[LBION] W. "A Modern Utopia." American Journal of
       Sociology 11 (Nov.):430-31.
       This work offers little more than good-natured satire.

269   "The Story of a Simple Soul." SR (London) 100 (18 Nov.):658,
       660.
       Focusing on present-day England, Kipps is remarkable in its
characterization and wit. The protagonist would hardly have been
a caricature if his defective speech had not been exaggerated.

270   [WARREN, THOMAS HERBERT.] "Books." Spectator (London) 95
       (21 Oct.):610-11. Reprinted in CH, pp. 117-21.
       Utopia presents some clever analyses of modern-day problems,
and the spirit of W's endeavor in this work deserves praise.

1906

271   ADAMS, JOHN. "The Future in America." Bookman (London) 31
       (Dec.):142-43.
       A fairly pessimistic work, this study deals less with the
future than with the present in America.

272   ADCOCK, A. ST. JOHN. "Mr. Wells's New Novel." Bookman
       (London) 31 (Oct.):38-39.

1906

> While interesting and imaginative, Comet presents an un-
believable, absurd idea.

273   "American Ideals." Athenaeum, no. 4125 (17 Nov.), pp. 614-15.
      Lucid and discriminating description is probably worth more
than prophecy in Future in America.

274   BETTANY, F.G. "The World of Books." Sunday Times (London), 30
      Sept., p. 2.
      One of his best, most delightful romances, Comet demon-
strates W's concern with the spiritual rather than the material
(as critics have charged him) comforts of mankind. He uses the
romance form, improved by his lucid style and wonderful insight
into middle-class life, to disseminate his ideas to a larger
audience than he could reach with scientific treatises.

275   "Books." Spectator (London) 97 (3 Nov.):683-84.
      W generalizes and exaggerates too much in Future in America.

276   "Books of the Day." Arena 36 (Dec.):683.
      Although at the outset Comet proves unconvincing, it is far
more than merely an interesting romance characterized by W's fine
literary style.

277   BROOKS, SYDNEY. "Mr. H.G. Wells and the American Sphinx."
      Living Age 251 (1 Dec.):565-69.
      Little of permanent consequence in the United States is
ignored in Future in America.

278   "Comment on Current Books." Outlook (New York) 84
      (3 Nov.):582.
      The latter part of Comet is not thoroughly worked out or
very interesting. W's solution in which two men happily love the
same woman is mystifying and ridiculous.

279   DANIELS, WINTHROP MORE. "Significant Books in Economics and
      Sociology." AM 98 (June):840-41.
      Utopia is a first class work in literary power and insight
into man's social nature.

280   DOTY, MADELEINE Z. "The Socialist in Recent Fiction."
      Charities and the Commons 17 (Dec.):487-88.
      Comet presents W's ideal imaginatively portrayed.

281   "Fiction." Academy 71 (15 Sept.):266.
      Comet expresses W's enthusiasm for human potentiality and
his impatience with the injustice and stupidity of the present
order of things.

282   "A Guide to the New Books." LD 33 (27 Oct.):596.
      Actually no more than a brilliant piece of descriptive
writing, Comet is fascinating but not W's best book.

283   "A Guide to the New Books." LD 33 (1 Dec.):814.
      Future in America is an able and earnest appraisal by a
modern thinker.

284   H., C.M. "A Modern Utopia." Journal of Political Economy 14
      (Nov.):581-82.
      As one reads this easy narrative, he is convinced that
utopia, like heaven, is within.

285   HENDERSON, CHARLES RICHMOND. "Partisans and Historians in
      Social Science." Dial 40 (1 May):296-97.
      Anyone who asks for facts in support of hypotheses will grow
weary of Utopia.

286   HOBSON, J.A. "The New Aristocracy of Mr. Wells." CR 89
      (April):487-97.
      Although W's notions about future society are unsound partly
because they are founded on mistaken ideas about human nature, his
courage, method, and skill in expressing them deserve consideration.

287   HOWELLS, W[ILLIAM] D[EAN]. "Kipps." NAR 183 (31 Oct.):795-98.
      Reprinted in CH, pp. 128-31.
      Mr. Lewisham is one of the very best books of the last few
years, and Kipps is only somewhat weaker. The latter work suffers
from too much plot, though the faults of the book, particularly
authorial intrusions, are less those of W than of the "bad English
school of fictional art."

288   "In the Days of the Comet." TLS, 14 Sept., p. 314.
      The readers of this book are advised to give it serious
attention as soon as the comet descending from the machine
appears.

289   ["Kipps."] CL 40:109-10.
      W's satire is superior to his pseudoscientific fiction, and
in this work it is sweetened by human interest. [Remarks on
reviews of the novel.]

290   LEE, VERNON. "On Modern Utopias: An Open Letter to H.G.
      Wells." FR 86 (Dec.):1121-37.
      While one might wish for the well-organized republic de-
picted in Utopia, the existence of a samurai implies its opposite,
thereby undercutting W's dream of the future. W overlooks "the
imperious now and the imperious self."

1906

291   "The Lounger." Critic (New York) 48 (May):394-95.
       [Relates W's visit and reaction to America.]

292   "Matters of the Moment." Daily Express (London), 19 Sept.,
       p. 4.
       [An editorial response to W's letter (printed in the same
    issue) countering reviews of Comet suggesting his allegiance to
    socialism.]

293   "Mr. Wells's Comet." Outlook (London), 18 (15 Sept.):351-52.
       Reprinted in CH, pp. 133-36.
       Like Kipling, W has slowly deserted art for the sermon; and
    in the case of Comet, one cannot escape the feeling that it was
    meant to be more of a story than a treatise. W's unquestionable
    artistry, so evident in the first part of the book, dissolves with
    the arrival of the comet.

294   "Modern Democracy and Its Problems." RR 34 (Dec.):760.
       Future in America is interesting, though deficient in its
    knowledge of American conditions.

295   "New Novels." Athenaeum, no. 4118 (29 Sept.), p. 362.
       On the whole Comet testifies to the imagination and intel-
    lect of one of the most original thinkers of the day.

296   "Notes on Authors." PW 69 (21 April):1215.
       [Reports itinerary and publication plans concerning W's trip
    to America.]

297   "Novels." Spectator (London) 97 (6 Oct.):496-97.
       A dramatized sociological treatise, Comet indicts many of
    the illnesses and much of the ugliness of our present social and
    political system.

298   "Novels with a Philosophy." EDR 203 (Jan.):64-84. Reprinted
       in LA 248 (24 March):724-40.
       In Kipps W insinuates ideas beneath the guise of drollery,
    successfully joining a humorous story and a tract on education.

299   PAYNE, WILLIAM MORTON. "Recent Fiction--Wells's Kipps." Dial
       40 (1 Jan.):17-18. Reprinted in CH, pp. 127-28.
       W possesses a Dickens-like gift for portraying eccentric
    traits and types of character.

300   "Two Important Books." Daily Express (London), 14 Sept., p. 4.
       Apart from its overemphatic, ineffective denunciations,
    Comet is a clever book.

301   "A Vision of a New World." SR (London) 102 (10 Nov.):581-82.
      Future in America is a good book, but its issues concern
present-day America rather than its future.

302   "Wells' Comet." SR (London) 102 (22 Sept.):365. Reprinted in
      CH, pp. 136-39.
      Comet represents at best only a clever kind of polemic; it
is a compilation of much that W has used before in magazine articles. Possibly the book satirizes women and socialism.

303   "Wells's New Story." Clarion (London), 21 Sept., p. 4.
      Comet is to date W's best story.

304   "Wells's Patent Comet." NYTSRB, 3 Nov., p. 719.
      W's union of imagination and scientific detail has achieved
better results in earlier works than in Comet.

305   Y., T.M., "Mr. Wells's New Novel." MG, 14 Sept., p. 3.
      Excellence and imperfection mark Comet. Only W could have
undertaken such a huge canvas, and even W is not wholly successful
in covering it with a real picture. Many readers prefer W's
gospel better than his way of proclaiming it and wish that his
attitude toward mankind "were rather less that of Olympian Jove
watching the struggles of a capsized beetle."

                              1907

306   de WYZEWA, T. "Le roman anglais en 1907." Revue des deux
      mondes 42 (15 Nov.):443-46 [not seen]. Extract translated in
      CH, pp. 142-45.
      Since W converted to socialism, the artist in him has given
way to the thinker, a sad transformation all too apparent in
Comet.

307   DROPPERS, GARRETT. "Book Reviews." Journal of Political
      Economy 15 (Feb.):174-77.
      [A favorable review of Future in America.]

308   "First Public Conference on Mr. H.G. Wells' 'Samurai.'" New
      Age, n.s. 1 (2 May):9-11.
      [Reports in detail the discussion of the samurai of Utopia
held at the New Reform Club on 11 April.]

309   "The 'Frozen Stride' as a Symbol of Boston's Culture." CL 42
      (April):404-6.
      [Discusses the controversy aroused in Boston by W's "The
Boston Enchantment" (later included in Future in America), espe-
cially as expressed in the Boston Evening Transcript, the New York
Evening Post, and the Boston Herald.]

1907

310   GALBRAITH. "H.G. Wells's New Life Study." <u>NYTSRB</u>, 12 Jan.,
       p. 19.
           Although W "takes himself, his mammouth rats, and his long-
       tailed comets with almost comic seriousness," his proposed study
       of race relations in America could be valuable.

311   "General Literature." <u>ALA</u> 3 (Feb.):50.
           Insight and sympathy characterize <u>Future in America</u>.

312   GUEST, L. HADEN. ["<u>In the Days of the Comet</u>."] <u>Fabian News</u> 17
       (Jan.):13-14. Reprinted in <u>CH</u>, pp. 140-41.
           This interesting and beautiful book should prove incendiary.

313   ["<u>In the Days of the Comet</u>."] <u>CL</u> 41:700-701.
           W is three novelists--realist, romanticist, and idealist--in
       one, and all three converge in this work. The result is interest-
       ing but unsatisfactory. [Remarks on reviews of the novel.]

314   "A Modern Prophet's Indictment of Our Civilization." <u>CL</u> 42
       (Jan.):78-80.
           [Primarily a descriptive review, with extensive quotations,
       of <u>Future in America</u>.]

315   MOSS, MARY. "The New Novels." <u>AM</u> 99 (Jan.):115.
           W wastes his talent as a genuine novelist in <u>Comet</u> by offer-
       ing unconvincing socialistic remedies.

316   MUIRHEAD, JAMES F. "Some Recent Books on the United States."
       <u>AM</u> 100 (Oct.):563-66.
           The attitude of <u>Future in America</u> is not the condescending
       one expected in such books written by British authors. One weak-
       ness, as in some of his other works, is W's apparent lack of
       interest in art.

317   "Mystery and Fantasy." <u>RR</u> 35 (Jan.):126.
           <u>Comet</u> is more sociological tract than a novel. Its ideas
       are fascinating even if not readily acceptable.

318   "Notes." <u>AAAP</u> 29 (Jan.):226-27.
           [Favorable review of <u>Future in America</u>.]

319   "The Novels of the Season." <u>ARR</u> 35:119-25.
           Sociological tract rather than a novel, <u>Comet</u> is unsuccess-
       ful as a story, though its ideas are presented with brilliancy.

320   PERRY, JOHN. "Social Problems in America." <u>Nature</u> 75
       (17 Jan.):265-66.
           <u>Future in America</u> is acutely observant, well-informed, and
       reasonable. The book marks a positive step in solving the prob-
       lems it discusses.

321   "A Prophet Abroad." Outlook (New York) 85 (2 March):526-27.
        Future in America is replete with quotable quotations.

322   "Reviews." Educational Review 34 (June):105.
        Instead of praise, Future in America warrants censure for
   its bad English and its superficiality.

323   "Socialism and Sex Relations." Spectator (London) 99
        (19 Oct.):558-59.
        Comet features free love as a principle facet of W's utopian
   state.

324   SPENDER, HAROLD. "H.G. Wells and His Work." PMM 40
        (Dec.):739-46.
        [A character sketch.]

325   UNWIN, GEORGE. "Socialism and the Family." International
        Journal of Ethics 17 (July):523-26.
        The danger in this book is W's premature formulation of his
   social philosophy.

326   VAN WESTRUM, A. SCHADE. "Mr. Wells's Future in America."
        Bookman (New York) 24 (Jan.):482-84.
        This book is hasty, superficial, and inconclusive.

                                    1908

327   BARRY, WILLIAM. "Forecasts of To-Morrow." QR 209 (July):1-27.
        [A somewhat skeptical discussion of Anticipations and New
   Worlds.]

328   BELLOC, HILAIRE. "A Letter to Wells." New Age, n.s. 3
        (17 Dec.):160-61.
        [Places Last Things primarily in the nominalist camp, yet
   notes elements intimating a realist position.]

329   BENNETT, ARNOLD. "Wells and His New Worlds." New Age, n.s. 2
        (14 March):391.
        [Unqualified praise for the book and extensive criticism of
   its reviewers.]

330   "Book Notes." Political Science Quarterly 23 (Sept.):556.
        Charm and grace of style add to the valuable content of New
   Worlds.

331   "Books on Socialism." Athenaeum, no. 4194 (14 March), p. 320.
        [A brief, gentle dismissal of New Worlds.

1908

332   BRUCE, H. ADDINGTON. "More Books on Socialism." Outlook (New
      York) 89 (20 June):388-89.
      [A gentle repudiation of the notion of socialism presented
in New Worlds.]

333   CANNAN, EDWIN. "New Worlds for Old." Economic Journal 18
      (Sept.):417-21.
      Where in principle is the difference between our present
condition and the socialistic world depicted in this book? Why
can't socialists be a little more courageous?

334   CHESTERTON, G.K. "On Wells and a Glass of Beer." New Age,
      n.s. 2 (25 Jan.):250.
      Whereas Dickens's imagination delved inside certain human
habits and saw them as large, W's imagination remains outside and
sees them as small. Unlike Dickens, W expresses a contempt for
mankind. Moreover, like so many socialists, W cites modern evils
that could not in the slightest be remedied by socialism.

335   "Current Fiction." Nation (New York) 87 (31 Dec.):655.
      Bert Smallways, a symbol of the average common sense of the
world, is a rich creation in the exciting War in the Air.

336   "Essays in Sociology." RR 37 (May):640.
      [Cites the clear style of New Worlds.]

337   FETTER, FRANK A. "New Worlds for Old." Economic Bulletin 1
      (April):53-55.
      This is the most sensible and least socialistic of recent
socialistic works, a good tract for social reformers.

338   "First and Last Things." TLS, 19 Nov., p. 419.
      Although W's philosophy tends to be eclectic, this incisive
book reveals his open-minded ability to disentangle facts from
irrelevancies and to stimulate thought.

339   FLOWER, B.O. "New Worlds for Old." Arena 39 (May):586-89.
      This work is the best popular treatment of socialism to
date.

340   "General Literature." ALA 4 (May):153.
      New Worlds is lucid, interesting, and open-minded.

341   "H.G. Wells's Confession of Faith." CL 45:648-52.
      Derived from lectures given to the Fabian Society, Last
Things recounts a skeptic's discovery of religious faith in life
and in himself. [Remarks on reviews of the novel.]

342   "The Ideas of Mr. H.G. Wells." QR 208 (April):472-90.
       In a striking manner W exhibits the virtues and defects of
the new English bourgeoisie. Superstitiousness is one trait he
shares with the barbaric mind, and his view of human life is
pagan. He has two moods: sometimes "he is the artificial creature of an education based on abstract science, to whose cold,
unmoved intelligence the life of humanity is a colourless specta-
cle"; at other times he is like Dickens. In the latter mood he is
a fine novelist, "the idiosyncrosy of whose genius resides in the
power of quick and winning sympathy with which he irradiates every
petty, commonplace detail in the life of the lower-middle classes."
In the former mood he inclines toward a frantic, fanatical sermon
presenting a Calvinistic socialism.

343   "Literature." Athenaeum, no. 4232 (5 Dec.), pp. 713-14.
       Last Things indicates that W is devoting his life "to the
cult of the Synthesis." Though he at times is diverted into
impassable paths, the book is vivid and stimulating.

344   M., A.N. "New Novels." MG, 28 Oct., p. 5.
       More didactic, more sociological, and less plausible that
War of the Worlds, War in the Air still presents a splendid narrative. Characteristically W lets us see all the events through
the eyes of a little Cockney.

345   MALLOCK, W.H. "Persuasive Socialism." NCA 63 (May):852-68.
       [Extensive refutation of W's views on socialism.]

346   "Mr. Wells in His Earlier Manner." NYTSRB, 14 Nov., p. 668.
       War in the Air entertains while it gently instructs. The
account of Bert Smallways's boyhood is most diverting.

347   MUSSEY, H.R. ["New Worlds for Old."] AAAP 32 (Sept.):467-68.
       [On the whole a very favorable review of the book.]

348   "New Heavens--While You Wait." SR (London) 106 (5 Dec.):700.
       [Criticizes W's advocation of socialism and free-love in
Last Things.]

349   "New Novels." Athenaeum, no. 4229 (14 Nov.), p. 602.
       Replete with vivid impressions, War in the Air is marred by
confusion and story-telling deficiencies.

350   "Notes." AAAP 28 (June):112.
       Comet fails as a serious study of social conditions and as a
story about love.

351   "Novel Notes." Bookman (London) 35 (Dec.):158.
       War in the Air is a typical W book, of which the life and
soul is the character Bert Smallways.

1908

352   "Novels." SR (London) 106 (14 Nov.):614, 616.
        War in the Air suffers from the fact that W tried to make it
   simultaneously a novel, a romance, a social study, and a prophetic
   anticipation.

353   "Novels." Spectator (London) 101 (12 Dec.):1001-2.
        War in the Air is an excellent example of W's mastery of the
   romance.

354   PALEY, G.A. "Conciliatory Socialism." New Quarterly 1
       (Oct.):563-78.
        W's idea of socialism in New Worlds depends on dubious
   assumptions about human nature and about economics.

355   "Reviews." Educational Review 36 (June):102.
        The content of New Worlds is grotesque and tiresome. The
   vogue enjoyed by W is a mystery.

356   S., P. "Theoretical Socialism." Academy 74 (9 May):759-60.
        The social optimism of New Worlds is ludicrous.

357   SETH, JAMES. "Reviews." HJ 6 (July):910-17.
        In New Worlds W manifests some irritating mannerisms, and
   his humor is not always in good taste.

358   SHARP, CLIFFORD. "Reviews." New Age, n.s. 2 (21 March):
       412-13.
        New Worlds marks an epoch in the history of English social-
   ism. Although it is not quite fair to the Fabian Society, it
   presents a dynamic rather than a static notion of socialism.

359   "A Sober Socialist." SR (London) 105 (28 March):405-6.
        In New Worlds W is pragmatic in his expectations of a so-
   cialist system. [Distinguishes between Marxist socialism and that
   of Wells.]

360   "Socialism and Its Critics." Nation (New York) 86
       (28 May):491.
        Little new in W's thinking is evident in New Worlds, a book
   that also suffers from its author's use of neologistic plurals.

361   "Soft Socialism." TLS, 19 March, pp. 89-90.
        New Worlds suffers from the lack of any coherent meaning or
   clearly thought out problem. W covers ground about which others
   know more than he.

362   "Three Books on Socialism." Spectator (London) 101
       (3 Oct.):471.

The society portrayed in New Worlds is alluring but not convincing.

363   "The War in the Air." TLS, 5 Nov., p. 390.
        This book may be powerful, terrifying, and suggestive, but
it finally amounts to "a boisterous piece of fiction." In spite
of its imaginative qualities, it fails as a serious work of art
because, like other of W's books, it sins aginst the first canon
of art—unity of tone.

364   X. "The Socialism of Mr. Wells." Academy 75 (22 Aug.):181-82.
        [Attacks W's praise of socialistic free love as expressed in
"My Socialism," an essay published in CR.]

365   Y., Y. "Apocryphal Apocalypses." Bookman (London) 34
        (April):27-29.
        New Worlds suffers from several defects, chiefly partial
views and unsound judgments.

366   YOUNG, FILSON. "On Shaw, Wells, Chesterton, and Belloc." New
        Age, n.s. 2 (7 March):370.
        W is not a revolutionary social reformer or even a good
socialist; he is simply a teller of tales.

1909

367   "Ann Veronica." Nation (London) 6 (23 Oct.):167-68. Reprinted
        in CH, pp. 165-69.
        Less a story than an honest and readable study of unrest,
this book lacks the intimacy and humor of Kipps or the epic sweep
of Tono-Bungay. W applies the dissector's scalpel to modern
English society.

368   "Ann Veronica." TLS, 7 Oct., p. 364.
        Rather formless, this novel is nonetheless actual and vivid.
The heroine represents a type of woman who "has never been so
keenly noted and courageously described as in this novel."

369   BARRY, WILLIAM. "The Story of Ann Veronica." Bookman (London)
        37 (Nov.):89-90.
        Advancing the notion of free love, Ann Veronica is "dan-
gerous to every woman into whose hands it is likely to fall."

370   BETTANY, F.G. "The World of Books." Sunday Times (London), 14
        Feb., p. 5.
        Strangely amorphous and subjective, Tono-Bungay lacks struc-
tural compactness and unity of design. Although W is too apt to
overshadow his characters, his book still manages to be interesting

1909

in many respects and possesses passages compelling in style and sentiment.

371 _____. "The World of Books." Sunday Times (London), 10 Oct., p. 5.
        Admirably lucid, insightfully thorough, albeit not a little coarse, Ann Veronica presents one of the most passionate and unconventional love stories in recent fiction. The book proves most perceptive concerning parent and sibling relationships.

372 BLAND, HUBERT. "Books of the Day: Something Like a Novel." DC (London), 9 Feb., p. 3. Reprinted in CH, pp. 146-47.
        Even more so than Kipps, Tono-Bungay suffers badly from W's attempt to be too inclusive. Too frequently essays interrupt the story.

373 "Books." Spectator (London) 102 (9 Jan.):59-60.
        W's quasi-religion in Last Things is unsympathetic to most of his readers. His brand of socialism and his optimism are also defective.

374 CHESSON, W.H. "Mr. Wells's New Novel." DC, 4 Oct., p. 3.
        In spite of the fact that it is nearly a perfect work of realism, Ann Veronica is bound to offend some readers. Thackeray would have admired the satire of this plotless, kindly audacious, adroitly written work. On the subject of love, W "is eloquent almost to newness."

375 CLARK, WARD. "H.G. Wells's Tono-Bungay." Bookman (New York) 29 (March):92-93.
        An amorphous tale, this book develops symphonically the themes of modern industry and finance.

376 CLEAR, CLAUDIUS. "The Correspondence of Claudius Clear." British Weekly, 18 Feb., p. 549.
        Tono-Bungay is an extremely clever book, the hero of which expresses views diametrically opposed to those of W. It attacks Christianity principally because the latter advocates chastity. Writing from the point of view of a B. Sc., W reduces his characters to animals without morals. There is no compunction as to the fate of the women in the book.

377 "Comment on Current Books." Outlook (New York) 91 (30 Jan.):243.
        Socialism is interesting but finally disappointing.

378 "Comment on Current Books." Outlook (New York) 91 (6 March):534.

1909

The narrative is too leisurely in Tono-Bungay, a book that also suffers from a tumultuous outpouring of concluding incidents. Its love story is not in the best taste.

379   COOPER, FREDERIC TABER. "Feminine Unrest and Some Recent Novels." Bookman (New York) 30 (Dec.):383-84.
Though thoughtful with regard to a young girl's education in the school of life, Ann Veronica suffers from bad logic, the use of chance, and unconvincing character development.

380   CRAUFURD, ALEXANDER H. The Religion of H.G. Wells and Other Essays. London: Unwin, 1909, pp. 111-15.
In some ways W's agnosticism tempered by pragmatism, as expressed in Last Things, is quite wise. He rejects scientific and philosophic dogmatism as readily as he does that of the theologian. With regard to the doctrine that there is a God, W is inconsistent; he admits purpose but not a purposing mind. Like Spencer, W is mistaken in rejecting Christ as being too mournful and not really human. The sort of religion W has defined is at best a temporary refuge lacking an assured permanence and an ethical coherence.

381   "Current Fiction." Nation (New York) 88 (18 Feb.):170-71.
Characters are more important than plot in Tono-Bungay, a book written somewhat in the Victorian manner.

382   "The Enthusiastic Mr. Wells." NYTSRB, 2 Jan., p. 9.
[Review of Socialism and Boots.]

383   "A Few Recent Novels." RR 39 (March):384.
Tono-Bungay is a vivacious novel of the familiar sort concerning life today.

384   "Fiction." ALA 4 (Jan.):27.
War in the Air is interesting but somewhat unpleasant.

385   "General Literature." ALA 4 (Feb.):53.
The sober chapters of Last Things are pervaded with lucidity of thought and a persuasive dynamic force.

386   "General Literature." ALA 5 (March):87.
Socialism gives an adequate view of the subject.

387   [GRAVES, CHARLES L.] "Novels." Spectator (London) 102 (27 Feb.):346. Reprinted in CH, pp. 151-53.
W identifies too closely with the narrator of Tono-Bungay. "In this strange go-as-you-please narrative which, in spite of its irregular and discursive method, is the most serious attempt at a

novel which he has hitherto undertaken, Mr. Wells has given us a strong, sincere, but in the main repellent work."

388   "H.G. Wells: Alarmist." <u>Bookman</u> (New York) 30 (Sept.):21.
      [Observes W's concern over the degeneration of the English people.]

389   HACKETT, FRANCIS. "The Modern: <u>Tono-Bungay</u>." <u>Chicago Evening Post Literary Review</u>, 26 March. Reprinted in <u>Horizons: A Book of Criticism</u> (New York: Huebsch, 1918), pp. 101-8.
      Although as a novel this work is too exuberant and too unsifted, it is rich and satisfying. Reflecting the views of the modernist—"hard on himself and others, dark with doubt, shot with aspiration, beauty and hope"—this work extends the frontiers of the novel.

390   HARRIS, G.W. "The Development of a Novelist." <u>RR</u> 40 (Oct.):508-9.
      American readers have not yet realized W's importance. [Includes biographical sketch of W.]

391   M., A.N. "Mr. Wells's New Book." <u>MG</u>, 4 Oct., p. 5.
      The protagonist of <u>Ann Veronica</u> does not appeal as a charming person or as an arresting human; nor does the book as a whole provide the exhileration that emerges from the fine art of <u>Tono-Bungay</u>.

392   _____. "Tono-Bungay." <u>MG</u>, 10 Feb., p. 5.
      This is a vastly entertaining book, in which the invention of Tono-Bungay serves as a symbol for a phase of human development. The book offers no easy solution, no smug socialist answer, and such inconclusiveness signifies the gropings of a great spirit. This is the saddest, strongest, and most intimate of W's works.

393   MASTERMAN, C[HARLES] F.G. <u>The Condition of England</u>. 1909 [not seen]. Reprint. London: Methuen, 1960, pp. xii, xiii-xiv, xxvi, 62, 72, 116-17, 129-30, 133-34, 170, 180-83, 196, 218, 220, 224-27, 229, 232-33.
      [Passing references to W and quotations from <u>Kipps</u>, <u>Last Things</u>, and <u>Tono-Bungay</u> to support Masterman's observations on the social conditions, attitudes, and values of pre-World War I England.]

394   "Mr. Wells As Feminist." <u>Glasgow Herald</u>, 5 Oct., p. 3.
      Unquestionably a good novel, <u>Ann Veronica</u> nevertheless disappoints after <u>Tono-Bungay</u>. There is little display of intensity of character, including the heroine who just misses truthfulness as a woman. The protagonist is really W in petticoats.

395   "Mr. Wells's Latest Book." <u>Glasgow Herald</u>, 9 Feb., p. 2.
        The best book W ever wrote and the most remarkable novel in
recent years, <u>Tono-Bungay</u> offers even a fuller measure of insight
and humor than <u>Kipps</u>. Its one fault is too much intellectualizing
and too little range of emotion, with a consequent dwindling of
W's humorous optimism.

396   MORSE, JOHN T. "The United States through Foreign Spectacles."
        <u>QR</u> 211 (Oct.):376-80.
        Although it seems audacious of W to prophesy in <u>Future in
America</u> after such a short visit, he manages to catch shrewdly the
nature of the situation.

397   "New Novels." <u>Athenaeum</u>, no. 4246 (13 March), p. 312.
        W's narrative style has become more abrupt and parenthetic
in <u>Tono-Bungay</u>, but his manner has grown along with his mannerisms. The novel is very fine.

398   "New Novels." <u>Athenaeum</u>, no. 4277 (16 Oct.), p. 456.
        <u>Ann Veronica</u> is an astonishingly brilliant story. It suf-
fers perhaps from a main character who seems the invention of the
author for the purpose of hanging his theories and cultivating his
plot.

399   "New York Book Announcements." <u>NYTSRB</u>, 16 Jan., p. 33.
        [Reports on <u>Tono-Bungay</u>, which W describes as an old-
fashioned novel unlike his previous scientific works.]

400   "Novels." <u>SR</u> (London) 107 (6 March):309-10.
        <u>Tono-Bungay</u> "is shrewd, amusing, melancholy, and almost free
from that indefinable quality for which no other word than 'cheap-
ness' has yet been devised." It is the best book W has written,
and it should be useful to future historians of English society.

401   "Novels." <u>Spectator</u> (London) 102 (27 Feb.):346.
        W identifies too closely with the narrator of <u>Tono-Bungay</u>.
"In this strange go-as-you-please narrative which, in spite of its
irregular and discursive method, is the most serious attempt at a
novel which he has hitherto undertaken, Mr. Wells has given us a
strong, sincere, but in the main repellent work."

402   O'LONDON, JOHN [pseud. of Wilfred Whitten]. ["<u>Ann Veronica</u>."]
        <u>JOL</u> 14 (22 Oct.):537-38. Reprinted in <u>CH</u>, pp. 160-64.
        The selfish protagonist of this book is not very real or
human but rather a typical embodiment of ideas. She invites women
"to run amuck through life in the name of self-fulfillment."

403   PAYNE, WILLIAM MORTON. "Recent Fiction--Wells's <u>The War in the
        Air</u>." <u>Dial</u> 46 (1 Feb.):85.
        The protagonist is the most effective aspect of this book.

1909

404   _____ . "Recent Fiction--Wells's Tono-Bungay." Dial 46
         (16 April):262-63.
             Its comedy and philosophy notwithstanding, this work fails
         to penetrate and its protagonist lacks heroic qualities.

405   R., E. "English Literature of Today." ER 3 (Nov.):666-68.
             W unconsciously revels in his own personality when writing
         fiction, with the result that at times he performs astonishingly
         well while at other times he performs atrociously. His preoccupa-
         tion with intellectual matters dampens his imaginative virtues,
         and aesthetically he is as artless as Dickens.

406   "Reviews." New Age, n.s. 5 (14 Oct.):447.
             A surprisingly poor book, Ann Veronica offers further proof
         that men can write of women only from the outside. One hopes it
         is a temporary aberration for W.

407   REYNOLDS, STEPHEN. "Mr. Wells's Confession." Bookman (London)
         35 (Jan.):193-94.
             Last Things represents another link in the chain of W's
         expression of his own self-education.

408   SCOTT-JAMES, R.A. "Woman." Daily News (London), 4 Oct., p. 3.
         Reprinted in CH, pp. 157-60.
             Although an excellent novel, Ann Veronica focuses on ideas,
         and it is at the level of its psychological notions that the book
         falters. Especially dubious is the solution W provides for his
         protagonist.

409   SHAW, BERNARD. "H.G. Wells and the Rest of Us." Christian
         Commonwealth (19 May). Reprinted in Pen Portraits and Reviews
         (London: Constable, 1932), pp. 279-83.
             [A satiric portrait of W, particularly concerning his views
         of the Fabian Society, beginning with W "is a spoiled child. His
         life has been one long promotion."]

410   [SHERWOOD, MARGARET ?] "A Survey of Recent Fiction." AM 103
         (May):705-6.
             Tono-Bungay is a prose epic written in a somewhat slipshod
         journalistic style. Although its manner lacks distinction, the
         book is wholesome.

411   "The Shop-Girl." SR (London) 108 (9 Oct.):444-45.
             An interesting study of human nature, Ann Veronica suffers
         from W's materialism and realism, particularly in the matter of
         sex.

412   S[HORTER], C[LEMENT] K. "A Literary Letter." Sphere 39
         (9 Oct.):vi.

In <u>Ann Veronica</u> W is still interesting but no longer an artist. Despite its good journalism, the book will prove pernicious in its influence. It also possesses a strain of vulgarity.

413 _____. "A Literary Letter." <u>Sphere</u> 39 (18 Dec.):268.
Although it is painful to disparage anything W has written, the sad fact is that in <u>Ann Veronica</u> he "has perpetrated the error of his life."

414 [STRACHEY, JOHN ST. LOE.] "A Poisonous Book." <u>Spectator</u> (London) 103 (20 Nov.):846-47. Reprinted in <u>CH</u>, pp. 169-72.
[Uses <u>Ann Veronica</u> as an excuse to lecture on Christian ethics, particularly concerning feminine self-restraint.]

415 ["<u>Tono-Bungay</u>."] <u>CL</u> 46:338-39.
[Remarks on several reviews of the novel.]

416 ["<u>Tono-Bungay</u>."] <u>DT</u>, 10 Feb., p. 15. Reprinted in <u>CH</u>, pp. 147-50.
One of the most significant of modern novels, this book is W's <u>David Copperfield</u>. Concerned with the theme of human waste, the novel displays a breadth and intensity far beyond W's previous writings.

417 "<u>Tono-Bungay</u>." <u>TLS</u>, 11 Feb., pp. 52-53.
The salient feature of this book is that it takes a comprehensive view of modern life. W's success in this work argues well for the use of the novel as a vehicle for ideas.

418 "Tono Wells." <u>Academy</u> 76 (16 March):845-46.
<u>Tono-Bungay</u> is so good that W's previous career may be conveniently forgotten.

419 TONSON, JACOB [pseud. of Arnold Bennett]. "Books and Persons." <u>New Age</u>, n.s. 4 (4 March):384-85. Reprinted in <u>Books and Persons: Being Comments on a Past Epoch, 1908-1911</u> (London: Chatto & Windus, 1917), pp. 109-16. Reprinted in <u>The Author's Craft and Other Critical Writings of Arnold Bennett</u>, ed. Samuel Hynes (Lincoln: University of Nebraska Press, 1968), pp. 198-202; and in <u>CH</u>, pp. 154-56.
<u>Tono-Bungay</u>, W's most powerful book, is an epic portraying the collision of George Ponderevo's soul with his epoch. No other "novelist ever more audaciously tried, or failed with more honour, to render in the limits of one book the enormous confusing complexity of a nation's racial existence."

420 "Wells Portrays the New Woman." <u>New York Times</u>, Autumn Book Number, pt. 1., 22 Oct., p. 622.

1909

Ann Veronica proves a surprisingly clever and able portrait
of a contemporary woman.

1910

421   "Ancient and Modern Stoicism." QR 212 (April):581.
       W's portrait of a modern utopia is reminiscent of European
stoicism.

422   ["Ann Veronica."] CL 48:108.
       [Remarks on several reviews of the novel.]

423   CAMPBELL, W.E. "H.G. Wells." Catholic World 91 (May):145-59;
       (June):312-25; (July):471-83; (Aug.):613-25.
       Based on good sociological observations, Anticipations seeks
to give man a gentle lead toward a more spiritual conception of
life. But W neglects the problem of free will, which seems merely
a vice in his vision of the future, and related factors concerning
human nature and desires. In place of the family unit, with its
emotional context, W offers the omnipotent state, with its rigid
and intellectual context.

424   CARTER, IRVING. "H.G. Wells's Latest Novel." NYTSRB, 25 June,
       p. 360.
       [Mistakenly reviews George Meek, Bath Chairman as W's book.]

425   CHESTERTON, G.K. "Interesting People: H.G. Wells." AM M 71
       (Nov.):32.
       No person alive today in England better deserves the name of
genius than W. His mind is not mechanical but has developed like
a living organism, its reliance less on reason than on instinct.

426   "Current Fiction." Nation (New York) 90 (6 Jan.):12-13.
       The protagonist of Ann Veronica represents the woman's move-
ment reduced to absurdity. The final scene is very remote from
the ingenious art W has created in the past.

427   "Current Fiction." Nation (New York) 90 (2 June):558-59.
       Although Mr. Polly is roughly analogous to The Old Wives'
Tale, W is no realist. The book represents W in his best mood,
and Mr. Polly's language may become "a new sort of art-tongue."

428   "Fiction." ALA 6 (May):356.
       Although it bears the marks of haste, Mr. Polly is as
acutely analytical and humorous as Kipps.

429 FINDLATER, JANE H. "Three Sides to a Question." National Review (London) 54 (Jan.):799-805.
     Everything is either black or white to W in Tono-Bungay, a book lacking any real solution to the major problems it discusses.

430 "A Guide to the New Books." LD 41 (17 Sept.):455-56.
     In Mr. Polly W has performed a difficult task well. The story is sincere, simple, and rich in humor.

431 "H.G. Wells on the Family." Academy 78 (18 June):585-87.
     [Takes exception to W's view of the family.]

432 "The History of Mr. Polly." Independent (New York) 68 (7 April):762-63.
     In this work W is too partial in his vision, presenting a distorted image out of proportion. If he had probed all the characters in the book and not merely the protagonist, W would have attained the exquisite art evident in Bennett's The Old Wives' Tale.

433 "The History of Mr. Polly." TLS, 21 April, p. 144. Reprinted in CH, pp. 175-76.
     This highly spirited, delightful tale exemplifies W's delicate artistry. W's method of construction gives a deceptive appearance of recklessness, as if the author were not concerned with style. Its chief fault lies in the fact that W has done this sort of thing before.

434 "Life and Letters." Academy 78 (25 June):603-5.
     [Continues the debate inaugurated in Academy 78 (18 June):585-87, with particular reference to Ann Veronica and Mr. Polly.]

435 "Literary and Trade Notes." PW 78 (30 July):600.
     [Reports, mostly in his own words, W's denial of authorship of George Meek, Bath Chairman.]

436 M., A.N. "Mr. Polly." MG, 20 April, p. 5.
     Hardly one of W's great books, Mr. Polly is brilliant and entertaining. W's ironic attitude is not quite flexible enough.

437 MENCKEN, H.L. "A Fictioneer of the Laboratory." Smart Set 31 (July):153-55. Reprinted in CH, pp. 178-80.
     Like Dickens, W is concerned with the lower middle class; unlike Dickens, he is a scientist rather than a sentimentalist in his treatment of his characters. This story, Mr. Polly, really a history of the protagonist's stomach, is replete with W's usual facility and humor but would have benefited from more polishing.

1910

438   "New Books Reviewed." NAR 192 (July):136-37. Reprinted in CH,
       p. 177.
           Whereas Tono-Bungay, in presenting an entire period, was
       vibrant with the current of contemporary life, Mr. Polly is a
       whimpering, incredible account.

439   "Novels." SR (London) 109 (7 May):602.
           Mr. Polly is better than many of W's previous works, espe-
       cially with regard to characterization. This book, like Wheels of
       Chance, Kipps, and Mr. Lewisham is better than W's tales of the
       future.

440   "Novels." Spectator (London) 104 (7 May):776.
           No one in Mr. Polly elicits the reader's interest. W looks
       upon Polly with affection, but in fact the character and ideals of
       this character fall far below the level of both Hoopdriver and
       Kipps.

441   "Our Library table." Athenaeum, no. 4318 (30 July), p. 124.
           [Takes exception to W's view of writing as expressed in his
       introductory comments to George Meek, Bath Chairman.]

442   PAYNE, WILLIAM MORTON. "Recent Fiction--Wells's Ann Veronica."
       Dial 48 (1 Jan.):17-18.
           This work is not to be taken seriously but to be read as a
       lark.

443   _____ . "Recent Fiction--Wells's The History of Mr. Polly."
       Dial 48 (1 June):393.
           This doctrinaire work worries its caricature to death.

444   REYNOLDS, STEPHEN. "What the Poor Want." QR 212 (Jan.):
       152-79.
           [Passing references to Last Things, particularly concerning
       the difference between how an educated man attempts to reason a
       matter out and how a poor man attempts "to weigh it up."]

445   S[HORTER], C[LEMENT] K. "A Literary Letter." Sphere 41
       (14 May):ii.
           Mr. Polly is a clever book and "will certainly make a rail-
       way journey a very pleasant affair." [Also praises W's introduc-
       tion to George Meek, Bath Chairman.]

446   T., A.M. "H.G. Wells." Glasgow Herald, 12 March, p. 12.
           What is most appreciated in such works as Kipps and Mr.
       Lewisham is the youthful gaiety of W's audacious self-revelations
       and his ability to transform daily trifles into poetry. W is to
       be read in the spirit of youth and joy, with an idealism mixed

with humor and free from snobbery, and with a faith in the possibility of human improvement. His artistry is particularly evident
in scenes of youthful lovemaking.

447 VAN WESTRUM, A. SCHADE. "Mr. Wells's The History of Mr.
     Polly." Bookman (New York) 31 (Aug.):631-32.
         W's socioeconomic moral, that society has not developed a
     collective intelligence and will to cope with Mr. Polly's human
     needs, detracts from the literary delight of this work.

1911

448 ADCOCK, A. ST. JOHN. "Short Stories." Bookman (London) 41
     (Oct.):52-53.
         Country is "by turns fantastic, humourous, supernatural,
     visionary, grimly terrible and sternly or tenderly realistic."

449 AUSTIN, MARY. "An Appreciation of H.G. Wells, Novelist." AM M
     72 (Oct.):733-35.
         W's work is understandably uneven. Even in Tono-Bungay, his
     best novel, there are entire chapters that could be omitted. W's
     male characters could be men anywhere, but his female characters
     are always English.

450 CLARK, WARD. "H.G. Wells's The New Machiavelli." Bookman (New
     York) 33 (March):101-2.
         The portrait of Richard Remington is almost an autobiography
     of the novelist's own spiritual evolution from socialism to a kind
     of Nietzschean aristocracy.

451 "Current Fiction." Nation (New York) 92 (9 March):244.
         Remington is a male Ann Veronica in Machiavelli, a book
     marred only by didactic passages and comment on English politics.

452 EMANUEL, WALTER. "Author and Artist Too." Strand Magazine 41
     (April):451-52.
         [Praises W's caricature drawings.]

453 "Fiction and Morals." Times (London), 29 March, p. 11.
         [Report on the banning of Machiavelli by the Free Libraries
     Committee of the Birmingham City Council.]

454 GIBBON, PERCEVAL. "The New Machiavelli." Bookman (London) 39
     (Feb.):238.
         This is the sort of book expected from W, one which has a
     well-developed and convincing main character. It is not safe to
     miss a work by W, if one wishes to keep in touch with the spirit
     of the time.

1911

455   HACKETT, FRANCIS. "The Political Comet: The New Machiavelli."
      Chicago Evening Post Literary Review, 20 Jan. Reprinted in
      Horizons: A Book of Criticism (New York: Huebsch, 1918), pp.
      109-17; and in CH, pp. 189-94.
         This book proves disappointing with regard to philosophy,
      character credibility, and artistic construction; yet it deserves
      some attention.

456   "History and Romance." Athenaeum, no. 4389 (9 Dec.), p. 731.
         Floor Games is full of excellent ideas on toys, how to play
      with them, and how to make them.

457   JACKSON, HOLBROOK. Romance and Reality. London: Richards,
      pp. 162-67.
         W brilliantly combines social concerns (like Dickens), sci-
      entific precision, and creative imagination. His gradual manner
      of storytelling is accented by an impressively punctilious style.
      The roots of his Marxiam socialism are evident in his science
      fiction works.

458   "Literature." Athenaeum, no. 4377 (16 Sept.), p. 318.
         W's definition of a short story, as argued in the introduc-
      tion to Country, is hardly acceptable. But the stories are artis-
      tically satisfying. The quality of W's gifts can still be found
      in his recent fiction; however, whereas they once engaged "in
      building castles," they now perform "the practical work of paving
      streets and laying drains."

459   M., A.N. "New Books." MG, 17 Jan., p. 4.
         A disturbing, moving, even inspiring book, Machiavelli
      represents W's search for clearness. It is not so much a story as
      a case in which the prosecution and defense are closely related.

460   "Mr. H.G. Wells Talks about His English Political Novel The New
      Machiavelli." NYTSRB, 21 Jan., p. 30.
         [A prepublication review noting that W uses real people in
      the novel only in an artistic fashion.]

461   "Mr. Wells and the Short Story." Academy 81 (26 Aug.):273-74.
         All the stories in Country are good. Although none of them
      match Henry James's "The Beast in the Jungle" or Joseph Conrad's
      "Typhoon," many are skillful in a way that these two authors could
      not produce.

462   "Mr. Wells' Don Juan." SR (London) 111 (28 Jan.):117-18.
         In Machiavelli W succeeds in characterizing many contempo-
      rary figures but he is too obsessed with talk about sex.

463   "Mr. Wells's Short Stories." TLS, 24 Aug., p. 310.
      In Country W shows that "he knows to a nicety the texture of
a dream, precisely where dream lours into nightmare. He knows the
magic that lurks in the ultra-usual when the right emotional
nerve--or some kind of mental funny bone--is tugged or rapped
patly and neatly."

464   "The New Books." Outlook (New York) 97 (4 March):514-15.
      Three parts dubious political philosophy and one part novel,
Machiavelli evinces only traces of W's narrative power.

465   [The New Machiavelli.] Nation (London) 8 (21 Jan.):690-92.
      Reprinted in CH, pp. 195-98.
      Inferior to Tono-Bungay and superior to Ann Veronica, this
book is weak in characterization but presents W's most powerful
sketch of social and moral discontent. Although its artistry is
weak and its explicit analogy to The Prince faintly absurd, the
book expresses an inquisitive and fiery spirit.

466   "The New Machiavelli." TLS, 19 Jan., p. 22. Reprinted in CH,
      pp. 186-88.
      While not the most entertaining or perfect of W's writings,
this book is his most important work. In general the arrangement
of the novel is masterly, though Remington's views and the narrative of the work are not quite completely fused. Margaret is
possibly "the most finely touched portrait" W has created.

467   "The New Machiavelli, Mr. H.G. Wells's Striking Political
      Romance of English Life in the Twentieth-Century." NYTRB, 5
      Feb., p. 55.
      Vividly imagined, this book unshrinkingly portrays the reac-
tion of personality to outward events.

468   "New Novels." Athenaeum, no. 4345 (4 Feb.), pp. 123-24.
      Not really a novel, Machiavelli presents a protagonist who
is too much an uninteresting abstraction. Its ideas, however, are
wonderfully stimulating.

469   "Novels." SR (London) 112 (16 Sept.):371.
      W's reputation will not survive on the strength of Country
because in general the book is based on the romantic possibilities
of science.

470   "An Odyssey of Discontent." Nation (London) 8 (21 Jan.):690,
      692. Reprinted in CH, pp. 195-98.
      Inferior to Tono-Bungay and superior to Ann Veronica,
Machiavelli is weak in characterization but represents W's most
powerful sketch of social and moral discontent. Although its

1911

artistry is weak and its explicit analogy to The Prince faintly
absurd, the book does possess an inquisitive and fiery spirit.

471   "Pan in Politics." Glasgow Herald, 17 Jan., p. 7.
        Although suggestive and revolutionary, Machiavelli is psy-
chologically and artistically disappointing. Problems surface
whenever characters are made to embody ideas. The book does,
however, make clear that W is the greatest sociologist among
novelists.

472   "Philosopher or Novelist?." Academy 80 (21 Jan.):72-73.
        Its limitations notwithstanding, Machiavelli is a remarkably
fine novel. Parts of it remind one of Henry James and Arnold
Bennett.

473   RANDALL, ALFRED E. "The Two Machiavellis." New Age, n.s. 8
        (9 Feb.):353-55; (23 Feb.):399-401; (20 April):598-99.
        Whereas Machiavelli left us The Prince, Remington offers
only "babies and bunkum" in Machiavelli. Another Frederick the
Great is not needed to refute this book.

474   ROSS, ROBERT. "The New Machiavelli: Mr. Wells's New Novel
        Read for the First Time." Bystander 29 (25 Jan.):172.
        This work is a brilliant piece of literature, its subject at
once modern and universal in appeal, its style a model for narrative. The most various novel since Vanity Fair, it evinces the
vigor of an Erasmus and should be indexed.

475   SCOTT-JAMES, R.A. "The Revenge of Mr. Wells." Daily News, 17
        Jan., p. 4. Reprinted in CH, pp. 183-86.
        The protagonist of Machiavelli is a product of his social
conditions and, because of W's critical genius in analyzing these
conditions, Remington may well become immortal in literature as
the twentieth-century Benvenuto Cellini or Jonathan Wild. Whereas
Galsworthy's fiction is illuminated by an underlying ideal, this
novel's informing center remains uncertain and unrealized.

476   SHERWOOD, MARGARET. "The Makers of Plots." AM 108 (Oct.):563-
        64. Reprinted in CH, pp. 201-2.
        Suffering from unconvincing politics and blurred, uncertain
characterization, Machiavelli bewilders rather than stimulates
understanding. W lacks the dramatic gift.

477   "Some of the Season's Best Fiction." RR 43 (June):757.
        Machiavelli is "a splendidly trenchant and superbly earnest
book."

478   STRAUS, RALPH. "A Select Conversation." Bodleian 2
        (Jan.):164-66.
        [An interview with W about Machiavelli.]

52

479   TONSON, JACOB [pseud. of Arnold Bennett]. "Books and Persons
       in London and Paris." New Age, n.s. 8 (2 Feb.):325;
       (16 Feb.):373; (27 April):613; 9 (25 May):85; (13 July):255.
       Reprinted in Books and Persons: Being Comments on a Past
       Epoch, 1908-1911 (London: Chatto & Windus, 1917), pp. 294-99.
           Machiavelli deserves a better reception than it has re-
       ceived. W's best books are always greeted with a lack of sponta-
       neity and by a mean reluctance. The novel is full of candor and
       generosity, but it is weak insofar as "the politically-creative
       part, as distinguished from the politically-shattering part, is
       not convincing."

1912

480   "Amateurs of Revolution." Nation (New York) 95 (11 July):
       27-28.
           Galsworthy, Shaw, and W are not really thorough or con-
       sistent in their philosophy. They believe in revolution but also
       believe that it will not do much good.

481   BEERBOHM, MAX. "Perkins and Mankind." In A Christmas Garland.
       London: Heinemann, pp. 33-46.
           [A short story mimicking W's style and ideas.]

482   "Chronicle and Comment." Bookman (New York) 36 (Oct.):106-8.
           Machiavelli is perhaps the most considerable novel of the
       decade, but its modernity is mere accident. [Refutes Wilbur Urban
       Marshall's "The Crisis of Taste," AM 90 (July 1912):53-59.]

483   CURLE, RICHARD. "H.G. Wells." Everyman 1 (20 Dec.):304.
           Tono-Bungay is W's best book, poetical in its realism. Its
       style represents the qualities and the limitations of W's mind.

484   _____. "Marriage." Bookman (London) 43 (Oct.):44.
           An energetic, remarkable achievement, this work suffers from
       the overextended philosophical monologues of the main character
       and the lack of a genuinely poetic command of words.

485   "The Difficult Art of Marriage." Nation (New York) 95
       (17 Oct.):358-59.
           In Marriage W criticizes many of the attitudes he previously
       held, with the result that he reveals a state of mind that is
       nearly Victorian. "He seems to be returning to the older and
       deeper view of love in marriage; but he cannot rid himself of the
       formulas and phrases he has gathered in the field of modern specu-
       lation."

1912

486   "Fiction." <u>ALA</u> 9 (Nov.):130.
        Although it is stimulating in thought and strong in charac-
terization, <u>Marriage</u> is inconclusive.

487   "Fiction." <u>Academy</u> 83 (21 Sept.):372-73.
        <u>Marriage</u> is nearly a great novel. We read W not for his
style or views but for the tale he tells and the part of himself
expressed in what he writes.

488   "Fiction." <u>ER</u> 12 (Oct.):490-92.
        In <u>Marriage</u> W's aim is as large as was that of Goethe in
<u>Faust.</u> Although he lacks the fine form, the precision, and the
economy of Goethe, he has wrestled brilliantly with the problems
of modern life, ignoring none of the impediments.

489   "Fiction." <u>Spectator</u> (London) 109 (12 Oct.):564.
        Though never lost, reader interest in <u>Marriage</u> follows an
uneven course; "the jerky manner of dividing long chapters into
numbered sections fits the inconclusive progress of the story."

490   GORDON, HOME. "The Popularity of H.G. Wells and Arnold
        Bennett." <u>Oxford and Cambridge Review</u>, no. 25 (Nov.),
        pp. 80-86.
        W and Bennett are alike in their use of detail, in their
attitudes toward religion, in their emphasis on segments of the
middle class, and in their dramatic use of prolonged silence.

491   "H.G. Wells, an Admirable Observer--Not Yet a Novelist."
        <u>NYTRB</u>, 6 Oct., p. 548.
        <u>Marriage</u> lacks fictive perspective; W is too much a scien-
tist in his fascination with process and problems rather than with
characters. [Compares certain of W's techniques to scientific
procedures.]

492   "H.G. Wells as a Playfellow." <u>BET</u>, 20 Nov., p. 25.
        [Notes <u>Floor Games.</u>]

493   "H.G. Wells Heads a Revolt against 'The Weary Giant.'" <u>CL</u> 52
        (Jan.):97-98.
        [Reports on W's view of the function of the novel as he
expressed it in a lecture delivered to the Times Book Club.]

494   "Happy Marriages in Fiction." <u>LD</u> 45 (16 Nov.):903-4.
        [Reports and cites from Harold Owen's reaction to <u>Marriage</u>
in the <u>DC</u> (not seen).]

495   JOURDAIN, PHILIP E.B. "Logic, M. Bergson, and Mr. H.G. Wells."
        <u>HJ</u> 10 (July):835-45.
        [A critical discussion of W's notion of logic.]

496   KENNEDY, J.M. English Literature 1880-1905. London: Swift,
       pp. 175, 206-52.
            Like Shaw, W spoils his work with ideas of social reform;
       even Tono-Bungay is more concerned with ideas and plot than with
       character. Possessing little artistic imagination, W creates
       unimportant and uninteresting characters who speak unrealisitc
       dialogue. W is a commercial writer who prostituted himself to the
       artistically ignorant middle class. [Takes vigorous exception to
       W's ideas about art.]

497   MABIE, HAMILTON W. "A Few Books of To-Day." Outlook (New
       York) 102 (23 Nov.):650.
            Too full of digressions and somewhat too clinical, Marriage
       is nevertheless interesting.

498   MACE, GRIFFIN. "H.G. Wells's Marriage." Bookman (New York) 36
       (Nov.):328-31.
            Approaching the leisurely style of Arnold Bennett, this book
       undertakes too broad an examination of contemporary social
       problems.

499   "Marriage." TLS, 12 Sept., p. 360.
            Not a provocative book, this novel represents a hybrid form.
       It is both dull and stimulating at times.

500   MARSHALL, WILBUR URBAN. "The Crisis in Taste." AM 90
       (July):53-59.
            W not only eschews tasteful indirection, he is doctrinaire
       on the matter of starkness.

501   "Mr. Wells Confessing." LD 44 (20 Jan.):119-20.
            [Reports W's autobiographic comments made for a projected
       Russian edition of his works, as reported in T.P.'s Magazine.]

502   "New Novels." Athenaeum, no. 4428 (7 Sept.), p. 241.
            Repetition, excessive length, and authorial self-indulgence
       mar Marriage.

503   "Novels." SR (London) 114 (7 Sept.):305.
            Marriage is a good book, and Marjorie the most important
       woman in W's novels.

504   "Other Books." Sun (New York), 2 Nov., p. 11.
            [Favorable review of Floor Games.]

505   "Reviews of New Books." LD 45 (7 Dec.):1081.
            [Rave review of Floor Games.]

1912

506   RIDER, FREMONT. "Marriage." PW 82 (19 Oct.):1364.
      This novel not only wonderfully questions many social con-
ventions but also represents a literary experiment "so sane, so
broad and deep and clear that it commands and impels conviction."

507   ROZ, FIRMIN. Le roman anglais contemporain: George Meredith,
      Thomas Hardy, Mme Humphry Ward, Rudyard Kipling, H.G. Wells.
      Paris: Librairie Hachette, pp. 227-71.
      There are many satiric elements in W's work; Dr. Moreau, for
instance, presents a parody of humanity. W's belief in socialism
derives from his sense of that doctrine's alignment to science.
For W social formalism, snobbery, and intellectual inertia are
consequences of the English social system. W became pessimistic
when he lost his confidence in the ability of reason to improve
man's condition.

508   SCOTT, DIXON. "Mr. Wells's New Novel." MG, 11 Sept., p. 4.
      The tone of parts of Marriage is somewhat priggish, pre-
sented in a "knuckle-rapping style." W's genius is too great to
be defined simply. His principal gift is a faculty for bold,
vivid improvization, for forging swift generalizations and powerful impromptus, and supporting them with life and validity, "with
images of an animal accuracy, phrases of pouncing precision, and
sudden epithets that leap like arrows to their mark."

509   SEGUY, RENÉ. "H.G. Wells et la pensée contemporaine."
      Mercure de France 95 (Feb.):673-99.
      Along with Durkheim, William James, and Bergson, W is part
of a new intellectual movement that is extending experimental
method to every philosophical and social area of inquiry. Though
he focuses on the individual, he is concerned with the general
physical and psychological forces that could be directed by science for the amelioration of mankind's economic, political, and
moral systems.

510   S[HORTER], C[LEMENT] K. "A Literary Letter." Sphere 50
      (21 Sept.):304.
      W and Bennett both lack the poetic vision found in the works
of great literary artists. In spite of some blemishes, however,
Marriage is a gripping book with many flashes of insight.

511   SLOSSON, EDWIN E. "London and Labrador." Independent (New
      York) 73 (10 Oct.):849-50.
      Marriage suggests that W's thought is moving into a new
phase, as if it were working toward some sort of belief in a
Bergsonian God. His craftsmanship, shrewd observation of human
traits, flexible style, and original ideas are all evident in this
book.

512   WEST, REBECCA [pseud. of Cicely Fairfield]. ["Marriage."]
Freewoman 2 (19 Sept.):346-48. Reprinted in CH, pp. 203-8.
      That Marjorie is presented as a normal woman and that she
should be "kept" by the community are the two major deceptions in
this novel, a work replete with W's infuriating mannerisms.

513   _____. "Mr. Wells on Marriage." Everyman 1 (8 Nov.):124-25.
      Marriage represents a protest against the spiritual dis-
satisfaction resulting from the dinginess of life supplanting the
reality of love.

                              1913

514   "Books for Boys." NYTRB, 9 Nov., p. 615.
      [Very favorable review of Little Wars.]

515   BRAITHWAITE, WILLIAM STANLEY. "Christmas Books for Children."
BET, 26 Nov., p. 26.
      [Favorable review of Little Wars.]

516   B[RAITHWAITE], W[ILLIAM] S[TANLEY]. "Contrasts in Time." BET,
12 April, pt. 3, p. 8.
      [Favorable review of Discovery.]

517   BROCK, H.I. "Wells in Toyland." NYTRB, 5 Jan., p. 5.
      [Glowing review of Floor Games and the most extensive the
book received.]

518   C., R.H. [Alfred Richard Orage]. "Readers and Writers." New
Age, n.s. 13 (16 Oct.):730. Reprinted in Selected Essays and
Critical Writings, ed. Herbert Read and Denis Saurat (London:
Nott, 1935), pp. 97-103; reprinted in part in CH, pp. 214-15.
      [Blistering attack on Boon (W makes himself evident "with
the regularity of the footprints of a buffalo on a tract of shin-
ing mud"), Research (the reductio ad absurdum of W's anarchic
notions of literary form), and Friends (in style and ideas as
loose and incontinent as a habitual writer could produce).]

519   "Can Man Discover the Future." CO 54 (June):481-82.
      [A summary of Discovery.]

520   COLBY, F.M. "H.G. Wells's Discovery of the Future." HW 57
(12 April):17.
      An ardent confession of faith, this book admirably clarifies
many of the ideas W presents in his novels. With regard to reality, however, it is more dubious. One may believe in W's fancies
but not in his facts.

1913

521 _____. "The Book of the Month." <u>NAR</u> 198 (Nov.):718-23.
     W has the gift of making old things seem new, and he is such
good company that one gladly goes with him in any direction he may
choose. A world of fancy and agreeable characters, rather than of
boldness or modernity, characterizes W's best work.

522 COURTNEY, W.L. "The Younger Novelists." <u>NAR</u> 198 (July):76-86.
     Probably W "is more responsible than anybody else for pretty
nearly all the latest developments of English fiction, so we may
as well give him the credit, or discredit, of the leisurely psychological development so much fancied at present."

523 CURLE, RICHARD. "H.G. Wells." <u>Bookman</u> (London) 45 (Oct.):58.
     Nearly a dull book, <u>Friends</u> presents characters who are
merely mouthpieces enunciating views that are not necessarily W's.

524 "Current Fiction." <u>Nation</u> (New York) 97 (4 Dec.):537.
     <u>Friends</u> shows that W "is but another victim, more intelli-
gent than some others, of that passing belief that somehow happiness is to result for humanity from setting the emotions free of
restraint rather than from the deliberate adjustment of the individual to the responsibilities imposed upon him."

525 DELL, FLOYD. "<u>The Passionate Friends</u>." <u>HW</u> 58 (13 Dec.):25.
     This quasi-novel tells a poor story because it passionately
presents an attack on romantic realism. The ethical ideal underlying the book deserves consideration.

526 E[DGETT], E[DWIN] F[RANCIS]. "H.G. Wells the Iconoclast."
     <u>BET</u>, 5 Nov., p. 24.
     Sadly serious, <u>Friends</u> is replete with reality, pathos, and
genuine sentiment. Whatever his shortcomings, W's sense of the
stage is always so developed that his characters prove convincing.
Few novelists can begin a story as effectively as can W.

527 "A Few Thought Compelling Novels." <u>RR</u> 47:242-44.
     <u>Marriage</u> is at once the most brilliant and least effective
of recent books on relations between the sexes. While it provides
an excellent picture of middle-class British life, it lacks value
as a study of social conditions.

528 "Fiction" <u>Academy</u> 85 (27 Sept.):398-99.
     [Commends the story and criticizes the style of <u>Friends</u>.]

529 "Fiction." <u>ALA</u> 10 (Dec.):158.
     <u>Friends</u> will interest thoughtful readers.

530   "Fiction." <u>Athenaeum</u>, no. 4481 (13 Sept.), pp. 248-49.
       In <u>Friends</u>, Mary is the most complex character W has ever
created. The weight of W's concerns has made his novels worthy of
attention, but as time passes his failure to have learned to write
will count against him.

531   FIELD, L[OUIS] M[AUNSELL]. "H.G. Wells." <u>NYTRB</u>, 2 Nov.,
       p. 593.
       Despite its tragic conclusion, <u>Friends</u> is finally a hopeful
book and ranks among the leading novels published this year. It
expresses many of the ideas that currently exist in nebulous form
in the minds of intelligent people. It may be considered as a
companion work to the remarkable <u>Marriage</u>.

532   FLEISHER, ALEXANDER. ["<u>The Discovery of the Future</u>."] <u>AAAP</u> 48
       (July):270.
       [Notes the interesting theory of the book.]

533   "General." <u>Athenaeum</u>, no. 4488 (1 Nov.), p. 495.
       <u>Discovery</u> reprints an address that is below W's usual stimu-
lating writing.

534   "General Literature." <u>ALA</u> 9 (Feb.):255.
       <u>Floor Games</u> appeals to intelligence and imagination.

535   "How They Do It." <u>NS</u> 2 (6 Dec.):275-76.
       [A series of quotations in W's later manner humorously
juxtaposed.]

536   HUEBSCH, B.W. "<u>The Discovery of the Future</u>." <u>Nation</u> (New
       York) 96 (22 May):521.
       [A letter from the publisher of the book explaining his side
of its publishing history.]

537   JACKSON, HOLBROOK. <u>The Eighteen Nineties: A Review of Art and
       Ideas at the Close of the Nineteenth Century</u>. [1913; not
       seen]. Rev. ed. New York: Knopf, 1922, pp. 27, 34, 35, 44,
       224, 225, 228-29, 274.
       Better than any other writer in his time, W introduces
reality into his novels without supplanting romance.

538   "Juvenile." <u>Athenaeum</u>, no. 4478 (23 Aug.), p. 181.
       <u>Little Wars</u> seems too dispassionate and artificial.

539   LAMBERTON, JOHN. "<u>The Discovery of the Future</u>." <u>Nation</u> (New
       York) 96 (1 May):440-41.
       [A letter discussing the publishing history of the book.]

1913

540   "Literature and ARt." CO 55 (Dec.):430-31.
       [Brief note on one critical response to Friends.]

541   LYND, ROBERT. "The World, the Flesh, and Mr. Wells." Daily
       News and Leader (London), 12 Sept., p. 2. Reprinted in CH,
       pp. 211-14.
          If pricked, the characters in Friends would bleed arguments.
       The work is an interesting if unimaginative study in the conflict
       of ideas.

542   "Mr. Wells' New Novel." NS 1 (20 Sept.):760-61.
          The characters of Friends scarcely come alive because they
       are not psychologically true to themselves. The plot and story of
       the book are the worst W has ever written; they do not even
       provoke thought.

543   "Mr. Wells, the Wanderer." Nation (London) 13 (27 Sept.):
       959-60.
          Friends indicates that W is most comfortable when free from
       artistry and indulging his diarist impulses. The book represents
       W at his later best, the author "of energetic and concentrated
       vision, with more feeling and less certainty than of yore, a more
       childlike, more religious spirit."

544   "Novels." SR (London) 116 (13 Sept.):339.
          The people in Friends continually talk, sometimes act, but
       never live.

545   "The Passionate Friends." TLS, 18 Sept., p. 387.
          W fails to make his heroine in this novel convincing. There
       is no grandeur, dignity, or tragedy in her fall.

546   "The Quality of Current Fiction." Nation (London) 13
       (12 July).
          W is nearly the only English novelist who generalizes boldly
       in examining modern problems, as Marriage demonstrates.

547   "Reviews of New Books." LD 47 (6 Dec.):1128.
       [Favorable review of Little Wars.]

548   S., B. "A New Novel by Mr. Wells." MG, 12 Sept., p. 5.
          In Friends W is perhaps too subtle. Conveying the idea that
       the ideal sexual relationship is one that includes every other
       kind of intimacy on equal terms could have been accomplished more
       successfully than by presenting a tale in which passion and
       friendship are so inextricably and wantonly entangled.

549   SCOTT-JAMES, R[OLFE] A[RNOLD]. Personality in Literature.
       London: Secker, pp. 151-69.

In Tono-Bungay W neglects style and form, ignoring selection and suppression; he writes in a slangy, cumbrous Latin-English that is still idiomatic. The social problems on which he focuses in the book arise naturally and inevitably as a part of human life. W's nervous, somewhat self-conscious manner is related to his personal experience with English national life. He tells his own story over and over again.

550   "Significant Novels of the New Season." RR 48:747-50.
       Friends contains W's "usual social and economic surprises."

551   "Sociology and Government." RR 48 (July):120.
       [Descriptive notice of Discovery.]

552   VAN LOON, H[ENDRICK] W[ILLEM]. "A Question of Publishing."
       Nation (New York) 96 (10 April):358; "Apropos of Sixty Cents."
       Nation (New York) 96 (1 May):441.
       [Correspondence objecting to the fact that virtually all of
       Discovery was printed in the New York Times.]

1914

553   ANGELL, NORMAN. "Mr. Wells and Anti-War Propaganda." Nation
       (London) 15 (5 Sept.):815-17.
       [A letter probing aspects of W's notions on propaganda.]

554   BAILEY, JOHN. "Mr. Wells's Pacifist State." Nation (London)
       15 (26 Sept.):887-88.
       [A letter taking exception to W's essay entitled "The Two
       Ways" and concluding that he misreads Englishmen and the lesson of
       the hour.]

555   BERESFORD, J.D. H.G. Wells. London: Nisbet.
       W's romances have little in common with those of Jules
       Verne, particularly concerning the means he employs in order to
       reach the intelligence and senses of the reader. War in the Air
       represents W's greatest achievement in fantasy. Men in the Moon
       is little more than a piece of sheer exuberance. Judged collec-
       tively W's romances provide a detachment and broad vision that
       might help promote a higher, more stable civilization. In con-
       trast to his romances, the position of W's novels is less certain.
       He creates illuminating phrases, but his characters tend to repre-
       sent some essential type of humanity and are less illuminating.
       Yet he has to some degree given the novel a new form.

556   "Books of the Week." Everyman 5 (13 Nov.):86-87.
       Isaac Harman is a vivid novel, particularly memorable in its
       portrait of Penrose.

1914

557   "The Character and Tendency of Contemporary Fiction."
      Athenaeum, suppl. (28 March), pp. 463-64. Reprinted in the Sun
      (New York), 18 April 1914, p. 9.
          W is perhaps the most interesting and representative of
      contemporary English novelists. In trying to reckon with progress
      and constructive thought, he has forged a peculiar discursive and
      autobiographical form of fiction. He also combines realism, ro-
      manticism, and social criticism, the three dominant elements of
      late Victorian writing.

558   "Chronicle and Comment." Bookman (New York) 39 (June):370-72.
          [Discusses aspects of the controversy between W's and Henry
      James's view of the novel.]

559   CLARK, WARD. "Mr. Wells's The Passionate Friends." Bookman
      (New York) 38 (Jan.):554-57. Reprinted in CH, pp. 216-19.
          Intellectually honest, this work represents W's most notable
      achievement. Especially in the character of Lady Mary Christian
      he presents a most complex and realistic creation, rather than a
      mere vehicle for the author's ideas.

560   "The Complex Personality of Herbert George Wells." Sun (New
      York), spring literary suppl., 4 April, p. 4.
          [Brief biographical sketch of W, emphasizing the paradoxical
      qualities of his personality.]

561   COOPER, FREDERIC TABER. "The Accustomed Manner and Some Recent
      Novels." Bookman (New York) 39 (May):320-28.
          A charlatan piece of work, World Set Free is more feeble
      than W's worst failures in the past.

562   _____. "Some Novels of the Month." Bookman (New York) 40
      (Dec.):435-37.
          Although an interesting novel, Isaac Harman suffers from
      a theatrical and radical conclusion contrary to the heroine's
      experience.

563   "Current Fiction." Nation (New York) 98 (16 April):433.
          Regarding W's World Set Free: "Heaven defend us from his
      Utopias! But we like his explosions."

564   "Current Fiction." Nation (New York) 99 (12 Nov.):581-82.
          Unlike the inimitable Mr. Polly, Isaac Harman presents humor
      and characterization too much overlaid with ideas.

565   "Current Literature." Spectator (London) 112 (25 April):681.
          Although sometimes prone to exaggeration, Englishman is
      suggestive and frequently just.

566   EAGLE, SOLOMON. "Books in General." NS 4 (31 Oct.):89.
        Isaac Harman is not W's best, particularly with regard to
the superficial travesties of familiar persons, but it does possess the incidental vivacities of W's style.

567   E[DGETT], E[DWIN] F[RANCIS]. "The Perversity of Mr H.G.
        Wells." BET, 28 Oct., p. 24.
        The great defect in Isaac Harman is that it seems to be a
composite of the three distinct moods evident in Tono-Bungay, Ann
Veronica, and Mr. Polly. The book is wise and witty, but its
ideas are beyond W's control. The purpose of the work remains a
mystery.

568   "Fiction." Academy 87 (31 Oct.):414.
        Shorn of discussions and digressions, Isaac Harman would
have been a better book.

569   "Fiction." ALA 10 (May):374.
        World Set Free is interesting and imaginative. [Cites a
review in the Nation (New York) 98 (16 April).]

570   "Fiction." ALA 11 (Nov.):125.
        Isaac Harman offers interesting ideas, vivid characters, but
a negligible story.

571   "Fiction." Athenaeum, no. 4515 (9 May), p. 652.
        World Set Free is not really fiction. An interesting book,
it is marred by certain dubious attitudes and some bad writing.

572   "Fiction." Athenaeum, no. 4539 (24 Oct.), p. 424.
        A certain loss of brilliancy is the welcome price paid for
restraint in Isaac Harman.

573   "Fiction." ER 17 (April):138-39.
        A little irritating and not written as well as it might be,
Englishman is generally lucid and prophetically imaginative.

574   "Fiction." Independent (New York) 80 (16 Nov.):243.
        W has never presented better social analysis and characteri-
zation than in Isaac Harman, a book marred by a dubious ending.
Its lesson is the same as that of Barrie's The Twelve-Pound Look.

575   "Fiction." Spectator (London) 112 (16 May):836-37.
        World Set Free is characterized by many of the merits and
all of the limitations of W's utopian romances.

576   "General Literature." ALA 10 (June):409.
        Many fresh, stimulating ideas are presented in Social
Forces.

1914

577 GRIBBLE, FRANCIS. "H.G. Wells." Everyman 4 (19 June):295-96.
Not the story but the ideas behind it fascinate W, a novelist who would have preferred some other medium. Unlike Jules
Verne, W's science is imaginative with little probability of
influencing future scientific discovery. For W human nature,
thought, and criticism are more important. The heroes in the
works of George Gissing and W are apt to be social outsiders
acutely aware of their personal superiority to their limited
environments; but whereas the Gissing protagonist never succeeds
or hopes to succeed, the W hero feels his potentiality and fights.

578 HAWTHORNE, HILDEGARDE. "Latest Works of Fiction." NYTRB, 1
Nov., pp. 473-74.
Deep insight into human nature accents Isaac Harman. In it
W's style escapes its usual faults. It will be the last work of
its sort about prewar England.

579 _____. "World Set Free." NYTRB, 29 March, p. 141.
A magnificent and skillful piece of workmanship, this sincere book is vigorous and picturesque.

580 HELLEMS, F.B.R. "Toward a Broader To-Morrow." Dial 56
(1 June):454-56.
In Social Forces W assails without pity and questions without ruth, yet he remains constructive. Although not free from
error, the book deserves wide circulation among thoughtful
readers.

581 JAMES, HENRY. "The Younger Generation." TLS, 19 March, pp.
133-34; 2 April, pp. 157-58. Reprinted in Notes on Novelists
(New York: Scribner's Sons, 1914), pp. 314-61; and in Henry
James and H.G. Wells: A Record of Their Friendship, Their
Dispute on the Art of Fiction, and Their Quarrel, ed. Leon Edel
and Gordon N. Ray (London: Rupert Hart-Davis, 1958),
pp. 178-215.
Like Bennett, W "is ideally immersed in his own body of
reference, and that immersion to any such degree and to the effect
of any such variety, intensity and plausibility is really among us
a new feature of the novelist's range of resource." In his works
W literally taps the reservoir of his own mind. W's later works
celebrate material itself rather than the use of material.

582 KEITH, BERNARD. "H.G. Wells's Social Forces in England and
America." Bookman (New York) 39 (June):461-63.
W is a penetrating and unprejudiced observer in this book.
He is the sanest living socialist.

583 KENTON, EDNA. "Manner in Modern Fiction." Bookman (New York)
38 (Jan.):491.

W manages, "often with a desperate wrenching of impedimenta, but always with a great resolve that commands admiration, to inject into his massive English settings a humanised world atmosphere."

584   "Knights of the Air." LD 49 (31 Oct.):841.
       [Reports comments in Aero and Hydro (Chicago) and the Aeroplane (London) reacting to W's proposal that fliers be knighted.]

585   "The Latest War Literature." Independent (New York) 80 (21 Dec.):476.
       [A short primarily favorable notice of War.]

586   LEE, VERNON. "'Vernon Lee's Message to Americans." Nation (New York) 99 (17 Sept.):345-46.
       [A letter responding to W's "Appeal to the American People" in the DC, 24 Aug. 1914; Lee's letter is responded to by Fred C. Conybeare, "Dr. Conybeare's Reply to 'Vernon Lee,'" Nation (New York) 99 (22 Oct. 1914):495-97.]

587   L[IPPMANN], W[ALTER]. "Mr. Wells Avoids Trouble." NR 1 (7 Nov.):27. Reprinted in CH, pp. 220-22.
       "A careless book written with comfortable facility out of the upper layers" of W's mind, Isaac Harman signals a recent change in its author, who in lieu of fresh adventure now seems to offer arm-chair creations. W no longer appears to be developing as a writer.

588   M., C.E. "Mr. Wells's New Book." MG, 23 Oct., p. 4.
       In a sense the first part of Isaac Harman is overpitched, but rightly so. "The wit of it romps without ever losing precision of thought, and always comes down with a sort of rollicking nicety on the diverting, unexpected, indispensable word." The last half of the book disappoints grievously, and it is hoped that W will realize this problem.

589   MIDDLETON, GEORGE. "War and Mr. Wells." Bookman (New York) 40 (Sept.):56-57.
       [Notes War in the Air and World Set Free.]

590   "The Mighty Atom." Nation (London) 15 (9 May):218-20.
       Sensitivity and audacity are joined in World Set Free.

591   "Mr. Wells Adjures Us." LD 49 (5 Sept.):416-17.
       [Reports excerpts from W's comments on the war.]

1914

592   "Mr. Wells at His Best." TLS, 29 Oct., p. 479.
      Each of W's novels reads as if it were his first with its
unpardonable faults of inexperience. Yet when such matters as
looseness of plot, too much preaching, and carelessly drawn characters are disregarded, even as one must do with Dickens's work,
then Isaac Harman can be appreciated for merits that readily
overshadow defects.

593   "Mr. Wells' Hypnosis of Himself." Sun (New York), 19 April,
      sec. 6, p. 14.
      [Descriptive mixed review of Social Forces.]

594   "Mr. Wells Loquitur." SR (London) 117 (28 Feb.):275.
      Although W's opinions on socialism and on the theory of the
novel are dubious, in Englishman he shows his ability to make
mundane topics interesting.

595   "Mr. Wells to His Countrymen." TLS, 26 Feb., p. 103.
      W's great ability to present imaginative new ideas is evi-
dent in Englishman.

596   "Mr. Wells's New Novel." Nation (London) 16 (24 Oct.):124,
      126.
      Both heroines of Isaac Harman are adeptly molded wax fig-
ures. Although W's satire is quite fine throughout the book, the
social message is less intrusive in the last part where his excellent impressionism and skill are much in evidence.

597   MUDGETT, BRIECE D. ["Social Forces in England and America."]
      AAAP 55 (Sept.):296.
      The major flaw in this book is W's attempt to enter fields
of study on which he is not sufficiently informed.

598   "Musings without Method." Blackwood's Magazine 195 (June):
      859-64.
      [Attacks W's notions of the future as revealed in World Set
Free, particularly objecting to his rejection of literary art and
painting.]

599   "New Books." Catholic World 100 (Dec.):398.
      As usual, in Isaac Harman every character depicted is pagan
to the core. Nowhere does W offer effective remedies for the
evils of modern social life.

600   "New Books on Religion and Philosophy." RR 49 (May):625.
      Social Forces is interesting even if one disagrees with it.

601   "New Books Seen through Reviews and Comments: Some Recent
      Novels." Sun (New York), 2 May, p. 8.

W's depiction of the savage response of English villagers to an angelic visitor overpowers the humor of Wonderful Visit, which could have been funnier.

602   "The New Novelist." Nation (London) 15 (11 July):571-72.
       Though their methods differ, both W and Bennett fail to portray genuine universals because they are too limited in their particulars.

603   "Novels of Significance." RR 50 (Dec.):764-65.
       W's intended literary method is obscure in Isaac Harman, which is really Marriage done again to the tune of Tono-Bungay. It is a tragedy presented as a farce.

604   "On the Eve of the Great War." Independent (New York) 79 (28 Sept.):449.
       Social Forces proves W to be England's prophet laureate.

605   "Out of Many Novels." Outlook (New York) 108 (4 Nov.):554.
       Isaac Harman is a literal translation of The Taming of the Shrew without any poetry, imagination, or humor.

606   P., R.T. "H.G. Wells the Prophetic." BET, 25 March, p. 24.
       Not a novel or romance, World Set Free is a stimulating epic of humanity with a well-done atmosphere of reality. Little incidents, presented in symbolic parallels, contribute collectively to the world movement that is the theme of the book.

607   "The Perfect World." SR (London), 117 (9 May):605-6.
       World Set Free evinces something of Defoe's and Swift's ability to make their stories plausible through the manipulation of detail. Objections might be raised to some of W's ideas.

608   "The Point of View." Scribner's Magazine 55 (May):660-61.
       W's advice in Friends concerning comradeship between father and son is unrealistic.

609   "A Prophet of Adventure." Nation (London) 14 (28 Feb.):892-93.
       [Discusses in detail the meaning of adventure in the modern world as presented in Englishman.]

610   "Recent Fiction." Dial 57 (1 Dec.):455.
       Though immensely interesting, Isaac Harman proves disappointing. The protagonist is an ineffectual wraith whose story should have begun at the point where it left off.

611   RIDER, FREMONT. "The Wife of Sir Isaac Harmon." PW 86 (17 Oct.):1287.
       [A very favorable review.]

1914

612 _____. "The World Set Free." PW 85 (18 April):1344-45.
Whether tract or novel, this work leaves the reader gasping
for more. The idea of atomic bombs is the most ingenious fabrica-
tion ever made by a writer of fiction.

613 ROBERTS, R. ELLIS. "Mr. Wells Let Loose." Bookman (London) 46
(June):131-32.
Offering science as the panacea of all current ills, World
Set Free shows again that in spite of his skill as an observer,
his real ingenuity of thought, and his sincere passion for prog-
ress, W has but little knowledge of the human heart.

614 "A Romance of the Atom." Independent (New York) 77
(30 March):454-55.
W has the most alert literary imagination of any modern
writer. He boldly bypasses the conventional novel plot and makes
a hero of cosmic energies. World Set Free is social prophecy with
a scientific motif.

615 SCUDDER, VIDA. "Book Reviews." Survey 32 (29 Aug.):548.
Social Forces is interesting but World Set Free is stimulating. In the latter W the idealist has free prophetic sway.

616 "The Season's New Fiction." RR 49 (April):499.
In World Set Free W succeeds Jules Verne and Edward Bellamy.
Although not entirely convincing, it is a clever book.

617 SECCOMBE, THOMAS. "H.G. Wells." Bookman (London) 46
(April);13-24. Reprinted in LA 282 (15 Aug.):392-405.
[An inaccurate literary biography of W, with a survey of
critical responses to and a general assessment of his work; suggests the close relation between the public work and the private
mind of W.]

618 SHERREN, WILKINSON. "The Everlasting Battlefield." Bookman
(London) 47 (Dec.):92-94.
As a mordant, subtle criticism of contemporary life, Isaac
Harman will probably remain supreme until W writes something
similar.

619 "Social Forces in England and America." Journal of Political
Economy 22 (Oct.):818.
Although its analysis is limited, originality and succinct
expression of growing feeling recommend this book.

620 WEST, REBECCA [pseud. of Cicely Fairfield]. "The Duty of Harsh
Criticism." NR 1 (7 Nov.):18-20.
Although W's mind works more steadily than Shaw's, it is
insufficiently aware of the readers and the nature of its stories,

indeed of everything save its own preoccupation with some problem. From <u>Friends</u> one might deduce that W "lived on the branch of a not too well organized railway system and wrote his books while waiting for trains at the main line junction."

621 ["<u>The World Set Free</u>."] <u>Sun</u> (New York), spring literary suppl., 4 April, p. 4.
    While W makes scientific possibilities seem plausible, his version of an ideal future without work, law, and religion disappoints. W may be tiring of socialism.

622 "<u>The World Set Free</u>." <u>TLS</u>, 14 May, p. 238.
    In spite of several ideas that may strike some as vague and unsatisfactory, this book in general demonstrates W's unrivalled artistic ability for this sort of story.

1915

623 "Adventures in the Research Magnificent." <u>NYTRB</u>, 12 Sept., p. 321.
    Less a novel than a biography of an idea embodied in a man, <u>Research</u> seems to indicate that W is shaken in his faith in the virtue of intellectual revolt. The book is replete with clever phrases and stimulating ideas, but it is not altogether clear as to W's viewpoint.

624 "<u>Bealby</u>." <u>TLS</u>, 8 July, p. 230.
    Nearly sheer tomfoolery, <u>Bealby</u> is a successful rollicking farce.

625 BLAND, J.O.P. "Self-Appointed Statesmen." <u>NCA</u> 77 (March):560-72. Reprinted in <u>LA</u>, 285 (8 May):331-41.
    Shaw and W are men who "have rushed into print with such flippant irresponsibility, combining an egregious display of swollen-headed vanity and lack of restraint with contemptuous indifference to the sentiments of the great mass of their countrymen."

626 _____. "Self-Appointed Statesmen." <u>NCA</u> 77 (May):1211-12.
    [A letter refuting W's response (<u>NCA</u> 77 [April]) to Bland's article (<u>NCA</u> 77 [March]).]

627 "Boon: H.G. Wells's Double-Barreled Satire on His Contemporaries." <u>CO</u> 59 (Aug.):122-23.
    [Primarily quotations from the book.]

628 BROOKS, VAN WYCK. <u>The World of H.G. Wells</u>. New York: Kennerley.

69

1915

        The world as presented by W is infinitely malleable, ready
to respond to whatever purpose or design, whatever ideas, the
human will imposes on it. This view underlies the real meaning of
W's socialism. For him the purpose of life is the development of
the collective consciousness of the race. In his opinion "there is
the static world, the normal, ordinary world which is on the whole
satisfied with itself, together with the great mass of men who
compose and sanction it; and there is the ever-advancing better
world, pushing through this outworn husk in the minds and wills of
creative humanity." An intellectual more than a novelist, W views
life in terms of ideas rather than in terms of experience--though
such a distinction should be made cautiously. He "has put before
us not so much a well-wrought body of artistic work, or a moral
programme, or an explanation of life . . . as a certain new
spirit, filled with all sorts of puzzled intimations of a new
beauty and even a new religion to be generated out of a new order
of things that is only glimpsed at present." At bottom W's socialism is a personal and mystical conception of life informing
his assumption that human nature can take care of itself.

629   COOPER, FREDERIC TABER. "Some Novels of the Month." Bookman
       (New York) 42 (Nov.):319-20.
          Thoughtful and insightful, Research is a psychological study
of mediocrity and uninspired lives.

630   "The Curiosity of Mr. Wells." TLS, 30 Sept., p. 329.
          Although studded with faults, Research possesses at least
the virtue of making the reader feel the protagonist's quest for
righteousness as genuine.

631   "Current Fiction." Nation (New York) 100 (8 April):387.
          Less successful than Mr. Polly, Bealby is comedy leaning
toward farce. The book would be merely silly were it not for the
Wellsian quality of the fun.

632   "Current Fiction." Nation (New York) 101 (7 Oct.):437.
          Research evinces several similarities to Boon. The pro-
tagonist is a new Quixote of the sort only W could have portrayed
with such affection and ridicule. Amanda is even more Wellsian
than Ann Veronica.

633   E[DGETT], E[DWIN] F[RANCIS]. "A Novelist's Escapades." BET,
       13 March, pt. 3, p. 8.
          In spite of its sprightly style, Bealby is an unsuccessful
serious attempt at farce. It is far removed from the manner of
Kipps.

634   _____. "H.G. Wells in Pursuit of an Idea." BET, 15 Sept.,
       p. 20.

Research displays the best of W as a thinker, a critic of man, a student of social crisis, and a novelist. The incidents of Benham's daily life are dexterously mingled with his ideas and aspirations.

635   _____. "H.G. Wells in the Role of Bernard Shaw." BET, 26 June, pt. 3, p. 8.
    [Very long favorable review of Boon, focusing on its shrewd humor.]

636   "Essays, Criticism, Portraiture." RR 52 (Sept.):375.
    Boon offers a series of delightfully witty and satirical sketches. The book is structured like the gift box that upon opening yields a smaller box until finally the last box is opened and found to be empty.

637   F., M. "Farce by Mr. Wells." NR 3 (8 May):22.
    As farce Bealby is unconscientious and ragged; the uniting, longed-for coincidence never arrives. Though tedious in places, it possesses some good attributes such as its large number of well-handled characters.

638   "Fiction." Academy 89 (3 July):28.
    Although the wit and wisdom of Bealby is resistible, the book can be read in a mood of lazy appreciation.

639   "Fiction." ALA 11 (April):367.
    Bealby is most entertaining.

640   "Fiction." ALA 12 (Dec.):140.
    To W's admirers Research is one of his most stimulating works.

641   "Fiction." Athenaeum, no. 4579 (31 July), p. 76.
    W is neither as amusing nor as instructive as usual in Bealby. The attack on the etiquette expected of a young officer is out of date.

642   "Fiction." Athenaeum, no. 4587 (25 Sept.), p. 207.
    The protagonist of Research is so futile that the account of his life will not help anyone with a modicum of common sense. Putting aside the wholly irrational Benham, there are several other characters who make the book worthwhile.

643   "Fiction." Spectator (London) 115 (17 July):85.
    Bealby may be a farce, but it is not humorous throughout. The main character and Lord Moggeridge are well done.

1915

644 "Fiction." Spectator (London) 115 (13 Nov.):670-71.
      There is less plot than usual in Research, but the attrac-
   tion and interest one expects from W's work are present.

645 "Film Fiction." Independent (New York) 82 (21 June):513.
      Bealby is pure fun and would make a fine motion picture.

646 "Fun as Acrobat." SR (London) 120 (31 July):115.
      Too thin for a long novel, Bealby is "a perfect orgy of wild
   irresponsibility."

647 GARDINER, A.G. Pillars of Society. London: Nisbet,
      pp. 316-24.
      W's work presents the fundamental conflict between hate and
   love. Philosophically he suggests Whitman, with the difference
   that Whitman offered prophetic vision whereas W provides mechanical ingenuity.

648 "General Literature." ALA 11 (March):310.
      [Notes War.]

649 "General Literature." ALA 12 (Nov.):80.
      Boon will please some as a masterpiece of philosophical
   satire; others will wonder what it is all about.

650 GILMAN, LAWRENCE. "Sartor Resartus Up to Date." NAR 202
      (Sept.):440-45.
      Boon is the most brilliant, engrossing, and savage satire
   since Sartor Resartus.

651 GOULD, GERALD "New Novels." NS 6 (9 Oct.):18.
      The main trouble with Research is its failure to focus.
   Since Kipps, W's characters have been unbelievable, "experimental,
   tentative, modes of thinking and finding out rather than flesh-
   and-blood."

652 "H.G. Wells on Holland." Outlook (New York) 109 (24 Feb.):
      411-12.
      [Discusses the suppression, in England, of W's article on
   Holland.]

653 HACKETT, FRANCIS. "Reshaping the World." NR 4 (25 Sept.):213-
      14. Reprinted in Horizons: A Book of Criticism (New York:
      Huebsch, 1918), pp. 118-24.
      Extremely eloquent, Research seems to lack a fundamental
   truthfulness. Finally it only contributes to the human muddle.

654 HALE, EDWARD E. "Mr. Wells and Reconstruction." Dial 58
      (1 April):247-50.

Scientific cooperation is crucial to W's system of reconstruction of society into a world state.

655   . "Recent Fiction--Wells's The Research Magnificent."
        Dial 59 (11 Nov.):421-22.
            This work is impoverished by the fact that the protagonist's
        search for knowledge is left unresolved.

656   HARVITT, HELEN J. "Wells' Passionate Friends and Fromentin's
        Dominique." Modern Language Notes 30 (April):125-26.
            [Remarks on a few similarities and contrasts between these
        two works.]

657   "Humor in War Time." NYTRB, 15 Aug., p. 292.
            W is at his humorous best in Bealby, a pure farce without
        serious content providing cheerful reading for a country at war.
        W has written better but seldom with a more accurate assessment of
        human needs at this particular time.

658   "Humors." Nation (London) 17 (24 July):548, 550.
            Bealby harkens back to the spirited Georgian novel. It
        shows, however, slight indications of lassitude.

659   JONES, W. HANDLEY. "The Message of Mr. H.G. Wells." London
        Quarterly Review 124 (July):19-36. Reprinted in LA 286
        (31 July):281-90.
            W is both an extraordinary story-teller and a successful
        interpreter of contemporary thought. The chief message of his
        work pertains to his belief that while material aspects of life
        have progressed, the spiritual aspects of man have not improved at
        the same pace. Liberty and education are the solutions, but these
        remedies are defective because W's notion of them is insufficient.

660   KELLY, FLORENCE FINCH. "H.G. Wells's Bealby." Bookman (New
        York) 41 (May):323-25.
            A warm satire, this carelessly written work details a hap-
        hazard succession of events jumbled together without much logic.

661   KERFOOT, J.B. "A Bewilderment and a Book." Everybody's
        Magazine 32 (Jan.):138-40.
            An astral body of meaning, Isaac Harman reveals W as "the
        personification of headlong optimism, gazing in ironic self-
        derision at the futility of his own impatience."

662   "Life and Letters." Academy 89 (14 Aug.):99.
            Concerning W's recent prosy opinions in the Nation (London),
        his falsetto voice might be used to sing soldiers asleep.

1915

663 M., A. [N.]. "A Book of Faith." MG, 21 Sept., p. 5.
A trumpet-call rousing generous youth, Research is probably
the most notable work produced in England during the war.

664 McKEE, DONALD. "Bealby." NYTRB, 22 Aug., p. 300.
[Objects to the praise of this book as genuine humor as
expressed in NYTRB, 15 Aug., p. 292.]

665 MELVILLE, LEWIS. "The Idealist." Bookman (London) 49
(Nov.):53-54.
A novel, yet not a novel, and a sociological treatise, yet
something more, Research is individual and charming.

666 "Mr. Wells Has His Fling." SSR, 18 July, pt. 2, p. 15.
Boon is W's latest joke, not altogether a good one because
it is too much preoccupied with literary circles and critics.
Unfortunately many of the features he attacks appear in his own
works.

667 "Mr. Wells Takes a Holiday." SSR, 11 April, pt. 2, p. 17.
Somewhat better in the beginning than in the later parts,
the humor of Bealby displays to excellent advantage the sharp barb
of W's satiric technique.

668 "Mr. Wells Writes Another." SDR, 16 Sept., p. 15.
The mind of the copybook idealist in Research, like that of
its author, seems confused and exhausted. Possibly the public has
had enough of W's formula of a hero who is merely a projection of
one aspect of his creator.

669 "Mr. Wells's 'Holiday in Book-Making.'" Dial 59
(30 Sept.):278-79.
W makes it clear that he is the protagonist of Boon. Actually all of the characters in the book represent phases of W's
mind. Like Carlyle, he employs straw men on whom he foists his
doubtful or inconclusive theories.

670 "More New Novels." Outlook (New York) 111 (27 Oct.):524-25.
Research is an able parable that will prove useful to future
historians in understanding the ferment of present times.

671 "New Books." Catholic World 101 (Aug.):692.
Bealby is well written and bubbling over with fun from
beginning to end.

672 "The New Books." Outlook (New York) 109 (24 March):237-38.
Bealby is an entertaining relief from W's elaborate attempts
to deal profoundly with social conditions.

673 "Our Library Table." Athenaeum, no. 4571 (5 June), p. 506.
"Mr. Wells, we are sure, will forgive us if the comparison
tends to his disadvantage," but Boon possesses a laughter unre-
stricted by the limitations of the novel or essay. It is the work
of a man of great literary ability. [The reviewer, taken in by
the title pages, believes W to be the editor only.]

674 PAYNE, WILLIAM MORTON. "Recent Fiction." Dial 58
(15 April):304.
Bealby is unadulterated farce free from digressions into
social homiletics.

675 "Provisional Thinking." NS 5 (5 June):210-11.
Although a poor book, Boon presents an apologia for W's
work. Doubtless his unfair attacks on Henry James, Joseph Conrad,
and Thomas Hardy are engendered by the thwarted artist in W.

676 "Reviews of New Books." LD 50 (17 April):886.
Engrossing entertainment, Bealby is pure fun, free from W's
usual weighty social questions and psychological discussions.

677 "Reviews of New Books." LD 51 (16 Oct.):848.
Research presents stimulating ideas and a fine analysis of
character; W's mastery of language has never been more evident.

678 RIDER, FREMONT. "The Research Magnificent." PW 88
(18 Sept.):782-83.
Although not worth missing, this book is scrappy with dis-
torted moral viewpoints of high intent leading nowhere.

679 SHERMAN, STUART P. "H.G. Wells and the Victorians." Nation
(New York) 100 (20 May):558-61. Expanded in On Contemporary
Literature (New York: Henry Holt, 1917), pp. 50-84; an extract
of the latter reprinted in CH, pp. 231-35.
Paradoxically, in spite of his scientific training, W throws
reason aside and advances a self-willed, egoistic, anarchical
imagination. Rather than relate him to Mathew Arnold, as Van Wyck
Brooks does, we might better note his connection with Shelley. He
is not a Victorian critic but a "Georgian angel." Since the war
that part of him that was a Utopian naturalist advocating the
harmonization of conscience with nature's laws has given way to a
recognition of human purposes and ideals that run counter to
biological purposes. In general, unfortunately, "his passion for
dynamiting his own rear and sallying out on that long march with
only his 'personal luggage' betokens not an intellectual leader
but an intellectual madcap."

680 _____. "The Realism of Arnold Bennett." Nation (New York) 101
(23 Dec.):741-44. Reprinted in On Contemporary Literature (New
York: Henry Holt, 1917), pp. 50-84.

1915

W has a theory of conduct, derived from a romantic yearning for a life of divine efficiency and ecstasy, that prevents him from writing a realistic novel. Pseudoscientific romances and fairy tales of contemporary society are his forte.

681   "Significant Novels." RR 52 (Nov.):631-32.
Research is a great novel because it reveals a human soul reflected in the troubles of modern life and because it raises the hope of spiritual regeneration.

682   "Some Books of the Week." Spectator (London) 114 (15 May):691.
An unelaborate satire on contemporary literature, Boon possesses more high spirits than subtlety.

683   SPARROW, WALTER SHAW. "Political Novelists and Their Humanity." SR (London) 119 (27 March):326-27.
W has failed to see how the war has improved the English people, a clue to the degree to which his views should be held suspect.

684   "The Superman and Wells." Independent (New York) 84
(11 Oct.):70.
Research is a curiously uneven book--W at his best and at his worst.

685   "This Puzzling World." Nation (New York) 101 (2 Sept.):293.
Boon superficially bears the earmarks of antebellum British humor. In it, however, is genuine humor that informs the suffering of today's world and heals it.

686   [W., A.U.] "Mr. Wells, Satirist." Nation (London) 17
(29 May):294, 296, 298. Reprinted in BET, 23 June 1915, pt. 3,
p. 4.
In Boon W fascinatingly alternates between playfulness and seriousness. "He kicks with the gusto of an infant, or a beetle on its back, or an untamed colt." The parody of Henry James is quite poor.

687   "Wells Himself." Independent (New York) 83 (13 Sept.):365-66.
Boon reveals W's fondness for satirizing his contemporaries, his ability to sketch a character in a few swift strokes ("but he does not care much for the character afterwards"), and his tendency to start better than he finishes ("he is apt to run out of breath before he comes to the end of a novel, and if he gets his second wind it is likely to be some other kind of wind").

688   WEST, REBECCA [pseud. of Cicely Fairfield]. "The Novel of
Ideas." NR (supplement) 5 (20 Nov.):3-5.

[A passionate defense of W against those who have faulted
him for mingling ideas and fiction. Cervantes, Dostoyevsky, Zola,
and Tolstoi figure in the argument, which includes a consideration
of the difference between W and Henry James regarding Research.

689   WHELPLEY, JAMES DAVENPORT. "English Characteristics." Century
(New York) 90 (July):379-83.
W may be responsible for much of the hysteria in England,
particularly as manifested in the organization of the last line of
home defense among women.

690   "The World of Books." Sunday Times (London), 26 Sept., p. 4.
Ideas are presented too much in the form of essays rather
than in terms of action in Research. Comedy and irony abound,
however, and the settings are so various that the book may be a
sign that English fiction has, with the war, been emancipated from
its insularity.

691   WYCKOFF, ELIZABETH PORTER. "Boon." PW 88 (21 Aug.):569-70.
This work is quintessential W, who is a second Jonathan
Swift.

1916

692   "Books." Spectator (London) 117 (29 July):133-34.
On the whole Coming provides cheerful reading, though one
needs much patience regarding W's views on marriage.

693   "Books." Spectator (London) 117 (21 Oct.):476-77.
A philosophical diary of World War I, Mr. Britling relates
the narrator's Hamlet-like tragedy.

694   BOURNE, RANDOLPH. "Seeing It Through." Dial 61 (28 Dec.):563-
65. Reprinted in CH, pp. 239-43.
W's use of religion in Mr. Britling signifies an "un-
stemmable plunge into the emotional abyss, with never a recovery
or hint of a recovery." It reveals W's despair as well as a sort
of wilful bankruptcy of intellect. [See also letter by John
Cotton Dana, "Seeing It Through." Dial 62 (25 Jan.):54]

695   BOYNTON, H.W. "Some Novels of the Month." Bookman (New York)
44 (Nov.):257-59.
A brilliant, warm story superior to the impotent ranting of
a Kipling or a Shaw, Mr. Britling presents a microcosm of the
essential England just prior to World War I.

696   _____. "Some Outstanding Novels of the Year." Nation (New
York) 103 (30 Nov.):508.

1916

A book of remarkable and intrinsic merit, Mr. Britling is a sincere, vivid impression of how the war has affected England.

697   _____. "Wells vs. Bennett Again." Nation (New York) 102 (3 Feb.):133-34.
       [A letter on the Sherman-Gerould controversy, Nation (New York) 102 (6, 20 Jan.).]

698   "A British Republican." Independent (New York) 87 (28 Aug.):313-14.
       W is well-equipped for the task he undertakes in Coming.

699   "Chronicle and Comment." Bookman (New York) 44 (Nov.):223.
       [Discusses some remarks on W made by Clement K. Shorter in the Sphere.]

700   COCKERELL, T.D.A. "The Europe of Tomorrow." Dial 61 (15 July):53-54.
       Although cynical, Coming is an important, thought-provoking book.

701   D., A.M. "Mr. Wells's War Novel." DC, 20 Sept., p. 4.
       In his prewar phase, the protagonist of Mr. Britling is a bore delivering tedious monologues; in his war phase, however, he becomes a congenial and sympathetic man. The book leaves the reader with a sense of dignity and toleration.

702   De la HIRE, JEAN. L'Europe future: Réponse à M.H.G. Wells. Paris: Albin-Michel.
       [Strongly disagrees with W's view of war and of Germany in War.]

703   de WYZEWA, T. "La conversion de M.H.G. Wells." Revue des deux mondes 36 (Nov.):457-68.
       The shock of the war has brought about a conversion in W away from the dogmatic insistence upon a social utopia derived from Karl Marx to the deep, immortal feelings of his race. This transformation is particularly clear in Mr. Britling.

704   DUTTON, GEORGE B. "The Wells-vs.-Bennett Controversy." Nation (New York) 102 (10 Feb.):9-10.
       [Another letter on the Sherman-Gerould controversy, Nation (New York) 102 (6, 20 Jan.).]

705   E[DGETT], E[DWIN] F[RANCIS]. "Mr. Wells Discourses on the War." BET, 23 Sept., pt. 3, p. 8.
       W the sociologist, reformer, historian, critic, romancer, humorist is epitomized in Mr. Britling. The work is journalistic

and therefore ephemeral, but it yields a valuable birdseye view of the war and is full of vigorous thought.

706 ENGLISH, HENRY. "Mr. Wells's New Novel." Daily News and Leader, 20 Sept., p. 4.
Lacking plot, Mr. Britling presents a dialogue of points of view. Even when W's "sympathies tug at him and bid him remain on one side, his intellect escapes and is off round the corner to investigate."

707 "European War." Wisconsin Library Bulletin 12 (July):321.
[Favorable notice of Coming.]

708 "Fiction." ALA 13 (Nov.):87.
Mr. Britling is compellingly vivid and tragic without despair.

709 "Fiction and the War." SSR, 8 Oct., pt. 2, p. 13.
Although parts of Mr. Britling make good reading, the novel is not art. Void replaces form, profusion supplants economy, and volubility overwhelms delicateness. The protagonist is a composite of several men of letters, including W and Lowes Dickinson.

710 "From the Bookman's Mailbag." Bookman (New York) 42 (Jan.):609.
[A letter complaining that W and Joseph Conrad were omitted from the Bookman's list of six great English novelists.]

711 "General Literature." ALA 13 (Oct.):28.
Coming is stimulating, if not conclusive.

712 GEROULD, KATHARINE FULLERTON. "Wells vs. Bennett." Nation (New York) 102 (6 Jan.):14-15.
[An angry letter reaction to Stuart P. Sherman Nation (New York) 101 [23 Dec. 1915]), arguing among other things the merits of Research. See also Carl Hoessler, "A Weather-Beaten Hat in the Ring," Nation (New York) 102 (10 Feb.):10.]

713 GILMAN, LAWRENCE. "The Man Who Would Be King." NAR 203 (Jan.):139-42.
At once epical and intense, Research is a masterpiece, the work "of a dreamer who is also a seer; a dramatist who is also a lyric poet; a philosopher who has walked among men."

714 GOULD, GERALD. "New Novels." NS 7 (23 Sept.):594.
In Mr. Britling the novelist and the sociologist meet. W has used the form of a novel to achieve a new form. The chief importance of the book is the fact that future historians will consult it.

1916

715   "H.G. Wells Forecasts the Future." NYTRB, 28 May, p. 221.
Although interesting, Coming is marred by sloppy writing.

716   H[ACKETT], F[RANCIS]. "Mr. Wells Discovers God." NR 8
(7 Oct.):248-49. Reprinted in Horizons: A Book of Criticism
(New York: Huebsch, 1918), pp. 125-30.
Mr. Britling, albeit not exempt from faults, is the finest
example of W's great ability to bring his age into focus.

717   HALE, EDWARD E. "Recent Fiction." Dial 61 (19 Oct.):314-15.
Judged as the writing of a publicist and not of a novelist,
Mr. Britling is excellent.

718   HOLMES, JOHN HAYNES. "H.G. Wells: Novelist and Prophet."
Bookman (New York) 43 (July):507-14.
W has passed through three stages: simple storyteller,
sociologist, and realist. Although consistent in his attack on
current disorder and the low state of the human mind, W has not
worked out a final philosophy of life and offers no perfect solutions. He combines the two apparently opposed ideals of aristocracy and socialism.

719   KELLY, FLORENCE FINCH. "Voices in the Wilderness." Bookman
(New York) 43 (Aug.):626-27.
Conveying many stimulating, penetrating ideas, Coming is
unfortunately stylistically sloppy, like most of what W writes.

720   "Light Exercises in War Prophecy." TLS, 25 May, p. 244.
In Coming W "rattles on agreeably" with no pretense of
original research or solid knowledge. The book does not warrant
serious criticism.

721   "Mr. Britling Sees It Through." Athenaeum, no. 4610 (Oct.),
p. 472.
The major problem with this book is W's acceptance of the
existence of people like Britling, whereas he must know that this
type should be made to see that they are obstructive to the
progress of democracy.

722   "Mr. Wells Sees It Through." Nation (New York) 103
(26 Oct.):397-98.
Despite some flaws, never before has W produced such an
engaging presentation of his ideas as in Mr. Britling. The war
has made W realize "the absurdity of clamoring for order, measure,
and control in the external world while reserving a silly and
sentimental little anarchy in the heart."

723 "Mr. Wells's New Novel." MG, 22 Sept., p. 3.
     A significant document of the period, Mr. Britling will
affect the peace that is to come in various subtle and valuable
ways.

724 "New Books." Catholic World 104 (Dec.):405-6.
     Mr. Britling is a wonderful study of character development.
This is the strongest of W's novels; it is more than fiction.

725 "New Books Reviewed." NAR 204 (Aug.):303-5.
     Coming is shrewd, plausible, and imaginative; its style is
clear and unmannered.

726 "New Books Reviewed." NAR 204 (Dec.):939-41.
     W's success in Mr. Britling derives in part from the fact
that he has little method as a novelist, that he is frankly dis-
quisitional. There may be some subtlety in this seeming off-
handedness, but basically W has few prepossessions as to what a
novel should be.

727 "The Novel and a Few Novels." Outlook (New York) 114
     (8 Nov.):570.
     An extraordinary book, Mr. Britling provides an unprece-
dented record of the psychology of a nation. Its tale of colossal
tragedy is related abruptly and unconventionally, with a searching
vividness.

728 "A Novel of the War by Mr. Wells." NYTRB, 24 Sept., p. 1.
     An accurate cross-section of contemporary English life, Mr.
Britling presents a penetrating study of the protagonist's mental
processes. The emotional intensity of the final chapter is une-
qualled in W's work.

729 "Other Books Worth While." LD 53 (18 Nov.):1344.
     What is involved in the change required in Coming is set
forth as if W were certain of his prophetic powers.

730 P[ERRY], J[OHN]. "Forecast by Mr. Wells." Nature 97
     (10 Aug.):478.
     [Descriptive review of Coming.

731 PHELPS, WILLIAM LYON. "The Advance of the English Novel, Part
     IX." Bookman (New York) 43 (June):404-13. Reprinted in The
     Advance of the English Novel. (New York: Dodd, Mead, 1916),
     pp. 252-54.
     A distinct contribution to modern art, Wheels of Chance
possesses a touch of spirituality very much obscured by the materialism of W's later works. W the artist is more admirable than W
the sociological preacher.

1916

732   "Prophesyings by Mr. Wells." Nation (New York) 103
      (17 Aug.):157.
           [A few questions are raised in reaction to Coming.]

733   R., A.B. "The Forecasts of H.G. Wells." BET, 31 May, pt. 3,
      p. 4.
           [Descriptive review of Coming, concluding that we may take
      W's latest prognostication for what it is worth.]

734   R[EEDY], W[ILLIAM] M[ORRIS]. "What I've Been Reading."
      Reedy's Mirror (St. Louis), 28 July, pp. 489-90.
           For the most part the views of society expressed in Coming
      are the same found in W's fiction.

735   RICHARDSON, HILARY G. "Wells's Appreciation of Bennett."
      Nation (New York) 102 (10 Feb.):10.
           [A final letter on the Sherman-Gerould controversy, Nation
      (New York) 102 (6, 20 Jan.).]

736   RIDER, FREMONT. "Mr. Britling Sees It Through." PW 90
      (16 Sept.):842.
           Pathos is a new note for W in this book, a work as stimu-
      lating as Research.

737   SAMPSON, GEORGE. "Mr. Wells at His best." Bookman (London) 51
      (Nov.):49-50.
           Containing some of the best and the worst of W's descrip-
      tions, Mr. Britling suffers from too much abstraction.

738   SHERMAN, STUART. "Mr. Sherman Returns to 'Wells vs. Bennett.'"
      Nation (New York) 102 (20 Jan.):74.
           [A letter responding to Katharine F. Gerould (Nation (New
      York) 102 [6 Jan.]).]

739   S[HORTER], C[LEMENT] K. "A Literary Letter." Sphere 66
      (30 Sept.):298.
           In spite of his limitations, W is trenchant and powerful in
      Mr. Britling. The book will no doubt have a permanent place as
      the best record of England in World War I.

740   SQUIRE, J.C. "Literary Affairs in London" Dial 61
      (5 Oct.):251.
           [Mere note that Mr. Britling is a conspicuous novel for
      autumn.]

741   "The Transfiguration of England." Independent (New York) 88
      (23 Oct.):162-63.
           Mr. Britling surpasses all of W's other books concerning the
      war.

742   "Views and Reviews of Current Fiction." <u>Trib</u>, 30 Sept., p. 9.
       Both a historical and a human document, <u>Mr. Britling</u> is a
tremendous, well-sustained masterpiece. The reader's reaction is
"like the momentary hush which is greater reward in the playhouse
and the concert-room than is the loudest of applause."

743   "War and Books." <u>NYTRB</u>, 5 Nov., p. 470.
       [Praises a letter written by an English father in <u>Mr.
Britling</u>.]

744   "The War in a Novel." <u>TLS</u>, 21 Sept., p. 451. Reprinted in <u>CH</u>,
       pp. 236-38
       <u>Mr. Britling</u> is not a great novel on the war, but its tone
is memorable.

745   WHITTEN, WILFRED. "Mr. Wells and Prophecy." <u>Bookman</u> (London)
       50 (July):108-9.
       W's projections in <u>Coming</u> tend to be cold and unrealistic.
He does not take human emotions into consideration when he con-
siders the future.

746   WOODLOCK, THOMAS F. "The Security of Democracy." <u>Catholic
       World</u> 103 (May):145-54.
       In his portrait of mankind W has borrowed from the Church's
concepts of human nature and has provided no significant solutions
to human problems. Although he makes the best possible argument
for socialism, his agnostic scheme only demonstrates its
impractability.

                              1917

747   ABBOTT, LYMAN. "Knoll Papers." <u>Outlook</u> (New York) 116
       (11 July):398-99.
       Despite his naive egotism, W is something of a mystic. Some
passages in <u>God</u> radiate spiritual illumination and inspiration.

748   ADENEY, D.D. "Mr. H.G. Wells's 'Modern Religion.'" <u>Biblical
       World</u> 50 (Oct.):220-26.
       Although it presents ancient gnostic notions as a new dis-
covery, <u>God</u> proclaims a reawakened sense of reality and of the
presence of a personal God in human life. On the whole, however,
W's ideas about theology and God are inconsistent, inaccurate, and
illogical.

749   "The Allies at War." <u>Bellman</u> 22 (31 March):358.
       [Short notice on <u>Britain at War</u>.]

1917

750   ARCHER, WILLIAM. God and Mr. Wells. London: Watts.
      God is an interesting, stimulating book marked by deep
poetic feeling, but it tends to soar gaily over the problems that
beset theological analysis.

751   BALLARD, FRANK. "The God of Mr. H.G. Wells." London Quarterly
      Review 128 (July):48-61. Reprinted in LA 294 (1 Sept.):543-51.
      A somewhat flamboyant work, God evokes some valid criticisms
but tends to suffer from too much confidence in assumptions of
infallibility, unfair accusations against Christianity, dogmatic
and often meaningless assertions, manifest fallacies, and unnecessary sneers. What appears as intellectual novelty in this work is
in fact a plagiarism of Christian concepts.

752   BELL, BERNARD IDDINGS. "The Meaning of Mr. Wells's New
      Religion." AM 120 (Nov.):620-25.
      In writing about God W shows he is bewildered, and it is
ironic that those who accept lines of theological belief most
antithetical to those of W are the very people who can best understand and appreciate God.

753   BLUNT, JOHN. "Britlingland." Bookman (New York) 45
      (Aug.):586-93.
      [Discusses the uplands of Essex as the source of many of W's
characters.]

754   "Books." Spectator (London) 118 (10 March):302-3.
      W is inconsistent in Britain at War. A pacifist would not
wish to see Germany broken or desire that the League of Nations be
armed to control all nations.

755   "Books." Spectator (London) 118 (16 June):674-75.
      A sincere pursuit of religion, God is too critical of other
faiths.

756   "Books." Spectator (London) 119 (27 Oct.):451.
      Vaguely drawn, the main character of Bishop is as limited as
W in understanding religious thought.

757   BOYNTON, H.W. "A Stroll through the Fair of Fiction." Bookman
      (New York) 46 (Nov.):338.
      Though sincere, Bishop is absurd in many respects.

758   _____. "Mr. Polly Being a Bishop." Bookman (New York) 46
      (Nov.):353-55.
      In Bishop W's conception of God is feeble, presenting the
deity as an indulgent confidant with little influence on the
actions of men. This "new deity is simply an apotheosis of that

eager, searching, dogmatic, well-disposed and unpractical personality, Mr. H.G. Wells."

759 ____. "Outstanding Novels of the Year." Nation (New York)
105 (29 Nov.):599-600.
Bishop is interesting but of little account as a novel. W
"has the world by the buttonhole still, but he may not be able to
hold it forever with that same old anecdote of his."

760 "Briefs on New Books." Dial 62 (17 May):445.
W's discussion of the yielding pacifist and of the religious
revival are weaknesses in Britain at War.

761 C., C.S. "The Soul of a Bishop." MG, 17 Sept., p. 3.
Bishop succeeds in making a stale theme interesting, but
readers who prefer the W of Kipps will not rank this work as even
second best.

762 "Casual Comment." Dial 63 (19 July):75-76.
[Brief attack on W's view of German aviation.]

763 "The Cheapjack in Religion." SR (London) (supplement) 123
(19 May):iii.
Neither philosophically nor scientifically sound, God re-
vives the old Manichaean heresy and introduces new problems that
leave the intellect and the heart dissatisfied.

764 CHESTERTON, G[ILBERT] K. "Mr. Wells as a Bishop." New Witness
10 (13 Sept.):466-67. Reprinted in LA 295 (3 Nov.):294-97.
In Bishop W really copies the Victorians he thinks he is
combating with regard to his imposition of a parochialism on the
universe.

765 "Chesterton Assails Wells's Attempted 'Simplification' of
Religion." CO 63 (Sept.):186.
[Report on G.K. Chesterton's attack on God in the Christian
Commonwealth (not seen).]

766 "Chronicle and Comment." Bookman (New York) 44 (Feb.):607-8.
Whereas Tono-Bungay is a prose epic of English civilization
at a point of stagnation, Mr. Britling records that civilization's
discovery of spiritual consciousness. Salvation lies within the
awakened individual rather than in socialistic ideology.

767 "Chronicle and Comment." Bookman (New York) 46 (Oct.):185.
The "God" presented by W in Bishop is a dissatisfying,
uninspiring deity, one too intellectually oriented.

1917

768   "Chronicle and Comment." Bookman (New York) 46 (Dec.):399–400.
      The main character of Bishop is unreal, merely a journal-
istic bundle of humanitarian ideas.

769   COLBY, ELBRIDGE. "Mr. Wells's New Book Unread." Bellman 22
      (14 April):409–11.
      [A prediction, derived from W's previous writings, as to
what he will argue in the yet unpublished God.]

770   D'ARCY, MARTIN. "The 'God' of Mr. Wells." Month 129
      (April):304–12.
      Mr. Britling is the best novel on the war to date. W's
notion of God somewhat resembles that of Shaw, though more rev-
erent. [Intricate discussion of W's theology, taking exception
with W's reduction of divine omnipotence.]

771   "De Maupassant War Tales." NYTRB 13 May, p. 188.
      [Notes that Swinburne and Comte advanced an idea of the
deity similar to that in God. This review is reported in "Mr.
Wells's 'Finite God,'" LD 54 (2 June):1706.]

772   "A Desperate Hope." TLS, 17 May, pp. 229–30. Reprinted in LA
      294 (27 July):234–39.
      In God W combines his own religious experience with a bio-
logical view of the universe. The deity presented is conceived so
that W could acknowledge him.

773   DEWEY, JOHN. "H.G. Wells, Theological Assembler." Seven Arts
      2 (July):334–39.
      In God W escapes his own tortured ego by creating an ulti-
mate alter ego as the deity of the modern world. [This review
reported in "Mr. Wells's God as the 'Projection' of His Own
Image," CO 63 (Aug.):112–13.]

774   "Difficulties Inherent in the Belief in a 'Struggling God.'"
      CO 62 (March):200–201.
      [Reports and quotes Rev. Carnegie Simpson's adverse remarks,
printed in the British Weekly (not seen), that refute W's notion
of God as presented in Mr. Britling.]

775   E[DGETT], E[DWIN] F[RANCIS]. "A Wellsian View of Man and His
      Soul." BET, 16 May, pt. 2, p. 6.
      God is not convincing, nor does it make clear what precisely
W really thinks. Albeit entertaining, the book is negatively
oriented, principally concerning W's disbelief.

776   _____. "The Fatal Verbosity of H.G. Wells." BET, 12 Sept.,
      pt. 2, p. 6.

The fictional basis of <u>Bishop</u> is extremely insecure. There are glimpses of reality, but W's characterization is unconvincing and reveals his lack of humor and resourcefulness.

777 "Fiction." <u>Athenaeum</u>, no. 4622 (Oct.), p. 529.
A thoughtful book written in a lucid style, <u>Bishop</u> may well fail to convince many readers.

778 "Fiction." <u>ALA</u> 14 (Dec.):99.
<u>Bishop</u> is not as interesting or as convincing as <u>Mr. Britling</u>.

779 "Fiction." <u>Outlook</u> (New York) 117 (10 Oct.):219.
More an argument than a novel, <u>Bishop</u> presents a well-wrought protagonist and many humorous touches.

780 FORREST, D.W. "The 'Modern Religion' of Mr. H.G. Wells." <u>Expositor</u> 14 (Dec.):437-46.
Although derived from a genuine religious experience, <u>God</u> contains several serious contradictions.

781 "General Literature." <u>ALA</u> 13 (April):310.
An excellent discussion, <u>Britain at War</u> is sane, philosophic, and practical.

782 "General Literature." <u>ALA</u> 13 (July):426.
From <u>God</u> some will conclude that W is still struggling in darkness; others will say he has expressed the only possible faith.

783 GILMAN, LAWRENCE. "A Divine Infatuation." <u>NAR</u> 206 (Nov.): 786-92.
The dope scenes in <u>Bishop</u> may be real, but it was "crass artistic tactlessness which made them an essential part of the machinery of a spiritual drama." Otherwise this unimpeachably sincere and at times poetic book might have been a genuinely moving spiritual adventure.

784 _____. "Mr. Wells and God." <u>NAR</u> 206 (July):123-30.
W's effort in <u>God</u>, to give us a deity acceptable to human reason fails, as it always has failed in the hands of others. It does not satisfy the deeper regions of the human self.

785 "The Gospel According to Wells." <u>Nation</u> (New York) 104 (14 June):710-11.
Compared to W's mellifluous egotism and insolence revealed in <u>God</u> "the Reverend Billy Sunday walks humbly and reverently before God and the history of human experience."

1917

786   "The Great European War." Athenaeum, no. 4615 (March), p. 156.
      [Brief, descriptive notice of Britain at War.]

787   "A Group of New Novels." SSR, 30 Sept., pt. 2, p. 15.
          Pretending to analyze the protagonist of Bishop minutely, in
      fact W resorts to blatant artificialities (e.g., a mysterious
      drug). The work resembles a novel only in its portrait of the
      main character, who nonetheless is not necessarily true to life or
      important.

788   H[ACKETT], F[RANCIS]. "Espousing God." NR 12 (22 Sept.):223-
      24. Reprinted in Horizons: A Book of Criticism (New York:
      Huebsch, 1918), pp. 131-38.
          A fascinating performance, Bishop develops a distinctive if
      somewhat thin character--"essentially a bobbin on whom the reli-
      gious thread is wound." No one writing today compares with W as a
      novelist of ideas.

789   HARRISON, FREDERIC. "A Very Invisible God." NCA 82
      (Oct.):771-81.
          [A discussion of God, presented in dialogue form, with
      apparently fictitious characters. W is accused of plagiarizing
      from Conte.]

790   HEDGES, M.H. "Seeing It Through." Dial 62 (25 Jan.):54.
          [A letter in rebuttal to R. Bourne's review (Dial 61
      [28 Dec. 1916]).]

791   HOLLAND, HENRY SCOTT. "A Book for the Month." Commonwealth
      (London) 23 (July):193-200.
          [Negative review of God, concluding that W cannot escape the
      Christian beliefs he attacks.]

792   "Humoring Mr. Wells." LD 55 (20 Oct.):29.
          [Reports critical comments from the Christian Century
      (Chicago) (not seen) and the Advance (Chicago) (not seen) con-
      cerning Bishop.]

793   "'I Have Been But Scribe to the Spirit of My Generation.'" PO
      111 (11 May):441-42.
          Although not new, the challenging yet constructive ideas of
      God are superbly well stated.

794   "The Impatient Idealist." Athenaeum, no. 4619 (July), p. 346.
          Aside from a cocksureness in God about many things wise men
      have left uncertain, "there should be joy among the angels of God
      for this novelist doing reverence to the ultimate reality, and
      standing where the great Augustine stood."

795   "Italy, France, and Britain." NYTRB, 11 Feb., p. 45.
       [Very favorable review of Britain at War.]

796   JACKS, L.P. "God the Invisible King." HJ 15 (July):683-89.
           W is much more indebted to past religions than he knows, and
       it is doubtful that his philosophy is any sounder than his
       history.

797   [JOHNSON, HEWLETT.] "Editor's Notes." Interpreter 13
       (Oct.):4-5.
           Unlike Nietzsche, W believes in prayers; unlike Shaw, he
       desires spiritual rather than economic change. Yet W dislikes any
       objective moral standards. He is somewhat confused concerning his
       view of the individual.

798   KELLY, FLORENCE FINCH. "Taking Thought for the Morrow."
       Bookman (New York) 45 (April):184-85.
           [Discusses W's view of America in Britain at War.]

799   KENNON, HARRY B. "Seeing It Through." Dial 62 (25 Jan.):54.
           [A letter commenting on R. Bourne's review (Dial 61
       [28 Dec. 1916]).]

800   "Kipling, Wells and the War." Independent (New York) 90
       (2 April):35-36.
           Whereas in Sea Warfare Kipling never rises above the level
       of a photographer, in Britain at War W reveals himself as a con-
       structive statesman and philosopher.

801   LACEY, T.A. Mr. Britling's Finite God. London: Mowbray.
           [A pamphlet presenting two lectures discussing the merits
       and errors of W's views in Mr. Britling and God.]

802   LAY, WILFRID. "H.G. Wells and His Mental 'Hinterland.'"
       Bookman (New York) 45 (July):461-68.
           The vast hinterland represents W's artistic term for the
       unconscious. W frequently portrays and satirizes the conflicts
       between the primordial cravings of the soul and the restrictions
       imposed by social life.

803   _____. "The Marriage Ideas of H.G. Wells." Bookman (New York)
       45 (Aug.):606-13.
           Without sacrificing charm or artistry, W includes in his
       works the insights of modern psychoanalysis. Especially with
       regard to marriage he demonstrates an awareness of the hidden
       factors involved in psychic conflicts.

804   L[IPPMANN], W[ALTER]. "Mr. Wells at the War." NR 10
       (17 March):201-2.
           [A favorable review of Britain at War.]

1917

805   M., D.L. "H.G. Wells at the Front." <u>BET</u>, 7 March, pt. 2,
       p. 8.
       [Descriptive review of <u>Britain at War</u>.]

806   MACY, JOHN. "Mr. Britling Sees Spooks." <u>Dial</u> 63 (28 June):
       13-15.
       <u>God</u> evinces the typical W weakness of incongruously mixing
       sociological and political problems with sheer fiction. Dis-
       cussing uncertainties in a tone of certitude, W writes of God the
       way he once wrote of flying machines.

807   M[AJOR], H.D.A. "A Modern Confession of Fatih." <u>Modern
       Churchman</u> 7 (June):131-37.
       Although in <u>God</u> W presents an unorthodox Christianity, he is
       not a formal heretic. The value of the message of the book is not
       diminished by W's bad attempt at interpreting the history of the
       Christian Church. Perhaps W is inclined to measure all religious
       experience by his own. He does, however, represent the tone and
       temper of modern England.

808   _____. "The Bishop That Did." <u>Modern Churchman</u> 7 (Dec.):
       485-88.
       W's advice in <u>Bishop</u> expresses the modern English tempera-
       ment, "which disposes men to withdraw from difficult and doubtful
       situations instead of urging them to remain and do their duty."

809   M[ILNE], J[AMES]. "A New Wells Novel." <u>DC</u>, 12 Sept., p. 2.
       Hardly a novel, <u>Bishop</u> is a tract by a man of vision with a
       style of romance.

810   "Mr. Wells and His God." <u>Trib</u>, 15 Sept., p. 6.
       The protagonist of <u>Bishop</u> suffers from an exaggerated ego,
       and one cannot imagine what he would do without his problems.

811   "Mr. Wells as Military Critic." <u>Glasgow Herald</u>, 22 Feb.,
       p. 12.
       The illuminating ideas in <u>Britain at War</u> are brilliantly
       expressed.

812   "Mr. Wells as Theologian." <u>SDR</u>, 3 Sept., p. 6.
       Hastily and crudely written, <u>God</u> is disappointingly inaccu-
       rate and unoriginal. It will contribute only to W's reputation
       for versatility.

813   "Mr. Wells Describes 'Renascent Religion.'" <u>NYTRB</u>, 13 May,
       p. 185.
       [Mixed review of <u>God</u>, noting its sincerity but doubting its
       representativeness of contemporary thinking.]

814   "Mr. Wells Discovers God." Independent (New York) 90
      (2 June):434-35.
          W's faith, as expressed in God, may be narrow and may in-
      clude too few articles of belief, but it is lucid and profound.
      This book marks a stage in W's religious development similar to
      that indicated by Shaw's preface to Androcles and the Lion.

815   "Mr. Wells Reasserts His Belief in a Struggling God." CO 63
      (July):40-41.
          [Reports reactions to God in several publications, including
      Public Opinion (London) (not seen) and Zion's Herald (Boston) (not
      seen).]

816   "Mr. Wells 'Sees It Through.'" LD 54 (10 Feb.):344.
          [Reports critical comments from the Christian Guardian
      (Toronto) (not seen) and Reedy's Mirror (St. Louis), 19 Jan.,
      1917, p. 37, in reaction to W's notion of God.]

817   "Mr. Wells's Experimental Novel." Nation (New York) 105
      (11 Oct.):401-2.
          The religious element "which bubbled up in Mr. Britling, and
      spouted up in God the Invisible King sinks to a shallow little
      surface pool in The Soul of a Bishop." The chief amusement of the
      book lies in the fact that Scrope is really W in bishop's dress.
      Herein also lies W's limitation: "he cannot find the way to the
      inside of any type of consciousness but his own."

818   "Mr. Wells's Latest Religion." SR (London) 124 (22 Sept.):228.
          W writes well only in fantastic tales and in no other form,
      least of all in Bishop. "It is one of the disadvantages of a
      'literary' education that one is pained by such a work."

819   "Mr. Wells's New Broom." LD 54 (26 May):1596.
          [Reports various responses to W's letter printed in the
      Times (London) concerning his alleged proposal to abolish the
      English dynasty.]

820   MOFFATT, JAMES. "The Soul of a Bishop." Bookman (London) 53
      (Oct.):19-20.
          Sacrificing drama to propaganda, W, the amateur theologian,
      has produced a work as close to a failure as anything he has
      written.

821   "New Books." Catholic World 105 (Sept.):832.
          Full of vague philosophy, God is a feeble attempt at
      religion.

822   "New Books Reviewed." NAR 205 (April):627-29.
          [A favorable review of Britain at War, focusing on W's
      lucidity and optimism.]

1917

823   NEWTON, C.B.   "Mr. Wells's Idea of God."   Bellman 22
      (2 June):608.
            Superficially W's ideas in God appear new; in essence they
      are the same as those of Christianity.   An inconsistency regarding
      tolerance and intolerance pervades his reasoning.

824   "Notes."   Nation (New York) 104 (31 May):661.
            W's description of the war fronts in Britain at War is more
      convincing than his generalizations and his remarks on the psycho-
      logical reactions of the belligerent nations.

825   "Notes on New Fiction."   Dial 63 (25 Oct.):402.
            The scenes and characters of Bishop are as bare as stage
      settings; it is the soul, not the action or the person, which
      interests W in this work.   The message is one of high inspiration.

826   OXON, C.   "A Book for the Month."   Commonwealth (London) 23
      (July):200-201.
            One hopes for W that the truth will overcome the mythology
      of God.

827   "Religion and Philosophy."   Outlook (New York) 116
      (20 June):305.
            Although frank and sincere, God is of little value.   W
      writes too much.

828   R[IDER], F[REMONT].   "'God, the Invisible King'--As a Churchman
      Sees Him."   PW 92 (15 Sept.):802.
            Bishop is an uncomplicated but very trenchant and stimu-
      lating work of fiction.

829   ROZ, FIRMIN.   "Les Anticipations de M. Wells."   Revue des deux
      mondes 41 (15 Sept.):445-56.
            W seems split between two opposing tendencies: belief in
      the power of the individual and nationalism and belief in a ra-
      tionalist utopia without nations, a society without classes, and a
      religion without churches.

830   SCHMALHAUSEN, SAM.   "The Joy of Misunderstanding, or the Reply
      Courteous."   Call (New York), 23 Sept., p. 15.
            [Replies to Blanche Watson's criticism (Call, 16 Sept.) of
      his review of God (Call, 2 Sept.).]

831   _____.   "The Renaissance of Superstition."   Call (New York),
      2 Sept., p. 15.
            Deficient in intellectual content, God is oracular but not
      illuminating.   It abounds in remarkable figures of speech.

832 SECCOMBE, THOMAS. "God the Invisible King." Bookman (London)
52 (July):122-24.
This work provides a humane notion of religion for those in
spiritual need.

833 SIMART, MAURICE. "Herbert George Wells: Sociologue." Mercure
de France 120 (March-April):193-221.
[Discusses the wide range of W's sociological views, particularly pertaining to the masses, women, and education, and
concludes that they are detailed rather than vague and both republican and socialist.]

834 SLOSSON, EDWIN E. Six Major Prophets. Boston: Little, Brown
& Co., pp. 56-128.
W's favorite theme is the reaction of society against a
disturbing force, its natural inertia in resisting any foreign
influence. W sympathizes with such new forces, though not always
confident of their victory. As a futurist he appraises everything
by what it will engender, sometimes with surprising accuracy. He
simultaneously hates the muddled, chaotic state of society and
distrusts a logical, orderly civilization.

835 "The Soul of a Bishop." Trib, 21 Oct., p. 4.
Although this book is not the most impressive work in years,
it testifies to W's alertness to new vistas. [Cites numerous
critical reactions to the book.]

836 "The Soul of a Bishop." TLS, 13 Sept., p. 438.
An interesting comment on the war, this book is an artistic
success but a theological failure.

837 TARGETT, A.B. "Marriage and Mr. Wells's Religion."
Englishwoman 35 (Sept.):205-11.
Contrary to W's notions, the universal experience of mankind
rather than mere religious bigotry or sexual prudery is the source
of the idea of the sanctity of marriage that W so frequently
laments.

838 THOMAS, PHILIP. "Mr. Wells's Essay in God-Making." Positivist
Review 25 (1 July):153-58.
In God W approaches but just falls short of the positivist
conception of humanity as the supreme being of man's life; for he
harks back to the theocractic stage.

839 "Vital Problems in Current Novels." NYTRB, 16 Sept., p. 341.
Not without power or interest, Bishop tends to be artificial
and unartistic. Using a hashish trance to free the soul is ludi-
crous, and Lady Sunderbund proves to be a mere piece of machinery.

1917

840   "War and the Future." TLS, 22 Feb., p. 89.
        Written by a layman for laymen, this book is only partially
trustworthy.

841   WARWICK, FRANCIS EVELYN. "The God of Mr. Britling--And of Our
        Fathers." Bookman (New York) 45 (April):145-47.
        If God works through moral laws that order the universe, if
at least some moral law pervades his creation, then Mr. Britling's
God is gentlemanly but rather small and helpless.

842   WATSON, BLANCHE. "Reviewing a Reviewer." Call (New York), 16
        Sept., p. 14.
        [Takes vigorous exception to Schmalhausen's review of God
(Call, 2 Sept.) and views the book as a stimulating, far-visioned
work.]

843   "With the Allies at War." SDR, 17 April, p. 6.
        [A favorable review of Britain at War.]

844   WOOD, CLEMENT. "War, God, Belgium, and Weak Women." Call (New
        York), 29 Dec., p. 15.
        A heavy theme is given life by W's invariable craftsmanship
in Bishop. "As a theological tract it is a good piece of fiction;
as a novel, it is an excellent treatise upon the Arian heresy."

845   WOOD, HERBERT G. "The Attitude of Mr. Wells towards Jesus
        Christ." Expositor 14 (Dec.):447-60.
        [Assesses W's negative views of Jesus Christ in God and
allows that he is still somewhat Christian in his views.]

846   WORSLEY, F.W. Letters to Mr. Britling. London: Scott.
        [A series of letters discussing, in personal and compas-
sionate terms, many of Mr. Britling's ideas about God.]

847   YARROW, VICTOR S. "H.G. Wells' Discovery of God." Reedy's
        Mirror (St. Louis), 19 Jan., p. 37.
        W's discovery of God under the pressure of war commands our
attention, but his notion that God sends war to perfect humanity
is naive.

1918

848   ABBOTT, LYMAN. "Knoll Papers." Outlook (New York) 118
        (28 June):467-60.
        Coming is less valuable for its accuracy than for its stimu-
lation of thought.

849   "Among the New Novels." Outlook (New York) 120 (6 Nov.):380.
      Aside from certain character portraits and the account of
the protagonists' childhood, Joan and Peter is disappointing. Its
theme is not very clear.

850   BALCH, EMILY GREENE. "Book Reviews." Survey 40 (20 July):457.
      Fourth Year exemplifies W's extraordinary gift for illumina-
tion and for inventive, constructive thinking.

851   BATES, HERBERT. English Literature. New York: Longmans,
      Green, pp. 519-20.
      In Kipps and Polly W uses language that conveys pictures; in
the later novels he seems to delve beneath the surface of realism.

852   BENNETT, ARNOLD. "The Fear of Knowledge." Bookman (New York)
      48 (Sept.):81-82.
      W makes good use of Samuel Butler's method of not merely
delineating but inquiring into the real nature of human character
and conduct. In general he manages the method intelligently and
scrupulously, but sometimes in his hands it is prone to a sentimental breakdown.

853   "Books." Spectator (London) 121 (10 Aug.):155.
      W's views of high officials and foreign policy in Fourth
Year are wrong-headed.

854   "Books." Spectator (London) 121 (16 Nov.):551.
      At once a novel and "a huge panoramic pamphlet," Joan and
Peter details British national incompetence resulting principally
from bad education and "fetish worship of the Hanoverian Monarchy."

855   BOURNE, RANDOLPH. "The Relegation of God." Dial 65
      (19 Sept.):215-16.
      W lacks "the slight skeptical weariness with which the
living remnant of a younger generation is beginning to view the
ease and blithness of political pragmatists." Yet Joan and Peter
is a vivacious narrative with characters who seem real in spite of
the fact that they are only types.

856   BOYNTON, H.W. "All Sorts." Bookman (New York) 48 (Dec.):
      490-91.
      Lacking solid action or characterization Joan and Peter
evinces fresh effusions of the most active and irresponsible mind
of this age.

857   DODGE, WALTER PHELPS. "Mr. Wells on the War." SR (18) 125
      (19 Jan.):50.
      [A letter attacking W's view of the war.]

1918

858   DOTTERER, R.H.   "The Doctrine of a Finite God in War-Time
       Thought."   HJ 16 (April):415-28.
          W manifests a curious atavistic preference for the image of
       kingship rather than that of fatherhood in presenting his idea of
       God.

859   E[DGETT], E[DWIN] F[RANCIS].   "The Undaunted Prolixity of Mr.
       Wells."   BET, 25 Sept., pt. 2, p. 6.
          More a discursive essay than a novel, Joan and Peter merely
       provides a vehicle for W's ideas.   Perhaps it will somehow become
       a best seller, but surely no novelist, not even one of W's reputa-
       tion, can survive the strain of such endless repetition.

860   "Fiction."   Athenaeum, no. 4634 (Oct.), p. 446.
          [Briefly, noncritically notes Joan and Peter.]

861   "Fiction."   ALA 15 (Nov.):72.
          Although Joan and Peter is interesting, it would have bene-
       fited from a blue pencil.

862   "Fiction."   OS, no. 11 (Dec.), p. 114.
          Joan and Peter is more interesting as criticism than as
       fiction.

863   FOLLET, H.T., and W. FOLLET.   Some Modern Novelists: Apprecia-
       tions and Estimates.   New York: Holt, pp. 235-63.
          Aside from a tendency toward inordinate repetition and melo-
       drama, W's work is exciting in its modernity.   It is infused with
       an instinct for truth that requires the sacrifice of tired
       conventions.

864   "The Fourth Year."   Independent (New York) 95 (13 July):64.
          [Remarks favorably on W's treatment of Wilson in Fourth
       Year.]

865   GEORGE, W.L.   A Novelist on Novels.   London: Collins,
       pp. 18-19.
          [Brief comment on Kipps and Machiavelli, as well-written,
       thoughtful books unstartling in form and content.]

866   GREY, J.C.   "War Book of the Month."   Bookman (New York) 47
       (Aug.):658-65.
          Fourth Year is plausible and often convincing.   But we look
       to W for literature, not for the millennium, and in this regard he
       is failing us.

867   H[ACKETT], F[RANCIS].   "A Novel of Opinion."   NR 16
       (5 Oct.):291-93.

The general estimate of the age presented in Joan and Peter is consummately interesting. The book is pamphleteering in flesh and blood. For W novels are principally a means whereby he gives kinetic form to his most recent ideas; rather than diverse personalities, they present a brilliant pattern of social and political convictions. This book "is triumphant beyond all decent expectation."

868   HUNTER, ALYMER D. That "Danse a trois" Mr. Wells. London: Caxton.
       [A pamphlet recognizing the sincerity but challenging the logic of God.]

869   "A Hymn of Hate." SR (London) 126 (5 Oct.):917-18.
       [A negative review of Joan and Peter that asks whether W is justified in raising the price of his books by fifty per cent.]

870   "Joan and Peter." NS 11 (28 Sept.):515-16.
       Interesting, if irritatingly unsatisfying, this work is more lecture than art. It suffers from sloppy writing, faulty characterization, satire pivoting on tired mechanical tricks, and a degeneration in thinking.

871   "Joan and Peter." WG [not seen]. Reprinted in LA 299 (9 Nov.):367-69.
       As a novel this book is padded and deficient, its story sacrificed for an inconclusive and nearly inchoate essay on education.

872   JOHNSON, WILLIS FLETCHER. "Morbid Problematizing." Trib 21 Sept., p. 7.
       Although clever and brilliant, Joan and Peter tends to sacrifice sincerity to sheer smartness. After reading W's "scintillating verbal pyrotechnics," one wonders if he approves of or believes in anything other than himself.

873   LASKI, HAROLD J. "The Literature of Reconstruction." Bookman (New York) 48 (Oct.):216.
       [Praises W's view of the League of Nations.]

874   L[ASKI?], H[AROLD] J. "Mr. Wells Thinks Aloud." NR 15 (6 July):295.
       [Favorable review of Fourth Year, taking exception only to W's eulogy of the Electoral College of the United States.]

875   "A League of the Nations." Nation (New York) 107 (19 Oct.):451.
       Fourth Year presents the League of Nations as an articulation of the blurred feelings and hopes that W symbolized by his God.

1918

876   "Literary Futures." <u>Nation</u> (New York) 107 (7 Sept.):
      245.
          "It is an interesting conjecture what will become of Mr.
      H.G. Wells, who mainly occupies himself with bringing water from a
      little way upstream when the mass of men have already camped at
      the source." [A passing reference.]

877   LOVE, BERT. "Eight Novels." <u>Reedy's Mirror</u> 27 (11 Jan.):25.
          <u>Bishop</u> leaves uncertain the significance of the new reli-
      gious views W expresses through his protagonist.

878   LYND, ROBERT. "Mr. Wells at Length." <u>Daily News</u> (London), 19
      Sept., p. 2.
          There are sufficient exciting episodes in <u>Joan and Peter</u> to
      balance W's social criticism. Best of all is W's dialogue
      technique.

879   M., J. "An Imperfect Deity." <u>TLS</u>, 2 May, p. 209.
          [A letter indicating that in 1904, B.A.G. Fuller expressed
      notions about God similar to those of W.]

880   MILNE, JAMES. "Mr. Wells Looks Back." <u>DC</u>, 19 Sept., p. 2.
          A book of value, <u>Joan and Peter</u> abounds in clever, sugges-
      tive things.

881   "Mr. Wells on World Peace." <u>SDR</u>, 27 June p. 8.
          Pungent comment, presented with humor, characterizes <u>Fourth
      Year</u>.

882   "Mr. Wells Outpours." <u>Nation</u> (New York) 107 (5 Oct.):377.
          Never has W been more eloquent, suggestive, whimsical, cock-
      sure yet less consistent or conclusive than in <u>Joan and Peter</u>.

883   "Mr. Wells Scolds England and Others." <u>NYTRB</u>, 22 Sept.,
      pp. 397-98.
          Less a story than an expression of W's theories and a gen-
      eral scolding of England, <u>Joan and Peter</u> is interesting even if it
      expresses W's bad temper and remains less rewarding than his study
      of Britling.

884   "Mr. Wells's <u>Anticipations.</u>" <u>TLS</u>, 13 June, p. 270.
          This book is instructive but deficient in an understanding
      of human nature.

885   "New Books." <u>Catholic World</u> 106 (Feb.):695-96.
          Seldom has propaganda been less beguilingly presented than
      in <u>Bishop</u>. W mistakenly identifies the mental with the spiritual.

886   "New Books Reviewed." NAR 208 (Nov.):776-78.
       Though not as fine as Mr. Britling or Research, Joan and
Peter offers fascinating characters and ideas. W is a caricatur-
ist with genius.

887   "The New 'Emile.'" Athenaeum, no. 4634 (Oct.), pp. 437-38.
       W sacrificed the future for the present when he failed to
choose between being a novelist or a teacher of social science.
He could not be both at the same time. Now and then Joan and
Peter gives clues to how great a novelist he might have been had
he not magnanimously chosen to serve the present.

888   "Our Library Table." SR (London) 125 (17 Aug.):755.
       Fourth Year is characterized by cleverness and a marring
cocksureness.

889   "Periodicals." TLS, 11 April, p. 175.
       W's concept of a finite God is well thought out.

890   PROTHERO, J.K. "The Two Voices of Mr. Wells." New Witness
       [not seen]. Reprinted in LA 299 (7 Dec. 1918):624-27.
       Time and again the story of Joan and Peter is interrupted by
W's attack on education. Whenever W is able to separate himself
from such arguments in the book, he demonstrates that earlier
artistic genius he has currently done so much to destroy.

891   RIDER, FREMONT. "Mr. Wells Again Comes Forward as Seer and
       Prophet." PW 94 (21 Sept.):847.
       Joan and Peter, not so much a story as propaganda, is an
intellectual feast. It will be W's biggest seller.

892   SAMPSON, GEORGE. "The New Émile." Bookman (London) 55
       (Nov.):60-61.
       The whole future of Britain depends upon the degree to which
the warnings W has woven into the absorbing story of Joan and
Peter are taken to heart.

893   "Some Novels of Present and Past." RR 58 (Nov.):553.
       Less successful in literary skill and in interest than Mr.
Britling, the story of Joan and Peter is a clothes-horse on which
W hangs various ideas. W the pamphleteer triumphs over W the
novelist.

894   W., A.S. "Mr. Wells's New Novel." MG, 19 Sept., p. 3.
       Although there is not a word in Joan and Peter one would
willingly forgo, nevertheless the reader grows impatient at times
at the mixture of two modes of writing: one in which the protagonists work out their very interesting natures, the other in which
they are shamelessly used as vehicles for W's ideas.

1918

895   "The War and Problems of a World Peace." NYTRB, 26 May,
       p. 241.
       [Favorable review of Fourth Year.]

896   "Wells on Education." NYT, 3 Nov., pt. 3, p. 1.
       [Reports W's ideas on education in Joan and Peter.]

897   "Wells's New Novel Presents an Inspiring Vision of World-
       Peace." CO 64 (Jan.):40-41.
       With Mr. Britling and God, Bishop forms a powerful trilogy.

898   WHITEFORD, ROBERT NAYLOR. Motives in English Fiction. New
       York: Putnam's, pp. 83-85.
       Men in the Moon imitates the humorous, tragically cynical
spirit of Swift's Gulliver's Travels.

899   WOOD, CLEMENT. "Wells and the Schoolroom." Call, 27 Oct.,
       p. 10.
       Greater than Tono-Bungay, Machiavelli, and Mr. Britling,
Joan and Peter offers "absorbing narrative, dazzling flashlights
of gossip, gripping skyrockets of philosophising."

900   [WOOLF, VIRGINIA]. "The Rights of Youth." TLS, 19 Sept., p.
       439. Reprinted in Contemporary Writers (London: Hogarth,
       1965), pp. 90-93; and in CH, pp. 244-47.
       W's great talent is his ability to visualize an entire world
in which his latest idea can grow. Flesh and blood have been
lavished upon the characters of Joan and Peter "but in crude lumps
and unmodelled masses, as if the creator's hand, after moulding
empires and sketching deities, had grown too large and slack and
insensitive to shape the fine clay of men and women."

                              1919

901   BINNS, LEONARD ELLIOTT. Mr. Wells' Invisible King: A Criti-
       cism. London: Society for Promoting Christian Knowledge.
       By character and training W is unfit to be a religious
teacher. Besides questionable arguments, God suffers from dogmatism. The book has some value in revealing something of the
lay mind and in bearing witness to what is good. Christianity
provides all and more than W promises his followers.

902   "Books of the Fortnight." Dial 66 (31 May):576.
       Fire is less a novel than an eloquent conversation that
becomes a sermon interrupted by an operation.

903   BOYNTON, H.W. "All Over the Lot." Bookman (New York) 49
       (Aug.):728-34.

Fire is a characteristic bit of improvisation on a congenial theme.

904   BRITTEN, CLARENCE. "The Ordeal of Reality." Dial 67
       (23 Aug.):140-44.
       Barrack, not Job Huss, should have been the hero of Fire.

905   BROUN, HEYWOOD. "The Undying Fire." Trib, 22 May, p. 10.
           The scheme of this book is too obtrusive and too regular.
       The characters whom W disfavors never have a chance against those
       whom he favors.

906   CAZAMIAN, LOUIS. "H.G. Wells: Jeanne et Pierre." Revue
       politique et littéraire 57 (31 May):340-43.
           This novel presents a complete image and a bold critical
       interpretation of English society. English destiny appears sus-
       pended in a profound complete reform of intelligence. Although
       artistically uneven, the book offers a rich gallery of social
       figures, suggestive historic presentations, and a congealing of
       ideas. All of W's novels sketch the same critique of English
       society, all express the same lesson of courage and reason; but
       never before has this lesson of organizaing reason been so di-
       rectly and systematically presented.

907   CHESTERTON, GILBERT K. Heretics. New York: Lane, pp. 68-91.
           W is a man of genius characterized by scientific humility.
       Unfortunately he is prone to the great scientific fallacy of
       beginning with protoplasm instead of with the human soul. Thus he
       mistakenly thinks that nothing endures and that in Utopia the
       idea of original sin will disappear. The heresy of immoral hero-
       worship "may perhaps still be prevented from perverting one of the
       best thinkers of the day."

908   "Condensed Classics." NYT, 1 June, pt. 3, p. 1.
           [Reflects somewhat negatively on the retelling of the bib-
       lical account of Job in Fire.]

909   "A Contemporary Job." TLS, 5 June, p. 305.
           Not as heretical as God, Fire suffers from W's notion that
       particulars should be lost in the universal.

910   CUNLIFFE, J.W. English Literature During the Last Half
       Century. New York: Macmillan, pp. 180-97.
           Clearly and artistically expressing vague popular discon-
       tents, W has widened the scope of the novel and reflects many
       typical trends in the thinking of his time. Although the main
       characters of Tono-Bungay are originally conceived and finely
       drawn, the minor ones, especially Beatrice, are much less success-
       ful. Likewise whereas W represents the lower forms of sexuality

1919

faithfully and sympathetically, he has no gift for expressing
passion in its higher moods.

911   DEAKIN, A. WALFORD. "Mr. H.G. Wells Pierces a Rood."
       Interpreter 17 (July):225-28.
            In God W propounds a theory about the purpose of suffering,
       whereas in Fire that theory is applied to a test case.

912   EAGLE, SOLOMON. "Books in General." NS 13 (7 June):240.
            Fire is one of W's best book since his early work, but its
       argument is curiously similar to that of Tennyson's In Memoriam.

913   _____. "Books in General." NS 14 (6 Dec.):280.
            The first installment of Outline may not offer new ideas or
       instruct the learned, but it bodes well for the entire work as an
       admirable masterpiece of popularization.

914   E[DGETT], E[DWIN] F[RANCIS]. "The Undying Fire of Mr. Wells."
       BET, 24 May, pt. 3, p. 10.
            Not a novel despite W's claims to the contrary, Fire is
       undeniably brilliant. Although its conclusion is lame and impo-
       tent, the book presents a vigorous discussion of many vital
       questions.

915   "Fiction." ALA 15 (June):358.
            [Quotes from the review in Dial 66 (31 May 1919):576.]

916   "Fiction." Outlook (New York) 123 (10 Sept.):59.
            Not very profound or satisfying, Fire amounts to something
       quite less than its biblical source.

917   "Fiction." Spectator (London) 122 (7 June):736.
            Free from the querulousness and personal attacks that marred
       Joan and Peter, Fire offers a stoical creed mixed with a mag-
       nanimous idealism not always present in W's works.

918   "Fiction." Wisconsin Library Bulletin 15 (July):184.
            There is more philosophy than plot in Fire.

919   GARROLD, R. "Open Letter to H.G. Wells." New Witness 15
       (22 Aug.):350-53.
            W's world is only a little larger than that of Jane Austen,
       an author to whom he is similar in several respects. [Argues with
       W's views on Catholicism.]

920   GILMAN, LAWRENCE. "Mr. Wells and Job." NAR 210 (July):122-27.
            A strange blend of burlesque extravaganza and spiritual
       allegory, Fire perpetrates "errors of discretion, gaucheries
       of humor, rough satires, exuberances of imagination, that any

Literary Editor could set right for him between the puffs of a
pipe." Moreover, his incessant talk about God has become boring,
though the book itself is impassioned.

921 H[ACKETT], F[RANCIS]. "Mr. Wells in the Pulpit." NR 19
     (7 June):188-89.
         The happy ending of Fire takes the edge off W's sermon, but
     it is "characteristic of his swift, experimental, sensational,
     superficial mind." Although W is trying to harness the existing
     religious impulse for social melioration, the world clearly needs
     another sort of remedy.

922 LEVINE, HYMAN. "Out of the Furnace." Public 22 (14 June):
     633-34.
         Fire will be read and reread for the wisdom and inspiration
     found on nearly every page.

923 LUNN, ARNOLD [pseud. of Henry Moore?]. Loose Ends. London:
     Hutchinson, pp. 137, 176, 182, 184, 188-89.
         Quirk, a schoolmaster, praises W and the moderns for getting
     nearer to life than any of the Victorian idols, especially com-
     mending them for their high general level of craftsmanship.
     Wheels of Chance is a little-known masterpiece.

924 M., A.N. "A Faith on Trial." MG, 6 June, p. 5.
         The eloquent fury of Fire forces the reader to face certain
     realities.

925 MENCKEN, H.L. "The Late Mr. Wells." Prejudices, First Series.
     New York: Knopf, pp. 22-35.
         W the artist is extinct. Such a work as the radiant Tono-
     Bungay has given way to the awful Joan and Peter. A few of his
     books will survive, as indeed they should.

926 "Mr. H.G. Wells: Eminent Victorian." SR (London) 128
     (13 Dec.):556-57.
         That W belongs to the era of Spencer and Tennyson is con-
     firmed by Outline, a work written a generation after its time.

927 "Mr. H.G. Wells's Great Forthcoming Book." JOL 2 (1 Nov.):101;
     (22 Nov.):182; (6 Dec.):217-18; (20 Dec.):322; (3 Feb. 1920):
     362; (27 March 1920):712.
         [An advance report on Outline, praising the work as the
     greatest, most important work W has yet written.]

928 "Mr. Wells and Evil." Athenaeum, no. 4648 (30 May), p. 398.
         [A mild, negative response to the ideas presented in Fire.]

1919

929   "Mr. Wells in the Land of Uz." Nation (London) [not seen].
       Reprinted in LA 302 (30 Aug.):532-35.
          Whereas the sincerity and the logic of Fire are unquestion-
       able, W's faith in the increase of knowledge as a remedy for the
       ills of mankind is dubious.

930   "Mr. Wells Presents the Universe." TLS, 27 Nov., p. 693.
          In the first volume of Outline W's gift for knowing what he
       wants to say and for being confident that it is worth saying is
       conveyed in an easy and vigorous style.

931   "Mr. Wells's Latest." Observer (London) [not seen]. Reprinted
       in SSR, 21 Dec., p. 15a.
          Outline is a good alternative to the specialist's treatment
       of history.

932   "Mr. Wells's Latest." SR (London) 127 (14 June):582-83.
          Fire "is called a contemporary novel. Heaven knows with
       what it is contemporary, and Hell knows that the thing is no
       novel."

933   "A Modern Version of 'Job' by Mr. Wells." NYTRB, 25 May,
       p. 294.
          Many of the arguments in Fire are put forth brilliantly.
       Part allegory, part philosophical treatise, the work may present
       somewhat contradictory ideas about God, but it remains an inter-
       esting piece of writing well worth reading.

934   "New Books." Catholic World 108 (Feb.):697.
          Not very human or appealing, Joan and Peter surpasses W's
       previous extravagant attacks on the Catholic Church.

935   "1918." Wisconsin Library Bulletin 15 (Jan.):34.
          W's customary vivid style is evident in Fourth Year.

936   "Notable Books in Brief Review." NYTRB, 6 April, p. 183.
          [Nonevaluative notice of Idea.]

937   "Our Literary Manners and Mr. Wells." LD 63 (27 Dec.):33.
          [Reports W's controversy over his alleged authorship of
       Barbellion's Diary and a reaction to this controversy printed in
       the Kansas City Star (not seen).]

938   "The Outline of History." Athenaeum, no. 4674 (28 Nov.),
       p. 1256.
          A better guide than W in this book (pt. 1) could not be
       desired, nor is it likely that he will be faulted in his facts.

939   PUGH, EDWIN. "Big Little H.G. Wells." New Witness 14
       (4 July):195-99.
          [An interesting personal account of the author's admiration
       for and meeting with W; remarks the possible prototype for
       Chitterlow in Kipps.]

940   PURE, SIMON. "The Londoner." Bookman (New York) 49
       (June):427-29.
          A recasting of the Book of Job in modern dress, Fire makes a
       pointed statement about the nature of human suffering, especially
       in modern times.

941   ROBERTS, R. ELLIS. "The Younger Novelists." Bookman (London)
       57 (Dec.):95.
          For W the novel is an instrument that can serve all kinds of
       ends; it becomes in turn essay, sermon, rhapsody and tract.

942   "Salvation by History." Nation (New York) 108 (28 June):1014.
          Only the fable is old in Fire; "the language belongs wholly
       to the elastic, colloquial, experimental generation of which Mr.
       Wells is the prophet furthest heard." The book is less triumphant
       as a result of its ideas and unsatisfying structure than on ac-
       count of the "swiftness, the energy, the serried tumult of vivid
       images, the easy and varied diction, the natural ranging from
       ironic comedy to the tragedy of profound despair—these no other
       living English novelist could have achieved."

943   SAMPSON, GEORGE. "Job the Undefeated." Bookman (London) 56
       (July):135-36.
          [Points out the ways in which Fire is similar to the Book of
       Job and Goethe's Faust.]

944   SCHOEN, MAX. "H.G. Wells on Education." Education 39
       (Feb.):325-34.
          In Joan and Peter W's scheme for future education is prac-
       tical and practicable. He stresses the need to bring the student
       into vital contact with himself as an individual, with his nation,
       and with mankind.

945   "Some Books of the Week." Spectator (London) 123 (22 Nov.):698.
          The first part of Outline is readable and spirited, an
       ambitious venture boding well for the remainder of the book.

946   "The Undying Fire." NS 13 (31 May):218-19.
          W is to be congratulated for his original and successful
       experiment in this work. A restatement of the theory presented in
       God, its doctrine is a readable and an integrated feature of the
       novel as a whole.

1919

947   "The War and After." OS, no. 9-10 (Sept.-Oct.), p. 90.
      Idea presents a clear direct statement of arguments favoring
the League.

948   WAUGH, ALEC. "World of Books." Sunday Times (London), 25 May,
      p. 7.
      Fire is an interesting, vital essay in which W demonstrates
that his collectivism is based on the individual rather than on
the state.

949   "Wells Pictures a Modern Job." SSR, 8 June, p. 19a.
      Although it does not define evil in all its modern manifes-
tations, the discussion in Fire is characterized by a penetration,
earnestness, and restraint not often found in W's works. The book
represents W's most considerable philosophical achievement.

950   WILLIAMS, HAROLD. Modern English Writers: Being a Study of
      Imaginative Literature, 1890-1914. New York: Knopf,
      pp. 357-64.
      Although an excellent storyteller for his generation, W
lacks the fervor of sympathy that inspires the great writer portraying simple and impulsive human beings.

951   [WOOLF, VIRGINIA.] "Modern Novels." TLS, 10 April, p. 189.
      Expanded in "Modern Fiction," in The Common Reader, 1st ser.
      [1925] (New York: Harcourt Brace & World, 1953), pp. 150-58.
      W, Bennett, and Galsworthy are more concerned with materi-
alism than with the spirit. In W a "great clod of clay . . . has
got itself mixed up with the purity of his inspiration."

                              1920

952   BELLOC, HILAIRE. "A Few Words with Mr. Wells." Dublin Review
      166 (Jan.):182-202.
      The adjectives, verbs, and adverbs of Outline testify to a
strong emotional bias in favor of a naturalistic view of the
universe. W's interpretation conflicts with reason.

953   _____. "Mr. Wells' Outline of History." LM 3 (Nov.):43-62.
      This work is factually defective. W saw a great task before
him, but he preferred to follow rather than to lead. The book
will have a prodigious vogue in its own time and an early grave in
the future. [See also a letter of disagreement: Warren H.
Lowenhaupt, "Mr. Belloc and Mr. Wells," LM 3 (Dec.):119-200.]

954   "Can Mr. Wells Write History?" Nation (London) [not seen].
      Reprinted in SSR, 8 Feb. 1920, p. 13A.

                              106

Over the years W has been forced to consider the ethical improvement of mankind, even as did the Victorians he despised. W's study of "universal" history attempts to impart a vision allowing for humanity's realization of its ideal potentiality.

955   "Discussing H.G. Wells." JOL 2 (21 Feb.):572.
        [A few remarks on W.H. Wilcockson's assessment of W's geological information in Outline.]

956   "Dr. Wells Dissects Russia." LD 67 (25 Dec.):16-18.
        [Reports responses in the New York Evening Post, the Seattle Times, the Chicago Daily News, the Weekly Review (New York), the Trib, the Call, the Schenectady Citizen, the St. Louis Post-Dispatch, the Troy Record, the Philadelphia Public Ledger, the St. Louis Globe-Democrat, and the NYT [all unseen] to W's articles on Russia.]

957   DOWNEY, RICHARD. "The Chronicles of Mr. H.G. Wells." Month 136 (Aug.):142-49; (Sept.):216-29; (Oct.):325-36. Reprinted in Some Errors of H.G. Wells (London): Burns Oates & Washbourne, 1921).
        [Detailed objection to inaccuracies in Outline, especially facts concerning religion.]

958   EDGETT, EDWIN FRANCIS. "A Novelist Becomes a Historian." BET, 24 Nov., pt. 3, p. 6.
        Outline is W's most important book, a work proving that the best historian is a man with imagination.

959   ERVINE, ST. JOHN. "Some Impressions of My Elders: H.G. Wells." NAR 212 (July):118-28.
        In a sense W is a personification of the past thirty years, "a questioning, variable, demanding person, with some impatience and testiness of temper, with, at times, a fantastic and wayward manner, but always superimposed on these superficialities, an eager and unthwartable desire for a true belief." Although his work manifests a "local pessimism," his "universal optimism" remains unimpaired.

960   FINGER, CHARLES J. "From the Workshop of H.G. Wells." Reedy's Mirror 29 (1 April):74.
        W's career falls into three phases: the production of fantasies, works of socioeconomic concerns, and novels on spiritual themes. He writes about three types of people: sheeplike followers, people with talent, and strong individuals who lead a complacent society toward a new order.

961   F[ORSTER], E.M. "A Great History." Athenaeum, no. 4705 (2 July), pp. 8-9; no. 4706 (9 July), pp. 42-43. Reprinted in CH, pp. 248-54.

1920

Volume one of Outline is a masterpiece, particularly regarding arrangement and selection of detail. Though the style is
journalistic, it is appropriate for the book. Yet individuals do
not come alive. W's history lives "by its fundamental soundness,
expressed through brilliant parallels and metaphors; not by imaginative reconstructions of individual people or scenes."

962   "General Literature." ALA 17 (Dec.):110.
       Outline will be very controversial.

963   GOLDRING, DOUGLAS. "H.G. Wells and the War." Nation (New
       York) 110 (1 May):589-90. Expanded in Reputations: Essays in
       Criticism (New York: Seltzer, 1920), pp. 79-98.
       We must be grateful to W for his wide influence, but since
the war he has lost touch with youth. He has fled from the task
of educating people, and his recent work reflects public opinion
rather than shapes it. "When he wakes again he will see the
forces he once led far in front of him."

964   GUYOT, EDOUARD. H.G. Wells. Paris: Payot.
       W applies the concept of evolution in order to give mankind
its just value and its true sense. Mixed with his evolutionary
notions is a strain of Puritanism, a haunting concern with salvation that becomes accentuated when W speculates about man's future. For W, adaptability to the conditions of life created by
civilization is a form of victory over nature; but increasingly he
stresses that evolution is less planned than willed and that the
natural conditions fixing the destiny of mankind are less important than those man creates himself. A pragmatic conception of
life humanizes W's idea of evolution (combining free will and
predestination), which idea includes two acts of faith: that
life has sense and that each mortal shares in the immortality of
the collective unconscious.
       In portraying the future W stresses the liberation from
contingencies, the spirit of anticipation, the creation of a
scientific and literary illusion, the examination of "operating
causes," the affirmation of a cold and rigid will, and the inevitability of an economic aristocracy forcing man to progress.
[Chapter five traces W's concept of aristocracy.] For W socialism
affirms a racial consciousness, a collective destiny affecting
both the individual and the human species through a transformation
of human mentality rather than through a metamorphosis of society's institutions.
       W's characters are receptacles for all the boredom, mental
laziness, and resistance to progress he perceives in England.
Unlike Dickens, W's attack is not localized. His belief in liberal sexual behavior and the emancipation of women is related to
his trust in the advancement of biology and free choice.

965   HARRIS, FRANK. Contemporary Portraits. 3d ser. New York:
       Harris, pp. 1-13.
            [Reflects on W's early works, which Harris edited, and
       concludes that W works too rapidly with a subsequent loss of
       quality in his later works and, as well, of the potentiality he
       had as a young man.]

966   "History from an Airplane." NS 15 (11 Sept.):624-25.
            In some ways provoking and admirable, Outline frequently
       presents erroneous or disputable opinions. Most fascinating is
       W's ability to perceive a unity in historical events.

967   "History with a Purpose." TLS, 23 Sept., p. 612.
            [Notes traces of Bossuet, Kant, and Berkely in Outline.]

968   JAMES, HENRY. The Letters of Henry James. Edited by Percy
       Lubbock. New York: Scribner's Sons, 1:298, 335, 388, 400,
       404; 2:37, 137, 180, 229, 261, 333, 485, 487.
            [Important letters, often amounting to private reviews of
       several of W's works, in which are reflected the controversy
       between W and James concerning the nature of fiction and art.]

969   JOHNSON, ALVIN. "World History According to Wells." NR 23
       (11 Aug.):309-12.
            Outline is a political work in which W seeks an impartial
       position between human brotherhood and the world state. Although
       weak with regard to certain specifics, the greater part of the
       work is interesting and illuminating.

970   McDONALD, PHILIP B. "World History by a Novelist." SSR, 21
       Nov., p. 7a.
            Even a reader who does not like W's novels can find interest
       in Outline.

971   "Mr. Wells on Himself." SR (London) 129 (3 Jan.):10.
            [A letter replying to W's letter (SR (London) 128
       [27 Dec .1919]:609 written in response to this anonymous author's
       review of Outline (SR (London) 128 [13 Dec 1919]:556-57).]

972   "Mr. Wells on Mankind." TLS, 1 July, p. 415.
            W's treatment of prehistory in Outline is more enjoyable
       than his discussion of history because in the former part his
       imagination had more play.

973   "Mr. Wells on the Outlook for Russia." TLS, 30 Dec., p. 883.
            An otherwise shrewd book, Russia suffers from cliché-ridden
       attacks on capitalism and a patronizing attitude toward Russia.

1920

974   "Mr. Wells Outline." Athenaeum, no. 4725 (19 Nov.):pp. 690-91.
      Certain inaccuracies and a certain esthetic blindness not-
withstanding, Outline is a wonderful achievement on the whole, not
likely to be superseded in our generation.

975   "Mr. Wells Turns Historian." NYTBM, 14 Nov., pp. 1, 24-25.
      Although readable and interesting, Outline is really too
broad in coverage and too narrow in its sources to be successful.

976   "Mr. Wells Unfolds His Panorama of World History." CO 69
      (Nov.):623-26.
      Outline is limited by what it neglects, such as the periods
of the Renaissance and the Reformation.

977   "Mr. Wells's Outline of History." Spectator (London) 124
      (12 June):798.
      [A favorable review of the first volume.]

978   "Mr. Wells's Visit to Russia." Spectator (London) 125
      (25 Dec.):854-55.
      In excusing the Bolsheviks, Russia presents some aston-
ishingly unconvincing judgments not easily reconciled with W's
cleverness.

979   O'LONDON, JOHN. [pseud. of Wilfred Whitten]. "How Mr. Wells
      Gets There." JOL 2 (20 March):683.
      In Outline one witnesses how things really happened.
"Grandiose conquests, immense marches and destructions, meet the
age, but 'raw humanity' and defects of character were working to
an equation." Yet W also realizes that great ideas had presented
themselves to man's vision.

980   "The Outline of History." Call, 29 Nov., p. 8.
      This work may indeed be faulted and might well have begun
with book 3, but it is a brave and earnest effort worthy of
attention. It will prove a significant paragraph in mankind's
declaration of intelligence.

981   PEARSON, EDMUND LESTER. "New Books and Old." Weekly Review 3
      (8 Dec.):558.
      Whatever the verdict of historical critics, Outline is ex-
traordinarily interesting.

982   PURE, SIMON. "The Londoner." Bookman (New York) 50
      (Feb.):544-51.
      [Discusses W.L. George's lecture on W and argues that W
stresses the practical and the immediate with regard to human
capacities.]

983   ____ . "The Londoner." Bookman (New York) 51 (June):417-18;
52 (Sept.):52; 52 (Nov.):222-23.
[Brief praise of Wi with comments on W's forthcoming visit
to New York and on his lecture method.]

984   RUDLAND, PERCY M. "The Courage of H.G. Wells." JOL 2
(14 Feb.):532.
The fearless truthfulness in W's work is nothing less than
courageous; courage, in fact, is a persistent theme throughout his
works. Especially with regard to the relationship between the
sexes, he has probably had a considerable influence on the younger
school of novelists.

985   "Russia As It Is." NS 16 (11 Dec.):296-97.
Realistic in its presentation, Russia is sympathetic to its
subject without being doctrinaire in a simple-minded manner.

986   SAMPSON, GEORGE. "Cursor Mundi." Bookman (London) 59
(Oct.):10-13. Reprinted in LA 307 (13 Nov.):413-15.
We finish Outline with admiration and amazement, but we have
learned less about man than about the voter. "In the beginning of
his story we hear the roar of chaos clearing into the music of the
spheres; in the end we hear nothing but the noise of politics; and
the sound is for all the world like the quacking of ducks."

987   SLOSSON, EDWIN E. "Wells on the World." Independent (New
York) 104 (11 Dec.):361-62.
Although Outline is necessarily inferior in comprehensiveness and scholarship, it benefits from readableness as well as
unity of style and viewpoint.

988   STEWART, HERBERT L. "The Prophetic Office of Mr. H.G. Wells."
International Journal of Ethics 30 (Jan.):172-89.
W provokes readers to independent thought, makes them laugh
at themselves rather than at the preceeding generations, and
inspires them to discover the unity between them. [Discusses many
of W's ideas.]

989   STUART, CAMPBELL. Secrets of Crewe House. London: Hodder &
Stoughton, pp. 61-81.
[Reports W's work on the Enemy Propaganda Committee and
reprints his "Memorandum on Propaganda Policy against Germany."]

990   "A 'Tour de Force.'" Nature 106 (30 Sept.):137-40.
Outline is a gift to education, a personal, selective,
entertaining, even great document.

991   WILLIAMSON, CLAUDE C.H. Writers of Three Centuries: 1789-
1914. Philadelphia: Jacobs, pp. 452-59.

1920

Paying little heed to style and form, W tends to be slangy and unselectively cumbrous. [Primarily focuses on W's notions of God.]

1921

992   "Another War?" SDR, 23 Sept., p. 8.
      Salvaging is typically Wellsian in its haste of composition and its avoidance of the facts of human frailty.

993   "An Authors' Battle." LD 71 (1 Oct.):28-29.
      [Reports the controversy between W and Henry Arthur Jones, whose forthcoming book entitled My Dear Wells says W hates England.]

994   BAKER, A.E. "The Religious Development of H.G. Wells." Church Quarterly Review 92 (April):69-105. Reprinted in LA 310 (16 July 1921):148-55; (23 July 1921):212-15; (30 July 1921): 277-83.
      Even allowing for certain shortcomings in the old Church of England, W's description of it is a short-sighted caricature, influenced by his nonconformist upbringing and training in natural science. W has moved from the position of an agnostic (1907) to a fervent apostle of a God who dwells in the heart of man (1917), a vague personification of humanitarian ideals. As with genuine prophets and mystics he combines the search for God and the terror of God; yet he avoids tackling the problem of evil, misunderstands the concept of omnipotence, and undercuts his position by attempting to discredit belief in the Trinity.

995   BECKER, CARL. "Mr. Wells and the New History." American Historical Review 26 (July):641-56. Reprinted in Everyman His Own Historian (New York: Crofts, 1935), pp. 169-90.
      Not designed as a reference book or as a contribution to knowledge, Outline is refreshing and enlightening. W may have read the past too close to his own desires, but his book serves as a powerful weapon employed in the war against hypocrisy, superstition, fanaticism, and tyranny. Strictly speaking this book may not be history, but its value is not depreciated as a result.

996   BELLOC, H[ILAIRE]. "Mr. Belloc and Mr. Wells." LM 3 (Feb.):422.
      [A letter in response to one by W (LM 3 [Jan. 1921]) replying to Belloc's article (LM 3 [Nov. 1920]).]

997   "Books." Spectator (London) 127 (6 Aug.):174-76.
      "If the capacities and temperaments of whole populations were, or might become, what Mr. Wells assumes them to be or to be

capable of becoming [in Salvaging], then there would be nothing left to do but to declare that nobody was ever more right than Mr. Wells and to carry out his programme with all possible speed."

998   BREWSTER, DOROTHY. "In Russia." Nation (New York) 112 (13 April):554-55.
      [Points up a few limitations in Russia.]

999   "Briefer Mention." Dial 70 (April):479.
      Russia deserves a better reception than it is likely to receive.

1000   "Briefer Mention." Dial 71 (Aug.):245.
       [Brief, basically negative notice of Salvaging.]

1001   BULLETT, GERALD. "Exuberance in Literature." NS 18 (26 Nov.):224-26.
       The finest example of exuberance in modern fiction is Mr. Polly, a book that successfully challenges Dickens.

1002   BURKE, JOHN BUTLER. "Mr. Wells and Modern Science." Dublin Review 169 (Oct.):222-36.
       Although a lucid work, Outline indicates that W is only an interested outsider. [Presents a theological discussion not immediately related to W.]

1003   "Churchill and Merezhkovsky Reply to Wells." CO 70 (Feb.): 216-18.
       [Reports the counterarguments of Winston Churchill and Dmitri Merezhkovsky in response to W's view of Bolshevik Russia.]

1004   "Contributions to History." RR 63 (Jan.):111.
       [Nonevaluative review of the first volume of Outline.]

1005   C[OOK] S[HERWIN] L[AWRENCE]. "Civilization." BET, 1 June, pt. 3, p. 4.
       Few books on the problem of world peace have been more readable, thoughtful, and logical than Salvaging.

1006   _____. "Wells in Russia." BET, 23 March, pt. 2, p. 8.
       Powerful and poignant, Russia properly emphasizes character and motives in the function of Soviet government.

1007   CROLY, HERBERT. "Hope, History and H.G. Wells." NR 29 (30 Nov.):10-12.
       W is "a parlor Bolshevik"; he recognizes the impotence of violence as a means for radical change. W is optimistic in his belief in human perfection.

1921

1008   DIXON, JAMES MAIN. "Wells Versus Kipling." Personalist 2
        (April):97-105.
            Outline suffers from an unsatisfactory treatment of the role
        of religion, which Kipling takes into account in his own works.
        Kipling's stress on human character is more pertinent than
        W's focus on an educational equivalent to mere intellectual
        inquisitiveness.

1009   E. "The Respectability of Mr. Wells." SR (London) 132
        (13 Aug.):203-4.
            W's age has triumphed over his mediocre mind, rendering him
        a professional tilter.

1010   ELLIOT, JOHN. "At Home with H.G. Wells." Bookman (New York)
        52 (Feb.):542-45.
            [Equates the characters of W's work, principally in Mr.
        Britling, to W himself and certain other people living in Essex
        County.]

1011   G., J.C.M. "Education and World Citizenship." Nature 107
        (4 Aug.):707-8.
            Clear and orderly, though marred by minor defects, Salvaging
        is an important book, especially with regard to W's ideas about
        education.

1012   "General Literature." ALA 17 (Feb.):178.
            Russia is a vivid presentation.

1013   GIBBS, PHILIP. More That Must Be Told. New York: Harper,
        pp. 59-63.
            W is more revolutionary in his ideals than most people
        suspect. He escapes detection because he possesses "the artful-
        ness of the 'restorer' of ancient monuments, who, by underpinning
        and other architectural dodges, produces a brand-new building
        without outraging public sentiment by obvious destruction of the
        old."

1014   GILLET, LOUIS. "Le dernier roman de M. Wells." Revue des deux
        mondes 61 (15 Feb.):870-82.
            In Outline W's pessimistic view of war and of political
        leaders provides the foundation for his optimism concerning man-
        kind's future. W rejects the notion of sin; there is no fall,
        only progression. He is a Darwinian who somehow believes in the
        goodness of human nature.

1015   GOMME, A.W. Mr. Wells as Historian. Glasgow: MacLehose,
        Jackson & Co.
            Throughout Outline W blunders by making confident statements
        at random, assertions too often derived from dubious sources or

114

from preconceived ideas. Such defects are especially apparent in
his treatment of ancient Greece and Rome, which sections reveal
carelessness in writing and confusion in thought. The book is
written in a flat, undistinguished style lacking edge and deci-
sion, and it is relieved only by an affected simplicity.

1016 _____. "Mr. Wells as Controversialist." FR 116 (July):124-30.
[Refutes attack on Mr. Wells as Historian in W's "History
for Everybody," FR 115 (June 1921):887-910.]

1017 "H.G. Wells' Views on Bolshevik Russia Challenged." CO 70
(Jan.):68-70.
[Reports the counterarguments of Henry Jones and John
Spargo.]

1018 HACKETT, FRANCIS. "A New Pass-Key." NR 27 (22 June):118-19.
Partly because he must be tired after having written
Outline, W depends in Salvaging on the old idea that the world
exists in a state of original sin. Perhaps this problem also
derives from his own depression, similar to that of his generation, over the alleged bankruptcy of civilization. A new Bible
will not solve the problems of the world.

1019 HELLEBERG, VICTOR E. "Russia in the Shadows. American Journal
of Sociology 27 (Nov.):405.
This work provides a moderate, sane, sympathetic account.

1020 HIND, C. LEWIS. Authors and I. New York: Lane, pp. 300-305.
There is no confusion, only development in W's work. His
thought is ever on the wing, never resting, always seeking.

1021 "History." TLS, 16 June, p. 390.
W has no trouble defending himself in The New Teaching of
History, but the resentful tone of parts of this pamphlet seem
unworthy of him.

1022 "History and Political Economy." Outlook (New York) 128
(3 Aug.):550.
Whether true or false, the remedies presented in Salvaging
are worth attention.

1023 "History and Travel." Wisconsin Library Bulletin 17 (April-
May):74.
Russia gives a vivid picture of its subject.

1024 "The Ills of Wells." LD 71 (17 Dec.):26-27.
[Reports the controversy between W and the Daily Mail
(London) concerning his reports from Washington.]

1921

1025   "Is Civilization Breaking Down?" <u>Overland</u> <u>Monthly</u> 77
       (Jan.):63-65.
          [A summary of W's pessimistic conclusions presented in his
       "State of the World" message of 1921.]

1026   JONES, H. STUART. "The Classics in Education." <u>EDR</u> 234
       (Oct.):312-13.
          [Favorably remarks on W's views on the classics.]

1027   JONES, HENRY ARTHUR. <u>My</u> <u>Dear</u> <u>Wells</u>. New York: Dutton.
          [A series of letters by the author on bolshevism, collec-
       tivism, internationalism, and the distribution of wealth charging
       W with confused thinking and vagueness.]

1028   _____. <u>Notes</u> <u>and</u> <u>Correspondence</u> <u>Concerning</u> "<u>My</u> <u>Dear</u> <u>Wells</u>."
       New York: Dutton.
          [A nineteen-page pamphlet, issued separately from the
       author's book, including W's letters of protest to the <u>Morning</u>
       <u>Post</u> and Jones's response.]

1029   LAPPIN, HENRY A. "The Latest Mr. Wells." <u>Catholic</u> <u>World</u> 112
       (Jan.):453-64.
          First a writer of scientific romances, then a tractarian
       novelist, and now the proclaimer of a provisional deity, W has
       become fatuous. [Attacks <u>Outline</u> from several angles.]

1030   L[ASKER[, B[RUNO]. "Book Reviews." <u>Survey</u> 47 (5 Nov.):222.
          Aside from frequent repetition and certain crudities,
       <u>Salvaging</u> is suggestive. The book does not confront larger
       problems in their full complexity.

1031   LLOYD, C.M. "Politics and Economics." <u>LM</u> 3 (March):570-71.
          [Favorable review of <u>Russia</u>.]

1032   _____. "Politics and Economics." <u>LM</u> 4 (Aug.):447-48.
          Too much confidence in mechanical shortcuts and too much
       optimism concerning the ability of men to agree mar <u>Salvaging</u>, the
       ideas and enthusiasm of which are nonetheless valuable.

1033   "Looking Forward." <u>TLS</u>, 2 June, p. 347.
          In <u>Salvaging</u> W's observations about the present world are
       realistic, but his solutions are romantically idealistic.

1034   LYND, ROBERT. "Mr. Wells and the World." <u>NS</u> 17 (4 June):
       246-48.
          A passionate syllabus for regaining Eden, <u>Salvaging</u> is like
       a Bible. Although the book renders a great service in reminding
       us of man's common origins and interests, its plan remains
       dubious.

116

1035   MEREJKOWSKI, DMITRI. "Lettre ouverte à Wells." Revue
       Hebdomadaire, n.s. 1 (Jan.):127-32.
           [Takes vigorous exception to W's idea that at present only
       the Soviet government is possible in Russia.]

1036   "Mr. Wells and Bolshevist Russia." NYTBM, 13 Feb., p. 18.
           [Descriptive review of Russia.]

1037   "Mr. Wells and the Daily Mail." NS 18 (3 Dec.):250-51.
           [Reports the controversy between W and the Daily Mail
       (London) over W's articles from Washington.]

1038   "Mr. Wells on 'History for Everybody.'" RR 64 (Aug.):215.
           Reports W's thoughts on Outline and his plans for a new
       edition.]

1039   "Mr. Wells on Russia." Athenaeum, no. 4732 (7 Jan.), p. 10.
           Although an interesting book, Russia suffers from W's lack
       of a definite point of view from which he could judge Russia's
       creative men.

1040   "Mr. Wells Revises His Outline." NYTBM, 27 Nov., p. 18.
           [Notes several revisions in the third edition.]

1041   "Mr. Wells's World State." Times (London), 24 May, p. 13.
           In Salvaging W trusts generalizations too much. Yet the
       fertility of his mind and his imaginative boldness redeem the
       book.

1042   MUMFORD, LEWIS. "The Russian Changeling." Freeman 3
       (27 April):165-66.
           [Discusses some of the views expressed in Russia.]

1043   MUZZEY, DAVID SAVILLE. ""Mr. Wells's Utopian Pessimism."
       Political Science Quarterly 36 (June):298-303.
           In Outline W makes history read like a novel; he is too
       preoccupied with characters and the succession of situations. His
       utopianism is really pessimism, for he focuses on the folly of man
       in history and looks toward the millennium. "The steeds of his
       imagination have broken the traces and left the chariot stranded."

1044   "New Books and Reprints: Sociology." TLS, 26 May, p. 343.
           [A brief note on Salvaging.]

1045   "New Books Reviewed." NAR 214 (Aug.):285-87.
           If not totally consistent logically, Salvaging is a stimu-
       lating presentation of several ordinary ideas greatly magnified.

1921

1046   "The New Books: World Politics." <u>ARR</u> 64:110.
      In <u>Salvaging</u> W anticipates the formation of a world state
and suggests that the future is hopeless until such a federation
comes into existence.

1047   NEWBERRY, JOHN STRONG.   "A Rhymed Review of <u>The Outline of
      History</u> by H.G. Wells." <u>LD</u> 69 (7 MAY):32.
      [Satiric poem.]

1048   PANGBORN, H.L. "History in a New Form." <u>Bookman</u> (New York) 52
      (Jan.):358-60.
      <u>Outline</u> is written by a seer with stupendous vision. To
find flaws in the work is petty; what matters is its stimulus
toward better education as a basis for world unity.

1049   PEARSON, HESKETH. <u>Modern Men and Mummers</u>. London: Allen &
      Unwin, pp. 183-84.
      A postimpressionist, W is "the literary Weather-Cock of the
age," pointing in the direction of the current popular wind.

1050   PETRUNKEVITCH, ALEXANDER. "Bolshevism: Its Critics and Propa-
      gandists." <u>Yale Review</u> 10 (April):661.
      Although the description is useful, the tone and conclusions
of <u>Russia</u> are unwarranted.

1051   PETRUNKEVITCH, IVAN. "Russia in Sun or Shadow." <u>Outlook</u> (New
      York) 127 (20 March):513-14.
      [Refutes <u>Russia</u>, concluding that the book was written as if
W had never left England.]

1052   "A Plain Story of Life and Mankind." <u>School Review</u> 29
      (Feb.):155-57.
      Despite the note of caution raised by the <u>Trib</u>, <u>Outline</u> is
to be commended and would make an excellent classroom text.

1053   PURE, SIMON. "The Londoner." <u>Bookman</u> (New York) 53
      (March):67.
      [Very brief reference to St. John Ervine's dramatization of
<u>Wonderful Visit</u>.]

1054   _____. "The Londoner." <u>Bookman</u> (New York) 53 (June):339-40.
      [Brief report on W's holiday in Italy (for his health) and
on his revision of <u>Outline</u>.]

1055   _____. "The Londoner." <u>Bookman</u> (New York) 53 (Aug.):539-40.
      [Comments on W's illness and announces <u>Salvaging</u>.]

1056   ROBERTS, RICHARD. "Architects of a New World." <u>Nation</u> (New
      York) 113 (3 Aug.):124-25.

Although it is well worth reading, Salvaging is too facile to be a reassuring guide. W does not know, or, perhaps, he refuses to pay attention to human nature.

1057 ROBINSON, JAMES HARVEY. "Mr. Wells's Gospel of History." Yale Review 10 (Jan.):412-18.
[A very favorable review of Outline that concludes that the book is wondrous.]

1058 "Russia, Mid-Europe, and International Relations." RR 63 (May):559.
Russia makes some observations that others have missed.

1059 SAMPSON, GEORGE. "The Impotence of Man." Bookman (London) 60 (July):176.
[Uses Salvaging as the springboard for an editorial.]

1060 SCHAPIRO, J. SALWYN. "Mr. Wells Discovers the Past." Nation (New York) 112 (9 Feb.):224-31.
W's profound sense of human relationships, unusual powers of imagination, and ability to write superlatively make Outline a fascinating book, original in point of view and method. Yet the book reveals W's fatal weakness, a good beginning soon followed by a slow fizzling out. This problem results from the fact that W may be the most imaginative man alive, but he is not the most intellectual. Consequently with regard to ideas, "he arouses, he stimulates, he throws out fine hints, he suggests new ways of looking at things; but he is utterly incapable of being the architect of any new system of thought."

1061 SHANKS, EDWARD. "Reflections on the Recent History of the English Novel." LM 4 (June):173-83. Reprinted in First Essays on Literature (London): Collins, 1923), pp. 172-91.
Early in his career W created poetic visions, of which War in the Air provides an excellent example. But after 1914, W the artist gave way to W the preacher and publicist, with a collateral degeneration in his style that "makes one think of a middle-aged man 'losing his figure.'"

1062 STEWART, HERBERT L. "The Probable Future of Mankind." Weekly Review 5 (6 Aug.):125-26.
Although instructive, Salvaging is below W's workmanship.

1063 STRUNSKY, SIMEON. "Mr. Wells and the Time-Sense." LR, 18 June, p. 5.
When it comes to the measurement of time in Salvaging W's arithmetic is bad. The note of aspiration is noble.

1921

1064   THOMPSON, CHARLES WILLIS. "The Next War and After." NYTBM, 29
        May, p. 3.
            [Remarks how Will Irwin's The Next War provides the factual
        details missing from Salvaging.]

1065   van LOON, HENDRICK WILLEM. "A Builder of History." Dial 70
        (Feb.):202-3.
            [Favorable comment on Outline.]

1066   "The War and After." Wisconsin Library Bulletin 17 (Oct.):154.
        Salvaging is stimulating and inconclusive.

1067   "The Wells History as Religion." LD 69 (9 April):30.
            [Cites reactions to Outline in the Christian Register,
        Christian Work (New York), the New York Christian Advocate, the
        Pittsburgh Christian Advocate (all not seen), and Catholic World
        112 (Jan. 1921):453-64.]

1068   "Wells on Russia." LR, 26 March, p. 8.
            As an honest portrayal by a man of genius, Russia is valu-
        able; as an argument for certain proposals, the book is dubious.

1069   "Wells Replies to the Critics of His History." CO 71 (Aug.):
        207-9.
            [Reports on W's argument with A. Gomme, H. Belloc, and Dr.
        Downey.]

1070   "Wells Tells How to Treat Russia." SSR, 3 April, p. 5a.
            Russia will interest even those who do not accept its con-
        clusions.

1071   WINDLE, BERTRAM C.A. "H.G. Wells on the Origin of Christian-
        ity." Catholic World 113 (Aug.):641-49.
            W can tell a good story, but there is great doubt that he
        can write history. His treatment of Christianity is inaccurate,
        and he fails to consider its status today.

1072   YORKE, GABRIEL. "A Shelf of New Books." Forum 65 (Jan.):
        98-103.
            Outline is a useful but hardly great work. Epic rather than
        historic in nature, it almost exclusively emphasizes men and
        political events.

                                1922

1073   BEARD, CHARLES A. "Hot Lovers and Hot Haters." Nation (New
        York) 114 (8 March):289-90.

Otherwise wise and suggestive, Washington is marred by W's savage attacks upon France.

1074   BLOCH, MARC. "H.G. Wells, historien." Revue de Paris, 15
        Aug., pp. 860-74.
        Outline is marred by W's tendency to pass judgments instead
of seeking knowledge. Too often partiality related to English
prejudice intrudes; W knows nothing about France.

1075   "Books." Spectator (London) 128 (4 Feb.):144-45.
        Washington is a well-intentioned, interesting, and able book
marred by the fact that everything in it is passionate, prayerful,
or scolding.

1076   BOYNTON, H.W. "Minor Prophecy." Independent (New York) 109
        (22 July):24-26.
        Most of the time W manages to be a journalist, prophet,
humorist, novelist, and scientist at the same time. Secret Places
reveals W's strength and weaknesses, and no novel reader will want
to miss this book.

1077   _____. "The Inexhaustible Playmate." LR, 10 June, pp. 714-15.
        "How childlike and harmless it [the world of Secret Places]
all is, a game of make-believe we can all enjoy because it has
nothing uncomfortable to do with reality!"

1078   "Briefer Notices." American Political Science Review 16
        (Aug.):528.
        [Favorable note on Washington.]

1079   BROUN, HEYWOOD. "It Seems to Me." World (New York), 2 June,
        p. 11.
        Although W is a writer whose work merits an enthusiastic
reception, Secret Places proves disappointing. Dr. Mortineau is
unrealistic and the women in the book do not fare well. If only W
would return to work like Mr. Polly!

1080   C[OOK], S[HERWIN] L[AWRENCE]. "A Novelist as Physician." BET,
        7 June, pt. 3, p. 4.
        Hardly a treatise and not quite a novel, Secret Places is a
dull failure. The strength and power of W's discussion should
have been applied in another fashion. W's tendency to decorate
immediate and perhaps ephemeral modern issues and theories makes
him fair game for good natured satirists.

1081   DARK, SIDNEY. An Outline of Wells. New York: Putnam's Sons.
        Who W is can be determined from his writings, the leading
characters of which represent phases of his development. He is a
man of courage, a crusader, a critic, a preacher with a gospel

1922

derived after many experiments and after testing many creeds. W
is less interested in literature as art than as a vehicle for
ideas. [A discussion of W's relation to his contemporaries, his
views of the world state, his novels as criticism of modern life,
his masterpiece Mr. Polly, his thoughts on socialism, his writings
during World War I, his notion of God, his postwar writings, and
his study of history.]

1082   DELINES, CLARA-MICHEL. "Le paradis de M. Wells." Bibliothèque
       universelle et revue suisse, 4th ser. 107:205-16, 263-77.
       W generalizes easily because he is more concerned with
possibilities than with logic. His theories are based more on
personal experience than on abstractions. [Surveys W's political,
economic, and social ideas.]

1083   DELL, FLOYD. "Non-Competitive Males." Nation (New York) 114
       (14 June):721-23.
       W's heroes are uniformly unhappy regardless of their eco-
nomic situation. They are angry that they must play a game or
compete for their happiness. Secret Places is actually a lecture
on the wickedness of being competitive, but the tragedy of its
protagonist is not convincing.

1084   "Don Juan Again." Weekly Westminster Gazette 1 (20 May):17.
       In Secret Places Richmond Hardy is an ignorant, loquacious
bore. W's grasp of character is slipping.

1085   DUTTON, GEORGE B. "Wells Again Mixes Love and Sociology."
       SSR, 28 May, p. 7a.
       Secret Places is a tract rather than a novel, journalism
rather than art. [Compares the techniques of W and John
Galsworthy.]

1086   "Fiction." SR (London) 133 (3 June):583.
       Considering the content, organization, and style of Secret
Places, W has finally written a really bad novel.

1087   FIELD, LOUISE MAUNSELL. "Mr. Wells Sketches a Golden Age."
       NYTBM, 21 May, pp. 4, 23.
       [Brief notice, focusing on the characters of Secret Places.]

1088   FISHER, W.E. GARRETT. "Christmas Books." SR (London) 134
       (25 Nov.):795.
       Short History succeeds because of W's flowing style and his
powers of visualization.

1089   FOX, W.A. "Fuel Control." Bookman (London) 62 (June):140.
       [Brief praise for Secret Places.]

1090   "The Greatest Intellectual Force in the English-Speaking
        World." CO 73 (July):94-96.
            W has written better novels than Secret Places. But he
        makes clear in it, in a way that will infect any sensitive reader,
        that matters may have to worsen before they improve. [Also re-
        ports on Sidney Dark's study of W.]

1091   HEWLETT, MAURICE. "Mr. Wells's Millennium." NA 30 (14 Jan.):
        584-86.
            In Washington W favors progress and efficiency over moral
        virtues.

1092   _____. "Mr. Wells on the Millennium." Forum 67 (March):
        185-91.
            W's "method has been like that of the gadfly which wings
        from rump to rump until he has the herd in violent commotion."
        Ignoring moral virtues, he conceives of peace solely in terms of
        matter and motion, of excitement and sensation.

1093   "History and Biography." English Review 35 (Dec.):578.
        [Rave review of Short History.]

1094   HOPKINS, R. THURSTON. H.G. Wells: Personality, Character,
        Topography. New York: Dutton.
            Of all current novelists W possesses the most progressive
        mind. This is one reason why it is difficult to delineate his
        final beliefs. Concerning his idea of God, for instance, he went
        through vacillations before arriving at the concept of a finite
        deity. His work, however, is always constructive, his message one
        of courage and good cheer. W's intentions are serious, which is
        why he avoids being cryptic or using paradox. His art is close to
        actual life, and his style, like that of Dickens, exemplifies a
        rare "power of diction that cuts and blazes a trail through the
        dense forest of custom." Tono-Bungay is his best novel. [A
        potpourri of various topics relating to W, including plot sum-
        maries and extensive quotations.]

1095   "International Problems." Wisconsin Library Bulletin 18
        (May):131.
            Washington is interesting but not necessary for the small
        library.

1096   J., G.W. "Mr. Wells Writes a Bad Novel." Greensboro Daily
        News (North Carolina), 23 July, p. 2.
            The treatise on psychiatry fails to make satisfying fiction
        in Secret Places, a work that is also neither good philosophy nor
        good propaganda. W takes himself too seriously, which is why the
        artist in him has been supplanted by the messianic impulse.

1922

1097   "Latest Books." Survey 47 (11 Feb.):769.
        Washington provides an interesting exhibit of the historian
turned newspaper reporter.

1098   LITTELL, ROBERT. "On the Trail of the Truth." NR 31
        (14 June):80.
        Secret Places starts out as a novel but soon becomes merely
another vehicle for W's ideas.

1099   LUBBOCK, PERCY. "Bennett and Wells." Independent (New York)
        108 (10 June):520.
        In spite of its merits Secret Places is precisely the sort
of book W wrote several times, only very much better, before the
war.

1100   M., A.N. "Mr. Wells's Novel." MG, 11 May, p. 5.
        Some will dismiss Secret Places as the spasmodic effort of a
bored, disillusioned man. The characters of the book remain mere
mouthpieces rather than become human beings. W is a great man who
resists the temptation to become a great novelist.

1101   MACY, JOHN. The Critical Game. New York: Boni & Liveright,
        pp. 269-76.
        W continually tries, without success, to blend the Jules
Verne romance and the novel of present-day life. His romantic
sense sometimes corrupts his sense of social and scientific fact.

1102   MARVIN, F.S. "Unified Human History." Nature 110 (30 Dec.):
        867-68.
        [Basically a favorable review of Short History.]

1103   MASTERMAN, C.F.G. "H.G. Wells." RR 65 (June):589-98.
        In Kipps and Mr. Polly a class emerges and becomes
articulate for the first time in literature. But of W's works
Tono-Bungay is most destined to be remembered. [A general review
of W's career with brief discussions of his encounter with World
War I, his relation to his novels, his sincerity, his life at
home, his relations with Lloyd George and Parliament.]

1104   "Mr. Wells at Washington." SDR, 29 March, p. 10.
        [Favorable review of Washington.]

1105   "Mr. Wells at Washington." TLS, 26 Jan., p. 50.
        In Washington W is too impatient with world affairs and
fails to see the need for gradual steps toward peace.

1106   "Mr. Wells on Washington." SR (London) 133 (28 Jan.):94.
        "Few journalists would be guilty of writing in a manner so
self-centered, so desultory, so completely at the mercy of the
irritations or enthusiasm of the moment" as is W in Washington.

1107   "Mr. Wells Presents the World." TLS, 23 Nov., p. 762.
       [Favorable review of Short History.]

1108   "Mr. Wells's Thesis." Times (London), 11 May, p. 16.
       W has deserted quality for inconclusive conclusions in
       Secret Places.

1109   "More Wells." Spectator (London) 128 (17 June):757.
       In Secret Places the views on psychoanalysis that W deems as
       advanced are not only not new but not particularly true. As a
       romancer W is praiseworthy; as a prophet he is behind the times.

1110   MUMFORD, LEWIS. The Story of Utopias. New York: Boni &
       Liveright, pp. 183-89.
       Utopia touches on all the important points raised by other
       studies on the subject and does so with deftness and humor. Un-
       like its predecessors, it is founded on reality.

1111   MURRAY, HENRY. "Mr. Wells's New Novel." Sunday Times
       (London), 14 May, p. 7.
       W's great theme of stultified social service peters out in
       Secret Places, a book illuminated with subsidiary ideas and ad-
       mirable writing. Although it does not rank with his best books,
       it could have been written only by W.

1112   N[OBLE], E[DMUND]. "H.G. Wells and the Riddle of Peace." BET,
       25 Feb., pt. 4, p. 7.
       In Washington W's plea is impassioned and at times
       desperate.

1113   PEARSON, EDMUND LESTER. "New Books and Old." Independent (New
       York) 108 (21 Jan.):61.
       [Quibbles over W's attitude toward France in Washington.]

1114   "Politics and Government." OS, no. 7-8 (July-Aug.), p. 54.
       Washington is written with a light touch for a newspaper-
       reading public.

1115   "The Problem of the Problem Novel." TLS, 18 May, p. 322.
       Secret Places does not entirely succeed as a novel of ideas.

1116   PURE, SIMON. "The Londoner." Bookman (New York) 56
       (Oct.):186-88.
       Men Like Gods combines the themes and methods of W's scien-
       tific romances and his later works.

1117   REID, FORREST. "A Novel with a Purpose." NA 31 (3 June):348.
       Whenever W forgets his social and economic ideas in Secret
       Places he rises to the higher level established in his earlier
       work. As a whole the book is admirable.

1922

1118 RICHTER, HELENE. "Herbert George Wells." Anglia 46 (April):
      97-136.
          [Discusses in detail W's socialistic notions in relation to
      the current situation, with some passing praise for his humor and
      irony particularly in the early scientific fantasies.]

1119 SHANKS, EDWARD. "Fiction." LM 6 (July):320-21.
          Probably the worst novel W has written, Secret Places yields
      "acres of talk" and only "a very few inches of thought or
      psychology."

1120 _____. "The Work of H.G. Wells." LM 5 (March):506-18.
      Reprinted in First Essays on Literature (London: Collins,
      1923), pp. 148-71; and in CH, pp. 255-57.
          By never neglecting the necessary consequences of his orig-
      inal thesis and by clothing his stories in vivid detail W raises
      the fantastic romance to the level of artistic storytelling.
      Compact, symmetrical, and economically written, his stories are
      better than good journalism; for in his early work W is a myth-
      maker who finds the material for his mythology in the scientific
      modern world. Since about 1906 his work, marked by impatience,
      has become didactic, propagandist, and controversial. W has
      shifted his focus from the human spirit to the problems that
      spirit encounters right now. Primarily the early work will sur-
      vive. [See also a letter: J.D. Beresford, "Mr. Beresford and Mr.
      Wells," LM 5 (April 1922):542.]

1121 "Shorter Notices." NS 20 (25 Nov.):250; abstracted in the
      supplement (2 Dec.):xx.
          Short History is in some respects better and weaker than its
      remarkable predecessor.

1122 TOWNSEND, R.D. "New Novels and Clever Tales." Outlook (New
      York) 131 (7 June):263.
          In Secret Places W appears to be more interested in the
      dramatic depiction of Sir Richmond, an inconsistent but very real
      person, than in presenting a particular theory.

1123 WALKER, CHARLES R. "What the Worker Reads." Bookman (New
      York) 54 (Jan.):417-18.
          [Speaks of W's appeal to the working man.]

1124 "Wells Boils It Down." NYTBR, 19 Nov., pp. 4, 23.
          [Favorable review of Short History.]

1125 "Wells in Washington." NYTBM, 12 March, p. 24.
          [Mixed review of Washington.]

126

1126   ZAMYATIN, YEVGENY. <u>H.G. Wells</u>. Petrograd: Epokha. Reprinted
as the preface to a Russian edition of the complete works of
Wells (Leningrad: Mysl, 1924 (not seen); expanded in <u>Litsa</u>
(Faces) (New York: Chekhov Publishing House, 1955) (not seen);
expanded version reprinted as "H.G. Wells," trans. Mirra
Ginsburg, <u>Midway</u> 10 (Summer 1969):97-126; extract reprinted in
<u>CH</u>, pp. 258-74.
    The modern city and the machine comprise the explicit or
implicit components of every fantastic work by W. The miraculous
atmosphere of the fairy tale informs these works, and typical of
the motifs of W's urban fairy tales are the invisible hat, the
flying carpet, dragons, giants, mermaids and carnivorous monsters.
Similarly to his fantastic romances, W's realistic works emphasize
the decline of European civilization, a special brand of socialism, a humanism that blames no one in particular, and the same
machine and city.

<u>1923</u>

1127   ADCOCK, A. ST. JOHN. <u>Gods of Modern Grub Street</u>. New York:
Stokes, pp. 303-10.
    [Praises W highly, in general terms, as a journalist,
prophet, and artist.]

1128   B., G. "Mr. Wells and the Reviewers." <u>Adelphi</u> 1 (Sept.):354.
    [Refutes W's notions about book reviewers.]

1129   BENNETT, ARNOLD. <u>Things That Have Interested Me</u>. New York:
Doran, pp. 166-78.
    In undertaking to write <u>Outline</u> W demonstrates great imagi-
nation and superlative courage.

1130   BERESFORD, J.D. "Utopias." <u>Adelphi</u> 1 (Aug.):241-42.
    [Compares briefly the utopian notes of W and Shaw, indicat-
ing that W's view is more popular though equally disagreeable to
certain people.]

1131   BERGENGREN, RALPH. "Another Wellsian Dip into the Future."
<u>BET</u>, 26 May, pt. 6, p. 2.
    That too much assurance of a public and too easy a command
of one's craft can be detrimental is evident in <u>Men Like Gods</u>.
Much remains unconvincing in the book.

1132   "Books." <u>English Review</u> 36 (May):494.
    [Brief, uncritical comment on <u>Men Like Gods</u>.]

1133   BRENNECKE, ERNEST, Jr. "H.G. Wells, Playboy of the Literary
World." <u>NYTBR</u>, 9 Sept., p. 6.

1923

[An interview with W, focusing on Mr. Polly, Wheels of Chance, and Men Like Gods.]

1134 BROWN, IVOR. H.G. Wells. London: Nisbet.
W contributed to the scientific romance a tenderness in humor, usually by means of adorning his picture "of a merciless mechanical progress with a rare bloom of human comedy." Similarly, in his lighter novels sympathy and boisterous comedy lift them "clear of farce into the keen air of true artistic vision." W's philosophic novels offer no simple solutions; the blend the essay and the novel in a fresh and generally successful literary method. Their characters are unforgettable in terms of their revelation of the comedy and agony of human limitations. Since World War I, W's work has mainly restated or reemphasized his views, adjusting them to the world situation. Of current literary figures W "is definitely the most radio-active, a spinning atom of suggestion warmed by satiric fire."

1135 CHESTERTON, GILBERT K. "The Patriot of the Planet." Century (New York) 105 (March):686-94.
[Responding to Salvaging, the author has some fun at W's expense and uses the work as a vehicle for his own ideas about nationalism.]

1136 COLUM, MARY M. "A Prophet of Main Street." LR, 7 July), pp. 809-10.
In Men Like Gods, probably W's worst book, "there is no turn of expression not easily achievable by a Hearst editorial writer or a single idea that might not have been arrived at by a bright high school boy or even by Mr. Babbitt of Main Street in his inspired moments." A plagiarism from his earlier work, this book is a natural consequence of W's literary notions and abilities.

1137 "Dreams and the Main Chance." Independent (New York) 110 (9 June):379.
[Short notice of Men Like Gods, remarking on W's casualness with regard to who acts as his spokesman in the book.]

1138 ERVINE, ST. JOHN G. Some Impressions of My Elders. London: Allen & Unwin, pp. 226-47.
[Personal reminiscences mentioning W at times.]

1139 "Fiction." ALA 19 (July):327.
Social ideas dominate story in Men Like Gods, though the style derives from W's early romances.

1140 "Fiction." OS, no. 7-8 (July-Aug.), p. 50.
Men Like Gods is amusing and interesting but not ingenious or as well sustained as some of W's earlier writings.

1141   "Fiction." <u>Spectator</u> (London) 130 (31 March):556-57.
       One of the most delightful novels W has ever written, <u>Men</u>
<u>Like Gods</u> is rich in humor and satire.

1142   FIELD, LOUISE MAUNSELL. "<u>Men Like Gods</u>." <u>LDI</u> 1 (June):54-55.
       Some clever characterization, amusing touches of satire, and
well-done description make this book readable. Some of the description, however, is repeated too often.

1143   FORMAN, HENRY JAMES. "H.G. Wells Skids into Utopia." <u>NYTBR</u>,
       27 May, pp. 1, 25.
       <u>Men Like Gods</u> is to date W's best portrait of utopia. Like
that of Isaiah, its narrative argues that mankind is losing as a
result of its apostasy.

1144   H[ALDANE], J. [B.] S. "Biology in Utopia." <u>Nature</u> 111
       (5 May):591-94.
       [Studies the probability of several of W's ideas in <u>Men Like
Gods</u>, concluding that he is correct in his premises.]

1145   _____. <u>Daedalus</u>. London: Kegan Paul, Trench, Trubner,
       pp. 9-11.
       Scientifically W is a generation behind the times.

1146   HANER, G.A. "Wells on Roman History." <u>Classical Journal</u> 18
       (March):360-68.
       W's section in <u>Outline</u> dealing with Roman history is inter-
esting and effective but not very accurate.

1147   KRUTCH, J[OSEPH] W[OOD]. "A Man of Faith." <u>Nation</u> (New York)
       117 (25 July):90.
       In <u>Men Like Gods</u> there is nothing that W has not said be-
fore; yet his unquenchable enthusiasm keeps the work from becoming
stale.

1148   LEO, Brother. "A Poet Frustrate: H.G. Wells." <u>Catholic World</u>
       118 (Dec.):295-305.
       W is generally misunderstood, even by himself. Possessing a
poet's fancy rather than a thinker's intellect, he expresses vague
and visionary theories derived not from rational analysis but from
emotional stress. <u>Outline</u> may be an epic, but it is not serious
history.

1149   "Life, Letters, and the Arts." <u>LA</u> 317 (April):244.
       [Reports on an amusing incident in which W is tried, in
person, by some students for crimes against art, particularly an
excessive use of dots in the emotional scenes of his novels.]

1923

1150   LYND, ROBERT. Books and Authors. New York: Putnam's Sons,
       pp. 206-13.
           Because of his love of the human race, W writes more as a
       philosopher and preacher than as a poet.

1151   M., C.C. "Men Like Gods." Dublin Review 173 (July):151-54.
           This is a very careless novel, fatiguing, academic, and
       mendacious.

1152   MacLEISH, ARCHIBALD. "Of Making Utopias." Yale Review 13
       (Oct.):165-69.
           Men Like Gods is a "romance of the Creative Impulse."

1153   "Men Like Gods." TLS, 8 March, p. 157.
           [Basically a descriptive review of this book, with some
       reference to the flaws in W's view of utopia.]

1154   "Mr. Wells Writes a Short World History." LDI 1 (March):40-41.
           Short History covers the same ground as Outline but in a
       more swiftly moving narrative.

1155   MORTIMER, RAYMOND. "New Novels." NS 20 (17 March):695.
           Men Like Gods presents no new ideas. A product of W's love
       of uniformity, its plan for utopia could not include humane,
       intelligent people.

1156   MUMFORD, LEWIS. "A One-Way Utopia." NR 35 (20 June):102-3.
           Fortunately W the satirist sometimes gets the upper hand in
       Men Like Gods. The utopia portrayed in this work is too exclu-
       sive, and in ruling out certain variations W behaves in the same
       way as a bureaucrat toward a culture of an "inferior" people.

1157   PATERSON, ISABEL. "The Too Perfect State." Trib, 20 May,
       pp. 17-18.
           Men Like Gods is less successful as a blueprint for society
       than as a guidebook to W. The lack of humor and individualism
       makes W's lazy notion of utopia appalling.

1158   PRIESTLEY, J.B. "Fiction." LM 8 (May):97.
           The best story by W in a long time, Men Like Gods reveals
       the artist in spite of himself. The book is not without
       weaknesses.

1159   PURE, SIMON. "The Londoner." Bookman (New York) 57 (April):
       186-87.
           [Responds to Wyatt Tilby's essay on W in the EDR 237
       (Jan. 1923) and justifies W's apparent artistic faults.]

1160 _____. "The Londoner." Bookman (New York) 57 (Aug.):618-19.
By using easily recognizable prominent personalities in Men
Like Gods, W has brought to the utopian novel a verisimilitude
hitherto unknown in the genre.

1161 ROYCE, EDWIN. "H.G. Wells." Manchester Quarterly 168
(Oct.):245-67.
Each new book from W goes off at a tangent from a preceding
one, and they all represent fascinating journeys. W is always on
the move. Few of W's characters, rarely analyzed, possess love-
ableness or charm--Mrs. Trafford in Marriage is an exception; few
of his women characters are attractive and in general they differ
from those found in the novels of Arnold Bennett. In spite of
inconsistencies, W's work manifests certain persistent tendencies.
W is not a pessimist; mingling hope with fear, he neither laughs
nor sorrows but passionately protests the human situation. Most
likely his early work will survive. [Presents biographical details and discusses W's writings chronologically.]

1162 R[UTLAND], A[RTHUR]. "Mr. Wells in Utopia." Bookman (London)
64 (April):32, 34.
Another view of W's utopia, Men Like Gods is timely.

1163 S., F. "Mr. Wells's New Novel." MG, 8 March, p. 16.
Men Like Gods is charming and absorbing, and only W could
have achieved such a triumph. W is always greater than his faults
because he is able to yield himself with candor, almost with
ecstasy, to his idealism.

1164 SELDES, GILBERT. "Mr. Wells' Ancients." Dial 75 (Sept.):
285-87.
The presentation of the real world in Men Like Gods is more
vigorous than that of the ideal, which lacks savour entirely.

1165 "Shorter Notices." NS 20 (10 March):672.
The fourth and definitive edition of Outline is the most
important book published in the English language in the last
decade.

1166 TILBY, A. WYATT. "Mr. H.G. Wells." EDR 237 (Jan.):113-32.
W writes too rapidly to be always top-notch. At his best he
is unique; at his worst he never falls into merely mechanical
fiction. The beginnings of his books are apt to be better than
the endings, and strangely his earlier work presents characters
who are more true to life than those in the later writings. W
knows that he is writing faster than he can think, that he has
written beyond his strength; "he might have been a greater novelist had he been a lesser man."

1923

1167   TOMLINSON, H.M. "Men Like Gods." Adelphi 1 (June):56-58.
        In this book W's art is such that we do not recognize it as
art but as life itself. In many respects W is like Dickens.

1168   "Wells' New Utopia." GDN, 29 July, p. 19.
        Hardly one of W's greatest books, Men Like Gods must rank as
the most beautiful work he has created.

1169   "Wells's Short History." SDR, 7 Feb., p. 8.
        W links together related incidents and influences interest-
ingly but sometimes does so too imaginatively.

1170   WOOLF, VIRGINIA. "Mr. Bennett and Mrs. Brown." LR, 17 Nov.,
        pp. 253-54. Reprinted in NA 34 (1 Dec.):342-43; LA 320
        (2 Feb.):229-32; expanded in Mr. Bennett and Mrs. Brown
        (London: Hogarth Press, 1924); The Captain's Death Bed and
        Other Essays (London: Hogarth Press, 1950), pp. 90-111;
        Collected Essays (New York: Harcourt, Brace & World, 1967),
        1:319-37.
        The fiction of Galsworthy, Bennett, and W is not suffi-
ciently self-contained and leaves the reader with a sense of
incompleteness and dissatisfaction. These writers, interested in
the world outside their books, require the reader to complete the
novel. In his imagined portrait of Mrs. Brown, W would concentrate on what she ought to be rather than on what she is. These
three Edwardian authors give "us a house in the hope that we may
be able to deduce the human beings who live there." [An address,
delivered 18 May 1924, before the Heretics, Cambridge.]

1171   Y[OUNG?], F[ILSON?]. "A Pilgrim's Progress." SR (London) 135
        (10 March):317-18.
        Men Like Gods is alike in spirit and literary quality to the
best of W's earlier work.

                                1924

1172   AAS, L. "H.G. Wells og hans verker" (H.G. Wells and his work).
        EDDA 21:105-23.
        [A survey of W's work from 1895 to 1918 with liberal refer-
ences to contemporary reviews and criticism to trace his development from novelist to prophet.] [In Norwegian.]

1173   ARMSTRONG, MARTIN. "The Utopian's Nightmare." Bookman
        (London) 66 (May):115.
        A competent story, Dream suffers from an unnecessary
contrivance.

                                132

1174   "Biography." Wisconsin Library Bulletin 20 (April):96.
        Schoolmaster is worth the attention of all American
    teachers.

1175   BIRON, CHARTRES. "Biography and Memoirs." LM 10 (June):223.
        Schoolmaster is interesting despite its controversial aims
    and methods.

1176   BOYNTON, H.W. "This Sorry Scheme." Outlook (New York) 137
        (7 May):31.
        Dream is dull; there can be no drama in perfection. W fails
    to transcend the boundaries of his didactic intent.

1177   BULLOCK, SHAN. "Wells on His (Literary) Death Bed." Chicago
        Evening Post Literary Review, 19 Dec., p. 4.
        [Negative response to W's pessimism in Prophesying based on
    advanced notices of the book.]

1178   [CANBY, HENRY SEIDEL?] "Mr. Wells in Utopia." LR, 26 April,
        p. 701.
        W's visions sometimes reveal more about W than about utopia.

1179   CHAPPELL, FRED A. Bibliography of H.G. Wells. Chicago:
        Covici-McGee.
        [An incomplete chronological list of works by and on W from
    1892-1924.]

1180   CRASHAW, WILLIAM H. The Making of English Literature. Rev.
        ed. Boston: Heath, pp. 433-35.
        W's scientific romances reveal his vivid imagination, story-
    telling skill, accomplished conception of natural characters,
    ready humor, and social and political interests.

1181   CUNLIFFE, J.W. "The Latest Wells Novel." LR, 10 May, p. 739.
        In spite of the bitterness of its censure of the present,
    Dream still evinces W's natural buoyancy of temperament.

1182   "The Dream." TLS, 10 April, p. 222.
        This work has little to distinguish it from any of W's
    earlier novels.

1183   "The Dream: Mr. Wells Accurately Describes the Current
        Century." Time 3 (12 May):14.
        Sarnac is a bore in this work, which presents impossible
    characters making unconvincing remarks. In general, however, it
    is done in W's best vein.

1184   "Elective System in the High School." SSR, 18 May, p. 5a.
        There is more interest and suggestion in Schoolmaster than
    in many ponderous volumes.

1924

1185   "Fiction." ALA 20 (June):341.
        Dream is graphic and readable.

1186   FIELD, LOUISE MAUNSELL. "The Dream." LDI 2 (June):552.
        This book would be more effective it it were less one-sided.
It is a well-managed book with a beautifully written conclusion.

1187   GOULD, GERALD. "New Fiction." SR (London) 137 (5 April):356.
        Aside from a naive view of the correctability of human
nature, Dream is as interesting as any of W's earlier adventures.

1188   _____. The English Novel of Today. London: Castle,
        pp. 60-63.
        General interest overshadows special interest in Mr.
Britling. W's use of real people as models for his characters is
ineffective in that "such realism destroys reality."

1189   GUEDALLA, PHILIP. A Gallery. London: Constable, pp. 63-71.
        Reprinted in Men of Letters (London: Hodder & Stoughton,
        1927), pp. 99-111.
        [A general appraisal of W stressing his focus on the present
rather than on the future and his preoccupation with subject
rather than with method.]

1190   GUÉRARD, ALBERT. "The 'New History': H.G. Wells and Voltaire."
        Scribner's Magazine 76 (Nov.):476-84.
        [Uses W's view of Voltaire as an opportunity to discuss the
French thinker, noting differences between the two writers but
describing W as Voltaire's younger brother.]

1191   "H.G. Wells." Catholic World 118 (Feb.):645-56.
        Overimagination and lack of rigorous scholarship invalidate
much of W's work, especially Outline. His attack on Christianity
is based on ignorance and his criticisms of it are inconsistent,
hypocritical, and prejudiced. W stresses education as a key to
survival, forgetting that one of the most educated nations in the
world deliberately brought about World War I.

1192   HARTLEY, L.P. "Visions and Warnings." Spectator (London) 132
        (12 April):604.
        Dream tells a good story but because it preaches continually
neither the author nor the reader can get really absorbed in it.

1193   "He Might Have Been Hurt." NYT, 13 May, p. 20.
        It is doubtful that any writer today other than W could aim
at lecturing in advanced sociology and produce such a good novel
as Dream.

1194   "History." TLS, 9 Oct., p. 633.
        Because there is nothing against which to compare it, Short
History is somewhat beyond criticism. Even though it is not great
history, it is interesting. Only W could have written it.

1195   HORWILL, HERBERT W. "The Vitalizing of Education." Nation
        (New York) 118 (6 Feb.):144-45.
        Schoolmaster might be advertized as a teacher's tonic.

1196   "How the Future May See Us." CO 76 (June):774-75.
        Dream, with its world of disorder, may be a retort to the
critics of Men Like Gods.

1197   KRUTCH, J[OSEPH] W[OOD]. "The Disinherited." Nation (New
        York) 119 (2 July):21.
        Though full of verve, Dream does not reveal any new side to
W's mind.

1198   LYND, ROBERT. "Humour." Quarterly Review 241 (Jan.):46.
        [A few lines remarking on Mr. Polly as W's masterpiece.]

1199   MACAULAY, ROSE. "Posterity Dreams." NA 35 (12 April):54, 56;
        longer version in NR 38 (7 May):292.
        W has told the story of Dream with more humor, wit, and
farce in his earlier work. Yet, despite its obvious thesis and
its inaccuracies (e.g., the details of the high Anglican morning
service), the book is readable.

1200   "Mr. Wells's Journalism." TLS, 25 Dec., p. 881.
        The strident side of W, a "fractious Peter Pan of modern
letters," dominates the human side in Prophesying.

1201   MORTIMER, RAYMOND. "New Novels." NS 23 (12 April):16-17.
        Dream contains something characteristic of each of W's
periods and is essentially marred by the narrowness of his arbi-
trary personal opinions. W is not realistic in his view of human
nature.

1202   N[OBLE], E[DMUND]. "A Great Schoolmaster." BET, 9 Feb., pt.
        7, p. 1.
        Schoolmaster is brief but impressive.

1203   O., C.B. "A Wellsian Vision of Us." BET, 23 April, pt. 3,
        p. 4.
        Dream is a typical modern autobiographical novel in which
the sad state of current civilization is portrayed by photographic
action rather than by direct comment. It is a good book of its
kind.

1924

1204   "Other Timely Works." RR 69 (April):448.
        [Short notice of Schoolmaster.]

1205   PATERSON, ISABEL. "A Troubled Dream." Trib, 27 April, p. 28.
        Dream is like a recurrent dream made dull through repeti-
tion. It is vague in its science and in its utopian portrait.

1206   PRIESTLEY, J.B. "Fiction." LM 10 (May):101.
        Dream is a notable exception to W's literary decline.

1207   PURE, SIMON. "The Londoner." Bookman (New York) 58
        (Feb.):641-42.
        In spite of his bad press, W is one of the geniuses of our
day.

1208   RAYMOND, E.T. "The Victorian Humorist." LM 10 (Aug.):383-84.
        W is typically neo-Georgian rather than Victorian in treat-
ing the parvenu with a certain dignity even when he disapproves of
him. [Kipps is contrasted with Samuel Warren's Ten Thousand a
Year.]

1209   "Sanderson of Oundle." SR (London) 127 (16 Feb.):162-63.
        [Somewhat sarcastic review of Schoolmaster.]

1210   "Sanderson of Oundle." TLS, 17 Jan., p. 37.
        Deficiency in facts pertaining to the history of education
in England and to the realities of public school life mar
Schoolmaster.

1211   "Shorter Notices." Spectator (London) 132 (5 April):566.
        Everyone interested in education or sociology should read
Schoolmaster.

1212   SOUČEK, FRANTIŠEK. "Náboženská zkusenost v díle H.G. Wellse"
        [Religious experience in the works of H.G. Wells]. Příspěvky k
dějinám řeči a literatury anglické od členů anglického semináře
při Universitě Karlově 1:83-126.
        World War I marks a decisive change in W's concern with
religion. Though he repudiates Christianity, his religious notions bear unmistakable and distinct traces of this faith, as, for
example, in his emphasis on man's military relationship to God,
the commander. W's God is powerless without men. [In Polish with
an English summary.]

1213   SPEARE, MORRIS EDMUND. The Political Novel. New York: Oxford
        University Press, pp. 268-86.
        W's characters are too individualistic, independent, and
disrespectful of the past, their passion treated too fatalisti-
cally. Yet W advances the political novel from where Mrs. Humphry

Ward left it, and his significance lies in his diagnosis of the political ills of his time. [Relates historical happenings to their counterparts in W's novels.]

1214 SPICER-SIMSON, THEODORE, and STUART P. SHERMAN. Men and Let-
       ters of the British Isles. New York: Rudge, pp. 127-28.
           W, whose fiction is a form of disguised autobiography,
       resorts to a basic recipe in his works: "Take equal parts of
       science, sex, and sociology. Mix thoroughly. Serve hot."

1215 STUART, HENRY LONGAN. "Mr. Wells Makes Up His Mind." NYTBR,
       27 April, pp. 1, 17.
           As good as anything W has done, Dream offers a rearrangement
       of several of his ideas in a book that is suggestive rather than
       instructive.

1216 TOMLINSON, PHILIP. "Mr. Wells's People." Adelphi 1
       (May):1112-13.
           In Dream W makes us hate the sin but love the sinner.

1217 TROTSKY, L. "H.G. Wells and Lenin." Labour Monthly 6
       (June):411-20.
           W's attitude toward Lenin "stinks of unwarranted smug self-
       conceit." W is indeed a petty bourgeois and a philistine.

1218 "The Universal Mind." SR (London) 138 (27 Dec.):655.
           In Prophesying W cannot cope with all of his ideas, which
       either fit together imperfectly or just contradict each other.

1219 "Utopian View of Us." SDR, 9 June, p. 6.
           A better book than Men Like Gods, Dream holds a mirror up to
       humanity.

1220 "Wells in Defeat." GDN, 27 July, p. 2.
           An appalling piece of preposterous tommy-rot, Dream implies
       that suicide is the only intelligent action open to man.

1221 WOOLSEY, DOROTHY BACON. "Utopia or Despair?" Independent (New
       York) 112 (7 June):317.
           Flashes of W's old humor and adroit characterization are
       evident in Dream, which is marked by self-interest.

1222 YOUNG, FILSON. "Wells's Novel Appears in London." NYTBR, 18
       May, p. 16.
           Dream echoes well the earlier W of Tono-Bungay and Mr.
       Polly.

1925

1223 AAS, L. "H.G. Wells og hans senere verker (1914-1924)." (H.G. Wells and his later works). <u>Edda</u> 24:182-206.
[A survey of W's later works from <u>Mr. Britling</u> to <u>Washington</u>. Certain titles are covered in detail with occasional judgments and an attempt to define central themes and preoccupations in the postwar production. There are numerous references to contemporary articles and reviews and liberal quotes from several.] [In Norwegian.]

1224 BEERBOHM, MAX. <u>Observations</u>. London: Heinemann, p. 35.
[Caricature of and alleged dialogue between the younger and the older W.]

1225 BOYNTON, H.W. "Another Wellsian Comedy." <u>SR</u> 2 (17 Oct.):209.
<u>Christina</u> is W's work nearest to the human interest of <u>Mr. Polly</u>. As usual the heroine is mechanical and unconvincing, and there is also a wistful, ineffective male like Mr. Polly.

1226 _____. "<u>Christina Alberta's Father</u>." <u>Outlook</u> (New York) 141 (Nov.):356.
As much romance as novel, this work is comfortably Wellsian. All the characters talk alike and frankly represent moods or aspects of W.

1227 CANBY, HENRY SEIDEL. "Outline of a Journalist." <u>SR</u> 1 (24 Jan.):473-75.
[A general sketch of W's career, focusing on the journalistic aspect of his work.]

1228 CHEVALLEY, ABEL. <u>The Modern English Novel</u>. New York: Knopf, pp. 156-66.
Caring little for beauty, W exteriorized the literary imagination. After 1905, the true novelist in him emerged; but by 1915, his literary influence was exhausted.

1229 "<u>Christina Alberta's Father</u>." <u>TLS</u>, 17 Sept., p. 598.
This book is interesting, but its protagonist is inconsistent.

1230 CHURCH, RICHARD. "H.G. Wells." <u>Calendar</u> 2 (Nov.):201-6. Reprinted in <u>LA</u> 328 (16 Feb.):154-57.
Throughout W's "work there is a quite strong suggestion of the lachrymose, a certain sponginess. But . . . it is also the moisture of fecundity." W's unparalleled portrayal of the love between parents and children in his work is an example of the emotional forces defining so much of what he writes.

1231   COOK, SHERWIN LAWRENCE. "A Prophetic Year with H.G. Wells."
       BET, 7 Feb., pt. 6, p. 4.
           Prophesying is a sort of admirable epilogue to the bulk of
       W's literary writings. It presents W's candid, accurate assess-
       ment of his previous work.

1232   DAVIS, ADA E. "H.G. Wells on Education." Education 46
       (Oct.):72-95.
           W sees education, when properly pursued, as a civilizing
       force directing men toward a collective life. It is presently in
       need of intellectual direction.

1233   "Fiction." ALA 22 (Dec.):120.
           Written in the inimitable style of his earlier works,
       Christina is a masterpiece of insight.

1234   FIELD, LOUISE MAUNSELL. "Mr. Wells Discusses the New Woman."
       LDI 3 (Nov.):793, 795.
           Christina begins delightfully and then becomes serious.
       Christina, not Mr. Preemby, dominates the book.

1235   G., S. "Mr. Wells's Output." SSR, 19 April, p. 7a.
           Prophesying has been compiled helter-skelter without
       editing.

1236   GILMAN, DOROTHY FOSTER. "A Modern Woman According to Wells."
       BET, 3 Oct., pt. 6, p. 4.
           A deftly constructed novel, Christina presents an inter-
       weaving of a "curious silken emotionalism, the sweetness of age
       and a tender charity." Preemby is a Christ figure. Although many
       will only be amused by the story, it is in fact a tremendous piece
       of work in implication, quite worthy of W's inherent and ripened
       genius.

1237   "H.G. Wells' New Novel Brings Ann Veronica Up to Date." NYTBR,
       27 Sept., p. 10.
           The heroine of Christina is really Ann Veronica years later.
       W's marvelous talent for presenting an individual as unique and
       yet at the same time as a type is evident in the work.

1238   "H.G. Wells Rebuked for His Pessimism." CO 78 (Feb.):168.
           [Cites comments from the Sunday Express (London) (not seen)
       and the Chicago Post (not seen) responding unfavorably to
       Prophesying.]

1239   "History and Political Economy." Outlook (New York) 139
       (1 April):504-5.
           In spite of some deficiencies, Prophesying is quite good,
       with many pages of pertinent satire and irony.

1925

1240   "In Brief Review." Bookman (New York) 61 (April):232.
       Prophesying is keen-witted, stimulating, and rational.

1241   KENNEDY, P.C. "New Novels." NS 25 (26 Sept.):665-66.
       Rich and delightful, Christina suffers from W's effort to
include too much. W is still at the height of his powers.

1242   LACON [pseud. of Edmund E.H. Lacon Watson]. Lectures to Living
       Authors. Freeport, N.Y.: Books for Libraries Press, pp. 31-39.
       [A general, quasi-psychological chronicle of W's life and
work, indicating that he made certain subjects available to modern
novelists.]

1243   LOVETT, ROBERT MORSS. "Ideas and Fiction." NR 44
       (18 Nov.):336-37.
       If Christina is not among the most significant fiction
currently, it is because it belongs to a type that is out of date
by about twenty years.

1244   MacDONALD, WILLIAM. "Mr. Wells on the Mountain." Nation (New
       York) 120 (15 April):434-36.
       [A favorable review of Prophesying.]

1245   McQUILLAND, LOUIS J. "Novels of the Day." G.K.'s Weekly 2
       (19 Sept.):21-23.
       W may be trying to differentiate between what is madness and
what is sanity in Christina, a novel marking his return to his
second best period.

1246   MENCKEN, H.L. "The English Novel." American Mercury 6 (Dec.):
       509-10.
       A thoroughly bad piece of work, Christina is poorly planned
and written and "full of characters that creak in every joint."
In contrast to young American writers, English novelists seem to
have lost their old capacity for working with material under their
noses.

1247   "Mr. Preemby." Observer (London), 20 Sept., p. 5.
       Christina takes the reader on a sort of journey without ever
arriving at a destination; but the journey is pleasant. In Mr.
Preemby W has created "a true Quixote, meaningful in his madness,
heroic in his disasters, and winning in his absurdities."

1248   "Mr. Wells Writes a Little More." NYTBR, 8 March, p. 5.
       [Favorable review of Prophesying.]

1249   "Mr. Wells's Mad Reformer." SSR, 27 Dec., p. 7a.
       Christina suffers from somewhat abstract and irrelevant
discussions, the sign of W's later work. Parts of the book remind

one of <u>Kipps</u>; and if W could maintain this style and approach, he would be working in a genre worthy of the art of English fiction.

1250   "Mr. Wells's New Novel." <u>Spectator</u> (London) 135 (19 Sept.): 459-60.
    <u>Christina</u> lends further evidence that W is the best contemporary writer of imaginative fiction in England.

1251   "Mr. Wells's Work." <u>TLS</u>, 15 Jan., p. 37.
    Unquestionably W is among the half-dozen great novelists of our time, especially in regard to his sympathy, humor, and insight in delineating characters. Yet his influence on contemporary thought has not been profound and his artistic significance has been supplanted by writers of lesser consequence. Perhaps his limitations as a thinker define his failings as an artist. <u>Kipps</u> and <u>Mr. Polly</u> will survive whereas <u>Marriage</u> and <u>Machiavelli</u> will not interest future generations. Although W believes that he contributes to literature as a thinker, the reader in fact is attracted to him as a humanist.

1252   MOULT, THOMAS. "H.G. Wells and <u>Christina Alberta's Father</u>." <u>Bookman</u> (London) 69 (Oct.):18-20.
    By means of excellent characterization, W succeeds in this book emphasizing the individual's godlikeness.

1253   "New Books at a Glance." <u>SR</u> (London) 140 (12 Sept.):291.
    <u>Christina</u>, if fifty pages are an indication, marks W's return to his best manner.

1254   "New Fiction." <u>SR</u> (London) 140 (26 Sept.):340.
    In <u>Christina</u> W the sociologist and prophet frustrates W the inspired storyteller. Moreover, "never was an author more completely duped by one of his creatures than Mr. Wells by Christina." W ought to harken to the promptings of his genius.

1255   PRIESTLEY, J.B. "H.G. Wells." <u>English Journal</u> 14 (Feb.): 89-97.
    W benefited from the reaction to the aestheticism of the 1890s and ever since has been struggling to hide the artist behind the moral prophet. But the artist is there, almost in spite of himself, and finds his best expression in the broad humor of W's best novels.

1256   R., D. "Mr. Wells, the Journalist." <u>Independent</u> (New York) 114 (21 Feb.):218.
    <u>Prophesying</u> is stimulatingly suggestive and intelligent as well as brilliantly written.

1925

1257   R., D. "The Romance of Madness." Independent (New York) 115
       (7 Nov.):533.
            Although not W's greatest book, Christina is done in the
       spirit of his most successful work.

1258   SAMPSON, GEORGE. "Christina Talks It Out." Weekly
       Westminster, n.s. 4 (19 Sept.):526.
            In Christina W prefers to let himself brim over instead of
       telling a story. The book, therefore, is merely an outline of the
       great work it could have been.

1259   "The Sanity of Mr. Wells." Spectator (London) 134 (24 Jan.):
       124.
            W is a supreme journalist in Prophesying. The book abounds
       in artful phrase making, particularly delightful aphorisms and
       similes. As prophecy the book is less successful.

1260   SHERMAN, STUART P. "Dreaming for the Future." Trib, 22 March,
       pp. 1, 2. Excerpted in RR 71 (May):535-36.
            Works allows us to reassess W, and clearly in spite of de-
       fects there is much to appreciate. The early tales, on rereading,
       are not purposeless but urge a new point of view and are burdened
       with moral meaning. Perhaps Dr. Moreau is a symbol for W himself.
       Unlike Thomas Hardy and Joseph Conrad, W is not a realist; he has
       little respect for chance and necessity.

1261   SMITH, HARRISON. "'The Mind of the Race." Trib, 4 Oct.,
       pp. 1-2.
            Anyone who thinks that because W failed as a prophet, he is
       also less a novelist will be corrected by Christina. [Reviews W's
       career too.]

1262   STANDARD, S.R. "Latest Wells Novel an Extremely Wellsian and
       Fascinating Tale." St. Louis Post-Dispatch, 24 Oct., p. 13.
            Although its story disappointingly leaves some of the most
       interesting characters with unresolved problems, Christina is
       fascinating and different. The protagonist is less interesting
       than the heroine, but he does represent something entirely new in
       modern fiction.

1263   T., W.O. "Mr. Wells' Masterly Tale of a Limpid Laundryman."
       LR, 7 Dec., p. 3.
            W is the greatest chronicler of English life since Dickens.
       Christina, in which humor and message are well joined, comes near
       to equalling Mr. Polly

1264   WALDMAN, MILTON. "Fiction." LM 12 (Oct.):658-59.
            In Christina interesting characters and a promising
       story are subordinated to ideas because for W the substance of

literature concerns the fortunes of the race rather than those of the individual.

1265   "Wells' Christina Alberta's Father Delightful Reading." St. Louis Daily Globe-Democrat, 26 Sept., p. 9.
         A clever, humorous style accents this novel, a book reflecting the mood of Kipps.

1266   WEYGANDT, CORNELIUS. A Century of the English Novel. New York: Century, pp. 404-14.
         Concerned with the issues of the hour rather than with essential matters, W is more a journalist than a novelist. Lacking a literary heritage, he differs in his treatment of life from genuine artists of either the romantic or the realistic schools. He can tell a story fairly well and manages a little humor, but he lacks style and can only approach characterization.

1267   WOOLF, LEONARD. "Mr. Wells and the Immortals." NA 37 (19 Sept.):734.
         The ease with which W brings his characters to life signifies an artist of the highest class. Frequently, however, he spoils his novels by indulging in propaganda. Fortunately the thesis of Christina is woven into the very texture of the novel, and only occasionally does W grow impatient and step before the curtain.

1926

1268   ADCOCK, ST. JOHN. "The End of William Clissold." Bookman (London) 71 (Nov.):136.
         Clissold is stimulating, entertaining, and variously interesting.

1269   _____. "A Man and His World." Bookman (London) 70 (Sept.):300.
         [Brief remarks on the first volume of Clissold.]

1270   _____. "The Progress of William Clissold." Bookman (London) (New York)71 (Oct.):31-32.
         A "familiar style" is part of W's literary gift evident in volume two of Clissold. W "handles abstruse and difficult subjects as he handles everyday topics, with a grasp of detail and an ease and clarity of diction, a gusto and wealth of humour and imagery that make interesting and alive themes that the orthodox scholar invests with dullness."

1271   AIKEN, CONRAD. "Bookshelf." AM 138 (Nov.):20; Reprinted in CH, pp. 275-76.

1926

   In Clissold, as elsewhere, W fails to select and synthesize
the elements of his character's self projection into "an aesthetic
and psychological envisagement of them as a unit." W explains
rather than depicts those scenes that should subtly convey these
elements.

1272   _____. "An Outline of the Modern Mind." Dial 81 (Dec.):503-6.
   Despite W's intention, the protagonist of Clissold never
comes to life. Part of the failure stems from the grandiosity of
what W has undertaken to do: to portray the entire intellectual,
emotional, and physical history of an individual. W has little
sense of character, which results in a lack of sensitivity to
proportion and arrangement in his book; he could have learned from
Tolstoi how to better manage these matters. Yet the book is a
landmark in the evolution of the novel, an instructive failure
opening vistas for a new technique.

1273   ARMSTRONG, HENRY E. "Education, Science and Mr. H.G. Wells."
   Nature 118 (20 Nov.):723-28.
   Clissold is not a novel but a medical treatise principally
on social pathology. W's views on education are particularly
pertinent.

1274   B., R. "A Notable Controversy." NS 28 (27 Nov.):202-4.
   Reprinted in LA 332 (1 Feb.):227-30.
   In his controversy with Belloc W has erred in defending an
outdated conception of natural selection.

1275   BELLOC, HILAIRE. A Companion to Mr. Wells's "Outline of
   History." London: Sheed & Ward.
   W's book is written sincerely, clearly, and with strong
imaginative power. But it is provincial insofar as W dismisses
whatever is outside his range of experience. Too often he re-
sponds rabidly to whatever is traditional and has blindly depended
on authorities without considering other points of view. [The
creation of the world, the fall of man, God, the nature of religion, genuine history, priesthood, Buddhism, the Incarnation, the
origins of the Roman Catholic Church, Islam, the Dark and Middle
Ages, and the Reformation are the chief areas discussed.]

1276   _____. Mr. Belloc Still Objects to Mr. Wells's "Outline of
   History." London: Sheed & Ward.
   [Continues the controversy between W and Belloc, focusing
specifically on W's notions of biology and his ignorance of the
Roman Catholic Church.]

1277   _____. "Mr. Wells v. Mr. Belloc." NA 40 (9 Oct.):18.
   [Letter regarding Woolf's review in NA 39 (25 Sept.):735.]

1278   B[ROWN[, I[VOR]. "Clissold Goes On." MG, 1 Oct., p. 9.
        Volume two of Clissold is rather clammy.

1279   _____. "First Phase of Mr. Clissold." MG, 1 Sept., p. 7.
        The first volume of Clissold is occasionally peppery, fre-
        quently profound, always intellectual. W's winged words have
        barbs.

1280   BULLETT, GERALD. Modern English Fiction. London: Jenkins,
        pp. 18-33.
        As a writer of allegorical scientific romances, W is bril-
        liantly entertaining; as a creator of comic characters, he is
        second only to Dickens; and as a proponent of sociology, he dis-
        turbs complacency. Unfortunately W cannot combine the roles of
        artist and prophet successfully.

1281   CALVERTON, V.F. "Ground Swells in Fiction." Survey 57
        (1 Nov.):159.
        Presenting a cross-section of contemporary life, Clissold
        captures, in its revolutionary motif, the new morality, religion,
        and economics. W is far more candid and revolutionary than George
        Meredith.

1282   "Citadels of Cosmopolis." Spectator (London) 137 (6 Nov.):819.
        Though not really a novel Clissold "is as great and daring
        in design as it is in achievement, a book that will live and help
        people to live."

1283   "Clissold in Love." NS 27 (2 Oct.):712-14.
        The second volume of Clissold, in contrast to the first,
        provides the substance of a real novel. Clissold's sex life is
        treated frankly.

1284   "Clissold's Last Words." TLS, 4 Nov., p. 760.
        The ideas expressed in Clissold are too generalized and
        unrealistic.

1285   COLUM, MARY M. "Mr. Wells's Emporium." SR 3 (13 Nov.):289-90.
        Reprinted in CH, pp. 277-81.
        More of an outline of opinion than a novel, Clissold fails
        to provide clarity of thought or even largeness of vision.

1286   CONNES, GEORGES. Etude sur la pensée de Wells. Paris:
        Librairie Hachette.
        The scientific orientation of W's work is more important
        than its superficial philosophy, though both are central to his
        writings. The notions of evolution and of Marxism (especially the
        inevitability of the split between the aristocracy and the prole-
        tariat) temper his imaginative enthusiasm. There are basically

four contradictory yet related veins of thought in W's works: the revolt against the misery of life and pity for the victims of an imperfect society (W's atrophied characters); the collective advancement of socialism as superior to individual effort and as the saviour of the downtrodden; the importance of sex to individual fulfillment and to the collective effort (via generations); the function of humor, not only in satire but in sheer fun, in obviating the despair of the philosopher. W views war optimistically but not without doubts; he seeks a personal God; he possesses a strong faith in education, implying the perfectability of man. W's ideas on education eventually supplant those on religion. He is the perennial optimist.

1287   COURNOS, JOHN. "Saul among the Prophets." LR, 9 Oct., pp. 1, 6.
        Clissold is a provocative, intellectual autobiography verging on a novel. As a whole it is not as coherent as it ought to be.

1288   "The Coyness of Mr. Wells." NA 39 (4 Sept.):643.
        The first volume of Clissold is really a collection of essays. W's ideas are too tentative and incoherent for him to present them in a genuine book of articles.

1289   DELL, FLOYD. "Mr. Wells Makes a Great Experiment." Bookman (New York) 64 (Nov.):336-40.
        Although journalistic in tone in the first part, the second part of Clissold brilliantly portrays a bewildered human groping for understanding in the darkness of life.

1290   EDGETT, EDWIN FRANCIS. "The World of an H.G. Wells Hero." BET, 2 Oct., pt. 7, p. 2.
        W is more thought provoking than ever in Clissold, a novel in which story and commentary do not interweave very well. Although not entirely satisfactory, the book is successfully interesting.

1291   EDMAN, IRVING. "A Man and His World." Trib, 10 Oct., p. 3.
        Although W never quite unites the passionate and the philosophical sides of his protagonist, Clissold is absorbing and successful. Mankind is part of Clissold's life.

1292   "The Encyclopedic Novel." NYT, 19 Sept., pt. 2, p. 6.
        [Attacks Clissold, concluding that if it is a novel then the Encyclopaedia Britannica is a poem.]

1293   "An English Babbitt." NS 27 (4 Sept.):584-85.
        The first volume of Clissold fails to present one new idea to readers familiar with W's work. One wonders why W bothered to invent such a tedious person as the main character of this book.

1294   FULLER, HENRY B. "Mr. Wells Insists on Making the World Over."
       LDI 4 (Oct.):755-56.
           Clissold is truly the book of books and succeeds as a novel
       of ideas.

1295   GAINES, CLARENCE H. "Self-Expression in the Novel." NAR 223
       (Dec.):725-28.
           Not a novel in the ordinary sense, Clissold disappointingly
       presents a somewhat discouraged view. In idea and in form the
       book is an imperfect synthesis.

1296   GOULD, GERALD. "Clissold Again." Observer (London), 3 Oct.,
       p. 6.
           The second volume of Clissold presents W almost at his best.
       The book seems to lack a note of deep tenderness; otherwise it is
       dexterous and brilliant.

1297   _____. "Mr. Clissold Objects." Observer (London), 31 Oct.,
       p. 7.
           Whatever the minor limitations of Clissold may be, only W
       could have raised so many issues and provoked one so readily to
       discussion and contradiction.

1298   _____. "A Splendid Hybrid." Observer (London), 5 Sept., p. 5.
           We owe W much for his inspiration and delight. The first
       volume of Clissold may be in several respects disappointing, but
       it manages to give a rich picture of the present time with laud-
       able variety, energy, and idealism.

1299   "H.G. Wells Diagnoses the Ills of Society." SSUR, 31 Oct.,
       p. 7f.
           Clissold ascends in interest even if its story is slight.

1300   HAMILTON, MARY AGNES. "Fiction on Crutches." TT 7
       (1 Oct.):875.
           Interest in Clissold and Arnold Bennett's Lord Raingo has
       been stimulated by the suggestion that certain characters are
       taken from real life. This development is not advantageous to the
       art of fiction.

1301   _____. "Looking at the World." TT 7 (3 Sept.):794-95.
           [Negative review of Clissold as something less than a
       novel.]

1302   _____. "William Clissold." TT 7 (5 Nov.):1006-7.
           The final verdict on Clissold must be that it is boring in
       its simplicity and vagueness.

1926

1303   HARTLEY, L.P. "New Fiction." SR (London) 142 (4 Sept.):263;
       (2 Oct.):388; (6 Nov.):558.
            The first volume of Clissold suffers in terms of content and
       characterization. Clissold is little more than his opinions. The
       second volume is not much better than the first. It is "thin,
       flacid, and unorganized." The memoir at the end gives the pro-
       tagonist some sympathetic qualities and should have appeared at
       the beginning of the book.

1304   "History." TLS, 7 Oct., p. 678.
            The polemic of Belloc Objects is witty but not always in the
       best of taste.

1305   HORWILL, HERBERT W. "H.G. Wells Ventures on Thin Ice." NYTBR,
       18 July, p. 12.
            [Reports W's ideas on the form of the novel and on his use
       of real personages as models for characters in Clissold.]

1306   "King George Is Ridiculed in New Wells Book as 'Uninteresting
       Son of Plump Old Edward.'" NYT, 2 Oct., p. 21.
            [Reports British response to comments in Clissold concerning
       King George.]

1307   KNOX, RONALD. "The Survival of the Rudest." Spectator
       (London) 137 (2 Oct.):535.
            [An attack on W's defense in Belloc Objects.]

1308   KRUTCH, JOSEPH WOOD. "Heavens Above and Earth Beneath."
       Nation (New York) 123 (24 Nov.):536-37.
            In Clissold "there are some clever things cleverly said, but
       they are all but lost in a flow of words and a flood of sentences,
       always competent, seldom distinguished." Buried in these two
       volumes are six good magazine articles. W has too much freedom
       from editorial restraint.

1309   LAWRENCE, D.H. "The World of William Clissold." Calender 3
       (Oct.):254-57. Reprinted in Phoenix: The Posthumous Papers of
       D.H. Lawrence (New York: Viking, 1936), pp. 346-50; and in
       Selected Literary Criticism, ed. Anthony Beal (London:
       Heinemann, 1955), pp. 133-38.
            Not good enough to be a novel, this book presents a protago-
       nist bored by his own story. Clissold "grinds on and on at the
       stale bones of sociology, while his actual living goes to pieces,
       falls into a state of irritable peevishness."

1310   le GALLIENNE, RICHARD. "The World and Mr. Wells." Forum 76
       (Dec.):956-58.
            Honest, didactic yet charming, Clissold is a work of spiri-
       tual and sociological value. The protagonist's single fault is

his denial of permanent elements in human nature, suggesting that he is outside life.

1311   LOVETT, ROBERT MORSS. "Mr. Wells's Newest World." NR 48 (6 Oct.):197-98.
          A story told in ununified chunks, Clissold fails to articulate theme and material. The protagonist seems an unreal aspect of a world of realities.

1312   McQUILLAND, LOUIS J. "Two Women Writers." Bookman (London) 70 (June):156-58.
          [Remarks on Margaret Storm Jameson's respect for W's work but criticizes W for his ignorance of the spiritual aspects of life, especially from a feminine point of view.]

1313   MELLERSH, H.E.L. "Shaw, Wells, and Creative Evolution." FR 125 (Feb.):178-88.
          Shaw and W both believe that human destiny lies in man's hands and that with effort, in conjunction with the Life Force, man will achieve control over himself and his surroundings.

1314   MENCKEN, H.L. "Wells Redivivus." American Mercury 9 (Dec.): 506-8. Reprinted in CH, pp. 282-85.
          An amazingly good book, Clissold reveals W the novelist and the seer as one and indivisible. W possesses a competent, original mind. He is the complete antithesis of the unimaginative, muddling traditional Briton. [The author readjusts his earlier views of W.]

1315   "Mr. Wells and the Novelist's Portrait Gallery." SR (London) 142 (28 Aug.):220-21.
          [Discusses aspects of W's use of real individuals as models for his characters.]

1316   "Mr. Wells As Ventriloquist." NYT, 6 Oct., p. 24.
          [Comments on the controversy over whether or not W should be identified with the protagonist of Clissold.]

1317   "Mr. Wells Looks Out His Window." Spectator (London) 137 (4 Sept.):340.
          [Discusses only the economic notions of Clissold.]

1318   MOODY, WILLIAM VAUGHAN, and ROBERT MORSS LOVETT. A History of English Literature. New York: Scribner's Sons, pp. 456-58.
          The humor of Kipps is Dickensian, and the form of Research is somewhat like that of Carlyle's Sartor Resartus. W is more optimistic about the future than are many of his contemporaries.

1926

1319 MURRAY, HENRY. "Mr. Wells's New Book." Sunday Times (London), 5 Sept., p. 6; 3 Oct., p. 9; 7 Nov., p. 8.
No novel, Clissold is too restricted in event and emotion, too devoid of human interest, too half-hearted in its cardboard characterization.

1320 "A Novel of Ideas." TLS, 2 Sept., p. 575.
Although its criticism of Marx is good, Clissold is redundantly Wellsian. It is doubtful that the book should have been written.

1321 OSBORN, E.B. "Mr. Wells's New Novel." Morning Post (London), 1 Sept., pp. 9, 14.
Apparently W is unaware of the degree to which he relies on autobiography in his works. Clissold evinces only the symptoms of a story, with a few good touches at characterization and several good phrases typical of W. Politically it seems W has moved toward the Right.

1322 "Our Bookshelf." Nature 118 (18 Dec.):872.
Although open to argument in a few places, the new edition of Outline is remarkable. In Belloc Objects W humorously makes short work of Belloc's criticisms.

1323 "Our Own Bookshelf." LA 331 (15 Nov.):375-76.
Although there is something in Clissold for everyone, no one will accept it in entirety with enthusiasm, for it is too much like life itself.

1324 "Outlined and Popularized." NYT, 26 Sept., pt. 2, p. 8.
[Refutes the idea that all histories prior to Outline were void of popular appeal.]

1325 PEARSON, EDMUND. "Heap Big Chiefs." Outlook (New York) 144 (6 Oct.):182-83.
Though long-winded, Clissold is replete with interesting and wise observations.

1326 PURE, SIMON. "The Londoner." Bookman (New York) 64 (Dec.):485-86.
Disappointment with W's new works, especially Clissold, stems from the critics' inability to preserve their freshness of taste.

1327 R., D. "The World of Mr. Wells." Independent (New York) 117 (23 Oct.):479.
Clissold is too rambling, too verbose, but it is intelligent and sometimes captures a certain genuine dramatic power.

1328   "Sensitiveness about the King." NYT, 5 Oct., p. 28.
       [Uses British response to views expressed in Clissold on
King George as the basis for an editorial.]

1329   SHANKS, EDWARD. "Fiction." LM 14 (Sept.):534-36.
       In spite of W's protests to the contrary, every novelist
draws from real people. W's work of the past years has almost
exclusively focused on a person very much like himself, observing
other people from the outside. His arguments possess "the air of
the fox who has lost his tail persuading all the other foxes to
dispense with theirs."

1330   _____. "Fiction." LM 15 (Nov.):96-97.
       Clissold is uninterestingly vague and unreal. Its main
character remains a mere mouthpiece for generalizations.

1331   SHERMAN, STUART. Critical Woodcuts. New York: Scribner's
       Sons, pp. 94-107.
       W's romances are religious myths and heroic fables or alle-
gories designed to serve as the new scriptures for the current
generation.

1332   STRUNSKY, SIMEON. "About Books, More or Less: Readers of
       Today." NYTBR, 1 Aug., p. 2.
       [Reports of W's use of real people in Clissold.]

1333   STUART, HENRY LONGAN. "H.G. Wells Surveys His World." NYTBR,
       26 Sept., pp. 1, 26.
       [Very long mixed and largely descriptive review of
Clissold.]

1334   STYLES, PETRONELLA. "Mr. Wells and the Novelist's Portrait
       Gallery." SR (London) 142 (4 Sept.):257.
       [A letter commenting on W's use of real people as models for
his characters.]

1335   "This Week's Books." Spectator (London) 137 (18 Sept.):431.
       Worth reading, Belloc Objects brings the Huxley-Gladstone
controversy up to date.

1336   WALPOLE, HUGH. "A Mouse from the Mountain and Other Fiction."
       Spectator (London) 137 (4 Sept.):349-50.
       The first volume of Clissold suffers from an inchoate repe-
tition of W's well-known opinions.

1337   WELBY, T. EARLE. "Conscientious Objectors." SR (London) 142
       (20 Nov.):617-18.
       [Review of Belloc Objects and Mr. Belloc Still Objects,
concluding that W has despised his own best gifts as a writer.]

1926

1338   WELLS, GEOFFREY H. "The Failure of H.G. Wells." <u>Adelphi</u> 3
        (Feb.):609-21. Reprinted in <u>CH</u>, pp. 290-99.
             Despite the fact that W is a great man, most of his novels
        will fall into oblivion. Most of his work fails to satisfy our
        deepest instincts, a problem arising from a conflict within him-
        self between reason and intuition. "He has rejected his truest
        knowledge for the judgment of the intellectual consciousness, and
        at the same time has lacked the courage . . . to follow to its
        bitter end the path of the intellectual consciousness." <u>Tono-</u>
        <u>Bungay</u> and <u>The</u> <u>History</u> <u>of</u> <u>Mr.</u> <u>Polly</u> will endure.

1339   _____. <u>The Works of H.G. Wells, 1887-1925.</u> London: Routledge
        & Sons.
             [Contains a bibliography of works by and on W, a dictionary
        relating to places, characters, and subjects treated by W, and a
        subject index.]

1340   "A Wells Three-Decker." <u>SSUR</u>, 26 Sept., p. 7F.
             [Cites a review of <u>Clissold</u> in the <u>Observer</u> (London),
        quibbling over how one can separate W's opinions from those of
        Clissold.]

1341   "Wells's New Novel Is on Living People." <u>NYT</u>, 2 Sept., p. 2.
             [Reports references to contemporary personages in <u>Clissold</u>.]

1342   "William Clissold." <u>TLS</u>, 7 Oct., p. 672.
             The women portrayed in <u>Clissold</u> are unreal; "they are objec-
        tives of an appetite rather than human beings existing in their
        own right."

                                1927

1343   ADCOCK, ST. JOHN. "<u>Meanwhile</u>." <u>Bookman</u> (London) 72
        (Aug.):271.
             Not strictly a novel, this work is a brilliant, intensely
        interesting exposition.

1344   ANTHONY, JOSEPH. "The Reading Room." <u>Century</u> (New York) 114
        (Sept.):636-37.
             Without the propaganda, which is bad enough, <u>Meanwhile</u> would
        be entirely unpalatable. W has sold his birthright for a pot of
        message.

1345   BRAYBROOKE, PATRICK. <u>Peeps</u> <u>at</u> <u>the</u> <u>Mighty</u>. London: Danegeld,
        pp. 9-25, 95-112.
             Replete with insights and delightful dialogue, <u>Christina</u>
        conveys an almost terrifying realism. In <u>Marriage</u> W writes

beautifully, "the type of writing that has something to do with wistfulness and human nature at its best."

1346   "Briefer Mention." <u>Dial</u> 83 (Nov.):444.
        Little more than a propagandist pamphlet, <u>Meanwhile</u> begins better than it ends.

1347   B[ROWN], I[VOR]. "<u>Meanwhile</u>." <u>MG</u>, 28 July, p. 7.
        Despite its good ideas, this book is not eminent among W's writings.

1348   BURT, STRUTHERS. "Furor Britannicus." <u>SEP</u> 200 (20 Aug.):6-7, 106, 111-12.
        [A sardonic rebuttal of views of America expressed in W's writings.]

1349   CHEVALLEY, ABEL. "H.G. Wells et son dernier livre." <u>Revue de Paris</u>, April, pp. 167-80.
        <u>Clissold</u> is a cemetary where the cadavers of noxious myths are arranged under various epitaphs. The attempt to realize a better world is the unique and constant aim of W's writing. Ironically his utopian concepts begin with an act of faith, and his ideal of equality between the sexes is undercut by the fact that Clissold must do without women.

1350   COOK, SHERWIN LAWRENCE. "Meanwhile We Listen to H.G. Wells." <u>BET</u>, 6 Aug., pt. 6, p. 2.
        In <u>Meanwhile</u> W prefers to talk almost as diffusely as Lewis Carroll's Walrus rather than to develop a firm fictional structure. He may be an able writer and a plausible thinker, but he is an awful craftsman with a tendency to create unrelated incidents and characters. W's ideas are not made sufficiently a part of the story. Sempack is W.

1351   CROSS, WILBUR [L.]. "The Mind of H.G. Wells." <u>Yale Review</u> 16 (Jan.):298-315. Reprinted in <u>Four Contemporary Novelists</u> (New York: Macmillan, 1930), pp. 155-93.
        W's scientific attitude distinguishes him from Victorian novelists. When it comes to the novel proper, W is thoroughly Victorian. Like Dickens, his primary aim is discursive characterization, not drama narrowly conceived. Usually he concentrates his attention on a single character who dominates a small group. These characters lack psychological analysis; they "wear, as it were, tags for identification."

1352   DANDIEU, ARNAUD. "Wells et Diderot." <u>Mercure de France</u> 194 (15 March):513-36.
        W and Diderot share a taste for natural science, a disdain for materialism, a belief in the interdependence of all beings, an

1927

optimism in the improvement of man's faculties, and a concern with
the conflict between reason and passion.

1353   "Dead and Live Issues." NS 29 (6 Aug.):540-41.
        Despite some useful insight into the general strike, Mean-
while is not very interesting. In fact W's reiteration of the
same ideas for over a quarter of a century has become irritating.
W really belongs to another age, the exciting years of 1895-1905.

1354   "Democracy Under Revision." TLS, 1 Sept., p. 582.
        [General favorable review.]

1355   DODD, LEE WILSON. "A Fighting Optimist." SR 4 (20 Aug.):54.
        Although the prophet and propagandist side of W is spoiling
the artistic side, Meanwhile manages to be a balanced, well-
planned novel.

1356   DOUGHTY, F.H. H.G. Wells: Educationist. New York: Doran.
        Contrary to many critical charges of inconsistency, W's
later work merely makes more evident the ideals underlying his
earlier writings, though it does accentuate the gap between artist
and thinker. A faith in evolutionary progress forms the hub of
W's views, which include the condemnation of the present forms of
education. The study of biology lies at the heart of his solution
to educational problems, but his treatment of the issue is unsys-
tematic and at times contradictory. W also stresses a racial
consciousness, currently being verified by psychological and philosophical inquiry, as well as the role of ethics. With such
grounds W's opinions are less dreams than pragmatic beliefs shaping an educational philosophy; but it is a point of view that is
frequently closer to propaganda than to a true education, which
should preserve the best of what genuine individualism has to
offer.

1357   ELIOT, T[HOMAS]. S. "Recent Books." Monthly Criterion 5
        (May):253-56.
        W, with his prodigious gift of historical imagination, has a
tactical advantage in his raging debate with Hilaire Belloc.

1358   "Fiction." ALA 24 (Nov.):70.
        An optimitic novel, Meanwhile provides shrewd criticism and
entertaining narrative.

1359   "Fiction." Outlook (New York) 147 (7 Sept.):26.
        It is doubtful that Meanwhile is a novel or that it is
readable.

1360   "Fiction." Wisconsin Library Bulletin 23 (Nov.):260.
        Meanwhile is shorter and lighter than most of W's novels.

1361   FLINT, F.S. "Books of the New Quarter." <u>New Criterion</u> 5
       (Jan.):114-17.
          The main character in <u>Clissold</u>, like W for whom he speaks,
       lets his imagination run away from him. His view of business
       magnates is totally unrealistic.

1362   FORSTER, E.M. <u>Aspects of the Novel</u>. New York: Harcourt,
       Brace & Co., pp. 31-34, 109-10, 231-33.
          W and Dickens are both humorists "who get an effect by
       cataloguing details and whisking the page over irritably."
       Neither has much taste, and the world of beauty that was partially
       closed to Dickens is entirely unavailable to W. W's characters
       are as flat as a photograph. [The author sides with W in his
       controversy with Henry James.]

1363   GATES, BARRINGTON. "Hammer and Tongs." <u>NA</u> 40 (15 Jan.):540.
          [Comments on the controversy between W and Belloc, favoring
       the former.]

1364   GILLET, LOUIS. "Le monde de M. Wells." <u>Revue des deux mondes</u>
       41 (1 Oct.):685-96.
          There are many parallels between W and the hero of <u>Clissold</u>.
       W's dreams of mankind's future are very naive.

1365   GOULD, GERALD. "Mr. Wells's New Novel." <u>Observer</u> (London), 31
       July, p. 4.
          <u>Meanwhile</u> may be faulted with regard to form and opinion but
       remains "gloriously readable." Whether it should be called a
       novel is open to debate.

1366   JENNINGS, RICHARD. "Mr. H.G. Wells' Pamphlet Novel." <u>Daily
       Mail</u> (London), 28 July, p. 4.
          The heroine of <u>Meanwhile</u> is never portrayed; she remains "a
       sort of ready postbox for others' communications." The book is
       not a novel but an often eloquent prolonged pamphlet.

1367   KEYNES, J.M. "One of Wells's Worlds." <u>NR</u> 49 (2 Feb.):301-3.
       Reprinted as "<u>Clissold</u>," <u>NA</u> 40 (22 Sept.):561-62; and in <u>CH</u>,
       pp. 285-90.
          Propaganda rather than a work of art, <u>Clissold</u> does not
       treat all of its themes equally well; some in fact inadvertently
       verge on caricature. Yet the book is a great achievement, "a huge
       meaty egg from a glorious hen."

1368   LEGOUIS, EMILE, and LOUIS CAZAMIAN. <u>A History of English
       Literature</u>. Translated by W.D. MacInnes and L. Cazamian. Vol.
       2. New York: Macmillan, pp. 468-73.
          W's early science fiction is written in a simple, straight-
       forward, natural style. <u>Kipps</u> and <u>Tono-Bungay</u>, W's best books,

1927

evince a single central impulse carrying them plausibly to their conclusion. W's later works fall victim to diffuseness, abstraction, and uncertainty. Though genial, W's humor is not exceptional.

1369   "Les lettres étrangères: Lettres anglo-saxonnes." Revue de
        France 7 (Aug.):568-74.
        Few writers have tried to solve the great problems of human-
ity more than W has. If, in many instances, he has adopted erro-
neous solutions, he has not lacked reflection. W has gone through
several stages, including a scientific phase, a socialistic phase,
and one in which the scientist and the socialist began to put
their knowledge at the service of W's convictions. W then began
to elaborate a new Bible. In Clissold W returns to the questions
that have always haunted him; unfortunately he repeats many of the
ideas expressed in other novels. Decidedly W was not made to
write philosophy, and he would have made a very dull professor.

1370   LEVY, H. "Science in Literature." Nature 120 (8 Oct.):503-4.
        In Short Stories W, unlike most authors of contemporary
fiction, conveys the dramatic element of scientific discovery and
its influence on human existence. He does not, however, provide
constructive answers to his view of the problems of human society
or fulfill the promise of these stories in his later work.

1371   "Life, Letters, and the Arts." LA 332 (1 May):835.
        [Report on W's address before the Sorbonne.]

1372   L[OVETT], R[OBERT] M[ORSS]. "Fiction Notes." NR 52
        (7 Sept.):79.
        A journalistic novel, Meanwhile is concerned less with story
than with W's ideas.

1373   MAYER, FREDERICK P. "The Real and the Unreal." Virginia
        Quarterly Review 3 (Jan.):127-42.
        Although not new, the adaptation of the biographical form to
storytelling represents one of the successful aspects of Clissold.

1374   "Mr. H.G. Wells's Delusions." Daily Mail (London), 28 July,
        p. 13.
        Its humor and charming heroine notwithstanding, Meanwhile
suffers from interminable political arguments and misinformation.

1375   "Mr. H.G. Wells's New Novel." DC, 28 July, p. 4.
        Although often penetratingly just, Meanwhile suffers from
unreality. It presents a tepid story with artificial characters,
but it is not without interest.

1376   "Mr. H.G. Wells's Short Stories." TLS, 15 Sept., p. 620.
        W is more accomplished than his predecessors in the art of
science fiction. [Discusses some of the scientific devices used
in Short Stories.]

1377   "Mr. H.G. Wells's World." SSUR, 11 Sept., p. 7F.
        Meanwhile has a slight plot that sluggishly and tenuously
makes it way through W's "mental everglades." The last third is
better than the rest of the book.

1378   MYERS, WALTER. The Later Realism: A Study of Characteriza-
        tion in the British Novel. Chicago: University of Chicago
        Press, pp. 5, 31, 104, 128-31, 146-48, 155.
        A late Victorian in his method of character portrayal, W
uses dialogue in the tradition of the eighteenth century: character traits and themes are exhibited in direct speech, most
frequently at a time of crisis. W is influenced by French natu-
ralism and belongs to the vitalist tradition of Goethe and Shaw.

1379   "New Novels." TLS, 28 July, p. 518.
        An entertaining book combining amusement and thought, Mean-
hile may irritate some. W's skill is evident in the book, but in
some respects it has worn a little thin.

1380   "Our Own Bookshelf." LA 333 (15 Sept.):563.
        The first third of Meanwhile is very entertaining whereas
the last part is boring.

1381   POYNTER, J.W. "Outlines of History." NA 40 (29 Jan):589.
        [A letter responding to Barrington Gates's article in NA 40
(15 Jan.), comparing Outline and Charles Stanton Devas's The Key
to the World's Progress.]

1382   PRIESTLEY, J.B. The English Novel. London: Benn, pp. 137-39.
        Although Invisible Man, Kipps, and Tono-Bungay will survive
the test of time, W has been too impatient with the art he prac-
tised. Combining the temperament of a romantic idealist with the
training of the scientist, W is a literary genius who arouses
people but who misses greatness as a novelist.

1383   RASCOE, BURTON. "Four New Works of Fiction." Bookman (New
        York) 66 (Sept.):89-90.
        Although the heroine of Meanwhile is charming, the book
itself lacks drama and arouses the suspicion of padding.

1384   "Reviews." SR (London) 144 (30 July):166-67.
        Although the analysis of the strike is extremely well
done in Meanwhile, the conclusions to be drawn from it are
questionable.

1927

1385   ROBERTSON, D.H. "A Symposium on Mr. Wells." <u>NA</u> 41 (30 July):
       581.
          [Reports several reactions to <u>Meanwhile</u> by acquaintances of
       the reviewer.]

1386   ROSE, DONALD F. "Meanwhile Here Is Wells." <u>Forum</u> 78
       (Nov.):797-98.
          <u>Meanwhile</u> proves weak in interest and strong in characteri-
       zation. "The meat of the book is the Wells philosophy, faintly
       sugared by this tabloid of current life."

1387   SCRUTATOR. "The Incredible Dullness of Mr. H.G. Wells."
       <u>Empire Review</u> 46 (Sept.):173-82. Reprinted in <u>LA</u> 333
       (15 Oct.):728-32.
          <u>Meanwhile</u> is devastatingly weary. W has ceased to be read-
       able; all that remains is malice, conceit, and ignorance.

1388   SHANKS, EDWARD. "Fiction." <u>LM</u> 16 (Aug.):430-31.
          Weak as a historical document, <u>Meanwhile</u> does succeed in
       presenting commentary and criticism in the language of its chief
       character.

1389   _____. "Fiction." <u>LM</u> 16 (Sept.):542.
          <u>Short Stories</u> indicates that once W preferred to write
       stories, but now he is content to give lectures.

1390   _____. "Mr. Wells's Stories." <u>SR</u> (London) 144 (27 Aug.):278.
          <u>Short Stories</u> is notable for its breadth of imagination.
       "The Country of the Blind" is the best short story ever written in
       English.

1391   S[HEEN], F[ULTON] J. "New Books." <u>Catholic World</u> 126 (Dec.):
       420.
          <u>Belloc Objects</u> indicates that W is not at his best when he
       must concern himself with reasoning, logic, and science. He is
       good at using personal abuse.

1392   "Shorter Notices." <u>Monthly Criterion</u> 6 (Oct.):379.
          Hardly a novel, <u>Meanwhile</u> presents lifeless characters and
       muddles thinking.

1393   SITWELL, OSBERT. "A Few Days in an Author's Life." In <u>All at
       Sea</u>, by Osbert and Sacheverell Sitwell. London: Duckworth,
       p. 40.
          <u>Meanwhile</u> is one of the most interesting books W has writ-
       ten. Its adverse critical reception is due to the perversity of
       critics who expect weak books from famous writers in their last
       years.

1394   SMERTENKO, JOHAN. "Really a Novel." Nation (New York) 125
        (7 Sept.):231-32.
            As an example of popular fiction Meanwhile is immeasurably
        superior to the inconsequential average English novel.

1395   SMITH, BEVERLY W. "Clissold on the General Strike." New York
        Evening Post, 20 Aug., Society section, p. 9.
            "With all its heavy cargo of sociological pontificating,
        [Meanwhile manages] to be very good stuff indeed." W comments on
        the general strike through his character, Philip Ryland, and the
        message appears to be that the intelligent, but mean, wealthy want
        to discredit the trade unions, while the unintelligent wealthy see
        Bolshevism in everything they feel is changing society too quickly.

1396   SMITH, HARRISON. "Mr. Wells Loses His Temper." Trib, 31 July,
        p. 3.
            If the prophet has disappeared, the novelist remains in W's
        recent work. Meanwhile, however, is a wholly uninspiring semi-
        tract and seminovel displaying a thoroughly bad temper.

1397   STRUNSKY, SIMEON. "About Books, More or Less; Belated Inven-
        tory." NYTBR, 9 Jan., p. 4.
            [Suggests that the lessened thrill in reading W's recent
        works, particularly Clissold, is more the fault of the reader than
        of the author.]

1398   STUART, HENRY LONGAN. "Mr. Wells Pleads for Leisure to Eval-
        uate Progress." NYTBR, 31 July, p. 4.
            A pamphlet for the times rather than a novel, Meanwhile is
        not very original. Too frequently confused and confusing theory
        interferes with human psychology in W's work.

1399   van LOON, HENDRICK, WILLEM. "The Wells of History Un-
        Belloc(k)ed." Forum 78 (Nov.):796-97.
            W and Belloc ought to give up their foolish feud; neither
        can gain anything by it. W should devote his energies to the
        world, which needs them.

1400   WARREN, C. HENRY. "Mr. Wells's Stories." Bookman (London) 73
        (Nov.):127-28.
            [Focuses principally on "The Door in the Wall" in Short
        Stories, mentioning its spiritual and possibly autobiographical
        elements.]

1401   WAY, OLIVER. "Wells and Maurois Grow Personal." Graphic 117
        (23 July):153.
            [Remarks on the outspokenness of Meanwhile.]

1927

1402   "Wells Versus Belloc." Trib, 2 Jan., p. 15.
        [Weary notice of Belloc Objects, tending to favor W in the
controversy.]

1403   WHIPPLE, LEON. "Some Like Them Hot." Survey 59 (1 Oct.):
        52-53.
             A warm but not great book, Meanwhile derives from W's Indian
Summer. Although it extends mathematics and reason to absurdity,
it presents people who are alive. W is better than Upton Sinclair
and Harold Bell Wright.

1404   WYATT, J.A., and HENRY CLAY. Modern English Literature, 1798-
        1935. London: University Tutorial Press, pp. 220-25.
             The style of W's best work, such as Kipps, is direct, vivid,
and colloquial. W's humor and realism are Dickensian.

1405   Y[EATS]-B[ROWN], F[RANCIS]. "Utopographers and Stupids."
        Spectator (London) 139 (30 July):193.
             A half-told and loosely knit book, Meanwhile can be read for
its occasional flashes of W's imagination.

1406   "Yesterday's Yeast." Time 10 (15 Aug.):31-32.
             Mostly "brainy petulance," Meanwhile is more cranky than
replete with a sense of life. It "snarls as well as chaffs at a
world with the gout."

                              1928

1407   BAKER, GEORGE. "H.G. Wells." Spectator (London) 141
        (28 July):127.
             [Presents the winning poem for an inscription on a bust of
W.]

1408   BIBESCO, ELIZABETH. "The Genius of Mr. Wells." NS, 31
        (22 Sept.):733-34.
             Simple, unenjoyable, and finally, Mr. Blettsworthy is a
tired satire. As a result of his unpruned writing, W conveys a
sense of the world but fails to create lifelike characters who act
in it.

1409   BIRREL, FRANCIS. "New Novels." NA 43 (25 Aug.):680.
             At times the satire of Mr. Blettsworthy is brilliant.

1410   BRAYBROOKE, PATRICK. Some Aspects of H.G. Wells. London:
        Daniel.
             Time Machine, War of the Worlds, and Food of the Gods pop-
ularize scientific thought; they are symbolic works informed by a
pessimistic philosophy. In his "suburban novels" W laughs with

                              160

and not at his characters. Most likely <u>Kipps</u>, <u>Mr. Lewisham</u>, and <u>Mr. Polly</u> will be judged as his best works. When W the prophet and the writer of middle-class comedy and tragedy turns to theology he is less successful because he is less knowledgeable in the area and cannot offer anything better than what has gone before. As a sociologist, most particularly in <u>Clissold</u>, W proposes an interesting world plan that fails to take into account certain essentials necessary to its well-being and tends too readily to consider everything in the present regime as bad. As <u>Utopia</u> indicates, W's talents as a writer surpass his ability as a thinker.

1411   BROWN, W[ILLIAM] SORLEY. <u>The Life and Genius of T.W.H. Crosland</u>. London: Cecil Palmer, pp. 172, 175, 210-11, 220, 244, 430, 442-43.
        [Passing remarks on W with regard to such issues as suburbanism, socialism, and the distinction between literature and journalism.]

1412   BURT, STRUTHERS. <u>The Other Side</u>. New York: Scribners' Sons, pp. 83-132.
        [Refutes W's criticism of America.]

1413   BYRON, MILTON. "A Way of Salvation." <u>Outlook</u> (New York) 150 (17 Oct.):995-96.
        In <u>Conspiracy</u> W has abandoned resourcefulness for messianic delusion.

1414   C.-S., A.M. "The Way the World Might Go." <u>Nature</u> 120 (7 July):3-6.
        In <u>Going</u> W admirably fulfills his role as prophet of the scientific method in the social field. In <u>Conspiracy</u> he is less successful, failing to state his case in the form of a novel intead of in that of an essay.

1415   CHAMBERLAIN, JOHN R. "H.G. Wells Once More Combines the Roles of Prophet and Entertainer." <u>NYTBR</u>, 11 Nov., p. 7.
        Although it offers nothing new, <u>Mr. Blettsworthy</u> is a very entertaining fantasy that becomes a parable. It excites after the fashion of W's early work.

1416   "Classified Books." <u>ALA</u> 25 (Dec.):107.
        <u>Conspiracy</u> offers stimulating ideas better presented elsewhere in W's work.

1417   "The Cosmopolis of Mr. Wells." <u>Morning Post</u> (London) [not seen]. Reprinted in <u>LA</u> 334 (July):1005-7.
        Vague with regard to specifics, <u>Conspiracy</u> is concerned only with dubious material comfort and with a dictatorship that would

1928

probably engender the worst tyranny ever known. The kingdom of
God is preferable to W's Cosmopolis.

1418   D., C. "The Wells Short Stories." Spectator (London) 140
        (25 Feb.):268-69.
        Short Stories indicates further that W's "interest in biol-
ogy has mated happily with his concern for the mass of human
nature to make him a general practitioner in the diseases of
creation: his consciousness of life as an organism has made him
the cosmic doctor."

1419   DUFFUS, R.L. "Mr. Wells Plans a New World." NYTBR, 16 Sept.,
        p. 1. Excerpted in SLP 27 (Jan.):9.
        [Unfavorable response to the freedomless and humorless world
portrayed in Conspiracy.]

1420   EDGETT, EDWIN FRANCIS. "About Books and Authors." BET,
        6 Oct., pt. 6, p. 7.
        [Negative review of Conspiracy with some cursory remarks
contrasting W and Kipling.]

1421   "Fiction." ER 47 (Oct.):491-92.
        Mr. Blettsworthy is a romance and adventure with an under-
lying allegory.

1422   GAMMACK, THOMAS H. "Mr. Wells and the Bankers." Outlook (New
        York) 149 (22 Aug.):673.
        [Defends bankers against W's remarks in the Banker
(London).]

1423   GOULD, GERALD. "Mr. Wellsworthy's Adventure." Observer
        (London), 2 Sept., p. 5.
        An astonishingly rich and various tale, Mr. Blettsworthy
presents a protagonist whose "adventures fall into sharp divi-
sions, each of which gives a different Wells his special opportunity; but a single purpose survives."

1424   H., A. "Sociology." SLP 26 (Sept.):273.
        Going is rapid, clear, and replete with humor.

1425   HARTLEY, L.P. "New Fiction." SR (London) 146 (1 Sept.):276.
        [A favorable review of Mr. Blettsworthy expressing a concern
over the lowering of moral standards suggested by W's work.]

1426   HOLMS, JOHN. "H.G. Wells." Calendar of Modern Letters 4
        (July):142-52. Reprinted in Scrutinies by Various Writers, ed.
        Edgell Rickword (London: Wishart, 1928), pp. 146-60; and in
        CH, pp. 299-307.

Though indebted to Dickens and lacking profound implications, W's small-scale figures represent an authentic comic and
artistic creation. Tono-Bungay, a fine symbolic novel, marks W's
substitution of the world he envisions for the world as it is.
If, as a result, his work suffers artistically, it gains
prophetically.

1427   JOHNSON, EDGAR. "H.G. Wells Views the Cannibal Island of New
       York." New York Evening Post, 10 Nov., sec. M, p. 9.
           Mr. Blettsworthy is not W's best novel but is far from being
       his worst. The "pity and shame are real, the drawing is clear and
       strong," but while W pretends to be modern his heart is with the
       country people like George Ponderevo "wishing that progress did
       not consist of Birmingham belching ever more black smoke into the
       air."

1428   KIRCHWEY, FREDA. "A Private Letter to H.G. Wells." Nation
       (New York) 127 (28 Nov.):576. Reprinted in CH, pp. 307-9.
           Galsworthy, Shaw, and W formed a sort of Unholy Trinity, a
       symbol of all that seemed daring, wicked, and promising in the
       prewar years. Though the younger generation has grown apart, this
       state of disagreement proves that W is an ideal father.

1429   LITTELL, PHILIP. "H.G. Wells, Committeeman." Bookman (New
       York) 68 (Nov.):355-56.
           [Expresses disappointment in being unable to praise
       Conspiracy.]

1430   LOVETT, ROBERT MORSS. "Mary and Martha." NR 56 (26 Sept.):
       156-57.
           [Compares Conspiracy and Clive Bell's Civilization.]

1431   MARBLE, ANNIE RUSSELL. A Study of the Modern Novel. New York:
       Appleton, pp. 136-41.
           Over the years W has lost much of his playful humor and his
       utopian vision. Tono-Bungay is W's first and best work of artis-
       tic fiction.

1432   "Mr. Blettsworthy on Rampole Island." TLS, 6 Sept., p. 630.
           This is an imaginative book with satire as effective as that
       of Gulliver's Travels.

1433   "Mr. H.G. Wells and Religion." NWA 1 (June):293-95.
           W's religious notions mistakenly emphasize intellect to the
       neglect of emotion.

1434   "Mr. Wells and the World." TLS, 8 March, p. 164.
           The blemishes in Going are trifling compared to the wide and
       inspiring vision.

1928

1435   "Mr. Wells Religion." TLS, 24 May, p. 388.
         In Conspiracy W's wisdom stops short with politics, a fea-
ture that will not satisfy the soul of man.

1436   MUNSON, GORHAM B. "The Quality of Readability." Bookman (New
         York) 68 (Nov.):338.
         An extraordinarily good novel, Mr. Blettsworthy pits the
hope of man against the depths of savagery with Swiftian force.

1437   MURRY, J[OHN] M[IDDLETON]. "Art and Society." NWA 2
         (Dec.):121-27.
         [Selectively supports and departs from ideas about contempo-
rary art expressed in Going.]

1438   M[URRY], J[OHN] M[IDDLETON]. "Rampole Island." NWA 2
         (Dec.):186.
         A creative counterpart to Conspiracy, Mr. Blettsworthy mag-
nificently blends tragedy and farce.

1439   PALMER, C.B. "Wells and the World Revolution." BET, 22 Sept.,
         pt. 6, p. 3.
         The importance of Conspiracy, a compelling book, cannot be
estimated at present.

1440   PARSONS, ALICE BEAL. "With Malice and Love." Trib, 11 Nov.,
         p. 7.
         Rarely boring, Mr. Blettsworthy resembles Candide. Ideas,
indebted to The Golden Bough and psychological researches in
Patagonia, get out of hand only at the end.

1441   R., R. "The Critics and Mr. Wells." NWA 2 (Sept.):61-62.
         [Remarks on Osbert Sitwell's prefatory praise of W in All at
Sea.]

1442   "Readers' Reports." Life and Letters 1 (Sept.):312-13.
         Realistic description, fantasy, sympathy with adolescence, a
sense of fun, and despair at human nature characterize Mr.
Blettsworthy, one of W's most entertaining stories.

1443   ROBERTS, R. ELLIS. "The Genius of H.G. Wells." Empire Review
         47 (April):237-46.
         In many of his most serious novels W is unable to keep his
mind on one subject. Although he has been ingenious in defending
his technique, he is not always successful in blending the imaginative and the factual. One also wonders if W's ideal republic
would admit him as a citizen.

1444   ROBERTSON, D.H. "Mr. Wells and the World." NA 42 (24 March):
         940.

164

If the essays in Going are not very novel, they are spar-
kling and stimulating.

1445 ROHÁČEK, VL. "H.G. Wells a věda" [Science in the thought of
H.G. Wells]. Příspěvky k dějinám řeči a literatury anglické od
členů anglického semináře Karlovy University v Praze 3:27-70.
Although trained in the sciences W engaged in subjective
criticism and does not reflect the cool indifference of the scientist. W evolved from a moderate, cautious naturalist to an inspired prophet of collective unity, who is willing to overlook
facts when they clash with his faith. Pure science led him to
pessimistic conclusions regarding mankind; so W came to believe
that science could not explain everything, particularly matters
concerning the psychic and moral aspects of man. This allowed for
a faith in free will and in a collective spirit. Scientists
figure prominently in W's vision of the collective growth of the
human race, but after World War I he realized that he had exaggerated the effect of mechanical progress on human moral and
social development and that advances in science might lead to
destruction without any commensurate development of man's moral
standard. Balance is effected chiefly through education. [In
Polish with an English summary.]

1446 ROSS, MARY. "'This Is My Religion.'" Trib, 9 Sept., pp. 3-4.
In Conspiracy W, like Moses, has not yet set foot on the
ground to be explored by those who will follow him.

1447 RUTLAND, ARTHUR. "Mr. Blettsworthy." Bookman (London) 74
(Sept.):309.
Chiefly regarding character development, Mr. Blettsworthy
shows W to be one of the few moralists of genius in our time.

1448 "Sacred Lunatic." Time 12 (19 Nov.):53.
Replete with symbolism, Mr. Blettsworthy provides excellent
readable satire. W is not afraid to satirize ideas he himself has
passionately advanced.

1449 SELDES, GILBERT. "The Road to Athens." Bookman (New York) 68
(Oct.):224-27.
W has dramatized the race between modern education and the
approaching apocalypse.

1450 SHANKS, EDWARD. "Fiction." LM 18 (Sept.):538-39.
Although the most readable story W has written in years, Mr.
Blettsworthy does reveal W's departure from his older, more suc-
cessful method.

1451 "Some Books of the Week." Spectator (London) 140 (19 May):769.
Although many of W's ideas are improbable and less desirable
than he thinks, Conspiracy is worth reading and marking.

1928

1452   VANČURA, ZD. "Filosofie vývoje u H.G. Wellse a G.B. Shawa"
        [The philosophy of evolution in the works of H.G. Wells and
        G.B. Shaw]. Příspěvky k dějinám řeči a literatury anglické od
        členů anglického semináře Karlovy University v Praze 3:1-24.
            W's early work is characterized by pessimistic determinism,
        but from the beginning of the twentieth century his writings
        reveal a more optimistic sense of human evolution. At first W was
        interested in the leaders of the new order he envisioned, but he
        came to recognize the important role of the average man who par-
        ticipates in the as yet unawakened collective spirit. During the
        years of the First World War W tends to see the world as a con-
        flict between nature and the spirit in the mind. [In Polish with
        an English summary.]

1453   "The Way of the Wells." SR (London) 145 (10 March):292.
            W's power to popularize, evident in Going should not be
        scorned; the publicist must speak the language of the drowsy
        multitude if he is to get their attention.

1454   "The Wells and Bennett Novel." TLS, 23 Aug., pp. 597-98.
            Novels, like those of W and Bennett, that provide "so satis-
        factory, so complete a panorama of the less delicate and impalpa-
        ble aspects of the world" are hard to find. Both men are
        fascinated by the multiplicity of events and their position in
        time, thus patiently accumulating material for generalization
        (though neither of them generalize with complete success). They
        differ, however, in regard to their method of dealing with the
        foreground of the novel and with the individuality of their
        characters.

1455   "Wells as a Religious Teacher." LD 99 (17 Nov.):32.
            [Reports Canon B.H. Streeter's remarks on W before the
        English Church Congress and the reaction of the NYT [not seen] to
        these comments.]

1456   Y[EATS]-B[ROWN], F[RANCIS]. "Our Modern World." Spectator
        (London) 140 (3 March):325-26.
            Going merits W "the laurels of immortality as regards intel-
        lectual pioneering, prophecy, invention, insight into the mind of
        the age."

1457   _____. "Our Sacred Lunatic." Spectator (London) 141
        (1 Sept.):269-70.
            Mr. Blettsworthy represents a return to the old manner of
        Mr. Polly and Kipps. Fantasy and philosophy are delightfully
        interwoven. "To the graces of genius are here added the insights
        of maturity."

1929

1458   BAKER, E.A. The History of the English Novel. Vol. 10,
        Yesterday. London: Witherby, pp. 247, 253.
              The real contrast in W's novels is between different ages
        and states of knowledge rather than between different worlds.

1459   BENNETT, ARNOLD. "The Progress of the Novel." Realist 1
        (April):3-11. Reprinted in The Author's Craft and Other Crit-
        ical Writings of Arnold Bennett, ed. Samuel Hynes (Lincoln:
        University of Nebraska Press, 1968), pp. 90-98.
              W's imagination is "wholesale" rather than "retail"; he
        creates societies before individuals. "Perhaps no novelist was
        ever so constructive" as W, and "few have been so destructive."

1460   BONNER, MARY GRAHAM. "Books for Children." NYTBR, 6 Oct.,
        p. 36.
              [Favorable notice of Tommy.]

1461   "The Book of a Film." TLS, 21 Feb., p. 136.
              [Discusses how the film of King came into existence.]

1462   "Books for the Holidays." Spectator (London) 142
        (29 June):1015.
              [Recommends King.]

1463   BRAYBROOKE, PATRICK. Philosophies in Modern Fiction. London:
        Daniel, pp. 71-76.
              [Discusses W's ideas, noting some contradictions.]

1464   BROWN, CHARLES S. "Mr. Wells Incorporates the World." Survey
        61 (1 Jan.):452-53.
              It is very doubtful that most of us will see the sound
        ground under W or hear his voice calling to us in Conspiracy.

1465   CANBY, HENRY SEIDEL. American Estimates. New York: Harcourt,
        Brace, pp. 147-51.
              W's novels all concern the theme of how to live. In every
        one of W's "serious books some simple rule of sociology, hygiene,
        or politics creates the possibility of a Utopia which, incident-
        ally, always has a cockney look and smell to it."

1466   [CANBY, HENRY SEIDEL?] "Simple Souls." SR 5 (12 Jan.):581.
              [Brief comment on W's tendency to cram his narratives with
        critical comment on everything in general.]

1467   "Classified Books." ALA 25 (March):243.
              Going is sober and serious.

1929

1468   COOK, SHERWIN LAWRENCE. "About The King Who Was a King." BET,
        25 May, pt. 6, p. 2.
            A better story than W has written in a long time, this novel
and well-wrought book would make a good movie.

1469   DARGAN, E. PRESTON. "Wells without End." SR 5 (13 July):1177.
            [Unpenetrating remarks on Mr. Blettsworthy and Conspiracy,
with some discussion of W's relation to eighteenth-century French
thinkers.]

1470   F., C.P. "Fiction Shorts." Nation (New York) 128
        (29 May):653.
            Short Stories recalls how tender and economical W's touch
once was. "The Country of the Blind" rereads remarkably well.

1471   "Fiction." ALA 25 (Jan.):168.
            Mr. Blettsworthy deftly combines pure adventure and social
criticism.

1472   FIELD, RACHEL. "A Sheaf of Picture Books." SR 6 (16 Nov.):
        403.
            Artistic skill is evident in the pictures and the text of
Tommy.

1473   "Five Novelists." Bookman (London) 76 (April):40-41.
            King would make a brilliant, powerful film.

1474   GOLDSMITH, SOPHIE L. "The Harvest of Children's Books."
        Nation (New York) 129 (20 Nov.):600.
            There is no hint of the well-known W in Tommy.

1475   HELLMAN, GEOFFREY T. "Mr. Wells's Moving Finger." Trib, 20
        Jan., p. 4.
            The epic qualities in Going differentiate W from men like
Robert Benchley and P.G. Wodehouse.

1476   HERRICK, ROBERT. "Fiction and Ideas." Bookman (New York) 69
        (July):546-57.
            As a cinema scenario King is too unpatriotic to be produced.
As an experimental literary work, it excellently presents gorgeous
images depicting W's arguments against war.

1477   HERRING, ROBERT. "The Old, the New and the Wells Worlds." LM
        19 (March):517-24.
            Set in the very romantic atmosphere it declaims, King is
behind the times with regard to cinematic audience and technique.
The writing, especially the dialogue, is slack.

1478   "Holy Ghost." Time 13 (25 March):49.
        [Discusses Shaw, Bennett, and W's refusal to give a testi-
monial for Harrods, a London department store.]

1479   IRVINE, LYN LLOYD. "New Novels." NA 44 (16 Feb.):692.
        King is trite in its psychology and mechanical in its drama
in spite of its exhausting symbolism.

1480   JAMESON, STORM. The Georgian Novel and Mr. Robinson. New
        York: Morrow, pp. 31-32.
        [Very brief mention of W in order to exemplify the transi-
tion between the solid characters of Victorian novels and the more
transparent creations of the Georgians.]

1481   KIRCHWEY, FREDA. "Screening Civic Virtue." Nation (New York)
        128 (29 May):649.
        Effective as a movie, King is tiresome as a book, "an
Anthony Hope romance gone wrong." The characters and story are
too simple and formalized.

1482   "The Leopard-Rampant of Clavery." Spectator (London) 142
        (16 Feb.):242.
        King is an excellent scenario, in which W the artist
triumphs over W the moralist. The greatness of the work lies in
its failure to provide any solution to the problems it propounds.

1483   LLOYD, C.M. "Politics and Economics." LM 19 (Jan.):333-34.
        Though inspiring, Conspiracy remains vague.

1484   "Mr. Wells and Peace." TLS, 23 May, p. 410.
        World Peace is clear in vision but impatient and
uncompromising.

1485   "Mr. Wells Preaches a Sermon on War." NYTBR, 26 May, p. 9.
        King is thin in presentation and in interest.

1486   MORTANE, JACQUES. "Ce que Edison et Wells pensaient de
        l'aviation après la travesée de la Manche." Annales politiques
        et littéraires 93 (Aug.):143.
        [Discusses W's warnings about Britain's apparent lack of
interest in flight.]

1487   P[RITCHETT], V.S. ""Mr. Wells in the Movies." CSM, 3 April,
        p. 14.
        King is a tiresome piece of sentimental propaganda, an
artistic failure.

1488   REDMAN, BEN RAY. "Old Wine in New Bottles." Trib, 24 March,
        p. 22.
        [Favorable notice of Short Stories.]

1929

1489 REDMAN, H. VERE. "Two English Journalist Authors. Kipling and Wells in Relation to the Types of Englishmen They Present." Studies in English Literature (Tokyo) 9 (July):371-88.
Less likely to carry the reader away on an imaginary flight than is Kipling, W is easier to criticize on the question of English types. He is more specifically associated with the lower middle-class misfits he portrays in his novels.

1490 "Science." TLS, 14 March, p. 211.
[Descriptive review of Science of Life.

1491 SEAVER, EDWIN. "Passing in Brief Review." New York Evening Post, 9 March, sec. M, p. 9.
Short Stories reveals W to be an "excellent man of ideas though not always a man of excellent ideas." Composed of pseudo-science and a dash of sociology cooked up over a reporter's flame, the stories evince a curiosity, but not of the sort that leads one to explore the depths of heart and mind. W tells us what happens next and in that he is, as a writer of short stories, "primarily a writer for boys."

1492 VAN de WATER, FREDERIC F. "F.F.V.: The Odds Are against a Critic." New York Evening Post, 15 June, sec. M, p. 7.
King is a "novel written like a movie scenario." Neither story nor picture plot are good, and the thesis is not plausible. It is "almost as dismal as its title."

1930

1493 ARROWSMITH, J.E.S. "Fiction-I." LM 22 (Oct.):560-61.
Though rich in satire, Mr. Parham suffers from a tedious overexpansiveness and indecision.

1494 "The Autocracy of Mr. Parham." TLS, 24 July, p. 608.
Some of W's best characterization can be found in this book as well as more pure narrative and less extraneous commentary than in any novel he has written since the beginning of World War I.

1495 "Blowing Bubbles." Spectator (London) 145 (26 July):137.
[A tongue-in-cheek review of Mr. Parham.]

1496 "Books in Brief." Nation (New York) 131 (20 Aug.):208.
A feeble farce, Mr. Parham proves dull in spite of a few touches of brilliance echoing Mr. Polly.

1497 CARTER, JOHN. "Mr. Wells Receives a Vision of the Next War." NYTBR, 29 June, p. 4.

Despite its common sense, the focus on current British politics is likely to reduce American interest in Mr. Parham.

1498   CLARKE, ALAN BURTON. "The Autocracy of Mr. Parham." Bookman (New York) 71 (Aug.);542-43.
       This is a good satire topped off with considerable moralizing; but its thesis is unsound.

1499   COOK, SHERWIN LAWRENCE. "Wells and The Autocracy of Mr. Parham." BET, 28 June, pt. 6, p. 4.
       Fascinatingly written, this book often reflects W at his satiric best, very near the peak of his writings. Its story is interwoven well with its treatise.

1500   CROSS, WILBUR L. Four Contemporary Novelists. New York: Macmillan, pp. 157-93.
       Unlike his Victorian predecessors, W offers solutions to social problems. Like Dickens, he aims at discursive characterization. The cosmic concerns of his work, especially Kipps, Tono-Bungay, and Ann Veronica, will cause it to endure.

1501   "The Fascist's Progress." RR 82 (Sept.):8.
       Mr. Parham is an amusing and philosophical essay in fascism.

1502   "A Future War." SSUR, 31 Aug., p. 7e.
       Frequently the humor in Mr. Parham succeeds. The book is intelligent light journalism.

1503   GRAHAM, GLADYS. "Wells in Boisterous Mood." SR 6 (19 July): 1203.
       The characters in Mr. Parham recall the ebullient type found in Mr. Polly and Tono-Bungay.

1504   HACKETT, FRANCIS. "The Post-Victorians." Bookman (New York) 71 (March):20-26.
       The modernity of W, Bennett, and Shaw has now faded. The First World War proved the touchstone of their limitations, revealing that they rarely touched or inspired the human imagination.

1505   HANSEN, HARRY. "The First Reader." World (New York), 21 June, p. 11.
       Mr. Parham [mistitled in the review] is a typical amusing, relevant W sermon.

1506   HYNDMAN, S.H. "An Aspect of H.G. Wells." Central Literary Magazine (Birmingham, Eng.), Jan., pp. 193-98.
       The creative artist in W is best measured in Wheels of Chance, Mr. Lewisham, Kipps, Tono-Bungay, Ann Veronica, Mr. Polly,

1930

and <u>Machiavelli</u>, in which the human comedy is given free expression and in which characters live unaided by the mechanics of
plot. "Although the author cannot resist an occasional bang upon
his secular pulpit, or restrain a muffled cry for order, at times
we are conscious of the play of words, the characterization, the
sympathetic observation, the music and the beauty that lift his
work beyond the levels of social instruction, and stamp it with
the mark of genius." In some respects <u>Tono-Bungay</u> may be compared
with Galsworthy's <u>The Forsyte Saga</u>.

1507   LASKI, HAROLD. "Four Literary Portraits." <u>Daily Herald</u>
       (London) [not seen]. Reprinted in <u>LA</u> 339 (Nov.):287–89.
            Despite his inconsistencies, W has had a greater influence
       on more people than any other writer of English prose. He is less
       introspective than Henry James, less exotic than George Meredith,
       less stylistically scrupulous that Virginia Woolf, but he "has
       realized the truth of Hazlitt's great dictum that to explain the
       nature of laughter and tears is to account for the condition of
       human life."

1508   McCALLUM, R.B. "History and Mr. Wells." <u>NCA</u> 108 (Sept.):
       407–16.
            W is a secularist humanitarian whose desire for reform stems
       from the moderate but firm idealism of Victorian evangelicism.
       [Defends the teaching of history at Oxford.]

1509   MELLERSH, H.E.L. "Religion & Mr. H.G. Wells." <u>Socialist
       Review</u> 2 (Sept.):259–67.
            In <u>Last Things, God</u>, and <u>Clissold</u> W defines his view of God,
       though recently he has become sensitive to the danger of using
       this word. W's view of the deity has remained consistent.

1510   "Men of No Nation." <u>NYT</u>, 7 Sept., pt. 3, p. 1.
            [Reports Henry W. Nevinson's adverse response in the <u>Week-
       End Review</u> [not seen] to the attack on tradition in <u>Mr. Parham</u>.]

1511   "Mr. Wells Argues." <u>NS</u> 35 (26 July):504–5.
            The trouble with <u>Mr. Parham</u>, as with so many of W's writ-
       ings, is his blind faith in human reason, as if no other factors
       are involved in the reformation of man. W's thinking is outdated,
       frequently generates boredom or contempt, and ultimately relies on
       the same spirit that directs wars.

1512   "Mr. Wells' Wonderland." <u>Time</u> 16 (7 July):63.
            Replete with argumentation and straw men, <u>Mr. Parham</u> is more
       pamphlet than novel.

1513   OLIVER, EDITH. "Mr. Wells, Mr. Parham, and Mrs. Markham." <u>NA</u>
       47 (2 Aug.):567.

Abounding in farce, caricature, and irony, Mr. Parham exhibits W's mastery of narrative art.

1514   SQUIRE, J.C. Sunday Mornings. London: Heinemann, pp. 55-63.
W's novels are the works of a poet lacking restraint and an interest in the differences distinguishing characters. His characters tend to be puppets, types illustrating an argument. Although Henry James is the better writer, the aesthetic ideas he represents should not exclude the legitimacy of W's artistic notions. [A compilation of essays written for the Observer (London).]

1515   TITTERTON, W.R. "H.G. Wells: Old and New." Bookman (London) 78 (Sept.):325-26.
Initially good, Mr. Parham loses quality in its unconvincing conclusion.

1516   WEST, GEOFFREY [pseud. of Geoffrey Wells]. H.G. Wells: A Sketch for a Portrait. London: Howe.
W's point of view derived principally from his sense of scientific dissociation from humanity. In his early tales circumstances are primary, the realistic characters little more than puppets displaying these circumstances. Yet, concurrently with the romances from 1895 onward, W wrote stories in which the characters themselves were largely the circumstances. His later works show detachment too, but frequently in these works his laughter at the incongruities of life includes himself. At the high point of his career W shifted to the novel of ideas. At the heart of this development is a central internal conflict between W's scientific detachment derived from his training and his artistic, intuitive sense of life. In general the former proved more influential as W followed the easier path; "he was a wiser man perhaps but certainly a sadder novelist." [A sympathetic but clearsighted portrait of W as a man and artist rather than as a thinker; a good biography with some penetrating commentary on W's writings, particularly Tono-Bungay and Mr. Polly.]

1517   "What War Does to Wells." LD 107 (22 Nov.):18.
[Reports the reaction of the Sunday Times (London) to W's remarks at Livingston Hall, Westminster.]

1518   WILSON, EDMUND. "The Academic Fascist." NR 64 (3 Sept.):79.
The encroachments of age have dulled W's imagination, but the fine chapters of Mr. Parham are as funny and shrewd as any satire he has ever written.

1519   "The Wisdom of the East." Quarterly Review 255 (July):164-78.
[Passing references to similarities and differences between W's views and Oriental thought.]

1931

1520   AMICUS. "Mr. H.G. Wells." Spectator (London) 146
       (14 Feb.):221-22.
           W is more interested in journalistic persuasion than in the
       carefully wrought form of the Jamesian artist. His work may not
       endure.

1521   BARTLETT, ROBERT MERRILL. "The Conscience of Europe." World
       Unity 7 (Feb.):307-11.
           [An interview with W.]

1522   BLUMENFELD, R.D. All in a Lifetime. London: Benn,
       pp. 173-78.
           [Remarks on W's inferiority complex, his big-minded humor,
       and his feminine intuition with a masculine viewpoint.]

1523   CHASE, STUART. "Mr. Wells' Monumental Trilogy Completed."
       Trib, 22 Nov., pp. 1, 4.
           Work excellently discusses the economic confusion portrayed
       in the epic Tono-Bungay, a book unmatchable in its account of the
       paradoxical folly of a pecuniary civilization.

1524   DAURAY, HENRY D. "Une romancier de notre epoque: H.G. Wells,
       maître du realisme et du merveilieux." Nouvelles littéraires,
       no. 439 (14 March), p. 6.
           [Relates biographical details, particularly pertaining to
       W's early association with Frank Harris.]

1525   Ford, Ford Madox [pseud. of Ford Madox Hueffer]. Return to
       Yesterday. London: Gollancz, pp. 20, 35, 186, 224, 377, 381,
       387, 393.
           [Reminiscences that include, among other items, W's advice
       to the author not to collaborate with Joseph Conrad.]

1526   GRATTAN, C. HARTLEY. "Good-Bye to H.G. Wells!" Outlook and
       Independent 157 (4 Feb.):178-79, 198.
           W is not in touch with the modern thoughtful public. He is
       ignorant of a variety of problems of which the new generation is
       aware. [Also a sketch of W's life and thought.]

1527   "H.G. Wells Here to Finish New Book." PW 120 (17 Oct.):1799.
           [Discusses Outline and refutes reports of W's alleged
       pessimism.]

1528   HAZLITT, HENRY. "The Wellsian Bible." Nation (New York) 133
       (30 Dec.):727-28.
           Haste, cocksureness of tone, and an implication that its
       audience is W's mental inferior damage Work, a book otherwise

superb controversial propaganda. With the possible exception of Shaw, W is the world's most eminent writing reformer.

1529 KNIGHT, GRANT C. The Novel in English. New York: Smith, pp. 313-20.
In a real sense W's novels are autobiographical and, in effect, represent his personal thinking performed in public. W does best when revealing himself; otherwise his didacticism, lack of imagination, and reliance on methods of a journalist constitute serious weaknesses.

1530 "Life of Life." Time 17 (2 Feb.):55.
[Favorable review of Science of Life.]

1531 MILLER, NATHAN. "Mr. Wells Sees It Through." SR 8 (5 Dec.):341, 344.
An instinct for phrasing and a buoyant humor contribute to Work, an interesting book.

1532 NOBLE, EDMUND. "Mr. Wells Pictures the Mankind of Today." BET, 28 Nov., pt. 6, p. 8.
[Favorable review of Work.]

1533 OCKHAM, DAVID. "People of Importance in Their Day." SR (London) 151 (20 June):896.
W has aged; his utopias, each increasingly unrealistic, are robotic and governed by bloodless supermen. As a prophet W is retrospective. Having failed to benefit from experience, he proclaims old ideals. Now W is "the sedulous ape of himself."

1534 PRIESTLEY, J.B. The English Novel. London: Benn, pp. 131-38.
W's particular genius in fiction stems from his temperament as a romantic idealist combined with his training and interests as a scientist.

1535 "Science." TLS, 26 March, p. 255.
[Favorable review of Science of Life.]

1536 SOULE, GEORGE. "Mr. Wells vs. the Human Race." NYTBR, 22 Nov., pp. 1, 18.
[Favorable review of Work, warning that not everything in the book is necessarily correct.]

1932

1537 "Blue Prints for Revolution." RRWW 86 (10 Sept.):24-28.
[Discusses an address given by W on the Independent Labour Party and some adverse responses to it.]

1932

1538   BRAILSFORD, H.N. "A Liberal Prophet." <u>World</u> <u>Tomorrow</u> 15
       (16 Nov.):465-66.
          [Discusses <u>After</u> <u>Democracy</u>.]

1539   "Classified Books." <u>ALA</u> 28 (Jan.):183.
          <u>Work</u> is challenging in its optimism.

1540   COLLINS, NORMAN. <u>The</u> <u>Facts</u> <u>of</u> <u>Fiction</u>. London: Gollancz,
       pp. 264-68.
          Critics too often focus on W's bungled, ungraceful sen-
       tences; but as <u>Kipps</u> indicates, W's sentences can move insistently
       with a sharpness and sureness. A less prolific W would have been
       more appreciated.

1541   "Dark Line." <u>Time</u> 20 (8 Aug.):12.
          [Reports W's attack on King George in a speech before the
       Liberal Summer School.]

1542   DAWSON, CHRISTOPHER. "H.G. Wells and History." <u>Criterion</u> 12
       (Oct.):9-16.
          Since 1910 W's works no longer manifest his earlier dualism
       between the world of supernatural science and the world of present-
       day suburban human nature. His subsequent monism has reduced the
       charm of his writings. W's proposed aristocracy is sterile, plac-
       ing value on qualities that make for nonsurvival.

1543   ENSOR, R.C.K. "Politics and Economics." <u>LM</u> 25 (April):603-4.
          <u>Work</u> is stupendous, an economic counterpart to <u>Outline</u>. The
       sweep of his imagination and his presentation are two lessons W
       teaches economists.

1544   FLANDERS, RALPH E. "The Plan of H.G. Wells." <u>Survey</u> 66
       (1 March):633.
          <u>Work</u>, a book in which W's literary gifts still enchant,
       represents an advancement in fundamental ideas and practical sug-
       gestions.

1545   FRIDAY, DAVID. "<u>The</u> <u>Work,</u> <u>Wealth</u> <u>and</u> <u>Happiness</u> <u>of</u> <u>Mankind</u>."
       <u>AM</u> 149 (May):10.
          [A favorable review.]

1546   HEARD, GERALD. "The World and Mr. Wells." <u>Spectator</u> (London)
       149 (5 March):335.
          "Because he seems so reasonable and yet his force is so
       titanic we must take care lest after the next revolution we may
       find that we are permitted no literary work save" <u>Work</u>.

1547   KINGSMILL, HUGH. "Remarks by Dr. Johnson on Certain Writers of
       the Present Age." <u>Bookman</u> (New York) 74 (March):604.

[Samuel Johnson's supposed remarks on W's work, focusing on the ignorance of W's characters.]

1548   _____. "Some Modern Light-Bringers: As They Might Have Been Extinguished by Thomas Carlyle." Bookman (New York) 75 (Dec.):766-68.
         [Caustic attack on W, Shaw, Proust, and Lawrence.]

1549   LEAVIS, F.R. "Babbitt Buys the World." Scrutiny 1 (May): 80-83. Reprinted in CH, pp. 315-18.
         Because it stresses only the ultimate value of efficient machinery Work tends to be trivial. The W man of the future will awaken to the arts but in the manner in which Bennett's characters do (e.g., the Imperial Palace Hotel). "We can respect him as we cannot respect Arnold Bennett, but it is significant that, for all his disinterestedness, he is not safe from the Arnold Bennett corruption."

1550   _____. "The Literary Mind." Scrutiny 1 (May):30-31.
         As a prophet W is deficient because he has missed or is incapable of the sort of education provided by humane letters.

1551   LEAVIS, Q.D. "A Middleman of Ideas." Scrutiny 1 (May):70-71
         W's presentation of information in Work is mere display.

1552   LLOYD, D.B. "The World and Mr. Wells." Quarterly Review 259 (July):49-61.
         Aside from the limitations of prejudice and an undisciplined fluency, Work raises important questions.

1553   LOVETT, ROBERT MORSS, and HELEN SARD HUGHES. The History of the Novel in England. New York: Houghton Mifflin, pp. 393-401.
         [Summary of W's career, with some interesting comparisons with his ideological Victorian precursors.]

1554   MAINE, BASIL. "Shaw, Wells, Binyon--and Music." Musical Quarterly 18 (July):375-82.
         [Uses a passage by W on vivisection to indicate two attitudes toward music.]

1555   MENKEN, JULES. "Mr. Wells Surveys Mankind." NCA 111 (April):500-12.
         Written with verve and gusto, Work could have been composed only by an author "with the imagination of the novelist, the knowledge of the historian and social psychologist and economist, the detachment of the scientist, and the inspired zeal of the social reformer."

1932

1556   MIRSKY, D.S. "H.G. Wells and History." Criterion 12 (Oct.):
       1-9.
          W is not an original thinker, and his ideas are essentially
       out of date. His writing shows a "profound philistinism, and
       self-satisfied ignorance, and a hatred of democracy." His style
       is vapid and loose, so bad in fact that it could not have been
       predicted from a member of the literary profession. That Outline
       was a success attests to the extraordinary low level of historical
       culture in the English speaking countries.

1557   _____. "Mr. Wells Shows His Class." Labour Monthly 14
       (June):383-87.
          W is an ideologist of imperialism with an inferiority com-
       plex concerning Marxism and communism.

1558   "Mr. Wells and the World." TLS, 3 Nov., p. 803.
          After Democracy revives old dogmatism in new terms. Some
       readers, who have a higher regard for the masses, will not agree
       with the book.

1559   "Our Workaday World." RRWW 85 (Jan.):6-7.
          Work is a scholarly book of magnificent scope.

1560   "A Panorama of Mankind." TLS, 25 Feb., p. 123.
          To read Work is to be overwhelmed by W's brilliant organiza-
       tion of massive material and his power of mind in shaping it so
       coherently. It is a courageous book.

1561   R[YAN], J[OHN] A. "New Books." Catholic World 134
       (March):752-53.
          Work may well delude half-educated and uncritical readers
       into thinking that they are encountering erudition, whereas in
       fact they will be assimilating half truths and pernicious
       principles.

1562   SCOTT-JAMES, R.A. "Mr. Wells's New World." SR (London) 153
       (27 Feb.):224, 226.
          Reading Work reminds one occasionally of Burton's Anatomy of
       Melancholy. It is a stimulating book addressed to the man of the
       street.

1563   _____. "Wells Surveys the World." CSM, 12 March, p. 5.
          Work is not without W's old faults of style or his old
       strength of provocative interest.

1564   SLICHTER, SUMNER H. "The World at Work and Play." NR 69
       (27 Jan.):300-302.
          Work is suggestive and stimulating but fails to penetrate
       the heart of our economic system.

1565   "Social Economics." <u>Nature</u> 129 (16 April):558-60.
       <u>Work</u> is a remarkable, stimulating, readable work.

1566   WOOLF, LEONARD. "Mr. Wells's Works and Days." <u>NSN</u> 3
       (27 Feb.):266.
       The merits of the trilogy to which <u>Work</u> belongs outweigh the
defects. Only W could have made a book of this kind readable and
valuable.

1933

1567   A., H.R. "Reviews." <u>America</u> 50 (4 Nov.):115.
       <u>Shape of Things</u> "is just another brain storm of this popular
writer who satisfies his egoism and intellectual vanity by re-
making history, revamping mores, upturning society, and now playing prophet of a new creation more weird than that of Dodgson in
his Wonderland."

1568   AGAR, HERBERT. "The Martyrdom of Man." <u>NSN</u> 6 (9 Sept.):299.
       W has never written more forcefully or lucidly nor in a more
compelling form than in <u>Shape of Things</u>; but the answers he provides are hideous. [See also letters by Dora Russell, <u>NSN</u> 6
(23 Sept.):349-50 and Herbert Agar, <u>NSN</u> 6 (30 Sept.):383.]

1569   ARMSTRONG, ANNE. "New Novels." <u>SR</u> (London) 155 (21 Jan.):70.
       <u>Bulpington</u> illustrates that W has lost much of his old skill
at writing.

1570   A[RMSTRONG], C[LAIRE]. "New Books." <u>Catholic World</u> 137
       (April):117-18.
       Much of what W has to offer by way of illumination in
<u>Bulpington</u> is rendered grotesque by his myopic vision. Three-
quarters of the way through the book he seems to have found the
project top-heavy and so decided to make a tragedy out of what was
left.

1571   ARROWSMITH, J.E.S. "Fiction-I." <u>LM</u> 27 (March):466-67.
       W's most indefatigable gifts are evident in <u>Bulpington</u>.

1572   BIRRELL, FRANCIS. "<u>The Bulpington of Blup</u>." <u>NSN</u> 5
       (4 Feb.):126-27; (18 Feb.):188-89.
       [Letters challenging W's intellectual fairness in the novel
and replying to W's rebuttal. See also letters by G.C. Allen,
David Garnett, Raymond Mortimer, and Dorothea M. Wright, <u>NSN</u> 5
(4 March):251-52.]

1573   "The Bookman's Table." <u>Bookman</u> (London) 83 (March):511.
       <u>Bulpington</u> presents good characterization but too much
pamphleteering.

1933

1574   "Books in Brief." Christian Century 50 (1 Feb.):163.
         W's satire, inventiveness, good conversation, and "ability
to toss ideas into the air so that they sparkle in the sun and to
catch them and toss them again" are all evident in Bulpington.

1575   "Books in Brief." Forum and Century 89 (March):vi.
         Bulpington is W at his amusing best and most characteristic,
though his irony has been more savage since Tono-Bungay.

1576   "Bottom of Wells." Time 21 (23 Jan.):51.
         W's triumph over his straw man protagonist in Bulpington is
embarrassing. The book offers only old exhibits. [See letters by
Joseph A. Ball, Robert H. Patton, and J. Stuart Neary, Time 21
(23 Jan.):51, challenging the label "second-class writer" applied
to W.]

1577   BRANDE, DOROTHY. "Four Novels." Bookman (New York) 76
         (Feb.):189.
         [Faults Bulpington, especially the conclusion.]

1578   "The Bulpington of Blup." TLS, 26 Jan., p. 56.
         W the novelist and W the theorizer are at odds in this book.
The former is better than the latter.

1579   BUTCHER, FANNY. "Tale of Brain Is Latest Novel by H.G. Wells."
         CDT, 21 Jan., p. 14.
         The first part of Bulpington is reminiscent of W's earlier
gift for fiction. The last half offers characters who lose their
life as they become mere representations of ideas.

1580   C., R.M. "War and Make-Believe." NY 8 (21 Jan.):54-55.
         Brilliantly fascinating, Bulpington is written in W's char-
acteristically lucid, free flowing style in which "each word,
unaffected and unambiguous, has an air of looking you straight in
the face and meaning just what it says it means." At the point
in the book when World War I begins, W seems to turn on his
protagonist.

1581   CHAMBERLAIN, JOHN. "Books of the Times." NYT, 7 Sept., p. 19.
         Everything works out all right in Shape of Things because W
stacks his cards.

1582   _____ . "H.G. Wells Returns to Satire." NYTBR, 22 Jan., pp. 1,
         17.
         Attacking the means whereby the pre-war generation refrained
from serious thinking, Bulpington ultimately loses its satiric
effect when it turns sad.

1583   CHILDS, MARQUIS W.   "Middle Class Millennium."   NR 76
        (11 Oct.):248-49.
        Shape of Things is marked by an understandable impatience in
its author. Although every contemporary implication would seem to
argue the contrary, W assumes that a technical education would
endow the middle class with insight and purity of purpose.

1584   CHILTON, ELEANOR CARROL.   "Two Good Novels."   ER 56 (Feb.):
        238-40.
        The protagonist of Bulpington is an artificial construction,
marred by the confusion of thought that produced him. The novel
constantly verges on reality but never achieves it.

1585   CUNLIFFE, J.W.   English Literature in the Twentieth Century.
        New York: Macmillan, pp. 139-60.
        W shifts from writing riotous romances told with verve and
technical skill to sociological novels. Tono-Bungay, one of his
best books, is well sustained and presents three finely drawn main
characters. Yet even in this book, as in Machiavelli, he fails to
portray real passion, for which in its more intense moments he
has no gift.

1586   DAVENPORT, BASIL.   "A Man Like Men."   SR 9 (11 Feb.):425.
        Bulpington presents a splendidly satiric portrait of man. W
seems to have settled finally on science rather than socialism or
education as the last fortress for hope. Wimperdick is a caricature of G.K. Chesterton.

1587   DENNIS, LAWRENCE.   "H.G. Wells Internationalism."   SR 10
        (9 Sept.):89-91.
        The outstanding feature of W's dream of the world state in
Shape of Things is its consistent universalism and repudiation of
individualism.

1588   DUFFUS, R.L.   "H.G. Wells Charts a New Course for the World's
        Future."   NYTBR, 10 Sept., pp. 3, 20.
        The narrative aspects of Shape of Things is good; the pre-
sentation of the worldplan proves tedious.

1589   EDGAR, PELHAM.   The Art of the Novel from 1700 to the Present
        Time. New York: Macmillan, pp. 217-28.
        Writing in an unsubtle yet effective style, W can penetrate
character, especially its comic aspects. Nevertheless, his lack
of conviction in the novel as an art form has led to uncontrolled
verbosity in, say, Clissold, which, along with Machiavelli, lacks
truly convincing characters.

1933

1590   ENSOR, R.C.K. "Politics and Economics." LM 29 (Nov.):94-95.
        Shape of Things may reflect some of W's bitterness over the
failure of mankind to profit by his years of prophesying.

1591   FAIRCHILD, EDWIN C. "The Persona, the Class Struggle and Mr.
        H.G. Wells." NWA 6 (April):58-60.
        If Marx's theory of class does not sufficiently take into
account the interplay between fear and courage, it reflects a truth
that escapes W, "who is so confounded by his theory of individual
temperament that action by vast numbers in concert becomes for him
an inexplicable circumstance."

1592   "Fiction." ALA 29 (Feb.):182.
        If Bulpington has a purpose, it is to contrast the romantic
with the scientific mind.

1593   "Fiction." PIFL, Summer, p. 38.
        Bulpington reflects W's characteristic blend of sarcasm and
clever observation.

1594   GARNETT, DAVID. "Books in General." NSN 5 (13 May):602.
        It is disappointing to note that, in general, W's early
romances now seem dated, overtaken by mechanical developments.
Time Machine and Men Like Gods escape this response because they
are simple, moving parables.

1595   GLASGOW, GEORGE. "Mr. Wells Looks Ahead." Observer (London),
        3 Sept., p. 5.
        Shape of Things lays bare current political nightmares but
oddly argues that the human spirit can be socialized and planned.

1596   GOULD, GERALD. "Mr. Wells's New Novel." Observer (London), 22
        Jan., p. 5.
        Shy humor and lyric rapture mark Bulpington, a book in which
W analyzes the times. By means of wit and excitement W entices us
to witness painful facts. That one may have to hurt in order to
heal is what W believes, combining the roles of surgeon and
artist.

1597   GRATTAN, C. HARTLEY. "Mr. Wells Again." Nation (New York) 137
        (20 Sept.):328.
        Sometimes wrongheaded, Shape of Things is fascinating, full
of interesting ideas and extraordinary insights into the present
and the future.

1598   GRAY, GEORGE W. "The Future of Science and Society." AM 152
        (Dec.):18, 20.

W's characteristic style and technique are evident in Shape of Things, as picture follows picture and whole movements are etched in terms of sharp profiles of personalities.

1599   H., L. "Mr. Wells Comes Back." Nature 132 (21 Oct.):620-22.
       The earlier part of Shape of Things is better done than the later sections. Though not a dull book, few intelligent people will read it without annoyance.

1600   H., W.E. "Mr. Wells Creates the Bulpingtons." BET, 18 Jan., pt. 4, p. 3.
       Some readers may readily dismiss Bulpington as confessional, but it does capture the details and substance of daily life.

1601   HAMILTON, MARY AGNES. Sidney and Beatrice Webb. Boston: Houghton Mifflin, pp. 79, 80, 86, 88, 154-57, 212.
       [Compares W unfavorably to the Webbs and particularly disparages Machiavelli.]

1602   HEARD, GERALD. "Mr. Wells' Apocalypse." NCA 114 (Oct.): 502-12.
       [A lengthy discussion of Shape of Things, noting its sobriety of tone.]

1603   KRUTCH, JOSEPH WOOD. "Prophet into Historian." Nation (New York) 136 (25 Jan.):97-98.
       Even if the writing and the entertainment in Bulpington are as good as ever for W, there are no surprises to the reader familiar with his work. In his later novels, W's strain of prophecy has dwindled, no longer predicting what his generation is going to do, only showing what it did. Consequently the tone is less confident or hopeful.

1604   LASKI, HAROLD J. "The Sinfulness of Daydreaming." NSN 5 (28 Jan.):105.
       Aside from flashes of contemporary insight, Bulpington bewilders the reader as to what W wanted to say. Some of the characters are not fully convincing, yet the work as a whole is alive, particularly when W attacks T.S Eliot. The work, "with its concrete vividness of imagery, its living sense of being right inside the belly of the universe," possesses W's old magic.

1605   M., A.N. "Mr. Wells's New Novel." MG, 20 Jan., p. 5.
       Full of eloquence, wit, and aptness, Bulpington unfortunately conveys a sense of a proposition overemphasized or overproved.

1606   MacKAY, L.A. "Liberal Surveys of Dictatorship." Canadian Forum 14 (Dec.):108-9.

1933

Even better than Shaw, W uses the epigram masterfully in Shape of Things, a book written in a style of persuasive actuality.

1607 MACKENZIE, COMPTON. Literature in My Time. London: Cowan, pp. 161-67.
      Although W is too didactic, subordinating characterization to ideology, he has been more profoundly influential than any other twentieth-century writer.

1608 MATTHEWS, T.S. "Five Recent Novels." NR 73 (25 Jan.):301.
      Never a neat writer, W is now merely messy. Bulpington is satire which unwittingly includes the author.

1609 MEARS, HELEN. "Education and the Good Life." Survey Graphic 22 (April):226.
      Bulpington is provocative; as a storyteller W has no contemporary superior.

1610 MILLIS, WALTER. "Mr. Wells Outlines the Future of History." Trib, 10 Sept, pp. 1, 6.
      [A lengthy favorable discussion of the ideas presented in Shape of Things.]

1611 "Mr. Wells's Novel." SSUR, 29 Jan., p. 7e.
      Bulpington is more successfully accomplished with regard to narrative and characterization than many of W's later works. Its satire recalls Tono-Bungay, still the best of W's "serious" writings.

1612 NEVINSON, HENRY W. "According to H.G. Wells." Spectator (London) 151 (1 Sept.):287.
      The optimism of W's prophesy in Shape of Things contrasts with the doom predicted by most others.

1613 "The Next Two Hundred Years." TLS, 7 Sept., p. 588.
      Not entirely successful, Shape of Things remains "a fascinating imaginative exercise, only too plausible in its earlier prophecies, effervescent with ideas, and containing much prose of as high quality as any its author has written for many years."

1614 N[OBLE], E[DMUND]. "H.G. Wells Dips into the Near Future." BET, 13 Sept., pt. 4, p. 2.
      Shape of Things is brilliantly written.

1615 "Outline of the Future." RRWW 87 (Oct.):4.
      Shape of Things offers logical insight vividly and imaginatively expressed.

1616   PRITCHETT, V.S. "Dreams and Mr. Wells." CSM, 18 Feb., p. 6.
        The satire of the first hundred pages of Bulpington is good,
written in a rosy and caustic style. The protagonist's dreams are
well managed, but the Jewish girl is the only living character in
the work.

1617   ROSS, MARY. "Mr. Wells Skilfully [sic] Pricks New Balloons."
        Trib, 22 Jan., p. 3.
        In Bulpington, a satiric yet tender work, W skillfully
wields "the lancet of science against overblown romanticism."

1618   SCHWIMMER, ROSIKA. "New Ways of Committing Suicide." World
        Tomorrow 16 (7 Dec.):668-69.
        Shape of Things repeats too much of what W has already said
elsewhere and is more idealistic than practical.

1619   "Scientific Romances." TLS, 3 Aug., pp. 517-18.
        [Uses The Scientific Romances of H.G. Wells as a means to
discuss the genre of science fiction, the differences between W
and Jules Verne, those of W's contemporaries who might have ri-
valed him had they continued to write, and the new novelists who
might carry on W's tradition.]

1620   SPENDER, STEPHEN. "The New Wells in a New World." Bookman
        (London) 85 (Oct.):48-49.
        Although the prognostication in Shape of Things is probable,
the solutions are not; "all we are given here is a hygenic,
cleaned-up, emasculated, utilatarian world, of the sort which was
the dream of mid-Victorian liberalism."

1621   STONE, GEOFFREY. "Two Theodores." Commonweal 18 (5 May):
        26-27.
        Bulpington is a ludicrous fable with a few interesting
passages in which W's ideas do not intrude.

1622   S[TRONG], L.A.G. "Mr. Wells's New Novel." Spectator (London)
        150 (27 Jan):122-23.
        Bulpington is not a great novel, but only a great man could
have written it.

1623   SUNNE, RICHARD. "Men and Books." TT 14 (2 Sept.):1036-37.
        Shape of Things should not be taken seriously even though
its strange philosophy is that of a humanist. [A mock-letter from
the future.]

1624   "The Tragedy of Mr. Wells." National Review (London) 100
        (Feb.):298-300.
        Although enormously clever, Bulpington fails to hold one's
attention. Whereas W's earlier works "start with the precision

1933

and assurance of a powerful car leaving home on a long run . . . a
driver at the wheel who has studied the road-map in advance," his
later works "start slowly and lethargically like an over-loaded
taxi-cab" with a driver who is not quite certain of the road.
Principally what is missing from the later works is a mystical
touch that gave a sublimity to the earlier writings.

1625 WEST, GEOFFREY [pseud. of Geoffrey Wells]. "Selected Fiction."
FR 139 (1 March):406-7.
Although not in the class with W's best work, Bulpington has
good moments.

1626 ____. "To-Morrow and To-Morrow." Yale Review 23 (Dec.):
399-400.
Shape of Things is as well written, as packed with thought
and invention as almost anything else W has written since World
War I.

1627 WILSON, P.W. "Books of the Month." Current History 39
(Oct.):iv.
Better late than never, W quotes the Bible in Shape of
Things.

1934

1628 BARBER, OTTO. H.G. Wells' Verhältnis zum Darwinismus.
Leipzig: Tauchnitz.
Darwinism, either directly or through its influence on other
thinkers, influenced W's purely scientific works as well as his
speculative fiction. Darwinian biology informs W's novels concerning the distant future and those indicating man's extinction
as a result of some catastrophe.

1629 BARTER, JOHN P. "The Stalin-Wells Talk." NSN 8 (17 Nov.):
713-14.
[A letter of disagreement with several of W's ideas expressed in his meeting with Stalin.]

1630 BINSSE, HARRY LORIN. "The Background of H.G. Wells." American
Review 4 (Nov.):110-17.
There are only brief passages of intellectual analysis in
Experiment; "the rest seems foggy, often deliberately irreverent,
often intolerably egotistical."

1631 "Biography." Wisconsin Library Bulletin 30 (Nov.):214.
In spite of apparent conceit and some dullness, Experiment
is interesting.

1632   BUTCHER, FANNY. "Wells Reveals Planned World as Key to Life."
       CDT, 27 Oct., p. 13.
       The first two parts of Experiment surpass the remainder. As
a whole the work is an important contemporary document.

1633   CHAMBERLAIN, JOHN. "Books of the Times." NYT, 26 Oct., p. 19.
       In Experiment W is admirably honest but mistaken in thinking
his novels of caricatures will not endure. W's permanent fiction
is his early work.

1634   COWLEY, MALCOLM. "Outline of Wells's History." NR 81
       (14 Nov.):22-23. Reprinted in Think Back on Us: A Contempo-
       rary Chronicle of the 1930's by Malcolm Cowley, ed. Henry Dan
       Piper (Carbondale and Edwardsville: Southern Illinois Univer-
       sity Press, 1967), pp. 244-47.
       Considering W's rapidly declining career, Experiment is an
artistic miracle, "the best of his novels." W is like "the sur-
vivor of a prehistoric time, a warm, ponderous, innocent creature
ill adapted to the Ice Age in which we live, and yet overshadowing
the smaller animals that shiver behind the rocks."

1635   DAVIS, ELMER. "Wells the Fantasiast." SR 10 (2 June):721,
       725.
       In Seven Famous Novels one can see how the evangelist in W
almost overcame the fantasiast. Apparently the example of Swift
inspired W to wed fantasy and social criticism. Although the
evangelist side deserves respect, only the artistic side as expressed in W's early works is likely to survive.

1636   EDGETT, EDWIN FRANCIS. "H.G. Wells Writes an Outline of Him-
       self." BET, 27 Oct., pt. 4, p. 1.
       At times Experiment reminds one of Rousseau, at other times
of Rabelais. It is informed and coherent but not always clear as
to what period of W's life it is describing. W's drawings could
have been deleted.

1637   ENSOR, R.C.K. "Mr. Wells on Himself." Spectator (London) 153
       (12 Oct.):529; "Mr. Wells Dissects Himself." Spectator
       (London) 153 (9 Nov.):722-23.
       [Brief remarks on Experiment; mentions W's modesty and his
liberal attitudes toward sex.]

1638   GARNETT, DAVID. "Books in General." NSN 8 (13 Oct.):472-73;
       NSN 8 (10 Nov.):664-65.
       Because it concerns people not manipulated for ulterior
purposes, the first volume of Experiment is the finest book W has
written. This work "is like the final great masterpiece, executed
in oils, for which many of the novels are studies in wash or
charcoal." Potentially the best autobiography written by an

1934

Englishman, it can be compared to The Education of Henry Adams.
Although not as intimate or objective as the first volume, the
second volume is full of charm and wit and, as well, generates
affection and gratitude for its author. [See also letter by V.H.
Porter, NSN 8 (17 Nov.):715.

1639   GARRISON, W.E. "Self-Revelation of H.G. Wells." Christian
        Century 51 (28 Nov.):1521-22.
            Although somewhat too prolix, Experiment is extraordinarily
        frank and fascinating.

1640   GORER, GEOFFREY. "Stalin and Wells." NSN 8 (10 Nov.):660.
            [A satiric poem on the meeting between Stalin and W.]

1641   GRABO, CARL H. "H.G. Wells: Chronicler, Philosopher and
        Seer." New Humanist (Chicago) 7 (July-Aug.):1-7.
            Generally one cannot reread W's works with undiminished
        interest; they are journalistic and ephemeral. W remains somewhat
        too insensitive to esthetic matters. It should be noted, however,
        that he is writing for a future that he believes will regard
        fiction less highly than do people today.

1642   H., T.Ll. "Mr. H.G. Wells Reveals Himself." Nature 134
        (13 Oct.):553-54.
            [A favorable descriptive review of the first volume of
        Experiment.]

1643   "H.G. Wells on Himself." RRWW 90 (Nov.):9-10.
            [Recommends Experiment.]

1644   "H.G. Wells Reviews Course of His Life." SSUR, 28 Oct., p. 7e.
            [Favorable descriptive review of Experiment.]

1645   HAZLITT, HENRY. "Thinker by Choice, Artist by Chance." SR 11
        (27 Oct.):233-35.
            A sort of valise of opinions, Experiment becomes increas-
        ingly garrulous, repetitious, irritating, and tedious.

1646   H[OLTBY], W[INIFRED]. "Wells without End." TT 15
        (3 Nov.):1388.
            Despite certain significant omissions and inaccuracies, the
        second volume of Experiment is superbly readable.

1647   "How Shaw Writes His Plays." Sheffield Telegraph, 15 Aug.
        Reprinted in Independent Shavian 10 (Winter 1971/72):6.
            [Shaw agrees with W's notion of the limitations of the
        stage.]

1648 JACK, PETER MONRO. "H.G. Wells' Outline of Himself." NYTBR, 28 Oct., pp. 1, 17.
The prodigious scope of Experiment is marvelous.

1649 KEUN, ODETTE. "H.G. Wells--The Player." TT 15 (13 Oct.):1249-51; (20 Oct.):1307-9; (27 Oct.):1346-48.
Despite the influence of Thomas Henry Huxley, W has not been able to transcend his impoverished Victorian upbringing. His motivation has primarily been the revolt of an outraged ego, which seeks gratification by demonstrating its own superiority--witness his gamelike skill at using various, even contradictory styles. W eventually repudiates everything he initially supported, including personal friends. His service to mankind is neither consistent nor enduring.

1650 "Kipps in the Kremlin." SR (London) 158 (25 Aug.):7.
[Imaginary satiric interview between W and Stalin.]

1651 L[EAVIS], F.R. "Progressive Schools." Scrutiny 3 (Sept.): 215-17.
[Comments on W's remarks in Manifesto, edited by C.E.M. Joad.]

1652 LEVY, H. "The Autobiography of H.G. Wells." Nature 134 (8 (8 Dec.):882-84.
Experiment raises the genre to a new level and unwittingly reveals how a false methodology in propaganda resulted in W's failure.

1653 "Literature." OS, no. 11-12 (Nov.-Dec.), p. 23.
Experiment is forceful.

1654 MENCKEN, H.L. "Wells Nearing Three Score." Nation (New York) 139 (14 Nov.):567.
W's novels will not long outlive him, and he would have been happier had he remained a biologist. W may have had fun writing his books, "but his inner pull was against them, and in the end he yielded to it."

1655 "Mr. Wells as Autobiographer." TLS, 8 Nov., pp. 761-62.
Less an artist than an intellectual in Experiment, W does not examine his ideas in the light of his life; he examines his life in the light of his ideas.

1656 "Mr. Wells Sees It Through." Books of the Month 4 (Nov.):11.
An astonishing feat of intellectual honesty, the first volume of Experiment presents a highly stimulating narrative. W's use of the comma, however, is irritating.

1934

1657   "Mr. Wells's Autobiography." TLS, 11 Oct., p. 685.
        Not a great work, albeit an interesting one, the first
volume of Experiment suffers from a casualness of style.

1658   NEVINSON, HENRY W. "A Prophet To-Day." FR 142 (Nov.):621-23;
        "An English Prophet." FR 142 (Dec.):753-54.
        In the second volume of Experiment W characteristically
discusses at length a subject of which he is ignorant or at least
mistaken: women's demand for equal citizenship. Otherwise shrewd
judgments abound in the book.

1659   "Persona Gratified." Time 24 (12 Nov.):69.
        [Favorable review of Experiment.]

1660   PRITCHETT, V.S. "Exhibit Wells, H.G." CSM, 27 Oct., p. 12.
        Experiment, written in a free-flowing style of freshness and
vitality, fulfills expectations. Its message is the same as
usual.

1661   _____. "The World and Mr. Wells." CSM Weekly Magazine, 21
Nov., p. 11.
        Every page of Experiment engenders enthusiastic agreement or
excited protest. W possesses the gift of tongues, otherwise his
influence on his generation would have been less. "One thinks of
him as some popular journalistic, art-hating Plato making Utopias
out of words of honey."

1662   RASCOE, BURTON. "H.G. Wells on the Adventures of H.G. Wells."
        Trib, 28 Oct., pp. 1-2.
        Experiment is a grave and honest effort at self-examination.

1663   SCOTT-JAMES, R.A. "Mr. Wells's Start in Life." LM 31
        (Nov.):68-69; "From Backyard to Cosmopolis." LM 31 (Dec.):
        177-78.
        The first volume of Experiment represents W's attempt to
make his past the substance of a new experience. The second
volume proves even more interesting than the first.

1664   SHAW, [GEORGE] BERNARD. "Stalin and Wells." NSN 8
        (3 Nov.):613-14; "Stalin and Wells Continued." NSN 8
        (17 Nov.):709-10; "Shaw and Wells." NSN 8 (8 Dec.):822-23.
        [Sees the meeting between W and Stalin (NSN 8 [27 Oct.]) as
comedy, describing W as a good talker but a terrible listener.
See also letters by J.M. Keynes, NSN 8 (10 Nov.):653-54; X. Y.,
NSN 8 (17 Nov.):714-15; Olivier, NSN 8 (17 Nov.):715; Dora
Russell, NSN 8 (17 Nov.); Julian Bell, NSN 8 (1 Dec.):787; Herbert
G. Wood, NSN 8 (1 Dec.):786-87.]

1665   SNOW, C.P. "H.G. Wells and Ourselves." Cambridge Review 56
        (19 Oct.):27-28; "H.G. Wells--Part II." Cambridge Review 56
        (30 Nov.):148.
            Volume one of Experiment is a magnificent book, one of the
        great autobiographies of the world and far more honest than those
        of Augustine and Rousseau. Like his characters, W possesses
        vividness, a well-marked persona, but sometimes fails to show the
        deeper urgencies of the inner life. This feature is one reason
        why his writings are often depreciated. Another reason lies in
        the fact that W's active and intelligent note of hope irritates
        those nurtured on nostalgic memories. The ending of Experiment
        will probably always be resented. The entire work, however, is
        one of the most vivid, glowing, and complete of books--the master-
        piece of a great writer.

1666   "Sociology." TLS, 6 Sept., p. 608.
        [Praises highly the new edition of Work.]

1667   TOLLER, ERNST. "Stalin and Wells." NSN 8 (3 Nov.):614-15.
        [Objects to certain of W's conclusions about Russia.]

1668   WEST, GEOFFREY [pseud. of Geoffrey Wells]. "The Burthen of
        Atlas." Yale Review 24 (Dec.):380-82.
            At least "the bones of a great book" are present in
        Experiment, a work "not so much planned as outpoured."

1669   WOLSELEY, R.E. "H.G. Wells." World Unity 15 (Oct.):5-9.
            W has tried to make the idea of a federated world popular.
        Though considered bourgeois by certain groups, to the tolerant
        type of intellectual he is a great prophet and social analyst.

1670   "Young Wells." Time 23 (18 June):72.
            [Disagrees with W's diminishment of the early works pub-
        lished in Seven Famous Novels.]

                                1935

1671   A[PP], A[UGUST] J. "New Books." Catholic World 140
        (Jan.):494-95.
            Experiment is a reasonably interesting, though often sordid,
        account. W is a gifted man devoting his talents to making immo-
        rality acceptable.

1672   BARNES, HARRY ELMER. "Whither America?" Nation (New York) 141
        (17 July):80-81.
            New America is pleasant and incisive, the product of a
        somewhat chastened W.

1935

1673   BELGION, MONTGOMERY. ["Experiment in Autobiography."]
        Criterion 14 (Jan.):315-22.
            The chief interest in this book lies in its story of a man
        who missed his opportunity and went off on a wild goose chase, a
        mistake repeated by the book itself. In a special way certain of
        W's novels made England intelligible, and it is a shame that he
        did not continue in this manner.

1674   BREYFOGLE, W.A. "Mr. Wells and Others." Canadian Forum 15
        (Jan.):156.
            [Descriptive review of Experiment, objecting to W's assess-
        ment of Joseph Conrad.]

1675   BRICKELL, HERSCHEL. "The Literary Landscape." NAR 239
        (Jan.):93.
            Experiment is outstanding, but parts of it prove tiresome
        and nonsensical.

1676   CECCHI, EMILIO. "Pentimenti di H.G. Wells (1926)." In
        Scrittori inglesi e americani. Milan: Guiseppe Carabbo,
        pp. 192-203.
            Lacking the verve and freshness of his early work, Clissold
        represents further unhappy changes in W. He now seems to be
        something of a conservative without any memory of socialism. His
        authoritarian tone is particularly offensive to a Latin intellect;
        but the embarassed stupor felt by the reader of this book is not
        limited to this side of the British Channel.

1677   CHAMBERLAIN, JOHN. "Books of the Times." NYT, 19 June, p. 17.
            [Negative review of New America.]

1678   _____. "The World in Books." Current History 42 (Aug.):
        vi-vii.
            The vagueness of W's generalities becomes irritating in New
        America.

1679   "Classified Books." ALA 32 (Sept.):12.
            New America is small but readable and incisive.

1680   COLUM, MARY M. "Personality and Autobiography." Forum and
        Century 93 (Feb.):84-86.
            Experiment is completely frank and evinces that power of
        observation that is infrequently revealed in W's novels.

1681   COWLEY, MALCOLM. "H.G. Wells in the Kremlin." NR 82
        (24 April):317. Reprinted in Think Back on Us: A Contemporary
        Chronicle of the 1930's by Malcolm Cowley, ed. Henry Dan Piper
        (Carbondale and Edwardsville: Southern Illinois University
        Press, 1967), pp. 84-86.

[Discusses the interview between Stalin and W in 1934, indicting W for not asking the right questions and for not listening—in short, for avoiding reality and clutching his own dream.]

1682   DANGERFIELD, GEORGE, HARRISON SMITH, and ROBERT HAAS. The Strange Death of Liberal England. New York: Smith & Haas, p. 168.
        [A very brief reference to Ann Veronica as a possible model for the women's movement.]

1683   DANIELS, JONATHAN. "Mr. Wells Still Has Hopes." SR 12 (22 June):5.
        In New America W writes exciting journalism, reducing complex life to simplicity and lifting it to drama.

1684   DAVY, CHARLES. "Mr. Wells Writes for the Screen." LM 33 (Dec.):239.
        Things to Come suffers from a division between the form of a short novel and that of a film script.

1685   E[DGETT, E[DWIN] F[RANCIS]. "Wellsian Portraits." BET, 3 July, pt. 3, p. 2.
        Clever characterization redeems New America, otherwise a rather unspectacular book.

1686   GARNETT, DAVID. "Books in General." NSN 10 (9 Nov.):677.
        Things to Come, the scenario version of Shape of Things, is a model of the genre. W's ultimate object is Druidism, that is to lead men toward engagement in gigantic enterprises. The problem with this propagandistic film is that it will convince people that war is inevitable and implant in their minds grandiose dreams that dictators can exploit. Though W's ideas are absurd, his imagination is that of a real artist.

1687   G[ARRISON], W.E. "Mr. Wells Diagnoses America." Christian Century 52 (31 July):992.
        [A favorable review of New America.]

1688   "H.G. Wells Looks at America." SSUR, 7 July, p. 5e.
        [Somewhat positive review of New America.]

1689   HAZLITT, HENRY. "Mr. Wells Reports on America." NYTBR, 23 June, pp. 1, 12.
        Avoidance of detail, albeit a weakness, increases the readability and the persuasiveness of New America.

1935

1690   "International Relations of the United States." Foreign
       Affairs 14 (Oct.):168.
            The essays in New America are in the best Wellsian style.

1691   LOW, [DAVID]. Lions and Lambs. New York: Harcourt, Brace,
       pp. 151-52.
            His proneness to cross beyond the boundaries of his knowl-
       edge notwithstanding, W possesses a dramatic genius for imper-
       sonating, faultlessly placing in the mouth of his characters the
       very words life would have put there.

1692   MATTICK, HEINZ. H.G. Wells als Sozialreformer. Leipzig:
       Tauchnitz.
            [Discusses the early social literature of England, partic-
       ularly that of Carlyle, Ruskin, and Morris, as it leads to the
       development of the Fabian Society. Indicates the influence of the
       Fabian Society on the works of Shaw and especially on W's Mr.
       Lewisham, Kipps, Tono-Bungay, and several books of nonfiction.]

1693   MAUROIS, ANDRÉ. "Wells: La religion de l'humanité." Revue
       hebdomadaire 8 (23 Feb.):406-33. Reprinted in Poets and
       Prophets, trans. Hamish Miles (London: Cassell, 1936),
       pp. 41-66.
            Precision, a coherent imagination, scientific knowledge, and
       the English art of combining the real with the marvelous charac-
       terize W's success in his romances. For W the world state is more
       a mystical hope than a clear idea. Insofar as he believes man can
       achieve a state of permanent perfection, W's doctrine becomes
       something of a religion.

1694   "Mr. Wells on America." TLS, 20 June, p. 386.
            In his fresh impression of the United States in New America
       W finds not a little of the gilt gone from the gingerbread.

1695   "Mr. Wells's Film of Things to Come." TLS, 2 Nov., p. 696.
            The film version of Shape of Things is less proportionate
       than the book. It is a hybrid work combining the defects of
       fiction and film.

1696   MURDOCH, WALTER. Three Popular Prophets. Sydney, Australia:
       Sands, pp. 3-9.
            W's characters are not great because his novels concern the
       common man, who lacks particular distinguishing traits. Unlike
       the characters of Victorian novelists, except Meredith, those of W
       think. We should be grateful to W for how much he has taught and
       delighted us. [A radio lecture, printed in pamphlet form by the
       Australian National Stations.]

1697   "The New America: The New World." Nature 136 (14 Sept.):414.
       This work is short but brilliant.

1698   PLOMER, WILLIAM. "'A Slant towards Optimism.'" LM 32
       (July):287-88.
           New America expresses some current and some original ideas.
       Though W's mind in this work is as ceaselessly active as ever, it
       is doubtful his arguments will do much good.

1699   RATCLIFFE, S.K. "Sad New World." Spectator (London) 155
       (5 July):24, 26.
           New America is as lucid and effective a work as W has
       written.

1700   READE. R.A. Main Currents in Modern Literature. London:
       Nicholson & Watson, pp. 30-36.
           Uncle Ponderevo and Aunt Susan are W's best realized char-
       acters, though in other respects Tono-Bungay initiates W's decline
       as a writer. W does best when drawing upon his imagination or his
       experience with the lower middle class.

1701   SELDES, GILBERT. "Mr. Wells to the Screen." SR 13
       (2 Nov.):11-12.
           Things to Come is a simple and effective presentation with
       tremendously moving visual images.

1702   STRAUSS, HAROLD. "A Wells Scenario," NYTBR, 10 Nov., pp. 18,
       20.
           Things to Come is pale compared to W's earlier works.

1703   SWINNERTON, FRANK. The Georgian Literary Scene. London:
       Hutchinson, pp. 64-86.
           Tono-Bungay is a great modern novel. If anyone objects that
       it is unaesthetic, his concept of art is too limited. [A general
       appreciative but penetratingly realistic survey of W's career.]

1704   W., A.M. "As Mr. Wells Sees the New America." CSM Weekly
       Magazine, 17 July, p. 11.
           Somewhat irritating because of authorial stance, New America
       is still worthy of attention.

1705   "Wellsian Future." Time 26 (4 Nov.):88.
           In Things to Come W's imagination flourishes in images of
       ruin; the productive side of his vision remains vague.

1706   WHIPPLE, LEON. "Concerning Revolutions." Survey Graphic 24
       (Jan.):38-39.
           Experiment is a great book in which W serves as an everyman
       for his age.

1935

1707   "World's Future." <u>SSUR</u>, 24 Nov., p. 7e.
        Vivid scenes and dialogue characterize <u>Things to Come</u>.

                            1936

1708   "Books in Brief." <u>Christian Century</u> 53 (1 July):942.
        [A descriptive mention of <u>Miracles</u> that implies
    disapproval.]

1709   BROWN, ALEC. <u>The Fate of the Middle Classes</u>. London:
        Gollancz.
        W has always been and still is acutely aware of his role as
    spokesman for the desires of the middle class, whose powers he
    unfortunately overestimates with regard to remodelling the world.
    W has been too unscientifically preoccupied with his belief in
    intellect to ask the obvious question concerning the effect of
    environment on how this intellect functions, if it can at all.

1710   BROWN, IVOR. "A Wellsian Film Script." <u>MG</u>, 12 May, p. 7.
        <u>Miracles</u> will make a good film, although its ending is not
    very satisfying.

1711   "Classified Books." <u>ALA</u> 33 (Sept.):16.
        <u>Miracles</u> is rollicking comedy with serious moments.

1712   COLUM, MARY M. "The Solitary Life." <u>Forum and Century</u> 96
        (Nov.):219.
        In <u>Anatomy</u> W is a mere grammarian of religion without knowl-
    edge of its ecstasy.

1713   "Current Literature." <u>Spectator</u> (London) 157 (23 Oct.):700.
        <u>Anatomy</u>, previously serialized in this journal, is an utter-
    ance of rare quality and vision.

1714   DAVIDSON, DONALD. "The Shape of Things and Men." <u>AR</u> 7
        (Summer):225-48.
        <u>Shape of Things</u> reveals that whereas W was once a happy
    prophet, he has become dogmatic and grim in his old age. Although
    his terminology is current, his "way of pretending to look bravely
    and nobly into the future is a trick for interpreting the past to
    suit the kind of scheming by which he hopes to modify the present.
    He is that most inferior kind of romanticist--a man who is retro-
    spective without knowing it."

1715   DAVIS, ELMER. "In the Image of Mr. Wells." <u>SR</u> 14
        (26 Sept.):6-7.
        <u>Anatomy</u> is a mental notebook and a missionary sermon.

1716   DOYAHN, ALFRED P. "H.G. Wells on Latin and Greek." Classical
        Journal 31 (March):374-75.
           [Notes W's remark about the classics in Dream.]

1717   "Encyclopedia as Panacea." Spectator (London) 157
        (27 Nov.):935-36.
           Childish optimism characterizes W's idea of a World Ency-
        clopedia, though the concept has serious implications. [Reports
        on a lecture W gave before the Royal Institution.]

1718   "A Film Scenario." TLS, 16 May, p. 409.
           Characters are vaguely drawn and the meaning is too un-
        artistically clear in Miracles, a scenario that should never-
        theless provide for an entertaining film.

1719   FORD, FORD MADOX [pseud. of Ford Madox Hueffer]. "H.G. Wells."
        American Mercury 38 (May):48-58. Reprinted in Mightier Than
        the Sword. (London: Allen & Unwin, 1938), pp. 145-65.
           [In-depth reminiscences, insightful and ironic, of W's rise
        to fame.]

1720   "A Frustrated World." TLS, 3 Oct., p. 779.
           Despite its vagueness concerning matters of practical appli-
        cation, Anatomy is vigorous in thought and lively in expression.

1721   GARNETT, DAVID. "Books in General." NSN 12 (12 Dec.):984.
           An unconventional and effective ghost story with an idea,
        Player represents W's return to the form of his early romances.
        It is a perfect little work of art.

1722   H., L.C. "Miscellaneous." SR 14 (23 May):16-17.
           Compared to Things to Come, Miracles will make a more satis-
        fying and effective film.

1723   HALL, A.D. "A Social Analysis." Nature 138 (7 Nov.):779-80.
           Anatomy is stimulating. "It is better to clear the mind
        than to trim it into a system."

1724   A JEW in ENGLAND. "Mr. Wells and the Jews." Spectator
        (London) 156 (24 April):749-50.
           [A letter commenting on W's analogy between the National
        Socialist Movement and the Zionist National Movement.]

1725   JOAD, C.E.M. "Wells and Steele." NSN 12 (10 Oct.):516, 518.
           The trouble with Anatomy, an inspiring book, lies in W's
        caginess regarding his protagonist. Does Steele speak for W? W's
        handling of his character gives the impression he is trying out
        ideas for which he wishes to avoid full responsibility.

1936

1726   MAUROIS, ANDRÉ. "Les 70 ans de H.G. Wells." <u>Nouvelles</u>
        <u>littéraires</u>, no. 729 (3 Oct.), p. 1.
            Like other great writers and painters W has shown a constant
        fidelity to several simple but important ideas throughout his
        works. He has gone through three cycles: works stressing utopias
        or anticipations, works using human reality in the construction of
        a future republic, and works of apprenticeship and experience
        presenting a hero who begins as a petty bourgeois but becomes a
        samurai. This last cycle combines the first two.

1727   "Mr. Wells's Croquet Player." <u>TLS</u>, 5 Dec., p. 1013.
            Although W may see himself as a prophet, his readers see him
        as an entertainer. It is difficult to know how seriously W re-
        gards the fears of Dr. Norbert in <u>Player</u>. Insecurity about the
        future has always existed and, consequently, is not as cata-
        strophic as W seems to imply.

1728   "Non-Fiction." <u>Time</u> 28 (12 Oct.):92.
            <u>Anatomy</u> is typically Wellsian, presenting ideas far more
        familiar than its author seems willing to admit.

1729   P., J. "Mr. Wells on Escaping Frustration." <u>MG</u>, 29 Sept.,
        p. 7.
            Some will enjoy <u>Anatomy</u> for passages as stimulating as
        anything W has recently written. Others will protest this effort
        to make "large problems disappear before floods of fluent general-
        isation like rabbits before a conjurer's patter."

1730   PLOMER, WILLIAM. "Fiction." <u>Spectator</u> (London) 157 (18 Dec.):
        1096.
            [Descriptive notice and possibly implied criticism of
        <u>Player</u>.]

1731   ROBERTS, MICHAEL. "Mr. Wells' Sombre World." <u>Spectator</u>
        (London) 157 (11 Dec.):1032-33.
            <u>Shape of Things</u> shows an impoverished world devoid of art
        and human kindness, a place where mechanical progress has replaced
        spiritual values.

1732   "'The Spectator' and Mr. Wells." <u>Spectator</u> (London) 156
        (10 Jan.):41-42.
            [A fulsome announcement of W's new work to appear in the
        journal.]

1733   S[TRAUSS], H[AROLD]. "Another Wells Film." <u>NYTBR</u>, 10 May,
        p. 19.
            As literature <u>Miracles</u> is a rehash of an excellent novel-
        ette; as film it is unoriginal.

1734   "Things to Come." Nature 137 (11 Jan.):50.
        This scenario emphasizes many of W's ideas more forcefully
than did Shape of Things.

1735   THOMPSON, RALPH. "Books of the Times." NYT, 22 Sept., p. 25.
        A book whose value will be disputed, Anatomy is W's boldest
work. Although vague and sometimes wearying, the book presents
interesting ideas that some subsequent generation will absorb in
elementary school.

1736   TOMLIN, E.W.F. "The Revolutionary Simpleton." Scrutiny 5
        (June):75-84.
        [Review of Alec Brown's The Fate of the Middle Class, indi-
cating several ways in which his views differ from W's.]

1737   WEST, GEOFFREY [pseud. of Geoffrey Wells]. "Exasperation, Yes;
        Melancholy, No." LM 34 (Oct.):561-62.
        Anatomy, a repudiation of Burton's Anatomy of Melancholy,
makes exciting and vivid reading.

1738   WHIPPLE, LEON. "Flares on the Road." Survey Graphic 25
        (Nov.):626.
        Anatomy is good for the heart and presents flashes that
always stir the mind.

1739   WILSON, P.W. "Mr. Wells in a Melancholy Mood." NYTBR, 27
        Sept., p. 4.
        Anatomy is less significant for what it says than for re-
vealing W as a man who has expressed and exploited a period of
time. The book is a mixture of balderdash and sagacity.

                              1937

1740   ASHLEY, C.A. "Well of Frustration." Canadian Forum 16
        (Jan.):33.
        The device used in Anatomy is clumsy because it irritates
the reader and screens out interest in the protagonist.

1741   BECKER, MAY LAMBERTON. "The Old Authentic Magic of H.G.
        Wells." Trib, 28 Feb., p. 5.
        Unlike most of W's later novels, Player not only starts
strong but continues to gather fury until the finish.

1742   BELITT, BEN. "Mr. Wells Picks a Bone." Nation (New York) 144
        (20 March):329-30.
        Expertly paced and adroitly done, Player proves that W is
too dapper a hand to succeed with his symbols. He employs poetic
symbols as if "they were propositions to be proved instead of

1937

projecting them with tangents and clarifying them with
refractions."

1743   BELL, ADRIAN. "Fiction." <u>Spectator</u> (London) 158
        (4 June):1064.
            In <u>Star Begotten</u> W "manages to relate a fantastic starry
        conception with the tensions of daily life among individual men
        and women."

1744   BERESFORD, J.D. "Mr. Wells and Miss Delafield." <u>MG</u>, 4 June,
        p. 7.
            The richness of W's imagination is evident in <u>Star Begotten</u>.

1745   BROOKS, V.E. "Mr. Wells's Thriller." <u>LM</u> 35 (Jan.):337.
            <u>Player</u> succeeds as a thriller and as a symbolic work.

1746   BROWN, IVOR. "Books and Ballyhoo." <u>MG</u>, 17 Sept., p. 7.
            A perfunctory story with occasionally brilliant pieces of
        description, <u>Brynhild</u> is easy to read and enjoy.

1747   BUTCHER, FANNY. "Novelist Hero of New Novel by H.G. Wells."
        <u>CDT</u>, 11 Sept., p. 12.
            Sometimes the heroine of <u>Brynhild</u> is a character, at other
        times a mere idea. But W succeeds in gripping the attention.

1748   _____. "Wells Develops Intriguing Idea in a New Novel." <u>CDT</u>,
        12 June, p. 12.
            <u>Star Begotten</u> echoes W's early fiction, but it "is a stick
        of lemon candy stuck in a dill pickle."

1749   CHURCH, RICHARD. "Mr. Wells Wrecks the School." <u>LM</u> 36
        (Oct.):585-86.
            Presenting W in an outrageous mood, <u>Brynhild</u> is too one-
        sided to be taken seriously.

1750   CLARK, WILLIAM H. "Wells as the Years Have Changed Him." <u>BET</u>,
        11 Sept., pt. 5, p. 2.
            Although satisfactory in its characterization, <u>Brynhild</u>
        fails as a novel because of the heavy burden of W's ideas which
        finally make the characters seem mere puppets.

1751   DAVIS, ELMER. "Supermen and Cosmic Rays." <u>SR</u> 16 (12 June):9.
            <u>Star Begotten</u> is not very new but nonetheless provides
        entertaining escapism.

1752   _____. "The Fame Business." <u>SR</u> 16 (11 Sept.):7.
            The plot of <u>Bulpington</u>, a book of limited appeal, is only a
        framework for comments by one of the most unfailingly entertaining
        authors of our time.

1753   DAVIS, H.J. "The Old and the Young." <u>Canadian Forum</u> 17
         (May):64-65.
              Amazingly the full force of W's thinking is conveyed in
         <u>Player</u>.

1754   DELL, FLOYD. "Oh, Mr. Wells, How Could You?" <u>Trib</u>, 12 Sept.,
         p. 2.
              Although the time of <u>Brynhild</u> is 1934, the satire is obvi-
         ously aimed at the boom era of 1927. "Maybe what our world's
         greatest living novelist needs is a copy of the World Almanac,
         with some recent significant American dates marked with red ink."

1755   _____. "Why Girls Grow Tall, and Other Ways of Cosmic Rays."
         <u>Trib</u>, 13 June, p. 14.
              Although it does not keep clear of the trammels of Wellsian
         social doctrine, <u>Star Begotten</u> is reassuring. There is some
         delightful satire and a genuine challenge to all utopia makers.

1756   "Dons in Disarray." <u>TLS</u>, 13 Nov., p. 861.
              It is ironic that <u>Camford Visitation</u> assaults the academic
         caste because Camford is one of the few places where a philosophy
         similar to that of Wells is held.

1757   DUFFUS, R.L. "A New Fantasia by H.G. Wells." <u>NYTBR</u>, 13 June,
         p. 2.
              Although not as interesting as some of W's earlier works,
         <u>Star Begotten</u> does present characters in whom the reader can
         believe. The work seems to be a satire on the old socialist W by
         his more realistic successor.

1758   "Fiction." <u>ALA</u> 33 (April):245.
              A compact allegorical novel, <u>Player</u> is limited in appeal.

1759   "Fiction." <u>ALA</u> 34 (1 Oct.):53-54.
              Rather long-winded, <u>Brynhild</u> is more cerebral than emotional
         in its appeal.

1760   "Fiction." <u>PIFL</u>, Summer, p. 40.
              A characteristic W story serves as a vehicle for social
         philosophy in <u>Player</u>.

1761   "Fiction." <u>Wisconsin Library Bulletin</u> 33 (May):101.
              <u>Player</u> is a short, effectively told fable.

1762   FIELD, LOUISE MAUNSELL. "Another Fantasy by H.G. Wells."
         <u>NYTBR</u>, 28 Feb., p. 6.
              Simultaneously a fantasy and an allegory, <u>Player</u> presents a
         vivid, impressionistic portrait.

1937

1763   GRUBE, G[WENYTH] M.A. "A Wellsian Lecture." <u>Canadian</u> <u>Forum</u> 17
       (Sept.):214-15.
            Unfortunately the manner of writing is limpid and imagina-
       tive pictures supplanted by conversation in <u>Star</u> <u>Begotten</u>.

1764   H., R.E. "Wells's Philosophy." <u>SSUR</u>, 3 Jan., p. 7e.
            Interest in <u>Anatomy</u> is dissipated by W's recapitulation of
       ideas he has presented many times before.

1765   H[ALDANE], J.B.S. "Messianic Radiation." <u>Nature</u> 140
       (31 July):171.
            If <u>Star</u> <u>Begotten</u> is read as a record of thoughts by a wor-
       ried intellectual, it is both an excellent piece of writing and a
       valuable historical document.

1766   HARRIS, WILSON. "What Mr. Wells Would Teach Us." <u>Spectator</u>
       (London) 159 (3 Sept.):371-72.
            W is correct in insisting on the need for scrapping tradi-
       tion in education, but there are some limitations based on human
       nature that need to be recognized.

1767   HAWKINS, A. DESMOND. "The Fortnightly Library." <u>FR</u> 148
       (Nov.):635.
            The failure of <u>Brynhild</u> as a novel can be explained in part
       by the fact that W has always advanced a crude and narrow ration-
       alism, replete with cocksure verities, which developed in the
       nineteenth century.

1768   "A London Diary." <u>NSN</u> 14 (20 Nov.):826-27.
            It is best to ignore <u>Camford</u> <u>Visitation</u>.

1769   MacAFEE, HELEN. "Outstanding Novels." <u>Yale</u> <u>Review</u> 27
       (Autumn):x-xi.
            <u>Brynhild</u> presents only the surface of things and characters
       in profile.

1770   "Man and His Masks." <u>TLS</u>, 18 Sept., p. 673.
            <u>Brynhild</u> is far inferior to W's early novels, albeit in the
       same mode. Its double theme is interesting, but the work is cut
       off too abruptly.

1771   NEAL, R.W. "<u>Star</u> <u>Begotten</u>." <u>SSUR</u>, 20 June, p. 7e.
            [Lukewarm review of the book, concluding that it is readable
       and interesting.]

1772   "New Books: A Reader's List." <u>NR</u> 91 (30 June):232.
            Less fantastic and exciting than W's earlier work, <u>Star</u>
       <u>Begotten</u> presents characters who are convincing even though they

are merely mouthpieces for their author. The directions for achieving utopia are fuzzy.

1773   "New Novels." National Review (London) 109 (Aug.):269.
        In Star Begotten W's notion of the regeneration of mankind "is a naive phantasy, a typical product of an active mind which has retained some of the characteristics of a precocious schoolboy."

1774   PHILLIPS, WILLIAM. "Shorter Notices." Nation (New York) 145
        (7 Aug.):157.
        A symptom of senility, Star Begotten shows that W's capacity to entertain is waning.

1775   PIERHAL, ARMAND. "Un nouveau roman de Wells." Annales
        politiques et littéraires, 10 June, pp. 575-81.
        Player exemplifies how W differs from Maupassant and Chekhov in his primary interest in ideological background over the story. In W's work the moral is not only primary but gives birth to the story, which is created to give expression to the message. Such thesis literature could be annoying were it not that W is gifted in making his narrative sufficiently realistic, even when fantastic, to contain the moral.

1776   PLOMER, WILLIAM. "Wells on Salvation." Spectator (London) 159
        (17 Sept.):472.
        As a novel Brynhild is spasmodic, and as a tract not very persuasive. W is beginning to resemble a Christian.

1777   P[RITCHETT], V.S. "Mr. Wells' Prophecies." CSM, 9 July,
        p. 14.
        Star Begotten is a shrewd political allegory.

1778   _____. "New Novels." NSN 13 (19 June):1007-8.
        W is the most persuasive of living writers, catching his audience on the full wave of its wish. W does not leave us so breathless in Star Begotten, the most mature of his fantasies. His ability to blast the present with a phrase is unsurpassed, even by Shaw.

1779   REID, FORREST. "Fiction." Spectator (London) 159
        (26 Nov.):966.
        Camford Visitation offers a warning to be heeded.

1780   "Return of the Martians." TLS, 5 June, p. 427.
        Star Begotten is basically identical to W's other utopian novels.

1937

1781   REYNOLDS, HORACE. "Wells the Novelist Again." CSM Weekly
        Magazine, 29 Sept., p. 11.
            Palace and Bunter fail to come alive in Brynhild, the pro-
        tagonist of which proves inconsistent. The book would make a good
        movie.

1782   RICHARDS, GERTRUDE R.B. "A Croquet Player Is Visioned by Mr.
        Wells." BET, 27 Feb., pt. 6, p. 2.
            Norbert is W's alter ego and the protagonist is a symbol of
        unthinking mankind in Player, a study in caricature or cartoon.

1783   SHACKLETON, EDITH. "New Novels." TT 18 (25 Sept.):1268.
            Instructive and provocative, Brynhild does not satisfy as a
        work of art or as social propaganda.

1784   SHAWE-TAYLOR, DESMOND. "New Novels." NSN 14 (18 Sept.):409.
            Brynhild, while thoroughly enjoyable, contains material for
        several short stories imperfectly joined together.

1785   STAPLEDON, OLAF. "Mr. Wells Calls in the Martians." LM 36
        (July):295-96.
            In Star Begotten, as elsewhere, W "is too ready to assume
        that an idealization of the positivistic, scientific mood, which
        is mainly the product of the nineteenth century, really can ade-
        quately suggest the essence of the truly adult human mentality."

1786   STEVENS, GEORGE. "Symbols of War." SR 15 (27 Feb.):10.
            Although skillfully told, Player fails to make one's flesh
        creep and lacks the compelling ingenuity of Time Machine.

1787   STRAUSS, HAROLD. "Wells Renounces (?) Prophecy and Writes a
        Good Novel." NYTBR, 12 Sept., p. 3.
            Sacrificing intensity to breadth and limited to the appre-
        hensions or language of its character, Brynhild is a brilliant
        satire of the public face of famous authors.

1788   THOMPSON, RALPH. "Books of the Times." NYT, 24 Feb., p. 21.
            Player is skillful if somewhat obvious sermonizing.

1789   _____. "Books of the Times." NYT, 19 June, p. 15.
            Star Begotten is a good story replete with shrewd
        observations.

1790   "Threat to Mankind in 'Ghosts' of Past." SSUR, 21 Feb., p. 7e.
            In Player W demonstrates a literary power long in abeyance.
        Its narrative, progressing by means of vigorous descriptive and
        psychological detail, presents a story symbolizing the ghost of
        man's animal inheritance.

1791   "UnWellsian Wells." Time 29 (1 March):69.
       Player is one more minor version of W's vision, except it
has fewer pages and presents an un-Wellsian ambiguous message.

1792   VAN GELDER, ROBERT. "Books of the Times." NYT, 9 Sept.,
       p. 21.
       Somewhat overlong, overleisured, old-fashioned, and defi-
cient in wit, Brynhild manages to sparkle with satiric comedy and
intelligence.

1793   VAUGHAN, RICHARD. "Mr. Wells Wiggles His Ears." NR 92
       (29 Sept.):222.
       [An ironic, disparaging mock interview concerning Brynhild.]

1794   WEBSTER, HARVEY CURTIS. "Mr. Wells in Arcadia." NR 90
       (14 April):300.
       Anatomy is inconsistent, neglects realistic considerations,
and tries to solve difficulties by overlooking them. Yet W's use
of the double-vision technique, a device borrowed from Carlyle,
enables him to avoid the tedium of such a tract novel as Marriage.
Player is a footnote to Anatomy.

1795   "Wells in Parvo." Time 29 (14 June):84-85.
       In Star Begotten, which offers a sample of nearly all of W's
tricks, straw men also "have the dubious gift of gabble. And for
every keen sentence he lets them blurt, he makes them babble a
tedious paragraph."

1796   "A Writing Man." SSUR, 10 Oct., p. 7e.
       Numerous amusing and sometimes brilliant flashes of wit help
the reader through the boggy places in Brynhild.

                              1938

1797   ASHLEY, C.A. "H.G. Wells." Canadian Forum 18 (June):89.
       World Brain is a stimulating book, but Brothers treats the
same theme in a way that announces that W is still our greatest
storyteller.

1798   BARRY, IRIS. "Wells on an Odious Woman." Trib, 6 Nov., p. 7.
       A very funny book, readily read out loud, Dolores is a most
successful blending of fiction and tract. The realistic protagonist is wonderfully observed and exposed. The novel undistortedly
mirrors humanity.

1799   BATHO, EDITH, and BONAMY DOBRÉE. The Victorians and After:
       1830-1914. New York: McBride, pp. 101-2.

1938

In spite of its loose prose and ideas, W's work is tremendously persuasive. His early fiction is most satisfactory artistically, and all of his works are influential less on other novelists than on a whole generation.

1800 BECKER, MAY LAMBERTON. "H.G. Wells and Some of the Spring Fiction." Trib, 10 April, p. 10.
Whereas in Brothers W was uncertain as to what to include, in World Brain he is very much on target.

1801 BERESFORD, J.D. "Five Novels." MG, 21 Jan., p. 7.
A wise and good story is presented in Brothers.

1802 "A Brain for Humanity." TLS, 19 Feb., p. 115.
World Brain flashes with sparks of observation, suggestion, and provocation. Yet W appears to be too much of an onlooker, not quite involved in the actual struggle for a happier society.

1803 BROWN, IVOR. "Plea for a Cosmic Brain." MG, 1 March, p. 7.
[Lukewarm review of World Brain, particularly emphasizing its vagueness.]

1804 CASSAL, GOULD. "Novel-with-a-Purpose." Nation (New York) 146 (9 April):420-21.
The story of Brothers tends to be sacrificed to preachment.

1805 CAUDWELL, CHRISTOPHER [pseud. of Christopher Sprigg]. Studies in a Dying Culture. London: Lane & Head, pp. 73-95.
W has created no art work of importance. It was impossible for W "to escape from the petty bourgeois hell, to accept art as an avocation, a social rôle, and be driven in on himself as an outcast from bourgeois values. He could only accept it as a means to success and the best road to cash."

1806 COURNOS, JOHN. "Mr. Wells Would Outline Everything." NYTBR, 8 May, p. 3.
[Tepid review of World Brain.]

1807 CRUSE, AMY. After the Victorians. London: Allen & Unwin, pp. 166-68.
[A cursory critique of W's science fiction.]

1808 DANGERFIELD, GEORGE. "The Obsolete Ego." SR 19 (29 Oct.):7.
In Dolores W shows he knows how to keep the reader moving from one notion to the next without giving him time to get bored. It is not clear, however, that W knows about what he was being serious in this book.

1809   DAVIS, ELMER. "Loose Leaf Wisdom for Seekers of Truth." SR 17
       (16 April):17.
          [Favorable, if qualified, review of World Brain.]

1810   "The Empire, the League and the World." TLS, 26 March, p. 211.
          W is somewhat too much of an onlooker in World Brain.

1811   F.-B., E. "Wellsian Dictatorship." CSM, 31 Jan., p. 14.
          Abounding in incisive criticism, Brothers is provocative and
       illuminating.

1812   FERGUSON, ALLAN. "Knowledge and World Progress." Nature 141
       (23 April):707-8.
          [Very favorable review of World Brain.]

1813   "Fiction." ALA 35 (15 Dec.):134.
          Admirers of W will find Dolores vivid and humorous; others
       will think it dull.

1814   "Fiction." NY 14 (5 Nov.):86.
          Dolores is not a novel but an easy and pleasant conversation
       with W.

1815   GARNETT, DAVID. "Books in Geneal." NSN 15 (26 Feb.):330.
          World Brain is extremely important. W "is like a boxer who
       hits some of the spectators."

1816   _____. "Books in General." NSN 16 (8 Oct.):532.
          The best novel W has written in years, Dolores reveals a
       mature mind and an undiminished creative force.

1817   GIBSON, WILFRID. "Mr. Wells and Others." MG, 7 Oct., p. 7.
          Besides acute characterization, richly humorous scenes, and
       pungent phrasemaking, Dolores is fertile with lively ideas.

1818   GILLETT, ERIC. "The Fortnightly Library." FR 149 (Feb.):250.
          W is at the top of his present form in the enjoyable Camford
       Visitation.

1819   HAWKINS, DESMOND. "The Fortnightly Library." FR 149
       (March):380.
          Reviving memories of Victorian liberalism, Brothers is not
       humorous unless one believes that W has never comprehended the
       underlying features of human behavior.

1820   "Infernal Feminine." TLS, 8 Oct., p. 641.
          Dolores is too much a protracted joke. W's "animation of
       mind carries a quality of obtuseness here that surely does him
       less than justice."

1938

1821   KAZIN, ALFRED. "Mr. Wells's Novel." <u>NYTBR</u>, 30 Oct., p. 7.
       W has outworn the novel as a means of expression. In
<u>Dolores</u> the heroine emerges as a specimen rather than as a
character.

1822   "Lady of Pain." <u>Spectator</u> (London) 161 (14 Oct.):624.
       The biological-sociological-philosophical treatise of
<u>Dolores</u> is uninteresting, but its character development is good.

1823   LEWIN, RONALD. "Mr. Wells's Allegory." <u>LM</u> 37 (March):555-56.
       A sparkling, vigorous allegory, <u>Brothers</u> reveals how ulti-
mately the aims of the political Right and Left converge.

1824   "Man and Marriage." <u>SSUR</u>, 4 Dec., p. 7e.
       [Uncertain, somewhat tepid short review of <u>Dolores</u>.]

1825   "Mr. Wells's Civil War Parable." <u>TLS</u>, 22 Jan., p. 59.
       Since men are divided by incidentals rather than essentials,
<u>Brothers</u> has creative meaning. "Lighted by deep feeling and
vision, it looks well beyond the horizon it depicts."

1826   "Mr. Wells's Parable." <u>NSN</u> 15 (12 Feb.):262.
       A readable, if only moderately exciting parable, <u>Brothers</u> is
a fable that falls short of successful fiction. W's fascist
leader is particularly unbelievable.

1827   "New Books: A Reader's List." <u>NR</u> 94 (4 May):406.
       A brilliant scheme is presented in <u>World Brain</u>.

1828   "New Books: A Reader's List." <u>NR</u> 94 (6 April):285.
       <u>Brothers</u> is a fantastic melodrama.

1829   "New Books: A Reader's List." <u>NR</u> 97 (7 Dec.):155.
       <u>Dolores</u> is a brilliant psychological study.

1830   P., F. "Fiction." <u>SR</u> 17 (9 April):21.
       Obvious symbolism and a weak solution mar the parable en-
titled <u>Brothers</u>.

1831   PRITCHETT, V.S. "New Literature." <u>LM</u> 39 (Nov.):73-74.
       Though a better book than many W has written, <u>Dolores</u> pre-
sents a "style so persuasive [it] makes no impression; an egotism
so impervious to half the experience of men and women leaves one
listless after the first excitement."

1832   RÉNIER, MARTINE. "Frère rouge et frère blanc par H.G. Wells."
<u>Annales politiques et littéraires</u>, 25 Aug., pp. 201-5.
       [A general, unpenetrating review of <u>Brothers</u>.]

1833   ROBERTS, MICHAEL. "The New Encyclopaedism." LM 37
       (March):545-46.
          W is "a very muddled liberal democrat," and in World Brain
       he unwittingly indicates that no one is in more need of an educa-
       tion than himself.

1834   S., J. "New Novels." Times (London), 21 Jan., p. 7.
          W's interest in ideas dominates his concern with narrative
       in Brothers.

1835   _____. "New Novels." Times (London), 7 Oct., p. 19.
          There is a masterly ease in Dolores, a book apparently
       written for the interest and enjoyment W had in his ideas.

1836   SCHRIFTGIESSER, EDWARD B. "Lesson from H.G. Wells." BET, 23
       April, pt. 3, p. 1.
          Brothers is cursory and never fully satisfying.

1837   SMITH, JAMES. "But Knowledge Is Not Enough." CSM Weekly
       Magazine, 6 April, p. 10.
          [Favorable review of World Brain.]

1838   "Some New Fiction." National Review (London) 110 (April):549.
          Brilliant in concept, Brothers is a feast for W's followers.

1839   STEPHENS, W.H. "The Muslim Protest against H.G. Wells." Great
       Britain and the East 51 (8 Sept.):263.
          [Reports and contributes to the adverse English Muslim reac-
       tion to W's references to Muhammad in Short History.]

1840   THOMPSON, RALPH. "Books of the Times." NYT, 26 April, p. 19.
          Brothers presents a provocative and satisfying fable, though
       its ideas are less adequate. World Brain is a sermon worth read-
       ing. [Counters the notion that it is not fashionable to read W.]

1841   TITTERTON, L.H. "A Political Fantasy by H.G. Wells." NYTBR,
       10 April, p. 7.
          Brothers is a moving and exciting book.

1842   WRIGHT, CUTHBERT. "Fiction." Commonweal 29 (25 Nov.):134-35.
          Passages in Dolores read like the travesty of W presented in
       Max Beerbohm's Christmas Garland; they are characteristic of their
       author and unwittingly funny.

1939

1843   BARRY, IRIS. "The Last of the Dictators--A Prophecy." Trib, 9
       April, p. 3.

1939

A keen humor and irreverence, an appealingly unaffected manner, and suspense characterize Terror, a lively, penetrating book. W's philosophical comments are effortlessly carried along by the plot.

1844   BARZUN, JACQUES. "How to Avoid Extermination." SR 21
        (4 Nov.):5.
        Fate is an unpedantic synthesis of a mass of facts organized in support of a single theme.

1845   BASSO, HAMILTON. "The Fate of H.G. Wells." NR 101
        (13 Dec.):234-35.
        Although one of W's most important works, Fate fails to meet the needs of the current times. "Sincerely anxious to help mankind, totally unable to believe in men, every last hope canceled by his conviction of human stupidity--this is the fate of H.G. Wells."

1846   BENNETT, HENRY. "Our Own Bookshelf." LA 356 (June):398-99.
        Haste and occasional superficiality mar Terror, an otherwise entertaining story replete with W's wit and epigrammatic bravura.

1847   BINDER, RUDOLPH M. "H.G. Wells Is Proposing a New World
        Order." NYTBR, 5 Nov., p. 5.
        Fate is a spiritual, controversial book presenting a well-written summary of W's philosophy.

1848   BROWN, HILTON. "Fiction." NCA 125 (May):611, 615.
        The characters in Terror are people, not mere talking machines. Especially fine is W's "adventurous nicety of phrase, . . . those inevitably apt Wellsian adjectives that are a lesson (and a despair) to us all."

1849   "Classified Books." ALA 36 (1 Dec.):127.
        The iconoclasm of Fate may offend devout readers.

1850   DAVIS, ELMER. "The First World Dictator." SR 19 (8 April):5.
        W's works present a single apocalypse "progressively revised on the Hegelian formula." Terror concentrates on the means rather than on the ends of the Golden Age.

1851   DAVIS, HASSOLDT. "Uppercut." BET, 15 April, pt. 4, p. 1.
        Although its conclusion may be too neat, Terror presents a superb, well-structured narrative with well-developed characters.

1852   DEAN of St. PAUL'S. "Plain Words to Homo Sapiens." Spectator
        (London) 163 (4 Aug.):189.

There is much in <u>Fate</u> with which every intelligent person must agree, but it is sad that W has never understood the nature of religion.

1853   DUFFUS, R.L. "The First World Dictator." <u>NYTBR</u>, 9 April, pp. 1, 16.
       In <u>Terror</u> W plays with an old idea in a new effective form, one that comes closer to the realities of human psychology and the present world situation.

1854   "Fiction Review." <u>Forum</u> 102 (July):iv.
       <u>Terror</u> is almost as clever as Saki's story of how the Kaiser conquered England.

1855   "General [Books]." <u>NY</u> 15 (4 Nov.):70.
       The last chapter of <u>Fate</u> is distinctly bearish.

1856   H., J.C. "The Future of Mankind." <u>Nature</u> 144 (2 Sept.): 397-98.
       <u>Fate</u> is a timely and sincere book written with courage.

1857   HOLMES, JOHN HAYNES. "Wells' Latest." <u>Unity</u> 124 (4 Sept.): 13-14.
       In <u>Terror</u> W writes badly, handles his material awkwardly, and seems uncertain of his purpose.

1858   JAMES, STANLEY B. "Meet Mr. H.G. Wells." <u>Catholic World</u> 149 (June):270-75.
       Mentally restless and inquisitive, W does not respect tradition. He is a prophet to a semieducated, newspaper-reading public. <u>God</u>, his attempt to synthesize many of his ideas, presents a thin, unsatisfying belief that any Christian thinker could refute.

1859   JOAD, C.E.M. "That We Are for It." <u>NSN</u> 18 (12 Aug.):251-52.
       In <u>Fate</u>, "so enlivened and exhilarated is the reader by the pyrotechnics and intellectual fisticuffs, that it is some time before he becomes sensible of the atmosphere of gloom." W has done his best and yet, as he tells us, he has failed.

1860   KINIERY, PAUL. "More Books of the Day." <u>Commonweal</u> 30 (28 April):24.
       An unbelievably dull and stupid book, <u>Terror</u> presents tiresome, pointless ideas that could have been summarized in a pamphlet of a dozen pages.

1861   "Man's Future: Mr. Wells on the Outlook." <u>Times</u> (London), 4 Aug., p. 17.
       In <u>Fate</u> W's diagnosis of the world situation proves masterly. He fails, however, with regard to the changes involved in

1939

the development of an adequate worldbrain and retreats to an
almost religious trust in science.

1862   MARRIOTT, CHARLES. "The New Novels." MG, 7 Feb., p. 7.
       Terror fuses W's power as a thinker and as a creative
artist, most evident previously in Anticipations and Kipps. The
second half of the work is as fine as anything W has written.

1863   MARTIN, KINGSLEY. "Out of the Strong Came Forth. . . ." NSN
       17 (11 Feb.):224.
       In Terror W's vitality and charm are as evident as ever. W
should not be chided for his moral--"that there is no hope for the
world until power is combined with intellect and benevolence,"--
even if he does not take into account the fact that power corrupts.

1864   "Mechanistic Utopia." TLS, 11 Feb., p. 87. Abstracted in
       "Echoes of the September Crisis," TLS (supplement), 25 March,
       p. xiii.
       Philistinism is the vice of modern and mechanistic utopias
such as the one W once again presents in Terror. W's notions are
obsolete.

1865   "Mr. H.G. Wells Fears for the World. TLS, 5 Aug., p. 462.
       W's solutions to the threat of the potential extinction of
man he remarks on in Fate are just as incapable of controlling the
human ego as any other method has been. Is there any difference
between W's idea of world citizen consciousness and the notion of
Christian brotherhood?

1866   "Modern Fairy Tale." TLS, 9 Dec., p. 719.
       The revised version of The Country of the Blind is less
satisfying than the original.

1867   PRITCHETT, V.S. "Best Sellers--Mr. Wells' Dictator." CSM
       Weekly Magazine, 11 March, p. 10.
       W is probably the greatest living propagandist, as Terror
makes clear. "He rises over the house with the blond suddenness
of an Edwardian balloon."

1868   ____. "Rearmament in Utopia." LM 39 (March):546-47.
       W's propaganda has reached a point of satiety, and even as
fiction Terror is tedious. The best of W's humor, a "withering
comicalness of a hurt and eloquent clowning," does appear in the
beginning of the book.

1869   SHUSTER, GEORGE N. "Evaluation for the Disillusioned." Trib,
       31 Dec., p. 6.

1940

There is no evidence to show that W is conclusively right in *Fate*. W "will go down into history as the John Bunyan who listened to Huxley but kept on looking for the New Jerusalem."

1870   SIEPMANN, ERIC. "Mr. Britling Is Seen Through." <u>NCA</u> 126 (Oct.):458-64.
        W has always been vague, idealistic, and unprecise, merely offering the bland suggestion that man must change. But man cannot change, and so in <u>Fate</u> W offers us only despair "in relays of 80,000 words at 8<u>s</u>.6<u>d</u>."

1871   VAN DOREN, CARL, and MARK VAN DOREN. <u>American and British Literature since 1890</u>. New York: Appleton-Century, pp. 207-12, 288-92.
        W's earlier novels are provocative studies, replete with ingenuity, humor, and wonderfully eloquent characters. <u>Clissold</u> is more discussion than fiction and its successors mere <u>trifles</u> when compared to W's earlier works of science fiction. But "the gusto of <u>Tono-Bungay</u> is enormous; the eloquence is overwhelming; the reporting of contemporary talk is well-nigh perfect." [Also a section on W as essayist.]

1872   W., J.D. "Mr. Wells and the Future of Man." <u>CSM</u> <u>Weekly</u> <u>Magazine</u>, 25 Nov., p. 12.
        [Very favorable review of <u>Fate</u>.]

1873   WAUGH, EVELYN. "Machiavelli and Utopia--Revised Version." <u>Spectator</u> (London) 162 (10 Feb.):234.
        Art is forsaken for philosophy in <u>Terror</u>. W tells a good story, but his characters are shallow.

1874   WOOD, MAX. "The Fortnightly Library." <u>FR</u> 151 (March):360-61.
        [Short, negative review of <u>Terror</u>.]

<u>1940</u>

1875   AARON, DANIEL. "Check." <u>BET</u>, 24 Feb., pt. 5, p. 2.
        <u>New World Order</u> is the most powerful tract W has written to date.

1876   "All at Sea on an Ark." <u>TLS</u>, 12 Oct., p. 521.
        <u>Ararat</u> commences brilliantly and then dwindles.

1877   "The Atlantic Bookshelf." <u>AM</u> 166 (Dec.):[xxxiv-xxxvii].
        <u>Babes</u> is tedious and ineffective as a novel.

1878   BARZUN, JACQUES. "No Royal Road." <u>SR</u> 21 (24 Feb.):6.
        [Favorable review of <u>New World Order</u>.]

1940

1879 BLYTON, W.J. "Brave New World Planning." Quarterly Review 274
      (April):263-77.
      [Passing references to W concerning utopias.]

1880 "Classified Books." ALA 36 (1 March):262.
      New World Order, vigorous in expression, merits the dis-
      cussion it will cause.

1881 "Collectivist States in World Federation." SSUR, 18 Feb.,
      p. 7e.
      When W tries to suggest solutions to real world problems in
      New World Order, his thinking hardly transcends semimystical,
      though sometimes searching, denunciations of confusion.

1882 CROWTHER, J.G. "Babes in the Darkling Wood." Nature 146
      (28 Dec.):822.
      This work is too discursive, but W's belief in the future
      and his wrestling with the present are inspiring.

1883 DAVIS, HASSOLDT. "Dialogue by Wells." Nation (New York) 151
      (28 Sept.):276.
      Although generally interesting, Babes is at times tedious
      and indicates, unfortunately, that W has not mastered his medium.
      "It is Wells worth borrowing."

1884 DENNIS, NIGEL. "H.G. Wells in Our Time." NR 103 (2 Dec.):
      761-62.
      The characters in Babes are shadowy. "Their thoughts are
      forever tripping over one another's feet, wearying the reader with
      a mixture of antagonistic interests."

1885 DINGLE, REGINALD J. "Our Secular Saviours." NCA 127
      (March):324-28.
      [Negative response to Fate.]

1886 _____. "The Tragedy of Kipps." NCA 128 (Nov.):474-78.
      Besides the fact that Ararat argues for the doctrine of
      totalitarianism, the book is in general full of mental confusion.
      W's "Ark will not reach Ararat or anywhere else and its log will
      not make pleasant reading."

1887 ELIOT, T.S. "Views and Reviews." New English Weekly 16
      (8 Feb.):237-38. Reprinted in CH, pp. 319-22.
      W's journalism succeeds because his bluntness and imagina-
      tive picture-book method make his arguments very real as well as
      impose no obstacle to the comprehension of the average person.

1888   E[VANS], I[FOR] B. "A New Noah." MG, 8 Oct., p. 7.
        Dull and almost pointless, Ararat falls far below W's
    earlier accomplishments.

1889   EVANS, IFOR B. "Mr. Wells's New Novel." MG, 1 Nov., p. 7.
        Babes magnificently converts contemporary circumstance and
    opinion into fictional form. Each opinion expressed is true for
    the character who is speaking and should not be confused with what
    W believes.

1890   FADIMAN, CLIFTON. "Chiefly War." NY 16 (28 Sept.):57-58.
        Although the reader is likely to agree with the notions
    expressed in Babes, the main characters "are such confounded
    little prigs that every idea they produce seems to lose some of
    its virtue as soon as uttered."

1891   "Fiction." ALA 37 (15 Dec.):156.
        Limited in appeal, Babes is a rambling novel of ideas.

1892   GREENE, GRAHAM. "The Second Deluge." Spectator (London) 165
        (18 Oct.):398.
        Even when vague W conveys an enormous creative drive.
    Ararat is humorous, evincing the poetic feeling that once made
    W a novelist of genius.

1893   GRIFFITH, GWILYM [O.]. "Mr. H.G. Wells as Gospeller." Baptist
        Quarterly 10 (July):146-53.
        W has not readily accepted science in lieu of religion; in
    fact he has tinged the former with a faded evangelicism. But
    clearly he now sees that his gospel of scientific humanism is
    exhausted--there is no man-god.

1894   GRUBE, GWENYTH. "The Shape of Things." Canadian Forum 19
        (March):398.
        New World Order is readable, useful, and illuminating.

1895   HARRIS, WILSON. "More Revolution." Spectator (London) 164
        (5 Jan.):23-24.
        Although not always convincingly analytic or constructive,
    New World Order laudably supplies ample materials for debate.

1896   HOBSON, J.A. "World Order." MG, 16 Jan., p. 3.
        [Positive review of New World Order.]

1897   HOWARD, BRIAN. "New Novels." NSN 20 (9 Nov.):472.
        Babes suffers from characters who talk too long, too much,
    and too unhumanly.

1940

1898   INGE, W.R.   "Victorian Socialism."   <u>Nature</u> 145 (13 Jan.):45-46.
        The utopia depicted in <u>New World Order</u> is utterly unrealiz-
able, but W's faith is admirable.

1899   JACKS, L.P.   "Mr. Wells on the Fate of Homo Sapiens."   <u>HJ</u> 38
        (Jan.):161-73.
        High purpose, clarity of thought, and freedom from cant are
the outstanding attributes of <u>Fate</u>.

1900   JOAD, C.E.M.   "An Open Letter to H.G. Wells."   <u>NSN</u> 20
        (17 Aug.):154-55.
        W's unflagging energy is admirable, but <u>War and Peace</u> only
points up again that he has not faced the ageold problem of how
the intellectual moves from thought to action in the real world.

1901   KAUFFMANN, STANLEY.   "Wells and the New Generation: The
        Decline of a Leader of Youth."   <u>College English</u> 1 (April):
        573-82.
        Since about 1925 W's influence has sharply declined.   His
style and technique are too classic to please modernists, while
his content is too modern to please classicists.

1902   KERWIN, JEROME G.   "More Books of the Week."   <u>Commonweal</u> 31
        (12 April):536.
        W's dream for a better earth in <u>New World Order</u> faintly
resembles a nineteenth-century utopia.

1903   L., P.   "H.G. Wells Looks Forward to a New World Order."   <u>CSM
        Weekly Magazine</u>, 17 Feb., p. 10.
        In spite of certain exaggerations, <u>New World Order</u> is pun-
gent, witty, and constructive.

1904   M., A.E.   "My Dear Mr. Wells!"   <u>NYTBR</u>, 29 Sept., pp. 22-23.
        In <u>Babes</u>, the "curious attempt at realistic thinking, half
copied from dull textbooks, half translated into Mr. Wells's
peculiar mixture of flippancy and vulgarity, ends with the
author's customary vague utopianism which contradicts the whole
theme of his book."

1905   MARSH, FRED T.   "At the End of an Era."   <u>Trib</u>, 25 Feb., p. 2.
        [Favorable review of <u>New World Order</u>.]

1906   _____.   "H.G. Wells's New Novel."   <u>Trib</u>, 6 Oct., p. 4.
        <u>Babes</u> provides food for thought, but W ought to avoid the
slovenliness evident in it.   His readers have accepted too much
too willingly, and W should set to work in earnest on the fine
novel of which he is capable.

1907   MARTIN, KINGSLEY. "The Rights of Man." NSN 19 (6 Jan.):15.
       New World Order presents W's familiar ideas with thoughtful
freshness and vigor.

1908   MERRIAM, CHARLES E. "The New World Order." American Journal
       of Sociology 46 (Nov.):402-3.
       Certain specifics in this work might be disputed, but on the
whole it is worth examining.

1909   "Mr. H.G. Wells's Plans." TLS, 16 March, p. 130.
       [Generally unfavorable review of Rights of Man.

1910   "Mr. Wells's Ideas." TLS, 2 Nov., p. 553.
       Babes is the sort of work W has written many times before.

1911   "Mr. Wells's World Plan." TLS, 6 Jan., pp. 6-7.
       More than any other writer, W has made the world aware of
change. Something of a pragmatist, his ideas are not merely
abstract; he is a scientist as well as a romanticist. [See letter
by E. Haigh Roscoe, TLS, 13 Jan., p. 19.]

1912   O'BRIEN, KATE. "Fiction." Spectator (London) 165
       (1 Nov.):452.
       The conflict between W the novelist and W the pedagogue
makes Babes unsatisfactory.

1913   PATON, DAVID M. "The World of God and the World of Wells."
       Theology (London) 40 (April):252-61; (May):349-56.
       W's world, especially in Shape of Things, reflects the
modern mind. It is an appalling conception of boredom, failing to
take into consideration such verities as man's radical evilness,
the unrelatedness of material and moral progress, the limited
purview of science, and the emptiness of happiness on earth.

1914   PRATT, FLETCHER. "A Wells without Remedy." SR 22
       (28 Sept.):5.
       In Babes W the social and moral philosopher is quite good,
but W the novelist is defunct. W offers no remedy here, looking
toward the past rather than toward the future.

1915   PRITCHETT, V.S. "Books in General." NSN 20 (5 Oct.):334.
       [Concerned with Noah Lammock as an apparent follower of W
who lacks several fundamental qualities found in his master.]

1916   "Shorter Notices." Nation (New York) 150 (16 March):371.
       The same Wellsian argument appears in fresh perspective in
New World Order.

1940

1917   THOMPSON, RALPH. "Books of the Times." <u>NYT</u>, 19 Feb., p. 15
       <u>New World Order</u> and <u>Travels</u> show W to be a more gifted
    preacher than was Shaw in his prime.

1918   "Tracts for the Time." <u>TLS</u>, 27 July, p. 358.
       <u>War and Peace</u> is vague and hortatory rather than factual.

1919   "Wandering Lights." <u>TLS</u>, 2 Nov., p. 555.
       <u>Babes</u> presents ideas insufficiently grounded in reality.

1920   "Why Great Britain Is Fighting." <u>TLS</u> (supplement), 16 March
    p. iii.
       Read out of the context of W's previous work, <u>New World
    Order</u> appears jejune and unoriginal.

<u>1941</u>

1921   BATES, H.E. <u>The Modern Short Story: A Critical Survey</u>.
       London: Nelson, pp. 105-18.
       Uniting Dickens and Poe, W writes fairy tales in scientific
    language. He evinces an artful artlessness in his careful use of
    apparently trivial items of fact and commonplace touches of formal
    style.

1922   FADIMAN, CLIFTON. "Mainly Winston Churchill." <u>NY</u> 17
       (19 April):73.
       <u>Ararat</u> offers diverting satirical conversation.

1923   GRIFFITH, GWILYM O. "Young Mr. Wells Anticipates." <u>Baptist
       Quarterly</u> 10 (Oct.):421-28.
       To reread <u>Anticipations</u> is to appreciate the accuracy of
    W's superficial foresights and to realize the degree to which he
    failed, then and now, to cope with the fundamental problems of the
    world.

1924   HAUSER, MARIANNE. "Mr. Wells's Tale of a Modern Noah." <u>NYTBR</u>,
       27 April, pp. 8, 26.
       Concerned with immediate problems, <u>Ararat</u> is funny and
    absurd yet also profound.

1925   HOBSON, HAROLD. Mr. Wells and the Novel--A London Letter."
       <u>CSM Weekly Magazine</u>, 4 Jan., p. 11.
       <u>Babes</u> presents stale, old-fashioned substitutes for
    thought. Is it possible, however, that the book is a subtle
    satire on Oxford and Cambridge?

1926   "Homo Tewler." TLS, 20 Dec., p. 641.
        The first two-thirds of Too Careful concentrates on charac-
ters more than on ideas, giving the work the quality of some of
W's better earlier writings.

1927   "Leaky Ark." Time 37 (21 April):108.
        After a splendid beginning, Ararat soon manifests an almost
unmitigated breakdown, as if its author realized his error in
midstream and tried simultaneously to finish and to back out of
it.

1928   LEWIS, SINCLAIR. Foreword to The History of Mr. Polly. New
        York Readers Club, pp. v-vii.
        No book before has been "so deeply reaching into contempo-
rary character, so funny yet so moving" as Mr. Polly.

1929   "Mr. Wells's New World." TLS, 31 May, p. 259.
        New World is imaginatively and incisively written, though
not without questionable ideas.

1930   ORWELL, GEORGE. "Wells, Hitler and the World State." Horizon
        (London) 4 (Aug.):133-39. Reprinted in Dickens, Dali, and
        Others: Studies in Popular Culture (New York: Reynal, 1946),
        pp. 115-123; The Golden Horizon, ed. Cyril Connolly (New York:
        University Books, 1955), pp. 28-33; Collected Essays, Journal-
        ism, and Letters of George Orwell, ed. Sonia Orwell and Ian
        Angus, vol. 2 (New York: Harcourt, Brace, 1968), pp. 139-45.
        W is too sane to comprehend the modern world. "The succes-
sion of lower-middle-class novels which are his greatest achievement stopped short at the other war and never really began again,
and since 1920 he has squandered his talents in slaying paper
dragons."

1931   SUGRUE, THOMAS. "A Cheerful H.G. Wells." Trib, (4 May), p. 3.
        The good-humored W of earlier times is evident in Ararat,
even poking fun at himself.

1932   "Wells on a Fresh Start for the Human Race." SSUR, 27 April,
        p. 7e.
        W's sincere forecast for man in Ararat restricts the flip-
pancy of the book.

1942

1933   "After-Man." TLS, 12 Sept., p. 448.
        Conquest of Time fails to replace Last Things.

1934   BOWEN, ELIZABETH. English Novelists. London: Collins,
        pp. 43-44.

1942

        W's "straight" novels depicting the consciousness of his time are preferable to his science fiction.

1935   BRIGHOUSE, HAROLD. "New Novels." MG, 9 Jan., p. 3.
        Too Careful is a stimulating, idiosyncratic work, somewhat less humorous than Kipps and Mr. Polly.

1936   COURNOS, JOHN. "'Ideers' and Tewler." NYTBR, 21 June, pp. 9-10.
        The first two-thirds of Too Careful marks the return of W the novelist, whereas the last third represents W the man of ideas at his deadliest.

1937   DANGERFIELD, GEORGE. "H.G. Wells Creates Tewler." SR 25 (27 June):7.
        As usual W disseminates characters or types and creates facts in Too Careful, which is a somewhat extensive prologue. The honesty and anger of the book, however, are worthwhile. W's final impression for posterity may be faint and perhaps even ludicrous, but it will be there.

1938   DUTT, R. PALME. "Mr. H.G. Wells and Communism." Labour Monthly 24 (Dec.):383-86.
        [Accuses W of attacking his political allies.]

1939   FADIMAN, CLIFTON. "Mixed Bag." NY 18 (20 June):57-58.
        Too Careful starts out as a novel and ends as a tract with characters. It is less interesting than the earlier W but it is sharper, truer, and more urgent.

1940   "Fiction." ALA 38 (15 July):443.
        Too Careful offers W's typical preaching on evils and reforms.

1941   G., R.M. "The Atlantic Bookshelf." AM 170 (July):110.
        Not subtle enough in its satire, Too Careful erupts with authorial intrusions. The chapters on Dooker's boarding house and Harold Thump are excellent.

1942   HAWKINS, DESMOND. "New Novels." NSN 23 (24 Jan.):60-61.
        Too Careful is a better novel than some W has recently written. W lacks Dickens's genius for the sublimely grotesque and for blending anger and tenderness.

1943   "Mr. Wells and the World." TLS, 25 July, p. 363.
        [A mixed review of Phoenix.]

1944   RUGOFF, MILTON. "Worm That Walks Like a Man." Trib, 21 June, p. 2.

W is too discursive in <u>Too</u> <u>Careful</u>. "Because it is the way of Showman Wells to mix circuses and bread, and because the Carlyle in him is leavened with the Dickens, he projects his ideas, exhortations and asides in the form of a novel full of pungent characters and juicy middle-class scenes."

1945   "Science." <u>TLS</u>, 31 Jan., p. 59.
    In <u>Science</u> <u>and</u> <u>the</u> <u>World-Mind</u> it is clear that although W possesses the method of our temporal salvation, he lacks the impulse.

1946   SYKES, W.J. "Is Wells Also among the Prophets?" <u>Queen's</u> <u>Quarterly</u> 49 (Autumn):233-45.
    W is not a major prophet, perhaps not even a minor one. Though some of his remarks are useful, he carries ideas to extremes and fails to ponder alternatives to his notions.

1947   "Tewleremia." <u>Time</u> 39 (22 June):88.
    Possessing mind but lacking in soul, <u>Too</u> <u>Careful</u> is a forceful, rather tortured tract deprived of the sort of clarity of design that could have made it an instructive parable. In emphasizing the remaking of Tewler's dim wits rather than his soul, W's program raises the question of whether the effort is worth it.

1948   TRILLING, DIANA. "The Tewlers." <u>Nation</u> (New York) 154
    (27 June):742.
    W's prose is satisfyingly vigorous in <u>Too</u> <u>Careful</u>. The book may not add anything new to what he has previously said, but modern weariness with W may betoken a more pervasive weariness of spirit on our part.

1943

1949   MOODY, W.V., and R.M. LOVETT. <u>A</u> <u>History</u> <u>of</u> <u>English</u> <u>Literature</u>. New York: Scribner's Sons, pp. 452, 456-58, 469-70, 478, 480.
    One of the four most significant social critics of the twentieth century, W is more optimistic than such critics are prone to be concerning the relationship between man and his environment. In <u>Research</u> W abandons traditional form for a loose narrative style in order to portray a changing character.

1950   NICHOLSON, NORMAN. <u>Man</u> <u>and</u> <u>Literature</u>. London: S.C.M. Press, pp. 9-10, 49-61.
    Often prosaic, unimaginative, and wordy, W represents the Pelagianistic view of man in his novels.

1943

1951   PRITCHETT, V.S. "Books in General." NSN 26 (4 Sept.):154-55.
       W's early work possessed an infectious sense of freedom
that was a fact in his environment. The later W escaped into a
dream world of using science "as a magic staircase out of essential social problems." The best W "is the destructive, ruthless,
black-eye dealing and house-burning Wells who foresaw the violence
and not the order of our time." But the early W of Time Machine,
his best piece of writing, did not escape. He failed to see the
strength of human resistance. Nevertheless, "we were and are just
as entranced as he was and he has given us the early part of our
scientific myth." [Also suggests similarities between W and
Jonathan Swift.]

1952   WEGENKNECHT, EDWARD. Cavalcade of the English Novel: From
       Elizabeth to George VI. New York: Holt, pp. 458-76.
       Though W disclaims great care in writing (his chief fault),
the appearance of his manuscripts argues otherwise. W destroyed
the gentility and widened the scope of the novel; as a pupil of
Samuel Butler, he felt free to do as he pleased with the form and
style of fiction. [Reviews several of W's works, particularly
noting the unsurpassed blend of humanity and ruthlessness in Mr.
Lewisham.]

                              1944

1953   BETTERANCE, WILFRED B. [pseud. of H.G. Wells]. "Alls Well
       That Ends Wells: A Complete Exposé of This Notorious Literary
       Humbug." Virginia Quarterly Review 21 (Summer):420-33.
       [Blistering assault on W, citing his atheism, lack of
tradition, pretentiousness, lack of education, and unreality.
Accuses W of plagiarizing Jules Verne.]

1954   "Books Received." Christian Century 61 (19 July):855.
       Prejudiced adjectives abound in Crux Ansata, a slashing
rather than judicious book. Further attention to it may be
warranted.

1955   BROOK, DONALD. Writers' Gallery. London: Rockliff,
       pp.154-63.
       [General, unpenetrating sketch of W's career.]

1956   EVANS, IFOR. "Mr. Wells at War." MG, 17 May, p. 3.
       [Negative review of '42 to '44.]

1957   JOHNSON, EDGAR. A Treasury of Satire. New York: Simon &
       Schuster, pp. 573-77.
       Too impatient to continue embodying social comment in imag-
inative literary form, W slowly eliminated the artistic side of

himself for the didactic side. The power of his satire lies in its pictorial features rather than in its intellectual scope. Men in the Moon recalls Swift.

1958   MILLETT, FRED B. Contemporary British Literature. New York: Harcourt, Brace, pp. 16, 21-24.
        Hardly a sensitive stylist and hardly to be taken seriously as a novelist, W is closer to the Victorians than are most of his contemporaries. His career warns of the danger of selling an artistic birthright for a mess of propaganda.

1959   "Mr. Wells on the World." TLS, 13 May, p. 232.
        '42 to '44 is horrible because it is unfair to its victims; it fascinates because seldom has the English language been used with such a wealth of merciless invective.

1960   "Mr. Wells Sees It Through." Time 43 (29 May):99-100.
        '42 to '44 is W at his most vigorous and entertaining.

1961   "Shorter Notices." Spectator (London) 172 (5 May):414.
        The old-fashioned catalogue of past indictments against the Roman Catholic Church will not persuade readers of Crux Ansata.

1962   STERN, JAMES. "The History of a Book." NR, 111 (6 Nov.): 600-604.
        [Discusses the publishing history and critical reception of Crux Ansata, concluding that it is a very poor book.]

1963   WOODWARD, E.L. "Angry Common Sense." Spectator (London) 172 (12 May):432.
        If not always scientific and if a little rattled and cruel, '42 to '44 is worth reading.

1964   WORSLEY, T.C. "The Dilemma of a Rationalist." NSN 27 (27 May):356.
        That '42 to '44 scolds too much may stem from W's sense of time running out and this underevaluation of the individual. W is puzzled by his own irrational behavior.

1945

1965   LERNER, MAX. "The Imagination of H.G. Wells." PM, 16 Nov. [not seen]. Reprinted in Actions and Passions (New York: Simon & Schuster, 1949), pp. 16-18.
        W knew the crucial truth "that there is an organic relation between man's tools and man's fate, that a world technology means either a world government or world suicide." The social meanings in his science fiction arise naturally from the story.

1945

1966   "The Pessimism of Mr. Wells." TLS, 24 Nov., p. 561.
       The pessimistic view of the world presented in Tether
probably has more to do with W's temperament than with his objective observations.

1967   UNDERWOOD, E. ASHWORTH. "The End of Man." Spectator (London)
       175 (9 Nov.):442, 444.
       Tether provides a serious biological contribution to the
scientific philosophy of the life process.

1968   "When the Sleeper Wakes: Mr. Wells's Journals of the Night."
       TLS, 3 March, p. 104.
       Turning lacks the quality of W's early works.

1946

1969   "About Two Authors." Scholastic 49 (11 Nov.):18.
       [Contrasts drawn between W and Shaw; however, both dis-
played "critical skepticism and reforming energy."]

1970   BABITS, SETH. "A Literary Miracle: H.G. Wells and the Atomic
       Bomb." Scholastic 49 (11 Nov.):21.
       W was proclaimed a prophet against his will and was annoyed
by the reaction to Orson Welles's radio broadcast of War of the
Worlds. He predicted the military strength of air power in War in
the Air and the atomic bomb in World Set Free.

1971   BENSUSAN, S.L. "'H.G.' and His Neighbours." FR 156
       (Oct.):280-83.
       While visiting R.D. Blumenfeld, editor of the Daily
Express, W decided he liked the countryside and leased the rectory
of Little Easton which he renamed Easton Glebe. Jane Wells made
the Glebe popular, and W spent much of his time working while she
took care of his guests. Character sketches of his friends and
neighbors can be seen in Mr. Britling, which was written there.

1972   "Body of Wells Cremated; J.B. Priestley Delivers Eulogy for
       Noted British Author." NYT, 17 Aug., p. 13.
       W was cremated at Golders Green Crematorium, 16 Aug.; Lord
Beaverbrook, Priestley, and David Low were present. Priestley:
"This was a man whose word was light in a thousand dark places.
When he was angry, it was because he knew, far better than we did,
that life need not be a sordid, greedy scramble."

1973   "Books: H.G. Wells, 1866-1946." Newsweek 28 (26 Aug.):82-83.
       Time will tell how much of W's work is great literature,
but no future critic will be able to deny him a place as one of
the giants in a particular era of English literature. [Obituary.]

1974   BROWN, E.K. "Two Formulas for Fiction: Henry James and H.G.
        Wells." College English 8:7-17.
            W was not sorry for what he had said about James in Boon,
        but sorry he had to say it. James felt the novel was an extension
        of life and that different experiences produced different novels.
        The picture of England in Portrait of a Lady differs from that in
        Tono-Bungay. W's charge that James "over-unified" his work is his
        "counter-attack on behalf of [his own] fiction," but W's discur-
        siveness has aged and dated his own work.

1975   C[ANBY], H[ENRY] S[EIDEL]. "The Superjournalist." SR 29
        (31 Aug.):10-11.
            W acted as a liaison between research science and the
        people who could benefit from its discoveries. He believed in a
        new society out of the industrial revolution creating a new way of
        life. His books were journalism, not literature. His reason was
        good, but his vision lacked warmth.

1976   CATLIN, GEORGE. "Prophet of Modernism." Commonweal 44
        (27 Sept.):572-73.
            For some W was a false prophet. He quarreled with people
        like Shaw and the Webbs because he was certain he was right.
        "With his confidence in progress Wells was a Victorian projected
        into the modern age. In morals he was an Edwardian gospeller for
        Dr. Stopes." He admitted in the end that the human race had
        disappointed him. In all his endeavors he was a man of his age,
        "a transitional writer of a transitional age; not so much a
        prophet as a tribune."

1977   CLEMENS, CYRIL. "Tea with H.G. Wells." Hobbies 51 (Nov.):
        141-42.
            Little is known of W as a man because he lacked the "vivid
        personality" of Chesterton or Shaw. He looked more like a pros-
        perous business man than a writer, and his voice reminded one of
        Calvin Coolidge, "pleasant, but not suited to oratorical effects."
        He felt he had "ruined a second rate reputation as a novelist" by
        his attack on war since 1918, and in fact critics were determined
        to find propaganda in everything he wrote.

1978   COLE, MARGARET. Beatrice Webb. (New York: Harcourt, Brace,
        pp. 67, 70, 124, 127-30, 136, 165, 180.
            The institutional basis of the Constitution for a Socialist
        Commonwealth came to Beatrice Webb during one of W's lectures.
        The confusion and discontent of Edwardian England are found in W's
        earlier novels. His attempts to reform the Fabians failed because
        he could not state his case in precise enough terms to be voted
        upon.

1946

1979   DAVIS, ELMER. "Notes on the Failure of a Mission." <u>SR</u> 29
       (31 Aug.):6-8.
            The turn of the century reformation of society failed for
       lack of enough disciples of people like Shaw and W. Generally, it
       was W who had his feet on the ground, but he had his visionary
       moments as well. He trained us to see better where and how he
       erred so that we could work out our own salvation for the human
       race.

1980   "De Mortuis." <u>America</u> 75 (24 Aug.):502.
            W may have bored and angered readers as adults with his
       "materialism and his prejudices," but he brought joy to our youth
       through his fantasies.

1981   FADIMAN, CLIFTON. "The Passing of a Prophet." <u>SR</u> 29
       (31 Aug.):3-6.
            Compared to the rest of mankind, W was a rational human
       being. His prophecies, no matter how catastrophic, had their
       origin in optimism. His work dates, but he intended it to do so,
       to remind us of the time in which we live. He wanted us to make
       his ideas a part of ourselves and to forget the being who gave us
       the ideas. He stifled the artist in himself that the teacher
       might survive, but his books were mostly experiments designed to
       lead the reader to come to certain conclusions. His fiction is
       not symbolic, but representative, for he could write fantasies,
       but could not create myths.

1982   "Funeral: Mr. H.G. Wells." <u>Times</u> (London), 17 Aug., p. 7.
            W was cremated at Golders Green Crematorium, where J.B.
       Priestley gave the address.

1983   GRAY, JAMES. "Four Rich Uncles." In <u>On Second Thought</u>.
       Minneapolis: University of Minnesota Press, pp. 36-58.
            W's talent as a writer has been used to reform society in
       the direction of liberalism. He lost his popular audience not
       because he was out of date, but because the popular audience
       always craves novelty.

1984   GREGORY, Sir RICHARD. "H.G. Wells: A Survey and Tribute."
       <u>Nature</u> 158 (21 Sept.):399-402.
            W's characters represent experiences of growth and the
       response of thought to those experiences. His field was always
       social biology, even in his science fiction, and he became the
       greatest teacher of science of his day.

1985   "H.G. Wells," <u>Times</u> (London), 14 Aug., p. 5.
            The world has lost an outstanding author and a vital per-
       sonality in the death of W. Much of what he wrote may have been

ephemeral, and he never found the means of redemption for humanity; but he may have kindled some fires for changes to come.

1986 "H.G. Wells." TLS, 17 Aug., p. 391. Reprinted in CH,
      p. 322-23.
         It was W who was responsible for the "popular intellectual
      climate" of the generation to follow him. His limitations are
      obvious now, and there is no question that his science fiction is
      his most original work. Popularizer and educator rather than
      original thinker, he belongs "somewhat narrowly" to his own time.

1987 "H.G. Wells Dead in London at 79; Forecast Atomic Age in 1914
      Novel." NYT, 14 Aug., pp. 1, 25.
         Prophet and profound sociologist, W sought to eliminate war
      and poverty. Differing from his contemporaries by his versatil-
      ity, he was without pose as prophet or man of letters and he
      "remained a typical Englishman of the lower middle classes."
      [Obituary.]

1988 "H.G. Wells' Last Journey into the Unknown." Christian Century
      63 (28 Aug.):1029-30.
         W was never motivated toward writing a perfect novel as a
      work of art. What was a defect (the extravagance of his fancy)
      was best suited for his real purpose of social criticism.

1989 "H.G. Wells Praised in Moscow." NYT, 18 Aug., p. 10.
         Izvestia praised W as "a contemporary English writer who
      showed the most concern over the future welfare of humanity."

1990 "H.G. Wells Urges King Abdicate; Fears Fascist Gold Tainted
      Throne." NYT, 6 July, p. 1.
         Contrary to the established practice of not attacking the
      Royal Family, W suggested in an article in the Socialist Leader
      that the fascist Sir Oswald Mosley had received money from
      Mussolini as a result of aid from the king and queen.

1991 HENKIN, LEO. "Problems and Digressions in the Victorian
      Novel." Bulletin of Bibliography 19, no. 1 (Sept.-Dec.):9; no.
      6 (May-Aug. 1948):158-59; no. 8 (Jan.-Apr. 1949):205.
         [Passing reference; annotated selections included under
      Socialism, Spiritualism and Theosophy, Science and Pseudo-science,
      and Utopia.]

1992 HORNSTEIN, GERRIG. "H.G. Wells in Petrograd." NSN 32
      (5 Oct.):247.
         [A letter to the editor commenting on a first impression of
      W and his Russia.]

1946

1993   HUXLEY, JULIAN. "H.G." Spectator 177 (16 Aug.):161.
        Like everyone else, W "had his gaps and defects." He liked
good music and pleasant paintings, but he was also convinced that
devoting all his energy to art was somehow inferior compared to
"the pursuits of knowledge or of ideas, or to the application of
ideas in practice." Both scientist and humanist, he may have done
more than any other man in the twentieth century to change "the
current of modern thought" in a "progressive direction."

1994   "Idols of the Market-Place." Canadian Forum 26 (Sept.):124-25.
        Apart from his other achievements, W was a major novelist,
in spite of the diminishing importance of his work in his last
years. Both he and Shaw reacted against the view of the artist
without social responsibility. W's range was narrower but more
intense than Shaw's, and this allowed him to see the implications
in social change.

1995   KAEMPFFERT, WALDEMAR. "Evangelist of Utopia." SR 29
        (31 Aug.):8-9.
        Verne was more practical than W in that he took the devices
described in popular scientific periodicals and used them as the
basis for thrillers, but it was W who was the more imaginative. W
had a social sense, which Verne lacked, and preached the application of the scientific method to government. He was a more specific planner in his design for world order than Marx who was only
concerned with a philosophy.

1996   _____. "Herbert George Wells: In Memoriam." NYTBR, 25 Aug.,
        p. 2.
        Much of his sociology is out of date, but W's own genera-
tion will not forget the scientific romances, social philosophy,
or the voice of progress which he represented.

1997   "Keeper of Royal Purse Amused." NYT, 6 July, p. 5.
        Sir Ulick Alexander denied W's suggestion that the Royal
Family helped Mosley or his organization.

1998   LANG, HANS J. "Die Weltanschauung H.G. Wells Urspruenge,
        Entwicklung, Kritik." Dissertation, University of Giessen,
        1946.
        [Listed in Lawrence F. McNamee, Dissertations in English
and American Literature (New York and London: Bowker, 1968).]

1999   LEWIS, SINCLAIR. "Our Friend, H.G." Trib, 20 Oct., pp. 1-2.
        Reprinted in A Sinclair Lewis Reader: The Man from Main
Street, Selected Essays and Other Writings, 1904-1950, ed.
Harry E. Maule and Melville H. Cane, assisted by Philip Allan
Friedman (New York: Random House, 1953), pp. 246-53.

More than any other man, W suggested to a generation that
education could bring about "cheerfulness, kindness, honesty,
plain decency," but it had to be education founded on imagination,
respect for known facts, and faith in the future. Tono-Bungay was
a warning of how dangerous and silly business could be, for W
understood economics as few novelists did. He was "a new and
livelier Plato."

2000   M., L. "La morte di Wells." Emporium 104 (Nov.):213-16.
       Recent scientific conquests and the horrible bestiality of
which man is capable have forced us to recall W, master of realism
and of the marvelous, who foretold both. With Love and Mr.
Lewisham W began a series of novels based on the marvelous and on
an exact perception of everyday life. He belonged to the phalanx
of writers grouped about Frank Harris and the Saturday Review,
even though he was no journalist. He teamed up with socialism and
the Fabians, as Shaw did, but with a more absolute dedication.
Giacomo Prampolini's assertion that W the sociologist and reformer
predominated over the artist is only partly true; he possessed at
the same time the perception of the realist and the imagination of
the poet.
       The conviction that reality cannot be abstracted is to be
found in all his writings. His most marvelous and fantastic tales
are first of all exact pictures of everyday life. Banal and
habitual circumstances of existence take on the role of principal
characters, the ineluctable forces of destiny. W's work is prophetic both of the future of civilization and of scientific discovery, and he foresaw world destruction such as that unchained in
Danzig in 1940. The prodigious visions of this implacable realist
spring from deepest observation; he divines the future by logical
deduction from the concrete present and projects it on the marvelous screen of his imagination. Whatever his artistic limitations,
with his death a figure of exceptional stature has passed from the
English and the world scene. Original, stimulating, never ortho-
dox, he had the courage to preach unpopular ideas and to speak to
the social conscience. Simple, direct, and clear, he pointed out
the way to salvation in a scientific era, and if man has failed to
follow it, that is no fault of W.

2001   MacCARTHY, DESMOND. "Last Words on Wells." Sunday Times
       (London) [not seen]. Reprinted in Memories (London and New
       York: Oxford University Press, 1953), pp. 137-40.
       W was a "writer of genius" obsessed by the problems of his
day. If the prophet had not been combined with the born novelist,
he would not have had such influence. He was the first author in
the scientific age to write imaginatively while saturated with
scientific ideas.

229

1946

2002   M[ARTIN], K[INGSLEY]. "H.G. Wells." <u>NSN</u> 32 (17 Aug.):115.
       The "philosophy of progress through science" reached its
end in W, who influenced his generation more deeply than any
writer in this century. "He was a man of infinite charm with whom
it was difficult for long to be annoyed."

2003   "Mr. H.G. Wells, Novelist and Thinker." <u>Times</u> (London)
       <u>Educational</u> <u>Supplement</u>, no. 1633 (17 Aug.), pp. 391.
       Whatever W's shortcomings there was a unity to his versa-
tile labor. He believed in planning for progress and in the doom
that would follow our not being ready for it.

2004   MURRY, JOHN MIDDLETON. "H.G. Wells." <u>Adelphi</u> 23
       (Oct./Dec.):1-5. Reprinted in <u>CH</u>, pp. 324-29.
       W can be seen as the embodiment of social upheaval in
England since 1906. <u>WG</u> refused to review his books because of his
treatment of the Webbs in <u>Machiavelli</u>. He contrasted an intellectual passion for a new order with an irrepressible irreverence,
and his greatness was his power to respond to the challenges of
his own times.

2005   NEWTON, DOUGLAS. "Literature and Art: The Untethered Mind of
       Wells." <u>America</u> 76 (12 Oct.):45-47.
       W's gift of vivid description and his powers as a popu-
larizer united with his ignorance of science and history to dis-
tort a whole generation by presenting a "new world order based on
false assumptions." He found his following in a generation robbed
of real faith.

2006   "Notes and Quotes; Died." <u>WLB</u> 21 (Oct.):106.
       W surpassed his contemporaries in versatility, making it
difficult to classify his work. <u>Outline</u> is his greatest
contribution.

2007   "Obituary: Mr. H.G. Wells, Novelist and Thinker." <u>Times</u>
       (London), 14 Aug., p. 7.
       Whatever his shortcomings as artist and thinker, his ver-
satility had a unifying force to it. He was novelist, fantasist,
analyst of society, amateur of science, popularizer of ideas. He
believed in the possibility of planning and shaping the progress
of mankind, and in the doom and destruction that awaited the
absence of control.

2008   "Obituary Notes." <u>PW</u> 151 (24 Aug.):824.
       Among the most prolific and versatile of English writers,
W ranks with Shaw and Kipling as a leading writer of the modern
era.

1946

2009   "Outline of Mystery." <u>Newsweek</u> 28 (15 July):45.
        In an article for the <u>New Leader</u>, W accuses the British
royal family of contributing money to Sir Oswald Mosley and suggests they "leave England free to return to her old and persistent
republican tradition." The Keeper of the Privy Purse denies the
accusation with laughter.

2010   "Passing of a Utopian." <u>NYT</u>, 14 Aug., p. 24.
        The voice of the fight for progress with a vision of sci-
ence as a servant of man, W underestimated his influence as the
"greatest public teacher of his time." [Editorial.]

2011   PRITCHETT, V.S. "The Scientific Romance." In <u>The Living
        Novel</u>. London: Chatto & Windus, pp. 116-24; New York: Reynal
        & Hitchcock, 1947, pp. 122-29. Reprinted in <u>CE</u>, pp. 32-38; and
        as "Wells and the English Novel," in "<u>The Time Machine</u>," "<u>The
        War of the Worlds</u>," ed. Frank D. McConnell, (New York: Oxford
        University Press, 1979), pp. 429-36.
        W's achievement was to install the "paraphernalia of our
new environment in our imagination." Once the artist has assimi-
lated life it becomes visible or tolerable to all of us. Ignorant
of the rooted, inner life of men and women, W foresaw the violence
of our world rather than its order.

2012   "Public Homage to H.G. Wells: Tributes of Friends." <u>Times</u>
        (London), 31 Oct., p. 6.
        [Memorial meeting, 30 Oct., sponsored by the British Asso-
ciation, the Society of Authors, P.E.N. (English Centre), and the
National Book League.]

2013   ROUTH, HAROLD VICTOR. <u>English Literature and Ideas in the
        Twentieth Century</u>. London: Methuen, pp. 16, 25-32, 45, 101,
        137.
        W made himself the prophet of the lower class, notable for
taking others' thoughts and popularizing them.

2014   S[HAW], G[EORGE] B[ERNARD]. "The Man I Knew." <u>NSN</u> 32
        (17 Aug.):115. Reprinted as "H.G. Wells Was a Man without
        Malice," <u>Scholastic</u> 49 (11 Nov.):17-18.
        No "conventional social station" fitted W, who remained
"entirely classless" and never behaved like anyone except himself.
Never having failed, he went straight up the ladder from poverty
to success. He may have raged against everyone, but no one re-
sented it because he was so amiable.

2015   "Shaw, Mosley Agree on Wells 'Nonsense.'" <u>NYT</u>, 7 July, p. 9.
        As an "anti-monarchist" W was welcomed as a contributor by
Douglas Rogers, editor of the <u>Socialist New Leader</u>. Shaw and

1946

Mosley both agree that W's charge that the Royal Family contributed to Mosley's Blackshirts was false.

2016   TINDALL, WILLIAM YORK. <u>Forces</u> <u>in</u> <u>Modern</u> <u>British</u> <u>Literature,</u>
        <u>1885-1946</u>. New York: Knopf, pp. 29, 39, 51, 54, 55, 69, 165,
        173-75, 195-96, 203, 209, 217, 221, 290, 301, 302, 325, 360.
            Although science shaped his view of humanity's precarious
        position, W's knowledge of science was superficial but greater
        than that of other literary men. In the later novels reality is
        replaced by the <u>idea</u> of reality. His religion was secular, benev-
        olent, and it focused on humanity. <u>William</u> <u>Clissold</u> is a monument
        to the fictional results of "social purpose inflamed by piety."

2017   "Topics of the Times." <u>NYT</u>, 26 Nov., p. 28.
            Unexpectedly reflecting the air of Victorian family rela-
        tionships, the wording of W's will is all the more comforting as a
        statement of the faith he had in his children.

2018   "Topics of the Times: Change Moves Slowly; Sharp but Cheer-
        ful." <u>NYT</u>, 14 July, sec. 4, p. 8.
            Shaw's calling W's statement about the Royal Family and the
        fascist movement in Britain "nonsense" is an example of the "one
        clear distinction between England's two most distinguished icono-
        clasts." W may feel deeply, while Shaw can only be irreverent.
        [Editorial.]

2019   "Topics of the Times: Fantasy Comes True." <u>NYT</u>, 13 June,
        p. 26.
            Verne is seen to have been the better prophet according to
        the older generation, but W's prophecies may yet come true.

2020   "Trotsky Data Asked of Nurenberg Tribunal; Check-Up on Moscow
        Is Sought in Nazi Files." <u>NYT</u>, 27 March, p. 12.
            W led a British group who asked the war crimes tribunal to
        use captured Nazi archives to check the 1936-38 charge that Leon
        Trotsky conspired with Hitler for the war.

2021   VAN GELDER, ROBERT. "H.G. Wells Discusses Himself and His
        Work." In <u>Writers</u> <u>and</u> <u>Writing</u>. New York: Scribner,
        pp. 127-31.
            W stopped writing short stories because he didn't have any
        more unusual, off the beaten path stories to tell. He considered
        himself primarily a journalist and not a storyteller. He revised
        his work up to seven times, and it was during the revisions that a
        work would take shape and form.

2022   "Voice of Reason." <u>Time</u> 48 (26 Aug.):28.
            W was the quintessence of the common man and may have been
        the greatest journalist since Defoe. The forces that scientific

research was loosing upon the world could "possibly liberate, and
might destroy it." To combat this, man had to accept the scientifically reasonable and reject the unreasonable. This belief was
altered in the end, and W decided either he or the human race was
wrong. [Obituary.]

2023　"Wells Left £59,811; Gifts Cut the Total." <u>NYT</u>, 23 Nov. p. 8.
　　　　W gave away most of his fortune, with all rights to <u>Outline</u>
and <u>Science</u> <u>of</u> <u>Life</u> going to his son, George, and other rights to
his son, Frank, and daughter-in-law, Marjorie, who was named as an
executor.

2024　WOODCOCK, GEORGE. "George Orwell, 19th Century Liberal."
　　　　<u>Politics</u> 3 (Dec.):384-88. Reprinted in <u>George</u> <u>Orwell:</u> <u>The</u>
　　　　<u>Critical</u> <u>Heritage</u>, ed. Jeffrey meyers (London and Boston:
　　　　Routledge & Kegan Paul, 1975), pp. 235-46.
　　　　W's influence on Orwell is clearest in <u>Animal</u> <u>Farm</u>, where
one hears echoes of Dr. Moreau's law in the rule of the farm.

2025　"The Worlds of H.G. Wells." <u>Nation</u> (New York), 163
　　　　(24 Aug.):201-2.
　　　　W outlived himself, and his last efforts were only part of
the real man. He will survive in a few of his stories, as Diderot
survives in "Rameau's Nephew." He was the last of the Victorians
in his trust in science and progress, attacking confusion because
he himself was confused.

<u>1947</u>

2026　BAILEY, J.O. <u>Pilgrims</u> <u>through</u> <u>Space</u> <u>and</u> <u>Time:</u> <u>Trends</u> <u>and</u>
　　　　<u>Patterns</u> <u>in</u> <u>Scientific</u> <u>and</u> <u>Utopian</u> <u>Fiction</u>. New York: Argus
　　　　Books, pp. 79-118; index.
　　　　The humor in W is either humor of character or irony. His
strengths are in his creation of characters (his people are real)
and his interest in the social consequences of advancing science.
There are utopian themes even in his science fiction. <u>War</u> <u>of</u> <u>the</u>
<u>Worlds</u> may be "the purest, the least sociological, as a romance of
science," but <u>Men</u> <u>in</u> <u>the</u> <u>Moon</u> is his first story to be "scientifically consistent" (with the exception of the antigravitation
device) and becomes satire on human specialization.

2027　BENTLEY, ERIC. <u>Bernard</u> <u>Shaw</u>. Norfolk, Conn.: New Directions,
　　　　pp. xiv, xvi, 2, 11, 20, 71, 190, 191, 194, 204, 212-13, 214.
　　　　W's observation of the passiveness of Fabians did not apply
to Shaw, who was also more realistic than W. W was gifted as a
storyteller, but disliked the novel as a medium.

1947

2028   CANTRIL, HADLEY. The Invasion from Mars: A Study in the
       Psychology of Panic. Princeton: University Press, pp. 3, 89,
       164.
           [A study of listener reaction to the 30 October 1938 broad-
       cast of War of the Worlds on Mercury Theatre based on detailed
       interviews with 135 people, most of whom had been upset by the
       play. Text of radio play. Passing references to W. Of 6,000,000
       who heard the broadcast, 1,200,000 took it literally.]

2029   COATES, J.B. Leaders of Modern Thought. London: Longmans,
       pp. 40-51.
           His early novels, both social and scientific, will make W
       immortal. His prospect of the future is filled with both hope and
       despair, but at the heart his teaching is sound.

2030   DUPEE, F.W. Introduction to The Question of Henry James: A
       Collection of Critical Essays. London: Allan Wingate, pp.
       vii-xiv.
           W's epigram about James's style reflected the attitude of a
       generation of British and American realists.

2031   "H.G. Wells, the Seer and the Artist." TLS, 19 July,
       pp. 357-59.
           As realistic as W was in many things, he was undecided
       about the means by which mankind should be saved. He seemed the
       victim of his whims; his importance is not as politician, sociolo-
       gist, or prophet, but as artist.

2032   HOUGH, GRAHAM. "Books in General." NSN 34 (19 July):53.
           W was not in fact a modernist but was firmly rooted in the
       past, especially in his stress on the conflict between social
       order and human passion.

2033   JONES, W.S. HANDLEY. "The World of H.G. Wells." London
       Quarterly and Holborn Review 172 (Jan.):26-34.
           W was considered by his own countrymen to be the "most
       lucid spokesman" of the contemporary world because he was "so
       thoroughly English in his outlook." He wrote of things he knew
       and used a protagonist who was really himself: "a bristly haired,
       irritable, humorous, restive product of London University or the
       South Kensington Colleges, a tentative socialist, a free-lance
       scientist; and he scampers round the universe like a miraculously
       intelligent terrier, pushing an inquisitive and irreverent nose
       into everything." W failed in his goal because he forgot that "a
       good world can only be built on moral foundations."

2034   MEYNELL, VIOLA, ed. Letters of J.M. Barrie. New York:
       Charles Scribner's, pp. 39-41, 65, 93, 223, 292.

1948

Barrie wanted to turn War of the Worlds into a play, but W refused.

2035   "Plumber Disputes Churchill's Son in Denver When Called to Fix
        Faulty Stopper in Bath." NYT, 3 Feb., p. 9.
            [American plumber, in dispute with Randolph Churchill,
        names W as the only intelligent Englishman.]

2036   "Sale of Mr. H.G. Wells's House." Times (London), 13 March,
        p. 7.
            W's Regent Park residence sold 12 March for 7,000 pounds.

2037   SALTER, Sir JAMES ARTHUR. "H.G. Wells, Apostle of a World
        Society." In Personality in Politics: Studies of Contemporary
        Statesmen. London: Faber, pp. 120-37.
            W was convinced the whole scope and character of government
        as well as the organization of society had to be changed to corre-
        spond to the human activities they controlled.

                                1948

2038   ALLEN, WALTER. Arnold Bennett. London: Home & Van Thal, pp.
        9-11, 16, 19-20, 22, 24-25, 31, 40-41, 49-51, 60, 71, 89, 102.
            Bennett's origins were not really the same as W's. W was
        of the servant class, while Bennett kept servants. W's account in
        Experiment is the best analysis of Bennett's dealings with women.
        W shared with Moore the responsibility of showing Bennett his
        subject matter. His Uncle Mesach is a "character" unlike those
        portrayed with such a delight in eccentricity by W.

2039   BIANCOLLI, LOUIS LEOPOLD, ed. Book of Great Conversations.
        New York: Simon & Schuster, pp. 551-66.
            W had found Lenin flexible, but Stalin took a fixed stand
        on Marxism. In their conversation in 1934, Stalin prolonged the
        interview out of a keen interest in W. (Text of interview
        follows.)

2040   CHURCH, RICHARD. British Authors. New ed. London: Longmans,
        pp. 45-48.
            W spoke for the technician and shopkeeper, but denounced
        those who thought the novel was only a means of relaxation.

2041   HEARD, GERALD. "H.G. Wells, the End of a Faith." SR 31
        (13 March):9-10, 31.
            W's end marked the end of utopianism, the faith of the
        modern era. His whole life was a struggle to be contemporary.
        "He chose to be right at once instead of right at the end, to be
        the illustrator rather than the creator." Like Kipling, he found

                                235

1948

the means and not the end as his goal, and he "advocated efficiency as a substitute for meaning."

2042   KOHLER, DAYTON. "Time in the Modern Novel." College English
       10 (Oct.):15-24.
          In fiction time is used as history, as method, as fantasy,
       as memory and myth, and as symbol. In Time Machine W employed a
       scientific background for his fantasy and managed time only as a
       concept to be measured in definite and predictable terms.

2043   NEVINS, ALLAN. "Travelers of the Fourth Period, 1870-1922."
       In America through British Eyes. New York: Oxford University
       Press, pp. 305-41.
          W's visit to America in 1906 was as a socialist with an
       interest only in the America of the future. He saw vigor and
       growth as "the fundamental attribute of the nation." Private
       wealth and reckless spending both amused and disgusted him. The
       chaos of American life, along with its lawlessness and disorder
       outraged him.

2044   NICOLSON, MARJORIE HOPE. Voyages to the Moon. New York:
       Macmillan, pp. ix, 3, 4, 5, 9, 47, 179, 237, 247-50.
          Fanciful accounts of lunar voyages, like Francis Godwin's
       Man in the Moone (1638) may have influenced W. His critique
       against science was really against those who pursue it narrowly
       for the wrong ends.

2045   Observer (London). Observer Profiles. London: Wingate,
       pp. 151-53.
          W was essentially the practical prophet, as a reading of
       Anticipations will indicate. As a socialist he preached coopera-
       tion more than he practiced it. His appeal to reason was flavored
       with a zest for the liberal, the salt of wit, and a peppery anger
       "against muddle and misrule."

2046   SCHORER, MARK. "Technique as Discovery." Hudson Review, 1
       (Spring):67-87. Reprinted in Mark Schorer, The World We
       Imagine: Selected Essays (New York: Farrar, Straus, & Giroux,
       1968), pp. 3-23.
          By his technique a writer discovers, explores, and develops
       his subject. W had no respect for technique, and his fiction
       suffers for it. Tono-Bungay has "the framework of Wells's ab-
       stract thinking, not of his craftsmanship," and the novel fails to
       meet the primary demands of the reader.

2047   SPENCER, SIDNEY. "H.G. Wells, Materialist and Mystic."
       Hibbert Journal 46 (July):358-61.
          W reflects the "intellectual gropings and perplexities of
       our age." He has a tendency to view the world as "the fundamental

reality" and still look beyond to "a greater Reality" revealed in consciousness. During his brush with religion, he saw God as finite and based on man; his faith did not go deep enough, and his utopia was not eternal.

2048   WEBB, BEATRICE. Our Partnership. Edited by Barbara Drake and Margaret I Cole. New York and London: Longmans, Green, pp. 33, 175, 226, 230-31, 289-90, 292, 305, 307-8, 311, 359-60, 366, 448-49.
         Like the Webbs, W thought administration should fit services. Anticipations was remarkable, the weak part being W's lack of knowledge of social organizations. His personality was unattractive, but he had an agreeable disposition and was a good "instrument for popularising ideas." He supplied the Webbs with "loose generalisations" as research instruments in exchange for "carefully sifted facts and broad administrative experience." He disliked the idea of collective provision of religious training or adult behavior.

1949

2049   BLACKSTONE, BERNARD. Virginia Woolf: A Commentary. New York: Harcourt, Brace, pp. 15, 17, 56, 186, 244.
         W, Bennett, and Galsworthy represent the settled traditions in literature. Woolf's criticism was not that women writers could do things men could not, but that the men were not doing what they ought to be doing--"penetrating by force of intellect into the nature of reality."

2050   "Education Notes: Bard--H.G. Wells Collection." NYT, 9 Jan., p. 9.
         Five hundred first editions of W's works as well as critical material are donated by Theodore Steinway, president of Steinway and Sons, to Bard College, Annandale-on-Hudson, N.Y.

2051   GEHMAN, RICHARD B. "Imagination Runs Wild." NR 120 (17 Jan.):16-18.
         W gave utopian fiction currency. Of all the writers of science fiction of his day, he had the best scientific training.

2052   GOLDRING, DOUGLAS. Trained for Genius: The Life and Writings of Ford Madox Ford. New York: Dutton, pp. viii, 83, 86, 87, 89, 90, 96, 131, 137, 139, 144, 163, 170, 172, 180-82, 201, 243.
         W linked Conrad and Ford as proponents of the importance of technique in writing, but felt that Conrad's idiom benefitted from their collaboration. W was among the few who saw Ford as a good but unappreciated poet. He was outraged by the attacks on The

1949

Good Soldier in the New Witness. It is uncertain whether Conrad
and W ever shared Ford's illusions over the commercial possibilities of the ER.

2053   HARDT, MARIA-AGNELIES. "Die Anthropologie H.G. Wells,
        Darstellung und Kritik Seines Utopischen Menschenbildes."
        Dissertation, University of Bonn.
            [Listed in Lawrence F. McNamee, Dissertations in English
        and American Literature (New York and London: Bowker, 1968).]

2054   HOLCOMB, CLAIRE. "The S-F Phenomenon in Literature." SR 32
        (28 May):9-10, 36-37.
            Atomic energy has been a favorite theme of science fiction
        since W's World Set Free forecast destruction of cities by atom
        bombs. At first he believed humanity would win the race for life
        against technology, but later wondered what a world of "human
        being gone sane" might be like.

2055   INNES, MICHAEL [pseud. of J.I.M. Stewart]. "Radio Notes." NSN
        38 (31 Dec.):779.
            W dismisses Gissing in Experiment as not being able to
        "look life squarely in the eyes." W was always able to face up to
        the world, according to Kingsley Martin's radio broadcast, "New
        Judgment." To a whole generation W was a beacon, and this broad-
        cast gave hope that future generations would continue to find
        delight in him.

2056   IRVINE, WILLIAM. The Universe of G.B.S. New York: Whittlesey
        House, pp. 61, 63, 109, 222, 265-69, 283, 329, 334.
            W thought the Fabians so concerned with small cities that
        they did not realize the need for large administrative units. He
        expected his ideas to be accepted immediately and was furious when
        it did not happen. The effect he had demonstrates how conserva-
        tive the Fabian Society really was.

2057   "Piccadilly Theatre." Times London), 21 May, p. 7.
            The dramatic version of Ann Veronica, by Ronald Gow, is
        given a light farcical treatment and sentimental ending despite
        indications that the theme is serious. Wendy Hiller plays Ann,
        but she is unable to give a characterization to a figure who has
        none.

2058   REICHARD, J. DAVIS. "Letters to the Editor: Kipling and H.G.
        Wells." SR 32 (18 June):22.
            A striking similarity exists between Kipling's "Aerial
        Board of Control" in "With the Night Mail" and W's "Air Dictator-
        ship" in Shape of Things, the basic difference being that Kipling
        was concerned with invasion of privacy and W was not.

2059   Swinnerton, Frank A. "H.G. Wells." In Tokefield Papers, Old
       and New. Garden City, N.Y.: Doubleday, pp. 121-23.
            W did not like adverse criticism but would accept candor
       from people he liked. He could have done more for literature, but
       he chose instead to be a teacher.

2060   WELLES, ORSON. "Can a Martian Help It If He's Colored Green?"
       In Invasion from Mars: Interplanetary Stories, selected by
       Orson Welles. New York: Dell, pp. 5-7.
            The people who fled to escape the Martians during the
       broadcast of War of the Worlds may have recovered, but Orson
       Welles became an addict of science fiction. While Verne was the
       genre's first well-known writer, W was "probably its most effec-
       tive one." [Book includes radio script of 1938 adaptation.]

2061   WEST, ANTHONY. "Did You Hear That? The Versatility of H.G.
       Wells." Listener 42 (8 Sept.):391.
            In a cartoon, David Low shows an important point about W:
       "Wells was a great many things, but not a great many things at the
       same time." W's various projects were not carried out simul-
       taneously, and past work was not allowed to obscure a current
       project. Friends and critics often missed the over-all point of a
       W novel by concentrating on details.

2062   WINSTEN, STEPHEN. Days with Bernard Shaw. New York: Vanguard
       Press, pp. 19, 24, 33, 35, 77, 98, 102, 148, 166, 174, 176,
       248, 249, 255, 289, 299.
            Shaw joked that Sidney Webb wrote his plays and W his
       prefaces. He had a habit of rushing to conclusions and leaving W
       to supply the evidence. Attacking him was "the special preroga-
       tive" of W, who was appointed dramatic critic because he'd never
       been in a theater. The two agreed about nothing--W taught every-
       thing and learned nothing.

1950

2063   EARLE, EDWARD MEADE. "H.G. Wells, British Patriot in Search of
       a World State." World Politics 2 (Jan.):181-208. Reprinted
       and expanded in Nationalism and Internationalism: Essays In-
       scribed to Carlton J.H. Hayes, ed. Edward Meade Earle (New
       York: Columbia University Press, 1950), pp. 79-121.
            With a faith in scientific method, W believed that reason
       and order were the guiding principles in building a better world.
       He disliked nationalism because of its disruptive and separatist
       tendencies, and he considered it a basic cause of war. In spite
       of this, he was a fervent patriot, and his patriotism can be
       measured in terms of his attitudes toward the German people. He
       stopped supporting the League of Nations because it was not moving

1950

fast enough in the direction he thought it should. Two world wars
only confirmed his opinions that a world state was necessary and
inevitable. His approach to world problems was that of the tech-
nician, not the politician.

2064   FLOWER, Sir NEWMAN. <u>Just as it Happened</u>. New York: Morrow,
       pp. 169-75.
              An untidy writer, W had his wife type his manuscript of
       "The Man Who Could Work Miracles," which the editor at
       Harmsworth's accidentally threw in the wastebasket and which
       Flower rescued. The second part of the title of <u>Mr. Britling</u> was
       supposed to be altered when W realized the war was not going to be
       over by the end of 1915, but he forgot to do it. [Anecdotes
       dealing with W's sense of humor.]

2065   FUSSELL, PAUL. "Iron Curtain." <u>American Speech</u> 25 (April):40.
              W was the first to use the term "iron curtain" in <u>Food of
       the Gods</u>. But in this novel it meant "an enforced breach of
       intercourse with society," thereby being of significance for an
       individual and not for a nation.

2066   KRUTCH, JOSEPH WOOD. "Two Prophets: Wells and Shaw." <u>Nation</u>
       (New York) 171 (16 Dec.):648, 650-51.
              Shaw was more than a teacher, whereas W never more than
       one. To judge either author requires the assessment of the aims,
       ideals, thinking of a half-century.

2067   MIZENER, ARTHUR. "The Novel of Manners in America." <u>Kenyon
       Review</u> 12:1-19.
              Young writers during World War I thought W had solved the
       problem of whether reality in fiction was best represented by
       political theory or by the "passionate, sensitive inner life." He
       managed to make the political novel personal and a sort of "pica-
       resque novel of ideas," but he was not concerned with the inner
       experience.

2068   NICHOLSON, NORMAN. <u>H.G. Wells</u>. Denver: Alan Swallow.
              W's fantasy has a solid base in actuality, and all of his
       greater works of the imagination begin with fact. In his scien-
       tific romances he uses the theme of disaster when science is
       divorced from humanity and wisdom. His comedies deal with changes
       in society and the type of man needed to bring about change. He
       was not a conscious artist and had no style, for his sentences are
       not "a pleasure in themselves."

2069   PEARSON, HESKETH. <u>G.B.S.: A Postscript</u>. New York: Harper &
       Bros., pp. 48, 89-90, 111-13.

Part of the reason for the Fabian debate was the vendetta between Hubert Bland and W after the Webbs warned him to keep daughters out of W's way.

2070   RUSSELL, BERTRAND. "George Orwell." World Review, n.s. 16 (June):5-7. Reprinted in George Orwell: The Critical Heritage, ed. Jeffrey Meyers (London and Boston: Routledge & Kegan Paul, 1975), pp. 299-301.
          Elderly radicals like W find the transition to a world of "stark power" difficult.

2071   RUSSELL, I. WILLIS. "Among the New Words." American Speech 25 (Oct.):224-26.
          While W may have used the term "iron curtain" in 1904, Churchill was not the next to use the phrase. George Crile's A Mechanistic View of War and Peace (1915) refers to an iron curtain on the frontier of France. [Russell speculates on the conditions under which a figure of speech becomes a dictionary term.]

2072   VALLENTIN, ANTONINA. H.G. Wells, Prophet of Our Day. New York: John Day.
          W's basic characteristic was optimism. Knowing little of human nature, he drew on what he had learned of science. Physical or biological possibilities were the springboard for his imagination. He was so sensitive to the changes of his time, and yet so far ahead of his time, that he is the sum of its content. "The contrast between his intense, acute enjoyment of life, which seemed to bubble up from the very fount of security, and his secret anxieties, lasted until the end of his days." [The criticism of this book as "a collection of book reviews" has been erroneously used as a description of its format in some sources.]

2073   WEST, ANTHONY. "Gissing and Wells." NSN 39 (14 Jan.):37-38.
          Gissing and W were better friends than the account rendered by Michael Innes (NSN, 31 Dec. 1949) would suggest. "Mr. Innes adroitly harshens Wells' final judgment on his friend by omitting its key phrase, the first part of the following sentence: 'He spent his big fine brain depreciating life, because he would not and perhaps could not look life squarely in the eyes.'" [Innes replies with a further portion of the same passage in Experiment and comments on how quickly W was to depreciate Gissing in spite of their friendship.]

1951

2074   BERNERI, MARIE LOUISE. "Modern Utopias." Journey Through Utopia. Boston: Beacon Press, pp. 293-317.

1951

<u>Utopia</u> is indebted to past utopian ideas and depends on the "assumption that laws are the best guardians of freedom," but his concept of freedom is narrow. In <u>Men Like Gods</u> he describes another sort of utopia without going into the practical aspects.

2075   BROME, VINCENT. <u>H.G. Wells: A Biography</u>. London: Longmans, Green.

W has never been surpassed as a writer of scientific romances. His important creative fiction stops at 1920, when the worldmaker replaces the man of literature. The rest of his life was spent in slaying paper dragons. The stresses between his three selves (scientist, artist, reformer) were enormous and account for the unevenness of his output. In years to come he may be seen to have prepared us for "the creative society."

2076   COSTA, RICHARD H. "H.G. Wells: Literary Journalist." <u>Journalism Quarterly</u> 28:63-68.

After 1910, W's novels show more structural evidence of his interest in journalism by exhibiting such standard devices as reporting and interviewing. Ideas and theories replace memorable characters, and the reader seems to be reading a daily newspaper instead of a novel. Aldous Huxley, Upton Sinclair, and John Hersey are other writers who worked in this genre.

2077   DAWSON, CHRISTOPHER. "Historians Reconsidered: IV. H.G. Wells and the <u>Outline of History</u>." <u>History Today</u> 1 (Oct.):29-32.

Not as superficial as critics claim, W's view of history does put details secondary to the "broad sweep of his historical vision." He overlooks actual achievement while criticizing mankind's failure to take advantage of opportunity to succeed. The treatment of recent history lacks depth because the journalist in him replaced the prophet and sociologist.

2078   HACKETT, FRANCIS. "Books and Men: Shaw--and Wells." <u>AM</u> 187 (May):73-76.

At the P.E.N. dinner celebrating W's seventieth birthday Shaw's tribute was to W as "a son, and as a brother, and as a father." Everyone laughed except W, who did not have the immunity to be able to laugh at himself.

2079   ISAACS, JACOB. <u>An Assessment of Twentieth Century Literature</u>. London: Secker & Warburg, pp. 21-24.

While W's influence on fiction in theme and form is extensive, <u>Experiment</u> may be the most important book of the twentieth century because it is "a parable of modern civilization."

2080   MEGROZ, R[ODOLPHE] L[OUIS]. "The Sacred Lunatic." In <u>Thirty-One Bedside Essays</u>. Hadleigh, Essex: Tower Bridge Publications, pp. 1-4.

1951

All his life, W "pitted his ideas of a civilised order against the disorder of our times." His final pessimism in Tether is best understood if one realizes he was a "visionary pessimist" even in Time Machine. While Bealby marks the division between the fantastic novels and those of contemporary life it is in Mr. Britling that the reader sees W in perspective. The novelist could not be completely obliterated by the social teacher and Mr. Blettsworthy "indirectly reveals the pressure of the contemporary world's insanities" on his mind.

2081   PATCH, BLANCHE. Thirty Years with G.B.S. New York: Dodd, Mead, pp. 18, 22, 25, 30, 31, 35, 104, 123, 128.
        [Passing reference.]

2082   PRITCHETT, V.S. "Books in General." NSN 91 (24 Feb.):220-21
        Behind the figure W presented to the world was a "wonderfully unpresentable collection of selves." He attained a sort of greatness in popular education but was a bad scientist. His failure as a novelist after Machiavelli may be attributed to "serious defects of character," especially the desire for power, money, and a too quickly inflated ego. Between teaching and creating he took the easy path. [Review of Vincent Brome's H.G. Wells: A Biography, which is "bright, slipshod, secondhand, and ingenuous . . . a hurried and sometimes atrociously written book, the work of an enthusiast who has jumped in too quick."]

2083   SCOTT-JAMES, ROLFE ARNOLD. "Ego and Kosmos." In Fifty Years of English Literature, 1900-1950. London: Longmans, pp. 22-33.
        W saw himself not merely as a representative Englishman, but a citizen of the world. He began with an instinctive perception that gave him the material for a wider vision. For him to see man as a part of a larger unit was an imaginative rather than intellectual feat. His function was to give "a picture of the consciousness of the changing England of his time." In science fiction he was interested in the social implications of the problems of science. His views were so thorougly absorbed they became truisms and platitudes.

2084   STEINBERG, MOSES W. "Formative Influence on the Thought of H.G. Wells." Dissertation, University of Toronto.
        [Listed in Lawrence F. McNamee, Dissertations in English and American Literature, supp. 1 (New York and London: Bowker, 1969).]

2085   TROUBRIDGE, ST. VINCENT. "Reviews and Letters: Iron Curtain." American Speech 26 (Feb.):49-50.
        "Iron Curtain" may have been coined by W in 1904, but its modern application first saw print in the London Sunday Empire

1951

News in "An Iron Curtain Across Europe," by St. Vincent
Troubridge, on 21 October 1945, an article on the difficulties of
military government.

1952

2086   BLACKSTONE, BERNARD. Virginia Woolf. Writers and Their Work.
        London and New York: Longmans, Green, p. 22.
           Politicians and theorists submerge the artist inside a
        frame within which life must be lived. For writers like W and
        Huxley, the frame is all that is remembered.

2087   CHANDLER, G. "The Literary Expression in H.G. Wells's Chief
        Novels of His Interest in Social Problems and Social Change,
        Excluding the Short Stories, the Scientific Romances, and the
        Fantasies." Dissertation, University of London.
           [Listed in Lawrence F. McNamee, Dissertations in English
        and American Literature (New York and London: Bowker, 1968).]

2088   CLARK, WILLIAM ROSS. "The Literary Aspects of Fabian Social-
        ism." Dissertation, Columbia University.
           [Listed in Dissertation Abstracts 12 (1952):615-16.]

2089   GORDON, J.D. "The Ghost at Brede Place." New York Public
        Library Bulletin 56:591-95.
           W was among those who collaborated on the play, The Ghost,
        performed in the schoolroom at Brede Village at Christmas 1899.

2090   GREEN, ROGER LANCELYN. A.E.W. Mason. London: Max Parrish,
        pp. 61, 80-82, 136.
           A ghost story told by Stephen Crane at a party at Brede
        Place was the source of a play (since lost), the collaborative
        effort of Henry James, Robert Barr, Rider Haggard, George Gissing,
        Conrad, H.B. Marriott-Watson, W, Edwin Pugh, Mason, and Crane.
        Mason only recalled that each wrote anything he liked and no one
        knew his part.

2091   LIBBEY, F.E. "Mr. Wells and Vernon Lee." Colby Library
        Quarterly 3 (Nov.):129-33.
           The files of Vernon Lee's correspondence indicate a more
        than casual acquaintance between W and Violet Paget. They ex-
        changed letters and books before World War I, when they disagreed
        over America's role in the war.

2092   MORTON, A[RTHUR] L[ESLIE]. The English Utopia. London:
        Lawrence & Wishart, pp. 129, 160, 182-95, 197-98, 201, 203,
        204.

1952

    W found it necessary to write of so many utopias because he
could not convince himself with any of them. His life was filled
with second thoughts. Socialism was only a means to achieve
utopia--and it would not be done through the working class. He
spent his life in a vain attempt to concoct a rival theory to
Marxism.

2093   NEGLEY, GLENN, and J. MAX PATRICK. The Quest for Utopia. New
        York: Abelard-Shuman, pp. 226-28.
            The utopian theme dominates much of the work of W, probably
        the "most aggressively progressive of all utopists." Centraliza-
        tion is "the keynote of efficiency for the future society," yet he
        does not expect any success until the aftermath of a world war has
        forced mankind to choose the scientific alternative to barbarism.

2094   PENZOLDT, PETER. The Supernatural in Fiction. London: Peter
        Nevill, pp. 50-53.
            Even if W did not "invent" science fiction, he made it
        popular in English. Poe's influence on W was as great as it was
        on Conan Doyle, but W outdid his mentor in quantity, if not in
        quality. He also created the prototype of the scientific ghost
        story in "The Inexperienced Ghost."

2095   POUND, REGINALD. Arnold Bennett: A Biography. London:
        Heinemann, pp. 2, 3, 5, 8, 16; index.
            W's personality may not have been "publicly attractive,"
        but in private circles he could be charming. Bennett, who under-
        took with W an abortive collaboration effort to write a detective
        play to be called "The Crime," was disturbed by the carelessness
        of his friend's writing. His ear for words did not warn him when
        he used "by us" and "bias" in the opening sentence of Tono-Bungay.
        Even though he received £3,000 for War in the Air, W could be
        discontented about money. He objected to literary agents, but got
        on well with Pinker. [Many passing references and incidental
        comments.]

2096   QUENNELL, PETER. "H.G. Wells." In The Singular Preference:
        Portraits and Essays. (London: Collins, 1952; New York:
        Viking, 1953), pp. 167-81.
            Tributes to W on his death were unsuccessful in supplying a
        balanced picture. He never conformed to the conventional pattern
        of the revolutionary socialist. He helped to build a new world on
        the ruins of the old and to open up new prospects for order and
        progress, but he died with the universe on the verge of collapse.

2097   SWAN, MICHAEL. Henry James. London: Arthur Barker,
        pp. 37-38.

1952

      James admired W's work but thought it was too formless.
When James was not sufficiently respectful of the younger novelists, W parodied him in <u>Boon</u>.

2098   SWINNERTON, FRANK. <u>The Bookman's London</u>. Garden City, N.Y.:
        Doubleday, pp. 9, 30, 38, 48, 52, 54, 59, 134, 136, 150.
      W had the proper touch of "impudent humour" which kept
breaking into his attempts to be a philosopher. He enjoyed the
stimulation of company, but preferred that it be in his own home.

2099   WARD, MAISIE. <u>Return to Chesterton</u>. New York: Sheed & Ward,
        pp. 55-60, 289-90.
      W agreed with the editors of the <u>New Age</u> on the benefit of
a socialist state, but their "dream of <u>bliss</u>" was a nightmare to
Chesterton and Belloc. W and Shaw had a bleak view of humanity
not shared by Belloc and Chesterton.

2100   WEEKS, ROBERT P. "H.G. Wells as a Sociological Novelist."
        Dissertation, University of Michigan.
      [Listed in <u>Dissertation Abstracts</u> 12:314.]

1953

2101   BELGION, MONTGOMERY. <u>H.G. Wells</u>. London and New York:
        Longman's Green.
      W is a complex blend of three figures: "Giant Wells," the
prolific writer and celebrity; "Baby Wells," the social reformer
with the outlook of an infant; and "Wells the sage" and author of
science fiction and social comedy. It is in the early novels that
we may find the answer to the question of how the modern world
came about.

2102   BENNETT, JOANN WAITE. "John Galsworthy and H.G. Wells." <u>Yale</u>
        <u>University Library Gazette</u> 28 (July):33-43.
      [First editions, inscribed copies, periodicals and manu-
scripts of the works of Galsworthy and W were acquired by Yale in
1953. Biographical sketch with notes on the scope of the
collection.]

2103   BRASE, GEORG. "Die Stellung der Realistischen Romane im
        Gesamtwerk von H.G. Wells. Im Lichte Seines Sozialist.
        Gedankengutes und Unter Bes Beruecks. Einiger Typ. Werke a.
        Mittleren Periode, 1905-1928." Dissertation, Marburg
        University.
      [Listed in Lawrence F. McNamee, <u>Dissertations in English</u>
<u>and American Literature</u> (New York and London: Bowker, 1968).]

2104   "Film Adaptation of H.G. Wells Story." Times (London),
        2 April, p. 2.
            George Pal's film of War of the Worlds departs from the
        original and so a potentially great film becomes a flawed work.
        The cast is defeated by the dialogue, but the special effects are
        the stars of the film.

2105   HAYNES, RENEE. Hilaire Belloc. London and New York:
        Longmans, Green, p. 5.
            Belloc, Shaw, Chesterton, and W were united in reacting
        against the complacency of their time: Belloc through satire,
        Shaw by reason, Chesterton through Christian paradox, and W by
        "angry, comic, compassionate fiction."

2106   HOPKINSON, TOM. George Orwell. London and New York:
        Longmans, Green, p. 9.
            Orwell viewed the future as an extension of the present and
        considered W's mistaken view of Hitler and the outcome of the war
        to be a result of his mind being rooted in the past.

2107   KETTLE, ARNOLD. An Introduction to the English Novel. Vol. 2.
        London: Hutchinson University Library, pp. 82-83, 89-95.
            Virginia Woolf objected to the novels of W, Bennett, and
        Galsworthy because they allowed life to escape their work. Slip-
        shod in construction, Tono-Bungay lacks pattern and fails as an
        adequate expression of W's own vision of life. W allows his
        opinions to intrude between the reader and the work, thus destroy-
        ing his effect.

2108   KRUTCH, JOSEPH WOOD. "The Loss of Confidence." American
        Scholar 12:141-53. Revised in The Measure of Man
        (Indianapolis: Bobbs-Merrill, 1954), pp. 18-22.
            Shaw and W truly represent "the temper of their age," but
        W's prosaic and literal mind and style make him a better illustra-
        tion of the transformation of twentieth-century optimism to
        despair.

2109   MAUGHAM, [W.] SOMERSET. "H.G. Wells." In The Vagrant Mood.
        London: Heinemann, 1952, pp. 209-19; New York: Doubleday,
        1953), pp. 218-28. Reprinted as "Remembrances of H.G. Wells,"
        SR 36 (11 April 1953):17-19, 68.
            W was "sharp-witted and, though apt to find persons who
        didn't agree with him stupid and so objects of ridicule, the humor
        he exercised at their expense was devoid of malice." Self-
        centered, he never idealized the women toward whom he was
        attracted and could not understand that they might really feel
        passion for him and be hurt when the relationship was broken off.
        Devoid of conceit, he treated people as equals and had no illu-
        sions about himself as an artist or author. He was unnecessarily

1953

verbose in his writing, but his theory of the short story was sensible. "It enabled him to write a number that were very good and several that were masterly." It was his theory of the novel-ist as teacher that made him digress in that form and his charac-ters' only function was to express his ideas.

2110   RUSSELL, BERTRAND. "Portraits from Memory--IV: H.G. Wells: Liberator of Thought." Listener 50 (10 Sept.):417-18. Reprinted as "H.G. Wells," in Portraits from Memory, and Other Essays (New York: Simon & Schuster), pp. 81-85.
        Russell shared a "political sympathy" with W over the anticipated war with Germany, although they differed on many issues. W was important as a "liberator of thought and imagination."

2111   SWAN, MICHAEL. "Henry James and H.G. Wells, a Study of Their Friendship Based on Their Unpublished Correspondence." Cornhill Magazine, Autumn, pp. 43-65. Reprinted in A Small Part of Time: Essays on Literature, Art, and Travel (London: Jonathan Cape, 1957), pp. 173-204.
        The friendship of W and James, which ended with the attack on James in Boon, can be traced through letters in the Houghton Library at Harvard.

2112   "Thoughts and Second Thoughts: 'Tono-Bungay': 1909. The World of Wells and Bennett." TLS, 28 Aug., pp. xxv-xxvi.
        At mid-century it is the early W that can still be read with pleasure while the later works are only of historic value. The same can be said of Bennett. The society that produced them has largely been destroyed, and W helped in that destruction. [Reprints TLS review of 11 Feb. 1909.]

2113   WALSH, J.H. "Set Books: IV: The History of Mr. Polly." Use of English 5, no. 2:82-86.
        Protesting against the commercialism, meanness, and love-lessness of his life, Mr. Polly avoids the ugliness by running away until confronted by it in the person of Uncle Jim at which time he makes an effort to face up to it.

2114   "A Wells Fantasy to be Filmed." Times (London), 10 Feb., p. 2.
        The proposed film of War of the Worlds, produced by George Pal, is unlikely to have the same effect as Orson Welles's radio version.

2115   WILSON, HAROLD. "Notes and Discussions: The Frustration of H.G. Wells." London Quarterly and Holborn Review 178 (Jan.):60-64.
        W was a frustrated individual in many ways. Ineffective in politics, his literary work shows the conflict of science,

propaganda, and art, while his "vain quest of Ideal Love" was
perhaps an even more vital frustration, as vital as his disappointment in not being able to create a World Federation. [Refers
to Vincent Brome's biography of W.]

1954

2116 ASQUITH, CYNTHIA. Portrait of Barrie. London: James Barrie,
      pp. 16, 75, 181-82, 215.
         Barrie found W entertaining in person, while W claimed he
learned about journalism by reading When a Man's Single.

2117 BROOKE, JOCELYN. Aldous Huxley. London and New York:
      Longmans Green, pp. 5, 22.
         Like W, Huxley was a scientific popularizer, prophet, revo-
lutionary, and a major influence on his younger contemporaries.
The difference between Men Like Gods and Brave New World is point
of view. For Huxley the utopia of W is dehumanized.

2118 BROPHY, LIAM. "Grave New Worlds." Catholic World 179
      (April):40-43.
         The aim of early utopian fiction was the portrayal of a
world of harmony. Its successor, science fiction, concerns itself
with destruction. W was the first to link science fiction with
social improvement.

2119 "Disposal of MSS by H.G. Wells." Times (London), 26 Jan.,
      p. 8.
         W's library, including manuscripts, letters, corrected
proofs and 1,000 copies of his books were sold to the University
of Illinois to provide material for Professor Gordon N. Ray to
write a biography.

2120 DONNELLY, MABEL COLLINS. George Gissing, Grave Comedian.
      Cambridge, Mass.: Harvard University Press, pp. 15, 143, 193,
      198-99, 214.
         W discerned the influence of Gissing's father on Gissing,
who came to find W's "blend of mysticism and science" irritating.

2121 HAFLEY, JAMES. The Glass Roof: Virginia Woolf as Novelist.
      Berkeley: University of California Press, pp. 8-9, 36.
         Woolf condemned W for falsifying life, but the division of
writers into Edwardian and Georgian is itself false.

2122 MOSKOWITZ, SAM. The Immortal Storm: A History of Science
      Fiction Fandom. Atlanta: Atlanta Science Fiction Organization
      Press, pp. 2, 3, 55, 75, 99, 195.

1954

[Passing references. W suggested as president of the Science Fiction Association in 1937.]

2123   NETHERCOT, ARTHUR H. Men and Supermen: The Shavian Portrait Gallery. Cambridge, Mass.: Harvard University Press, pp. 36, 111, 131, 279.
Reading W convinces Clara Hill to become a New Woman, while Henry Straker in Man and Superman is a version of W's future for man.

2124   S[MITH], H[ARRISON]. "Utopian Nightmare." SR 37 (21 Aug.):22.
W's prophecies of postwar concern over leisure time in World Set Free are coming true in 1954.

2125   WEEKS, ROBERT P. "Disentanglement as a Theme in H.G. Wells's Fiction." Michigan Academy of Science, Arts, and Letters 39:439-44. Reprinted in CE, pp. 25-31.
W's heroes are caught in a network of limitations from which they must disentangle themselves. The typical hero in W has a free will and a desire for freedom. The special world W created influenced our attitude toward the real world, but when he turned from depicting the real world to arguing about it, his novels lost their significance.

2126   WELLS, FRANK. Introduction to Love and Mr. Lewisham. London: Collins, pp. 11-16.
The theme of the novel is "domestic claustrophobia" and Mr. Lewisham's fear of it, a theme to recur in many of W's later works. It is in Utopia that the author comes closest to a possible cure for the phobia.

1955

2127   CASS, CASHENDEN. "A Matter of Fact." NR 133 (17 Oct.): 19-20.
Anthony West's novel Heritage is an antidote to the misrepresentation of W by St. John Ervine in "Portrait of H.G. Wells," but the knowledge that Max Town is really W distracts from the writer's work.

2128   DAVENPORT, BASIL. Inquiry into Science Fiction. New York: Longmans, Green, pp. 5-7, 19, 27.
W was versed in plausible scientific double-talk that made it possible to evade the impossible. Some of the most fertile ideas in science fiction (time travel, interplanetary warfare, the detached brain) are found in his work.

2129   ERVINE, ST. JOHN.   "Edwardian Authors: Portrait of H.G.
        Wells."   Listener 54 (25 Aug.):291-92.
            W played Sancho Panza to Shaw's Don Quixote.   "He had none
        of G.B.S.'s fineness of character or loyalty either to friends or
        causes, though he could be beautifully generous when he was in the
        mood, which was not often."   Mr. Polly is a portrait of W's
        father, and it was his father's failure as a shopkeeper (and not
        any shrewd prophecy) that led W to predict the "speedy extinction
        of the retail trader as a result of combines."   Had he been less
        of a sociologist he might have been as great a comic writer as
        Dickens.   Disliking mankind in the concrete prevented him from
        being a genius.

2130   GERBER, RICHARD.   Utopian Fantasy.   London: Routledge & Kegan
        Paul.   Reissued, with expanded list of utopian fiction.
        London: Routledge & Kegan Paul; New York: McGraw-Hill, 1973,
        pp. xiv, 10, 11, 13; index.
            W is the most important representative of twentieth-century
        utopian writing.   He depicts ideal man as well as ideal society,
        and the former is suggested rather than explicitly described.   In
        common with Olaf Stapledon, W expresses the ideas that a longer
        life will lead to a higher mentality and that man becomes godlike
        when he can experience many more things steadily and wholly.   Time
        is the enemy since the whole struggle for progress may become
        meaningless.

2131   GERHARD, WILFRIED.   "Der Fortschritts-gedanke in den
        erzählenden Werken von H.G. Wells."   Dissertation, University
        of Köln.
            [Listed in Lawrence F. McNamee, Dissertations in English
        and American Literature (New York and London: Bowker, 1968).]

2132   HARPER, Mr.   "After Hours: Utopias You Wouldn't Like."
        Harper's Magazine 210 (April):87-88.
            Science fiction today is social satire, "a literature of
        nightmare and polemic" that has "turned against science."   In the
        days when W was writing science fiction "it exuded a contented
        faith in Progress and the Machine; it was Utopian at least to the
        extent that it imagined the Future to be an improvement on the
        Present."

2133   RAKNEM, INGVALD.   "H.G. Wells Fiction from 1887 to 1920 in the
        Light of the Literary Criticism of His Age."   Dissertation,
        University of London.
            Published as entry 2286.

2134   SHIVELY, JAMES ROSS.   "Fantasy in the Fiction of H.G. Wells."
        Dissertation, University of Nebraska (Lincoln).
            [Listed in Dissertation Abstracts 15 (1955):1402.]

1955

2135   UNTERMEYER, LOUIS. "H.G. Wells." In <u>Makers of the Modern</u>
       <u>World</u>. New York: Simon & Schuster, pp. 345-51.
           W wrote the most candid summary of his own life in an
       "auto-obituary" printed in the <u>Living Age</u> in 1936 as well as in
       <u>Experiment</u>. He wrote of his extramarital affairs not out of
       exhibitionism but in an effort to understand his sexual appetites.
       "A product of the English liberal-rationalist movement, he filled
       his work with social ideals, envisioning a better world than the
       world in which he lived."

2136   WEST, ANTHONY. <u>Heritage</u>. New York: Random House.
           Like his Grub Street namesake, Richard Savage is illegiti-
       mate, the son of world-famous actress Naomi Savage and world-
       famous novelist Max Town. His story is his struggle to find his
       own identity. [The author is portraying himself and his own
       parents, W and Rebecca West.]

1956

2137   COLE, G.D.H. <u>History of Socialist Thought: The Second Inter-</u>
       <u>national, 1889-1914</u>. Vol. 3. London: Macmillan; New York:
       St. Martin's Press, pp. x, 201-6, 214, 216, 218, 219, 243, 982.
           Much of W's plan for the Fabians was not practical--he
       wished the organization to do more than it was financially capable
       of doing. His passion for order in his writing contrasted with
       "the disorderliness of his own mind and behaviour." His best
       writing came out when large numbers of young people were turning
       to socialism. The Fabian debate was not a clash of ideas but of
       personalities.

2138   ERVINE, ST. JOHN. <u>Bernard Shaw: His Life, Work and Friends</u>.
       New York: William Morrow, pp. 90, 95, 118, 125-27, 185; index.
           The Fabian Society declined after W convinced it to become
       a club of socialists instead of a research facility. W met his
       match in the Fabian debate with Shaw because he did not have the
       training or patience to be effective in the sort of revolution he
       imagined. His revenge in <u>Machiavelli</u> was a poor one, and his
       posthumously published obituary of Shaw was best left unpublished.

2139   GRANSDEN, K.W. "The S.S. Koteliansky Bequest." <u>British Museum</u>
       <u>Quarterly</u> 20:83-84.
           The correspondence of Koteliansky that was given to the
       British Museum includes letters from W and other modern writers.

2140   GRIGSON, GEOFFREY, and C.H. GIBBS-SMITH, ed. <u>People</u>. New
       York: Hawthorn, pp. 455-56. Second U.S. ed., pp. 423-24.
           W faced the world with all the answers, convinced that what
       he wrote was journalism, only valid for his own time.

2141   HENDERSON, ARCHIBALD. <u>George</u> <u>Bernard</u> <u>Shaw:</u>   <u>Man</u> <u>of</u> <u>the</u> Cen-
       tury. Rev. ed. New York: Appleton-Century-Crofts, pp. 87,
       88, 250-57, 306-7, 310, 337, 338, 350, 351, 352, 355; index.
           W intended his paper "This Misery of Boots" to serve as a
       model for Fabian Society tracts. His controversies with Shaw were
       marked by a tone of patronizing superiority on the one hand and
       outbreaks of ungovernable fury on the other. In <u>Machiavelli</u> he
       satirized Beatrice Webb's monopolization of conversation and de-
       bate, and in <u>The</u> <u>Science</u> <u>of</u> <u>Life</u> he disparaged Shaw's biological
       speculations. W felt he had anticipated Einstein in some articles
       in the <u>Fortnightly</u> <u>Review</u>.

2142   HOLLIS, CHRISTOPER. <u>A</u> <u>Study</u> <u>of</u> <u>George</u> <u>Orwell,</u> <u>the</u> <u>Man</u> <u>and</u> <u>His</u>
       <u>Works</u>. London: Hollis & Carter, pp. 16, 182, 185, 186.
           Orwell read all of W, Shaw, and Galsworthy at an early age
       and believed that W's assumptions that science would lead to world
       order were false. He preferred Kipling who, at least, faced some
       of the facts.

2143   HYDE, WILLIAM J. "The Socialism of H.G. Wells in the Early
       Twentieth Century." <u>Journal</u> <u>of</u> <u>the</u> <u>History</u> <u>of</u> <u>Ideas</u> 17:217-34.
           The ultimate objectives of W's socialism are the future of
       civilization and the world state. His socialism did not conform
       to a particular party but was more of a "creative idea." His
       clash with the Fabians was over power and a conflict in ideals.
       The primary concern of his socialism was improvement of the race
       through such things as marriage insurance, a minimum standard of
       child welfare, enforced parental responsibility, the abolition of
       private property (except for very personal items), a new middle
       class, elimination of the laboring class, and automatic sickness
       and age insurance. "His was the appeal for a social order of
       'constructive design,' an end in which every self-seeking aim
       would be subordinated in a State devoted to collective aims and
       racial well-being."

2144   MEYER, M[ATHILDE] M. <u>H.G.</u> <u>Wells</u> <u>and</u> <u>His</u> <u>Family</u> (As <u>I</u> <u>Have</u>
       <u>Known</u> <u>Them)</u>. Edinburgh: International Publishing Co.
           [Memoir of W as family man by the Swiss governess of Frank
       and G.P. from 1908 to 1913. Anecdotal and definitely partisan in
       spite of the candid accounts of W losing his temper. A portion is
       based on Memorandum Book kept from 15 August 1912 to 21 July 1913,
       with amplification from memory. The relationship was kept up by
       correspondence and occasional visits to W's home until the death
       of his wife. Frank justifies to his old governess the sending of
       the archives to Illinois.]

2145   MOTTRAM, R.H. <u>For</u> <u>Some</u> <u>We</u> <u>Loved:</u>   <u>An</u> <u>Intimate</u> <u>Portrait</u> <u>of</u> <u>Ada</u>
       <u>and</u> <u>John</u> <u>Galsworthy</u>. London: Hutchinson, pp. 36, 54, 78, 100,
       102, 103, 104, 105, 140, 231, 275.

1956

W had the storyteller's delight in words that made him write autobiography, correspondence, and newspaper pieces as well as his regular works. He was smiled at for writing of new and better worlds, for he was known to be a socialist. He and Shaw countered Belloc's and Chesterton's insistence that humanity had gone astray by saying it had only begun to go right. He had to be a cockney, not an Englishman, in order to survive. His was a fixed creed, and he felt that people erred in not believing him. Ada thought the heroine in Tono-Bungay only a "peg to hang theories upon."

2146   PEARSON, HESKETH. "Snapshots of My Seniors: H.G. Wells and Frank Harris." Listener 56 (5 July):15-16. Revised in Hesketh Pearson by Himself (New York: Harper, 1960).
       W was the poet of the Age of the Little Man and looked the part. He came to dislike his early creations and argued with anyone who praised them. He claimed Harris was a blackmailer and proceeded to prove it.

2147   ROPPEN, GEORG. Evolution and Poetic Belief: A Study in Some Victorian and Modern Writers. Oslo Studies in English. Oslo: Oslo University Press, pp. 345-46, 349-50, 402-57.
       Utopia is the most representative, but not of the whole range, of W's prophetic force. It is the most carefully thought out and steady vision if not the most fascinating. His search into evolutionary ideas comes from a different intuitive source with an emotional basis of fear and anxiety. He gave an ethical significance to Darwin and replaced Nature with homo sapiens, in theory coming close to fatalism. The immediate effect of the war on his utopian dream was a desire to escape from man and his world. In the books that follow, W still appears to believe in moral and intellectual evolution, even though realizing the inadequacy of man for the task.

2148   STYLITES, SIMEON. "H.G. Wells Meets the Twelve." Christian Century 73 (12 Dec.):1451.
       St. John Ervine's biography of Bernard Shaw relates a fantasy of W berating Jesus for wasting his time with the twelve disciples in trying to change the world.

2149   SWINNERTON, FRANK A. "Three Older Novelists." In Background with Chorus: A Footnote to Changes in English Literary Fashion between 1901 and 1917. New York: Farrar, Straus, pp. 185-203.
       W was a simple man; Kipps and Mr. Polly are in a sense portraits of their creator. He continued his revisions of his books right up to the galley proofs. His novels were often "expositions of recent happenings, with commentaries upon individuals

involved." He had an insatiable curiosity and stored up observations for future use. Even in his reading he "skimmed cream from their surfaces and adapted it to his own use."

2150   WILSON, COLIN. The Outsider. Boston: Houghton Mifflin; London: Victor Gollancz, pp. 15-20.
       In Tether W affirms the fundamental attitude of the outside in not accepting the continuation of human society. It is the existentialist problem: "Must thought negate life?"

2151   WOODCOCK, G[EORGE]. "Books and Comment: Five Who Fear the Future." NR 134 (16 April):17-19.
       Shaw, Wells, Huxley, Orwell, and Koestler, "men of the Left, with quite different standpoints from the conservatives" who used to criticize progress, were all critical of world developments in this century because there was peril for the "old radical ideals" of freedom and equality. The loss of hope for men like W means that progress has come to an end for man as he is and only miracles can provide solutions.

2152   WOODCOCK, GEORGE. "Utopias in Negative." Sewanee Review 64:81-97.
       In Time Machine W predicted that the misuse of science might make mankind atrophy toward "physical ineptitude or mental brutalization."

2153   YOUNG, KENNETH. Ford Madox Ford. London and New York: Longmans, Green, p. 11.
       Though he worked briefly with Ford on the English Review W saw him as only a "poseur."

1957

2154   CAMBERTON, ROLAND. "The Vision of H.G. Wells." Humanist 72:11-13.
       The essence of W is the free inquiring spirit. Not just a view of utopia, his hope for a world government is necessary in his opinion for the survival of the human race.

2155   CLARKE, I.F. "Science Fiction: Past and Present." Quarterly Review 295:260-70.
       Science fiction began long before W, but examples are rare until the nineteenth century. The earliest examples all expect social perfection to come from scientific progress. W gave the genre the shape it has today, and Time Machine is his most vivid and convincing use of Darwinian ideas.

1957

2156   "The Desert Daisy." NYTBR 24 Sept., p. 5.
       As an early effort, Desert Daisy demonstrates that W was
not a writer for the squeamish nor was he one to respect royalty,
the army, the government, or conventions. He even poked fun at
himself in this "gaily tragic tale." [Notice of the publication
of the ms.]

2157   GLASS, BENTLEY. "The Scientist in Contemporary Fiction."
       Scientific Monthly 85 (Dec.):288-93.
       Novels with scientist-heroes fall into three categories:
science fiction and mystery fiction, novels of science as a social
force, and novels about the personal struggle of the scientist. W
is in the second category where the scientist is "the dedicated
tool, the impersonal means to a magnificent end."

2158   GREGORY, HORACE. "H.G. Wells: A Wreath for the Liberal Tradi-
       tion." In New World Writing. New York: New American Library,
       pp. 100-11. Reprinted in Spirit of Time and Place (New York:
       Norton, 1973), pp. 217-24.
       The living W may be found in three books, Time Machine, Men
in the Moon, and Tono-Bungay. British "internal social revolutions" since World War II followed his pattern instead of one of
Marxian open class warfare. In his science fiction he implies a
rejection of the past lest mankind repeat its mistakes in the
future.

2159   HILLEGAS, MARK R. "The Cosmic Voyage and the Doctrine of
       Inhabited Worlds in Nineteenth-Century English Literature."
       Dissertation, Columbia University.
       [Listed in Dissertation Abstracts 17 (1957):2001.]

2160   "In Brief." Times (London), 12 Dec., p. 13.
       The original manuscript of Desert Daisy, written when W was
12, was reproduced in facsimile with an introduction by Gordon N.
Ray. "More amusing than most juvenilia."

2161   JEAN-AUBRY, GERARD. The Sea Dreamer: A Definitive Biograpohy
       of Joseph Conrad. Garden City, N.Y.: Doubleday, pp. 98, 221,
       235, 242, 245.
       W reviewed An Outcast of the Islands so favorably that
Conrad wrote to thank him.

2162   [LOW, DAVID.] Low's Autobiography. New York: Simon &
       Schuster, pp. 103-6, 108, 175, 250, 281-86, 294, 338-39, 354,
       368-70.
       In spite of an enthusiasm for his works, the first visit
with W was not an event of which to boast. Later encounters were
more enjoyable. As a talker, W had the rare ability to make
himself clear, excite curiosity, and prompt inquiry, but his

suggestions for the subject of cartoons were usually impractical. In illustrating Mr. Parham care had to be taken not to make the figures too recognizable to avoid libel actions.

2163   McCORMICK, JOHN. Catastrophe and Imagination: An Interpretation of the Recent English and American Novel. New York and London: Longman's, pp. 149, 158-59, 217.
    W is to the comic novel what Hardy is to the tragic novel. He perceived the end of the Victorian order but took his "technical equipment" from the Victorians.

2164   PADOVER, SAUL K., ed. Confessions and Self-Portraits. New York: Day, pp. 241-45.
    W was a literary giant of the Age of Science and War who predicted that mankind was racing between education and catastrophe.

2165   PURDOM, C.B., ed. Bernard Shaw's Letters to Granville Barker. New York: Theatre Arts Books, pp. 68, 111, 148, 149, 191, 192. [Passing references.]

2166   RAY, GORDON N. Introduction to "The Desert Daisy." Urbana, Ill.: Beta Phi Mu, pp. vii-xvii.
    "Desert Daisy," written when W was 12 or 13, is a remarkable achievment considering the circumstances under which the young author was raised. His dismal boyhood led him to dream of being a great leader and to set down some of his dreams. His favorite children's book was Struwwelpeter (Slovenly Peter), and "Daisy" may have been modelled on this in both text and drawings. His gift as a humorist and a hint of the mature skeptic to come are both revealed in much of the work.

2167   SIEVEKING, LANCE. "The Vitality and Kindliness of H.G. Wells." Listener 57 (17 Jan.):103-4.
    Though not a Christian W worked to enlighten his fellow men in a manner not unworthy of the founder of Christianity. He was not afraid of death since he had faced it so often while a young man. Quick to anger, soon to forget, he aided the dramatization of some of his stories for radio and film. [Reminiscences of a friend and BBC writer.]

2168   SPEAIGHT, ROBERT. The Life of Hilaire Belloc. New York: Farrar, Straus & Cudahy, pp. 253-54, 307, 364, 397-403.
    Belloc thought W had a good scientific imagination and wrote well. The controversy over Outline was a duel between "a European mind and a provincial imagination," with the mind winning "because it had forced the imagination to fight on ground of its own choosing."

1957

2169   STARR, WILLIAM T.   "Romain Rolland and H.G. Wells."   French
        Review 30:195-200.
            The mutual esteem that Rolland and W felt for each other
        was based on both of them being reformers (in their way) as well
        as writers.

2170   SWINNERTON, FRANK.   "Never Meet an Author."   SR 40 (2 March):
        7-9.
            There is a disillusioning difference between a "modern
        author's persona as conveyed to the public and his character as
        seen by his intimates."   W was uneasy around Sinclair Lewis's
        tense personality and loud voice.   Others found W himself "common-
        place, cheap, quarrelsome."   W's "lovable mischief" made
        Swinnerton forget his defects.   On the other hand, W's books are
        never easy to read for their "too obviously unrealized" ideas and
        are totally unlike their author.

2171   VALLETTE, JACQUES.   "Une amitié littéraire et sa fin."   Mercure
        de France 333 (1957-58):706-8.
            In the literary debate between W and Henry James, W vied
        for the rejection of exclusive rules and writing styles; he argued
        for literature as a means rather than as an end, with James on the
        side of the traditionalists.

2172   WEEKS, ROBERT P.   "Bibliography, News, and Notes: H.G. Wells."
        EFT 1:37-42.
            [Seventy-six items not included in Geoffrey West's bibliog-
        raphies (1926 and 1930) or Vincent Brome's bibliography in his
        1951 biography; largely unannotated.]

2173   WEST, ANTHONY.   "The Dark World of H.G. Wells."   Harper's
        Magazine 214 (May):68-73.
            As early as Time Machine W dealt with the mechanistic view
        of the universe, "the ideological basis of pessimism," in which
        the human mind is a sort of accident.   In Dr. Moreau the conse-
        quences of "the Darwinian intellectual revolution . . . will be
        moral collapse."   The intellectual is isolated in both Invisible
        Man and "Country," and the protagonists are corrupted by their
        special knowledge.   W's later optimistic works go against his
        natural tendencies and may be accounted for by his wider social
        experience and his success in life.   His real view of human nature
        was opposed to the romantic utopia that figured so much in his
        later writing.   In his last pessimistic phase, he was being true
        to his own ideas.   [Greatly rewritten version of essay published
        in entry 2174; omits anecdotes of family life.]

2174   _____.   "Men and Ideas: H.G. Wells."   Encounter 8 (Feb.):52-
        59.   Reprinted in Anthony West, Principles and Persuasions
        (London: Eyre & Spottiswoode, 1958) [Note: this essay does

not appear in the U.S. edition of this book]; in CE, pp. 8-24; and in "The Time Machine," "The War of the Worlds," ed. Frank D. McConnell. (New York: Oxford University Press, 1977), pp. 437-55.

The popular view of W as an optimist certain of the inevitability of progress is wrong. In reality he began as a pessimist and his whole life was a struggle with pessimism. His undisciplined mind led him to contradict himself, or appear to do so, and this has led to the assumption of his optimism. His abundant spirit in his writing makes it easy to miss the intensity of his struggle. From Croquet Player on he tried to recapture the spirit of his early work, but found it was too late. [Anecdotes of family life and of W's opinions; greatly rewritten version appeared in entry 2173.]

2175   WINSTEN, STEPHEN. Jesting Apostle: The Private Life of
       Bernard Shaw. New York: Dutton, pp. 104, 133, 134, 153, 158,
       181, 197, 198, 204, 209-10.
       W fell into Shaw's trap in debate over the Fabians and used
the language of a street brawl. In spite of their quarrels they
were in sympathy with each other, but Shaw was afraid of a post-
humous attack from W in the manner of his attack on James.

1958

2176   Allen, Jerry. The Thunder and the Sunshine: A Biography of
       Joseph Conrad. New York: G.P. Putnam, pp. 10, 213-14, 218.
       W's criticism of Conrad's style did not prevent him from
calling An Outcast of the Islands the finest bit of fiction of
1896.

2177   BERGONZI, BERNARD. "An Early Wells Review of Henry James."
       TLS, 18 April, p. 216.
       W reviewed fiction (anonymously) for Frank Harris's
Saturday Review from March 1895 to 1897. On 1 June 1895 he
reviewed Henry James's Terminations as having "a ground-glass
style. By close application you can just discern men and women as
trees walking. Nevertheless, they are living men and women."

2178   _____. "Notes and Reviews: Another Early Wells Item."
       Nineteenth Century Fiction 13:72-73.
       W's article "Man of the Year Million" was revised and
included in his collection, Personal Matters, as "Of a Book Un-
written." Another essay in that collection, "The Extinction of
Man," contains ideas later used in Time Machine (the giant crabs),
"The Sea Raiders" (the giant octopus), and "The Empire of the
Ants." This latter essay is "evidence of Wells's early pessimistic period."

1958

2179   _____. "The Novelist and His Subject-matter." <u>Listener</u> 60
         (18 Sept.):426-27.
            W was making a false distinction between literature as an
         end in itself and as a means to an end in his debate with Henry
         James. As a novelist he was "a thorough-going Victorian, but his
         genius for caricature and comic creation placed him closer to
         Dickens than to Trollope." His scientific romances gain much from
         the reportorial detail of their settings. The isolation of
         James's characters "suggests obliquely the common condition of
         life for innumerable people in the middle of the twentieth cen-
         tury." W had certain intimations of this but could not expand on
         them since his "moral perceptions were of the crudest."

2180   BRADY, CHARLES A.   "Lunatics and Selenophiles." <u>America</u> 99
         (27 July):448-49.
            <u>Men in the Moon</u> is the only moon adventure to rival Verne's
         <u>From the Earth to the Moon</u>. Where Verne's voyagers find a dead
         world, W's find one inhabited by thinking ants. Reality has put
         stories of moon travel aside in favor of stories about Mars and
         Venus.

2181   BROME, VINCENT. <u>Six Studies in Quarrelling</u>. London: Cresset
         Press.
            W clashed with Shaw over the policies of the Fabian Soci-
         ety, and his paper, "Faults of the Fabians," read on 17 January
         1906, brought matters to a head. The debate soon turned to per-
         sonal and sweeping attacks by W and witty rebuttals by Shaw. They
         never lost sight of their friendship in spite of continued differ-
         ences in print over socialism, vivisection, capitalism, Marxism,
         and the role of religion in the scientific age. The issues over
         which they fought have been largely reconciled today, but many
         later debatable issues had their foundations in their discussions.
         The two were on the same side for part of the quarrel between W
         and playwright Henry Arthur Jones, who persisted in misinterpret-
         ing everything W said or wrote. W was attacked in print for his
         patriotism, his views on the Bolshevik government in Russia, and
         his supposed conversion to Marxism. When Churchill and W argued
         over points in <u>Russia</u>, Jones felt he had a new ally. W tried to
         ignore Jones's fixation as well as the voluminous letters that he
         wrote him. In 1921, Jones published his collected attacks in <u>My
         Dear Wells</u>, which Shaw reviewed. W clashed with Henry James over
         their respective views of what the novel should be. W spoke
         scornfully of James in private, but praise from him really mat-
         tered to W. Next to James, he seemed vulgar, and talks between
         them were tortured. The final blow came with the publication of
         the parody of James's style in <u>Boon</u>. Hilaire Belloc attacked the
         <u>Outline</u> in a series of articles in the Catholic <u>Universe</u> in 1926.
         W offered a six-part reply, which the magazine did not wish to
         print. The complete account of their debate was later published

in Belloc's <u>A</u> <u>Companion</u> <u>to</u> <u>Mr.</u> <u>Wells'</u> <u>Outline</u> <u>of</u> <u>History</u>, W's <u>Belloc</u> <u>Objects</u>, and Belloc's <u>Mr.</u> <u>Belloc</u> <u>Still</u> <u>Objects</u>. "Both men had torrential nervous energy, both could be savagely tenacious, both were freshly enraged by each new statement of the other." [Liberal excerpts from letters and other publications setting forth the points of debate; Brome furnishes running commentary and links between documents.]

2182   CLARKE, I.F. "The Nineteenth-Century Utopia." <u>Quarterly</u> <u>Review</u> 296:80-91.
        The utopias of the 1890s all present serious criticism of the current state of society and the world. W's visions of the future are "uniformly pessimistic," and his characters view Victorian England with nostalgia. His future has everything the people of the 1890s could wish, except liberty and equality. With the coming of the Edwardian age his tone changed to one of optimism.

2183   EDEL, LEON, and GORDON N. RAY, eds. Introduction to <u>Henry</u> <u>James</u> <u>and</u> <u>H.G.</u> <u>Wells:</u> <u>A</u> <u>Record</u> <u>of</u> <u>Their</u> <u>Friendship,</u> <u>Their</u> <u>Debate</u> <u>on</u> <u>the</u> <u>Art</u> <u>of</u> <u>Fiction</u> <u>and</u> <u>Their</u> <u>Quarrel</u>. Urbana: University of Illinois Press, 1958) pp. 15-41.
        James, dedicated to his craft, attracted young writers, including W. Their basic differences were ones of beauty (James) contrasted with function (W). They were at cross-purposes in their letters: James was creating an avant-garde form of fiction while W accepted the novel for what it had always been. He sent James copies of his new books and waited for the criticism so he could reply. While working on <u>Boon</u>, W read James's article on "The Younger Generation" and added a new chapter mocking James. The older writer responded by ending their association, but W could never quite forget what he had done to him.

2184   GREEN, ROGER LANCELYN. <u>Into</u> <u>Other</u> <u>Worlds:</u> <u>Space-Flight</u> <u>in</u> <u>Fiction,</u> <u>from</u> <u>Lucian</u> <u>to</u> <u>Lewis</u>. London and New York: Abelard-Schuman, pp. 73, 118-21, 131, 138-42, 151, 182, 184.
        Joseph Atterley's means of getting to the moon in <u>Voyage</u> <u>to</u> <u>the</u> <u>Moon</u> (1827) requires a new substance for propulsion, a forerunner of W's "Cavorite." On its own level, <u>War</u> <u>of</u> <u>the</u> <u>Worlds</u> is brilliant as sensational invention, but must be supplemented with "The Crystal Egg" for W's idea of Mars itself. It is Bedford's ignorance of science in <u>Men</u> <u>in</u> <u>the</u> <u>Moon</u> that saves W from having to make the scientific background plausible. There may have been an influence from Verne on the Selenites living inside the moon, while W certainly influenced Burroughs's inner moon world in <u>The</u> <u>Moon</u> <u>Maid</u>. Humphrey Davy's <u>Consolations</u> <u>in</u> <u>Travel</u> (1830) probably had an influence on the description of the Martians in <u>War</u> <u>of</u> <u>the</u> <u>Worlds</u>.

1958

2185   GUÉRARD, ALBERT J. Conrad, The Novelist. Cambridge, Mass.:
        Harvard University Press, pp. 265, 300.
            Chance may have been partially suggested by W's "image of a
        financial structure built on advertising alone."

2186   HAIGHT, GORDON S. "H.G. Wells's 'The Man of the Year
        Million.'" Nineteenth Century Fiction 12 (March):323-26.
            It is W's own article on man's future physical appearance
        from the Pall Mall Budget (16 Nov. 1893) to which he refers in
        book 2, chapter 2, of War of the Worlds. The caricature in Punch
        that he mentions is also real (25 Nov. 1893) and was accompanied
        by a set of verses.

2187   HOLMEBAKK, GORDON. "Romanen som redskap eller erkjennelse.
        Noen notater om forholdet mellom Henry James og H.G. Wells"
        [The novel as tool or vehicle of self-awareness. Some remarks
        on the relationship between Henry James and H.G. Wells].
        Vinduet 12:170-78.
            An examination of the letters exchanged between Henry James
        and W over a period of seventeen years indicates that the conflict
        between the two grew out of their irreconcilable views of art,
        more specifically their different views of the novel form. [In
        Norwegian.]

2188   McCARTHY, HAROLD T. Henry James: The Creative Process.
        Rutherford, Madison, Teaneck, N.J.: Fairleigh Dickinson Uni-
        versity Press, pp. 47, 76, 82, 138-39.
            James admired W, but recognized the difference in their
        views on art. He was hurt by W's parody because it meant W could
        not accept someone else's personal view.

2189   REXROTH, KENNETH. "The Screw Turns on Mr. James." Nation (New
        York) 187 (16 Aug.):76-77. Reprinted as "Henry James and H.G.
        Wells," in Assays (New York: New Directions, 1961),
        pp. 114-17.
            The subjects of all W's major novels are the same as those
        of D.H. Lawrence—matrimony, "the mysteries and difficulties and
        agonies and tragedies and—rarely—the joys of the search for a
        true 'life of dialogue.'" James was a snob writing unrealistic
        fiction, while W was a part of the "literary world of Huckleberry
        Finn or Don Quixote." [Review of Henry James and H.G. Wells: A
        Record of Their Friendship.]

2190   ROBSON, W.W. "Spring Books: The Documents in the Case."
        Spectator 200 (28 March):397.
            It was once customary to assume James was wrong to react
        the way he did to Boon. The collection of correspondence indi-
        cates that W may have been wrong to write it. The critical issue
        raised by their views of art has never been resolved.

2191   STREATFEILD, NOEL. Magic and the Magician: E.F. Nesbit and
       Her Children's Books. London: Benn, pp. 12, 17-18.
       The Nesbit of the children's books is far-removed from the
personality that W wrote about in Experiment, and his account of
the Blands conflicts with that of others.

2192   "Those Martians Land Again." NYT, 27 June, p. 51.
       A radio adaptation of War of the Worlds in Carcavelos,
Purtugal, was cut off the air after panic began.

2193   WATSON, JOHN G. "The Role of the Writer." HJ 56 (July):
       371-76.
       W deliberately used the novel as a vehicle for ideas, but
he did not realize that he was most successful when he showed the
reality behind abstract ideas of society by conveying his own
experience (as in Mr. Polly).

1959

2194   BROME, VINCENT. Frank Harris. London: Cassell, pp. 4, 50,
       57, 75-76, 80, 82, 85; index.
       W, calling on Harris after submitting "The Rediscovery of
the Unique," had cleaned his hat with water which made it curl and
warp as he stood with it in his hand. [This anecdote should have
referred to "The Universe Rigid."]

2195   CALDER, RITCHIE. "Herbert George Wells." In Dictionary of
       National Biography, 1941-50. London: Oxford University Press,
       pp. 944-49.
       W's origins and upbringing influenced his work and social
attitudes and explain the contradictions in his public image.
[Biographical sketch with list of selected references.]

2196   DAVENPORT, BASIL, ed. The Science Fiction Novel: Imagination
       and Social Criticism. Chicago: Advent, pp. 12, 28, 32, 39,
       81, 102, 103.
       [Passing references to W; four essays by Robert A.
Heinlein, C.M. Kornbluth, Alfred Bester, and Robert Bloch.]

2197   GORDAN, JOHN D. "New in the Berg Collection: 1957-1958." New
       York Public Library Bulletin 63 (April):205-15.
       [A set of Outline in twenty-four parts with corrections
by W and his wife as well as letters from them to the indexer
Strickland Gibson were on exhibit at the New York Public Library.]

2198   KRUEGER, JOHN R. "The Impact of Russian and Western Literature
       on Mongolia." Slavic and East European Journal 17 (Spring):
       25-34.

1959

In the early 1920s, adventure stories and fantastic literature began to have an appeal for the Mongols, especially works of
Jack London, Jules Verne, W, and Edgar Allan Poe.

2199   MIROIU, MIHAI. "Critica sociala in romanele de moravuri ale
       lui H.G. Wells: Tono-Bungay" [Social criticism as reflected in
       the novels of H.G. Wells: Tono-Bungay]. Analele Universitatii
       "C.L. Parhon" (Filologie) (Bucharest) 15:389-410.
            That the contradictions in Wells's novels reflect those of
       contemporary society is especially apparent in Tono-Bungay's
       satire on a commercial and superannuated social order. W experi-
       enced the economic crisis in England during 1886-1895. Despite
       occasional vacillations and skepticism, W is optimistic. [In
       Romanian with an English summary.]

2200   "New B.B.C. Serial on Television." Times (London), 4 April,
       p. 10.
            The B.B.C. production of Love and Mr. Lewisham is "fair to
       the original and entertaining in its own right." Alec McCowen is
       the perfect embodiment of the W hero, shabby and socially insecure
       with an occasional awkward charm.

2201   RAYMOND, JOHN. "Books in General: Alive and Kicking." NS 57
       (10 Jan.):46-47.
            W was fascinated by politicians, though he never tried to
       conceal his distrust of them. The one he most admired was
       Theodore Roosevelt, but there is much he had in common with Lloyd
       George. Both were geniuses who did not care for their media--the
       novel and power. W was the first writer to use science fully in
       imaginative literature, and that part of his work is
       indestructible.

2202   STYLITES, SIMEON. "Let H.G. Wells Be Right!" Christian
       Century 76 (9 Sept.):1039.
            W's prediction of "people of all nations joined to abolish
       war" in World Set Free should come true.

2203   "Visual Trickery the Be All and End All." Times (London), 11
       March, p. 13.
            Douglas Cleverden's BBC-TV adaptation of "The Truth About
       Pyecraft" is more interesting for the special effects than for the
       story.

2204   WAUGH, EVELYN. The Life of the Right Reverend Ronald Knox.
       London: Chapman & Hall, p. 232.
            W probably did not write Outline as an attack on Chris-
       tianity and was surprised when Belloc responded. He was even more
       surprised that the popular press found the debate unimportant.

2205   "A Wellsian Film." <u>Times</u> (London), 7 Feb., p. 10.
         <u>Island</u> <u>of</u> <u>Lost</u> <u>Souls</u> is available for showing in England
for the first time in twenty years. The fine points of W's story
still hold up, as does the chilling effect created by Charles
Laughton.

2206   AMIS, KINGSLEY. <u>New</u> <u>Maps</u> <u>of</u> <u>Hell</u>: <u>A</u> <u>Survey</u> <u>of</u> <u>Science</u> <u>Fic</u>-
         tion. New York: Harcourt Brace, pp. 15-41. Reprinted as
"Starting Points," in <u>Science</u> <u>Fiction</u>: <u>A</u> <u>Collection</u> <u>of</u> <u>Crit</u>-
<u>ical</u> <u>Essays</u>, ed. Mark Rose (Englewood Cliffs, N.J.: Prentice-
Hall, 1976), pp. 9-29.
         W's most influential work was written before science fic-
tion had become separated from the mainstream of literature.
While he was mainly interested in the effect of scientific advance
on human life, the stories that had the most effect on the development of the genre were not dependent on extrapolation. He did
not use his wonders merely to point up moral lessons for society.

2207   BAILEY, J.O. "Is Science-Fiction Art? A Look at H.G. Wells."
         <u>Extrapolation</u> 2:17-19.
         Scholars have been unjust to W because they only see the
surface of his science fiction, a consequence primarily of the
reputation of science fiction as "juvenile fantasy." <u>Sleeper</u>
<u>Wakes</u> is no longer a realistic forecast but a "synthesis of how
men of science saw the world in the 1890's" along with some observations on human nature. W's science fiction stories are allego-
ries that may be superior to his later novels.

2208   BAINES, JOCELYN. <u>Joseph</u> <u>Conrad</u>: <u>A</u> <u>Critical</u> <u>Biography</u>. New
         York and London: McGraw-Hill, pp. 144, 165-67, 215-16, 230-34;
index.
         Conrad saw W as an original writer with individual judgment
and imagination. While W's review of <u>An</u> <u>Outcast</u> <u>of</u> <u>the</u> <u>Islands</u>
was favorable, he criticized Conrad for wordiness. The two re-
mained friends until a basic difference in outlook and temperament
caused the friendship to cool.

2209   BEHRMAN, S.N. <u>Portrait</u> <u>of</u> <u>Max</u>: <u>An</u> <u>Intimate</u> <u>Memoir</u> <u>of</u> <u>Sir</u> <u>Max</u>
         <u>Beerbohm</u>. New York: Random House, pp. 87, 91, 109, 123, 223,
237, 238, 255.
         It was Hardy who insisted that "Maltby and Braxton" were
modeled after W and Bennett. Beerbohm caricatured W, whom he
found nice and not vindictive.

2210   BERGONZI, BERNARD. "The Publication of <u>The</u> <u>Time</u> <u>Machine</u>, 1894-
         1895." <u>Review</u> <u>of</u> <u>English</u> <u>Studies</u>, n.s. 11:42-51. Reprinted in

1960

SF: The Other Side of Realism, ed. Thomas D. Clareson (Bowling
Green, Ohio: Bowling Green University Press, 1971),
pp. 204-15.
   Extensive revisions made by W in Time Machine suggest that
the younger writer was as scrupulous an artist as Henry James.
[Detailed comparisons between texts of periodical and book
versions.]

2211   _____. "The Time Machine: An Ironic Myth." Critical
      Quarterly 2:293-305. Reprinted in CE, pp. 39-54.
         Concerning W's early work, critical emphasis should be on
      the romance and not on the scientific. As with other forms of
      literary romance, his are distinguished by their symbolic quality.
      The myth in Time Machine is biological and cosmological as well as
      social, with the symbolic element "inherent in the total fictional
      situation." Reflecting the views of the eighties and nineties,
      the central narrative of this book depicts opposing images of
      paradise and hell. Its tensions are imaginatively, but not intel-
      lectually, resolved, and a note of irony becomes apparent in the
      traveler's explorations.

2212   BIBBY, [HAROLD] CYRIL. T.H. Huxley: Scientist, Humanist and
      Educator. New York: Horizon Press, pp. 120, 140, 141.
         W's mother was reassured to learn Huxley was a Dean and not
      merely a "notoriously irreligious man." W complained that he
      learned only science and not teaching method from Huxley, but he
      later claimed that year of study to have been his most
      educational.

2213   BOGGS, W. ARTHUR. "Looking Backward at the Utopian Novel,
      1888-1900." New York Public Library Bulletin 64:329-36.
         Sleeper Wakes is among the better novels of the nineteenth
      century that were influenced by Edward Bellamy's Looking Backward.

2214   BORINSKI, LUDWIG. "Amerika im Spiegel der Englischen Literatur
      des Zwanzigsten Jahrhunderts." Neuren Sprachen, no. 10 (Oct.),
      472-85.
         W is the only English writer of the early twentieth century
      to deal with America thoroughly and repeatedly. Future in America
      is impressionistic, superficial, and biased, but perceptive.

2215   BUCKSTEAD, RICHARD CHRIS. "H.G. Wells, Arnold Bennett, John
      Galsworthy: Three Novelists in Revolt Against the Middle
      Class." Dissertation, Iowa State University.
         [Listed in Dissertation Abstracts 20 (1960):4652-53.]

2216   CHUKOVSKY, KORNEI. "H.G. Wells's Phantasmagoria." Anglo-
      Soviet Journal 21 (Spring):10-11.

1960

W stayed in Maxim Gorky's flat when he visited the Soviet Union in 1920. He was warmly greeted by school children familiar with his science fiction, but he refused to believe they had not been coached to respond to him in this manner.

2217   DRINKWATER, F.H. "Writer as Prophet: H.G. Wells and War." *Commonweal* 73 (30 Dec.):362-64.
     W was a great storyteller "before he took to reforming human society." War in the Air is undeservedly forgotten, perhaps because its prophecies were too accurate for some, not accurate enough for others.

2218   ELLMANN, RICHARD. "Two Faces of Edward." In Edwardians and Late Victorians. New York: Columbia University Press, pp. 188-210. Reprinted in Literary Criticism: Idea and Act, ed. W.K. Wimsatt (Berkeley: University of California Press, 1974) pp. 560-75; and in Richard Ellmann, Golden Codgers: Biographical Speculations (New York and London: Oxford University Press, 1973), pp. 114, 118, 1 22-23, 126, 127, 153.
     W followed some of the themes in common use in Edwardian times. Religious terms were in use by believer and unbeliever alike. W's terms "finite God" and "king of man's adventures in space and time" are part of this as well as the use of secular miracles in his fiction (Kipps and Ponderevo are reflections of his favorite myth of human achievement). In W the essential terms are "science" and "truth." Reexamining W is somewhat disillusioning; he seems less than we had expected.

2219   FIELDING, K.J. "Dickens and the Novel." Dickensian 56 (Sept.):160-64.
     The critics here are so respectful of Henry James's theories of the novel "that criticism may be lulled to rest." W's comments have not been included in Allott, but should have been because his practice as a novelist bears out James and also has much to contribute to a discussion of the novel. W is much closer to a link between Dickens and the modern novel. All three, Dickens, James, and W required freedom to develop the novel to suit themselves. [Review article of Richard Stang's The Theory of the Novel in England, 1850-1870 and Miriam Allott's Novelists on the Novel.]

2220   FREMANTLE, ANNE. This Little Band of Prophets: The British Fabians. New York: New American Library, pp. 16, 28, 40, 45, 50, 52, 53, 101, 111, 114-16, 141, 148, 153-66; index.
     W sincerely wanted to make the Fabians into his samurai, whereas the Webbs hoped he would popularize their visions. Had he been a more effective speaker the Fabian Society might have had a different history. In spite of the breach, he did make their views well known, especially in America.

1960

2221   GERBER, H[ELMUT] E. "H.G. Wells at English Institute." EFT
       3:15-16.
           Gordon Ray's paper, "H.G. Wells Tries to Be a Novelist,"
       read at Conference 2, focused attention of W's theory of fiction
       from 1895 to 1910. "Realism . . . in the sense of life seen
       whole, both in its tragic and in its comic aspect, was his key-
       note." One reason W rejected the idea of the novel as a work of
       art was the reaction of critics to Ann Veronica.

2222   _____, ed. "Some Letters of H.G. Wells (From a Private Collec-
       tion)." EFT 3, no. 1:1-11.
       [Eighteen letters, many written by W to Ralph D.
       Blumenfeld, editor of the Daily Express, 1902-1932, "reflect
       significantly on Wells' work, on his opinions on literature and
       politics, and on the vicissitudes of his family and friends."
       Notes by the editor and the collector.]

2223   HILLEGAS, MARK R. "The First Invasions from Mars." Michigan
       Alumnus Quarterly Review 66 (Feb.):107-12.
           The myth of the superior Martians began with stories about
       earthmen traveling to mars to view the wonders of the advanced
       civilization. By the mid-1890s the situation was reversed, and
       the stories were of invasions of earth by beings so advanced that
       friendly contact was impossible. Kurd Lasswitz's Auf Zwei
       Planeten (1897) and W's War of the Worlds were the first stories
       in this cycle, the latter raising the myth to a new level by
       portraying human reaction to an alien force.

2224   JEFFERSON, D.W. Henry James. Edinburgh and London: Oliver &
       Boyd, p. 97.
           W's satire of James is the most obvious example of a fail-
       ure to understand what an older writer was trying to do.

2225   MOORE, HARRY T. Foreword to Tono-Bungay. New York: New
       American Library, pp. vii-xiii.
           All three aspects of W as writer are present in Tono-
       Bungay: "educational reformer, science fictionist, and the tradi-
       tional novelist somewhat in the vein of Dickens." Since he spent
       three years writing it, W may have tried harder to be an artist in
       Tono-Bungay.

2226   OSTROWSKI, WITOLD. "Imaginary History." Zagadnienia Rodzajow
       Literackick 3, no. 2:27-38.
           The "imaginary history" as a distinct literary genre is an
       exacting form that demands attention to content as well as style.
       W was the first writer to produce a fully realized example in
       Shape of Things although most of the necessary requirements are
       also present in World Set Free. In doing so, he may have been

aware of Olaf Stapledon's own example of the genre, <u>Last</u> <u>and</u> <u>First</u> <u>Men</u>.

2227   PRIESTLEY, J.B. <u>Literature</u> <u>and</u> <u>Western</u> <u>Man</u>. New York: Harper
        & Row, pp. 317, 319, 342, 344-48, 352, 355, 425.
            W's literary reputation would have been greater had he had
        a shorter life, for his best work as a novelist appears before
        World War I. His training and conscious outlook were scientific,
        but his temperament and natural genius were literary. The con-
        flict between these two was the key to his success.

2228   RAY, GORDON N. "H.G. Wells Tries to be a Novelist." In
        <u>Edwardians</u> <u>and</u> <u>Late</u> <u>Victorians</u>. Edited by Richard Ellman.
        (New York: Columbia University Press, pp. 106-59. Reprinted
        with slight changes, as "Introduction: The Early Novels of
        H.G. Wells," in <u>The</u> <u>History</u> <u>of</u> <u>Mr.</u> <u>Polly</u>, ed. Gordon N. Ray
        (Cambridge, Mass.: Houghton Mifflin, 1960), pp. v-xlix.
            In his reviews for <u>Saturday</u> <u>Review</u> (1895-97) W worked out
        his concept of what the novel should be. <u>Mr.</u> <u>Lewisham</u> is his
        "most carefully constructed" novel, but its aims are limited. He
        was "the most ambitious and successful anatomist of the Edwardian
        social order in fiction."

2229   REXROTH, KENNETH. "The Students Take Over." <u>Nation</u> New York
        191 (2 July):4-9.
            At the end of his life, W saw "a perverse lust for physical
        and moral violence and lack of respect for integrity of the per-
        sonality invading everyday life." [Passing reference.]

2230   RÜHLE, JURGEN. <u>Literature</u> <u>and</u> <u>Revolution:</u> <u>A</u> <u>Critical</u> <u>Study</u>
        <u>of</u> <u>the</u> <u>Writer</u> <u>and</u> <u>Communism</u> <u>in</u> <u>the</u> <u>Twentieth</u> <u>Century</u>.
        Translated and edited by Jean Steinberg from <u>Literatur</u> <u>und</u>
        <u>Revolution</u>. German Fed. Republic: Kiepenheuer & Witsch.
        English translation. New York: Praeger, 1969, pp. 315-18,
        467, 473.
            W's generalizations about world peace are so broad the
        Communists find no difficulty adapting it to their rhetoric in
        spite of their criticism of <u>Russia</u> as naive. W was impressed by
        Lenin but not by Stalin.

2231   STEVENSON, LIONEL. <u>The</u> <u>English</u> <u>Novel:</u> <u>A</u> <u>Panorama</u>. New York:
        Riverside Press; Boston: Houghton Mifflin, pp. 434-36, 440-41,
        450-51, 453-54, 457, 463-64, 468, 472, 474-75, 477-78, 493,
        514, 531.
            W's early books came at a time when education was spreading
        and science was in the news. His work cast an imaginative glamor
        over the new knowledge. <u>Kipps</u> established him in the central
        tradition of the English novel, and <u>Mr.</u> <u>Britling</u> reassured those
        readers who had been repelled by <u>Ann</u> <u>Veronica</u>.

1960

2232   STROUSE, NORMAN H.   Introduction to Tono-Bungay.   New York:
       Heritage Press, pp. vii-xiii.
          W was a prolific but uneven writer.   Tono-Bungay's interest
       for modern readers is its criticism of aspects of contemporary
       life as well as the characterization and "subtle outcroppings of
       philosophical thought that provoke the reader to a reassessment of
       his own standards and aims."

2233   "The Uses of Comic Vision."   TLS 9 Sept., ix.
          Many British novelists use humor to "express their social
       feelings, or their attitude towards a moral situation."   W is in
       the same company as Aldous Huxley, Kingsley Amis, Wyndham Lewis,
       and Anthony Powell, though their type and use of humor differ.
       The humor in the books of W's "finest period" (Kipps, Mr. Polly,
       Tono-Bungay) "sprang from love and optimism" though his attitude
       did not survive World War I.   After 1920, W "did not really under-
       stand the sort of world he was living in," according to Orwell.
       W's humor is "too perfectly of its time, and the faintly self-
       congratulatory air with which Wells viewed his Little Man heroes
       has seemed to later generations uncommonly near to smugness."

2234   WEEKS, ROBERT P.   "Wells Scholarship in Perspective."   EFT 3,
       no. 1:12-15.
          W's reputation has declined since 1946, but there is still
       a need to study his work and place it in perspective.   A defini-
       tive biography is needed as well as studies of various aspects
       of his work, the influence of Darwin and Huxley on his thought,
       his influence on a whole generation, his contribution to science
       fiction and a study of his middle-class novels.   [Informal report
       at Conference on English Fiction in Transition, New York City, 29
       Dec. 1958.]

2235   Wellsian 1, no. 1 (Oct.).
          [The first issue sets forth the objectives of the society:
       to preserve the memory, ideas, and vision of W without worshipping
       the man.   Contents include: "Why an H.G. Wells Society?" by H.H.;
       correspondence and reminiscences of M.M. Meyer; list of Books and
       Pamphlets by W; list of Books by Other Writers with Prefaces by W;
       account of a visit to Easton Glebe by Eric N. Simons; "H.G. Wells:
       An Appreciation" by John R. Hammond; "Wells and Science" by
       Hammond; an appreciation of Mr. Blettsworthy; and "The Reality of
       Wells: The Unappreciated" by Peter Donoghue.]   [Articles in
       issues of the Wellsian, n.s., annotated individually.]

2236   WILSON, HARRIS.   Introduction to Arnold Bennett and H.G. Wells:
       A Record of a Personal and a Literary Friendship.   Edited by
       Harris Wilson.   Urbana: University of Illinois Press; London:
       R. Hart-Davis, pp. 11-31.

Despite similarities between their backgrounds, there were basic differences in experience and viewpoint between W and Bennett. Their differing views are best seen in a series of letters in 1905 when they accuse each other of either missing the point in their respective writings or of a lack of "social perspective." The reasons for their amicable relationship lies in personality and character. Bennett seemed to consider W a genius "both as a novelist and as a social philosopher." He kept urging him to be careful of details in his writing, but W paid no attention. Both were candid critics of each other's work, and in 1905, Bennett accurately predicted the direction that W's career would take. No break occurred in their relationship, merely a break in their correspondence, due partly to twentieth-century methods of communication that made writing unnecessary.

1961

2237   "Amends to a Prophet." Times (London), 8 Aug., p. 9.
    The safe return of cosmonaut Major Titov prompts some editorial comments on the impact of W's prophecy.

2238   "Backwards and Forwards." TLS 20 Oct., p. 751.
    W betrayed his artistic imagination when he accepted irrelevant ideals such as those of the Fabians. "The Door in the Wall," in which the hero turns his back on his career and dies, can be read as representative of W's career. Even the revised editions of Outline are still essentially W's work and "an adult successor to Time Machine and Sleeper Wakes." [Review of the rev. ed. of Outline as well as Bergonzi's The Early H.G. Wells.]

2239   BERGONZI, BERNARD. The Early H.G. Wells: A Study of the Scientific Romances. Manchester: University Press.
    W's literary home is not in some "Wellsian future" but fin de siècle Europe, characterized by an ambivalence toward the advent of the new century. In his day he was compared to storytellers like Stevenson and Haggard and praised for his skills when his subject matter (as in Dr. Moreau) was disturbing. The key to his story structure in Time Machine is the collision of the exotic and the commonplace and the marooning of the hero in an alien environment, a structure that recurs in his later works. A new social awareness in Invisible Man leads to War of the Worlds and beyond. Up to 1901, W was able to define himself against a scientific outlook, but after that he was false to himself; and the "Fabian ideal of 'social service' destroyed the autonomy of his imagination." (Includes texts of "A Tale of the Twentieth Century" and "The Chronic Argonauts.")

1961

2240   CARGILL, OSCAR. The Novels of Henry James.. New York:
        Macmillan, pp. 166, 380, 488.
            It is ingenious, but not valid, to consider The Sense of
        the Past as a time machine just because James admired W's science
        fiction.

2241   CASSELL, RICHARD A. Ford Madox Ford: A Study of His Novels.
        Baltimore: Johns Hopkins Press, pp. 4-5, 21, 47, 72.
            For a time W was among those writers who introduced England
        to the fictional art of the French realists and Turgenev. He
        thought Conrad was in danger of losing his own style by collabo-
        rating with Ford.

2242   CHURCHILL, R.C. "The Comedy of Ideas: Cross-Currents in the
        Fiction and Drama of the Twentieth Century." In The Modern
        Age. Edited by Boris Ford. Pelican Guide to English Litera-
        ture, vol. 7. Baltimore: Penguin, pp. 221-30.
            W had "the Dickensian gift for comic speech" so that his
        characters are remembered more for their idiom than for their
        personalities. In the best of his social comedies, scientific
        romances, and short stories he becomes a minor but original liter-
        ary artist.

2243   CLARKE, I.F. The Tale of the Future: From the Beginning to
        the Present Time. London: Library Association, pp. 5-6;
        index. 2 ed. 1972.
            Since after 1918 progressive and evolutionary ideas ceased
        to be complementary, W was the last exponent of the union of
        Darwinism and progress. All the major forms of the tale of the
        future can be found in his work. [Chronological arrangement of
        titles with brief annotations; includes fourteen by W.]

2244   GARNETT, DAVID. "Some Writers I Have Known: Galsworthy,
        Forster, Moore, and Wells." Texas Quarterly 4:190-202.
            W was a remarkable, but not a great writer. Much of his
        best work is found in his early "lighthearted" scientific stories.
        His later novels tend to be autobiographical, and while Player (a
        parable of the Nazis) is among the best things he wrote, it made
        no impact.

2245   GETTMANN, ROYAL A. Introduction to George Gissing and H.G.
        Wells: Their Friendship and Correspondence. Edited by Royal
        A. Gettmann. Urbana: University of Illinois Press, pp. 11-31.
            There were many similarities between W and Gissing in their
        life and attitudes of mind, but W rose to prosperity and fame whie
        Gissing did not. Their attitude toward journalism primarily ac-
        counts for this difference. W had no difficulty adjusting his
        writing for a market, and his interests were wide. Gissing may

1961

have been "perplexed and uncertain" in his ideas of art, an issue
that did not interest W.

2246   GROSS, JOHN. "History of Mr. Wells." NS 62 (13 Oct.):516-17.
        W was his own literary reputation's greatest opponent. He
claimed so often not to be an artist that people believed him.
The revised edition of Outline still contains the qualities that
made it a classic. [Review of Outline and Bergonzi's Early H.G.
Wells.]

2247   "The H.G. Wells Society." Times (London), 14 June, p. 14.
        The formation of the H.G. Wells Society to study W's works
and encourage dissemination of them was announced.

2248   HENDERSON, ARTHUR. "Internationalists: One Planet Indivisi-
        ble." SR 44 (3 June):25, 40.
        W's contemporaries find it difficult to consider him as
less than a major prophet in letters. All his life he was a
prophet of world order and took advantage of his reputation to
exaggerate dilemmas. One of the most characteristic features of
his writing was his insistence that the planned world order depended on education and on humanity thinking as one.

2249   HILLEGAS, MARK R. "Cosmic Pessimism in H.G. Wells's Scientific
        Romances." Michigan Academy of Science, Arts, and Letters.
        Papers 46:655-63.
        The early novels reflect W's attempts to shock readers out
of their complacency about the inevitability of progress by presenting T.H. Huxley's pessimistic view of the evolutionary process
in imaginative terms.

2250   _____. "Dystopian Science Fiction: New Index to the Human
        Situation." New Mexico Quarterly 31:238-49.
        Science fiction is distantly related to the utopian litera-
ture that is optimistic about science. Among these is W's Utopia.

2251   HOFFMAN, FREDERICK J. "Howards End and the Bogey of
        Progress." MFS 7 (Autumn):243-57.
        The view of progress in Forster's novel is seen more
clearly by contrasting his approach to human situations to that of
W. Forster's "conscientious irony" is radically different from
the "excessive simplicity" in W's extrapolations of society's
present condition to explain the utopian future.

2252   HOUGH, GRAHAM. The Last Romantics. London: Methuen; New
        York: Barnes & Noble, pp. 263-74.
        [Imaginary dialogue--"Conversation in Limbo"--between W and
Yeats; science vs. poetry.]

1961

2253   JONES, DAVID. "Letter; 'Amends to a Prophet.'" <u>Times</u>
        (London), 12 Aug., p. 7.
            W, the one man who saw the future most clearly, was not a
        profound thinker.

2254   LANSFORD, W. DOUGLAS. "The Secret World of H.G. Wells."
        <u>Climax</u> 7 (Feb.):58-68.
            [Fictionalized biography with emphasis on the women in W's
        life.]

2255   MASUR, GERHARD. <u>Prophets of Yesterday: Studies in European
        Culture, 1890-1914</u>. New York: Macmillan, pp. 277, 285, 287-
        89, 291, 381, 397.
            <u>Experiment</u> presents a representative picture of its author,
        "a radical and nonconformist turned socialist and international-
        ist. His attitude always preserved the confidence that animated
        the world before 1914." It was also a representative picture of
        his age.

2256   MEYER, KARL E. <u>The New America: Politics and Society in the
        Age of the Smooth Deal</u>. New York: Basic Books, pp. 171-72,
        175.
            W personified the utopian tradition.

2257   NEWELL, KENNETH B. "The Structure of H.G. Wells' <u>Tono-Bungay</u>."
        <u>EFT</u> 4, pt. 2:1-8.
            Two recurring metaphors (the flight of a skyrocket and the
        life cycle of an organism) in <u>Tono-Bungay</u> parallel the idea of
        "the transformation of reality into illusion," and together they
        suggest the "unifying idea of Change" that becomes the structure
        of this supposedly unstructured novel.

2258   RAY, GORDON N. "H.G. Wells's Contributions to the <u>Saturday
        Review</u>." <u>Library</u> 16 (March):29-36.
            While he began writing scientific and educational articles
        for the <u>SR</u> (London) W soon turned to reviewing novels. He par-
        ticularly enjoyed reviewing the fictional masters of the day and
        as a result developed criteria that would influence his own no-
        vels. [Checklist of 111 contributions by W to the <u>SR</u> (London)
        between 1894 and 1898.]

2259   SCHORER, MARK. <u>Sinclair Lewis: An American Life</u>. New York:
        McGraw-Hill, pp. 95, 181-82, 186, 197, 202; index.
            Lewis was influenced by the satirical aspects of W's novels
        and tried to get Morrow to publish W's work and later proposed him
        for the Nobel Prize. (Morrow felt W was "too intellectual.") The
        central figure in <u>Our Mr. Wrenn</u> was drawn from <u>Mr. Polly</u>. Lewis's
        talkativeness made it difficult for him to become close friends
        with W, since the latter hated noise.

2260   STEVENSON, ELIZABETH. The Crooked Corridor: A Study of Henry
        James. New York: Macmillan, pp. 18, 139, 157.
            James may have been overgenerous toward W and received only
        misunderstanding in Boon.

2261   VOORHEES, RICHARD J. The Paradox of George Orwell. Lafayette,
        Ind.: Purdue University Studies, pp. 73, 85, 99, 109-10.
            W liked to think of the world as a place where the scien-
        tist could represent sanity. Coming Up for Air is part Kipps and
        part Mr. Polly.

2262   WAGER, W. WARREN. H.G. Wells and the World State. New Haven:
        Yale University Press.
            Most of W's best books "overflow with ideas . . . supplying
        the intellectual historian with invaluable clues to the mental
        climate of the years of their publication." In his later writings
        he sought to convert world crisis into world order. Set apart
        from the later prophets by his roots in the nineteenth century,
        his analysis of man's predicament developed naturally from his
        analysis of nineteenth-century English society. He was inclined
        to see life in terms of mental activity instead of economics,
        politics, or geography. The failure at Versailles was a result of
        poor knowledge of history and the closed minds of the treaty
        makers, a belief from which he developed his three Outlines and
        his idea for a world encyclopedia. Distrustful of democracy, he
        proposed a system of rule by "a service aristocracy" responsible
        to "the evolving mind of the race."
            His failures included spreading himself so thin he lost the
        attention of the younger generation. An inconsistent thinker
        experiencing difficulty in working with others, he advanced sound
        theories but could not put them into practice in his own work.
        His success lay in the assimilation of his ideas so completely
        into society that they began to sound like platitudes. He was the
        first twentieth century writer "to predict and dramatize the po-
        litical, economic, social, and religious crisis in contemporary
        Western civilization." He would have to have been "a consummate
        hypocrite" to have been a total pessimist all his life, as some
        claim.

2263   Wellsian 1, no. 2 (Jan.).
            [Statement of aims and objectives of the Society with
        discussion of future activities. Contents include: "The End of
        Oil by H[enry] Zalica; "Wells and the Unconscious" (W was con-
        cerned with the unconscious of society and not Freudian matters);
        "Wells Is a Historical Landmark" by Rupert Pennick (W's ideas are
        his lasting legacy); Addenda to the Books and Pamphlets by H.G.
        Wells.] [Articles in the Wellsian, n.s. annotated individually.]

1961

2264   Wellsian 1, no. 3 (Feb.).
        [Progress Report; Minutes of London Branch Meeting;
        "Wellsian World Citizens" by Hugh J. Schonfield (W's dreams in
        Phoenix find their reality in the Commonwealth of World Citizens);
        "A Wellsian Pamphlet" (the necessity for a concise statement of
        W's ideas); "The Editor's Piece" (What this magazine should
        include).]

2265   Wellsian 1, no. 4 (April ?).
        [Members Forum; "Religious Attitudes in the Novels of H.G.
        Wells," by Michael H. Briggs (W exercised his greatest influence
        on contemporary thought about religion through his imaginative
        writing); "'Little Wars' and General H.G.W.," by Eric N. Simons
        (correspondence with W over a rule of play in the war game);
        "There Is No Substitute for Wool--or Is There?" by P. Lewyckyj
        (reply to article on oil in no. 2); "Proposal--an Institute for
        Comparative Wellsianism," by P.R. Lawton; "Quotations by H.G.
        Wells"; London Branch Meeting; "The Ideas of H.G. Wells," by John
        R. Hammond (world government and a new world through education;
        the socialist idea of a planned world is underlying all his think-
        ing; the adaptation of mankind before he perishes).]

2266   Wellsian 1, no. 5 (July).
        [Contents include: "The Next Steps for the Society"; "The
        Analysis of the Questionnaire (sent to the members)" (included in
        a separate supplement); "Wells and World Government," by Patrick
        Marlowe (the motivating force of W's last years was the idea of
        World Government to permit civilization to survive); "The Morning
        After," by G.F. Smith (W's range of interests and ideas was enor-
        mous, but he had a blind spot in economics and politics); "The
        House Where The Time Machine Was Born," by John R. Hammond (a
        description of Uppark); Members' Forum; Topical Comments.]

2267   Wellsian 1, no. 6 (Nov. ?).
        [Contents include: "Food Unfit for Gods: A Note on the
        Dietary History of H.G. Wells," by W.R. Aykroyd (W didn't realize
        what boyhood malnutrition had done to him until he was an adult);
        "'Anticipations' in Retrospect," by G.F. Smith (W's book is dated
        but useful to the student of the development of his ideas); "News
        Item" (concerns a letter from W to Lidiya Kislova dated 5 Jan.
        1944, dealing with Russian language and literature); "H.G. Wells
        and Religion: Prophet of Humanism or Mystic Manque?" by Patrick
        Marlowe (in spite of his public utterances, W had an intensity of
        vision that amounted to a missionary religion.)]

2268   WILLS, GARRY. Chesterton, Man and Mask. New York: Sheed &
        Ward, pp. 80, 88, 153, 180-83, 184, 186, 194, 195, 199, 231,
        232-33, 235.

Chesterton's review of Outline comprises the entire argument of The Everlasting Man. He did not attack the observed facts of evolution, but the areas of confusion. Chesterton's reply to the Outline was a philosophy of history.

2269 YOUNG, ARTHUR C., ed. The Letters of George Gissing to Eduard Bertz, 1887-1903. London: Constable, pp. x-xi, xxi, xxxiv, xxxvi, 25, 227, 245, 250, 280, 293, 295-96; [index not totally accurate].
W's "memories" of Gissing in Experiment are not reliable. [Passing reference and quotations from W in letters and notes.]

1962

2270 BERGONZI, BERNARD. "The Last Heirs of Dickens." Essays in Criticism 12 (July):314-21. Reprinted as "The Correspondence of Gissing and Wells," in The Turn of a Century: Essays on Victorian and Modern English Literature. New York: Barnes & Noble, 1974; London: Macmillan, 1973), pp. 64-71.
There is little of literary interest beyond the trivial in the letters of Gissing and W. The editor of this collection is "adequate" in his comments on Gissing but "conventional and perfunctory" on W. the most interesting material is contained in W's critical essays on Gissing that appear in the appendices to this collection. The two writers, dissimilar though they were, were also "the last direct heirs of Dickens in serious English fiction." [Review article on George Gissing and H.G. Wells, edited by Royal Gettmann.]

2271 BLAND, D.S. "An Early Estimate of H.G. Wells." EFT 5:21-22.
W was included in a survey of Victorian novels published as no. 77 of the Penny Popular Novels in 1897. Time Machine was an attempt to speculate on the future of the human race while War of the Worlds "affords a fair example of the latest style of fin de siècle romance."

2272 BREWSTER, DOROTHY. Virginia Woolf. New York: New York University Press, pp. 22, 33, 36, 55, 103, 154.
W's views on women irritated Woolf, who labeled him and his contemporaries "materialists" for making the trivial seem important.

2273 BROME, VINCENT. "My Most Unforgettable Character." Reader's Digest 80 (Feb.):134-38.
W was a "man without sham, untroubled by those small hypocrises" in others. He had courage and "taught men not to be blinded by the traditions of the past, but to use their own reasons."

1962

2274   CHAPPELOW, ALLAN. Shaw the Villager and Human Being: A Bio-
        graphical Symposium. New York: Macmillan, pp. 1, 11, 24, 46,
        107-8, 131, 180, 221.
            [Passing references.]

2275   CLARKE, ARTHUR C. "Invisible Men and Other Prodigies."
        Profiles of the Future: An Enquiry into the Limits of the
        Possible. New York: Harper & Row.
            W was writing fantasy, not science fiction, in Invisible
        Man. It is easy to demonstrate why the optical properties of air
        (which Griffin's drug gives him) would not bring about invisibility.

2276   COUSTILLAS, PIERRE. "George Gissing et H.G. Wells." Etudes
        Anglaises 15 (April):156-66.
            The content of Gissing's correspondence with W and the
        German, Eduard Bertz, clarifies our understanding of Gissing's
        family life.

2277   GURKO, LEO. Joseph Conrad: Giant in Exile. New York:
        Macmillan, pp. 105, 121, 146, 155, 247.
            Conrad discussed writing problems with W, who found
        Conrad's "life performance" in the face of adversity "preten-
        tious." Conrad, wanting to challenge Shaw to a duel after an
        attack on his work, was placated by W.

2278   KAGARLITSKIĬ, ÎU. "Uells i Dziul' Vern" [Wells and Jules
        Verne]. Voprosy Literatury (Moscow) 6, no. 6:116-33.
            Jules Verne's novels were fantasies of the past, those of
        W, of the future: so W has more technical and concrete detail
        than Verne. [In Russian.]

2279   KROOK, DOROTHEA. The Ordeal of Consciousness in Henry James.
        Cambridge: University Press, pp. 177, 185, 290, 409.
            [Passing references to James's letter to W that "Art makes
        life. . . ."]

2280   LAND, MYRICK EBBEN. Fine Art of Literary Mayhem. New York:
        Holt, pp. 98-117.
            Part of the attraction between James and W may have been
        their fundamental differences. James was truly concerned that his
        friend was capable of writing trash and told him exactly what he
        thought.

2281   LIGHT, MARTIN. "H.G. Wells and Sinclair Lewis: Friendship,
        Literary Influence, and Letters." EFT 5, no. 4:1-20.
            In their correspondence, Lewis can be seen as a disciple of
        W, deriving a background of social ideas and shaping them into
        fiction. Lewis even nominated W for the Nobel Prize. [Texts of
        eleven exchanges of letters between 1922 and 1937.]

2282   MARSHALL, PETER. "A British Sensation." In Edward Bellamy
        Abroad: An American Prophet's Influence. Edited by Sylvia E.
        Bowman. New York: Twayne, pp. 87-118; index for passing refs.
            W made few references to Bellamy in Utopia, but the
        latter's suggestion that machines free mankind could have had an
        influence on W's utopian thought.

2283   MEIXNER, JOHN A. Ford Madox Ford's Novels: A Critical Study.
        Minneapolis: University of Minnesota Press, pp. 3-4, 12, 202.
            Ford's generosity to young authors made W call him the
        "only Uncle of the Gifted Young." Ford did not think the novelist
        should distort life (as W did) into an image of what the society
        ought to be. W thought Ford's manner "omniscient."

2284   NICKERSON, CHARLES C. "Some Neglected Opinions of H.G. Wells."
        EFT 5, pt 5:27-30.
            W's critics either claim he believed the artist to have a
        moral duty or that he regretted not perfecting his skills instead
        of being didactic. His writings contain many passages that do not
        fit either assertion. He disliked "mediocre taste" and shared
        with his generation "the quest for an exoticism which would hint
        at the sublime." He believed one should cultivate the ideal as a
        rest from the sordid, but also as enabling one to face the real
        world. He writes in "The Lost Inheritance" of a writer who cannot
        keep from worrying about his surroundings being correct for writ-
        ing. His statement about "the war that will end war" has been
        misinterpreted to be a reflection of his own optimism, while his
        parody of James in Boon is really a parody of James's disciples.

2285   OHMANN, RICHARD M. Shaw: The Style and the Man. Middletown,
        Conn.: Wesleyan University Press, pp. 127, 137.
            Richness of illustration makes Shaw's writing interesting.
        In a reply to W's letter on vivisection, which used abstract
        reasoning, Shaw used specific examples.

2286   RAKNEM, INGVALD. H.G. Wells and His Critics. Oslo:
        Universitetsforlaget: London: George Allen & Unwin.
            Few critics of W's fiction paid any attention to his form,
        technique, or style, concentrating instead on his skill as a
        storyteller, his use of science in fiction, his preoccupation with
        the repulsive, the vulgar, and indecent, as well as his work as a
        social novelist, the autobiographical elements in his fiction, his
        characters, lack of psychological insight, and his place in tradi-
        tions of literature typified by writers like Dickens and Verne.
        The early critics missed the point of works like Dr. Moreau and
        Invisible Man, but praised his short stories and his power to
        create the illusion of scientific accuracy. As the social critic
        replaced the narrator in his work it became apparent that he would

1962

never fulfill his early promise as a first-rate novelist. [Surveys the contemporary reaction to W's fiction through examining newspaper and periodical reviews; some attention to later critical studies through 1953; extensive bibliography of reviews and other sources; no index.]

2287   REES, RICHARD. George Orwell, Fugitive from the Camp of Victory. Carbondale: Southern Illinois University Press, pp. 10, 14, 15, 53, 63, 120-23.
     Sensible men may agree with W over the world state, but are powerless to act. The British "angry young man" is manifested differently in W, Orwell, and John Osborne. It was the sheltered English life that made W underrate Hitler's power. Conrad may have carried on James's tradition, but it was W and Shaw who represented the main intellectual current.

2288   SCHWALBE, DORIS JEANNE. "H.G. Wells and the Superfluous Woman." Dissertation, University of Colorado.
    [Listed in Dissertation Abstracts 23 (1962):2120.]

2289   TIMKO, MICHAEL. "H.G. Wells Dramatic Criticism for the Pall Mall Gazette." Library 17:138-45.
     While he did not enjoy being a dramatic critic, W took the task seriously. His work in this field complements his general theories of art and life and add to our understanding of him. [Checklist of thirty-three items from the Pall Mall Gazette attributed to W.]

2290   WALSH, CHAD. From Utopia to Nightmare. New York and Evanston: Harper & Row, pp. 25, 35-36, 39, 54-54; index.
     W's utopia is a more rational and humane world than ours and it strives for greater perfection, yet its creator does not suggest perfection can be achieved. His samurai are Plato's philosopher-rulers, far more complex people than most critics realize. Utopia depicts one of the most plausible future societies ever imagined.

2291   Wellsian 1, no. 7.
    [Contents include: "Cause and Some Effect," by P.R. Lawton (W predicted the breakdown of order before World War I and it was a major concern of his for years explaining his attempt to develop a technology of the future); "Desert Island Wellsianism," by G.F. Smith (a list and discussion of the essential titles by W); "Prophet of World Order," by John R. Hammond (review of H.G. Wells and the World State); "Towards a Wellsian Science Policy," by Alan Mayne.]

2292   Wellsian 1, no. 8 (June).
        [Contents include: "The Successors," by H.D. Baecker (an
injunction for members of the society to read more science fiction
in order to better understand W); an obituary of Frank Horrabin,
illustrator of Outline; "The War of the Germs," by Patrick Marlowe
(plea for total disarmament); notes on Phoenix and War in the Air;
"Wells as Others Saw Him" (quotations); "A Special H.G. Wells
Collection" (University of London's need for certain first editions); "Functional World Authorities" (follow-up to some comments
in vol. 1, no. 7); "The Lesser Known Wells," by John R. Hammond;
and "Wells--the Magnificent Philistine" by William V. Calvert (W
had no scientific discipline).]

2293   Wellsian 1, no. 9.
        [Contents include: "Apostle of Progress," by William V.
Calvert (W's belief in progress is the summation of the man; "H.G.
Wells and Science Fiction," by Arthur C. Clarke (reprint of the
introduction to the Washington Square Press edition of Invisible
Man and War of the Worlds); "The World Encyclopedia," by L.E.C.
Hughes; "The Amateur's Place in Science"; "The Study of the New in
Human Affairs"; "Some Aspects of H.G. Wells," by John R. Hammond
(W's inconsistencies and limitations should be balanced by the
generally positive view of his achievements).]

2294   WILEY, PAUL L. Novelist of Three Worlds: Ford Madox Ford.
        Syracuse, N.Y.: Syracuse University Press, pp. 14, 41, 151,
295.
        Mr. Apollo is close in tone to some of W's scientific
romances, but without his geniality. Ford lacked the "English
place sense" that came so easily to W.

2295   WILSON, COLIN. The Strength to Dream: Literature and the
        Imagination. Boston: Houghton Mifflin; London: Gollancz, pp.
xxii, 50, 97-100, 106-8, 111, 114-15, 116, 117, 121, 122, 125,
126, 129, 182-83, 189, 192, 193, 194, 196, 199-200.
        The weakness in W's scientific optimism is most apparent in
Men Like Gods, where utopia becomes stifling and mechanical.
Reading it makes anti-utopian books comprehensible.

                                    1963

2296   AMIS, KINGSLEY. "H.G. Wells: A Foreword." In H.G. Wells:
        "The War of the Worlds," "The Time Machine" and Selected Short
        Stories. New York: Platt & Munk.
        In W's frightening predictions of what man might become, we
are made to feel his marvels are possible because he united the
fantastic with everyday experience. Striking in the early romances are the variety, the realism, and the poetic feeling.

1963

2297 BARKER, DUDLEY. The Man of Principle: A View of John
Galsworthy. New York: London House & Maxwell; London: Allen
& Unwin, pp. 82, 118, 122, 143, 150.
W wrote a polite note about the characters of Villa Rubein.
Though on occasion W could be complimentary, an instinctive per-
sonal and literary antipathy existed between Galsworthy and him.

2298 DUNBAR, JANET. Mrs. G.B.S. a Portrait. New York: Harper &
Row, pp. 180, 188, 191-94, 222, 258-59.
W might have been of service to the Fabian Society, if he
could have kept his temper. The eulogy at Mrs. W's funeral was
totally false to her character.

2299 HAY, ELOISE KNAPP. The Political Novels of Joseph Conrad.
Chicago and London: University of Chicago Press, pp. 214, 215.
Conrad objected to the "literary truth" and not the general
truth in W, Bennett, and Galsworthy. His fundamental difference
from W was a moral, not an artistic one.

2300 HEPBURN, JAMES G. The Art of Arnold Bennett. Bloomington:
Indiana University Press, pp. 12, 14, 18, 19, 35, 134, 229,
230, 233, 238.
As a realist, Bennett is a more genuine artist than W. The
Pretty Lady is not a patriotic novel in the same way as Mr.
Britling. [Passing references.]

2301 HILLEGAS, MARK R. "Science Fiction as a Cultural Phenomenon:
A Re-Evaluation." Extrapolation 4 (May):26-33. Reprinted in
SF: The Other Side of Realism, ed. Thomas Clareson (Bowling
Green, Ohio: Bowling Green University Press, 1971),
pp. 272-81.
The two greatest examples in twentieth-century fiction of
the use of plausible other worlds to criticize human life are Men
in the Moon and C.S. Lewis's Out of the Silent Planet. W poses
the problem of how the world can achieve stability without dehu-
manizing the individual.

2302 HUGHES, DAVID Y. "An Edition and a Survey of H.G. Wells's The
War of the Worlds." Dissertation, University of Illinois
(Urbana-Champaign).
[Listed in Dissertation Abstracts 23 (1963):2914.]

2303 HURLEY, RICHARD J., ed. "A Word to the Reader." In "The Time
Machine" and Other Stories. New York: Scholastic Book Ser-
vices, pp. iii-vi.
In his rise from obscurity to world fame, W can be called
"the Horatio Alger of speculative fiction and English letters."
His persuasiveness and perception won him an audience. He tricks
the reader into accepting his fantasy in Time Machine by using

ordinary people and places in the opening section. As both narrator and main character, the author is able to present his own
views. He liberated science fiction from the formula of Verne.

2304   KATEB, GEORGE. Utopia and Its Enemies. New York: Free Press,
        pp. 115, 198-99, 220-21; index.
        W excels in writing of the "advantages of adversity and
strife to human nature." In Utopia he is at his most practical.
Modern utopianism denied the doctrine of original sin, and W was
prepared to deny it, aware that his utopia was unique in granting
liberty and privacy. His utopia was unusual in suggesting a
society that corrects the world's follies.

2305   KORG, JACOB. George Gissing: A Critical Biography. Seattle:
        University of Washington Press, pp. 16, 206-7, 209-10, 211,
        222-23; index.
        Gissing, like W may have found himself overworked and
underpaid as a teacher. Their origins only superficially similar,
W must have seemed proletarian to Gissing, who admired him for
being self-educated. W objected to the ideal of scholarly refinement in Gissing's work and he tried to care for Gissing during the
latter's dying days. His suppressed introduction to Veranilda was
published in a revised form in the Monthly Review, but the references to personal matters met with general indignation.

2306   LANGNER, LAWRENCE. G.B.S. and the Lunatic. New York:
        Atheneum, pp. 113-14.
        W's attack on Shaw in the NYT in 1927 irritated his
friends, but not Shaw himself.

2307   MILLER, WALTER J., ed. "Reader's Supplement." In The Invis-
        ible Man. Reader's Enrichment Series. New York: Washington
        Square Press, pp. 1-36. [Pagination separate from novel.]
        W's simple formula to make his science fiction real was to
mix small portions of fantasy with large ones of real life. Like
Griffin, he had been a teacher, had experienced poverty, was
blunt, and disliked trivia. Like Kemp, he had a "keen sense of
the social ethics of science. [Contains a biographical sketch,
historical background, analysis of W's style, analysis of characters, vocabulary exercise, and questions for discussion.]

2308   MOSKOWITZ, SAM. "The Wonders of Wells." In Explorers of the
        Infinite: Shapers of Science Fiction. Cleveland and New York:
        World, pp. 128-41.
        W is the answer to the question; "Is science-fiction lit-
erature?" It isn't his ideas, or his sensationalism, or even his
warnings to civilization that keep his stories alive, but "the
word-mastery of a literary genius, who took the elements of the

1963

scientific 'boys' tales' and 'thrillers' and created permanent and
enduring literature."

2309   NULLE, STEBELTON H.   "The General Education of H.G. Wells."
       University College Quarterly 8 (March):22-26.
       The thoughtful educator in the first half of the twentieth
century is in debt to W. His plan for general education included
the preparation of the citizen for the world state he anticipated,
but it was "too utopian, too authoritarian, too remote" from a
world that was not ready for knowledge.

2310   PRITCHETT, V.S.   "The Prognosticators."   NS 66 (20 Sept.):360.
       There has been no master of science fiction since W, only
literacy, more experience and knowledge, much inventiveness, but
little imagination. Wonder was possible in his day, and he could
squeeze the most from "ironical doubt." When he became journalistic and depended upon mere notions he failed. Time Machine is
"one of the most assured and intense short fantasies in the language." He always had a "shrewd eye for the imponderables," as
one may see in War of the Worlds when the Martians win yet die
anyway. "Being a master, he has a warm narrative style and a view
of human life."

2311   SCHORER, MARK.   Sinclair Lewis.   Minneapolis: University of
       Minnesota Press, p. 41.
       Lewis wove the "diluted optimism" he found in W's novels
into the positive element in his otherwise negative view of American life.

2312   SMART, J.I.C.   "Is Time Travel Possible?"   Journal of
       Philosophy 60 (April):237-41.
       Since space-time cannot be treated as a space in the con-
tinuant sense, W's time machine could not remain at the same point
on the Earth's surface while moving up and down the Earth's world
line.

2313   STEVENSON, LIONEL.   "The Artistic Problem: Science Fiction as
       Romance."   Extrapolation 4 (May):17-22.
       W combined a journalist's curiosity and intelligence with a
disregard for tradition to transform Verne's boys' adventures into
a new type of story.

2314   STEWART, J.I.M.   Eight Modern Writers.   London: Oxford Uni-
       versity Press, pp. 11-12.
       W dramatized the impatience and aspirations of a genera-
tion. If he did not give wisdom, he gave exhilaration.

2315   Wellsian 1, no. 10.
       [Contents include: "Towards a Science of Invention and
Innovation" (editorial); "Wellsiana," by John R. Hammond (notes on
Penguin ed. of Moreau and Fremantle's Little Band of Prophets;
"Humanists and Mystics"; "Living Religion as a Section of the
World Encyclopedia," by J.H. Ovenden; "H.G. Wells Award Essay: An
Appreciation of The Time Machine," by Andrew R. Cherry (W must be
allowed poetic license in his description of the machine itself);
"H.G. Wells as a Political Thinker," by P. Yarr (W had a consis-
tent political philosophy and unified the whole of nineteenth and
early twentieth-century thought).]

2316   WHITTEMORE, REED. "The Fascination of the Abomination--Wells,
       Shaw, Ford, Conrad." In The Fascination of the Abomination:
       Poems, Stories, and Essays. New York: Macmillan, pp. 129-66.
       Much of the art in W is "the art of argument." Mr.
Britling, confronted by the abomination of war, tries to view it
through rose-colored glasses until the hard facts make it impossible. It is important for W to set up a scheme to "weed out the
abominations" so that any reality in his fiction is tidy and well-
groomed. Shaw follows this pattern, while Conrad and Ford tend to
become more deeply involved with the problems in their books.

                              1964

2317   BERGONZI, BERNARD. "Before 1914: Writers and the Threat of
       War." Critical Quarterly 6 (Summer):126-34.
       War in the Air is "a shapeless book" but "contains a fairly
good anticipation of the horrors of aerial bombardment." In World
Set Free, war is "prelude to utopia" but reflects the international alliances of 1914. War of the Worlds conveys "an apocalyptic vision."

2318   BORGES, JORGE LUIS. "The First Wells." In Other Inquisitions
       1937-1952. Austin: University of Texas Press, pp. 86-88.
       Reprinted in CH, pp. 330-32.
       W was an admirable storyteller before he became "a socio-
logical spectator." He wrote for all ages in contrast to Jules
Verne who wrote for young people. His first books "tell a story
symbolic of processes that are somehow inherent in all human des-
tinies." W's doctrines were all right, but he should not have put
them into his narrative fiction.

2319   CAMPBELL, ALEX. "Between Education and Catastrophe." NR 151
       (31 Oct.):19-20.
       Ideas grew in W's presence, flowing naturally from his
grasp of science. His final pessimism may have a sound basis.

1964

2320   EDWARDS, OLIVER. "At the Villa Jasmin." Times (London), 3
       Sept., p. 13.
           Clissold has something to offer the reader who will take
       the time to look for it. Clissold himself is a more real char-
       acter than Mr. Britling, although the pleasure in reading the book
       today may be in seeing him against the glamour and illusions of
       the 1920s.

2321   GEMME, FRANCIS R. Introduction to The War of the Worlds. New
       York: Airmont, pp. 3-6.
           The plausibility of the novel results from the author's
       knowledge of evolution in depicting the Martians. In the story, W
       is a prophet of the anxieties that mankind would face in the atomic
       and space age. [Biographical sketch.]

2322   H.G. Wells Society Bulletin, n.s., nos. 1-20 (Feb. 1964-
       Autumn 1971).
           [News and notes on matters of interest to the Society: new
       editions of W's works, special collections, doings of members of
       the Society in matters considered to be Wellsian or of which W
       would have approved, reviews of current books.]

2323   KETTERER, DAVID. New Worlds for Old: The Apocalyptic Imagina-
       tion, Science Fiction, and American Literature. Garden City,
       N.Y.: Anchor Books, pp. x, 16, 18n, 21, 32, 50, 67; index.
           W may owe something to Poe's "The Conversation of Eiros and
       Charmion" for his "The Star" and Comet. He may have originated
       the "terminal beach" myth (the end of man comes on a beach as life
       once came from the sea) in Time Machine and "The Star." His
       suggestion of time as the fourth dimension sets the rationale for
       time travel, but it becomes accepted as a convention for the sake
       of the story rather than as a realistic possibility. The alien
       threat in War of the Worlds, where it is not technology but bac-
       teria that wins, points up the destructive potential of human
       pride.

2324   LID, R.W. Ford Madox Ford: The Essence of His Art. Berkeley
       and Los Angeles: University of California Press, p. 11.
           The hallmarks of the artist are eccentricity, whimsey, and
       fantasy, but W was offended by Ford's poses.

2325   LOWNDES, ROBERT A.W. Introduction to The Invisible Man. New
       York: Airmont, pp. 3-8.
           The central feature of W's character and work is "univer-
       sality." His humor is that of "understanding, without the bitter-
       ness of the great satirists like Swift." The themes of his
       science fiction concern the ways in which reaching the moon or
       becoming invisible affect characters.

1964

2326   MADOW, PAULINE. "The Horse's Mouth." Nation (New York) 199
       (7 Dec.):444-46.
          W may have considered himself a journalist but this is "too
       impoverished a label to describe prophetic genius, historical
       understanding, psychological and sociological insight." [Review
       of H.G. Wells: Journalism and Prophecy 1893-1946, edited by W.
       Warren Wager.]

2327   MERRIAM, RAY BYRON. "The Educational Theories of H.G. Wells."
       Dissertation, New York University.
          [Listed in Dissertation Abstracts 25 (1964):2380.]

2328   NOWELL-SMITH, SIMON, ed. Edwardian England: 1901-1914.
       London: Oxford University Press, pp. 141, 153-54, 182, 188,
       211, 297-300, 309, 310, 312, 325, 365.
          W's novels have provided characteristic portraits of the
       domestic lives of the middle classes. While the public identified
       Shaw and W with the Fabians, both were too individualistic to be
       so neatly labeled. W's connections were to lead him more and more
       into planning utopian societies. Any student of the social life
       of the time must read W, Bennett, and Galsworthy.

2329   RAMSAYE, TERRY. A Million and One Nights: A History of the
       Motion Picture. New York: Simon & Schuster, pp. 147-62.
          Robert Paul saw in Time Machine a chance to use motion
       pictures as an effective means of narration. The changes of scene
       described by the Time Traveller are precisely the same as watching
       images move backwards or forwards on film.

2330   SCHULZ, JOAN EVELYN. "A Study of H.G. Wells's In the Days of
       the Comet." Dissertation, University of Illinois.
          [Listed in Dissertation Abstracts 24 (1964):4200.]

2331   STONE, EDWARD. The Battle and the Books: Some Aspects of
       Henry James. Athens: Ohio University Press, pp. 5-6, 19, 45-
       46, 150, 172-73, 195, 198-99.
          The unsettling caused by the Great War may have been partly
       the stimulus for W's attack on James in Boon. Time travel had
       been a theme of literature before W, but he was the first to
       create a scientific basis for it.

2332   TAINE, JOHN. "Writing a Science Novel." In Of Worlds Beyond:
       The Science of Science Fiction Writing. Edited by Lloyd Arthur
       Eshbach. Chicago: Advent, pp. 23-36.
          It is the unusual writer who can write fiction based on the
       physical, biological, and engineering sciences. W had the educa-
       tion for the first two and imagination enough for the third. He
       also had to keep up with the changes in science.

1964

2333   TIMKO, MICHAEL. "H.G. Wells and 'The Most Unholy Trade.'"
       English Language Notes 1:280-84.
           Increased royalties and the tightening of copyright laws
       made many writers turn to playwriting as a short cut to wealth in
       the later nineteenth century. W reflects this road to riches as a
       recurrent theme in many novels, and he may have regretted not
       making more of an effort in this direction himself.

2334   _____, ed. "H.G. Wells and the Theatre." In Hoopdriver's
       Holiday. Lafayette, Ind.: English Literature in Transition,
       Special Series, pp. iv-xiii.
           W's interest in the theater has been largely ignored by the
       critics. His knowledge of the dramatic conventions of the time
       dates from his brief period as dramatic critic for the Pall Mall
       Gazette. He dramatized Wheels of Chance as Hoopdriver's Holiday
       and attempted an original play, "The Tail of the Comet." His
       failure to get Hoopdriver produced and his growing success in
       other fields led to his loss of interest in drama. The play sheds
       some light on his developing art and thought because in it criti-
       cism of society becomes the dominant theme.

2335   WEIAND, HERMANN. "H.G. Wells: 'The Country of the Blind.'"
       In Insight II: Analyses of British Literature. Edited by
       John V. Hagopian and Martin Dolch. Frankfurt: Hirschgraben,
       pp. 344-55.
           A close examination of the symbolic meaning of light and
       darkness in W's story suggests an awakening of man to higher
       truths found in the realm of the spirit.

1965

2336   ALLEN, JERRY. The Sea Years of Joseph Conrad. Garden City,
       N.Y.: Doubleday, pp. 2, 14, 29-30, 62, 299, 301-3, 308.
           Conrad admired W enough to dedicate The Secret Agent to
him.

2337   AMIS, KINGSLEY. "Party of One. Science Fiction: A Practical
       Nightmare." Holiday 37 (Feb.):8-15.
           W created most of the themes of science fiction and used
       them "in prose of greater force and energy than any of his suc-
       cessors. . . . His mythic power, his ability to allegorize in
       striking terms some of our deepest instincts and wishes and fears,
       is unique."

2338   BORRELLO, ALFRED. "H.G. Wells: Art of the Novel."
       Dissertation, St. John's University (Brooklyn).

[Listed in Lawrence F. McNamee, Dissertations in English and American Literature, supp. 1 (New York & London: Bowker, 1969).] Published as entry 2588.

2339   BROWN, IVOR. Shaw in His Time. London: Nelson, pp. 70, 106, 139, 141, 143, 158, 194.
        [Passing references, mostly on W's influence and satires on the Fabians.]

2340   CANNING, JOHN, ed. 100 Great Modern Lives. New York and London: Hawthorn, pp. 311-16. Reprinted. London: Souvenir Press; New York: Crown/Beekman House, 1972.
        Like all great novelists, W was a man with a message. His writings make him one of the most powerful influences of his time. [Brief biography.]

2341   CECIL, DAVID. Max: A Biography. Boston: Houghton Mifflin, pp. 145, 180, 244, 251, 252, 270, 367, 441.
        Beerbohm thought W's utopias "cheap and unlovely" and his habit of putting friends in his novels insensitive.

2342   CLAES, V. "De invloed van Wells' 'God the Invisible King' op het werk van Pär Lagerkvist" [The influence of Wells' "God the Invisible King" on the work of Pär Lagerkvist]. Studia Germanica Gandensia 7:287-97.
        W's personal theology was most clearly expressed in God, which contrasted God the Creator with a finite, personal God of the Heart. This theology struck a responsive chord among followers of the livstro ("faith in life") movement in Sweden, which included Pär Lagerkvist. Although the primary influence on Lagerkvist was undoubtedly Ellen Key, W's essay contains imagery that reappears in some of Lagerkvist's poetry, in his drama Den Osynlige ("The Invisible One"), and in the essay Det besigrade livet ("The Vanquished Life"). Most striking among the parallels are the image of God as a youth, God as an impotent king, and God as invisible. The distinction between a lordly, eternal Being and a personal Deity made manifest only through the works of man reappears as well in Lagerkvist's work. [In Dutch.]

2343   EVANS, I.O. Jules Verne and His Work. London: Arco, pp. 11, 63, 84, 140, 155-60, 161.
        Verne contrasts sharply with W, who gave his imagination free range and was not as scrupulous about the factual basis of his science fiction. He is less documentary than Verne but goes into detail in his real flights of fancy.

2344   GUIGUET, JEAN. Virginia Woolf and Her Works. New York: Harcourt, Brace & World, pp. 38, 43, 118, 137, 244, 358.
        [Translated from Virginia Woolf et son oeuvre (1962).]

1965

       W disappoints because life eludes him. He is representa-
tive of a trend or theory in Woolf's criticism, not a subject of
critical study.

2345   HOEL, SIGURD. "Om Nazismens vesen" [On the nature of Nazism].
       In Essays I Utvalg. Edited by Nils Lie. Oslo: Gyldendal,
       pp. 9-37.
       The methods and ideology of Nazism are reminiscent of the
worst excesses described by W in Dr. Moreau. [In Norwegian.]

2346   HUGHES, DAVID Y. "H.G. Wells: Ironic Romancer."
       Extrapolation 6 (May):32-38.
       Three early short stories ("The Sea Raiders," "Aepyornis
Island," and "The Empire of the Ants") have their sources in
scientific writings read by their author. The stories begin with
the excitement of scientific progress, which is balanced by the
irony of human insignificance at the end. This change of perspective helps to keep the early work from being dated.

2347   KACZ-PALCZEWSKI, JULIUSZ. "O zainteresowaniu H.G. Wellsa
       przyszłoscią" [On H.G. Wells' interest in the Future].
       Przegląd Humanistyczny (Warsaw) 9, no. 2:73-84.
       For W, the future was something more realistic than the
present, which is only the shadow of a dream. [In Polish.]

2348   LEBOWITZ, NAOMI. The Imagination of Loving: Henry James's
       Legacy to the Novel. Detroit: Wayne State University Press,
       pp. 11, 12, 15, 50.
       There are still critics who will agree with W's description
of a James novel; only James's example can refute it.

2349   LEEPER, GEOFFREY. "The Happy Utopias of Huxley and Wells."
       Meanjin Quarterly 24 (March):120-24.
       The horrible utopias of Orwell and Huxley remain in fashion
while the happy ones of W do not. Huxley's last novel, Island,
was an attempt to depict a happy utopia and may have been influenced by Men Like Gods. [Passing comment that C.P. Snow forgot
about W when he wrote of the Two Cultures; almost alone of men in
the twentieth century, W belonged to both.]

2350   LUDWIG, RICHARD M., ed. Letters of Ford Madox Ford.
       Princeton, N.J.: Princeton University Press, pp. 18, 21, 22,
       25, 26, 28, 31-38, 42-43, 53, 56, 63, 119-22, 123, 154, 157-58,
       169, 237, 248-50.
       Mankind is delightful reading, but W errs in upholding
Elizabethanism as a model for English and in undervaluing Latin.
While taking issue with parts of Utopia the book succeeds in
presenting a memorable picture. Kipps is W's best novel, and
Tono-Bungay has all the qualities of the classic English novel. W

broke his word to Ford repeatedly during the English Review incident, and Ford annoyed W by writing to his wife and by treating it like a business affair. W disputed Ford's claim that he had ever instructed Ford in writing.

2351   LUPOFF, RICHARD A. *Edgar Rice Burroughs: Master of Adventure.* New York: Canaveral Press, pp. 3, 23, 31, 32, 93, 94, 105, 186, 273.
         The Morlocks and Eloi may have been an influence on the Hither and Thither people in Edwin Lester Arnold's *Gulliver of Mars* just as *Men in the Moon* may have influenced *The Moon Maid.*

2352   MacSHANE, FRANK. *The Life and Work of Ford Madox Ford.* New York: Horizon Press, pp. 31, 37, 38–39, 51–53, 56–57, 60–63, 65, 75–77, 82–83, 86, 90, 119, 129–30, 156, 164, 187, 206.
         After being exposed to Ford's enthusiasm about the mechanics of style, W was content to call himself a journalist and not a novelist. Ford even chided W for "nostalgia" in *Mankind.* By Jan. 1908, they planned starting a magazine together which would have serialized *Tono-Bungay.* The cause of their disagreement was financial, but Ford's abusive letter to Mrs. W did not help. Only W remained loyal to Ford during Ford's marital difficulties. In their respective early work, W's characters and situations are real while Ford's are not. [Passing references.]

2353   PEARCE, T[HOMAS] M. *Mary Hunter Austin.* New York: Twayne, pp. 39–40, 69.
         Mary Austin reported W's conversation with her about his domestic problem in the first printing of *Earth Horizon*, but she removed it at his request from the later printings.

2354   PEARSON, ANTHONY. "H.G. Wells and *Pincher Martin.*" *Notes and Queries*, n.s. 12 (July):275–76.
         William Golding may have remembered W's story "The Remarkable Case of Davidson's Eyes" when writing *Pincher Martin.* There are several parallels--e.g., "The idea of one area of the mind building up an image that the rest refuses to accept"--between the two, although the themes are quite different.

2355   PEARSON, HESKETH. *Hesketh Pearson by Himself.* New York: Harper & Row, pp. 266–70.
         A prophet may contradict himself by nature, but no one was more contradictory in his statements than W. His "concern with humanity had completely vitiated his understanding of human beings." He disliked praise for his early novels and couldn't control his temper. "Wells was a lesser Dickens, small and tubby and easily offended; Shaw was a greater Voltaire, tall and lean and impervious to insult."

1965

2356 POSTON, LAWRENCE, III. "Tono-Bungay: Wells's Unconstructed
Tale." College English 26:433-38.
In the story of George Ponderevo W shows "a society moving
from an established tradition to a doubtful future."

2357 "Quick Guide to New Reading." Times (London), 26 Aug., p. 11.
Short History (1922) has been revised and brought up to
date by Raymond Postgate and G.P. Wells. The last chapters cover
the Russian Revolution to the 1963 Nuclear Test Ban Treaty.

2358 SMITH, J. PERCY. The Unrepentant Pilgrim: A Study of the
Development of Bernard Shaw. Boston: Houghton Mifflin, pp.
96, 97, 101.
Shaw won the Fabian Society debate partly by his style and
squelched W with a joke.

2359 TAUBMAN, HOWARD. "The Theater: 'Half a Sixpence' Opens."
NYT, 26 April, p. 38.
With script by Beverly cross, music and lyrics by David
Heneker, Kipps has been freely adapted into a Victorian soap opera
with music. The plot cannot be taken seriously, and the music is
largely responsible for the show's virtues.

2360 TIMKO, MICHAEL. "Entente cordiale: The Dramatic Criticism of
Shaw and Wells." Modern Drama 8:39-46.
The differences between Shaw and W often obscure their
mutual admiration for each other. A close examination of their
drama reviews of Jan.-May 1895 indicates similar attitudes toward
the theater. W disagreed with Shaw in his approach to writing in
general and not on any specific theory of drama.

2361 WAGAR, W. WARREN. Introduction to H.G. Wells: Journalism and
Prophecy, 1893-1946. Boston: Houghton Mifflin, 1964; London:
Bodley Head, 1965), pp. xv-xxvi.
W wrote a little of everything and is thus unclassifiable.
After 1910 journalism ruined his novels as works of art. Whatever
art and craftsmanship he possessed he gave to "the cause of an
integrated world civilization." His essays are documents in contemporary history, but contrary to popular belief he was not a
very good prophet and was often "preposterously wrong." The true
disciple of W is the man who comes to his own conclusions.

2362 WOLLHEIM, DONALD A. Introduction to The Food of the Gods. New
York: Airmont, pp. 1-5.
W's message in Food of the Gods is to concentrate on the
great things in life and the reason for their greatness and to
forget one's immediate problems.

1966

2363   ADLER, HENRY. "Letters to the Editor: H.G. Wells." Listener
       76 (4 Aug.):168.
       [List of contradictions in Taylor, "The Man who Tried to
Work Miracles," Listener, 21 July 1966.]

2364   "The Arts." Times (London), 1 Aug., p. 6.
       Horizon on BBC 2 concentrated its tribute to W on his role
as a man of science, with Professor Ritchie Calder remarking on
the influence of his novels on the present generation of scientists and with Professor G.P. Wells speaking of his father's
aspirations.

2365   "As It Happens: Chez Kipps." Times (London), 14 May, p. 11.
       Spade House, Folkestone, built by W in the 1890s, is to be
the center of some centenary events.

2366   "As It Happens: War of Knife and Fork; Mr. Polly in the
       Lords." Times (London), 14 Sept., p. 11.
       Conflicts in scheduling leave W's birthplace, Bromley,
without a major commemorative dinner, while a plaque at Hanover
Terrace and a dinner in the House of Lords seem set for the near
future.

2367   BARKER, DUDLEY. Writer by Trade: A Portrait of Arnold
       Bennett. New York: Atheneum, pp. 29, 31, 53, 60, 97, 98, 101,
       112, 113; index.
       Bennett thought W was one of the most stimulating men he
knew. W introduced him to the literary agent J.B. Pinker and
reproached him for not being bold enough in Leonora. However
frequently they quarreled on literary matters, they were close
correspondents until Bennett's death.

2368   BERGONZI, BERNARD. Introduction to Tono-Bungay. Boston:
       Houghton Mifflin, pp. v-xxiii. Reprinted as "Tono-Bungay," in
       The Turn of a Century: Essays on Victorian and Modern English
       Literature (New York: Barnes & Noble, 1974; London:
       Macmillan, 1973), pp. 72-98.
       Tono-Bungay was almost the last and most ambitious work of
tribute W made to the art of the novel. As a novel of ideas it
functions by turning problems into "imaginative entities." The
vitality and humor of the early chapters compensate for W's failure to relate the lives of the characters to the social action.

2369   BROME, VINCENT. "H.G. Wells as a Controversialist." Univer-
       sity of Windsor Review 2:31-45.

1966

W's controversies with the figures of his days—James, Shaw, Belloc—reflect not only his own personal troubles, but the conflicts of his time.

2370   BUCKLEY, JEROME HAMILTON. The Triumph of Time: A Study of the Victorian Concepts of Time, History, Progress, and Decadence. Cambridge, Mass.: Harvard University Press, pp. 67, 86-88, 89, 113-14, 170.
Though known as prophet of science and progress, W had experienced a darker view, and his theme of decadence links late Victorians with the later generation. The symbolism and implication of "The Door in the Wall" is "patently sexual."

2371   CALDER, NIGEL. "Wells and the Future." NS 72 (23 Sept.):427.
W tried to persuade us to take the future seriously, but we have barely begun to look for answers to the important questions.

2372   CHAPPELOW, ALLAN. "Memoir: To H.G. Wells—In Heaven or Hell. A Centenary Tribute." CR 209 (Dec.):305-8.
W's frail body was "scarcely more than a vehicle for [his] amazing mind." He was the man of his age, as Voltaire was the man of his. He underestimated the irrational elements in human nature and placed too much value on externals, but he taught an age to dream.

2373   CLARKE, I.F. Voices Prophesying War. London and New York: Oxford University Press, pp. 3, 73, 91-92, 93-103, 178, 206.
War of the Worlds conveys the perfect nineteenth-century myth of the imaginary war. W's imagination worked out three principle ideas: the violence of colonial warfare, the Darwinian struggle between competing groups, and the potential of advanced military technology. His story transcends all the limitations of the mass of imaginary war fiction.

2374   COLLINS, CHRISTOPHER. "Zamyatin, Wells and the Utopian Literary Tradition." Slavonic and East European Review 44:351-60.
Zamyatin wrote a parody of W in his novel We, yet their utopian visions coincide. W "combined the social satire of Swift, the Utopianism of Plato, the science fantasy of Verne, and the English travel-adventure novel of Defoe." Zamyatin introduced conflict into utopian fiction, but conflict engendered from within the self.

2375   COSTA, RICHARD HAUER. "Wells and the Cosmic Despair." Nation (New York) 203 (12 Sept.):222-24.
A reassessment of W must begin with his earlier books and not dwell on his later years. His major works "form a catalogue of foreboding" and warnings to mankind. One of his final pieces of writing was a revision of "The Country of the Blind," making

its ending express his later pessimism. He could never resolve the conflict between artist and educator.

2376   "Diversity of Views on Wells." Times (London), 16 Sept., p. 14.
        Christopher Burstall's script for BBC 1's tribute to W ("Whoosh") covered so much territory that no strong portrait emerged. Everyone interviewed had a different view of him.

2377   EDWARDS, JULIETTE. "Letters: Prophetic Wells." TLS, 21 July, p. 635.
        Edward Ponderevo called a house "a machine you can live in" more than ten years before Le Corbusier used the phrase.

2378   ELTON, JOHN. "How Well Have They Worn?-15: Mr. Britling Sees It Through." Times (London), 14 April, p. 15.
        The story of Mr. Britling's love for his son is a masterpiece of storytelling. W's interruptive "dissertations" are unreadable today and make the book into a museum piece, saved only by the superb writing in the final chapter.

2379   FRYE, NORTHROP. "Varieties of Literary Utopias." In Utopias and Utopian Thought. Edited by Frank Manuel. Boston: Houghton Mifflin, pp. 25-49.
        W created both serious and satirical utopias, and his writing demonstrates that a view of man as good by nature does not lead to a "good-natured view" of man. The scientists in charge are a new version of the priestly elite.

2380   "H.G. Wells, A Backward Look at a Prophet." Illustrated London News 249 (24 Sept.):14-15.
        [Some of the milestones in W's life as recorded in past issues of Illustrated London News.]

2381   HAYNES, RENEE. "Letters to the Editor: H.G. Wells." Listener 76 (28 July):132.
        W's "impossibilities" are really more possible than Taylor suggests. [Reply to A.J.P. Taylor: "The Man Who Tried to Work Miracles," Listener, 21 July 1966.]

2382   HEINLEIN, ROBERT A. "Pandora's Box." In The Worlds of Robert A. Heinlein. New York: Ace, pp. 7-31. Reprinted in Damon Knight Turning Points: Essays on the Art of Science Fiction (New York: Harper & Row, 1977), pp. 238-58.
        As prophecy W's stories are dated, but they are still spellbinding because he never forgot to be entertaining. His method was to take a basic new assumption and examine its consequences in human terms.

1966

2383   HUGHES, DAVID Y.   "H.G. Wells and the Charge of Plagiarism."
       Nineteenth Century Fiction 21:85-90.
          Ingvald Raknem in H.G. Wells and His Critics accuses W of
       plagiarism, but the charge is difficult to prove. The similari-
       ties between Wonderful Visit and Grant Allen's The British Bar-
       barians are coincidental, both writers borrowing from a recogniz-
       able and common literary tradition.

2384   _____. "The War of the Worlds in the Yellow Press."
       Journalism Quarterly 43:639-46.
          The Mercury Theatre adaptation of War of the Worlds was
       viewed by W as an infringement of copyright in the same way as
       were the sensational versions of the original story that the New
       York Journal and Boston Post serialized in 1898.

2385   HUTCHINSON, GERTRUDE. "Letters to the Editor: H.G. Wells."
       Listener 76 (4 Aug.):168.
          W hoped some day the stronger and the better sides of human
       nature would unite. His characters are more real than one imag-
       ines, and the television commercial of today is but an extension
       of the advertisements for Tono-Bungay. [Reply to Taylor, "The Man
       Who Tried to Work Miracles," Listener, 21 July 1966, by former
       secretary to W.]

2386   KADZ-PALCZEWSKI, JULIUSZ. "Utopia eksperymentalna H.G. Wellsa"
       [H.G. Wells's experimental utopia]. Kwartalnik Neofilologiczny
       (Warsaw) 13, no. 3:311-17.
          Although W created a modern framework for utopia, he could
   not always give it a modern content. [In Polish.]

2387   KAGARLITSKY, JULIUS. "H.G. Wells in Russia." Soviet Litera-
       ture, no. 9, pp. 150-55.
          W probably never knew how popular he was in Russia. War of
       the Worlds appeared in 1897, and collected editions of his works
       in translation have appeared at intervals ever since. His visits
       helped promote interest, but it was his thinking in terms of
       epochs and making heroes of entire social classes that attracted
       Russians the most.

2388   _____. The Life and Thought of H.G. Wells. London: Sidgwick
       & Jackson. [Translated from the Russian, Gerbert Uells
       (Moscow: Gosizdat, 1963).]
          W was "a great prophet and the grand daredevil of modern
       literature" who needs to be evaluated on a large scale. He needed
       to be in the center of controversy because nothing left him indif-
       ferent. If his "shots" seemed to miss the target, it was because
       people were impatient to see immediate results. The tendency of
       art to generalize as well as to be specific fascinated him; art
       was for him a separate form of activity that was only part of the

whole existence of mankind. His thought served as the instrument
of generalization by which to portray the diversity of the world.
His place in the literary world was determined by his attitude
that one cannot describe the present without considering the
future.

2389 KANIN, GARSON. Remembering Mr. Maugham. New York: Atheneum,
      pp. 23, 101, 144, 147, 149.
      W dealt with "burning issues" that eventually disappeared.

2390 KOVALEV, IŨ . V. "Gerbert Uells v sovetskoĭ kritike 1920-kh
      godov" [H.G. Wells in Soviet criticism of the twenties].
      Vestnik Leningradskogo Universiteta (seriĩa istorii, ĩazyka i
      literaturу) (Leningrad) no. 20, pp. 89-97.
      In the early twenties, W's basic themes coincided with
      vital questions in the Soviet Union, including the liquidation of
      the consequences of World War I. But W was also attacked by
      Soviet critics as "a real bourgeois who does not believe in the
      future happiness of mankind." Other critics protested against
      these attacks, finding in his work genuine values that might be
      placed at the service of the Revolution. [In Russian with an
      English summary.]

2391 _____. "Pomoshch' Uellsa russkim uchenym" [Wells' assistance
      for Russian scholars]. In Russko-Evropeiskie literaturnye
      sviãzi. Moscow: "Nauka," pp. 378-85.
      Gorky wrote to W (13 Aug. 1920) asking for material help
      for Soviet scholars. After W visited the Soviet Union he arranged
      for the despatch of scholarly literature. [In Russian.]

2392 LEVIDOVA I.M., and B.M. PARCHEVSKAĨA. Gerbert Dzhordzh Uells.
      Bibliografiĩa Russkikh Perevodov i kriticheskoi literatury na
      Russkom ĩa zike, 1898-1965 [Herbert George Wells. Bibliography
      of Russian translations and critical literature in the Russian
      language]. Moscow: "Kniga."
      [Eight-hundred-sixty-seven entries, some of many volume
      editions. Seven "collected works" of W (the first in 1909),
      several with good "apparatus," have been published in Russian.
      Between 1945 and 1954, W was not published in the Soviet Union,
      corresponding to a general decline of interest in his works. The
      latest "complete works" in Russian (1964) was printed in 300,000
      copies.] [Abstract of review by Iu. Kagarlitskii, "Uells v
      Rossii" [Wells in Russia], Voprosy Literatury (Moscow) 7
      (1966):242-43.] [In Russian.]

2393 LODGE, DAVID. "Tono-Bungay and the Condition of England." In
      Language of Fiction. New York: Columbia University Press, pp.
      214-42; London: Routledge & Kegan Paul. Reprinted in CE,
      pp. 110-39.

1966

In Tono-Bungay the central character is not George
Ponderevo but England itself. The theme is "the condition of
England," in which W shows England as an organism undergoing a
process of change and decay. He achieves this through his topo-
graphical and architectural descriptions. His style may not be
that of Henry James, but it "has its own kind of expressive effectiveness" to make the fantastic credible.

2394   LOWNDES, ROBERT A.W.   Introduction to In the Days of the Comet.
        New York: Airmont, pp. 5-10.
            A broken leg as a child made W turn to reading while re-
        covering. This put him ahead in school, while a later accident
        forced him out of teaching into journalism. These "lucky breaks"
        made him a writer who drew on his own life for his early work,
        particularly the early chapters of Comet. In his role as a modern
        prophet, he proclaimed that something be done to avert disaster.

2395   _____.   Introduction to The Island of Dr. Moreau. New York:
        Airmont, pp. 5-10.
            W's imagination was developed early in his life, but the
        facts of his life are too improbable to fit into a work of fic-
        tion. His own fiction became a series of vehicles for his
        thoughts on the human condition. Dr. Moreau is both allegory and
        horror story, and it foretold some of the dilemmas involved when
        science interferes with life.

2396   MANUEL, FRANK.   "Toward a Psychological History of Utopias."
        In Utopias and Utopian Thought. Edited by Frank Manuel.
        Boston: Houghton Mifflin, pp. 69-98.
            W's utopia was not setting a new style, but was among the
        last of the nineteenth-century utopias.

2397   MARTIN, KINGSLEY.   Father Figures. London: Hutchinson, pp.
        77, 114-15, 124, 155, 176.
            Martin read W on the train. Beatrice and Sidney Webb
        showed good humor to W in spite of his attack on them in
        Machiavelli.

2398   MENZLER, F.A.A.   "Letters to the Editor: H.G. Wells."
        Listener 76 (4 Aug.):168.
            Contrary to Taylor's assertion, W had more than elementary
        training in biology and held a B.Sc. with first place honors.
        [Reply to Taylor, "The Man Who Tried to Work Miracles," Listener,
        21 July 1966.]

2399   MOORE, DORIS LANGLEY.   E. Nesbit: A Biography. Rev. ed.
        Philadelphia and New York: Chilton, pp. xiv-xv, xviii, xxiv-
        xxvi, 137, 176, 177, 178-79, 182, 187.

W may have been "paying off an old score" in his attacks on Hubert Bland, but evidence suggests that what he said had substance. W may have repaid a "churlish reception" of Moore by his praise of her work in Experiment. He thought Nesbit's stories in Thirteen Ways Home overly sentimental; she replied the stories were fairy tales in the same sense as Utopia. Thinking she was a man, W addressed her as "Ernest," a convention he continued for a time even after meeting her.

2400   "More Vivid Impression of Wells." Times (London), 22 Sept., p. 6.
        Granada television used extracts from W's writings as background for the visual scenes in its strong centenary tribute.

2401   MOSKOWITZ, SAM. Introduction to Masterpieces of Science Fiction. Cleveland and New York: World, pp. 1-26.
        War of the Worlds belongs to the category of future-war stories with planets instead of nations. It was the most literary work of its type at the time of first publication. W was greatly influenced by Hawthorne, a fact that is evident in "The Chronic Argonauts." The greatest science fiction writer of all time, W either created or popularized the basic themes of the genre.

2402   _____. "The Jew in Science Fiction." Worlds of Tomorrow 4 (Nov.):109-22. Reprinted as "Anti-Semitism: The Day of the Messiah," in Strange Horizons: The Spectrum of Science Fiction (New York: Charles Scribner's Sons, 1976), pp. 22-49.
        Science fiction writers "appear to be more reactionary and intolerant than mainstream writers" in their use of Jewish characters. The characterization of a Polish Jew in Invisible Man is a deliberate bit of anti-Semitism, but the covetous Jew escaping the invading Martians appears only in the original magazine version of War of the Worlds.

2403   NEWHOUSE, NEVILLE H. Joseph Conrad. London: Evans, pp. 16-17, 22, 24-26, 39.
        W lamented the intensity with which Conrad adopted a "literary" persona. W wanted the novel and all art to improve the social order.

2404   PARRINDER, PATRICK. "Letters to the Editor: H.G. Wells." Listener 76 (28 July):132.
        W was not the fool Taylor contends. Arguments used by Taylor against him may be found in W's own works. [Reply to A.J.P. Taylor, "The Man Who Tried to Work Miracles," Listener, 21 July 1966.]

2405   PRIESTLEY, J.B. "Light in a Thousand Dark Places." Horizon (New York) 8 (Winter):33-37. Translated as "Les paradoxes de H.G. Wells," Nouvelles littéraires, 15 Dec. 1966, pp. 1, 11.

1966

The paradox of W was that he was a literary genius who
never considered himself enjoying a literary career. He was a
science instructor at heart, as deeply divided in his intellectual
life as in his emotional life. His divisiveness can be seen as
early as 1897 in War of the Worlds. The best of his later novels,
Kipps, Tono-Bungay, and Mr. Polly, represent his "most personal
and lasting contribution to the English novel." Machiavelli marks
the beginning of his decline as he "sacrificed himself to a bad
formula" and wrote journalistic fiction. It was outside western
Europe (with Outline) that he had his greatest influence as world
educator.

2406   PRITCHETT, V.S. "Wells Marches On." NS 72 (23 Sept.):433-34.
        W was an "effusive romantic" whose magic touch was in books
concerned with the desire for personal freedom. His genius was in
fantasy and not in reality. In the long run he was "the expression of a real liberation in English life of which we have all
been the beneficiaries." His was an eighteenth-century spirit and
not a nineteenth-century one.

2407   "Report on a Disappointed Genius: H.G. Wells Talked of Suicide
        at 72." Times (London), 6 Dec. p. 12.
        Lord Snow's H.G. Wells Centenary Lecture recounts a 1938
conversation in which W admitted thinking of suicide in his later
years, because his influence and hopes seemed finished. To the
end of his days he wished he had been a professional scientist and
might have made a very good professor of zoology.

2408   SAID, EDWARD W. Joseph Conrad and the Fiction of Autobiog-
        raphy. Cambridge, Mass.: Harvard University Press, pp. 40-41,
        49-50, 54, 91, 93.
        [Passing references; Conrad's letters to W quoted.]

2409   SCHONFIELD, HUGH J. "Letters to the Editor: H.G. Wells
        Memorial." Times (London), 3 May, p. 17.
        Plans for the centenary celebration include the first
annual H.G. Wells Lecture.

2410   SEYMOUR-SMITH, MARTIN. "Wells--the Gloomy Dreamer."
        Spectator, no. 7214 (30 Sept.), p. 420.
        W's centenary finds him "persistently underrated, neglected
and, above all, misunderstood." His imaginative power was greater
than Shaw's with a "self-regenerative creative integrity." He was
never an optimist but a "gloomy dreamer" with a feeling of social
inferiority.

2411   SHKLAR, JUDITH. "The Political Theory of Utopia: From Melan-
        choly to Nostalgia." In Utopias and Utopian Thought. Edited
        by Frank Manuel. Boston: Houghton Mifflin, pp. 101-15.

W realized his utopia had nothing in common with its prede-
cessors since his perfect model was in the future, was "world-
wide, devoted to science, to progress, to change," and allowed for
individuality. He was aware of the necessity to discard the
closed social order of classicism.

2412   SMITH, GODFREY. "An Outline of H.G. Wells." NYT Magazine, 21
        Aug., pp. 30-31, 39-40, 42, 44.
            "In the direct and literal sense [W's] books do not per-
        meate our lives very much." His science fiction has lasted and is
        used by both Oxford and Cambridge in General Certificate of Educa-
        tion exams in English for fifteen-year-olds. His name, however,
        is still a "part of the literate sub-conscious." For all his
        socialism, he was never in complete sympathy with the working
        class.

2413   STEWART, J.I.M. Rudyard Kipling. New York: Dodd, Mead,
        p. 155.
            W considered "The Moral Reformers" to be an indictment of
        the wickedness of the British Empire.

2414   TAYLOR, A.J.P. "The Man Who Tried To Work Miracles."
        Listener 76 (21 July):81-84.
            At his centenary no one bothers about W as thinker and few
        as prophet. He was more representative than originator. As a
        writer, two qualities keep him alive: a gift for social comedy
        and an ability to pretend and then show how the pretense could
        work. As a prophet he was an inspired guesser with a lively
        imagination. As a thinker he imagined man's nature could be
        changed overnight. He regarded society as subject to the same
        laws as human nature and took sweeping generalizations seriously.
        Outline was intended to show how all recorded history was moving
        toward a planned world state, but it shows instead only that men
        have always been in conflict and that the rich have exploited the
        poor. W is read today for fun, not for guidance.

2415   "Time for Wells." TLS, 29 Sept., p. 893.
            Popular taste has kept W's early fiction in print, whereas
        Utopia and Shape of Things are forgotten. The stories are highly
        readable, evincing the "quality of immediate conviction." He was
        even capable of "great aesthetic concentration and symbolic intri-
        cacy" in "Country of the Blind" and "The Hole [sic] in the Wall."
        [Review of new ed. of Complete Short Stories.]

2416   TOMLIN, E.W.F. "The Prose of Thought." In The Modern Age.
        Edited by Boris Ford. The Pelican Guide to English Literature,
        vol. 7. Baltimore: Penguin, pp. 231-44.

1966

        The "incandescent quality" of W's early work overcame his
undistinguished style. By the time he wrote <u>Clissold</u> his dis-
illusionment replaced that quality with invective and sarcasm.

2417   URNOV, M. "Uells protiv Dzheimsa" [Wells contra James].
        <u>Voprosy Literatury</u> (Moscow), no. 7, pp. 92-112.
        The dispute between W and Henry James on the future of the
novel symbolizes the frontier of a new stage in the development of
literature, revealing characteristic features of the transitional
period, which were echoed in later disputes and in the critical
practice of leading English and American writers. [In Russian.]

2418   VERNIER, J[EAN]-P[IERRE]. "H.G. Wells critique." <u>Etudes
        anglaises</u> 19:424-38.
        W took advantage of his brief career as a critic for the
<u>Saturday Review</u> to deepen his views on the novel and to develop
his demanding conception of the role of modern literature. His
fundamental literary principles were: the novel is a work of art
that adheres to certain literary rules while propagandizing an
idea would never make a good novel; the exactitude of the author
is essential with fictional or nonfictional vision; the style must
be concise and simple; and the point of view of the author must
appear in his work.

2419   <u>Wellsian</u> 2, no. 2 (Dec.).
        [Centenary Issue: Contents include: Editorial (the best
memorial is to work for a new world without war and want but with
creative fulfillment for all); "H.G. Wells and the Modern Mind,"
by Richard Clements (an overview of the life and accomplishments
reprinted from the <u>Ethical Record</u> of Dec. 1966); "A Centenary
Impression," by Brian Ash (the unveiling of the plaque at Hanover
Terrace); "H.G. Wells and the Shape of Things to Come," by C.J.
Colmer (his prophecies may have won him fame, but he took it upon
himself to be his own debunker in <u>Experiment</u>); "Writers Who Have
Influenced Me--H.G. Wells," by J.R. Hammond (reprinted from <u>Coop-
erative Consumer</u>, March 1963, a survey of the work of the man with
a "unique place in English literature as a prophet, a visionary,
and an apostle of a better world"; "H.G. Wells--An Assessment," by
Peter Lonsdale (W's efforts were defeated by the stupidity of
humanity); "Outing to Uppark," by W.L. George (notes on a tour of
the world of the early writings).]

2420   "The Wells That Will Last for Another 100 Years." <u>Times</u>
        (London), 21 Sept., p. 11.
        W will live for a handful of characters (not always major
ones) in his early novels. His greatness derives from his romantic search for the joy in life.

1967

2421 WILLIAMSON, JOHN STEWART. "H.G. Wells, Critic of Progress: A Study of the Early Fiction." Dissertation, University of Colorado, 1964.
[Listed in <u>Dissertation</u> <u>Abstracts</u> 26 (1966):5420.] Published as entry 2650.

2422 WOODCOCK, GEORGE. <u>The</u> <u>Crystal</u> <u>Spirit:</u> <u>A</u> <u>Study</u> <u>of</u> <u>George</u> <u>Orwell</u>. Boston: Little, Brown, pp. 82, 176, 209, 213, 236, 238, 245, 247-48, 291, 302, 315-318.
Like's W's Morlocks, the Burmese seemed a sort of underground people to Orwell. W belonged to an age of sanity and could not understand fascism, while Spanish anarchists and left-wing socialists had not read him and so had little trust in utopia.

2423 WOODRING, CARL. <u>Virginia</u> <u>Woolf</u>. New York and London: Columbia University Press, p. 5.
Woolf's criticism of deficiencies in Galsworthy, Bennett, and W helped her define her own approach to fiction.

2424 WREN-LEWIS, JOHN. "The Agnostic Prophet." <u>MG</u>, 8 Sept., p. 6.
W articulated Wren-Lewis's frustration of "living in a working-class home dominated by prejudice and superstitious fear." He challenged theologians to consider whether they might be advocating subservience to the world, and he asserted that creativity could triumph over conservative forces in nature and society.

2425 ZOLOTOW, SAM. "Comedian's Play Due Here in Fall: 'Sixpence' in Circulation." <u>NYT</u>, 9 June, p. 55.
"Half a Sixpence," the musical version of <u>Kipps</u>, is to close at the Broadhurst Theatre after the 512th performance. It is scheduled to open in San Francisco for a seven-week run, then to Los Angeles for another seven weeks before beginning its national tour.

<u>1967</u>

2426 ARAUJO, VICTOR de. "The Short Story of Fantasy: Henry James, H.G. Wells, and E.M. Forster." Dissertation, University of Washington, 1965.
[Listed in <u>Dissertation</u> <u>Abstracts</u> 27 (1967):200A.]

2427 ARMYTAGE, W.H.G. "Superman and the System." <u>RQ</u> 2 (March): 232-42.
W considered his early novels to contain a new system of ideas of "kinetic utopianism" based on Nietzsche and Darwin. He left novel writing for sociological tracts in an effort to change the future.

1967

2428   BERGONZI, BERNARD. Introduction to The Invisible Man. New
        York: Heritage Press, pp. xiii-xviii.
            W's genius in science fiction was his ability to combine
        legend and myth with rational, scientific explanation. Griffin
        has something in common with the narrator in Dostoyevsky's Notes
        from Underground, in that they both feel a sense of superiority to
        others and are isolated. They both are aware of a gap between
        aspiration and achievement.

2429   BURGESS, ANTHONY. "Utopias and Dystopias." In The Novel Now:
        A Guide to Contemporary Fiction. New York: W.W. Norton, pp.
        38-47.
            W was a progressive writer whose earlier works were ab-
        sorbed and whose later books were rejected. Whereas the contempo-
        rary novelist accepts that man is imperfect, W expected too much
        of man.

2430   COSTA, RICHARD HAUER. H.G. Wells. Twayne English Authors
        Series, 43. New York: Twayne.
            The part of W's work that will live is the early science
        fiction and comic novels. As utopian and historian W wore "hats
        that ill-fitted him." His sociological and political novels were
        the by-products of his life as artist. His apparently sudden
        pessimistic turn at the end of his life was in reality a return to
        the skepticism of his early and most creative years. Though he is
        misunderstood, he is really one of the most representative writers
        of the twentieth century. [Selected and annotated bibliography of
        criticism; chronology of W's life and career.]

2431   _____. "H.G. Wells's Tono-Bungay: Review of New Studies."
        ELT 10:89-96.
            The panorama of Tono-Bungay is important to note, as well
        as its satire on advertising. W may have been out of touch with
        the new generation studying individuals, but he forecast a time
        when objects would be "dramatized by the graphic arts and deified
        by hucksters" at the expense of the individual.

2432   CROWLEY, C.P. "Failure of Nerve: H.G. Wells." UWR 2:1-8.
            The influence of Darwin's thought carried W for most of his
        life, but he lost faith in it just as the rest of the world began
        to see its possibilities for modern life. His "basic mistake was
        in accepting change as though it were inevitable."

2433   DE TURRIS, GIANFRANCO. "Il centenario di Wells." Italia che
        scribe 50 (Feb.-March):32.
            Surprisingly little notice has been taken in newspapers and
        journals of the centennial of the initiator of science fiction and
        the harbinger of some of the most significant scientific discov-
        eries of our time. His own works, however, are well represented

on Italian newsstands in pocket editions. W's production falls
into two periods: "fantasy" from 1895 to 1910, and his more
openly "social" work that followed. Each work contains an idea
later to become fundamental in science fiction. True voyages in
time already existed in Twain and Dickens, but W introduced the
pseudoscientific element. The idea of invisibility was also not
new, but W's use of it for ethical instruction was. With Moreau W
introduced the mad scientist since elaborated in many films and
books. In Food of the Gods began the theme of giants and insects,
which was to become so dear to the makers of second-rate films.
With War of the Worlds W presented for the first time terrestrial
invasion by Martians, bent on destroying human civilization.
     Not only have his novels given key ideas to four genera-
tions of writers, but his short stories are mines of original
invention: intelligent insects out to conquer the world, monsters
produced from prehistoric eggs, a celestial body threatening to
collide with earth, a drug for speeding up time, interplanetary
communications, the existence of worlds like our own on other
dimensional planes, urban revolution, obsessive publicity, and the
rise of psychoanalysis. The surprising thing is that W remains so
eminently pleasurable to read after all these years and after the
gigantic strides science has taken. This is because W is in the
truest sense a true writer.

2434   EURICH, NELL. Science in Utopia: A Mighty Design. Cambridge,
       Mass.: Harvard University Press, pp. 260, 271-72.
       W is no more interested in techniques than any other
utopian dreamer. He wants results and benefits. Though people
may be numbers in his system, they are free to develop themselves.

2435   FARRELL, JOHN K. "H.G. Wells as an Historian." UWR 2
       (Spring):47-57.
       While W's idea of a world history is commendable, his
history was oversimplified. Some of his foresight in Outline was
short of the mark, but had insight and a grasp of the patterns of
human history. [H.G. Wells Centennial Issue.]

2436   GOLD, HERBERT. "The Art of Fiction XL: Vladimir Nabokov, An
       Interview." Paris Review, no. 41 (Summer-Fall), pp. 92-111.
       W was Nabokov's favorite writer as a boy. Friends, Ann
Veronica, Time Machine, "The Country of the Blind" "are far better
than anything Bennett, or Conrad, or, in fact, any of Wells's
contemporaries could produce. His sociological cogitations can be
safely ignored, of course, but his romances and fantasias are
superb." [Anecdote of the time W was at a dinner in St.
Petersburg and a guest confused War of the Worlds with Conan
Doyle's The Lost World.]

1967

2437   HILLEGAS, MARK R. The Future as Nightmare: H.G. Wells and the
       Anti-Utopians. New York: Oxford University Press.
          W originated many of the main and peripheral themes used in
       later anti-utopian writing because these writers both continue his
       ideas and react against them. His early stories present visions
       of man and science that do not resemble the so-called "Wellsian
       vision" prominent in the 1930s. There was in his early work a
       "cosmic pessimism" rebelling against Victorian complacency and
       social injustice. He uses a mythic technique in Time Machine and
       Dr. Moreau and a satiric technique in Sleeper Wakes and Men in the
       Moon. He believed that "the greatest enemy of progress was faith
       in inevitable progress," but he turned from trying to shock people
       out of complacency to showing them the future toward which they
       could strive. [The anti-utopians are represented by E.M.
       Forster's "The Machine Stops," Capek's R.U.R., Zamyatin's We,
       Huxley's Brave New World, Orwell's 1984, C.S. Lewis's Out of the
       Silent Planet, Perelandra, and That Hideous Strength.] Later
       science fiction waters down the Wellsian elements, but the anti-
       utopian theme is still present; some of the better examples are
       Ray Bradbury's Fahrenheit 451 and Kurt Vonnegut's Player Piano.
       Even William Golding's The Inheritors borrows from W and is re-
       lated to the anti-utopian novel. The final strain seems to be the
       apocalyptic novel predicting the doom of mankind.

2438   _____. Introduction to A Modern Utopia. Lincoln: University
       of Nebraska Press, pp. v-xxv.
          Utopia is a revolutionary book whose prophecies have not
       yet been realized. W's greatest impact occurred during the first
       two decades of the twentieth century, when the book was treated
       with respect. His two chief characters are just real enough to
       make the utopian world convincing. Influenced by the "social and
       economic unrest" of 1905 and his attempt to control the Fabian
       Society, the key to W's utopia is the "Wellsian imagination" of
       world order. More powerful and efficient controls are required
       than appear in the democratic process. His was the first utopia
       in the tradition to allow for change.

2439   HOLROYD, MICHAEL. Lytton Strachey: A Critical Biography.
       Vol. 1, The Unknown Years. London: Heinemann, pp. 10, 13,
       427.
          W was seen as a rebel, opposing everything the Stracheys
       had upheld. Rupert Brooke was criticized for admiring him.

2440   KNIGHT, DAMON. In Search of Wonder: Essays on Modern Science
       Fiction. Rev. ed. Chicago: Advent, pp. 8, 35, 72, 91, 178,
       179, 207, 252, 253, 276.
          [Passing references. W's influences on later writers in
       whose work his themes are repeated.]

2441   LeMIRE, EUGENE D. "H.G. Wells and the World of Science Fic-
       tion." UWR 2 (Spring):59-66.
           W suggested the basic impermanence of all things in his
       science fiction, which owes something to his three artistic
       motives: "to entertain simply, to teach ironically, to describe
       objectively."

2442   LEWIS, C.S. "On Science Fiction." In Of Other Worlds: Essays
       and Stories. New York: Harcourt, Brace & World, pp. 59-73.
       Reprinted in Turning Points: Essays on the Art of Science
       Fiction, ed. Damon Knight (New York: Harper & Row, 1977), pp.
       119-31; and in Science Fiction: A Collection of Critical
       Essays, ed. Mark Rose (Englewood Cliffs, N.J.: Prentice-Hall,
       1976), pp. 103-115.
           W's use of cavorite makes Men in the Moon speculative as
       well as scientific. This choice of an implausible substance
       centers the focus of the story less on the method of reaching the
       moon than on what the moon is like.

2443   LEY, WILLY. Introduction to The First Men in the Moon. New
       York: Dell, pp. 7-12.
           The discovery, in 1895, of helium, coupled with the 1898
       publication of Kepler's Somnium in German, may have had some
       influence on W's novel. While cavorite is an impossibility, one
       must remember the author was not writing a scientific treatise.
       (One difference between Verne and W is that the hero is the active
       agent in Verne's works, whereas he is not in complete control in
       W's works.)

2444   LODGE, DAVID. "Men and Ideas: Assessing H.G. Wells."
       Encounter 28:54-61. Reprinted in The Novelist at the Cross-
       roads, and Other Essays. Ithaca (New York: Cornell University
       Press, 1971), pp. 205-20.
           At the time of his death, W was "a discredited thinker,"
       the father of science fiction, and an author of "lightweight sub-
       Dickensian comedies." By the time of the centenary of his birth
       there was something of an attempt to redefine his position, and
       several collections of his writings (including his letters) ap-
       peared. The conflict in him between optimism and pessimism "is
       more or less the natural condition of the modern intellectual."
       As a writer of fiction, his principal gift resided in his ability
       to be persuasively concrete in his speculations about changes in
       life and society.

2445   MAISKIĬ, IVAN MIKHAĬLOVICH. "Gerbert Uells" [Herbert Wells].
       In B. Shou i drugie: Vospominaniĭa [B. Shaw and others:
       Memoirs]. Moscow: Iskusstvo, pp. 54-102.
           In 1927, W told Maisky that Marxists believed only the
       proletariat could and must achieve the socialist revolution, but

1967

he believed it could be achieved by an "elite" of engineers,
technicians, etc. Maisky explained the Marxist viewpoint to W.
When Maisky met W in the thirties, he saw that the latter's views
of revolutionary Russia had evolved considerably. After W visited
the Soviet Union (1934), he was impressed by material progress and
by the "Americanization" of the Russian people, who were more
active and practical than during his 1920 visit. After 1934, his
relationship with Maisky altered for the worse: W protested
against the repressions in the Soviet Union (1936-38) and the cult
of personality. After 1941, they became more cordial. Since W
was not a Marxist, he made many mistakes in trying to serve the
happiness of mankind: he was a great utopianist. This was why he
failed to establish any school or followers. [In Russian.]

2446 MATTHEISEN, PAUL F., and ARTHUR C. YOUNG. "Gissing, Gosse, and
      the Civil List." Victorian Newsletter, no. 32 (Fall),
      pp. 11-16.
         By writing Edmond Gosse, W took the first step to get a
      pension from the Civil List for George Gissing's two sons. He
      also tried to get a grant from the Royal Literary Fund for
      George's brother, Algernon, who was supporting himself by his
      novels.

2447 McNAMARA, EUGENE. "H.G. Wells as Novelist." UWR 2
      (Spring):21-29.
         W's reputation as a novelist has suffered because of the
      condescension of the generation that followed his. He saw the
      novel as a means to a greater end, not as an end in itself (as
      James did). Tono-Bungay may be his best novel.

2448 MEYER, BERNARD C. Joseph Conrad: A Psychoanalytic Biography.
      Princeton, N.J.: Princeton University Press, pp. 134, 142,
      154, 208, 288, 322.
         W had to prod Violet Hunt to call on Ford Madox Ford to
      submit some stories to the English Review. Conrad responded to
      W's criticism of his style by noting that while it might be bad,
      it was effective and recognizably individual.

2449 MULLEN, RICHARD D. "H.G. Wells and Victor Rousseau Emmanuel:
      When the Sleeper Wakes and The Messiah of the Cylinder."
      Extrapolation 8 (May):31-63.
         The Messiah of the Cylinder is no literary classic and is
      justifiably forgotten, but its intellectual content ought to in-
      terest students of science fiction. It is an early anti-utopian
      novel, a forerunner of 1984 and imitates W's Sleeper Wakes. In
      spite of its flaws, W's novel is easily in the second rank of
      science fiction novels.

2450 _____. "H.G. Wells: The Old Orthodoxy and the New." RQ 3 (Aug.):66-68.
The "old orthodoxy" calls W's later works his masterpieces and ignores the scientific romances, while the "new orthodoxy" reverses that, but extends his period of artistic success to 1910. The neglect of the later work is shown by the inaccuracies and misreadings found in Richard H. Costa's H.G. Wells.

2451 NEWELL, KENNETH B. "Structure in H.G. Wells's Dickensian Novels." Dissertation, University of Pennsylvania, 1964.
[Listed in Dissertation Abstracts 28 (1967):239A.] Published as entry 2486.

2452 NORWOOD, W.D., Jr. "C.S. Lewis, Owen Barfield and the Modern Myth." Midwest Quarterly 8:279-91.
W's concepts of outer space may be outmoded and may be contrasted with those of Lewis in Out of the Silent Planet.

2453 PARR, J. GORDON. "H.G. Wells: His Significance in 1966." UWR 2 (Spring):67-76.
From the vantage point of 1966 W's significance seems to reside in his recognition of the integration of technology and the evolution of society. [H.G. Wells Centennial Issue.]

2454 PHILLIPPS, K.C. "H.G. Wells: A Possible Debt to Trollope." Notes and Queries 14 (July):244-45.
The train episode of chapter 6 in Mr. Polly resembles chapter 45 of Small House at Allington. A comparison of the two offers a "contrast in method and speed of narrative."

2455 POLI, BERNARD J. Ford Madox Ford and the "Transatlantic Review." Syracuse, N.Y.: Syracuse University Press, pp. 4, 32, 40, 54, 76, 78, 89, 133, 142, 164.
W's relations with Ford were somewhat confused due to the past experience with the English Review. W praised Ford as a poet, and although the latter disapproved of W's political comments, Ford was an old friend of Catherine Wells. The Transatlantic Review might have been a financial success if W and many others had written for it.

2456 PRINTZ-PÅHLSON, GÖRAN. "Den melankoliska utopin" [The melancholy utopian]. Bonniers litterära magasin 36:49-52.
W's shortcomings (stylistic carelessness and political naivete) were voiced by people like Henry James, Jules Verne, and George Orwell. He is still, however, very current, perhaps more so than during his lifetime, and so his position in literature ought to be reconsidered. He was farsighted and perceptive, addressing himself not to the elite, but to individuals. His writings exhibit a balance: the pessimistic view of civilization

1967

is countered by his fairytalelike delight in the infinite possibilities of beginnings. [In Swedish.]

2457   ROTHSTEIN, ANDREW. "Cultural Relations 1917-1967." Anglo-
Soviet Journal 28:14-20.
       Russia is both misleading and badly informed. W vigorously
defended the Bolsheviks and after his visit arranged to send many
scientific works to the Soviets.

2458   SHAYON, ROBERT LEWIS. "Which H.G. Wells was Right?" SR 50
(28 Jan.):30.
       BBC production of W's life story on Spectrum fails to
explain why he disavowed his former writings and optimistic pre-
dictions in his later years.

2459   SNOW, C[HARLES] P[ERCY]. "H.G. Wells." In Variety of Men.
New York: Scribner, pp. 63-85. Reprinted as "The Unwitting
Rival; Or, How Not to Advise the Lovelorn," SR 50 (1 April
1967):48-49.
       W had read Snow's The Search with interest, but persisted
in considering it autobiographical and asked Snow for advice in
his difficulties with his latest mistress. If teaching had not
been a part of W his best novels would certainly have turned out
differently. "He wanted a society into which his life would fit,"
and he was impatient that it took so long to reshape.

2460   SQUIRE, EDGAR LARRY. "The Necessity for Self-Awakening in the
Scientific Romances and Early Social Novels of H.G. Wells."
Dissertation, University of California (Davis), 1966.
       [Listed in Dissertation Abstracts 28 (1967):243-44A.]

2461   STEINBERG, MOSES W. "H.G. Wells as Social Critic." UWR 2
(Spring):9-20.
       W's iconoclasm and positive ideas are based on his early
experiences, which include the social changes of the last part of
the nineteenth century, and are reflected in his early writings.
His idea of socialism was constructive and based on a desire for
an orderly and planned scientific society. His most intense
concern centered on conditions that would allow the greatest
development of the individual, though his belief in a Collective
Mind would have denied variety and interest in life.

2462   STEVENSON, LIONEL. The History of the English Novel: Yesterday and After. New York: Barnes & Noble, pp. 11-59.
       W's faults include writing too much too fast and a depend-
ence on his journalistic facility. His fiction served only as a
medium of propaganda in which he repeated and contradicted himself. Yet he had the makings of a great novelist, for he could

tell a good story, invent memorable characters, and "was profoundly concerned with the major themes of human nature and human
relationships." In his science fiction he mingled the commonplace
with "the eerie conquests of physical limits" to intensify the
"atmosphere of terror." In all literary respects he was a tradi-
tionalist, even though he wrote on controversial "modern" topics.
His view of the novel was the Victorian one: "a picture of society and an instrument for influencing social improvement." The
nonobsessive use of sex in his books comprised an indictment of
the maladjustment of human relations. He seemed unaware of the
European writers whose influence was reshaping English literature.

2463   WALSH, JOHN. "H.G. Wells: He Was a Seer, but a Disappointed
        Scientist." Science 155 (13 Jan.):181-82.
        There is evidence during the centenary of W's birth that
his achievements are being acknowledged by scientists in a manner
denied him during his life when he was disappointed not to have
become a member of the Royal Society. His advice to adopt an
"attitude of constructive pessimism" is one of his lessons for the
modern reader.

2464   WARD, J.A. The Search for Form: Studies in the Structure of
        James's Fiction. Chapel Hill: University of North Carolina
        Press, pp. 20, 56.
        Freedom from convention led to carelessness in W and
Bennett. James tried to explain to W some of the confusion that
had arisen over Turn of the Screw.

2465   WATTS, C.T. "Joseph Conrad, Dr. MacIntyre, and The
        Inheritors." Notes and Queries 14 (July):245-47.
        Conrad's recent reading of Time Machine, discussions of the
secret of the universe, and a demonstration of an X-ray machine
may have influenced the scientific mechanism of The Inheritors,
the novel he was to write with Ford Madox Ford.

2466   ZGÓRZELSKI, A. "Elementy realizma i fantastyki w Niewidzialnym
        czlowieku H.G. Wellsa" [Elements of realism and the fantastic
        in H.G. Wells's The Invisible Man]. Acta uniwersyteta M.C.
        Slobowskiej (Lublin) (seria F) 22:85-100.
        Despite realistic elements (use of vernacular, homely de-
tails, etc., for plausibility), the fantastic element dominates in
W's work, as is evident in characterization, theme, and composition. [In Polish.]

1968

2467   APPEL, ALFRED, Jr. "Vladimir Nabokov." Contemporary Lit-
        erature 9 (Spring):236-45.

1968

Nabokov read W's science fiction as a boy and made his own contributions to the genre in Bend Sinister and Invitation to a Beheading as "future-scene fiction."

2468   ARMYTAGE, W.H.G. Yesterday's Tomorrows: A Historical Survey of Future Societies. London: Routledge & Kegan Paul; Toronto: Toronto University Press, pp. 12, 29, 34, 72, 90-91, 112-13, 116, 151-52, 161, 182, 212, 215, 251.
W may have been influenced by Camille Flammarion, though he never mentions reading the works of the French astronomer (esp. La Fin du monde). Chesterton's The Napoleon of Notting Hill was an answer to W's view of science guiding the future. Olaf Stapledon thought W's view of human nature superficial. [Passing references and quotes.]

2469   BEACHCROFT, THOMAS OWEN. The Modest Art. London and New York: Oxford University Press, pp. 119, 150, 156, 160.
W may have been the most famous short story writer after Kipling and used the form to explore strange ideas instead of developing the style he used in Kipps.

2470   BORRELLO, ALFRED. "Bibliography, News and Notes: H.G. Wells." ELT 11:56-64.
[Annotated bibliography of items about W not listed in West (1926, 1930) or Brome (1951). Forty-six items published 1957-1967.]

2471   CHRISTOPHER, JOHN. "Not What-If But How-He." Writer 81 (Nov.):15-17.
W was the initiator of the Old English school of science fiction, in which the familiar world encounters a new scientific development or other external force. The American school depicts a world that is alien to our own.

2472   CLARENS, CARLOS. An Illustrated History of the Horror Film. New York: Capricorn Books, pp. 5, 32, 46, 65, 84, 85, 119, 124, 125, 150, 162, 165.
W thought Fritz Lang's film, Metropolis, was silly and borrowed from his own stories; A Blind Bargain (Goldwyn, 1922) was freely based on Dr. Moreau; Invisible Man was ideal for filming, and the movie has good dialogue; nothing in the film version of Dr. Moreau from Paramount (Island of Lost Souls) approaches the climactic terror of the original, and W thought it "a vulgarization." The Martian war machines in War of the Worlds (1953) have hardly been surpassed, but the sight of a Martian is disappointing. The film succeeds in its depiction of convincing destruction. The films supervised by W himself Things to Come and Miracles) "resulted in ponderous dogmatic bores."

2473   CROFT-COOKE, RUPERT. <u>Feasting</u> <u>with</u> <u>Panthers:</u>   <u>A</u> <u>New</u> <u>Considera-</u>
        <u>tion</u> <u>of</u> <u>Some</u> <u>Late</u> <u>Victorian</u> <u>Writers.</u>   New York: Holt, Rinehart
        & Winston, pp. 9, 167, 178, 285, 288.
            W was one of the "hearty men" in the movement that super-
        ceded Oscar Wilde and the decadent nineties. Decadence being a
        upper-class weakness, the new fictional heroes were of the lower
        middle-class like Kipps and Mr. Polly.

2474   DONAGHY, HENRY J.   "Love and Mr. Wells: A Shelleyan Search for
        the Epipsyche." <u>SLI</u> 1:41-50.
            A struggle to find the epipsyche (ideal love) is part of
        the work of both Shelley and W. In <u>Mr.</u> <u>Lewisham</u>, <u>Kipps</u>, <u>Tono-</u>
        <u>Bungay</u>, and <u>Mr.</u> <u>Polly</u> realistic approaches to love turn into
        cynicism. When the love is found, the ideal disappears.

2475   GARD, ROGER, ed. <u>Henry</u> <u>James:</u>   <u>The</u> <u>Critical</u> <u>Heritage.</u>   London
        and Boston: Routledge & Kegan Paul, pp. 15, 373, 517-26, 527-
        30, 534.
            W's attack on James in <u>Boon</u> was a more refined version of
        George Moore's remark about "James the eunuch." [W's essay,
        James's letters in reply reprinted.]

2476   HARRIS, WENDELL V.   "English Short Fiction in the Nineteenth
        Century." <u>Studies</u> <u>in</u> <u>Short</u> <u>Fiction</u> 6 (Fall):1-93 [esp. pp. 71-
        73].
            W, like Kipling, was a "master at giving a sense of depth
        and significance to what were basically anecdotes. The short
        stories are more striking than the novels, and the variety of
        periodicals in which he appeared shows the expanding market for
        the short story. The application of logic to the "paradoxes
        inherent in the theory" of time as the fourth dimension in <u>Time</u>
        <u>Machine</u> demonstrates the essence of his method.

2477   HOLROYD, MICHAEL. <u>Lytton</u> <u>Strachey:</u>   <u>A</u> <u>Critical</u> <u>Biography.</u>
        Vol. 2, <u>The</u> <u>Years</u> <u>of</u> <u>Achievement.</u>   London: Heinemann, pp. 145,
        184, 438, 469, 560, 628.
            Strachey tried to forget the war by reading <u>Boon</u> and
        Virginia Woolf's <u>The</u> <u>Voyage</u> <u>Out.</u>   He ceased to think of W when the
        latter became a thinker, yet could not help enjoying <u>Men</u> <u>Like</u> <u>Gods</u>
        in spite of its author.

2478   HYNES, SAMUEL. <u>The</u> <u>Edwardian</u> <u>Turn</u> <u>of</u> <u>Mind.</u>   Princeton, N.J.:
        Princeton University Press, pp. 87-131; index.
            While W had used science to make statements about social
        forces in his early books, not until be began writing sociology
        did he come to the attention of the Webbs and the Fabian society.
        The combination of a knowledge of science with the novelist's
        imagination made his social and political thinking seem unique.
        He could make socialism sound both simple and touching. Mrs. Webb

1968

considered him "a useful contact with the lower classes" who was
also ignorant of the workings of society. Tono-Bungay, Ann
Veronica, and Machiavelli reflect aspects of his experiences with
the Fabians, whom he misread as a result of his trying to turn a
political philosophy into a religion.

2479 HYNES, SAMUEL. William Golding. New York: Columbia University Press, pp. 16-23.
Lord of the Flies makes use of R.M. Ballantyne's Coral
Island as "the embodiment of an attitude--a symbol out of childhood of a whole set of wrong beliefs about good and evil." In The
Inheritors, Golding uses W's Outline in the same manner when he
depicts the extermination of Neanderthal man from the point of
view of the Neanderthal man. In simple terms W had barely mentioned the arrival of Homo sapiens and the effect on Neanderthal
man. The Inheritors reverses W's "rationalist gospel."

2480 JACOBS, ROBERT G. "H.G. Wells, Joseph Conrad, and the Relative
Universe." Conradiana 1 (Summer):51-55.
Conrad shows the influence of W not only in The Inheritors
but also in Heart of Darkness and Lord Jim when he uses the
relativity of time.

2481 KAZIN, ALFRED. "Reappraisals: H.G. Wells, America and 'The
Future.'" American Scholar 37:137-44.
On visiting America in 1906, W was interested less in the
future than in portraying history as constant movement, "the
movement of [his] own mind." The contrast between Henry James and
W can be seen in their respective works, American Scene and Future
in America, one with the sense of the past, the other with a sense
of the future.

2482 KEYNES, GEOFFREY, ed. The Letters of Rupert Brooke. New York:
Harcourt, Brace & World, pp. 44, 61, 119, 173; index.
While W's serial in the Chronicle (1906) "has a delightful
main idea," the love-interest is not pleasant. To rank Mr.
Lewisham with Kipps is a mistake. Last Things encourages inac-
curate thinking.

2483 MARDER, HERBERT. Feminism and Art: A Study of Virginia Woolf.
Chicago: University of Chicago Press, pp. 8, 118-20.
In spite of dealing with advanced ideas, events in Ann
Veronica unfold predictably. Woolf thought W's attempts to com-
bine art and propaganda to be misguided. Unlike W, Joyce was
aware life involved more than externals.

2484 MORGAN, DEAN LUCIEN. "Scientific Method and Vision of Reality:
The Short Stories of H.G. Wells." Dissertation, University of
Southern California, 1967.
[Listed in Dissertation Abstracts 28 (1968):4182A.]

2485   MOSKOWITZ, SAM. Science Fiction by Gaslight: A History and
        Anthology of Science Fiction in the Popular Magazines, 1891-
        1911. Cleveland and New York: World, pp. 24-29, 203-4.
            The appearance of Time Machine in the New Review in 1895
        paved the way for a policy of including science fiction in most
        popular magazines. W was not the first to predict the use of
        tanks, but he better understood their tactical use than any ear-
        lier writer, and he may have been the first to anticipate the need
        for caterpillar treads.

2486   NEWELL, KENNETH B. Structure in Four Novels by H.G. Wells.
        The Hague: Mouton.
            Structural analysis of Mr. Lewisham, Kipps, Tono-Bungay and
        Mr. Polly reveals meanings in each novel that differ from conven-
        tional interpretations. Themes of deception, vanity, illusion,
        change and "multiple forms of the idea of 'indigestion'" indicate
        W's novels do not lack organization as is commonly thought. The
        four novels are "antideterministic" in theme and "non-pessimistic"
        in tone, which sets them apart from other fiction of their time.
        [Slightly condensed version of entry 2451.]

2487   PHILMUS, ROBERT M. "Into the Unknown: The Evolution of Sci-
        ence Fiction in England from Francis Godwin to H.G. Wells."
        Dissertation, University of of California (San Diego).
            [Listed in Dissertation Abstracts 29 (1968):1545A.] Pub-
        lished as entry 2553.

2488   RAINER, DACHINE. "Rebecca West: Disturber of the Peace."
        Commonweal 88 (10 May):227-30.
            Rebecca West's talent seems to have come fully developed as
        though it were drawn from both of her mentors, W and Shaw. She
        thought of W as "the most bubbling creative mind . . . since the
        days of Leonardo da Vinci." Her style came from Shaw, her think-
        ing from W.

2489   RICKS, CHRISTOPHER. "Games People Play." New York Review of
        Books 10 (14 March):32-34.
            Hillegas belabors the obvious when he describes W's por-
        trayal of the future as a nightmare. W views life through books,
        like spectacles that need adjusting. All that remains of Utopia
        is a joyless game, while Experiment is depressing in its demon-
        stration of how much was lost when W turned to social science.
        [Review of Mark Hillegas, The Future as Nightmare.]

2490   SCHEICK, WILLIAM J. "The Thing That Is and the Speculative If:
        The Pattern of Several Motifs in Three Novels by H.G. Wells."
        ELT 11:67-78.
            Tono-Bungay, Machiavelli, and Comet are partly built on W's
        concept of the spirit of man and the motifs of his innate nobility,

1968

sense of beauty, creative imagination, and capacity for love,
which find fulfillment in a "creatively directed science." For W
the present world is a dream from which humanity will awaken to
reality.

2491   SMITH, WARREN SYLVESTER. The London Heretics, 1870-1914. New
        York: Dodd, Mead, pp. 254-56.
            Despite a hidden guilt about his reluctance to "plunge
        directly into the turbulence of life," W deeply influenced the
        heretical spirit before and after World War I.

2492   STEWART, J.I.M. Joseph Conrad. London: Longmans, pp. 9, 25,
        132, 134.
            Although he had a limited contact with English society,
        Conrad was able to get along with W, whose outlook was alien to
        him.

2493   SUSSMAN, HERBERT L. Victorians and the Machine: The Literary
        Response to Technology. Cambridge, Mass.: Harvard University
        Press, pp. 3, 7, 10-12, 95, 97, 128, 133, 144, 169-93; index.
            W used the machine as a symbol of the interrelationships of
        technological change, psychic well-being, and mechanistic thought,
        but also of the specifically scientific mind. The scientific
        romances use the machine as both cause and symbol of social ex-
        ploitation. Like Rider Haggard's heroes battling in exotic sur-
        roundings, W's fight against machinery. "For all their symbolic
        weight, the scientific romances are adaptations of the imperial-
        istic adventure story to the problem of the machine."

2494   VAUGHAN, GILBERT LEE. "Humor in the Early Fiction of H.G.
        Wells." Dissertation, University of Arkansas.
            [[Listed in Dissertation Abstracts 29 (1968):278-79A.]

2495   WELLS, G[EORGE] P[HILIP]. Introduction and Appendix to The
        Last Books of H.G. Wells: The Happy Turning and Mind at the
        End of Its Tether. London: H.G. Wells Society, pp. 7-17,
        79-84.
            Tether was a reworking and expansion of material previously
        used in the revised edition of Short History. To understand
        properly W's final outlook, these last writings need to be ex-
        amined together and against the background of his earlier work. W
        was not a total pessimist in his final days. [Appendix: Textual
        history of the books as reconstructed from papers in the H.G.
        Wells Archive in the library of the University of Illinois,
        Urbana.]

2496   "Wells Novel as a Play." Times (London), 17 Oct., p. 19.
            A musical version of Ann Veronica will have its premiere 6
        Feb. The adaptation is by Frank Wells and Ronald Gow, with music

by Cyril Ornadel and lyrics by David Croft. Dorothy Tutin has
been signed to play the lead.

2497   Wellsian 2, no. 3.
        [Contents include: Editorial; "Science and the World
Order" (a short version of W's paper for the British Association
for the Advancement of Science of 1941); "Wellsian Poetic Devices," by V.B. Leyland (a catalog of examples of W using poetic
passages or suggestions of poetry in his prose as excerpted from
Leyland's thesis, "The Visible Man"); "Russian Critical Attitudes," by Professor Y.V. Kovalev (a translation by Baroness Moura
Budberg of the introduction to the bibliography of W's work as
translated into Russian and of criticism published in Russia); "On
Human Rights," by the Rt. Hon. the Lord Ritchie-Calder (a digest
of his speech); "Three Satirical Novels," by John Hammond (Dr.
Moreau, Blettsworthy, and Croquet Player are strongly satirical
and allegorical, but must be read several times before the full
meaning of these parables of man's folly can be understood);
"Wells Versus Shaw," by Brian Ash (the exchanges between the two
writers comprise "a lifetime of inspired bickering".]

                              1969

2498   BORRELLO, ALFRED. "Bibliography, News and Notes: H.G. Wells."
        ELT 12:49-54.
        [Annotated bibliography (31 items) of material about W
published 1954-68.]

2499   BROGAN, DENIS. "M. Britling commence à voir claire."
        Spectator 222 (31 Jan.):139.
        Mr. Britling can withstand rereading, and W's reputation
has suffered unjustly. The novel is really an account of the
awakening of society from complacency about the old order in
England.

2500   DAVENPORT, W.A. To the Lighthouse (Virginia Woolf). Notes on
        English Literature. Oxford: Basil Blackwell, p. 8.
        Woolf's search for new conventions resulted in criticism of
the established writers like Bennett, W, and Galsworthy.

2501   DICKSON, LOVAT. H.G. Wells: His Turbulent Life and Times.
        New York: Atheneum.
        A concentration on the early years of W's career with only
a glance at the last thirty years is intentional since Machiavelli
was the end of an era. His passion for science activated his
artistic vision and led to his acceptance as a writer of genius by
a broad spectrum of the public as well as by the society represented by James, Gosse, Crane, Ford, and Conrad. His utopian

visions and criticism of the existing social order soon replaced
the scientific romances and led him into controversy. His talents
were lost to art when he turned to education and reform. One
basic flaw in his character seems to be the absence of moral
values, i.e., the "moral resources of humanity." [For discussion
of contradictions in Dickson, see Stanley Kauffmann, "The Man Who
Couldn't Work Miracles," New Republic 161 (9 Aug.):20-23; includes
very selective bibliography and identifies few sources; still, a
valuable account by an editor and director of W's principal
publisher.]

2502   EDEL, LEON. Henry James, 1895-1901: The Treacherous Years.
        Philadelphia: J.B. Lippincott, pp. 68-72, 74, 76, 78, 80, 87,
        213, 333, 337.
            W was assigned to review Guy Domville because he was not
        part of the regular reviewing clique. His review noted the char-
        acters moving like "rabbits in a warren" and cited the writing as
        beautiful but too delicate for acting.

2503   GLIKIN, GLORIA. "Through the Novelist's Looking Glass."
        Kenyon Review 31:297-319. Reprinted as by Gloria Glikin Fromm,
        CE, pp. 157-77.
            W portrayed himself from different angles in his novels and
        projected all the angles in Experiment. In Pilgrimage, Dorothy
        Richardson caught his essential qualities in the character of Hypo
        Wilson. Like W, he is convinced the world can be improved and
        demands the whole stage while explaining. Miriam proofreads
        Wilson's books the way Arnold Bennett did W's. Despite a tendency
        to dwell on his deficiencies, she realizes the psychological
        conflict--he is an artist suppressed by a teacher.

2504   GROSS, JOHN. "Reassessment--1: H.G. Wells: The Road to
        Utopia." NS 78 (25 July):108-9.
            There is irony in the fact that W's visions of the future
        are gathering dust and that "The man who encouraged his generation
        to jettison the past has been consigned to the scrap-heap him-
        self." The part of him that matters as a writer will stand out as
        the propagandist dwindles. Outline still seems better than most
        universal histories of its day, but it is Time Machine and Mr.
        Polly that deserve reading.

2505   HYDE, H. MONTGOMERY. Henry James at Home. New York: Farrar,
        Straus & Giroux, pp. 63, 87-8, 91, 114, 128, 140, 150, 164,
        179, 186-91, 241, 248, 250, 251, 268-70, 281, 293, 294.
            James and Gosse called on W when he was ill and tried to
        learn if he needed financial help. James was not amused or con-
        vinced by W's arguments in Boon or by the resulting
        correspondence.

2506   [HYNES, SAMUEL.] "H.G. and G.B.S." TLS (London), 27 Nov.,
        pp. 1349-50. Reprinted as "The Higher Journalism: Edwardian
        Polymaths," in T.L.S., Essays and Reviews from the Times
        Literary Supplement, 1969 (London: Oxford University Press,
        pp. 27-34, and reprinted in part in Edwardian Occasions (New
        York: Oxford University Press, pp. 18-23.
            Shaw and W were both the best-known writers of their day
        and both have unstable reputations. In addition, both used per-
        sonal elements from their lives in their writings or created
        public characters for themselves. They can be best regarded not
        as playwright and novelist, but as polymaths because they believed
        they could embrace knowledge and affect the future of the species.
        The comparison between W and Dickens is legitimate since both had
        "a gift for particularizing ordinariness and imagining new
        actualities."

2507   KARL, FREDERICK R. A Reader's Guide to Joseph Conrad. Rev.
        ed. New York: Farrar, Straus & Giroux, pp. 16, 36-37, 145,
        187.
            As a journalist W made fidelity to fact and fidelity to
        truth identical.

2508   LAUN, EDWARD C. "The Self-Made Gentleman as a Hero in
        Victorian Fiction." Dissertation, University of Wisconsin,
        1968.
            [Listed in Dissertation Abstracts International 29
        (1969):4496A.]

2509   LODGE, DAVID. "Utopia and Criticism: The Radical Longing for
        Paradise." Encounter 32 (April):65-75. Reprinted in The
        Novelist at the Crossroads and Other Essays (Ithaca, N.Y.:
        Cornell University Press, 1971), pp. 221-36.
            W influenced Orwell and Zamyatin, while himself being in-
        fluenced by existing traditions of utopian fantasy. He reversed
        the usual trend by writing anti-utopian fiction before writing
        utopian fiction. It is in Men in the Moon that his "'progressive'
        ideas began to pull damagingly against his pessimistic intui-
        tions." In Utopia he imagines the kind of social structure that
        would make his own kind of success available to everyone. He
        disarms most criticism by anticipating it. One can discover myths
        and archetypes in the structure of the utopian fiction, and behind
        War of the Worlds may be seen some of the same elements in
        Milton's Paradise Lost.

2510   MECKIER, JEROME. Aldous Huxley: Satire and Structure.
        London: Chatto & Windus, pp. 7, 112, 121-22, 124, 159-60, 176-
        77, 185-86, 197, 200.
            Brave New World confronts W's "scientific future" with
        Lawrence's "primitive past" and "repudiates" both. W himself is

1969

satirized as "Mr. Scogan" in Crome Yellow, and his ideas are
satirized in Brave New World. Like W in Clissold, Huxley often
puts himself into a novel in order to comment on the era.

2511   MINNEY, R.J.   Recollections of George Bernard Shaw.   Englewood
       Cliffs, N.J.:   Prentice-Hall, pp. 28-29, 67-68, 72, 169, 176.
            W's mental range was wider than Shaw's, and he felt serious
       subjects required a serious tone.   He once suggested Shaw shave
       his beard so he could go about unrecognized.

2512   MONTEIRO, GEORGE.   "Harold Frederic: An Unrecorded Review."
       Papers of the Bibliographical Society of America 63:30-31.
            W wanted to review Gissing's The Whirlpool for SR (London),
       but he was beaten to it by Harold Frederic.

2513   MOORE, HARRY T.   Preface to The Wealth of Mr. Waddy: A Novel.
       Carbondale: Southern Illinois University Press; London:
       Feffer & Simons, pp. vii-ix.
            As an unfinished novel, Mr. Waddy has some of the fascina-
       tion of The Mystery of Edwin Drood, The Weir of Hermiston, and The
       Last Tycoon.

2514   MÜLLENBROCK, HEINZ-JOACHIM.   "Gesellschaftliche Thematik in
       E.M. Forsters Roman Howards End."   Anglia 87:367-91.
            Forster's Howards End, Galsworthy's The Patrician and W's
       Tono-Bungay are examples of fiction that focuses on contemporary
       social conditions in turn-of-the century England.   Unlike W's
       earlier works describing the petty bourgeois, Tono-Bungay portrays
       a panorama of the entire English society.

2515   _____.   "Nationalismus und Internationalismus im Werk von H.G.
       Wells."   Neuren Sprachen, n.s. 18:478-97.
            W's viewpoint shifts from nationalist to internationalist
       in his works before 1914.   The two opposing views come together in
       a psychological compromise in which W embraces a cosmopolitanism
       without denying his concessions to patriotism.   Anticipation rep-
       resents the first phase, Utopia and Comet represent the second
       phase, while Machiavelli is the third phase.

2516   "Musical's Relapse."   Times (London), 18 April, p. 15.
            The musical version of Ann Veronica is "tame and
       lacklustre."

2517   PHILMUS, ROBERT M.   "The Time Machine; Or, The Fourth Dimension
       as Prophecy."   PMLA 84 (May):530-35.
            W's vision of the future in this book runs counter to the
       assumption that evolution was for the benefit of mankind.   It is a
       critique of pre-Wellsian utopian romances, the idea of striving
       toward "ease and delight."   The Traveler's viewpoint is even more

limited than the viewpoint of his audience and he returns to the future to prove he has been there.

2518 PLATZNER, ROBERT L. "H.G. Wells's Jungle Book: The Influence of Kipling on The Island of Dr. Moreau." Victorian Newsletter, no. 36 (Fall):19-22.
       The borrowings of W from Kipling for Moreau are extensive, and the relationship between the two works includes both philosophical and literary satire. W found the Jungle Book "grotesquely false, biologically and morally."

2519 POTTS, WILLARD C. "H.G. Wells on the Novel." Dissertation, University of Washington, 1969.
       [Listed in Dissertation Abstracts 30 (1969):2544A.]

2520 PRITCHETT, V.S. "The History of Mr. Wells." NS 78 (14 Nov.):698-99.
       It may be that W's restlessness, temper, and the scandals in his life saved him from pomposity. "He was very representative of the emerging lower middle class in the Edwardian age, a regiment of bubble-blowing dreamers, believers in the prosperity of the species, who had thrown off late-Victorian doubt, but to whom bitter early struggle had given a touch of aggressive nastiness." There is a strong sense of moral values in his early work through Mr. Polly (contrary to the view of Lovat Dickson). He lost his material for art when he became prosperous, and this may be dated from the success of Anticipations--for "journalism pays and art does not." The social historian will find much in his work. [Review of Lovat Dickson, H.G. Wells: His Turbulent Life and Times.]

2521 SCHEICK, WILLIAM J. "Reality and the Word: The Last Books of H.G. Wells." ELT 12:151-54.
       The predominant motif in Turning is the dream representing human potential. The real world in Tether is shown to be no more real than a motion picture. W meant to wake up humanity from the dream of reality to this greater reality of human potential, but he recognized this desire as his own private dream.

2522 SMITH, PAGE. "The Millenial Vision of H.G. Wells." Journal of Historical Studies 2:23-24.
       W's reflections on "The Next Stage of History" from Outline seem "touching and naive," for he sees progress as "an accelerating process" without hindrances. He does serve to remind historians of the proper orientation to the future.

2523 STRAUSS, SYLVIA. "H.G. Wells and America." Dissertation, Rutgers University, 1968.
       [Listed in Dissertation Abstracts 29 (1969):2199A.]

1969

2524   THIBAULT, ALBERT A. "H.G. Wells et la France." Revue de
       l'Université d'Ottawa 39:562-76.
            The French have been generally favorable toward W, and he
       toward them. Their love of his fantasies and his concern with
       national and international problems show why they considered him
       Jules Verne's English counterpart. Although W often omitted any
       mention of France in his writings, he was influenced by many
       French writers.

2525   "The Times Diary: The Wells Father and Son Musical." Times
       (London), 15 April, p. 10.
            Frank Wells recalls his father saying that Ann Veronica was
       the best female character he ever wrote about. In the musical,
       her soliloquies "click when turned into songs." Frank and his
       father used to talk about his writing, and a discussion of "The
       Country of the Blind" resulted in W rewriting the story. (Mary
       Millar will portray Ann Veronica in the Cambridge Theater opening
       of the musical.)

2526   WARNER, HARRY. All Our Yesterdays: An Informal History of
       Science Fiction Fandom in the Forties. Chicago: Advent, pp.
       5-6, 7, 9, 37, 103, 117, 149.
            W appears to have wanted to be a "fan" but was too success-
       ful in all his ventures to remain at that level. With no real
       association with fandom, he eventually was the focus of a society
       designed to stimulate interest in his ideas.

2527   WILLIAMSON, JACK. "H.G. Wells, Critic of Progress." RQ 3
       (1967-68):6-31, 96-117, 187-207, 272-93; 4 (1969):24-33.
            W's method of writing science fiction was to introduce
       novel elements into familiar situations. In his early work he is
       "a second Swift, sadly aware of the animal heritage and all the
       hostile forces that oppose our dreams of progress." The idea of
       progress for W symbolized universal conflict. "Challenging the
       hope of progress, he was perhaps unconsciously expressing the
       inevitable resistance of social tradition to all the impulses of
       the individual ego." [Reprinted, with alterations, by Mirage
       Press, 1973.]

2528   WILSON, COLIN. Bernard Shaw: A Reassessment. New York:
       Atheneum, pp. 16, 28, 86, 107, 114, 149, 150, 203, 206, 207,
       208, 210, 211, 214, 220, 228, 230, 238, 239, 261, 264, 285,
       293.
            W's relations with his mother were similar to Shaw's. Like
       W's hero in "The Country of the Blind," Shaw could see the distant
       point and thus was thought mad. Unlike Shaw, W never bothered
       with a public image. Far from being "squelched" by Shaw's quip
       during a Fabian debate, W was elected to the executive committee.
       Compared to W, Shaw was the pampered one. There is a sense of

repetition and futility in <u>Machiavelli</u> and <u>Marriage</u>, but his trilogy (<u>Outline</u>, <u>Science of Life</u>, <u>Work</u>) shows a mind aiming at the universe.

2529   WILSON, HARRIS. Introduction to <u>The Wealth of Mr. Waddy</u>: <u>A Novel</u>. Carbondale: Southern Illinois University Press; London: Feffer & Simons, pp. xi–xxiii.
        <u>Mr. Waddy</u> was written at the peak of W's career and throws light on his literature development. Part of it later became the published novel, <u>Kipps</u>, which is only half the length he projected for <u>Mr. Waddy</u> The most important difference between the two versions is the development of the characters of Waddy, Citterlow, and Muriel. One significant part that disappeared in the transition satirized contemporary fiction. In the subsequent novel, <u>Kipps</u>, W unsuccessfully attempted to superimpose one type of novel onto another.

2530   WOOD, JAMES PLAYSTED. <u>I Told You So!</u> <u>A Life of H.G. Wells</u>. New York: Pantheon Books.
        [A brief biography written for "young people."]

                              <u>1970</u>

2531   ATHELING, WILLIAM [pseud. of James Blish]. <u>More Issues at Hand</u>. Chicago: Advent, pp. 14, 25, 26, 30, 31, 35, 45, 47, 48, 50, 58, 76, 98–102, 103, 104–5, 144.
        W's method in fantasy was rigid: only one miracle per story and that to be used logically. Although his themes involve the future of progress as human degradation, he was always precise about how it could happen, something later writers often ignore. All the early science fiction is cautionary in tone. When it became visionary, it lost its impact.

2532   BAXTER, JOHN. <u>Science Fiction in the Cinema</u>. New York: A.S. Barnes, pp. 47–48, 51–65, 109–10, 148–50.
        Despite the liberties taken with the original romance and W's own repudiation of the film, <u>The Island of Lost Souls</u> remains "one of the cleverest Hollywood adaptations of his work." The film version of <u>Invisible Man</u>, with Claude Rains, reflects some of W's own amusement over the theme and is one of the best adaptations of a W story. <u>Things to Come</u>, in spite of some good moments, is a flawed film, marred by W's "simple-minded and often shoddy pamphleteering." Little of the original idea is left in George Pal's film of <u>Time Machine</u> and of <u>War of the Worlds</u>.

2533   BEJA, MORRIS. <u>Virginia Woolf</u>: <u>To the Lighthouse, a Casebook</u>. London: Macmillan, pp. 18, 64, 66–68, 85.

                              323

1970

It is ironic that Woolf should have criticized W, Bennett, and Galsworthy for the faults she found in their work since her own work is often criticized for not dealing with real life.

2534   BELLOW, SAUL. <u>Mr. Sammler's Planet</u>. New York: Viking Press, pp. 19, 27-30, 41, 71-72, 98, 106-7, 112-13, 128-29, 130, 136, 196, 198-200, 207, 210-13, 264-65.
        Artur Sammler, who spoke with W in his last days, plans to write a memoir someday of that "horny man of labyrinthine extraordinary sensuality." His daughter imagines the conversations lasted over a period of several years and that the memoir will astonish everyone, for "Wells had communicated things to Sammler that the world didn't know." She steals the manuscript to a book on the future of the Moon because she thinks her father should know if W had been correct. Sammler recalls that W "in his seventies was still obsessed with girls," but "that tough brave little old fellow . . . had had prophetic visions after all. . . . In those days my own ideas didn't amount to much so I listened to his. Scientific humanism, faith in an emancipated future, in active benevolence, in reason, in civilization, Not popular ideas at the moment. . . . Still, you know, Schopenhauer would not have called Wells a vulgar optimist. Wells had many dark thoughts. Take a book like <u>War of the Worlds</u>. There the Martians come to get rid of mankind. They treat our species as Americans treated the bison and other animals, or for that matter the American Indians. Extermination."

2535   BERGONZI, BERNARD. <u>The Situation of the Novel</u> London: Macmillan, 1970; Pittsburgh: University of Pittsburgh Press, 1971, pp. 23, 72, 84, 162-63, 176-78, 195-97, 199, 208, 210.
        W was following various traditions in English literature in many of his stories. He foreshadowed "the common state of individual alienation in mass urban society" in <u>Invisible Man</u>, but "A Story of the Stone Age" is derivative. The symbolic role of the English mansion in fiction is seen in Bladesover in <u>Tono-Bungay</u>. A number of later writers were influenced in part by W: Kingsley Amis's <u>Lucky Jim</u> is in the same tradition of Edwardian comic fiction as <u>Kipps</u>, and if Evelyn Waugh's <u>Love Among the Ruins</u> and L.P. Hartley's <u>Facial Justice</u> seem to reflect Orwell, they also reflect W's <u>Sleeper Wakes</u> in satirizing an imaginary totalitarian England. Wanting to change the shape of the novel, W wrote dialogues and monologues in which to discuss contemporary issues.

2536   BLEICH, DAVID. "Utopia: The Psychology of a Cultural Fantasy." Dissertation, New York University, 1968.
        [Listed in <u>Dissertation Abstracts International</u> 30 (1970):4935A-36A.]

2537   BOJARSKI, EDMUND A. "Wells on Conrad." TLS, 28 May, p. 586.
[Letter.] W's review of Conrad's An Outcast of the Islands
began "the ambivalent friendship between the two writers." His
early reviews may have influenced other writers and ought to be
studied with some care.

2538   BUCKLEY, JEROME. "Autobiography in the English Bildungsroman."
In The Interpretation of Narrative: Theory and Practice.
Edited by Morton W. Bloomfield. Cambridge, Mass.: Harvard
University Press, pp. 93-109.
Like Wordsworth's Prelude, Tono-Bungay is a Bildungsroman,
a story of apprenticeship designed as an exercise in self-
justification (or self-understanding), which traces the char-
acter's move from a provincial life to cosmopolitan London.
George Ponderevo is more seriously alienated from society than W
was until his old age.

2539   CHAPPIE, J.A.V. Documentary and Imaginative Literature.
London: Blandford; New York: Barnes & Noble, pp. 22, 29, 30,
110, 113-14, 121, 145, 146-49, 154, 221, 225, 229, 238, 248,
258, 263-65, 268-78, 280, 303, 327, 329, 332, 338, 343, 350.
W was more in tune with "preliminary movements of sensi-
bility in his time" than were other writers. He was afraid his
utopia might be built on quicksand. His criticism of women's
suffrage in Ann Veronica concerns the "militant manifestations"
and not the cause itself. His imaginative invention in War in the
Air is based on "reasoned speculation." He was the sort of writer
who was involved to the fullest in the events of his own age.

2540   DUNBAR, JANET. J.M. Barrie: The Man Behind the Image.
Boston: Houghton Mifflin, pp. 157, 221-23, 226, 229-30, 231,
388.
Barrie and W were occasional correspondents and dinner
companions. W was among those who tried to lessen press comment
on Barrie's divorce. [Letter of W to Mary Barrie.]

2541   EDWARDS, G. JOHN. "Filmbook: The Island of Lost Souls."
Famous Monsters of Filmland, no. 81 (Dec. 1970), pp. 12-21; no.
82 (Feb. 1971), pp. 14-23.
[Detailed synopsis with fifteen photos of the 1932 film
version of Dr. Moreau.]

2542   ELLIOTT, ROBERT C. The Shape of Utopia: Studies in a Literary
Genre. Chicago: University of Chicago Press, pp. 85-86, 113-
16, 118n, 132.
W's utopian speculations were based on the assumption that
scientific analysis of the present can help man control the future. His optimism got out of control, and he now seems merely
pathetic. The bold conception of Utopia, part fiction, part

1970

essay, is marred by his "clumsy entanglement with the subjunctive
mood"; W "cannot dissolve the incompatibility of the materials he
was working with: the large generalities of the ideas, the in-
sistent specificity of the characters."

2543   FARMER, DAVID. "The Bibliographical Potential of a 20th Cen-
       tury Literary Agent's Archive: The Pinker Papers." Library
       Chronicle (University of Texas at Austin), Nov., pp. 26-35.
       [Correspondence to and from literary agent J.B. Pinker, in
the Pinker papers at the University of Texas at Austin, includes
letters of W.]

2544   GOEWEY, HERBERT J. "The Apology for Death and the Rejection of
       Extended Life in Nineteenth- and Twentieth-Century British
       Visionary Fiction." Dissertation, Wayne State University,
       1969.
       [Listed in Dissertation Abstracts International 30
(1970):3942A.]

2545   HILLEGAS, MARK R. "Martians and Mythmakers: 1877-1938." In
       Challenges in American Culture. Edited by Ray B. Browne, Larry
       N. Landrum, and William K. Bottorff. Bowling Green, Ohio:
       Bowling Green University Popular Press, pp. 150-77.
       Myths are created all the time, one of which is the myth of
superior aliens invading earth. There are four interpretations of
this myth, which has its roots in the late nineteenth century:
(1) we fear to be alone in the universe, (2) historical events may
suggest future wars, (3) the rapid advance of science and technology generates fear, and (4) a scientific, post-Christian age
requires a search for new gods. Percival Lowell's 1895 study,
Mars, started much of the speculative writing about the planet.
The first major treatments of the myth were Kurd Lasswitz's Auf
Zwei Planeten and War of the Worlds. W's story conveys the arche-
typal form of the myth, which may be seen in later writings by
C.S. Lewis, Robert Heinlein, Arthur C. Clarke, and Edgar Rice
Burroughs. The climax of the myth came in 1938 with Orson
Welles's Mercury Theatre broadcast of War of the Worlds. After
that, it was no longer credible, though Martian stories were still
being written. The myth itself can still be found in a film like
2001.

2546   HUNTLEY, H. ROBERT. The Alien Protagonist of Ford Madox Ford.
       Chapel Hill, N.C.: University of North Carolina Press, pp. 8,
       9, 11, 12; index.
       W's impressions of Ford in Experiment are vague. W looked
to a "shaky fusion" of Schopenhauer and Darwin to answer his fears
of personal extinction and Edwardian political anarchy. The meta-
physics of evolution expressed in Mankind in the Making assume
naively that man is implicitly the apex of the process. "A Story

of the Stone age" focuses on the discovery of the flint-headed axe, the moment when paleolithic man became fit to survive. W's distrust of traditional guides irritated Ford, who publicly denounced imperialism.

2547   HUXLEY, JULIAN. Memories. Vol. 1. New York: Harper & Row, 1970, pp. 149, 151, 155-74, 259. Vol. 2. New York: Harper & Row, 1973, pp. 145, 242.
    W was a philistine and genius whose knowledge of biology was old-fashioned. The scientific material in The Science of Life was the work of Huxley and W's son, Gip. His petulant letters to Huxley over the amount of work to be produced for the book was due in part to worries about Jane's health. The work went on despite stormy incidents between W and Odette Keun. The book had the effect of creating in the general public an interest in its subject that was reflected in the greater attention given to biology in education curricula. In the course of writing it Huxley learned a great deal about the ways to popularize difficult ideas. W refused to allow him to insert a statement about the length of red corpuscles if placed end to end because no one would believe it and might be skeptical of the rest of the book. [Ten letters of W quoted in full or at length; Huxley appears to believe Laughton's film Island of Lost Souls was never released due to the ghastly subject matter.]

2548   KOCH, HOWARD. The Panic Broadcast: Portrait of an Event. Boston: Little, Brown.
    In 1938 when John Houseman gave Koch a copy of War of the Worlds to dramatize for the Mercury Theatre, he found very little of the original that he could use. A New Jersey map was the source of the setting for the invasion, Grovers Mills. The lesson for the "survivors" of the invasion is to doubt and test everything on the air or in print. [Text of the radio play with reminiscences by its author on its creation, broadcast, and the aftermath; photos, newspaper facsimiles.]

2549   MULLER, HERBERT J. "A Note on Utopia." The Children of Frankenstein. Bloomington and London: Indiana University Press, pp. 369-83.
    W's utopian visions were based on science, and W had more concern for common people than most writers. His dark fears for the future stemmed from his high hopes for man, and he was a major source for the revolt against utopianism.

2550   PANSHIN, ALEXEI. "A Basic Science Fiction Collection." Library Journal 95 (15 June):2223-29.
    Though many of Verne's prophecies have come true, W's "dreaming of great dreams" best represents science fiction. [Annotated bibliography includes all of W's science fiction.]

1970

2551   PARRINDER, PATRICK. H.G. Wells. Edinburgh: Oliver & Boyd.
        The theme of W's novels seems to be the need for rising
above given social conditions. He seems to have tried to give
humanity his own instincts for growth and survival, and his writings reflect ideas on man's consciousness of the species as an
entity with "a common, collective purpose." He is "a sociological
novelist who relates the individual lives he presents to general
patterns and classifications." [Originally John P. Parrinder,
"H.G. Wells and the Social Novel," unpublished dissertation,
Cambridge University, 1970; listed in Lawrence F. McNamee,
Dissertations in English and American Literature, supp. 2
(New York & London: Bowker, 1974).]

2552   _____. "Wells on Hardy." TLS 23 April, p. 455.
        W's anonymous review of Hardy's Jude the Obscure is noted
as having been reprinted in two collections of reviews of Hardy
without being attributed to him.

2553   PHILMUS, ROBERT M. Into the Unknown: The Evolution of Science
        Fiction from Francis Godwin to H.G. Wells. Berkeley and Los
        Angeles: University of California Press, pp. 2, 5-6, 12, 31-
        34, 101-2, 124-25; index.
        Science fiction shows the earliest high consciousness of
myth in W's early romances. These works satirized accepted ideas
and ideals by "depicting their consequences as cosmic principles
or demonstrating their partiality by embodying as myth the 'opposite idea.'" Time Machine becomes a "commentary on complacency
and dogmatism" because it places in doubt the distinction between
the actual and the possible. Invisible Man is a modern Faustian
myth, whereas Dr. Moreau embodies the myth of man's partial ani-
mality as a force motivated by fear and desire. W anticipates the
dilemma of technological progress that has been explored by later
science fiction writers, while his own later works can be seen as
logical developments from the early fantasy.

2554   PIPER, D.G.B. "Yuriy Olesha's Zavist: An Interpretation."
        Slavonic and East European Review 48 (Jan.):27-43.
        That Zavist was inspired by Invisible Man is generally
ignored by critics, who consider Olesha's novel to be concerned
with the clash of old and new worlds. In Zavist the protagonists
inhabit a fantasy world of the imagination that is as invisible to
the real world as is the protagonist in W's novel.

2555   ROBSON, W.W. Modern English Literature. London and New York:
        Oxford University Press, pp. 8-12, 14, 18, 20-22, 26, 28, 40,
        74, 102, 126, 153.
        W is the most characteristically English writer in the
twentieth century. Impatient, impulsive, inaccurate, often superficial, he grasped the possibilities of modern science with imagination. His early commercial success was due to his writing on

topical subjects, primarily the practical application of science. The reader is never concerned with his books as a whole but in what will happen next. Invisible Man is entertaining, but W never went beyond the comic or thriller aspects of his idea. It is in "The Country of the Blind" that he comes closest to uniting intellect and imagination, while "The Door in the Wall" hints at another dimension of meaning, like a myth.

2556 ROSE, LOIS, and STEPHEN ROSE. The Shattered Ring: Science Fiction and the Quest for Meaning. Richmond, Va.: John Knox, pp. 31-39.
 The root of the alienation of youth is "political impotence" and the origins for this may be found in W's writings, "the first science fiction master to use the literary form for polemical purposes."

2557 SAVESON, JOHN E. "Conrad's View of Primitive Peoples in Lord Jim and Heart of Darkness." MFS 16:163-84.
 W had an influence on Conrad's "intellectual and moral sophistication" from the time he wrote an unfavorable review of Outcast of the Islands for Frank Harris's SR (London). Conrad read W (fiction and nonfiction) and struck up a correspondence. W warned Ford Madox Ford against collaborating with Conrad for fear he would spoil his "wonderful Oriental style."

2558 SCHEICK, WILLIAM J. "If Not a Window, At Least a Peephole." ELT 13:86-88.
 Harris Wilson's edition of W's unfinished novel, Mr. Waddy, demonstrates certain aspects of the novelist at work, particularly his "accretive approach to writing" in developing his characters.

2559 THATCHER, DAVID S. Nietzsche in England, 1890-1914. Toronto: University of Toronto Press, pp. 6n, 7, 11, 33, 81-3, 109, 143n, 170-1, 190, 207, 209, 221, 227-29, 231, 267, 269, 299n, 304n.
 W was fully aware of the subversive implications of Darwinism, and motifs from Nietzsche (repudiation of the idea of original sin, insistence on the law of change, premonitions of world wars) appeared in his work long before Nietzsche was available in English. Dr. Moreau suggests Nietzsche's "transvaluation of values," whereby traditional ethics are abandoned and a new type of man is advocated. Nietzsche's idea of a superman was expressed by W in a way designed to appeal to the English practical mind.

2560 TONKIN, HUMPHREY. "Utopias: Notes on a Pattern of Thought." Centennial Review 14:385-95.
 The impulse to create utopias is as old as man. The danger of utopian idealism seems to include a lack of flexibility and a

1970

sacrifice of the individual to society. In Utopia, W analyzes
utopian writings and proposes a model society, which is subject to
change, and thereby avoids the failures of the past.

2561   VERNIER, J[EAN]-P[IERRE].   "The New Machiavelli, roman de la
confusion." Etudes anglaises 23:62-71.
Machiavelli was one of W's first works to use fiction as a
vehicle for propaganda by incorporating the author's own ideas
into the novel. A number of incidents in W's life became part of
the novel, which has two primary themes: order and discipline,
and the paradox of the unity to be found in "love and fine
thinking."

1971

2562   BELLAMY, WILLIAM. The Novels of Wells, Bennett and Galsworthy,
1890-1910. London: Routledge & Kegan Paul.
The view of the Edwardian period as "out-moded Neo-
Vitalism" soon overturned by science and the First World War is
valid, but there is also an "underlying problem of disengaged
consciousness" that renders culture obsolete. Edwardian beliefs
grew out of late-Victorian moods, and what was lacking in the
1890s was supplied in the Edwardian period. W, Bennett, and
Galsworthy in their novels helped "institutionalize the thera-
peutic imagination of modern man."

2563   _____. "Wells, Bennett and Galsworthy." TLS 23 July, p. 861.
The Novels of Wells, Bennett and Galsworthy is "not inconsistent with a valuing of great literature" in its concern with
"the historical sequence of literary works" but an example of
"critical realism" which insists that "literature tends and always
has tended towards the undermining of coherent culture, and this
is its perennially 'modernist' function and this is why readers
value it." [Response to review of Bellamy's book in TLS, 9 July
1971.]

2564   BERGONZI, BERNARD. "H.G. Wells," In The Politics of Twentieth
Century Novelists. Edited by George Andrew Panichas. New
York: Hawthorn, pp. 3-14. Reprinted as "Wells, Fiction and
Politics," in The Turn of a Century: Essays on Victorian and
Modern English Literature (New York: Barnes & Noble, 1974;
London: Macmillan, 1973), pp. 99-113.
At socialist meetings in the 1880s W became interested in a
"milennial world" and began thinking of events on a global scale.
In his earliest work he is content to reflect on the world as it
is and as it might become without saying anything about what
should happen. His detachment was important in his early literary

development, emphasizing humanity in the mass instead of individuals. Since no class existed with which he could identify, he tried to create one, an idealized version of himself.

2565 BRADBURY, MALCOLM. The Social Context of Modern English Literature. New York: Schocken; Oxford: Blackwell, pp. 28, 32n, 45, 47n, 50–52, 56, 57, 59n, 78, 79, 89, 249n, 254.
As reflected in Tono-Bungay, the city is at once the place for confusion and stress and a source for the stimulating and exotic.

2566 ELWIN, MALCOLM. "Wells, Bennett and Galsworthy." TLS, 23 July, p. 861.
W, Bennett, and Galsworthy were discussed together in several publications before Virginia Woolf did so, the earliest was in Ford Madox Hueffer's Critical Attitude in 1911. [Letter in response to review of Bellamy, The Novels of Wells, Bennett and Galsworthy.]

2567 GIFFORD, DENIS. Science Fiction Film. New York: E.P. Dutton.
[Stills and brief notes on film versions of W's science fiction: Men in the Moon, Things to Come, War of the Worlds, Time Machine. See also the index to film titles.]

2568 GREEN, BENNY. "The History of Mr. Wells." Spectator 227 (14 Aug.):242–43.
Experiment is "too ingenious an exercise in self-dramatization to be a reliable biographical guide." W is hardly mentioned by the literary gossips except in comments on his temperament. By nature he was an optimist, by training a pessimist; and he fought to reconcile this conflict all his life.

2569 HODGART, MATTHEW. "From Animal Farm to Nineteen-Eighty-Four." In The World of George Orwell. Edited by Miriam Gross. (London: Weidenfeld & Nicolson, 1971; New York: Simon & Schuster, n.d.), pp. 135–43.
Orwell disliked W's Shape of Things and Huxley's Brave New World for being "lacking in a sense of political reality." His preference was for Jack London's The Iron Heel and Zamyatin's We.

2570 KAGARLITSKI, JULIUS. "Realism and Fantasy." In SF: The Other Side of Realism. Edited by Thomas Clareson. (Bowling Green, Ohio: Bowling Green University Press), pp. 29–52.
Realistic or "scientific" fantasy is indebted to Jules Verne and his "positivist convictions." W opposes the Verne approach in Time Machine and felt that "a materialistic civilization, developing within the framework of an unjust society would lead to the destruction of mankind." W was the Balzac and Dickens of fantasy.

1971

2571   KATEB, GEORGE, ed. Introduction to <u>Utopia</u>. New York:
        Atherton Press, pp. 1-28.
            W may be the greatest utopian writer after Plato, yet he
        never explored the method of making social change an institution.
        He took seriously the dangers of passivity that the utopian life
        poses.

2572   LOWNDES, SUSAN, ed. <u>Diaries</u> <u>and</u> <u>Letters</u> <u>of</u> <u>Marie</u> <u>Belloc</u>
        <u>Lowndes,</u> <u>1911-1947</u>. London: Chatto & Windus, pp. 25, 26, 126,
        183, 218, 222-23, 242, 255.
            At a lunch W said he felt the war of 1939 would not last
        long. He was bitter that the <u>Times</u> (London) would not print his
        letters, in which he abused the government. He doted on the
        Baroness Budberg, who refused to marry him.

2573   LUNDWALL, SAM J. <u>Science</u> <u>Fiction:</u> <u>What</u> <u>It's</u> <u>All</u> <u>About</u>. New
        York: Ace, pp. 16, 17, 21, 24, 36, 37, 39, 40, 52, 53, 59, 89,
        171.
            W has never been accepted into English literature because
        he advocated change and was therefore considered subversive. Ini-
        tially writing anti-utopian works, he later became increasingly
        reactionary. [Originally in Swedish.]

2574   MIZENER, ARTHUR. <u>The</u> <u>Saddest</u> <u>Story:</u> <u>A</u> <u>Biography</u> <u>of</u> <u>Ford</u> <u>Madox</u>
        <u>Ford</u>. New York and Cleveland: World Publishing, pp. xxi,
        xxii, 26, 40, 41, 44, 154-55, 161-64, 283-84; index.
            Ford's poems in <u>The</u> <u>Face</u> <u>of</u> <u>the</u> <u>Night</u> were praised by W.
        W felt the Webbs, Bland, and Shaw were not imaginative enough to
        lead the Fabians in an important socialist movement. Ford had
        been impressed by <u>Sea</u> <u>Lady</u>, and his <u>Mr.</u> <u>Apollo</u> shows the influence
        of that as well as of <u>Wonderful</u> <u>Visit</u>. Beatrice, in <u>Tono-Bungay</u>,
        is based on Violet Hunt. At the beginning of the arrangement over
        <u>ER</u> W was full of energy and enthusiasm, but he soon withdrew both
        editorial and financial support since one-fifth of the profits
        would not be enough for <u>Tono-Bungay</u>. Ford also had a habit of
        losing manuscripts. His portrait of Ford in <u>Bulpington</u> is mild
        compared to Ford's portrait of him in <u>The</u> <u>New</u> <u>Humpty-Dumpty</u>. W
        came to Ford's financial rescue with a check for 2,000 francs.
        [Many passing references.]

2575   NEWELL, KENNETH B. "<u>Kipps</u> and the Masterman Episode." <u>PMLA</u>
        86:1035-36.
            The success of Chitterlow's play in <u>Kipps</u> is part of
        the pattern of chance that structures the novel. The reason for
        W's suppression of the episode of Masterman's visit and death
        cannot have been commercial or he would also have omitted other
        examples of Masterman's social criticism. By omitting the final
        appearance W made the "strong social criticism largely implicit"

in the narrative and thus strengthened the novel. [Response to Wilson, PMLA 86:63-69.]

2576   RHODES, CAROLYN H. "Intelligence Testing in Utopia." Extrapolation 13 (Dec.):25-47.
       The application of intelligence tests in novels about the future is the most obvious use of psychological techniques in utopian fiction. Men Like Gods is vague about psychology as a scientific study.

2577   SMITH, M.P. "The Treatment of Money in Five Novels Between 1875 and 1914: The Way We Live Now, The Awkward Age, Born in Exile, Tono-Bungay, and Howard's End." Dissertation, University of London.
       [Listed in Lawrence F. McNamee, Dissertations in English and American Literature, supp. 2 (New York & London: Bowker, 1974).]

2578   WEINTRAUB, STANLEY. Journey to Heartbreak: The Crucible Years of Bernard Shaw, 1914-1918. New York: Weybright & Talley, pp. 29, 35, 38, 40-41, 76-78, 86, 103, 106, 158, 159, 166-67, 172, 174, 193, 199, 200, 213-14, 218, 232, 238, 240, 254.
       One symptom of W's mind giving way was his attack on Shaw for being "muddle-headed." W had second thoughts about the war and reestablished his friendship with Shaw. Shaw sent him a copy of Androcles and the Lion, to which W replied at length. W's suggestion that the Kaiser be thrown out and the monarchy replaced by a republic was a safeguard against possible puppet monarchies to fill vacant thrones. All of his ideas were not accepted during the war; one that was rejected was the "telphrage system."

2579   "Welles's War of Worlds Still Stirs Consternation." NYT 1 Nov., p. 82.
       Buffalo radio station WKBW adapted War of the Worlds and used a local suburb, Grand Island, as a setting. City police switchboard received one-hundred calls in reaction.

2580   WILLIAMS, RAYMOND. George Orwell. New York: Viking, pp. 33, 43, 82, 89.
       The quarrel between James and W came at a time when the development of the novel was an important issue. Though grounded in W, Joyce, Gissing, and Maugham, Orwell's early novels set the style for the English novel of the 1950s.

2581   _____. The English Novel from Dickens to Lawrence. New York: Oxford University Press, pp. 120, 121, 125-31, 133, 135, 136; index.
       Changes in the novel between 1895 and 1914 are evident in W's fiction, especially in Tono-Bungay where there is a

1971

consciousness of the end of an era. He wrote of a traditional
community (symbolized by the world of Bladesover) breaking down.
He was unique in seeing clearly the scope of the change and that
it could not be covered in any single literary form.

2582   WILSON, HARRIS. "The Death of Masterman: A Repressed Episode
in H.G. Wells Kipps." PMLA 86:63-69.
        The manuscript of Kipps is the most extensive example of
W's writing methods and includes an entire section of 11,000
words that was omitted from the final version of the novel. This
was due to aesthetic and commercial considerations. The importance and influence of Masterman on Kipps would have changed the
novel's structure and made it too long for serialization and book
publication. [Lengthy excerpts and paraphrases of the Masterman
section included.]

2583   WILSON, JOHN T. "Is Utopia Possible?" English (London) 20
(Summer):51-55.
        W's utopia allowed room for imperfection, progress, change
and innovation. Utopia relates the individual to the whole of
society.

2584   WOLLHEIM, DONALD A. The Universe Makers: Science Fiction
Today. New York: Harper & Row, pp. 18-21, 23, 31, 80.
        Unlike Verne's, W's themes included future prediction and
social satire, even in War of the Worlds and Dr. Moreau. Many of
his concepts seem to be firsts in modern science fiction. In his
short stories he set down the premise that a good science fiction
story would gain impact by having only one unknown factor against
a background of what is known. For him "sociology and human
relations merging with modern science are necessary ingredients of
science fiction," and thus he continues to influence the world by
his science fiction.

2585   WRIGHT, WALTER F. Arnold Bennett: Romantic Realist. Lincoln:
University of Nebraska Press, pp. 9, 20, 21-22, 27-28, 33, 55,
87, 89, 93, 98, 101, 102, 113, 121.
        W judged Bennett from personal impressions and not from a
study of the serious novels. W was a favorite of Bennett's in
spite of his sense of W's lack of artistic craftsmanship. W was
interested in remodeling the world, while Bennett was concerned
with self-discipline.

1972

2586   AYLESWORTH, THOMAS G. Monsters from the Movies. Philadelphia
and New York: J.B. Lippincott, pp. 20, 70, 79, 83, 116, 128.

334

The Island of Lost Souls may have been the source of the phrase, "the natives are restless tonight," spoken by Charles Laughton as Dr. Moreau.

2587   BELL, QUENTIN. Virginia Woolf: A Biography. New York: Harcourt, Brace; London: Hogarth Press, 1:161; 2:104-5. (London ed. published in 2 vols).
        Woolf felt like a character in a novel by W when working in an office. The new novelist, she felt, should look beyond W's moralizing and approach reality. In meeting with W she got along well but thought him an odd mixture of "bubble and solidity."

2588   BORRELLO, ALFRED. H.G. Wells, Author in Agony. Carbondale: Southern Illinois University Press.
        At first W optimistically relied on the force of individuality to provide the panacea for human limitation and suffering; then he shifted this faith in the individual to the idea of a dedicated superior group; eventually he abandoned even this belief to the despair of his last years. He failed to realize that the root of man's problems lies in his own nature; thus in his works characters are "merely puppets for their creator to move as he willed" and human nature is reduced to "rigid, immutable, and predictable patterns."

2589   CASSELL, RICHARD A. Introduction to Ford Madox Ford: Modern Judgements. London: Macmillan, pp. 13, 14, 15.
        W thought Ford's accumulation of personae and poses bordered on madness, but he defended his impressionistic memoir of Conrad and thought him an "unrecognized great poet."

2590   CLARESON, THOMAS D., ed. A Spectrum of Worlds. Garden City, N.Y.: Doubleday, pp. 23-24, 58-60.
        The texture of the imagined worlds before World War I is thin; W overcame the limitations of the science fiction genre and transformed its concepts into a vision of the future. In "The Sea Raiders" he "fused together the familiar and the mythic to achieve a metaphysical statement of man's frail place in the universe."

2591   CONNELY, WAYNE C. "H.G. Well[s]'s The Time Machine: Its Neglected Mythos." RQ 5 (Aug.):178-91.
        W's story is interpreted as a scientific allegory, while its socialistic aspects are ignored. Time Machine suggests what would happen to society and power after the revolution.

2592   COUSTILLAS, PIERRE, and COLIN PARTRIDGE. Introduction to Gissing: The Critical Heritage. London and Boston: Routledge & Kegan Paul, pp. 1-46. [See also Index to entire volume].

1972

W's survey of Gissing has some serious misinterpretations, especially the question of imperialism. W's preface to <u>Veranilda</u> was rejected and replaced by Frederic Harrison's.

2593 EDEL, LEON. <u>Henry James, 1901-1916: The Master</u>.
Philadelphia: J.B. Lippincott, pp. 23-24, 40-41, 49, 57-59, 63-66, 96, 196, 318, 365-67, 449, 493-94, 496-98, 533-38, 556.
W and James began as good friends and exchanged copies of each others' books, with James replying to W's gifts with full-scale critiques. Although he objected to the autobiographical form of W's novels, James always felt their discussions were between professionals. He found W's personal attack in <u>Boon</u> difficult to understand in the light of friendship.

2594 EGAN, MICHAEL. <u>Henry James: The Ibsen Years</u>. New York: Barnes & Noble, pp. 23, 60, 124.
W detected the unevenness of <u>Guy Domville</u> when James got away from using Ibsen as a model.

2595 EISENSTEIN, ALEX. "Very Early Wells: Origins of Some Major Physical Motifs in <u>The Time Machine</u> and <u>The War of the Worlds</u>." <u>Extrapolation</u> 13 (May):119-26.
W used his imagination to change common objects from his past into fundamental images in fiction. Underground areas in his boyhood home as described in <u>Experiment</u> became the subterranean world of the Morlocks in <u>Time Machine</u>. A telescope that he found in the attic at the age of fourteen may have served as inspiration for certain aspects of the Martians in <u>War of the Worlds</u>.

2596 FELSTINER, JOHN. <u>The Lies of Art: Max Beerbohm's Parody and Caricature</u>. New York: Knopf, pp. 85, 103, 118, 158.
In keeping with other specialists, W lacked sympathy with human nature. He responded to Beerbohm's caricature of himself with another one. In a series "The Old and the Young Self" (1925) W appears as both an "ambitious biologist" and a "monger of the future." Beerbohm's parodies of W indicate he had nothing good to say of him.

2597 FIRCHOW, PETER. <u>Aldous Huxley: Satirist and Novelist</u>. Minneapolis: University of Minnesota Press, p. 120.
<u>Brave New World</u> is specifically a parody of <u>Men Like Gods</u>, depicting horror at W's utopia and a revolt against it.

2598 FRIEDELL, EGON. <u>The Return of the Time Machine</u>. New York: DAW Books.
[A sequel to W's <u>Time Machine</u> originally published in 1946 as <u>Die Reise mit der Zeitmaschine</u> (Munich: R. Piper & Co. Verlag), translated by Eddy C. Bertin.]

2599   GILL, RICHARD. Happy Rural Seat: The English Country House
       and the Literary Imagination. New Haven and London: Yale
       University Press, pp. 97-110, 115-16, 119, 121, 125, 128, 131,
       138, 201, 211.
            In Tono-Bungay, Bladesover is the key to an understanding
       of "the hierarchical structure of English society." In a chang-
       ing world the country house offered "the possibility of dramatiz-
       ing the failures of a whole social order." W, of all Edwardian
       writers, was not interested in symbolism and he made the signifi-
       cance of Bladesover explicit in contrast to the symbolic house in
       Forster's Howards End.

2600   GLOVER, WILLIS B. "Religious Orientations of H.G. Wells: A
       Case Study in Scientific Humanism." Harvard Theological Review
       65:117-35.
            Any importance that W may have as a scientist is as a
       popularizer and protagonist of scientific humanism, that "faith in
       science as a historical movement in which man will learn to con-
       trol both himself and the world and so impose his will upon nature
       as to bring solutions to all his problems." A study of God and
       Last Things among other works, indicates his religious nature in
       searching for "whatever made life meaningful and significant."
       His faith was humanism with a "distinct theology."

2601   HARRIS, WENDELL V. "Beginnings of the True Short Story in
       England." ELT 15;269-72.
            Kipling, W, and a few other writers realized that the short
       story gave the reader a vignette to consider, whereas the novel
       was the entry to the world. The point from which the reader sees
       that vignette is important and must be fixed early in the story.

2602   HERBERT, LUCILLE. "Tono-Bungay: Tradition and Experiment."
       Modern Language Quarterly 33 (June):140-55. Reprinted in CE,
       pp. 140-56.
            Tono-Bungay is of special interest as an example of the way
       in which some themes and techniques in the nineteenth-century
       novel become "irrelevant" to "the expressive needs of the nar-
       rator."   There is a difference between the concepts of society and
       the self in his novel and in those of traditional writers. The
       unifying form of the novel is a search for expression that can be
       seen in George Ponderevo's attempts to "purge his consciousness of
       the delusions and maladies of the existing social order so that,
       as he writes, he is in the process of becoming what Wells would
       have us believe is a man of the future."

2603   HYNES, SAMUEL. "Mr. Pember's Academy." In Edwardian
       Occasions. New York: Oxford University Press, pp. 199-200.

1972

> Asked to join the Royal Society of Literature, W refused.
> "I am hostile to any attempts to organize art and literature,
> which are things necessarily wild and free."

2604 JOHNSTON, DILLON. "The Recreation of Self in Wells's Experiment in Autobiography." Criticism 14 (Fall):345-60.
Experiment exemplifies the autobiography genre as "a dynamic interplay of confessional, apologetic, and memoirist inten-
tions." While W denies the concept of his having an "essential
self," he makes his own self-image his subject. He interprets the
incidents of his life according to this image and omits anything
that is "extraneous to this organizing principle."

2605 Journal of the H.G. Wells Society: Incorporating the Wellsian
and the Bulletin, nos. 1-5 (Spring 1972-Winter 1973/74); unnum-
bered issues dated Winter 1974 and Spring 1975.
[Brief reviews and articles. Contents include: "Mr.
Brownlow's Newspaper" (summary); "Orwell and Wells"; "Spade House,
Folkeston"; "The Outline of History--A Contemporary Re-
Assessment"; "Filming The Invisible Man"; "The Edwardians--A
Revival of Interest and the Scope of the Society," by Eric F.J.
Ford; "The Humour of Jerome K. Jerome and H.G. Wells," by J.H.
Ovenden (Jerome depicted the world of 1889-1910 as a Golden Age
while W serves as a corrective); "On Space Monsters," by P.
Lonsdale (world problems define us as our own space monsters);
Index to nos. 1-5; "A Wellsian View of World Crisis," by Lloyd
Canonbury; notes on forthcoming books; Corrigenda to the numbering
of issue 4 as issue 3, and the issuing of the true no. 3
(Vernier's paper) in two versions, one as Occasional Paper no. 1.
Editor of nos. 1-4 was J.H. Ovenden, subsequent issues edited by
Eric Ford.]

2606 MacKENZIE, NORMAN. "Kipps or Homo Sapiens." NS 84
(1 Dec.):824-25.
During W's lifetime there was never any doubt about his
importance or his influence as a popular writer. His indecision
about the focus of his career gave critics difficulty because even
his best novels were part of greater projects. [Review of H.G.
Wells: The Critical Heritage.]

2607 MARTIN, KINGSLEY. Foreword to H.G. Wells: A Comprehensive
Bibliography. St. Albans: Flarepath Printers, for the H.G.
Wells Society, p. v.
W's many publishers and variety of writings pose special
problems for the bibliographer. There has never been a definitive
edition of his works. [Annotated listing of one-hundred-fifty-six
separately published works, seventy-five short stories with original sources, secondary works, etc.]

2608   MAY, KEITH. <u>Aldous Huxley</u>. New York: Barnes & Noble, pp. 99, 102-3, 108, 178, 183, 198.
As a good storyteller, W can hold the reader's interest in an expansive and leisurely book like <u>Men Like Gods</u>, which <u>Brave New World</u> was intended to parody.

2609   NEWELL, KENNETH B. "Science Fiction and the Merging of Romance and Realism." <u>Extrapolation</u> 14:6-12.
In following W's tradition modern science fiction explores the resources of romance while possessing a "necessary realism."

2610   PARRINDER, PATRICK. Introduction to <u>H.G. Wells: The Critical Heritage</u>. London and Boston: Routledge & Kegan Paul, pp. 1-31.
The role of the literary artist was restrictive to W, and he relished the larger roles of journalist, social prophet, educator, and communicator. At his peak he had the gift of arousing the energies revolutionaries try to harness. No writer has equalled his ability to combine imaginative appeal with political and ideological relevance. The importance of the scientific romances and the pessimism of those books have become more apparent in recent years. [Individual articles entered according to original year of publication.]

2611   SAVESON, JOHN E. <u>Joseph Conrad: The Making of a Moralist</u>. Amsterdam: Rodopi NV, pp. 9-13, 17-18, 118.
W and Conrad may have fallen out due to the unflattering look at socialists in <u>The Secret Agent</u>. The two were opposed in social philosophies and temperament. W was an influence on some of Conrad's work; he may have been a model for Marlow in "Heart of Darkness," and <u>Victory</u>, like <u>Dr. Moreau</u>, is a parable of evolution.

2612   SHERRY, NORMAN. <u>Conrad and His World</u>. London: Thames & Hudson, pp. 70, 79-81.
W recognized Conrad's originality and genius in his review of <u>Outcast of the Islands</u>, but their friendship was never a close one.

2613   SMITH, GROVER. <u>Ford Madox Ford</u>. New York and London: Columbia University Press, p. 13.
<u>The Inheritors</u> has elements of Conrad as well as W's fourth dimensional beings and bits of the social satire of <u>Tono-Bungay</u>. The discussion with W over starting a new literary review finally ended in a quarrel.

2614   STEINMANN, THEO. "The Second Death of Nunez in 'The Country of the Blind.'" <u>Studies in Short Fiction</u> 9:157-63.

1972

"Country" is actually one of the rare examples of "post-mortem consciousness" in English literature, since Nunez really died during his first fall and the story is only in his mind as he rolls down the mountainside. Circumstantial and internal evidence as well as certain references to time bear this out.

2615   THOMPSON, HOWARD. "Stage: <u>Dr. Moreau</u>." <u>NYT</u>, 3 Dec., p. 85.
        Five performers off Broadway use the power of suggestion to bring W's novel to life "more succinctly and literately" than the old film. The acting is "chillingly credible," and W's reminder that we are all part of the animal kingdom comes through clearly.

2616   TORNQUIST, THOMAS EMMONS. "Art, Science and Propaganda in the Works of H.G. Wells." Dissertation, Columbia University.
        [Listed in <u>Dissertation Abstracts</u> 30 (1972):768-69A.]

2617   TRILLING, LIONEL. "Mind in the Modern World." <u>TLS</u>, 17 Nov., pp. 1381-85.
        Old, ill, despairing over World War II, W wrote <u>Tether</u>, "the whole import of the essay [being] contained in its title." In it he repudiated his belief that humanity could be saved by reason. In later years, some may find it even more relevant than in 1946.

2618   WHITMAN, ALDEN. "A World History by 42 Professors." <u>NYT</u>, 18 July, p. 23.
        The <u>Columbia History of the World</u> was inspired by <u>Outline</u>. That it took forty-two men to write it shows how historical knowledge has grown since W's day.

2619   WILLIAMSON, JACK. "H.G. Wells: The Man Who Discovered Tomorrow." <u>SR</u> 55 (1 Jan.):12-15.
        W's central intellectual achievement is his discovery of the principles that led to the science of futurology, his "discovery of the future." His forerunners did not use the right approach, "the notion of inevitable and systematic change, observed in the past and projected upon possible tomorrows."

2620   W[OLLHEIM], D[ONALD]. A. "H.G. Wells and Egon Friedell." In <u>The Return of the Time Machine</u>. New York: DAW Books, pp. 11-16.
        <u>Time Machine</u> may be W's "single finest work of creation." The ending of the story implied a sequel that was supplied by Egon Friedell (1878-1938), a Viennese dramatist. Nothing is known of the circumstances of its writing and why its publication was delayed until 1946, when it appeared in Munich as <u>Die Reise mit der Zeitmachine</u>.

2621   ALDISS, BRIAN W. Billion Year Spree: The True History of
        Science Fiction. Garden City, N.Y.: Doubleday; London:
        Weidenfeld & Nicolson, pp. 113-33, 134, 142, 145, 156-59;
        index.
            W's autobiography reveals much of his negative and positive
        sides. Time Machine is "very nearly his most perfect" book, in
        which there are bits of the despair of Hardy as well as the
        "submerged nation" theme found in British writing. W admitted his
        debt to Hawthorne, Poe, and Swift; whereas he lacks depth of
        characterization, he excels in imagination and inventiveness. His
        virtues also include the enquiring spirit of Swift and the ability
        to see his own world clearly. His three principles of story
        construction are: draw a recognizable picture of the time, in-
        clude the latest scientific principles as a story hinge, and let
        the social criticism arise from the story itself. In science
        fiction he "elevated the freak event . . . into an artistic
        whole," extended both scope and power of such events, and gave the
        genre popularity and distinctiveness.

2622   BARKER, DUDLEY. G.K. Chesterton: A Biography. New York:
        Stein & Day, pp. 141, 172, 176, 182-84, 210, 235, 239-40, 256-
        57, 262, 264.
            Chesterton attacked the attitude of modern science in the
        person of W, while Belloc was odd man out in the quartette writing
        for the New Age. The arguments were predictable, and what is
        entertaining is to look for the most telling points of debate. W
        had written to Chesterton to complain about the attacks on Ford
        Madox Ford in the New Witness, though Chesterton had had nothing
        to do with them. The Everlasting Man was a more effective reply
        to Outline than Belloc's because, while serious, it was not
        solemn.

2623   BECK, ART. For[e]ward to Mind at the End of Its Tether. San
        Francisco: Millett Books, pp. [iii-iv].
            In Tether W says that the central fact of our existence is
        the insufficiency of humanity, a statement neither positive nor
        negative.

2624   CLARKE, ARTHUR C. Introduction to "The Invisible Man" and "The
        War of the Worlds." New York: Pocket Books, pp. xi-xix.
            The theme of Invisible Man may also be found in "The Coun-
        try of the Blind"--a great gift may also be an intolerable curse.
        W may possibly be responsible for the science fiction creed that
        anything alien is likely to be terrible. He was not blind in his
        belief in the capability of men to someday build sane societies.

1973

2625   COLE, Dame MARGARET. "Letters from. . . ." Books and Bookmen
        18 (August):8-9.
            W was "really an impatient schoolteacher, yearning to hit
        children over the knuckles" when they could not follow his in-
        structions. Doubts any significance to the revival of interest in
        W. [Response to Colin Wilson's review of MacKenzie biography.]

2626   COUSTILLAS, PIERRE. Henry Hick's Recollections of George
        Gissing. London: Enitharmon Press, pp. 3, 4, 11, 12, 13, 22,
        23, 34, 35, 38, 39, 43, 47, 48, 49, passim.
            Hick's suggestion that Gissing died of "gross incompetence"
        may be due to W's prejudice and ought to be questioned. Gissing's
        difficulties in learning to ride a bicycle are exaggerated in
        Experiment. [Mostly passing references to visits between W and
        Gissing.]

2627   DESSNER, LAWRENCE JAY. "H.G. Wells, Mr. Polly, and the Uses of
        Art." ELT 16:121-34.
            Mr. Polly can be read as the story of "the possibilities
        and consequences of the aesthetic impulse." Despite his equivocal
        relationship to art, W demonstrates in this book what "literary
        art" can accomplish. He knew the limits of art and refused to be
        a Mr. Polly.

2628   FINK, HOWARD. "Coming Up for Air: Orwell's Ambiguous Satire
        on the Wellsian Utopia." SLI 6 (Fall):51-60. Reprinted as
        "The Shadow of Men Like Gods: Orwell's Coming Up for Air as
        Parody," in H.G. Wells and Modern Science Fiction, ed. Darko
        Suvin and Robert M. Philmus (Lewisburg, Pa.: Bucknell Univer-
        sity Press; London: Associated University Press, 1977), pp.
        144-58.
            Orwell's anti-utopian satire is ambiguous because its dark
        conclusion reflecting an idea of progress through science revives
        the vision of utopia by describing an ideal that is found in one
        of W's early novels.

2629   FORD, ERIC F.J. "H.G. Wells." Times (London), 23 June, p. 13.
            The current readers of W's works are people who read English
        literature (particularly the Edwardians) as well as anyone inter-
        ested in the times in which W lived. [Letter.]

2630   _____. "H.G. Wells." TLS, 20 July, p. 835.
            While the best-seller status of The Time Traveller, by
        Norman and Jeanne MacKenzie, indicates an interest in W's life, it
        ought to be followed up by the publication of a standard collected
        edition of his works and more scholarship. [Letter.]

2631   HARSON, ROBERT R. "H.G. Wells: The Mordet Island Episode."
        Costerus 8:65-76.

The Mordet Island expedition in <u>Tono-Bungay</u> is not (as many
critics suggest) a superfluous episode, but an "integral part of
the novel's structure and meaning" as well as the climactic event.
The theme of the loss of illusion in the first half and the shift
in the perception of the absurd culminate in George Ponderevo's
discoveries about himself.

2632   HUGHES, DAVID Y., and R.M. PHILMUS. "The Early Science Jour-
       nalism of H.G. Wells: A Chronological Survey." <u>SFS</u> 1
       (Fall):98-114. [Reprinted as "A Selective Bibliography (with
       abstracts) of H.G. Wells's Science Journalism, 1887-1901," in
       <u>H.G. Wells and Modern Science Fiction</u>, ed. Darko Suvin and
       Robert M. Philmus (Lewisburg, Pa.: Bucknell University Press;
       London: Associated University Press, 1977), pp. 191-222.
       [Abstracts of ninety items attributed to W that appeared in
periodicals between 1887 and 1904. The essays are divided into
three categories: Education and Popularizations; The Wonders and
Mysteries of Science; Unorthodox Speculation.]

2633   JOHNSON, ROY R. "A Critical Study of H.G. Wells' Development
       and Reputed Decline as a Novelist." Dissertation, University
       of Exeter, 1973.
       [Listed in Lawrence F. McNamee, <u>Dissertations in English
       and American Literature</u>, supp. 2 (New York & London: Bowker,
       1974).]

2634   KARL, FREDRICK R. "Conrad, Wells, and the Two Voices." <u>PMLA</u>
       88 (Oct.):1049-65.
       The imprecision of art is a counter to the rationality of
science, as demonstrated in the correspondence of W and Conrad.
Their letters involve "profound assumptions about man and the
world . . . the question of preservation" of elements of the past
and deciding how much of the present is worth continuing.

2635   LAUTERBACH, EDWARD S., and W. EUGENE DAVIS. <u>The Transitional
       Age: British Literature 1880-1920</u>. Troy, N.Y.: Whitson,
       pp. 297-300.
       Symbolism and myth added depth to W's entertaining fan-
tasies. In spite of his serious nonfiction and "earnest propaganda novels," his best work lies in the realms of science fiction
and social comedy. [Selected bibliography of primary and secondary works.]

2636   LUCKETT, RICHARD. "Review of Books: Richard Luckett on the
       History of Mr. Wells." <u>Spectator</u> 230 (23 June):785-86.
       The philosophy of Thomas Huxley in his 1889 article "Agnos-
ticism" could have served as the text for all of W's "lay sermons"
as well as "the basis of a reading of his own life." <u>Tono-Bungay</u>
is proof that he worked best when he "evolved his own conventions"

1973

in the novelist's art. [Review of The Time Traveller: The Life of H.G. Wells, by Norman and Jeanne Mackenzie.]

2637   MacKENZIE, NORMAN, and JEANNE MacKENZIE. "How H.G. Harried His Publishers." Bookseller, 26 May, pp. 2574-77.
Anxiety made W send his publishers letters about terms, editions, and promotion schemes. He lost as much as he gained by switching publishers (for a new advance) before his previous publisher had earned back the investment on his last book. He quarreled with his agent and made separate deals with publishers himself. His very eccentricity is fascinating, and his publishing career is the story of the book-trade itself.

2638   _____. The Time Traveller: The Life of H.G. Wells. London: Weidenfeld & Nicolson. [Published in America as H.G. Wells: A Biography. (New York: Simon & Schuster, 1973).]
Novelist, social critic, historian, visionary--the biography of W is told in the context of the social and intellectual milieu of his time. His total output of publications defies classification. Not a great artist or thinker, nevertheless he cannot be dismissed; he was an influence and phenomenon of his time. His scientific romances and early novels are still his best, but he never worked a fictional problem through to the end in strictly novelistic terms. Essentially an Edwardian who lived beyond his era, W's life and work made their crucial turn about 1910. [Rich in intimate detail to the point of trivia, this may be considered the standard biography. Extensive, but selective bibliography.]

2639   MANVELL, ROGER. "H.G. Wells and the Modern Utopia." New Humanist 89 (Oct.):196-98.
Had it not been for writing and for women W would have "driven himself mad," for he was compulsive in both roles as writer and lover and he was a creature of impulse. [Review of MacKenzie, The Time Traveller.]

2640   MEYER, MICHAEL. "Memories of George Orwell." In The World of George Orwell. Edited by Miriam Gross. New York: Simon & Schuster, pp. 128-33.
Orwell and his wife lived in quarters over the garage of W's house in Regent Park until W evicted them. W thought Orwell had been "saying unkind things about him behind his back." Orwell invited W to dinner to patch things up, where W insisted on eating curry and plum cake in spite of his bad stomach and then accused Orwell of trying to poison him.

2641   MULLEN, R.D. "The Books and Pamphlets of H.G. Wells: A Chronological Survey." SFS 1 (Fall):114-35. Reprinted as "An Annotated Survey of Books and Pamphlets by H.G. Wells," in H.G.

<u>Wells</u> and <u>Modern</u> <u>Science</u> <u>Fiction</u>, ed. Darko Suvin and Robert M. Philmus (Lewisburg, Pa.: Bucknell University Press; London: Associated University Press, 1977), pp. 223-68.
[Annotated bibliography of one-hundred-thirteen publications.]

2642   PARRINDER, PATRICK. "Imagining the Future: Zamyatin and Wells." <u>SFS</u> 1 (Spring):17-26. Revised as "Imagining the Future: <u>Wells</u> and Zamyatin," in <u>H.G.</u> <u>Wells</u> <u>and</u> <u>Modern</u> <u>Science</u> <u>Fiction</u>, ed. Darko Suvin and Robert M. Philmus (Lewisburg, Pa.: Bucknell University Press; London: Associated University Press, 1977), pp. 126-43.
Zamyatin never doubted that science fiction was a major literary genre, whereas W created masterpieces without believing they were masterpieces. The difference between <u>Time</u> <u>Machine</u> and <u>We</u> involves two distinctly different kinds of imagination. W is concerned with facing the unknown; Zamyatin is concerned with being the unknown.

2643   PRITCHETT, V.S. "Ego and Apocalypse." <u>NS</u> 85 (15 June):885-86.
The biographer of W should capture both the person and the many separate worlds he inhabited. W was preoccupied with apocalypse, but his prose suggests the sensibleness of the eighteenth-century narrative writer. [Review of MacKenzie, <u>The</u> <u>Time</u> <u>Traveler</u>.]

2644   SAMUELSON, DAVID N. "<u>Childhood's</u> <u>End</u>: A Median Stage of Adolescence?" <u>SFS</u> 1 (Spring):4-17.
Arthur C. Clarke's <u>Childhood's</u> <u>End</u> is not a utopian novel, as Mark Hillegas suggests in <u>The</u> <u>Future</u> <u>as</u> <u>Nightmare</u>. Clarke is a commercial writer whose roots are in the British literary tradition represented by Blake, Hardy, W, Doyle, Stapledon, C.S. Lewis, and Orwell, among others who treat science and technology as potentially demonic.

2645   SCARFE, FRANCIS. "H.G. Wells: A Soured Idealist." <u>Etudes</u> <u>anglaises</u> 26:309-11.
Although Vernier's study, <u>H.G.</u> <u>Wells</u> <u>et</u> <u>son</u> <u>temps</u>, deals competently with W's relationship to the world and his society, his sociological approach tends to diminish W's contributions and underestimate his creative writing. He should have said more about W's ideas on education and spent less time on the negative assessments of other people.

2646   SHERRY, NORMAN, ed. <u>Conrad:</u> <u>The</u> <u>Critical</u> <u>Heritage</u>. London and Boston: Routledge & Kegan Paul, pp. 7-8, 9-10, 38, 53, 73-76, 181, 368-69, 372.
Conrad was pleased by W's review of <u>An</u> <u>Outcast</u> <u>of</u> <u>the</u> <u>Islands</u>, though W made much of his wordiness. W thought Conrad

looked like Svengali and Cutcliffe Hyne's Captain Kettle. [W's reviews of <u>Almayer's Folly</u>, <u>An Outcast of the Islands</u> reprinted.]

2647 SUVIN, DARKO. "<u>Time Machine</u> versus <u>Utopia</u> as a Structural Model for Science Fiction." <u>Comparative Literature Studies</u> 10 (Dec.):334-52. Reprinted as "A Grammar of Form and Criticism of Fact: <u>Time Machine</u> as a Structural Model for Science Fiction," in <u>H.G. Wells and Modern Science Fiction</u>, ed. Darko Suvin and Robert M. Philmus (Lewisburg, Pa.: Bucknell University Press; London: Associated University Press, 1977), pp. 90-115; as "<u>Time Machine</u> versus <u>Utopia</u> as Structural Models for SF," in <u>Metamorphoses of Science Fiction</u>, by Darko Suvin (New Haven and London: Yale University Press, pp. 222-42.
The Time Traveller's visions of the future are inverted versions of the Victorian reader's class consciousness and "belief in linear progress." This feature is symbolized by biological regression and the polarization of light and darkness. In <u>Utopia</u> the reader's world is the inversion. Later science fiction is a variation on W's plan.

2648 VERNIER, JEAN-PIERRE. "H.G. Wells at the Turn of the Century: From Science Fiction to Anticipation." <u>Journal of the H.G. Wells Society</u>, no. 3 (Winter/Spring), pp. 25-34. Reprinted as <u>Occasional Papers</u> (supplement to the <u>Journal of the H.G. Wells Society</u>, no. 1 (1973).
W's shift from science fiction to "straight" novels was motivated by a desire on his part to strengthen his reputation. He had written the fantasies to make money, but did not realize that steeped as he was in the trends of his time his imagination made the fantasies more representative of his day than his more intellectual writing. It was the change in attitudes at the end of the Victorian era that marked the turning point in his career when he turned to prophecy and more conventional fiction. [Originally a paper read at a meeting of the H.G. Wells Society on 22 Sept. 1972 at Imperial College, South Kensington.]

2649 WAGER, W. WARREN. "H.G. Wells and the Radicalism of Despair." <u>SLI</u> 6 (Fall):1-10.
The despair found in W's novels emanates less from a fear of no breakthrough to the sanity of a scientifically ordered world than in the prevalence of traditional methods of "democratic and liberal-pacifist action."

2650 WILLIAMSON, JACK. <u>H.G. Wells: Critic of Progress</u>. Baltimore: Mirage Press.
[Reprints, with alterations, five articles from <u>RQ</u> 3-4 (1967-69); prefatory chapter added.]

2651   WILSON, COLIN. "A Time for Wells." Books and Bookmen 18
       (July):54-56.
          The MacKenzie biography of W is the first book to give the
       key to W--his lifelong sexual obsession, his love of parties, and
       his wide circle of friends. Each of these was "a kind of perma-
       nent leak in his creative energies." He wrote to get the misery
       and frustration of his love affairs out of his system. The book
       is not definitive because it takes a standard view of its subject,
       does not recognize the greatness of the later novels, and does not
       realize that his importance "still lies in the future."

2652   WOODCOCK, GEORGE. "The Darkness Violated By Light: A Revi-
       sionist View of H.G. Wells." Malahat Review, no. 26 (April),
       pp. 144-60.
          W's books give the reader an "attitude towards life and
       society." While inaccurate generalizations make contemporary
       historians reject Outline, the reader remembers its "great sweep
       of the human story." The image of man as optimist detracts from
       the essence of W's best work, but at the end he returns (in
       Tether) to the central attitude of skepticism that marks his most
       creative period and the work for which he will be remembered.

1974

2653   ALLEN, L. DAVID. Science Fiction: An Introduction. Lincoln,
       Neb.: Centennial Press, pp. 15, 16-17, 19, 24, 30-40; Re-
       printed as Science Fiction Reader's Guide, 1974.
          W was the "archetypal practitioner of Extrapolative Soft
       Science Fiction." Many of the devices he used to create plausi-
       bility in Time Machine are still in practice. The novel still has
       a "thematic relevance" on a psychological level in the split
       between dominant approaches to life. His reputation rests on his
       treatment of ideas as well as on the ideas themselves.

2654   APPEL, ALFRED. Nabokov's Dark Cinema. New York: Oxford Uni-
       versity Press, pp. 26, 167-68, 170.
          Nabokov admired W as a writer, and his influence may be
       seen in Invitation to a Beheading. Nabokov's Cincinnatus is a
       science fiction figure: the Last Man in the World, which suggests
       War of the Worlds or "The Country of the Blind."

2655   ASIMOV, ISAAC, ed. Before the Golden Age: A Science Fiction
       Anthology of the 1930s. Garden City, N.Y.: Doubleday, p. 539.
          War of the Worlds was the first science fiction story to
       treat extraterrestrial aliens realistically.

2656   BAYLEN, JOSEPH O. "W.T. Stead and the Early career of H.G.
       Wells, 1895-1911." Huntington Library Quarterly 38:53-79.

1974

As editor of Review of Reviews, Stead had high praise for
W's early works, both as serials and books, due as much to his
interest in the occult as to his abilities as an editor. Stead
was convinced that W received his inspiration through spiritual-
istic means. In a letter he compared parts of Anticipations to
the ideas of Cecil Rhodes, which displeased W. Stead's criticism
of Machiavelli was responsible for their break, and any reconciliation was prevented by Stead's death on the Titanic in 1912.
[Liberal excerpts from Stead's reviews and letters.]

2657   BEDFORD, SYBILLE. Aldous Huxley: A Biography. New York:
Knopf, Harper, pp. 188, 200, 244, 253, 316, 338, 541, 660, 685.
Brave New World was intended as a satire on W until Huxley
"got caught up in the excitement of his own ideas." Only the
scientific romances did not disappoint Huxley on rereading.

2658   BOWEN, ROGER. "Isolation, Utopia, and Anti-Utopia: The Island
Motif in the Literary Imagination. A Selective History of the
Archetype and Its Characteristics, with Special Studies in H.G.
Wells, Joseph Conrad, and William Golding." Dissertation,
Harvard University, 1972.
[Listed in Lawrence F. McNamee, Dissertations in English
and American Literature, supp. 2 (New York & London: Bowker,
1974).]

2659   BUCKLEY, JEROME HAMILTON. "H.G. Wells: The Hero as Scientist." In Season of Youth: The Bildungsroman from Dickens to
Golding. Cambridge, Mass.: Harvard University Press,
pp. 186-203.
Tono-Bungay has most of the elements of the Bildungsroman:
a fatherless boy, alienated from his unsympathetic mother, who
finds a friend at school, discovers substitute parents during
apprenticeship, and finally acquires mental and physical maturity.
W must have been familiar with his antecedents in the genre since
many of their themes and details are present. George Ponderevo
turns to science to save himself from despair, and his mature
vision is as disillusioned as that of his creator.

2660   COLE, MARGARET. "H.G. Wells and the Fabian Society." In
Edwardian Radicalism: 1900-1914. Some Aspects of British
Radicalism. Edited by A.J.A. Morris. London: Routledge &
Kegan Paul, pp. 97-113.
The picture of W as "genuine and generous Radical whose
ideas were shipwrecked on the reactionary rock of the Fabians" is
inaccurate. There was little difference between them in general
ideas; the quarrel lay in style and method.

2661   CURTIS, ANTHONY. The Pattern of Maugham: A Critical Portrait.
New York: Taplinger, pp. 3, 13, 26, 124, 143-44, 218-19, 237,
238, 239.

W may have been more prolific than Maugham, but he did not
have his variety. In Cakes and Ale, Driffield is partly a portrait of W, at least initially, as much as of Hardy; and the
atmosphere is much like Wheels of Chance. Maugham's view of the
art of fiction differed from that of W, though he did like Tono-
Bungay and thought Trafford in Marriage to be a portrait of both
the man W thought he was as well as the man he wanted to be.

2662   DOOLEY, D.J. Compton Mackenzie. Twayne's English Authors
       Series, 173. New York: Twayne, pp. 24, 35-36, 38-39; index.
       Sinister Street was intended to tell the story of a public
school boy contrasted to the lower-class youth found in W. Jenny
Pearl in Carnival is a real person rather than a sociological
phenomenon like Ann Veronica.

2663   DRABBLE, MARGARET. Arnold Bennett. New York: Knopf, pp. 6,
       33, 36, 59, 72, 74; index.
       W claimed Bennett's productivity was caused by the belief
that idleness was wicked. The two were friends from the time they
met and defended and praised each other's works. W's gloom was
profound while Bennett achieved happiness. They worked together
on a play (unfinished) called "The Crime." W was enthusiastic
about The Old Wives' Tale, but Bennett was not so impressed with
Ann Veronica. Ann Veronica and Bennett's Hilda Lessways represent
totally different worlds though they lived in the same era.
Bennett came to W's defense in the storm over Machiavelli.
Bennett did not share his attitude over the role of the army in
World War I. Beaverbrook offered knighthoods to both of them, but
both refused. Bennett had some reservations about Clissold, but
he enjoyed it and objected to D.H. Lawrence's "literary manners"
when he reviewed it in the Calendar. W later praised Lord Raingo.
In later years W claimed he and Bennett had cooled in their
friendship, but the record does not support this, and W was
considerably moved by Bennett's death.

2664   _____. "Rebecca West." Listener 92 (28 Nov.):716.
       Gordon Ray's H.G. Wells and Rebecca West is an embarrassing
book in its discussion of the sexual relationship of the two
writers and their babytalk. It is also a depressing book as it
bears witness to the obstacles of love. It may have needed to be
written, but "it is impossible to read it without feeling a fris-
son of true fear."

2665   EISENSTEIN, ALEX. "Wells, Verne, and Science." SFS 1
       (Fall):305-6.
       The observation that Men in the Moon is scientifically
inaccurate has been made by readers (Verne among them) who misread
his text. [Response to Darko Suvin, "H.G. Wells and Earlier SF."]

1974

2666   ESPEY, DAVID B. "George Orwell vs. Christopher Caudwell:
        Politics and Literary Criticism." Illinois Quarterly 36
        (April):46-60.
             Both Orwell and Caudwell typify the concern of writers with
        politics in the 1930s and both were led to the Republican side in
        the Spanish civil War. W's pacifism made him a target for both
        men, Caudwell viewing him in terms of class and Orwell seeing
        beyond W's prejudices to appreciate the writer.

2667   FIDO, MARTIN. "Mr. Biswas and Mr. Polly." Ariel 5, no. 4:
        30-37.
             The existence of parallels between V.S. Naipaul's A House
        of Mr. Biswas and Mr. Polly does not imply plagiarism by Naipaul,
        but an attempt to apply W's themes to Trinidad culture.

2668   FURBANK, P.N. "Chesterton the Edwardian." In G.K. Chesterton:
        A Centenary Appraisal. Edited by John Sullivan. New York:
        Barnes & Noble, pp. 16-27.
             In Mr. Polly W glories in the little man's rebellion
        against the humdrum in a condescending tone.

2669   GREEN, ROGER LANCELYN, and WALTER HOOPER. C.S. Lewis: A
        Biography. New York and London: Harcourt Brace Jovanovich,
        pp. 27, 163-64, 167, 178, 244.
             Lewis's taste for Haggard outlasted that for W. Contrary
        to opinion, W was not the model for Jules in That Hideous
        Strength.

2670   HAMILL, PAUL. "Conrad, Wells, and the Two Voices." PMLA
        89:581-82.
             Frederick Karl misreads the differences between Conrad's
        humanism and W's social criticism. Conrad's wisdom was more
        rigorous than W's.

2671   HANSOT, ELISABETH. Perfection and Progress: Two Modes of
        Utopian Thought. Cambridge, Mass., and London: MIT Press, pp.
        146-68; index.
             Utopia can be best understood as a commentary on contempo-
        rary society and not as a standard by which to judge that society.
        W's utopian ideal "differs only in degree, not in kind, from the
        rationale that sustains existing social organizations." Utopians
        may value the individual, but the significance of developing
        individuality is left unclear. The samurai have no purpose other
        than to create the utopia.

2672   HARDY, ALISTER. "A Quotation from Wells." TLS, 13 Dec.,
        p. 1417.
             A request for the source of W's statement that religion was
        like a fictive net to give a mountaineer confidence.

2673   HELLMAN, LILLIAN.   "H.G. Wells and Rebecca West." <u>NYTBR</u> 13
       Oct. pp. 4-5.
           Can we trust the memories of a lady over eighty on her love
       affair to fill in accurately the gaps of what remains of the
       correspondence? Does anyone need to preserve all material, how-
       ever irrelevant, about the famous if it does not help evaluate the
       writer's work? [Review article on <u>H.G. Wells and Rebecca West</u>, by
       G.N. Ray.]

2674   HOCKS, RICHARD A. <u>Henry James and Pragmatistic Thought</u>.
       Chapel Hill: University of North Carolina Press, pp. 42-43,
       44, 45, 66, 93.
           W's view of James's work is now generally repudiated.

2675   INGLE, STEPHEN J. "The Political Writing of H.G. Wells."
       <u>Queen's Quarterly</u> 81:396-411.
           Socialism as W understood it, both stimulated and gave a
       thematic unity to his best novels. Eventually this made him
       abandon the novel as an art form and concentrate on the novel as
       an educational, social, and political tract.

2676   _____. "Socialism and Literature: The Contribution of Imagi-
       native Writers to the Development of the British Labor Party."
       <u>Political Studies</u> 22:158-67.
           Shaw, Orwell, and W each consciously wrote in order to
       bring about a socialist society, though their definitions of the
       concept differed.

2677   KIRLIN, THOMAS MICHAEL. "H.G. Wells and the Geometric Imagina-
       tion: A Study of Three Science Fiction Novels in the Nine-
       ties." Dissertation, University of Iowa.
           [Listed in <u>Dissertation Abstracts International</u> 35
       (1974):2276-77A.]

2678   KLEIN, MARY ANNE. "Conceptual and Artistic Limits of Eight
       Nineteenth Century British Literary Utopias." Dissertation,
       Marquette University, 1973.
           [Listed in <u>Dissertation Abstracts International</u> 35
       (1974):1048-49.]

2679   LEEPER, G[EOFFREY] W. "The Impact of H.G. Wells on His Cen-
       tury." <u>Meanjin Quarterly</u> 33 (June):214-19.
           Vernier, in his study of W, follows the fashionable beliefs
       that he was a pessimist and that his last 30 years show a decline
       in his influence. On the contrary, the anti-fascist novel, <u>Mr.
       Parham</u>, and his talks with Stalin are examples of his optimism and
       his attempts to establish a better-ordered world.

1974

2680   LUCAS, JOHN. <u>Arnold Bennett: A Study of His Fiction</u>. London:
        Methuen, pp. 31, 56, 61, 64, 67, 72, 78, 155-57, 167, 178.
            Bennett was so ashamed of <u>Teresa of Watling Street</u> ("this
        sub-Buchan story") that he considered asking W if he might stop
        its publication. <u>A Great Man</u> lacks the exuberance of <u>Mr. Polly</u>,
        but it is better written. Bennett, George Moore, and W deliber-
        ately try to prove to Europeans that English novelists can write
        of real women with real feelings. <u>Ann Veronica</u> succeeds because W
        convinces us that freedom for Ann means more than the freedom to
        be passionate.

2681   MAGILL, FRANK N., ed. <u>Cyclopedia of World Authors</u>. Rev. ed.
        Vol. 3. Englewood Cliffs, N.J.: Salem Press, pp. 1873-76.
            W sacrificed art to propaganda, but his sincerity, elo-
        quence, and conviction cannot be doubted. [Biographical sketch
        with list of principal works and secondary sources.]

2682   MELLERSH, H.E.L. "H.G. Wells: An Episode." <u>Contemporary
        Review</u> 224 (June):306-12.
            A scheme for a "thoroughly Wellsian" periodical gained
        support from W himself, but never saw print through the inexperi-
        ence in journalism of its editor. The influence of W on Mellersh
        and his generation was profound.

2683   MOORE, HARRY T. <u>Henry James</u>. New York: Viking Press, pp. 74,
        85, 104-6.
            <u>Marriage</u> was the subject of a discussion with James.

2684   PHILMUS, ROBERT M. "Wells and Borges and the Labyrinths of
        Time." <u>SFS</u> 1 (Fall):237-48. Reprinted as "Borges and Wells
        and the Labyrinths of Time," in <u>H.G. Wells and Modern Science
        Fiction</u>, ed. Darko Suvin and Robert M. Philmus (Lewisburg, Pa.:
        Bucknell University Press; London: Associated University
        Press, 1977), pp. 159-78.
            Each writer, Borges says, has created his own precursors,
        because we would not have known of them as precursors had the
        writer not refashioned the earlier material as he did. Despite
        Borges's praise for W and his admitted debt to "The Crystal Egg,"
        he has not "created" W in the same way by refashioning him. In
        discussing <u>Time Machine</u> Borges does invert W by making space an
        episode of time. He can do this only by considering the flower
        brought back by the Time Traveler as a symbol of despair.

2685   PLUMMER, KATHLEEN C. "The Streamlined Modern." <u>Art in America</u>
        62 (Jan.):46-54.
            The 1930s design of round corners, sheer horizontal sur-
        faces banded with chrome, machine-green tile, black Vitrolite,
        etc., has become respectable again. It is possible to view the

1974

style as the ultimate expression of W's visionary love of gadg-
etry and the machine.

2686   PRITCHETT, V.S. "Mr. Wells's New Woman." NS 88 (22 Nov.):
       742-43.
          The raw material for future biographers of W is too raw.
       The loss of West's letters to W results in a distorted picture of
       their relationship. [Review of H.G. Wells and Rebecca West.]

2687   RAY, GORDON N. H.G. Wells and Rebecca West. New Haven, Conn.:
       Yale University Press; London: Macmillan.
          A miracle they stayed together for ten years (1913-23), W
       and Rebecca West were locked into an impossible situation by their
       profound attachment for each other. The letters they exchanged
       document both their attraction and growing estrangement. W gained
       happiness during this decade of his life, and West was influenced
       in her future life and career by the experience. More of W's
       letters survive than Rebecca West's, but liberal excerpts from his
       and reconstructions of hers help document their story. [Some
       reviews of this book suggest that the texts of the British and
       American editions differ. They are the same and used the same
       plates so that the pagination is identical.]

2688   ROCKWELL, JOAN. Fact in Fiction: The Use of Literature in the
       Systematic Study of Society. London: Routledge & Kegan Paul,
       pp. 93, 105.
          Jack London's Valley of the Moon is an exposé of social
       conditions with the same moral to be found in W, "the main thing
       about the working class is to get out of it." Ann Veronica,
       Galsworthy's Man of Property, and Alan Sillitoe's A Start in Life
       are examples of fiction in which the writers used their own expe-
       rience of a challenge to the norm resulting in success.

2689   RYAN, J.S. "The Two Pincher Martins: From Survival Adventure
       to Golding's Myth of Dying." English Studies 55:140-51.
          Golding used Outline not for its "plot," but its attitude
       as the "rationalist gospel in excelsis," in writing The
       Inheritors. By contrast, Golding's view is that of the moralist-
       humanist. Pincher Martin may have been influenced by "The Remark-
       able Case of Davidson's Eyes," since the plots are related and the
       naval officer in charge of corpse disposal in Golding's book is
       named Davidson.

2690   SHENFIELD, MARGARET. "Mr. Biswas and Mr. Polly." English
       (London) 23:95-100.
          The protagonists of Mr. Polly and Naipaul's A House for Mr.
       Biswas are both small men who have stomach trouble and yearn after
       romance. W is more patronizing toward Mr. Polly than Naipaul is
       toward Mr. Biswas.

1974

2691   SMITH, JANE SCHUR. "Identity as Change: The Protean Character
        in Nineteenth- and Twentieth-Century Fiction." Dissertation,
        Yale University.
        [Listed in <u>Dissertation Abstracts International</u> 35
        (1974):2955A.]

2692   STABLEFORD, BRIAN M. "Science Fiction: A Sociological Per-
        spective." <u>Fantastic</u> 23 (March):101-7, 110.
        Science fiction, as a social phenomenon, is a product of
        the twentieth century. W's visions of the future were not fic-
        tional but utopian philosophy and not written within "the SF
        paradigm." When <u>Time Machine</u> was written, the paradigm did not
        exist, thus only after this paradigm came into being can it be
        read as science fiction.

2693   S[UVIN], D[ARKO]. "In Response to Mr. Eisenstein." <u>SFS</u> 1
        (Fall):306-7.
        W preferred to keep science subordinate to story, but
        though his theory for the distinction between science fiction and
        fantasy may be basic, his insistence on only one impossibility in
        a story is "theoretically unclear." The theory behind cavorite
        and the working of the shutters remains difficult to grasp. A
        search for further sources of his inspiration is necessary.

2694   _____. "H.G. Wells and Earlier SF." <u>SFS</u> 1 (Spring):221-22.
        Parallels exist between <u>Men in the Moon</u> and an 1864 novel,
        <u>The History of a Voyage to the Moon, with an Account of the</u>
        <u>Adventurers' Subsequent Discoveries</u>, including dual protagonists,
        a "'mineral-repellant' mixture of clays which they use to coat
        their space vehicle," and the doubts of what future invasions of
        the moon may be like. Evidence suggests that W was more familiar
        with earlier examples of science fiction than has been suspected.
        A study of subliterary science fiction of the nineteenth century
        (including dime novels) should reveal more antecedents and help us
        to better understand W's significance.

2695   THORBURN, DAVID. <u>Conrad's Romanticism</u>. New Haven and London:
        Yale University Press, pp. 7-8, 11, 18-19, 77, 79, 120.
        W's praise of <u>An Outcast of the Islands</u> was as strong as
        his criticism. He considered it a serious work and appreciated
        Conrad's grasp of character. On meeting Conrad, W was impressed
        by his foreignness and politeness.

2696   TINDALL, GILLIAN. <u>George Gissing: The Born Exile</u>. New York
        and London: Harcourt Brace Jovanovich, pp. 20, 28, 47, 87,
        103, 126, 156, 164-67, 175, 238, 241, 248-49, 260-61.
        W soon perceived Gissing's neurotic anxieties over his
        association with Nell. Gabrielle thought W's giving Gissing
        broth, wine, and coffee killed him. [Many passing references.]

1974

2697   TRILLING, DIANA. "The Jaguar and the Panther." TLS, 22 Nov.,
       pp. 1301-2.
          The history of the love affair of W and Rebecca West has a
       particular relevance in reminding us of the "emotional complex-
       ities" of trying to remedy the "uneven situation of the sexes."
       [Review article of H.G. Wells and Rebecca West, by G.N. Ray.]

2698   WATKINS, A.H., ed. Catalogue of the H.G. Wells Collection in
       the Bromley Public Libraries. Bromley: London Bureau of
       Bromley Public Libraries.
          [A list of material by and about W in the Bromley Library.
       The catalogue is divided into nine sections: The Works of H.G.
       Wells; Bibliographies, Catalogues, Dictionaries; Biography; Books
       and articles relating to Wells, other than biography; Reviews (of
       books by and about Wells); Periodicals; Letters; Pictorial Mate-
       rial; Miscellany. Illustrated; index. Briefly and selectively
       annotated.]

2699   WEST, ANTHONY. "Love and Mr. Wells." Books and Bookmen 20
       (Dec.):10-11.
          In H.G. Wells and Rebecca West, Gordon Ray takes sides in
       "a family row" and portrays W as a "much colder, nastier and more
       calculating man than [Anthony West] ever knew him to be." By
       slighting references to W's affair with Amber Reeves, Ray throws
       the West/Wells relationship into a different perspective. The
       book "has been written without regard to . . . obligations as a
       scholar" and thus has not added to the understanding of its
       subject.

2700   YOUNG, KENNETH. H.G. Wells. Writers and Their Work no. 233.
       London and New York: Longmans, Green.
          Whereas Time Machine has the flaw of hasty and awkward
       writing, Dr. Moreau is "tautly constructed" as a black fantasy and
       a critique of the nature of humanity. Invisible Man lacks both
       the poetry and various levels of meaning of Time Machine, and
       Griffin is not as effective a portrait of the amoral scientist as
       is Moreau, but it was appreciated by early readers. The Martians
       in War of the Worlds are based on current scientific hypothesis,
       and the documentary style contributes to the plausibility of the
       story; the book appealed to its contemporary readers' fears of
       invasion from France or Germany. Kipps is one of W's three best
       novels, while Comet is either a final fantasy, a fictional vehicle
       for the ideas in Utopia, or a satire on politicians--or all three.
       Mr. Britling is the last real novel in which W employs his great-
       est gifts. While it is possible to write propaganda that is also
       good fiction, W did not, and one of the reasons his ideas may not
       seem so original as they did to his contemporaries is that they
       have been accepted as part of modern thinking. He finally real-
       ized that human nature was the greatest obstacle to his objective

1974

in reforming the world. Frequently his ideals were undesirable as
well as unattainable; people did not want a central world government. In the final analysis, however, the best of his fiction is
still worth reading for itself.

2701   ZWERDLING, ALEX. Orwell and the Left. New Haven and London:
       Yale University Press, pp. 35, 41, 43, 96, 117, 145, 193, 198,
       207.
          W's version of socialism grew out of his hatred for "anar-
       chic mess" and was obsessed with planning. He thought the Fabian
       Society as exclusive as a London Club. He could not understand
       the "primitive passions" that dominated the 1930s and 1940s.
       Orwell deliberately rationed his fantasy in Animal Farm, unlike W
       in Time Machine.

1975

2702   ADAM, RALPH. "Pulling Minds of Social Scientists Together
       Towards a World Social Science Information System." Inter-
       national Social Science Journal 27:519-31.
          W's approach to the unification of knowledge was an objec-
       tive world encyclopedia as a standard source of information for
       educational institutions and a synthesis of what was being pro-
       duced by those institutions. His idea led to the World Informa-
       tion Synthesis and Encyclopedia (Kochen, 1972) and the Universal
       Reference System.

2703   ASH, BRIAN. Faces of the Future: The Lessons of Science
       Fiction. New York: Taplinger, pp. 10-11, 40-63, 107-8, 133-
       34; index.
          The scientific implausibility in Men in the Moon does not
       matter if we consider the story as a warning about human enslave-
       ment to the state through applied biology, just as Sleeper Wakes
       is a prototype of "anti-utopian nastiness" and Dr. Moreau warns
       that we may have trouble overcoming our animal nature. Time
       Machine expresses Huxley's philosophy as well as that of W. This
       thread of pessimism runs through most of the scientific romances.
       W's greatest contribution to science fiction was his extrapolation
       from existing trends to what might come. The "willing suspension
       of disbelief" is easy for his readers because of the familiar
       backgrounds in which stories like Invisible Man and War of the
       Worlds are set. In later works, like Mr. Blettsworthy and Player,
       W returns to the theme of Dr. Moreau, the "beast inherent."

2704   BERGONZI, BERNARD, ed. Introduction to H.G. Wells: A Collec-
       tion of Critical Essays. (Englewood Cliffs, N.J.: Prentice-
       Hall, pp. 1-7.

W was an "inconsistent, impulsive thinker and the writings of his old age are particularly incoherent," his hope for mankind destroyed during the Second World War. His optimism was an escape from reality, and his writings are so self-contradictory they can be used to depict him on any side of a controversial question. As a product of an age of transitions and new frontiers he enjoyed disturbing readers with apocalyptic visions of the future. He cared nothing for the past. His most enduring work was produced when he took himself seriously as a critic and writer. [Individual articles annotated under date of first publication.]

2705 CHAPPELL, FRED. "The SF Film: Metropolis and Things to Come." SFS 2 (Nov.):292-93.
    W's screenplay was intended to be "radically antithetical" to Fritz Lang's 1927 film, Metropolis. W felt Metropolis was "merely cheap melodrama and that Lang's vision of the future was absurd." He was correct in calling the Lang film "technological gothic," since it represents the horror story tradition in science fiction films. Things to Come belongs to the "rationalist" tradition but takes itself too seriously.

2706 CRISTENSEN, JOHN MICHAEL. "Utopia and the Late Victorians: A Study in Popular Literature, 1870-1900." Dissertation, Northwestern University, 1974.
    [Listed in Dissertation Abstracts International 35 (1975):6705-6A.]

2707 COSTA, RICHARD HAUER. "Edwardian Intimations of the Shape of Fiction to Come: Mr. Britling/Job Huss as Wellsian Central Intelligence." ELT 18:229-42.
    In his "dialogue novels," like Mr. Britling and Undying Fire, W set a standard for a hybrid fiction, part novel and part journalism, which forecast a time when the journalist would replace the novelist.

2708 DE CAMP, L. SPRAGUE. Lovecraft: A Biography. Garden City, N.Y.: Doubleday, pp. 3, 62, 176-77, 267, 377, 424, 437.
    A childhood copy of Dr. Moreau was confiscated by Lovecraft's mother, who thought it was too gruesome for him to read. He enjoyed W's work at first, then decided W's social satire impaired the plausibility of his fantasy. He read and reread Science of Life because it was "the greatest single exposition of biological knowledge" he had seen.

2709 _____, and CATHERINE CROOK. Science Fiction Handbook, Revised. Philadelphia: Owlswick Press, pp. 1-2, 15-16, 19, 36, 77, 107, 130.
    W adopted the view of many intellectuals of his time that a combination of science and socialism would cure mankind's ills.

357

1975

Welles's radio adaptation of War of the Worlds focused attention
on science fiction and eventually led to the first world science
fiction convention in 1939. W was the subject of C.S. Lewis's
caricature, Jules, in That Hideous Strength.

2710   "F.C.C. Cites Station for Martian 'Scare.'" NYT, 18 July,
        p. 61.
            The F.C.C. admonished Providence, Rhode Island, radio sta-
        tion WPRO for broadcasting an updated version of W's War of the
        Worlds, which frightened listeners.

2711   GILL, STEPHEN M. Scientific Romances of H.G. Wells: A Crit-
        ical Study. Cornwall, Ont.: Vesta Publications.
            W's reputation will probably not remain constant since the
        role of a prophet is usually forgotten once the prophecy is ful-
        filled. While many of his scientific romances can be dismissed as
        "mere fantasies" his "unique thoughts" will continue to be an
        inspiration as well as an entertainment. It is as a progenitor
        that he will survive.

2712   GUNN, JAMES. Alternate Worlds: The Illustrated History of
        Science Fiction. Englewood Cliffs, N.J.: Prentice-Hall, pp.
        87-101; index.
            W's early short stories exhibit characteristics of his
        later, best-selling work: the uninvolved narrator, the basis in
        science of natural history, the philosophy that mankind's domi-
        nance is an illusion and that the pursuit of knowledge is danger-
        ous. The legacy he left to science fiction is enormous, not only
        in ideas that became traditional to the genre, but by his shift of
        its focus from the individual to society. The possibilities for
        the genre as a literary and a popular form were established
        through his example.

2713   HARPHAM, GEOFFREY GALT. "Cultural Degeneration and the Gro-
        tesque in H.G. Wells and Jack London." Dissertation, Univer-
        sity of California (Los Angeles), 1974.
            [Listed in Dissertation Abstracts International 35
        (1975):5345-46A.]

2714   HARRIS, MASON. "Science Fiction as the Dream and Nightmare of
        Progress." West Coast Review 9, no. 4:3-9.
            W founded the "alienated tradition" in science fiction and
        foreshadowed some of the weaknesses in the genre. His insistence
        on physical reality in the Time Machine made it possible to dis-
        cuss social and psychological themes that would not have been
        possible in a story of pure fantasy.

2715   _____. "Science Fiction as the Dream and Nightmare of Prog-
        ress: 2b, The Island of Dr. Moreau and Later Wells." West
        Coast Review 10 (June):19-26.

Although W encourages us to find a social dimension in Dr. Moreau, his reference to the book as a "theological grotesque" implies a satire on religion. Moreau's godlike role as well as the bizarre Christianity ("the Law") of the Beast Folk seem to bear this out. Two decades later, Freud's Civilization and Its Discontents would work out some of the same problems W approaches in fantasy in this and later stories.

2716   H.G. Wells Society Newsletter 1, nos. 1-15 (April 1975–
        Feb. 1979).
        [News and notes on activities of the H.G. Wells Society, with lists of new editions of his works, forthcoming works on W, work in progress, and related matters. "The newsletter will aim to provide news and information of Wellsian interest and will also serve to keep members in touch with one another."--vol. 1, no. 1.]

2717   HILLEGAS, MARK R. "Victorian 'Extraterrestrials.'" In The Worlds of Victorian Fiction. Edited by Jerome H. Buckley. Cambridge, Mass.: Harvard University Press, pp. 391-414.
        War of the Worlds represents the climax of the development of the Martian romance in English. While the plot is superficially like that of Lasswitz's Auf zwei Planeten, W elevates the material to the level of literature. The Selenites in Men in the Moon are one of his greatest inventions, going beyond the usual concept of imagining extraterrestrials as anthropoids and seeing them as antlike.

2718   HUGHES, DAVID Y., and ROBERT M. PHILMUS. "The Early Science Journalism of H.G. Wells: Addenda." SFS 2 (March):98-99.
        [Annotated list of five articles omitted from the list of W's science journalism in SFS 1 (Fall 1973):98-114.]

2719   KOVALEV, ĨU. "Uells v borbe protiv fashizmu 1941-45" [Wells in the struggle against fascism 1941-45]. Vestnik Leningradskogo Universiteta (Leningrad) 8, no. 2:104-7.
        W's interest in Russia intensified after the 1917 Revolution because he believed in the unavoidable downfall of capitalism and the transformation of the world on socialist principles. An important part of his activity during World War II was cooperation with many Soviet institutions and publishing houses, despite his bad health. [In Russian.]

2720   LEHMANN, JOHN. Virginia Woolf and Her World. New York and London: Harcourt Brace Jovanovich, pp. 45, 48.
        Woolf decided the works of W, Bennett, and Galsworthy were not a true reflection of life, and she intended to capture a different reality in her fiction.

1975

2721 LEONARD, JOHN. "TV: 'The Invisible Man.'" NYT, 8 Sept.,
      p. 62.
         The NBC TV series based on Invisible Man is an "exercise in
      witlessness" and an "insult to H.G. Wells" as well as to the
      memorable films based on his novel.

2722 MEYERS, JEFFREY. Introduction to George Orwell: The Critical
      Heritage. London and Boston: Routledge & Kegan Paul,
      pp. 1-36.
         Orwell had Mr. Polly and Mr. Britling in mind when he
      explained that Coming Up for Air was "watered down" W. Orwell
      appears to some critics to be in the tradition of English radical
      writers like W.

2723 _____. A Reader's Guide to George Orwell. London: Thames &
      Hudson, pp. 64, 107, 172.
         W had an influence on Orwell's early fiction, Coming Up for
      Air suggesting Mr. Polly and Mr. Britling.

2724 MONTEIRO, GEORGE. "Addenda to the Bibliographies of Hardy,
      Wells, and T.S. Perry." Papers of the Bibliographical Society
      of America 19:272-73.
         "A Statement from Mr. Wells" from NYTSRBA, 8 July 1905, p.
      454, should be added to Geoffrey H. Wells's bibliography.

2725 MUMFORD, LEWIS. "Reflections: Prologue to Our Time." NY 51
      (10 March):42-63.
         In early life, Mumford considered W one of his patron
      saints. W predicted disaster for mankind all his own life, even
      in the midst of his most exuberant fantasies of the future.

2726 NEULEIB, JANICE. "Technology and Theocracy: The Cosmic Voy-
      ages of Wells and Lewis." Extrapolation 16 (May):130-36.
         In style and technique, C.S. Lewis's Out of the Silent
      Planet parallels Men in the Moon. Lewis's theme of moral superi-
      ority contrasts with the satire of W.

2727 "Night the 'Martians' Landed Recalled." NYT 26 Oct., p. 101.
         [Account of the spread of hysteria throughout New Jersey
      and the rest of the U.S. on 30 Oct. 1938, when Orson Welles's
      production of War of the Worlds was broadcast on CBS radio.]

2728 O'CONNOR, JOHN J. "TV Review." NYT, 6 May, p. 79.
         David McCallum, as Daniel Weston, stars in a television
      film loosely based on W's novel, Invisible Man. The plot is
      tired, and the characters exist in a vacuum with little logic and
      reality.

2729   PARRINDER, PATRICK. "The 'English Jules Verne,'" SFS 2
       (March):98.
          Arthur H. Lawrence was the first to call W "the English
       Jules Verne" in Young Man (August 1897), although reviewers of
       Time Machine suggested the comparison earlier.

2730   PHILMUS, ROBERT, and DAVID Y. HUGHES, eds. H.G. Wells: Early
       Writings in Science and Science Fiction. Berkeley, Los
       Angeles, London: University of California Press.
          Twenty-eight essays, reviews, stories, follow the outline
       of W's intellectual development, his discovery of the principle of
       "complementarity" as well as the value of using both the human and
       cosmic viewpoint. [Grouped into categories: Enormous Repudia-
       tions; Revisions of the Future; the Opposite Idea; Precarious Man;
       Evolution and Ethics; A Selective Bibliography (with abstracts) of
       H.G. Wells's Science Journalism, 1887-1901.]

2731   PIRIE, GORDON. Henry James. Literature in Perspective.
       Totowa, N.J.: Rowan & Littlefield, pp. 25, 28.
          Guy Domville failed in spite of favorable notices by Shaw,
       W, and Bennett. Boon was a clever, but malicious attack on
       James's work.

2732   POOLE, ADRIAN. Gissing in Context. Totowa, N.J.: Rowan &
       Littlefield; London: Macmillan, pp. 3, 5, 6, 18, 25, 48, 59,
       113, 128, 133-34, 198-99, 202-3, 204, 205.
          W is the character "N" in The Private Papers of Henry
       Ryecroft. His remarks on The Whirlpool contributed vitally to the
       critical recognition of Gissing, but W misinterpreted the "import
       of the scene at the end of the novel. [Passing references com-
       paring W and Gissing.]

2733   PORGES, IRWIN. Edgar Rice Burroughs: The Man Who Created
       Tarzan. Provo, Utah: Brigham Young University Press, pp. 129-
       30, 388.
          There is no logical evidence that W was an influence on
       Burroughs.

2734   RAY, GORDON N. "All in the Family." Harper's Magazine 250
       (April):18, 22.
          West's review of Ray's edition of W's letters to his
       mother, Rebecca West, has "no real authority" and is "marked by an
       aggressive bias." W and Rebecca West's disagreement had ended
       long before W's death, but West revived the fight in his novel
       Heritage. [Rebecca West quoted that Anthony West was not con-
       ceived intentionally; AW replies that his mother is writing fifty-
       eight years after the event.]

1975

2735   RESTON, JAMES. "What Do We Stand For?" NYT, 31 Oct., p. 33.
       America's responsibility for world leadership in the
twenty-first century will depend largely upon the ability to
overcome a drift from dynamism, something W attempted to do for
England before World War I.

2736   SCHEICK, WILLIAM J. "The Womb of Time: Spengler's Influence
       on Wells's Apropos of Dolores." ELT 18:217-28.
       The structure of Apropos of Dolores is "wholly organic" to
its themes if it is read with Spengler's distinctions between
culture and civilization in mind. W considered his novel to be
his statement of an emerging culture as opposed to James's fiction, which represented a declining civilization.

2737   SHAPIRO, BARBARA LINDA. "Autobiography and the Fiction of H.G.
       Wells." Dissertation, Harvard University, 1973.
       [Listed in Dissertation Abstracts International 35:5363A.]

2738   SHIPPS, ANTHONY. "A Quotation from Wells." TLS, 10 Jan.,
       p. 36.
       A passage comparing the mountaineer's net with religion
(TLS, 13 Dec. 1974) is traced to chapter 2 in God.

2739   SKORBURG, MARY E. "Adlerian Interpretation of H.G. Wells's The
       Invisible Man." Journal of Individual Psychology 31:85-96.
       Like Alfred Adler, W is primarily concerned with the unique
personality of the criminal, Griffin, rather than with his actions. Griffin died because he cooperated with no one and contributed nothing.

2740   STERRENBURG, LEE. "Psychoanalysis and the Iconography of Revo-
       lution." Victorian Studies 19 (Dec.):241-64.
       The analogies between revolution and cannibalism found in
Carlyle, Dickens, and W were taken up by Freud as part of his
"framework for interpreting group and mass psychology." For W, a
by-product of the capitalist and industrial order is the reversion
to barbarism. Great cosmic and social forces overwhelm the iso-
lated individual, who is helpless to affect the world around him.

2741   SUVIN, DARKO. "Wells as the Turning Point for the SF Tradi-
       tion." Minnesota Review, n.s. 4:106-15. Reprinted in Darko
       Suvin, Metamorphoses of Science Fiction (New Haven and London:
       Yale University Press, 1979), pp. 208-21.
       W is still the central figure in the development of science
fiction. He took all of the major ingredients of earlier writers,
added the time-travel theme, and reshaped them into the elements
of the modern tradition. He was the "first significant writer to
write SF from within the world of science, and not merely facing
it."

2742   WATKINS, A.H.   "Charles Dickens and H.G. Wells."   Occasional
       Papers no. 2).   Journal of the H.G. Wells Society (supp.).
       Dickens and W began life with "similar temperaments and
intellectual ability, subjected to surprisingly similar environments, grew to manhood each with a sensitive social conscience,
and each sought to right the wrongs which he recognised in his own
time."   The influence of Dickens is, of course, strongest in the
comic novels, especially in the characters.   [Essay based on a
paper read at a joint meeting of the Dickens Fellowship and the
H.G. Wells Society, London, 12 Feb. 1970.]

2743   WATT, DONALD.   "The View from Malacandra."   Bulletin of the New
       York C.S. Lewis Society 6, no. 8:5-7.
       Despite vivid descriptions in Men in the Moon, W never
achieved the "critical perspective upon human kind from the alien
view" that C.S. Lewis managed in the last scenes in Out of the
Silent Planet.

2744   WEBB, MAX A.   "The Missing Father and the Theme of Alienation
       in H.G. Wells's Tono-Bungay."   ELT 18:243-47.
       Tono-Bungay belongs to the tradition of novels about found-
lings in English literature, but its author has altered the literary conventions to depict the disorder of post-Victorian English
society.

2745   WELLMAN, MANLY W., and WADE WELLMAN.   Sherlock Holmes's War of
       the Worlds.   New York: Warner Books.
       [Elements from "The Crystal Egg" and War of the Worlds are
blended in a fantasy in which Sherlock Holmes and Professor
Challenger become the central characters in a sort of pastiche of
W's work.]

2746   WELLS, G.P.   "H.G. Wells and His Wife Jane."   Books and Bookmen
       20 (April):28.
       Contrary to accounts in Norman and Jeanne MacKenzie's biog-
raphy of W and Gordon Ray's H.G. Wells and Rebecca West, Jane
Wells was not present when Frau Gatternig attempted suicide in W's
London flat in 1923.   She was serving as hostess at Little Easton
at the celebration after G.P. Wells received his B.A. from
Cambridge.

2747   WEST, ANTHONY.   "The Mystery of My Birth."   Harper's Magazine
       250 (Jan.):82-86.
       Professor Ray's edition of W's letters to Rebecca West is
"little more than a partisan statement extending the running fight
between [the two] that should properly have been ended with [W's]
death."   By leaving out the Amber Reeves incident, Ray has made
the circumstances of the Rebecca West liaison "inexplicable."   The
MacKenzies appear distressed by the contradiction of a rational

363

1975

man who was unable to have adult relationships. [Review of H.G. Wells and Rebecca West and MacKenzie's H.G. Wells.]

2748   WEST, REBECCA. "G.P. Wells and Gordon Ray." Books and Bookmen 20 (April):27.
        While she gave Gordon Ray permission to see letters from W to her, Rebecca West did not give final approval to the book H.G. Wells and Rebecca West and disagreed with some of its author's interpretations. Prime objection is with inaccurate information about the attempted suicide of Frau Gatternig. [See also G.P. Wells's "H.G. Wells and Jane."]

2749   _____. "All in the Family." Harper's Magazine 250 (April):22.
        The picture Anthony West gives of his grandmother in his review of Ray's H.G. Wells and Rebecca West is false. Likewise, Jane Wells never gossiped about W's love affairs. [Anthony West's reply quotes a passage from the book that leaves a different impression.]

1976

2750   AQUINO, JOHN. Science Fiction as Literature. Washington, D.C.: National Education Association, pp. 36–39.
        As a science fiction story, "The Star" concerns an incident of an imagined future rendered with scientific plausibility and detail through a detached omniscient narrator.

2751   ASH, BRIAN. Who's Who in Science Fiction. New York: Taplinger, pp. 204-7.
        W did more than anyone else to establish the basic plot structures and thematic material of the modern science fiction genre.

2752   BERMAN, JEFFREY. "Forster's Other Cave: The Platonic Structure of The Machine Stops." Extrapolation 17 (May):172–81.
        The Machine Stops, as the first of the serious twentieth-century anti-utopian novels, may have been a satire on W's Time Machine, but it was more heavily influenced by Plato's Republic.

2753   BOWEN, ROGER. "Science, Myth, and Fiction in H.G. Wells's Island of Dr. Moreau." Studies in the Novel 8 (Fall):318-35.
        W was stimulated by discoveries in biological science and the growing evidence of human alienation. In Dr. Moreau he adapted myths for a new age and rediscovered the island as the symbol for human isolation. Differing from his other fantasies in not having a familiar and reassuring setting, the literary antecedents of this movie include The Jungle Book, The Narrative of Arthur Gordon Pym, Dr. Jekyll and Mr. Hyde, and Frankenstein.

2754   BUITENHUIS, PETER. "The Selling of the Great War." <u>Canadian</u>
        <u>Review</u> <u>of</u> <u>American</u> <u>Studies</u> 7:139-50.
            W was among the few to realize the "all-embracing nature"
        of the First World War and the role that propaganda was to play in
        it.

2755   BUSZA, ANDRZEJ. "Rhetoric and Ideology in Conrad's <u>Under</u> <u>West-</u>
        <u>ern</u> <u>Eyes</u>." In <u>Joseph</u> <u>Conrad:</u> <u>A</u> <u>Commemoration</u>. Edited by
        Norman Sherry. New York: Barnes & Noble, 1977; London:
        Macmillan, 1976, pp. 105-18.
            <u>The</u> <u>Secret</u> <u>Agent</u> is an ironic look at W's "utopian
        illusions."

2756   CANBY, VINCENT. "Huge Creatures Roam in <u>Food</u> <u>of</u> <u>the</u> <u>Gods</u>."
        <u>NYT</u>, 17 July, p. 9.
            Based on W's novel, the film of <u>Food</u> <u>of</u> <u>the</u> <u>Gods</u> mixes
        science fiction and horror cliches, failing to realize the impor-
        tant theme of clean environment.

2757   CHRISTIANSON, GALE E. "Kepler's <u>Somnium</u>: Science Fiction and
        the Renaissance Scientist." <u>SFS</u> 3 (March):79-90.
            As the origin of modern science fiction, Kepler's <u>The</u>
        <u>Somnium;</u> <u>or,</u> <u>The</u> <u>Dream</u> was known to many writers, including Verne
        and W.

2758   DUPRE, CATHERINE. <u>John</u> <u>Galsworthy:</u> <u>A</u> <u>Biography</u>. New York:
        Coward, McCann & Geoghegan, pp. 124, 135, 137, 219.
            W disliked <u>The</u> <u>Country</u> <u>House</u>; Woolf's bracketing him with
        Bennett and Galsworthy is a distortion.

2759   EISENSTEIN, ALEX. "<u>The</u> <u>Time</u> <u>Machine</u> and the End of Man." <u>SFS</u>
        3 (July):161-65.
            W often reworked old stories and essays into new ones,
        sometimes inverting the ideas of the first for a fresh view in the
        new work. The model for the evolution of humanity in "The Man of
        the Year Million" is the same as that in <u>War</u> <u>of</u> <u>the</u> <u>Worlds</u>, while
        that in <u>Time</u> <u>Machine</u> has been depicted as "little more than a
        giant polyp."

2760   FIRCHOW, PETER. "Wells and Lawrence in Huxley's <u>Brave</u> <u>New</u>
        <u>World</u>." <u>Journal</u> <u>of</u> <u>Modern</u> <u>Literature</u> 5 (April):260-78.
            Huxley identified W with the "doctrine that man can live by
        technology alone" and someday be like a god. W was offended by
        what he considered the personal attack upon him in <u>Brave</u> <u>New</u>
        <u>World</u>. Huxley questioned the bad conclusions, not the good inten-
        tions, behind W's version of the future. W was unrealistic with a
        false estimate of human nature, and this made his prophecies
        misleading. <u>Brave</u> <u>New</u> <u>World</u> may have begun as a parody of <u>Men</u>
        <u>Like</u> <u>Gods</u>, but the results were quite different.

1976

2761   "The Mars Attack." NYT 24 Oct., p. 41.
        Howard E. Koch plans a full-length theatrical adaptation of
his radio script of W's War of the Worlds.

2762   GARFIELD, EUGENE. "The World Brain as Seen by an Information
        Entrepreneur." Current Contents, no. 48 (29 Nov.), pp. 5-12.
        Reprinted in Essays of an Information Scientist, vol. 2
        (Philadelphia: ISI Press, 1977), pp. 638-45.
        Science Citation Index and the Institute for Scientific
Information had their origin in the type of "world brain" suggested by W in 1937.

2763   GILBERT, JAMES B. "Wars of the Worlds." Journal of Popular
        Culture 10 (Fall):326-36.
        Both the 1938 radio play and the 1953 film version of War
of the Worlds preserved the "decisive narrative mechanics" of the
original story while disguising and modifying scenes and characters. Orson Welles and Howard Koch eliminated the pessimism and
didacticism of W and transformed the soldier into a "proto-
Fascist." The adaptation for radio emphasized drama and propaganda, whereas the film, using the shell of the novel, created a
new drama for a new audience, changing it to a "metaphoric vehicle
to explore World War III."

2764   GILLIATT, PENELOPE. "The Inseparables." NY 52 (26 July):46,
        48.
        The driving idea in Food of the Gods is similar to the
"drink me" warning in Alice in Wonderland. The film version is a
horror film full of commonplace modern discussion.

2765   HAMMOND, J[OHN] R. "The Scenic Background of Tono-Bungay."
        Wellsian, n.s., no. 1, pp. 3-5.
        The house where W stayed when his mother was housekeeper
stimulated his imagination and appears in several of his stories,
but nowhere so vividly as in Tono-Bungay.

2766   HIGHET, GILBERT. "The Illusion of Progress." In The Immortal
        Profession: The Joys of Teaching and Learning. New York:
        Weybright & Talley, pp. 21-29.
        Food of the Gods is a modern myth based on the idea that
little people are mean and big people are noble, and the assumption that power is good. His other works suggest a belief in
progress through scientific development.

2767   HODGENS, RICHARD. "Book Notes." C.S. Lewis Bulletin 7, no.
        3:8-12.
        A comparison of passages suggests that Lewis's writings
contain echoes of W. Lewis intended Jules in That Hideous

strength to be a portrait of W, no matter what his biographers have said.

2768   HUGHES, DAVID Y. "Bergonzi and After in the Criticism of
       Wells's SF." SFS 3 (July):165-74.
          The six most significant contributions to an understanding
       of W in the years 1961-75 have been Bergonzi, The Early H.G.
       Wells; Hillegas, The Future as Nightmare; Parrinder, H.G. Wells;
       Philmus, Into the Unknown; MacKenzie, H.G. Wells: A Biography;
       and Bergonzi, H.G. Wells: A Collection of Critical Essays.
       [Individual titles abstracted under date of first publication.]

2769   HUTCHINSON, TOM. "Fantasias of Possibility." Times (London),
       2 Oct., p. 7.
          To read W after an interval of time is to realize how much
       science fiction owes to him.

2770   KOVALEV, IÛ. V. "Russkiĭ perevodchik Gerberta Uellsa" [H.G.
       Wells's Russian translator]. Sovetskie arkhivy (Moscow) 1:
       73-80.
          Seventeen letters to W from Mikhail Likiardopolou (W's
       Russian translator) are preserved at Urbana, Ill. W's letters to
       him are lost. Likiardopolou was instrumental in placing W's work
       (in his own translation) in Russian and Soviet periodicals. The
       last letters are dated 1925. [In Russian.]

2771   LOCKE, GEORGE. "Wells in Three Volumes? A Sketch of British
       Publishing in the 19th Century." SFS 3 (Nov.):282-86.
          W's science fiction was a product of publishing methods of
       his day, particularly periodicals. The science fiction story
       flourished when magazine publication replaced the traditional
       three decker novel. Basically a fiction of ideas and often only
       one major idea per story, science fiction never suited the three-
       volume novel.

2772   MORTON, PETER R. "Biological Degeneration: A Motif in H.G.
       Wells and Other Late Victorian Utopianists." Southern Review
       9:93-112.
          Victorian biology considered waste to be part of the nat-
       ural order. Time Machine was written to expose the inadequacy of
       such temporal utopias as W.H. Hudson's A Crystal Age. W returned
       to the image of the degenerated man in War of the Worlds and Men
       in the Moon.

2773   MOSKOWITZ, SAM. "Warrior of If." In Strange Horizons: The
       Spectrum of Science Fiction. New York: Charles Scribner's
       Sons, pp. 182-217.
          As a writer, George Griffith was popular and influen-
       tial during his era, but has not survived because he was not

1976

innovative. W admitted reading and admiring Griffith's work when
they were contemporaneous contributors to Pearson's Magazine, and
War of the Worlds may have been inspired by Griffith's serial "The
Syren of the Skies" (1893).

2774   PALCZEWSKI, JULIUSZ K. "Powieści obyczajowe i powieści-
        traktaty H.G. Wellsa" [H.G. Wells's novels of manners and
        treatise-novels]. Przegląd humanistyczny (Warsaw) 20, no.
        7:31-40.
        W's novels of manners continue the conventions of Dickens,
particularly good humor and a tendency to caricature. Tono-Bungay
was W's greatest artistic success. The "discussion" novels range
from Mr. Britling to Dolores, in which W remains "engaged" despite
loss of self-control in construction and composition. [In
Polish.]

2775   PARRINDER, PATRICK. "H.G. Wells and Beatrice Webb: Reflec-
        tions on a Quarrel." Wellsian, n.s., no. 1, pp. 11-17.
        Had W been more of a politician than a prophet, educator,
and artist, he might have made peace with the Webbs. Their quarrel concerned utopianism and social science.

2776   _____. "News from Nowhere, The Time Machine, and the Break-up
        of Classical Realism." SFS 3 (Nov.):265-74.
        There is a fusion of propaganda and dream in News from
Nowhere and Time Machine. Morris inverts the Dickensian view of
degradation and presents a world of mutual trust and fulfillment,
whereas W presents a satire on utopia with a romantic hero in a
menacing future. Reacting to the break-up of mid-Victorian realism in fiction, they both used fantasy to assert the place of
visions and expectations.

2777   PATTERSON, ALICE C. "Cyril Povey: The Emblem of Social
        Change." ELT 19:248-64.
        George Ponderevo symbolizes social rebellion in Edwardian
England, just as does Philip Bosinney for Galsworthy in The Man of
Property and Cyril Povey for Bennett in The Old Wive's Tale.
Unlike the others, Ponderevo is the main character in Tono-Bungay.

2778   PHILMUS, ROBERT M. "Revisions of the Future: The Time
        Machine." Journal of General Education 28:23-30.
        The Heinemann edition of Time Machine brings together ideas
dealt with by W in separate publications: time travel, an apocalyptic theory of evolution, and the human/cosmic viewpoints that
link the rationale for time-travel with the prophetic vision.

2779   POHL, FREDERICK. "The Innovators." Journal of General Educa-
        tion 28:43-49.

W contributed the greatest number of original ideas to science fiction.

2780   PULLAR, PHILIPPA. Frank Harris: A Biography. New York: Simon & Schuster, pp. 148, 165-67, 169-71, 173, 190, 241, 246, 264-65, 296, 316, 318, 346, 380.
Harris is depicted as Alfred Butteridge in The War in the Air. W offended Harris by asking which half, the tawdry or the good, of The Bomb had been written by him, and he never quite got over having Harris imitate his speech mannerisms.

2781   RABKIN, ERIC S. The Fantastic in Literature. Princeton, N.J.: Princeton University Press, pp. 21, 22, 61, 110, 122, 140-41, 144, 147, 153-55. Chapter 4, "The Fantastic and Genre Criticism," reprinted as "Genre Criticism: Science Fiction and the Fantastic," in Science Fiction: A Collection of Critical Essays, ed. Mark Rose (Englewood Cliffs, N.J.: Prentice-Hall, 1976), pp. 89-101.]
Time Machine uses fantasy to give a vivid social warning based on contemporary biology and political science. From the standpoint of both fields, it can be compared to Bellamy's Looking Backward. Because he was a Victorian W showed how new mechanisms could destroy mankind. After 1900 his literary ambivalence toward science disappears, and he recommends the "benevolent despotism of the engineers."

2782   ROSE, MARK. Introduction to Science Fiction: A Collection of Critical Essays. Englewood Cliffs, N.J.: Prentice-Hall, pp. 1-7.
Time Machine depends on magic rather than science, but it is "informed with a scientific vision" in its "meditation" on implications of Darwinian discovery.

2783   RYDEL, CHRISTINE. "Bulgakov and H.G. Wells." Russian Literature Triquarterly 15:293-311.
W was published in Russian translation as early as 1899 and has never been out of print. His greatest popularity was during the 1920s when he influenced a number of writers, including Bulgakov. Moscow in the twenty-third century in Bliss is the twenty-second century of "A Story of the Days to Come" and When the Sleeper Wakes. "The Fatal Eggs" follows Food of the Gods; and The Heart of a Dog completely reverses Dr. Moreau.

2784   SANCTON, ANDREW. "British Socialist Theories of Division of Power by Area." Political Studies 24:158-70.
W's paper to the Fabians in 1903 was the beginning of the development of policies in local government for the Society. He was primarily concerned with the efficiency of the system.

1976

2785   SARGENT, LYMAN TOWER. "Themes in Utopian Fiction in English
        Before Wells." SFS 3 (Nov.):275-82.
            There have been about 1500 works on utopias published
        between 1516 and 1975, and W's impact was significant. The works
        before his can be divided into five periods: the sixteenth cen-
        tury, which emphasized authority and religion; the seventeenth
        century, with more concern with education and the first positive
        statements about democracy; the eighteenth century, with the dis-
        trust of lawyers and the legal and the significant place given to
        reason; the nineteenth century before Bellamy, with its equitable
        economic system, the "communitarian movement," and the rule of
        women; and the period from Bellamy to W, which continues most of
        the earlier themes but is largely reactions to Looking Backward.

2786   SAVATER, FRANCIS. "Los habitantes de los astros." In La
        infancia recuperada. Madrid: Taurus Ediciones, S.A., pp. 93-
        103. Translated as "Dwellers in the Stars," in Childhood
        Regained (New York: Columbia University Press, 1982),
        pp. 91-103.
            The lesson to be drawn from War of the Worlds and Men in
        the Moon is that meetings with interplanetary beings bring about
        conflict either because our passions are uncontrollable or because
        extraterrestrials have no passions.

2787   STRAUSS, SYLVIA. "Women in 'Utopia.'" South Atlantic
        Quarterly 75 (Winter):115-31.
            Like Bellamy and Morris, W wrote from a patriarchal bias
        and a middle-class perspective. His main concern in Utopia is
        eugenics, so that while he sets up a theoretical equality between
        his sexes, his reflections on women reveal his true attitudes. To
        be samurai women must produce children.

2788   "Timing Devices." TLS, 24 Sept., p. 1208.
            A reading of the current issue of the Wellsian suggests that
        studies of W appear to have fallen into "the hands of a cabal of
        Canadian New Critics," especially R.M. Philmus of Loyala Univer-
        sity, Montreal, and Darko Suvin of McGill.

2789   VERNIER, J[EAN]-P[IERRE]. "Remington as Time Traveller:
        Wells's Treatment of Time in The New Machiavelli." Wellsian,
        n.s., no. 1, pp. 6-10.
            The impression that the perspective is wrong in Machiavelli
        comes from W's deliberate confusion of "historical and narrative
        times" to overcome the difficulty of compressing twenty years of
        Remington's life into a "clearly defined historical period" for
        the purposes of critical examination of that period.

2790   WEST, ANTHONY. "My Father's Unpaid Debts of Love." Observer
        (London), 11 Jan., p. 17.

W's tangled relationship with the five women in his life in the 1920s was a source of disturbance to Anthony, but as he grew older his appreciation of W grew as well. In <u>Boon</u>, W attacked the elitist culture as an enemy of civilization and he chose the path of the new social order.

1977

2791   BLOOM, ROBERT. <u>Anatomies of Egotism: A Reading of the Last Novels of H.G. Wells</u>. Lincoln: University of Nebraska Press.
As a novelist, W always wrote about himself, life as he saw it. His rejection of James's views did not mean he took the novel lightly. At first he used the novel as a framework for ideas; later ideas dominated the characters, and what they said was more interesting than what they were. A reading of <u>Bulpington</u>, <u>Brynhild</u>, <u>Dolores</u>, and <u>Babes</u> reveals how he managed to join extensive motifing and intensive characterization to convey a message about "the characteristics and consequences of egotism."

2792   BREEN, JON L. "World of Mysteries--Plus." <u>WLB</u> 52 (Dec.): 306-7.
Two recent paperback editions of <u>Dr. Moreau</u> are deceptively packaged to cash in on the second movie version. Signet's "Special Movie Edition" has nothing to do with the film beyond the cover legend, while Ace's edition is a novelization by Joseph Silva [pseud. of Ron Goulart] of the screenplay based on the original novel.

2793   BRITIKOV, A.F. "Uells i revolutsionnaia Rossiia" [Wells and revolutionary Russia]. <u>Russkaia literatura</u> (Leningrad) 2: 37-53.
When W wrote a preface to the third edition of his collected works in Russian (St. Petersburg, 1909-17), he was already well known in Russia for his fantastic and utopian novels, sociological treatises, and scientific and technical prognoses. Until 1917, he had regarded Marxism as merely a theory of the destruction of the capitalist system, and he considered the Soviet government (after 1917) as morally superior to its opponents. The work of the Marxist critic S. Dinamov left an important mark on Soviet studies of W; in his preface to <u>Clissold</u> Dinamov examined W's literary traditions and the technique of his fantastic fiction, based on content. Lunacharskii was more objective in his criticism and pointed out the strong and weak sides of W's fiction from the point of view of critical realism. The first Soviet monograph on W was that by Kagarlitskii (1963), who showed W expressing the unavoidable movement of mankind toward communism. W's visits to the Soviet Union and correspondence with Maxim Gorky encouraged his belief in the possibilities of a better world,

1977

starting with the Soviet Union. He also admired Turgenev and L. Tolstoi, whose influence can be seen in World Set Free (though the character Karenin has nothing to do with Tolstoi's Karenin). The successes of socialism in the Soviet Union often assisted W to overcome his mistaken prognoses. [In Russian.]

2794   CARTER, PAUL A. The Creation of Tomorrow: Fifty Years of Magazine Science Fiction. New York: Columbia University Press, pp. 7, 8-9, 31-32, 91-96, 233-34; index.
"The Man Who Could Work Miracles" is science fiction only by a stretch of definition. The effectiveness of W's novels derives from their prosaic British setting, Time Machine emerging as one of the great parables of Western civilization. Pulp writers elaborated on many of his themes, including those in Shape of Things, which assumed that World War II would end in a stalemate followed by starvation and disease that would destroy Europe.

2795   CHERNYSHEVA, TATYANA. "The Folktale, Wells, and Modern Science Fiction." In Modern SF, pp. 35-47.
Elements of the folktale rather than of scientific knowledge dominate W's early fiction, a feature still valid in modern science fiction where science and the folktale "interact in still imperfectly known ways" and wonder has not lost its power.

2796   CLARESON, THOMAS D. "Many Futures, Many Worlds." In Many Futures, Many Worlds: Theme and Form in Science Fiction. Kent, Ohio: Kent State University Press, pp. 14-26.
W's warnings about the precarious position of man in the natural order came as early as Time Machine and "Sea Raiders."

2797   CLARKE, I.F. "From Prophecy to Prediction: The Ideologies of Ideality." Futures 9:432-34.
Pessimism about the future reflected in Brave New World was renewed after World War II when W's Short History of the World proclaimed the story of humanity to be at an end.

2798   COOKE, ALISTAIR. "Bertrand Russell." In Six Men. New York: Knopf, p. 165.
A vain man with some original ideas, W was spoiled by his ambition to be thought upper class.

2799   EVERED, ROGER D. "Interest in the Future: A Search for Useable Measures." Futures 9:285-302.
W was the first true futurologist. [Only brief mention.]

2800   FETZER, LELAND. "H.G. Wells' First Russian Admirer." Foundation: Review of Science Fiction 11:39-48.

The first Russian writer to be influenced by W was not Zamyatin, but Alexander Kuprin whose novellas, Liquid Sunshine and Every Wish, are reflections of the scientific romances.

2801 GARFIELD, EUGENE. "Negative Science and 'The Outlook for the Flying Machine.'" Current Contents, no. 26 (27 June), pp. 5-16.
       W's reference to "Professor Simon Newcomb" in Time Machine concerned a paper on a possible fourth spatial dimension he had read in Nature (1 Feb. 1895).

2802 GUNN, JAMES. "The Father of Modern Science Fiction." In The Road to Science Fiction: From Gilgamesh to Wells. New York: New American Library, pp. 380-83.
       W brought to science fiction many new ideas and elaborated on older ones. His technique as well as the number and excitement of those ideas helped broaden the audience for the genre. [Biographical sketch.]

2803 HAMMOND, JOHN R. Herbert George Wells: An Annotated Bibliography of His Works. New York: Garland Publishing.
       [Part One, Fiction: Novels, Romances, Short Stories, Essays; Part Two, Non-Fiction: Books, Pamphlets; Part Three, Collected Editions; Part Four, Posthumously Published Works; Part Five, Letters; Part Six, Books By Other Writers Containing Prefaces By Wells; Part Seven, Books By Other Writers Containing Contributions by Wells; Part Eight, Illustrations; Appendixes: Works Chronologically arranged; Note on Unreprinted Writings; Critical Biographical and Bibliographical Studies; Principal Collections of H.G. Wells Material; The H.G. Wells Society; Index. References to secondary literature relating to specific works.]

2804 HUGHES, DAVID Y. "The Garden in Wells's Early Science Fiction." In Modern SF, pp. 48-69.
       The prevailing metaphor in W's scientific romances is a biological one, the "self-ordering garden of nature." Through this metaphor the limits of the human condition are revealed in the quests and attempted conquests of the narrators.

2805 _____. "McConnell's 'Critical Edition' of Time Machine and War of the Worlds." SFS 4:196-97.
       "McConnell is irresponsible textually and untrustworthy in matters of fact . . . [as well as] erratic in his literary judgments." [Review article of McConnell.]

2806 _____. "The Mood of A Modern Utopia." Extrapolation 19 (Dec.):59-67.

1977

> The subjunctive mode is used in Utopia, thereby inviting
> the reader to participate in and also to question what he
> discovers.

2807 HUMBLE, M.E. "Breakdown of a Consensus: British Writers and
Anglo-German Relations, 1900-1920." Journal of European
Studies 7:41-68.
Mr. Britling is probably the most significant of the "home
front" novels of the first World War in its reflection of the
attitudes of the liberally educated.

2808 HYNES, SAMUEL L., and FRANK D. McCONNELL. "The Time Machine
and The War of the Worlds: Parable and Possibility in H.G.
Wells." In "The Time Machine," "The War of the Worlds."
Edited by Frank D. McConnell. New York: Oxford University
Press, pp. 345-66.
Like parables, W's science fiction contains moral judgments
as well as "dark, anxious feelings about the nature of science and
about the human consequences of the scientific vision of reality."
He is not concerned with science itself but our feelings about
science. The gloomy parable of the social consequences of science
in Time Machine was deflected to one of the possibilities of the
future in War of the Worlds.

2809 INGLE, S[TEPHEN] J. "Politics and Literature: Unconsummated
Relationship." Political Studies 25:549-62.
The themes of social rebellion and the sublimation of the
self to new social values dominate much of W's writing but are
bridged by the science, toward which he had an ambivalent
attitude.

2810 KING, J. NORMAN. "Theology, Science Fiction, and Man's Future
Orientation." In Many Futures, Many Worlds: Theme and Form in
Science Fiction. Edited by Thomas D. Clareson. Kent, Ohio:
Kent State University Press, pp. 237-59.
Utopia is a typical example of the theme (carried on in
Asimov's Foundation) that an elite leadership, using the best
scientific and technical information, can lead to an ideal
society.

2811 KNIGHT, DAMON, ed. "What Is Science Fiction?" In Turning
Points: Essays on the Art of Science Fiction. New York:
Harper & Row, pp. 62-69.
Stableford's argument (Fantastic, March 1974) that Verne
and W are not part of science fiction as a social phenomenon
requires interpretation. There is a crude, basic type of science
fiction that appeals to the desire for the pseudoscientific mar-
vel, but does not appeal to any other part of the intellect.

Since no audience for this type of work existed in W's day, Time Machine was not science fiction when he wrote it.

2812 KOMATSU, SAKYO. "H.G. Wells and Japanese Science Fiction." In Modern SF, pp. 179-90.
      A low opinion of science fiction, the absence of a scientific world view, military nationalism, and narrow-minded ideological disputes prevented the serious consideration of W in Japan until the 1960s. Modern technology led to an appreciation of Verne, but it took the recognition of man as a species with a place in universal space and time for W's ideas to be appreciated.

2813 LEE, HERMIONE. The Novels of Virginia Woolf. New York: Holmes & Meier, pp. 15, 18, 23, 84, 86.
      Woolf rejected Bennett, Galsworthy, and W in favor of the "Georgians"--Forster, Lawrence, Joyce, Strachey, Eliot, Dorothy Richardson. She wanted to be a more realistic novelist than W, but she preferred her own kind of reality.

2814 LODGE, DAVID. The Modes of Modern Writing. Ithaca, N.Y.: Cornell University Press, pp. 41-44, 46, 51, 55, 125.
      James passed the same judgment on Arnold Bennett as he did on W. Impressed by the subject matter in the novels of both writers, he still disliked their waste of space. Virginia Woolf in 1919 had similar reservations but expressed them more directly.

2815 McCONNELL, FRANK D., ed. Introduction to "The Time Machine," "The War of the Worlds": A Critical Edition. New York: Oxford University Press, pp. 3-10.
      The view of science fiction as a bridge between popular and high culture is demonstrated in W's early novels. His imagination had its foundation in the literature of his day.

2816 MacKENZIE, NORMAN, and JEANNE MacKENZIE. The Fabians. New York: Simon & Schuster, pp. 283, 290, 322-72, 409-10.
      W first came to the notice of the Fabians when Beatrice Webb read Anticipations and saw that his "vision of a future society run on collectivist lines by a managerial elite was very close to Fabian thinking." His life had reflected his gloomy view of the extinction of the human race, but success had led him to try to apply science to social problems. He wished to impress the Webbs as a social scientist, but the bohemian life of the Blands attracted him as well. The Fabians did not want to lose a writer who could present their ideas so pleasantly in fiction as he did in Utopia in 1905. W's debate with Shaw over the future of the Society was welcomed by those members who felt that Shaw and the Webbs had been using the organization for political gain, a debate soon deteriorating into a takeover bid by W who had no idea what he would do if he won control of the Fabians. Eventually he

1977

decided his role as prophet was more interesting than his role as a member of Fabian committees. Undertaking a serious attempt to change, the Society experienced the threat of losing its distinctive character. Even the reformers could not agree on a coherent plan. The entire episode served as the basis for Machiavelli, as his affair with Amber Reeves had done for Ann Veronica.

2817   MULLEN, RICHARD D. "'I Told You So': Wells's Last Decade, 1936-1945." In Modern SF, pp. 116-25.
The topics of conversation of the 1970s (ecology, conservation, war, the sexual revolution, etc.) were the subject of W's work before they were fashionable. The theme of the later works is frustration. W's optimism and pessimism are based on the concept of man as two species: one capable of adapting to his new environment and one incapable of adapting.

2818   NETTELS, ELSA. James and Conrad. Athens: University of Georgia Press, pp. 5-8, 13, 16-17, 191, 251.
James's and Conrad's enthusiasm for W faded when they realized he was indifferent to the art of the novel.

2819   OWER, JOHN. "Theme and Technique in H.G. Wells's 'The Star.'" Extrapolation 18 (May):167-75.
The events in "The Star" are determined by the characters, with the result that irony and pathos are generated by an emotional and intellectual tension. Through this narrative technique W treats man and universe ambivalently.

2820   PHILMUS, ROBERT M. "H.G. Wells as Literary Critic for the Saturday Review." SFS 4 (July):166-93.
The reviews that W wrote for the Saturday Review are a clear record of his views on literature as well as of the reading that may have influenced him as a writer. [Abstracts of ninety-two literary reviews arranged chronologically.]

2821   PURDY, STROTHER. The Hole in the Fabric: Science, Contemporary Literature, and Henry James. Pittsburgh: University of Pittsburgh Press, pp. 37, 57, 60, 80, 83, 85-86, 93, 129, 162.
W's prediction of World War II in Shape of Things is not far-fetched considering Hitler's activities at the time. Lewis parodied W in order to "undo what he saw as his baneful influence." The psychological and motivational aspects of Time Machine are stunted since it only "gives flesh to scientific speculation."

2822   SCHOLES, ROBERT, and ERIC S. RABKIN. Science Fiction: History, Science, Vision. London and New York: Oxford University Press, pp. 14-26, 155-56, 167-68, 200-204; index.
W's success in Time Machine derives from his reliance on a machine (rather than dream) for time travel and his introduction

of Darwinian thought to fiction. His ability to combine the fantastic and the plausible, while dramatizing truths about the human condition comprises his greatest contribution to science fiction. In Time Machine he gave the genre the potential for both "social and metaphysical speculation."

2823   STORM, MELVIN G. "Thematic Parallelism in Tono-Bungay: 'Night and the Open Sea' as Structural Device." Extrapolation 18 (May):181-85.
       The concluding chapter of Tono-Bungay is a unifying factor rather than a negation of the values toward which the plot was moving. The trip down the Thames provides a panorama of the social history of England as well as a panorama of the novel itself. The connection between George Ponderevo's own experience and his society is reinforced by the reminders of his past. This view also gives insight into the quap episode, which marks the collapse of the Ponderevo empire.

2824   SUVIN, DARKO. Introduction to Modern SF, pp. 9-32.
       W's most lasting contribution to science fiction is his earliest work, in which the protagonist is the scientific-adventurer who disregards common sense and received opinion in his search for the New. Time Machine and Men in the Moon become paradigms of science fiction that display W's outlook and limitations.

2825   VERNIER, J[EAN] P[IERRE]. "Evolution as a Literary Theme in H.G. Wells's Science Fiction." In Modern SF, pp. 70-89.
       A simple pattern characterizes W's scientific romances: the protagonist who represents the species faces a situation as a result of an evolutionary change. Evolution was for W an imaginative device for the creation of "plausible visions of the future." This visionary approach keeps his work alive and modern, and it forms the "ideological basis" for twentieth-century science fiction.

2826   WELLS, FRANK. H.G. Wells: A Pictorial Biography. Introduction by Frank Swinnerton. London: Jupiter Books.
       Swinnerton had little personal contact with W until he reviewed Swinnerton's study of Gissing. From 1912, he was a frequent invited guest at W's home. W was a generous man who "helped to mould his age," but he never forgot his origins. [Nearly eighty pages of photos; brief captions; chronological list of W's writings.]

2827   WHEATLEY, DENNIS. The Time Has Come . . . The Memoirs of Dennis Wheatley: The Young Man Said, 1897-1914. London: Hutchinson, pp. 81, 193.

1977

W's science fiction was not exciting, although the glimpses of the future were unrivalled.

2828 WYKES, ALAN. H.G. Wells in The Cinema. London: Jupiter Books.
Films made from W's stories have not been numerous (only thirty to date), but they have an appeal to the "Everyman" in their viewers. ("The common touch is everywhere evident in Wells.") They span the history of the cinema itself and range from a lost version of Invisible Man ("The Invisible Thief") in 1909 to a 1977 version of Food of the Gods. Moreau has been filmed twice, Kipps three times. [Brief discussion of each film with over 100 stills; cast and credits.]

1978

2829 ALDRIDGE, ALEXANDRA BERTASH. "Scientising Society: The Dystopian Novel and the Scientific World View." Dissertation, University of Michigan.
[Listed in Dissertation Abstracts International 39 (1978):3560-61A.]

2830 ALEXANDER, P.H. "A Man Who Built a Real Time Machine." In Scrapbook, pp. 44-45.
[Brief account of Robert W. Paul's discussion of the Kinetoscope with W.]

2831 BOWEN, ROGER. "Mr. Blettsworthy of Rampole Island: 'The Story of a Gentleman of Culture and Refinement.'" Wellsian, n.s. 2, pp. 6-21, 5.
The Boston trial of Sacco and Vanzetti is an important background source for Mr. Blettsworthy, in spite of a seemingly "casual reference" in the fourth chapter. Thirty-two years after Dr. Moreau, the novel is "sombre evidence of unchanged human nature, of an unchanged species."

2832 BRUZENAK, KEN. "The Shape of Things to Come." Mediascene, no. 34 (Nov.-Dec.), pp. 18-21.
The remake of the 1936 film, Things to Come, is retitled H.G. Wells's The Shape of Things to Come and newly plotted as a space opera in which "good," in the persons of Jason Cabell and his father, fight "evil," personified by a man named Omus. [Twenty-three stills and production designs for the film illustrate the article.]

2833 CARTHEW, JOHN. "Adapting to Trinidad: Mr. Biswas and Mr. Polly Revisited." Journal of Commonwealth Literature 13:58-64.

378

Naipaul's article "Jasmine" indicates that he read W in a manner which makes it possible for <u>Mr. Polly</u> to have had an influence on <u>A House for Mr. Biswas</u> in spite of the dissimilarity of the two novels.

2834   CLEARY, MICHAEL J., and HORACE W. LANFORD. "Evolution of Technology Assessment." <u>Industrial Marketing Management</u> 7: 26-31.
        Interest in the study of the effects that may occur when technology is introduced or improved may be traced to the work of Verne and W.

2835   COPPER, BASIL. "Ecstasy and Time Travel in Sevenoaks: The Genesis of Modern Science Fiction." In <u>Scrapbook</u>, pp. 36-42.
        Rural Sevenoaks was the home of W and Jane at the time he wrote <u>Time Machine</u>.

2836   COSTELLO, PETER. <u>Jules Verne: Inventor of Science Fiction</u>. New York: Charles Scribner's Sons, pp. 185-89, 206, 214.
        Verne greatly admired W's work, regarding it as different from his own. Verne thought about possible developments; W, the trained scientist, was the more imaginative.

2837   DRAPER, MICHAEL. "News from Somewhere: Competing Viewpoints in <u>The Wheels of Chance</u>." <u>Wellsian</u>, n.s., no. 2, pp. 22-30.
        The idea of travel to a world where everyday events are seen from a different perspective is presented in "topical present-day terms" instead of those of the future, as in <u>Time Machine</u>.

2838   EVANS, ROBERT O. "The Inheritors: Some Inversions." In <u>William Golding: Some Critical Considerations</u>. Edited by Jack I. Biles and Robert O. Evans. Lexington: University of Kentucky Press, pp. 87-102.
        <u>The Inheritors</u> is a deliberate distortion of <u>Outline</u>, which provides "the anthropological skeleton upon which the tale is based."

2839   FAIRLIE, HENRY. "An Idea Whose Time Is Never." <u>NR</u>, 178 (14 Jan.):12-15.
        <u>Little Wars</u> not only suggests that real wars be replaced by miniature war games, but acknowledges the combative instinct in humans. (See reply by R.D. Mullen, "H.G. Wells," <u>NR</u> 178 [28 Jan. 1978]:4.)

2840   GIFFORD, DENIS. "The Man Who Did Work Miracles--in the Movies." In <u>Scrapbook</u>, pp. 119-34.

1978

W's influence on the cinema has been greater than many realize, and some of the films adapted from his work are deservedly considered classics. [Survey of the films from 1902-76.]

2841 GOTTMANN, JEAN. "Urbanisation and Employment: Towards a General Theory." Town Planning Review 49:393-401.
      When W predicted pleasure cities along the Mediterranean by the twenty-second century in Sleeper Wakes, urban growth caused by seasonal tourism had already begun.

2842 GREEN, BENNY. "Poisoned Wells." Spectator 240 (23 Sept.): 45-46.
      Ann Veronica, once the focus of shock and indignation on the part of the critics, is now considered to be a second-division novel, interesting today only because W wrote such better books in Kipps, Tono-Bungay, and Mr. Polly. It might have been a better book had W waited and allowed his imagination to transform the reality of his private affairs into fiction.

2843 HAINING, PETER, ed. The H.G. Wells Scrapbook. London: New English Library, 1978; New York: Clarkson N. Potter, 1979.
      ["Articles, essays, letters, anecdotes, illustrations, photographs and memorabilia about the prophetic genius of the twentieth century." Includes contemporary reviews as well as current material, some of it peripheral.] Contents: "The Fables of H.G. Wells," by Jorge Luis Borges (1946); "Baron Munchausen's Trip to the Moon," by R.E. Raspe; "A Voyage to the Planets," by Sir Humphrey Davy; "War Fantasies" (from Experiment), by H.G.W.; "A Tale of the Twentieth Century," by H.G. Wells (1887); "The Man of the Year Million," by H.G. Wells (1893); "Canals on the Planet Mars," by Richard A. Proctor (1892); "The Truth About Mars," by H.P. Lovecraft (1917); "Intelligence on Mars," by H.G. Wells (1896); "Ecstasy and Time Travel in Sevenoaks: The Genesis of Modern Science Fiction," by Basil Copper; "A Man of Genius," by W.T. Stead (1895); "A Man Who Built a Real Time Machine," by P.H. Alexander; "A Loathsome and Repulsive Book" (1896); "Cheap Horrors," by Chalmers Mitchell (1896); "[Letter:] Scientific Justification for The Island of Dr. Moreau," by H.G. Wells (1896); "The Island of Professor Menu," by James F. Sullivan (1896); "The Prophetic Powers of Mr. Wells," (1897); "The Invisible Man" [review], (1897); "Earth Invaded by Martians," (1898); "A Novel of London Devastated" (1898); "The War of the Wenuses," by Charles Graves and E.V. Lucas [n.d.]; "In the Wake of the Martians" (1899); "The Finding of Laura," by Jules Castier (1899); "A Lunar Romance" (1902); "The Queer Story of Brownlow's Newspaper," by H.G. Wells (1932); "Scientific Romances" (1933); "Mr. Wells' Apocalypse," by Gerald Heard (1933); "Radio Listeners in Panic--War Drama Taken as Fact!" (1938); "The Man Who Did Work Miracles--in the Movies," by Denis Gifford; "Filming War of the Worlds," by

George Pal (1953); "Wells the Science Fiction Fan" (1959); "Science Fiction That Endures," by Hugo Gernsback (1967?); "Mars Probe Furrows Scientists' Brows" (1977).

2844   HARPHAM, GEOFFREY GALT. "Minority Report: Tono-Bungay and the Shape of Wells's Career." Modern Language Quarterly 39 (March):50-62.

An apocalyptic formula characterizes much of W's works, one that emerged gradually. He began by predicting degeneracy and decay in the future and ended by describing imminent holocaust to purge and regenerate humanity. Tono-Bungay symbolically depicts England as a diseased organism cured through the certainties of science.

2845   HILL, ELDON C. George Bernard Shaw. Twayne's English Authors Series, 236. Boston: Twayne, pp. 79, 126, 142.

Straker is a dramatic sketch for W's efficient engineer. Shaw's views on World War II were opposite to those of W.

2846   HUTCHINSON, TOM. "A World Made Clean." Times (London), 8 April, p. 11.

W is able to convince even the most skeptical reader that his story in Comet is possible. The most compelling parts are his descriptions of the dispossessed lower middle-class at the turn of the century and the drudgery of unrequited love.

2847   MacKENZIE, NORMAN, ed. The Letters of Sidney and Beatrice Webb. Vol. 1, Partnership, 1892-1912. London: Cambridge University Press, pp. 143-45, 170, 172, 199, 202-3, 207-8, 210, 215-16, 235-38, 243, 248, 250-51, 254-57, 262-64, 273, 291-92, 294, 302, 308, 315-17, 323-27, 334-35, 338.

W saw the man of science in too narrow terms, overlooking the need for administrators. There was a distance between his ideas and those of the Webbs that the latter recognized. W was convinced the Webbs had gossiped about him over Amber Reeves, and this led to his estrangement from them.

2848   _____, ed. The Letters of Sidney and Beatrice Webb. Vol. 2, Pilgrimage, 1912-1947. London: Cambridge University Press, pp. 48, 80, 140-41, 294-95, 299, 380-81, 404-6, 409-10, 415, 419-20, 422, 429, 437-38, 452-53, 458-59, 463-64.

The Webbs were reconciled to W in 1920, although they did not agree with all of his ideas. Beatrice objected to the title of Open Conspiracy, but not to the content. She was interested in his ideas of the "vocation of leadership" in the samurai. He still seemed obsessed with the notion of a Brain Trust or World Brain and encyclopedia of all knowledge, a notion that Beatrice felt was outworn.

1978

2849   MACKERNESS, E.D. "Nathan Benjulia, a Prototype of Dr. Moreau?"
       Wellsian, n.s., no. 2, pp. 1-5.
         Dr. Nathan Benjulia, the specialist in brain disease and
nervous complaints in Wilkie Collins's Heart and Science, may have
been the model for Dr. Moreau.

2850   MONICK, STANLEY. "G.K. Chesterton and H.G. Wells: Part 1, The
       Hell at the Centre of the Cosmos; Part 2, Myth and Creative
       Balance." Lantern (Pretoria) 27 (July):24-29; 28 (Dec.):77-82.
         Chesterton and W viewed literature as a means to express
ideas primarily through myth. The acceptance of limitation in
dealing with the inner self gave Chesterton a feeling of balance,
while the rejection of the same was responsible for an imbalance
in W.

2851   NIEDERLAND, WILLIAM G. "The Birth of H.G. Wells's Time
       Machine." American Imago 35:106-12.
         An analysis of the themes, influences, and fantasies of
Time Machine shows how W worked the story of his tuberculosis and
struggle with death into the pages of the novel.

2852   PAGETTI, CARLO. "H.G. Wells: The First Men in the Moon." In
       Studi Inglesi: Raccolta di saggi e richerche. Edited by
       Agostino Lombardo. Bari: Adriatica, pp. 189-210. Translated
       as "The First Men in the Moon: H.G. Wells and the Fictional
       Strategy of His 'Scientific Romances,'" SFS 7 (July 1980):
       124-33.
         Men in the Moon represents not a transition between W's
scientific romances and his sociological novels, but a new formal
structure that includes comedy of manners, didactic novel, gothic
horror, and utopian novel with a satire on both society and the
narrator.

2853   PARADIS, JAMES G. T.H. Huxley: Man's Place in Nature.
       Lincoln and London: University of Nebraska Press, p. 134.
         The concept of a primitive self influences a wide range of
writers, including Stevenson, Conan Doyle, and W, in such characters as Mr. Hyde, the Nottingham Murderer, and the Morlocks.

2854   PEROSA, SERGIO. Henry James and the Experimental Novel.
       Charlottesville: University of Virginia Press, pp. 108, 157.
         W was among the collaborators on a play given at Brede
Place. Because James admired W's scientific romances, one cannot
suggest he too was imagining a time machine.

2855   PHILMUS, ROBERT M. "Revisions of His Past: H.G. Wells's
       Anatomy of Frustration." Texas Studies in Literature and
       Language 20 (Summer):249-66.

Contrary to the generally held opinion, W's later books
display an advanced craftsmanship and a revision of ideas expressed in his earliest days. The combination of fictional biography and discussion of ideas in Anatomy provides a link between
the creative artist and the journalist.

2856   ROSE, PHYLLIS. Woman of Letters: A Life of Virginia Woolf.
        New York: Oxford University Press, pp. 46, 97-98, 102, 208,
        232.
        "Modern Fiction" is both a discussion of the contemporary
literary scene and a "self-justifying statement" on Woolf's own
writing, though she realized the attack on W was not the real
attack on realism she intended.

2857   SCHEICK, WILLIAM J. "The Fourth Dimension in Wells's Novels of
        the 1920's." Criticism 20 (Spring):167-90.
        Throughout his career W was irritated by the limitations of
the novel for expressing his artistic and social ideas, and he
sought new ways to present them. The structure and form of fictional "space" are modified through W's literary experiments with
time as the fourth dimension, the dimension open to the imagination. W's novels of the 1920s utilize the concept of human relativity to transform the limits of conventional fiction.

2858   SWINNERTON, FRANK. Arnold Bennett: A Last Word. London:
        Hamish Hamilton, pp. 3, 6, 13-14, 18, 28, 34, 42, 48-49, 51,
        74, 76, 81, 87-88, 93, 113.
        [Passing references principally anecdotal.] Bennett appar-
ently felt at a disadvantage, since W was a good conversationalist
and he was not. W was greatly moved by Swinnerton's tribute to
Bennett in the Evening News.

2859   "Time After Time." Mediascene, no. 34 (Nov.-Dec.), pp. 26-27.
        The Warner Brothers film, Time After Time, which stars
Malcolm McDowell as W and Mary Steenburgen as Amy Robbins, is a
"science-fiction, thriller, comedy romance." [Illus. with nine
stills from film.]

2860   TUCK, DONALD H. "Wells, H.G." In The Encyclopedia of Science
        Fiction and Fantasy Through 1968. Vol. 2. Chicago: Advent,
        1978, pp. 449-52.
        [Brief biography with bibliography of W's works, periodical
appearances, later editions, contents of short story anthologies;
some annotations of plots.]

2861   WHEATLEY, DENNIS. The Time Has Come . . . The Memoirs of
        Dennis Wheatley: Officer and Temporary Gentleman, 1914-1918.
        London: Hutchinson, pp. 100, 145-46.

1978

Tono-Bungay predicted changes in Britain's social structure, but W's characters are unsympathetic.

2862 WILLIAMSON, JACK. Foreword to The H.G. Wells Scrapbook.
Edited by Peter Haining. London: New English Library, 1978;
New York: Clarkson N. Potter, 1979, pp. 6-9.
W is often slighted by those who cannot appreciate how
varied were his achievements. His textbooks may be out of date,
but his science fiction still holds our attention with its gripping action and arresting themes.

1979

2863 ALEXANDER, KARL. Time After Time. New York: Dell.
[W, as a character in this novel, creates a time machine
which is stolen by Dr. John Leslie Stephenson, alias Jack the
Ripper. W pursues him to twentieth-century San Francisco (the
machine is part of an exhibition of Wellsiana there) and meets
Catherine Amy Robbins. She returns with him to the nineteenth
century. Novelization of the Warner Bros. film. Original mss
title: "The Time Travellers."]

2864 ASH, BRIAN. Who's Who in H.G. Wells. London: Elm Tree Books,
Hamish Hamilton.
W is "a bridge between the Victorian scene . . . and the
twentieth-century era of speculative fiction." His characters
fall into three main categories: the little man, the liberated
woman, and scientists and other "dreamers for mankind," as well as
a fourth category apart from these: the allegorical figure. By
using extensions of himself as his characters W reflected his
times more than any other writer in his generation. [Alphabetically arranged sketches of the major figures in W's fiction with
a synopsis of each story given under the name of the lead
character.]

2865 BEAUCHAMP, GORMAN. "The Island of Dr. Moreau as Theological
Grotesque." Papers on Language and Literature 15:408-17.
Moreau can be interpreted as a "theological grotesque" only
when we reverse the usual assumption that the title character is
playing God and view the novel as a microcosm for the "macrocosmic
process of evolutionary creation through suffering."

2866 BRAENDLIN, BONNIE HOOVER. "Bildung and the Role of Woman in
the Edwardian Bildungsroman: Maugham, Bennett, and Wells."
Dissertation, Florida State University, 1978.
[Listed in Dissertation Abstracts International 40
(1979):866-67A.]

2867   DEL REY, LESTER. The World of Science Fiction: 1926-1976.
        The History of a Subculture. New York: Ballantine, pp. 19-20,
        23, 30, 35, 43, 44, 129, 130, 152, 254, 263, 309, 337, 343,
        345, 386.
            W did more than any writer before him to make science
        fiction an acceptable literary type. In the future he depicted,
        man's base desires or lack of control over technology bring dis-
        aster. Utopia is interesting because he avoided a completely
        static culture. [Passing references.]

2868   DENBY, DAVID. "Time Out of Joint." New York 12 (8 Oct.):86.
            Time After Time, Nicholas Meyer's film of time travel with
        W and Jack the Ripper, is a "conventionally manipulative suspense
        film" that is not always "clearly staged."

2869   GUNN, JAMES. "On the Road to Science Fiction: From Heinlein
        to Here." Isaac Asimov's Science Fiction Magazine 3
        (March):100-121. Reprinted as the Introduction to The Road to
        Science Fiction: From Heinlein to Here (New York: New
        American Library, 1979), pp. 1-22.
            Verne objected to having W referred to as "the English
        Jules Verne" since he thought W's work was not "based solidly on
        science." W agreed they were not the same type of writer. It was
        John W. Campbell who tried to combine their two types of story in
        Astounding Science Fiction: plausible stories with a scientific
        setting.

2870   _____. "On the Road to Science Fiction: From Wells to
        Heinlein." Isaac Asimov's Science Fiction Magazine 3
        (Jan.):64-81. Reprinted as the Introduction to The Road to
        Science Fiction #2: From Wells to Heinlein (New York: New
        American Library, pp. 1-16.
            W's focus of concern on the species and not the individual
        was the beginning of modern science fiction.

2871   _____. "Science: The New Accelerator." In The Road to
        Science Fiction #2: From Wells to Heinlein (New York: New
        American Library, pp. 17-20.
            W exhausted all the possibilities of depicting change, from
        the hope of utopia to the threat of extinction. As usual, the
        central idea in "The New Accelerator" is treated casually, but it
        is obvious he was aware of its implications.

2872   HAMMOND, J[OHN] R. An H.G. Wells Companion: A Guide to the
        Novels, Romances and Short Stories. London: Macmillan; New
        York: Barnes & Noble.
            [Divided into six parts: Background and W's Literary Repu-
        tation; An H.G. Wells Dictionary; The Short Stories; The Romances;
        The Novels; and a Key to the Characters and Locations, with an

1979

Appendix listing twenty-one film versions of his novels, References (i.e., footnotes to the previous sections), Select Bibliography, with annotations, and Index. The Wells Dictionary is an alphabetical guide to titles in book form, with synopses and much other data, but not the place and publisher of the books. Of the short stories (discussed in part 3) the overriding factor they have in common is that they are disturbing. Much biographical detail throughout. W emerges as "the enfant terrible of English letters" whose supreme contribution to the novel in the accepted sense is Tono-Bungay.]

2873   HARRISON, HARRY, and MALCOLM EDWARDS. Spacecraft in Fact and Fiction. New York: Exeter Books, pp. 10, 13, 14, 31, 41.
He may have "fudged" his science in Men in the Moon, but W's spaceship was well designed. The barrels within cannon barrels in the film Things to Come looked practical as well.

2874   HENNELLY, MARK M., Jr. "The Time Machine: A Romance of 'The Human Heart.'" Extrapolation 20 (Summer):154-67.
The full meaning of Time Machine as an allegory is intelligible when the book is read as a "romance," in which the scientific is an externalization of the psychological. Hawthorne expressed it in simpler terms as "the truth of the human heart."

2875   HUGHES, DAVID Y. "Criticism in English of H.G. Wells's Science Fiction: A Select Annotated Bibliography." SFS 6:309-19.
[Eighty-five items published through 1977 with a few for 1978; most of the items have appeared since 1960 and the revival of critical interest in W; abstracted individually under original publication in this bibliography.]

2876   HUNTINGTON, JOHN. "The Science Fiction of H.G. Wells." In Science Fiction: A Critical Guide. Edited by Patrick Parrinder. London and New York: Longman, pp. 34-50.
W never avoids conflict or defends a point of view, but sets up contradictions in order to explore alternatives. His early work is "profoundly disturbing" because of the way in which he probes situations and maintains a skeptical openness while developing structures that illuminate as they reflect. The complexity in his science fiction is the mark of its genius.

2877   JONES, WILL. "After Last Night: Time After Time Could Be Sitcom Rerun." Minneapolis Tribune, 2 Oct., p. 58.
W's ideas, advanced for his time, seem old-fashioned in the twentieth century. The dialogue sometimes seems like social commentary, but also often like banter in a television situation comedy. [Review of the film Time After Time.]

2878   KARL, FREDERICK R. Joseph Conrad: The Three Lives. New York:
        Farrar, Straus & Giroux, pp. 108, 322, 371-75, 387, 389; index.
            W's notices of Conrad are reviewing at its best. Conrad
        thought W too selective in his readership for Utopia, that he only
        addressed the converted and could not change minds. Though Conrad
        suggested translating Invisible Man into Polish, it was inevitable
        the propagandist and the aesthete would eventually part
        friendship.

2879   KAY, JOSEPH. "H.G. Wells Revival: The Shape of Things to
        Come." Future Life, no. 10 (May), pp. 26-30.
            The Canadian film, The Shape of Things to Come, is not a
        remake of the 1936 Korda film, but a sequel with W's sociology
        replaced by spaceships and special effects. The original film
        could not be remade without being dated, since W's future vision
        was conditioned by what he knew about his present. [Illustrated
        with stills and production art.]

2880   LAKE, DAVID J. "The White Sphinx and the Whitened Lemur:
        Images of Death in The Time Machine." SFS 6:77-84.
            White as a color and variations on it (such as grey and
        silvery moonlight) are used expertly by W to indicate death and
        decay. This appears not only in Time Machine but throughout many
        other early works.

2881   LAURSEN, BYRON. "Time After Wells." Ampersand, Jan./Feb.,
        pp. 12-13.
            [Interview with the director and principal players in the
        film Time After Time, based on a superficial version of W's char-
        acter and an unpublished (at the time) novel by Karl Alexander,
        The Time Travelers. "Beyond that, research was not really impor-
        tant for the story," . . . which is intended to be an "ironic
        fable" of the lack of real progress in the twentieth century.]

2882   LEONOV, VALERIJ P. "On the Concept of Automated Encyclopedia."
        International Forum on Information and Documentation 4, no.
        1:6-11.
            The concept of an automated encyclopedia may owe something
        to W's World Encyclopedia of 1936 as well as to the later Westrand
        Extelopaedia of Stanislav Lem.

2883   LEWIS, BARBARA. "H.G. Wells Revival: Return of the Time
        Traveler." Future Life, no. 10 (May), pp. 30-31.
            In Nicholas Meyer's film, Time After Time, W appears as a
        time traveler in pursuit of Jack the Ripper.

2884   LUNDEGAARD, BOB. "At the Movies." Minneapolis Tribune, 7
        Oct., p. 9G.

1979

Though implausible, the film Time After Time has the power
to hold an audience. It is essential to the development of the
film and its chief message that utopia is tarnished and that W is
not portrayed as he really was.

2885 MAGILL, FRANK N., ed. Survey of Science Fiction Literature. 5
vols. (Englewood Cliffs, N.J.: Salem Press, pp. 782-86, 807-
12, 1057-61, 1079-83, 1375-79, 1429-34, 1902-7, 1967-72, 2287-
92, 2407-10, 2416-23, 2459-62.
[Plot synopses with critical comment on Men in the Moon,
Food of the Gods, Invisible Man, Dr. Moreau, Men Like Gods,
Utopia, Shape of Things, Short Stories, Time Machine, War in the
Air, War of the Worlds, and Sleeper Wakes; includes bibliographical references to selected criticism.]

2886 MASSEY, RAYMOND. A Hundred Different Lives: An Autobiography.
Boston: Little, Brown, pp. 185, 191-92, 194, 198.
A difficult and uncomfortable film to make, Things to Come
occupied Massey for a year. The wit and emotion of the novel were
replaced by speeches filled with socialistic theory. W had complete auithority in the making of the film, but all he knew of
filmmaking was what he had picked up on a tour of the Disney
studios. Apart from his attention to women's costumes, he left
the film to the professionals. The film survives in cut versions
because of the cinematic technique.

2887 MORSON, GARY SAUL. "The War of the Well(e)s." Journal of
Communication 29 (Summer):10-20.
The illusion of reality created for the fiction of Orson
Welles's 1938 radio adaptation of War of the Worlds is something
of a parody of the illusion of reality that W created for the
original story.

2888 NACHMAN, GERALD. "Time Machine Has a Few Kinks in It." SFC,
28 Sept., p. 70.
The clash of cultures and eras in Time After Time is too
farfetched and shifts from comedy to horror. W is portrayed too
meekly for credibility.

2889 PARKER, DAVID B. "Invasion from Mars." Yankee 43 (Oct.):118-
23, 148.
While W protested the adaptation of War of the Worlds (a
misleading title, since there is no real "war") as a news story
for radio in 1938, there was no other way to tell it. There were
too many characters and too much action for a straight dramatiza-
tion. The reaction to the broadcast was symptomatic of the time
when Americans were wary of the coming European war and insecure
after the Depression.

2890   PEARCE, THOMAS, M., ed. Literary America 1903-1934: The Mary
        Austin Letters. Westport, Conn.: Greenwood Press, pp. xi, 48-
        49, 53, 56, 58, 102-3, 104-8, 114, 135-37, 155, 220, 250-53.
            Mary Austin and W shared many attitudes and points of view
        on religion, education, and marriage, but on the issue of freedom
        from sexual restraint they differed.

2891   RABKIN, ERIC S. "Metalinguistics and Science Fiction."
        Critical Inquiry 6 (Autumn):79-97.
            The narrator's self-reflexive gesture (so common in science
        fiction) to take Time Machine as fiction allows the reader to
        "enter into the reality of the novel."

2892   REED, JOHN R. "The Future According to H.G. Wells." NAR 264
        (Summer):53-56.
            It was W's triumph to attempt an identification of fiction
        with the history of the race, but the story he told did not
        capture his audience's imagination. After Outline he designed his
        work to create "a new cosmogony for modern man."

2893   _____. "The Literary Piracy of H.G. Wells." Journal of Modern
        Literature 7:537-42.
            W's novels were often "contradictory responses" to contem-
        porary works by other writers. Sea Lady is an attempt to arrange
        a different ending to the plot of Ibsen's The Lady from the Sea,
        for example. In the later novels (such as Babes, which takes its
        plot from Rebecca West's The Return of the Soldier) the method is
        a self-indulgent borrowing to give structure to his polemic.

2894   [RUSSELL, A. KINGSLEY], ed. "A Golden Era of Science Fiction
        and Fantasy." In Science Fiction by the Rivals of H.G. Wells.
        Secaucus, N.J.: Castle Books, pp. vii-ix.
            Even as the founding father of science fiction, W had to
        compete with others writers in the mass market periodicals, writ-
        ers who are "barely known today, let alone read." [Omnibus of
        thirty stories and one novel by writers (primarily British) from
        1896 to 1905.]

2895   SCHEICK, WILLIAM J. "Marketable Footle: Bennett and Wells's
        'The Crime.'" Cahiers Victoriens et Edouardiens, no. 9/10
        (Oct.), pp. 165-80.
            W and Bennett exhibited a typical Edwardian interest in the
        theater through their attempted collaboration on a detective play
        that reveals characteristics about their differing literary atti-
        tudes. [Prints the text of "The Crime" from Bennett's manuscript.]

2896   SEARLES, BAIRD, MARTIN LAST, BETH MEACHAN, and MICHAEL
        FRANKLIN. A Reader's Guide to Science Fiction. New York:
        Avon, pp. 191-94, 249-50.

1979

W was as much a synthesizer as an innovator of science
fiction, bringing together many earlier ideas with intelligence,
literary grace, and wit. He was not so much the father of science
fiction as its mentor and guide.

2897   SUVIN, DARKO. Metamorphoses of Science Fiction: On the
       Poetics and History of a Literary Genre. New Haven and London:
       Yale University Press, pp. 5, 9-10, 12, 206-42; index.
          In defining science fiction as "the fiction of cognitive
       estrangement," with the cognitive concept meaning science and the
       concept of estrangement meaning fiction, the genre is set apart
       from naturalistic fiction or the supernatural as expressed in
       fantasy, myths, folktales, or fairy tales. W provides various
       points of comparison or contrast. Dislike of being labelled "the
       English Verne" led W to try to go him one better. Whether science
       fiction's status changed at the time of W and as a result of his
       work is uncertain.

2898   WEINTRAUB, STANLEY. London Yankees: Portraits of American
       Writers and Artists in England, 1894-1914. New York: Harcourt
       Brace Jovanovich, pp. 102, 105, 147, 169-71, 173, 175-76, 241,
       254, 266, 288, 332, 376.
          The ghost play in which W participated at the Brede house
       party was a "last hurrah" for Stephen Crane. W bicycled to Rye
       for the doctor when Crane had a lung hemorrhage. [Quotations and
       passing references.]

2899   WERTHEIM, STANLEY. "H.G. Wells to Cora Crane: Some Letters
       and Corrections." Resources for American Literary Study 9
       (Fall):207-10.
          Four letters from W to Mrs. Stephen Crane (1900) serve to
       correct some of the myths about the relationship between the two
       writers.

2900   WHEATLEY, DENNIS. The Time Has Come . . . The Memoirs of
       Dennis Wheatley: Drink and Ink, 1919-1977. London:
       Hutchinson, p. 118.
          W was chairman when Wheatley joined the PEN Club, but few
       well-known authors seemed to be members.

2901   WOLFE, GARY K. "The Rocket and the Hearth." In Selected
       Proceedings of the 1978 Science Fiction Research Association
       National Conference. Edited by Thomas J. Remington. Cedar
       Falls: University of Northern Iowa, pp. 22-29.
          The spaceship in science fiction can be viewed from two per-
       spectives: the alien view from outside the ship or the domestic
       view from inside. The second image is a kind of habitat, a harbor
       of safety, such as the warm and habitable sphere in Men in the
       Moon.

1980

2902   ANDERSON, LINDA R.   "Self and Society in H.G. Wells's <u>Tono-Bungay</u>."   <u>MFS</u> 26 (Summer):199-212.
Like James, W registered a severe imbalance between the demands of the individual self and the incompatible forms of society.   Unlike James, W did not discover a solution in art as subjective contemplation; rather he located the problem in an art that reflects historical context, which for W determined the pattern of art.

2903   BENGELS, BARBARA.   "Flights Into the Unknown: Structural Similarities in Two Works by H.G. Wells and Henry James."   <u>Extrapolation</u> 21 (Winter):361-66.
There are great similarities in style and format between <u>Time Machine</u> and <u>The Turn of the Screw</u>.   The differences only illustrate the fine line between the emphasis on the character of the human race in the first work and a sense of individual characterization in the second.   W focuses on the sociological, while James is concerned with psychological implications.

2904   BJORNSON, RICHARD.   "Future History: The Rhetoric of Utopian Narrative in H.G. Wells' (shape of) Things to Come."   In <u>Purdue University Fifth Annual Conference on Film</u>.   West Lafayette, Ind.:   Purdue University, pp. 31-36.
To maintain the same verisimilitude established in <u>Shape of Things</u> by contrasting the values of contemporary society with those of utopia, W needed a new rhetoric for the film made with Korda.   He retained the dual function of future history, but by narrowing the focus to a moral parable about John Cabal and his grandson and by dramatizing the action, the abstract ideas of the book become concrete.   Even so, the film version is not completely successful and the utopian world is one of sterile plexiglass.

2905   BUTLER, COLIN.   "<u>Mr. Britling Sees It Through</u>:   A View from the Other Side."   In <u>The First World War in German Narrative Prose: Essays in Honour of George Wallis Field</u>.   Edited by Charles N. Genno and Heinz Wetzel.   Toronto: University of Toronto Press, pp. 118-37.
<u>Mr. Britling</u> was written as a response to the First World War in an attempt to reconcile that episode in history with W's idea of a world state.   The cosmopolitan Heinrich expresses his creator's criticism of the English.

2906   CARMAN, BARRY.   "H.G. Wells and the BBC."   <u>Listener</u> 104 (18 and 25 Dec.):822-24.
It was Hilda Matheson, the BBC's Director of Talks, who was able to persuade W to make his first radio broadcast in 1929. Afterwards he threw himself into broadcasting with his usual

1980

customary enthusiasm for new projects. He was continually at odds
with the official attitude of the BBC, who considered him "too
awkward in his views."

2907 CONRAD, PETER. Imagining America. New York: Oxford University Press, pp. 130-158; index.
America represented the technocratic future for W. Its
society was not seen as an organism, but as a machine.

2908 COSTA, RICHARD HAUER. Edmund Wilson: Our Neighbor from
Talcottville. Syracuse, N.Y.: Syracuse University Press, pp.
11-12, 22-26, 42-43, 61-62, 75-77, 159-160; index.
Wilson read the James-Wells correspondence and seemed to be
on W's side. A reference to Anthony West in any book on W would
mean it could have no British publication while Rebecca West was
still alive. W and Shaw both had a tremendous influence on
Wilson's generation, but it may not have been positive--they were
"too Rousseauvian."

2909 GRIFFITHS, JOHN. Three Tomorrows: American, British and
Soviet Science Fiction. Totowa, N.J.: Barnes & Noble; London:
Macmillan, pp. 40-42; index.
W is remarkable for having anticipated so many science
fiction themes, including the thread of pessimism that runs
through so much of the genre.

2910 HAMMOND, J[OHN] R., ed. H.G. Wells: Interviews and Recollec-
tions. London: Macmillan.
[An anthology of items by contemporaries of W, selected
from books and periodicals, to present the author as a human being
apart from his roles as novelist and father of science fiction.
Includes some previously unpublished sections of reminiscences.
Contributions by Elizabeth Healey, Arthur H. Lawrence, Geoffrey
West, M.M. Meyer, Berta Ruck, Compton Mackenzie, Margaret Cole,
Frank Swinnerton, Fenner Brockway, Bertrand Russell, Lance
Sieveking, Arthur Salter, Julian Huxley, Ernest Benn, Kingsley
Martin, Fredric Warburg, Francis Williams, J.L. Hodson. Includes
excerpt from W's "The Betterave Papers," (Cornhill Magazine, July
1945) and "My Auto-Obituary."]

2911 HAMPSON, R. "H.G. Wells and the Staffordshire Potteries."
Wellsian, n.s., no. 3, pp. 1-5.
The Potteries made a deep impression on W in his early
life, the result of which may be seen in the background of Comet
and other stories.

2912 HAYNES, ROSLYNN D. H.G. Wells: Discoverer of the Future. New
York and London: New York University Press.

W's scientific training influenced his thinking and writing, not just in the scientific romances, but also in the sociological novels, the utopian works, and virtually everything else he wrote. His approach to the traditional themes of fiction and his viewpoint on traditional values as well as his choice of subjects and issues on which to write were likewise affected. The most far-reaching effect of his work was a new awareness of the future. For his nineteenth-century reading public he not only anticipated the twentieth-century climate of thought and feeling but "fostered" it. He realized that anyone attempting to participate completely in modern society needed to rely on scientific principles. His "synthetic way of thinking" gave a unity and philosophical dimension to his work and made it possible to see each entity in relation to every other. His experiments with form and style had their origin in the scientific truth that hypotheses may be discarded by the presence of a single contrary fact. This "transitoriness" of science accounts for his reply to James's criticism of his style.

2913   HENNELLY, MARK M., Jr. "Reader Vivisection in The Island of Dr. Moreau." Essays in Arts and Sciences 9:217-33.
        Contemporary reader reaction to Dr. Moreau may have reflected the controversy over vivisection "raging [in the tabloids] since the eighteen-seventies" and the public concern over the 1888 accounts of Jack the Ripper. Readers then and now find confusion over Prendick's attitude toward vivisection that reflects the ambivalence of the author.

2914   HUNTER, JEFFERSON. "Orwell, Wells, and Coming Up for Air." Modern Philology 78:38-47.
        Orwell's treatment of the past through the use of W's Polly in his novel becomes a device for indicating his own break with traditional fiction.

2915   LAKE, DAVID J. "The Drafts of The Time Machine, 1894." Wellsian, n.s., no. 3, pp. 6-13.
        The 1894 manuscript versions of Time Machine in the library of the University of Illinois support most of Bergonzi's conclusions about the writing of the novel. [Description of the different drafts.]

2916   MORGAN, CHRIS. The Shape of Futures Past: The Story of Prediction. Exeter, Eng.: Webb & Bower, pp. 17-18, 67-69, 92-93, 107-8, 111-12, 173-74.
        W's predictive fiction included satirical accounts of business and politics set in the future, a utopia coming into being overnight, and intelligent forecasts of the restrictions of aerial warfare. His nonfiction work, Anticipations, was responsible for the science of futurism.

1980

2917   NORTON, DAVID. "Lawrence, Wells and Bennett: Influence and
        Tradition." Aumla: Journal of the Australasian Universities
        Language and Literature Association 54 (Nov.):171-90.
            Machiavelli had a distinct influence on Lawrence's novels,
        Women in Love and The Rainbow, not only because Lawrence read W's
        novel at the right time, but because it belonged to a tradition of
        thought with which Lawrence was familiar and sympathetic. To
        Lawrence, Machiavelli represented England and the idea of what
        would effect a cure for the nation.

2918   PARRINDER, PATRICK. "Science Fiction as Truncated Epic." In
        Bridges to Science Fiction. Edited by George E. Slusser,
        George R. Guffey, and Mark Rose. Carbondale: Southern
        Illinois University Press; London: Feffer, pp. 91-106.
            Events in a science fiction novel can be epic in their
        magnitude, dealing as they do with the future of entire societies,
        but presented in a brief, allegorical, frustrated, or truncated
        manner for the greatest effect. A major example is Time Machine,
        where thirty million years are described in only 30,000 words.

2919   _____, and ROBERT M. PHILMUS, eds. H.G. Wells's Literary
        Criticism. Brighton, Eng.: Harvester Press; Totowa, N.J.:
        Barnes & Noble.
            W's work as a reviewer for journals like Saturday Review
        affected his conception of his own role in literature. He was
        particularly successful at recognizing talent and reviewed the
        early works of Buchan, Conrad, and Stephen Crane. His stance
        toward literature was never as simple as the controversy with
        Henry James suggests. [Collection divided into five sections:
        Drama Criticism for Pall Mall Gazette; Literary criticism for the
        Saturday Review; Gissing, Crane, and Joyce; W and James; Science
        Fiction, Utopian Fiction, and Fantasy; includes general introduc-
        tion and prefaces to each section.]

2920   PARSONS, DAVID. "H.G. Wells and the Psychology of Utopianism."
        Stand 22:40-47.
            W's combination of optimism and pessimism developed natur-
        ally into an interest in utopianism. His model for the ideal
        citizen in Utopia was the human psyche and its possibilities,
        individual and collective.

2921   PRIEST, CHRISTOPHER. "Wells's Novels, Imagination or Thought?"
        Wellsian, n.s., no. 3, pp. 14-24.
            In tribute to W's early work, which contains "a meta-
        phorical life" not found in the later work, Priest's The Space
        Machine assumes that Time Machine and War of the Worlds are jour-
        nalistic accounts of real events. W's role in the history of
        science fiction is a "seminal" one.

2922   ROULSTON, ROBERT. "Notes and Comment: Traces of Tono-Bungay in The Great Gatsby." Journal of Narrative Technique 10 (Winter):68-76.
Nick Carraway's function as critical yet sympathetic observer to Gatsby mirrors that of George Ponderevo to his uncle in W's novel. The techniques Fitzgerald had absorbed from other authors did not replace his earlier lessons from W.

2923   RUDE, DONALD. "Mr. Wells and Conrad's Nigger: A Note and Some Queries." American Notes & Queries 18:73-75.
A request for the complete text and source of a review of Conrad's novel, The Nigger of the Narcissus. A portion of the review, presumably written by W, is preserved in Conrad's own press clippings in the Beinecke Rare Book Room, Yale University Library.

2924   SCHEICK, WILLIAM J. "Schopenhauer, Maori Symbolism, and Wells's Brynhild." SLI 13 (Spring):17-29.
Critics can only assess W's artistic achievement adequately if they recognize the continuities as well as his experiments with convention and novelistic form. The mundane plot of Brynhild tends to conceal his concern with "modes of perception of reality." A careful reading will reveal "modified Schopenhauerian notions (which) provide a philosophical basis for its artistic effects." The concrete illustration of this abstract theme can be seen in his adaptation of Maori archetypes and sacred symbols, especially the water imagery of the "eddy" as it spirals around a fixed center. Like the "eddy," Brynhild turns aside from "the main current of fictional conventions."

2925   SIMMONS, HARVEY G. "H.G. Wells as Futurologist." English Studies in Canada 6:212-31.
Writing about the future creatively was part of W's plan to educate the public to think differently about the social problems of the age.

2926   VERNIER, J[EAN]-P[IERRE]. "H.G. Wells, Writer or Thinker? From Science Fiction to Social Prophecy." Wellsian, n.s., no. 3, pp. 24-35.
It is pointless to regret W's choice of prophet over novelist, since science fiction was a kind of dead end and the concern with social forces seemed endless. Perhaps his prophecies are still readable because they are "so profoundly fiction."

2927   WASSON, RICHARD. "Myth and the Ex-Nomination of Class in The Time Machine." Minnesota Review 15 (Fall):112-22.
By turning class difference into biological difference, W pointed the way toward the displacement, or "ex-nomination," of the rhetoric of class in fiction.

1980

2928   WOLFE, G. JOSEPH. "War of the Worlds and the Editors."
        Journalism Quarterly 57 (Spring):39-44.
            Newspaper editorials following the 1938 broadcast of War of
        the Worlds were critical of public gullibility as well as radio's
        need to recognize the relationship between freedom and
        responsibility.

                                1981

2929   BALLARD, MICHEL. "Dualité et duplicité dans The Wheels of
        Chance." Etudes Anglaises 34 (April/June):153-64.
            In Wheels of Chance the aspirations or frustrations of the
        characters are manifested in examples of duplicity and duality.
        Hoopdriver and Jessie Milton are the prototypes for Mr. Polly and
        Ann Veronica.

2930   HAYNES, R.D. "Wells's Debt to Huxley and the Myth of Dr.
        Moreau." Cahiers Victoriens et Edouardiens, no. 13 (April),
        pp. 31-41.
            The fascination and subtlety of Dr. Moreau lie in the
        combination of Moreau as scientist with the allegory of the proc-
        ess of evolution. The meaning and implication of evolution as
        well as the dual nature of man are clearly stated in the novel,
        which extends the expression of Huxley's arguments in his essay,
        "Evolution and Ethics."

2931   HUNTINGTON, JOHN. "Thinking by Opposition; The 'Two-World'
        Structure in H.G. Wells's Short Fiction." SFS 8 (Nov.):240-54.
            A fundamental structural element in all of W's early fic-
        tion is the coexistence of opposites, which often takes the place
        of plot or moral. The device allows the author to meditate on
        those contradictions and tensions to be found in humanity.

2932   HUTCHINGS, WILLIAM. "Structure and Design in a Soviet
        Dystopia: H.G. Wells, Constructivism, and Yevgeny Zamyatin's
        We." Journal of Modern Literature 9 (1981/82):81-102.
            Zamyatin was familiar enough with W's work, especially
        Comet, from his own translating, to learn from the older writer.
        In We he consolidates and simplifies elements from W's narrative
        structure while eliminating such standard devices as the second
        intermediary narrator.

2933   KAHN, SUSAN. "The Intellectual and Aesthetic Evolution of the
        British Satiric Novel, 1879-1928: A Comparative Study of Works
        by George Meredith, H.G. Wells, and Aldous Huxley." Disserta-
        tion, University of Wisconsin at Madison.
            [Listed in Dissertation Abstracts International 42
        (1981):2142A.]

2934   LAKE, DAVID J.   "The Whiteness of Griffin and H.G. Wells's
       Images of Death, 1897-1914."   SFS 8 (March):12-18.
            The color white (equated with death) and the motif of
       invisibility are retained in W's fiction beyond their use as
       symbols for Griffin's damnation in Invisible Man.

2935   _____.   "Wells's Time Traveller: An Unreliable Narrator?"
       Extrapolation 22 (Summer):117-26.
            Inconsistencies and too many loose ends in Time Machine
       suggest we cannot trust the observations of its narrator to be
       accurate.   The situation of an unreliable narrator merely empha-
       sizes the complex, Swiftian ironies of the story.

2936   LEVINE, SUZANNE JILL.   "Science versus the Library in The
       Island of Dr. Moreau, La Invencion de Morel, and Plan de
       evasion."   Latin American Literary Review 9 (Spring/Summer):
       17-26.
            The echoes of W in the work of Bioy Casares go beyond
       theme, plot, and character to variations of narrative devices such
       as the first-person account of extraordinary events.

2937   MacKERNESS, E.D.   "Zola, Wells, and 'The Coming Beast.'"   SFS 8
       (July):143-48.
            Resemblances between Germinal and Time Machine suggest a
       common concern with some concepts of Social Darwinism: a life of
       interminable struggle in which the strong devour the weak for the
       survival of the species.

2938   McCONNELL, FRANK.   The Science Fiction of H.G. Wells.   New York
       and Oxford: Oxford University Press.
            W may not have been an original thinker, but there was
       nothing wrong with his imagination and even his most didactic,
       least artistic, novels fulfilled and kept alive the tradition of
       fiction as a public forum.   His science fiction was a variation on
       the central themes of a man of the present finding himself in a
       possible future, or the future somehow testing the man of the
       present.   [Critical comment focuses on Time Machine, Moreau,
       Invisible Man, War of the Worlds, First Men in the Moon, Food of
       the Gods, In the Days of the Comet.]

2939   PHILMUS, ROBERT M.   "The Satiric Ambivalence of The Island of
       Dr. Moreau."   SFS 8 (March):2-11.
            The original draft of Moreau reveals W's inspiration to be
       closer to that of Stevenson in Dr. Jekyll and Mr. Hyde than to the
       satire of Swift.   His reading of Frank Challice Constable's The
       Curse of Intellect may have suggested the basic revisions that
       appear in the final version: the Swiftian view of man as civil-
       ized animal and the ambivalent emphasis on natural man or artifi-
       cial man as the object of the satire.

1981

2940   P[HILMUS], R[OBERT] M., ed.   "Women and Primitive Culture."
        SFS 8 (March):35-37.
            [Introduction to a previously unattributed essay of W's,
        which treats women and the ethnology of Mason Otis Tufton; the
        essay has been traced to the Saturday Review 79 (22 June
        1895):815.]

2941   ROSE, MARK. Alien Encounters: Anatomy of Science Fiction.
        Cambridge, Mass.: Harvard University Press, pp. 10-11, 24-33,
        69-77, 99-105.
            W's indirect procedure of implying credibility to his sci-
        entific romances works by invoking the incredible and denying that
        the work is unscientific. Thus, the relationship of the familiar
        to the unfamiliar, the ordinary to the extraordinary, with form
        inseparable from content, becomes the subject of science fiction.
        The presence of the machine in Time Machine indicates that the
        central concern of the story is power, but reveals that man's hope
        to dominate time is a false one.

2942   _____.   "Filling the Void: Verne, Wells, and Lem." SFS 8
        (July):121-42.
            Science fiction has a basic concern with the relationship
        between the human and the nonhuman. A story like W's "The Star"
        depends on a sense of alienation even when it does not present the
        problem of how to portray aliens that War of the Worlds raises.

2943   SCAFELLA, FRANK. "The White Sphinx and The Time Machine." SFS
        8 (Nov.):255-265.
            While this novel cannot be considered an allegorical ver-
        sion of the story of Oedipus' meeting with the Sphinx on the road
        to Thebes, there are enough parallels to suggest an allegory of
        the role of the scientist in the modern world.

2944   SCHEICK, WILLIAM J. "Toward the Ultra-Science-Fiction Novel:
        H.G. Wells's Star Begotten." SFS 8 (March):19-25.
            Though largely ignored by critics, Star Begotten was viewed
        by its author as an advance toward "the ultra-SF novel." Its
        structural open-endedness and realism suggest the capacity of the
        genre to "accommodate countless beginnings as each new clarifying
        ideological framework within such works generates from within
        itself successive enlargements of parallel dimensions of human
        possibility." It was, for W, a new species of fiction.

2945   SPERBER, MURRAY A. "The Author as Culture Hero: H.G. Wells
        and George Orwell." Mosaic 14 (Fall):15-29.
            With similar psychological traits, both W and Orwell were
        able to convert private concerns into public issues, articulate
        communal fears and beliefs, and shape the culture of their times.

W's "apocalyptic personality," part of which was paranoia, combined with his scientific education to communicate with an audience he never fully understood.

2946   SULLIVAN, JOHN.   "The Everlasting Man: G.K. Chesterton's
       Answer to H.G. Wells." Seven: An Anglo-American Literary
       Review 2 (March):57-65.
          A much neglected work, Chesterton's book is a careful and
       well-reasoned argument reacting to W's view of world history and
       the development of man.

2947   WASSON, RICHARD.   "Myths of the Future." In The English Novel
       and the Movies. Edited by Michael Klein and Gillian Parker.
       New York: Frederick Ungar, pp. 187-96.
          There is a continuity between W's Time Machine as a novel
       and George Pal's 1952 film version. The first dealt with
       nineteenth-century concerns over class struggle, while the second
       reflected mid-century anxiety over the atom bomb and the cold war.

1982

2948   ALDISS, BRIAN W.   "H.G. Wells, 1866-1946." In Science Fiction
       Writers: Critical Studies of the Major Authors from the Early
       Nineteenth Century to the Present Day. Edited by Everett
       Franklin Bleiler. New York: Scribner's, pp. 25-30.
          W was very nearly the greatest science fiction writer at
       the time of his death. His best fiction contains stimulating
       ideas that remain enjoyable, while his spirit still lives today.
       His ultimate critical reception may remain in doubt, but not his
       continued popularity.

2949   ASKER, D.B.D.   "H.G. Wells and Regressive Evolution." Dutch
       Quarterly Review of Anglo-American Letters 12:15-29.
          W's imagination was fired by T.H. Huxley's notion of the
       possibility for humans to regress into animal behavior, a theme he
       expressed in four short stories: "The Sea Raiders," "The Empire
       of the Ants," "In the Abyss," and "The Aru Observatory," as well
       as in the novels Time Machine and Dr. Moreau.

2950   BARKER, JOHN.   The Super Historians. New York: Scribner's,
       pp. 300-330.
          The viewpoint on the human epic found in Outline has become
       common to most of us. It is a view of the future that can be
       traced throughout all of W's writings from Time Machine, with its
       Huxleyan conclusion to the question of human destiny, to the later
       romances, with their common "prophetic pessimism." As a whole
       they throw doubt on the dream of progress that W tried to replace
       with his own vision of a Federation of Mankind. His simple survey

1982

of all of mankind became his greatest bestseller and the history book that has had the hardest impact. In its view of progress, Outline was history tied to a biological foundation. That events did not bear W out was the tragedy of his later career.

2951   BATCHELOR, JOHN. The Edwardian Novelists. New York: St. Martin's Press, pp. 119-49; index.
The dominant feature of W's Edwardian books is a drive toward freedom, as individual characters are disentangled from their disadvantageous positions, making "flight and escape" the central feature of the author's "Edwardian temperament."

2952   BLOCK, ED, Jr. "James Sully, Evolutionist Psychology and Late Victorian Gothic Fiction." Victorian Studies 25 (Summer): 443-67.
Evolutionary concepts from the work of James Sully, a late nineteenth-century psychologist, are suggested artistically in gothic fiction. Stevenson's Dr. Jekyll and Mr. Hyde is perhaps the best-known example, with the exception of Dr. Moreau.

2953   CROSSLEY, ROBERT, ed. "The Correspondence of Olaf Stapledon and H.G. Wells, 1931-1942." In Science Fiction Dialogues. Edited by Gary Wolfe. Chicago: Academy Chicago, pp. 27-57.
Thirty-three extant letters, all that remain of the intermittent correspondence between W and Olaf Stapledon between 1931 and 1942, shed light on their relationship as science fiction writers. The correspondence reflects a tension between the certainties of W and the uncertainties of Stapledon.

2954   _____. "Famous Mythical Beasts: Olaf Stapledon and H.G. Wells." Georgia Review 36 (Fall):619-35.
The correspondence of Stapledon and W documents a fascinating literary association. Readings of their fiction support what the letters assert. Stapledon was truly ignorant of all of W's science fiction, and their fiction is fundamentally different in spite of similarities in ideas. W's anxieties seem eccentric, while Stapledon's represent our own.

2955   DALE, ALZINA STONE. The Outline of Sanity: A Biography of G.K. Chesterton. Grand Rapids, Mich.: William B. Eerdmans, pp. 111-12, 116-17, 212-13, 222-23, 248-51, 283-84; index.
Chesterton had a genuine fondness for W, and the two often invented games together, the point of one of which was that it had no point. Chesterton's view of history was at odds with that of W, and one of his major works, The Everlasting Man, began as part of the public debate between W and Belloc over Outline. Chesterton showed the Incarnation as a real event in human history.

2956   DELBANCO, NICHOLAS. Group Portrait: Joseph Conrad, Stephen
        Crane, Ford Madox Ford, Henry James and H.G. Wells. New York:
        Morrow, pp. 32-33, 66-67, 88-89, 137-79; index.
            W was part of a distinct literary community as significant
        as Bloomsbury. With Stephen Crane, he represented a new approach
        to fiction, and his break with James is a break with the past in
        literature and the assertion of his own independence. The strong-
        est link among all five writers was their conviviality.

2957   ELKINS, CHARLES L. "George Orwell, 1903-1950." In Science
        Fiction Writers: Critical Studies of the Major Authors from
        the Early Nineteenth Century to the Present Day. Edited by
        Everett Franklin Bleiler. New York: Scribner's, pp. 233-41.
            One of the primary literary influences on 1984 was W's
        Utopia, although Orwell thought the author painted too optimistic
        a picture of the progress of society through science and
        technology.

2958   HARRISON, JOHN R. "Gissing's Friendship with H.G. Wells."
        Gissing Newsletter 18 (Jan.):9-40.
            Common backgrounds were partly responsible for the friend-
        ship between George Gissing and W, which began when they met at
        dinner in 1896. W's wit and good humor attracted Gissing, and he
        found the Wells home a temporary refuge from overwork and an
        unhappy marriage.

2959   _____. "The Rejected Veranilda Preface: Wells's View of
        Gissing as a Novelist." Gissing Newsletter 18 (Oct.):24-33.
            W's essay, "George Gissing: An Impression" in the Monthly
        Review (August 1904), was intended as a preface to Gissing's
        Veranilda, but was rejected by Gissing's family. W felt his
        friendship with the man made him the only authority on his life
        and work.

2960   HINKLE, JAMES. "Seeing through It in A Farewell to Arms."
        Hemingway Review 2 (Fall):94-95.
            The discussion of belief in God in Hemingway's novel sprang
        from a mistake in translation of the title of a French edition of
        W's Mr. Britling.

2961   HUNTER, JEFFERSON. Edwardian Fiction. Cambridge, Mass.:
        Harvard University Press, pp. 4-6, 41-43, 62-65.
            W's view of the Edwardian age opposed the nostalgic, and
        inaccurate, view of it as a golden era. The best fiction forced
        the Edwardians to examine their ideas, but W failed to devise a
        form that suited his purposes. His own discursiveness and acute
        sense of character are too often in conflict. The differences
        between him and the disciplined novelist are most apparent in his
        correspodence with Henry James. W's novels serve as a reliable

1982

guide to the major intellectual, political, and scientific developments of the age, and his ability to see things as though no one
had seen them before was a quality praised by many of his
contemporaries.

2962   HUNTINGTON, JOHN. The Logic of Fantasy: Science Fiction and
        H.G. Wells. New York: Columbia University Press.
        Neither the claims of prophecy nor a sense of wonder are
sufficient to an understanding of W's achievement in science
fiction. Despite such claims, the prophetic value of the genre is
minimal, and the actual does not live up to its advance billing.
The whole body of W's early romances and stories focuses on crucial issues of the future of civilization, yet uncommitted to any
specific solution. W's career became a movement from the "undi-
rected thought" of the romances to the "directed thought" of his
later work. His logical system was devised from the evolution-
ethics debate of Darwin and Thomas Huxley.

2963   _____. "Utopian and Anti-Utopian Logic: H.G. Wells and His
        Successors." SFS 9 (July):122-46.
        W's later work is recognizably more prophetic and utopian
than his early writings, but also involve structures that are
anti-utopian (a conscious attempt to dismember a world instead of
putting one together and endorsing it). Such writers as Zamyatin
in We, Orwell in 1984, Bradbury in Fahrenheit 451, and Huxley in
Brave New World carry W's structures even further. In Utopia W
shows that the two-world system of the scientific romances is a
balanced one without the clear choices present in the later work.

2964   KALBOUSS, GEORGE. "Russian Symbolism Breaking Away: Sologub's
        Legend in Creation." Perspectives on Contemporary Literature
        8:115-21.
        Fedor Sologub (1863-1927) attempted to integrate the im-
agery of W's science-fantasy with themes from Russian symbolism
in his trilogy, Legend in Creation (1907-12), as a break with
tradition.

2965   KEMP, PETER. H.G. Wells and the Culminating Ape: Biological
        Themes and Imaginative Obsessions. New York: St. Martins.
        W's training in biology provided a homogeneous theme that
runs through his most diverse publications. His stress on the
importance of the species over the individual and his concentra-
tion on "biological imperatives"--food, sex, habitat--and survival
are apparent from a close reading of his work. Images of eating,
digestion, and reactions to food may be found throughout, although
there may be more examples in his fiction than his nonfiction.
His characters enjoy their food. His fascination with sex comes
from an interest in the renewal of energy rather than the renewal
of life. Women appear as goddesses or children in whom egotism

1982

must be suppressed lest they distract the male from his proper pursuit of masculine intellectual interests. Habitat and environment shaped the species, while survival was manifested in his life and works in terms of fighting, escape, and cooperation. His healthy image of himself in his early life swelled to a size where it "squashed his creativity," if not his imagination.

2966   KETTERER, DAVID. "Notes and Correspondence: Oedipus as Time
        Traveller." SFS 9 (Nov.):340-41.
        Time Machine has analogous ties to the Oedipus myth; the
myth of origin in the older work is a myth of ending in the later,
and both stories end in "moments of appalled recognition." That
the Time Machine is open to psychological interpretations is
suggested by the fact that among the group to witness the demonstration is a psychologist.

2967   KLAUS, H. GUSTAV, ed. "Silhouettes of Revolution: Some Ne-
        glected Novels of the Early 1920s." In The Socialist Novel in
        Britain, Towards the Recovery of a Tradition. New York: St.
        Martins, pp. 89-109.
        W recognized the enemies of progress with a greater clarity
than he did its potential allies. He could see only the deficiencies in the prevailing system. He fleshed out his concepts with
his own brand of meaning. Men Like Gods fails as a vision of the
future, but not as an "exposure of imperialism."

2968   McDORMAN, KATHRYNE S. "Tarnished Brass: The Imperial Heroes
        of John Galsworthy and H.G. Wells." North Dakota Quarterly 50
        (Winter):37-45.
        Britain's imperial mission was a trust that required dedi-
cated, selfless service, not the commercialism of a Ponderevo.

2969   MELLA, JOHN. "On Innovative Writing." Chicago Review 33, no.
        2:13-27.
        The break with James indicated a deep schism in W's nature,
and he turned away from the 10% of his works that have proved most
durable. He was not a realist in the usual late Victorian sense,
but in the sense that he followed the reality of the structure of
experience.

2970   P[HILMUS], R[OBERT] M., ed. "Utopias." SFS 9 (July):117-21.
        A radio talk over the Australian Broadcasting Co., 19
January 1939, shows that W was aware of the coming war.

2971   REED, JOHN R. The Natural History of H.G. Wells. Athens,
        Ohio: Ohio University Press.
        W's world view was more coherent and consistent than that
of most men of letters because it was rooted in his "private fears

1982

and desires," which found their expression in images that reinforced his "intellectual constructions." He was a divided man,
part idealist and part pragmatist; but he was also the product of
a divided time. W's ideas were not unique or original, but they
were presented in a unique and original manner.

2972   ROEMER, KENNETH M. "H.G. Wells and the 'Momentary Voices' of A
       Modern Utopia. Extrapolation 23 (Summer):117-37.
          W's use of several different narrative voices in Utopia was
       intended to represent different aspects of his own personality and
       to overcome the problem of presenting the incredible with credi-
       bility and detachment.

2973   SCHEICK, WILLIAM J. "Yours, H.G.: Some Missing Wells Letters
       to Arnold Bennett." ELT 25:10-20.
          In spite of their differences, W and Bennett maintained
       their relationship over the years as revealed by the correspond-
       ence in the archives of the Academic Center Library of the Univer-
       sity of Texas at Austin. [Texts of sixteen letters with notes and
       comment included.]

1983

2974   ALDRIDGE, ALEXANDRIA. "Origins of Dystopia: When the Sleeper
       Awakes and We." In Clockwork Worlds: Mechanized Environments
       in SF. Edited by Richard D. Erlich and Thomas P. Dunn.
       Westport, Conn.: Greenwood Press, pp. 63-84.
          Sleeper Wakes provides more of the major themes and imagery
       of the great dystopias than any of W's other writings. Zamyatin's
       We owes much to it, but as an advanced view of society where the
       emphasis is on the internal consciousness of self.

2975   CROSSLEY, ROBERT. "Parables for the Modern Researcher."
       Malahat Review 64 (Feb.):173-188.
          Of W's five best science fiction novels, Time Machine, War
       of the Worlds, and Men in the Moon are futuristic travelogues,
       while Dr. Moreau and Invisible Man are parables of the philosoph-
       ical debate over the ethics of research.

2976   DAVIS, KEN. "The Shape of Things to Come: H.G. Wells and the
       Rhetoric of Proteus." In No Place Else: Explorations in
       Utopian and Dystopian Fiction. Edited by Eric S. Rabkin,
       Martin Greenberg, and Joseph D. Olander. Carbondale: Southern
       Illinois University Press, pp. 110-24.
          W's vision of utopia is not limited to a single work, but
       exists in his entire output. The fullest realization may be found
       in Shape of Things, but the failure of his vision is found in the
       subsequent film of the book.

2977 FERRELL, WILLIAM R., III. "Man and Machines: Two Visions of the Future." In Sixth International Conference on Computers and the Humanities. Edited by Sarah K. Burton and Douglas Short. Rockville, Md.: Computer Science Press, p. 164.
       W felt that man would not rise to the challenge of technology, but succumb to it.

2978 HOLLOW, JOHN. Against the Night, the Stars: The Science Fiction of Arthur C. Clarke. New York: Harcourt Brace Jovanovich, pp. 1-29.
       Clarke is an inheritor of the tradition of science fiction defined by W. He works within the future as anticipated by W in Time Machine, War of the Worlds, and "The Star," and his themes are often typically Wellsian.

2979 HUME, KATHRYN. "The Hidden Dynamics of The War of the Worlds." Philological Quarterly 62 (Summer):279-92.
       Scientific, social, and psychological values generate a war within the narrator's mind in War of the Worlds that corresponds to the visible battles with the Martians. There is a compelling sense of malaise in the novel that is derived from W's ambivalence about the issues he raises and that gives the work a continuing potency.

2980 McLEISH, KENNETH. "The Rippingest Yarn of All." In J.R.R. Tolkien: This Far Land. Edited by Robert Gildings. London: Vision; Totowa, N.J.: Barnes & Noble, pp. 125-36.
       The Martian battles of War of the Worlds, the satanic creatures of Dr. Moreau, and the terrors of Shape of Things are possible sources for Tolkien's Lord of the Rings.

2981 MARIZ, GEORGE. "The Fabians and the 'Episode of Mr. Wells.'" Research Studies (Pullman, Wash.), 51 (June):83-97.
       W's attempts to reform the Fabian Society exposed the shortcomings of that organization and antagonized the membership so that he lost its support. An account of the "incident" of his membership can explain the Society's tolerance of dissent whether one sees W as an interloper or the Fabians as a closed society.

2982 RAINWATER, [MARY] CATHERINE. "Encounters with the 'White Sphinx': Poe's Influence on Some Early Works of H.G. Wells." ELT 26:35-51.
       Poe's influence on W falls in three areas: "symbolic settings and spatial metaphors suggesting psychological terrain, a questioning of conventional ideas of objective reality and individual identity, and the role of language in creating, sustaining, or destroying both. The "white sphinx" in Time Machine suggests the "white god" at the end of The Narrative of Arthur Gordon Pym

1983

and "implies much about the complex relationship between the human mind and phenomena."

2983 _____. "Twentieth-Century Writers in the Poe Tradition: Wells, Bowles, and Nabokov." Dissertation, University of Texas at Austin, 1982.
[Listed in <u>Dissertation</u> <u>Abstracts</u> <u>International</u> 43 (Jan. 1983):2342A.]

2984 RAY, MARTIN. "Conrad and Wells: Yet Another Dated Letter." <u>Notes</u> & <u>Queries</u> 30 (Aug.):323-25.
An undated letter to W from Conrad seems to refer to <u>Discovery</u> and can thus be dated for February 1902, correcting the date assigned in <u>Joseph</u> <u>Conrad</u>: <u>Life</u> <u>and</u> <u>Letters</u>, by Georges Jean-Aubry.

2985 SCHEICK, WILLIAM J. "Exorcising the Ghost Story: Wells's <u>The</u> <u>Croquet</u> <u>Player</u> and <u>The</u> <u>Camford</u> <u>Visitation</u>." <u>Cahiers</u> <u>Victoriennes</u> <u>et</u> <u>Edouardiennes</u>, no. 17 (April), pp. 53-62.
W revises the traditional ghost story in two novellas he wrote in the 1930s by replacing its typical sensationalism for its own sake with structural devices pertaining to the realities of modern life. These stories shatter reader insularity by means of W's technique of the splintering frame, which not only correlates life and fiction but also evokes an aesthetic fourth dimension by including the reader within the structural frame of the texts.

2986 _____. "Lost Places in Dreams and Texts: H.G. Wells's <u>The</u> <u>Autocracy</u> <u>of</u> <u>Mr.</u> <u>Parham</u>." <u>Kentucky</u> <u>Review</u> 4 (Winter):56-64.
W's novel begins like a latter-day <u>Satyricon</u>, but is revised in a manner to violate reader expectations based on fictional conventions. W thereby creates a self-awareness in the reader that invades his normal sense of reality and that permits "open-ended possibilities for an evolutionary transformation of human existence."

2987 SHELTON, ROBERT FREDERICK. "Forms of Things Unknown: The Alien and Utopian Visions of Wells, Stapledon, and Clarke." Dissertation, University of California (Berkeley), 1982.
[Listed in <u>Dissertation</u> <u>Abstracts</u> <u>International</u> 44 (July):178A.]

<u>1984</u>

2988 BEGIEBING, ROBERT J. "The Mythic Hero in H.G. Wells's <u>The</u> <u>Time</u> <u>Machine</u>." <u>Essays</u> <u>in</u> <u>Literature</u> (Macomb, Ill.) 11 (Fall): 201-10.

W's hero in Time Machine follows the pattern of the mythic
hero described by Joseph Campbell: an extraordinary individual
who undertakes a quest (a voyage into self as much as a physical
journey), whose survival is due to force and cunning, who carries
life-energy (fire), gains wisdom, and returns with a message.
Much of W's work builds on this hero with earned wisdom.

2989   BUITENHUIS, PETER. "After the Slam of A Doll's House Door:
       Reverberations in the Work of James, Hardy, Ford, and Wells."
       Mosaic 17 (Winter):83-96.
          The literary world discussed the implication of Ibsen's
play, A Doll's House, until early in the twentieth century. W
used his novels to discuss the social questions raised by Ibsen
and to attempt to solve them.

2990   GREEN, BENNY. Introduction to Kipps. Oxford: Oxford Univer-
       sity Press, pp. 1-10.
          Kipps is unquestionably the finest of the "three great
comedies of haberdashery" that W wrote between 1896 and 1910, the
other two being Wheels of Chance and Mr. Polly. Artie Kipp's
liberation is made the most convincing, since W used his own
experiences and drew on them artistically.

2991   HUGHES, DAVID Y. "Recent Wells Studies." SFS 11 (March):
       61-70.
          [Recent works by R.D. Haynes, John Huntington, Peter Kemp,
and John R. Reed are discussed.]

2992   MAYHEW, PAULA HOOPER. "Narrative Theory: Henry James and H.G.
       Wells." Dissertation, Princeton University.
          [Listed in Dissertation Abstracts International 45
(Dec.):1760A.]

2993   PEER, WILLIE van. "Pulp and Purpose: Stylistic Analysis as an
       Aid to a Theory of Texts." Dutch Quarterly Review of Anglo-
       American Letters 14:229-248.
          A stylistic comparison of popular stories (for example, C.
Mortimer's The Tempestuous Flame and literary stories (Time
Machine) highlights contrasts in uniformity and complexity that
relate to the purpose of the story as entertainment or creativity.

2994   SCHEICK, WILLIAM J. The Splintering Frame: The Later Fiction
       of H.G. Wells. Victoria, B.C.: University of Victoria.
          The aesthetic design of W's late fiction conveys the new
reality of the notion of relativity, which evokes hope rather than
despair concerning human potentiality. This concern in his work
is reinforced by techniques related to, yet distinct from, other
modernist experiments with open form; these techniques were to

1984

make this reality thematically pertinent to each reader's perspective. Specifically, W's technique of the splintering frame employs certain fictional conventions in a way designed (1) to frustrate expectations aroused by the conventions, (2) to draw attention to the artificiality of and the ideology behind these conventions, and (3) to point away from the "exhausted" text as a self-contained, finished artifact and toward the self-aware reader, who ideally participates within the expanded boundary of the text and discovers within himself a capacity for a heightened awareness of and control over human fate.

2995　SCHULTZ, BRUNO. "Herbert George Wells: A Modern Utopia (1905)." In Die Utopie in der Angloamerikanischen Literatur: Interpretationen. Düsseldorf: Bagel, pp. 161-75.
　　　Utopia was the first work to present a positive future society in which social problems are addressed and solved. Ironically, it is also an anti-utopian work in its satirical approach. The book is the watershed between the works of W's youth (the scientific romances) and the problem novels of his mature years.

2996　SHELTON, ROBERT. "The Mars-Begotten Men of Olaf Stapledon and H.G. Wells." SFS 11 (March):1-14.
　　　The careers of W and Stapledon can be compared most effectively by discussing W's use of Martians in War of the Worlds and Star Begotten, and Stapledon's manner in Last and First Men. While differing in approach, both use Martians to reveal the nature of the Other, which leads to self-knowledge

2997　WEST, ANTHONY. H.G. Wells: Aspects of a Life. London: Hutchinson; New York: Random House.
　　　W has been misrepresented by such individuals as Dorothy Richardson and Rebecca West. W had his faults, but he was a very human individual who blundered into a career as a novelist. W's most lasting contributions to society were explaining and disseminating ideas that influenced thousands.

2998　WILLIAMSON, JACK. Wonder's Child: My Life in Science Fiction. New York: Bluejay Books, pp. 3, 16, 29, 50, 110, 122-23, 209-10, 248.
　　　Williamson's father still believed in the dream of progress, but at the time Williamson began reading science fiction that dream had been under intellectual assault for years by writers such as W. By 1914, W was no longer as critical of progress, but an evangelist for progress who feared world collapse. The only writer in the genre to equal W's influence was John W. Campbell, editor of Astounding. Williamson shared W's essential problem in his own writing and thought: the conflict between society and the individual, which is "the stuff of most fiction."

2999   WOOLF, VIRGINIA. The Diary of Virginia Woolf. Edited by Anne
        Olivier Bell. Vol. 5, 1936-1941. New York: Harcourt Brace
        Jovanovich, pp. 52-53; index.
            An amused piece on the elderly W, who had pronounced opin-
        ions on T.S. Eliot and who gave the impression of being detached,
        satisfied, and conscious of his own lack of distinction.

                               1985

3000   BATCHELOR, JOHN. H.G. Wells. Cambridge, Mass.: Harvard Uni-
        versity Press.
            W was complex and contradictory both as a writer and per-
        son. While discussion of his work tends to focus on the scien-
        tific romances and his early years, he was a greater artist than
        he has been given credit for. His theory of fiction was both
        coherent and responsible, and it was the foundation of his best
        work. Unconsciously he took the side of his adversaries by not
        defending his literary theories as vigorously as he could have.

3001   COLEMAN, ARTHUR. "The Americanization of H.G. Wells: Sinclair
        Lewis' Our Mr. Wrenn." MFS 31 (Autumn):495-501.
            Structurally and thematically, Our Mr. Wrenn is an echo of
        Kipps and Mr. Polly. Lewis reiterates W's thesis that society has
        a responsibility to deal with its imperfect citizens in practical
        terms.

3002   COSTA, RICHARD HAUER. H.G. Wells. Rev. ed. Twayne's English
        Authors Series, 43. Boston: Twayne.
            [Revision of the original edition of 1967. Overview of
        Wellsian universe which consists of three parts: Mythopoeic
        Wells, Poet-Fantasist Wells, and Ordinary-Sage Wells. Discusses
        the best of the secondary literature since 1967 and surveys the
        critical reception of the author from 1915 to 1985. A comparison
        of readings of Time Machine conveys the sense of what is happening
        in the W criticism.]

3003   _____. "The Rescue of H.G. Wells." ELT, special ser., no. 3,
        pp. 42-58.
            The literary salvaging of W's career in recent years was
        made necessary by the damage his image as a celebrity had done to
        his reputation. The campaign waged by critics such as John
        Batchelor, Roslynn Haynes, Kenneth Newell, Mark Hillegas, and
        Patrick Parrinder has been joined by Anthony West's necessarily
        biased reassessment (H.G. Wells: Aspects of a Life) and by W's
        own retrieved postscript to Experiment, H.G. Wells in Love.
        [Similar, but not identical, to material in the revised edition of
        Costa's H.G. Wells (Boston: Twayne, 1985).]

1985

3004   DICKSON, L.L. "H.G. Wells Upside Down: Fantasy as Allegory in
        William Golding's Inheritors." In The Scope of the Fantastic--
        Theory, Technique, Major Authors. Edited by Robert A. Collins
        and Howard D. Pearce. Westport, Conn.: Greenwood Press,
        pp. 151-57.
            Golding's novel can be read as the reverse of W's belief
        that the Neanderthal subhumans were subdued by the superior race.

3005   KEESEY, DOUGLAS. "So Much Life (So to Speak) So Little Living:
        The Literary Side of the James-Wells Debate." Henry James
        Review 6 (Winter):80-88.
            Many critics have seen the argument between W and Henry
        James as a paradigm of the split between different kinds of art-
        ists and novels in the twentieth century. Neither side has a
        monopoly on the truth, but represents different kinds of truth and
        perspectives with varying means of achieving the desired effect in
        the finished work of art.

3006   LINDSAY, CLARENCE. "H.G. Wells, Viktor Shklovsky, and Paul de
        Man: The Subversion of Romanticism." In The Scope of the
        Fantastic--Theory, Technique, Major Authors. Edited by Robert
        A. Collins and Howard D. Pearce. Westport, Conn.: Greenwood
        Press, pp. 125-33.
            W's science fiction renewed romantic conventions at the
        same time that it subverted the conventions through which romantic
        consciousness had been expressed.

3007   MILLING, JILL LANGSTON. "The Ambiguous Animal: Evolution of
        the Beast-Man in Scientific Creation Myths." Dissertation,
        University of Texas at Dallas.
            [Listed in Dissertation Abstracts International 46
        (Dec. 1985):1617A.]

3008   PARRINDER, PATRICK. "Utopia and Meta-Utopia in H.G. Wells."
        SFS 12 (July):115-28.
            Utopia is a synthetic resumé of the utopian tradition that
        fails for three reasons: nostalgia for the Earthly Paradise, the
        perpetuation of aggression, and its note of apocalyptic prophecy.
        The prophetic strain is not in tune with the premises of the
        classical style.

3009   PRIEST, CHRISTOPHER. Introduction to Christina Alberta's
        Father. London: Hogarth Press, pp. 1-6.
            While dismissive about most of his fiction from the 1920s,
        W defended Christina, which has proved a more substantial work
        than most. It has a narrative structure that does not depend on
        the ideas expressed to make it succeed.

3010   RAY, MARTIN. "Conrad to Wells: An Undated Letter." English
        Language Notes 23:48-61.
             Jean-Aubrey's Joseph Conrad: Life and Times dates a letter
        from Conrad to W as 1904, but a textual analysis suggests it must
        have been written earlier because it discusses Mankind as a new
        work.

3011   SOMMERS, JEFFREY. "Wells's Tono-Bungay: The Novel within the
        Novel." Studies in the Novel 17 (Spring):69-79.
             The experimental aspects of Tono-Bungay show that it was
        intended as an autobiographical novel rather than an autobiog-
        raphy. W is thus on a continuum between Trollope and Joyce.
        George Ponderevo is a fictional character allowing the reader to
        read the novel he is writing and thus to accept his ideas as if he
        were something more than fictional. By not being overt propa-
        ganda, as in an essay, W's message is more effective.

3012   STEFFEN-FLUHR, NANCY. "Paper Tiger: Women and H.G. Wells."
        SFS 12 (Nov.):311-29.
             W's work still generates excitement because of himself, not
        because of his ideas. [A review-essay.]

                                1986

3013   GLENDINNING, VICTORIA. Introduction to Marriage. London:
        Hogarth Press, pp. (1-7).
             The novel is still enjoyable and absorbing, although W
        fails to transcend his male perspective and egotism.

3014   _____. Introduction to The Passionate Friends. London:
        Hogarth Press, pp. i-vi.
             The true subject of the novel is jealousy. The ambiguous
        ideas W expressed about the relation between the sexes make for
        lively reading.

3015   HUNTINGTON, JOHN. "Rethinking Wells." SFS 13 (July):200-206.
             Critics must concentrate on W's detailed ideas and polit-
        ical stances. [A review-essay.]

3016   McCARTHY, PATRICK A. "Heart of Darkness and the Early Novels
        of H.G. Wells: Evolution, Anarchy, Entropy." Journal of
        Modern Literature 13 (March):37-60.
             Conrad's later works reflect none of the simple enthusiasm
        for utopias that exists in W's later writings. Conrad and W are
        kin in their management of entropy, atavism, anarchy, and disease;
        but wheras W satirized energy, empire, science, and progress,
        Conrad treated them with more complex irony.

1986

3017   OREL, HAROLD. The Victorian Short Story: Development and
        Triumph of a Literary Genre. Cambridge: Cambridge University
        Press, pp. 172-83.
            W's short stories were not written to formula, but influ-
        enced hundreds of writers who found them easy to analyze and imi-
        tate. They were profitable for him as a writer since they could
        be republished in books after the initial magazine appearances.

3018   ROSE, JONATHAN. The Edwardian Temperament, 1895-1919. Athens,
        Ohio and London: Ohio University Press, pp. 97-98, 105-6, 110-
        11, 123-27, 131-38, 141-53, 161-62; index.
            W.E. Henley asked W to add a postscript to Time Machine to
        defuse its dismal fatalism. W had preached the same moral as
        Rebecca West (some years before they met) in his novel Ann
        Veronica. Efficiency was a political program for W and the other
        Fabians as well as a means of organizing daily life. (It cer-
        tainly accounts for his own impressive productivity.) The credo
        of the brain worker, efficiency, was ridiculed by the writers who
        considered themselves to be artists. It was W's "technocracy"
        that E.M. Forster satirized in "The Machine Stops" in 1908. W
        substituted a priesthood of engineers for religion in his life,
        and as a scientist he was horrified by the prospect of scientific
        progress coming to an end.

3019   SMITH, DAVID C. H.G. Wells, Desperately Mortal: A Biography.
        New Haven: Yale University Press.
            W's life divides into four periods. The first, spanning
        the 1860s and the 1890s, is characterized by W's studies; the
        second, from the 1890s to 1918, is marked by W's effort to become
        an author; the third, including the 1920s and the 1930s, is dis-
        tinguished by W's role as a teacher; the fourth, the 1940s, is
        demarcated by W's role as prophet. There were three times of
        great stress and great productivity: learning to write in the
        1890s while facing medical predictions of a short life for him,
        trying to force a faith to aid humanity in facing World War I, and
        attempting desperately to design a keel of reason for the preser-
        vation of humanity from World War II.
            W's contemporaries considered him to possess one of the
        most brilliant minds of his time and thought he radiated energy
        while waiting for the coming events he had foretold. His legacy
        remains his direct influence on Western thought and action. He
        translated the doctrine of evolution (as well as other scientific
        ideas) first into textbooks and articles, then into his teaching,
        his fiction, and even his concept of writing. Education, he
        believed, was the certain cure of the follies and insanities of
        this world. His fiction reflected hope for the middle and lower
        classes, and his use of didactic fiction opened up the modern
        novel to previously unexplored possibilities. His was a major
        role in the early days of modern feminism. In short, he believed
        that the human species could live up to its potential.

Index

Included here are authors, editors and translators of articles and books on Wells as well as any writers mentioned in the abstracts. Numbers after each name refer to the item(s) in the bibliography where the name occurs.

Index

Blunt, Frank, 214
Blunt, John, 753
Blyton, W.J., 1879
Boggs, W. Arthur, 2213
Bojarski, Edmund A., 2537
Borges, Jorge Luis, 2318, 2684, 2843
Borinski, Ludwig, 2214
Bonner, Mary Graham, 1460
Borrello, Alfred, 2338, 2470, 2498, 2588
Bottorff, William K., 2545
Bourne, Randolph, 694, 855
Bouton, Emily S., 92
Bowen, Elizabeth, 1934
Bowen, Roger, 2658, 2753, 2831
Boynton, H.W., 695-97, 757-59, 856, 903, 1076-77, 1176, 1225-26
Bradbury, Malcolm, 2565
Bradbury, Ray, 2437, 2963
Brady, Charles A., 2180
Braendlin, Bonnie Hoover, 2866
Brailsford, H.N., 1538
Braithwaite, William Stanley, 515-16
Brande, Dorothy, 1577
Brase, George, 2103
Braybrooke, Patrick, 1345, 1410, 1463
Breen, Jon L., 2794
Brennecke, Ernest, Jr., 1133
Brewster, Dorothy, 998, 2272
Breyfogle, W.A., 1674
Brickell, Herschel, 1675
Brighouse, Harold, 1935
Briggs, Michael H., 2265
Britikov, A.F., 2793
Britten, Clarence, 904
Brock, H.I., 517
Brock, L.G., 240
Brogan, Denis, 2499
Brome, Vincent, 2075, 2082, 2105, 2172, 2181, 2194, 2273, 2369
Brook, Donald, 1955
Brook, Jocelyn, 2117
Brooke, Rupert, 2439, 2482
Brooks, Sydney, 93, 279
Brooks, V.E., 1745
Brooks, Van Wyck, 628
Brophy, Liam, 2118
Broun, Heywood, 905, 1079

Brown, Alec, 1709, 1736
Brown, Charles S., 1464
Brown, E.K., 1974
Brown, Hilton, 1848
Brown, Ivor, 1134, 1278-79, 1347, 1710, 1746, 1803, 2339
Brown, William Sorley, 1411
Browne, Ray B., 2543
Bruce, H. Addington, 332
Bruzenak, Ken, 2832
Buckley, Jerome Hamilton, 2370, 2538, 2659, 2717
Buckstead, Richard Chris, 2215
Buitenhuis, Peter, 2754, 2989
Bulgakov, 2783
Bullett, Gerald, 1001, 1280
Bullock, Shan, 1177
Burgess, Anthony, 2429
Burke, John Butler, 1002
Burroughs, Edgar Rice, 2351, 2545, 2733
Burstall, Christopher, 2376
Burt, Struthers, 1348, 1412
Burton, Robert, 1562, 1737
Burton, Sarah, 2977
Busza, Andrzej, 2755
Butcher, Fanny, 1579, 1632, 1747-48
Butler, Colin, 2905
Butler, Samuel, 1952
Byron, Milton, 1413

C., C.S., 761
C., R.H. See Alfred Richard Orage
C., R.M., 1580
C.-S., A.M., 1414
Calder, Nigel, 2371
Calder, Ritchie, 2195, 2364
Calvert, William V., 2292-93
Calverton, V.F., 1281
Camberton, Roland, 2154
Campbell, Alex, 2319
Campbell, John W., 2998
Campbell, Joseph, 2988
Campbell, W.E., 423
Canby, Henry Seidel, 1178, 1227, 1465-66, 1975
Canby, Vincent, 2756
Cannan, Edwin, 333
Canning, John, 2340
Cantril, Hadley, 2028
Capek, Karel, 2437

Index

H., J.H., 246
H., L., 1599
H., L.C., 1722
H., R.E., 1764
H., T. Ll., 1642
H., W.E., 1600
Hackett, Francis, 389, 455, 653,
    716, 788, 867, 921, 1018, 2078
Hafley, James, 2121
Haggard, Rider, 2090, 2239, 2493
Haight, Gordon S., 2186
Haining, Peter, 2843
Haldane, J.B.S., 1144-45, 1765
Hale, Edward E., 654-55, 717
Hall, A.D., 1723
Hamill, Paul, 2670
Hamilton, Mary Agnes, 1300-2, 1601
Hammond, John R., 2235, 2265-66,
    2291-93, 2315, 2419, 2497,
    2765, 2803, 2872, 2910
Hampson, R., 2911
Haner, G.A., 1146
Hansen, Harry, 1505
Hansot, Elisabeth, 2671
Hardt, Maria-Agnelies, 2053
Hardy, Alister, 2672
Hardy, Thomas, 675, 2163, 2644
Harper, Mr., 2132
Harpham, Geoffrey Galt, 2713, 2844
Harris, Frank, 965, 1524, 2000,
    2146, 2177, 2194, 2780
Harris, G.W., 390
Harris, Mason, 2714-15
Harris, Wendell V., 2476, 2601
Harris, Wilson, 1766, 1895
Harrison, Frederic, 789
Harrison, Harry, 2873
Harrison, John R., 2958-59
Harson, Robert R., 2631
Hartley, L.P., 1192, 1303, 1425,
    2535
Hauser, Marianne, 1924
Harvitt, Helen J., 656
Hawkins, A. Desmond, 1767, 1819,
    1942
Hawthone, Hildegarde, 578-79
Hawthorne, Nathaniel, 12, 2621
Hay, Eloise Knapp, 2299
Haynes, Renee, 2105, 2381
Haynes, Roslynn D., 2912, 2930,
    2991
Hazlitt, Henry, 1528, 1645, 1690

Heard, Gerald, 1546, 1602, 2041,
    2843
Hedges, M.H., 790
Heinlein, Robert A., 2382, 2545
Helleberg, Victor E., 1019
Hellems, F.B.R., 580
Hellman, Geoffrey T., 1475
Hellman, Lillian, 2673
Hemingway, Ernest, 2960
Henderson, Archibald, 2141
Henderson, Arthur, 2248
Henderson, Charles Richmond, 285
Heneker, David, 2359
Henken, Leo, 1991
Hennelly, Mark M., Jr., 2874, 2913
Hepburn, James G., 2300
Herbert, Lucille, 2602
Herrick, Robert, 1476-77
Hersey, John, 2076
Hewlett, Maurice, 1091-92
Highet, Gilbert, 2766
Hill, Eldon C., 2845
Hillegas, Mark R., 2159, 2223,
    2249-50, 2301, 2437-38, 2489,
    2545, 2644, 2717, 2768
Hind, C. Lewis, 1020
Hinkle, James, 2960
Hobson, Harold, 1925
Hobson, J.A., 286, 1896
Hocks, Richard A., 2674
Hodgard, Matthew, 2569
Hodgens, Richard, 2767
Hoel, Sigurd, 2345
Hoessler, Carl, 712
Hoffman, Frederick J., 2251
Holcomb, Claire, 2054
Holland, Henry Scott, 791
Hollis, Christopher, 2142
Hollow, John, 2978
Holmebakk, Gordon, 2187
Holmes, John Haynes, 718, 1857
Holms, John, 1426
Holroyd, Michael, 2439, 2477
Holtby, Winifred, 1646
Hooper, Walter, 2669
Hope, Anthony, 1481
Hopkins, R. Thurston, 1094
Hopkinson, Tom, 2106
Hornstein, Gerrig, 1992
Horrabin, Frank, 2292
Horwill, Herbert W., 1195, 1305
Hough, Graham, 2032, 2252

Index

Kemp, Peter, 2965, 2991
Kennedy, J.M., 496
Kennedy, P.C., 1241
Kennon, Harry B., 799
Kenton, Edna, 583
Kepler, Johannes, 2443, 2757
Kerfoot, J.B., 661
Kerwin, Jerome G., 1902
Ketterer, David, 2323, 2966
Kettle, Arnold, 2107
Keun, Odette, 1649
Keynes, Geoffrey, 2482
Keynes, J.M., 1367, 1664
Kiniery, Paul, 1860
King, J. Norman, 2810
Kingsmill, Hugh, 1547-48
Kipling, Rudyard, 7, 84, 230, 293,
    800, 1008, 1420, 2008, 2058,
    2142, 2469, 2476, 2518, 2601,
    2753
Kirchwey, Freda, 1428, 1481
Kirlin, Thomas Michael, 2677
Klaus, H. Gustav, 2967
Klein, Mary Anne, 2678
Knight, Damon, 2382, 2440, 2442,
    2811
Knight, Grant C., 1529
Knox, Ronald, 1307
Koch, Howard, 2548, 2761
Kohler, Dayton, 2042
Komatsu, Sakyo, 2812
Korg, Jacob, 2305
Kovalev Iu. V., 2390-91, 2497,
    2719, 2770
Krook, Dorothea, 2279
Kruegar, John R., 2198
Krutch, Joseph Wood, 1147, 1197,
    1308, 1603, 2066, 2108
Kuprin, Alexander, 2800

L., A.H., 64
L., P., 1903
Lacey, T.A., 801
Lacon. See Edmund E.H. Lacon
    Watson
Lagerkvist, Pär, 2342
Lake, David J., 2880, 2915, 2934,
    2935
Lamberton, John, 539
Land, Myrick Ebben, 2280
Landrum, Larry N., 2545
Lanford, Horace W., 2834

Lang, Fritz, 2472, 2705
Lang, Hans J., 1998
Langner, Lawrence, 2306
Lankestes, E. Ray, 188
Lansford, W. Douglas, 2254
Lappin, Henry A., 1029
Lasker, Bruno, 1030
Laski, Harold J., 873-74, 1507,
    1604
Lasswitz, Kurd, 2223, 2545, 2717
Last, Martin, 2896
Laun, Edward C., 2508
Laursen, Byron, 2881
Lauterbach, Edward S., 2635
Lawrence, Arthur H., 2729
Lawrence, D.H., 1309, 1548, 2189,
    2917
Lawton, P.R., 2265, 2291
Lay, Wilfrid, 802-3
Leavis, F.R., 1549-50, 1651
Leavis, Q.D., 1551
Lebowitz, Naomi, 2348
Lee, Hermione, 2813
Lee, Vernon, 290, 586, 2091
Leeper, Geoffrey W., 2349, 2679
le Gallienne, Richard, 1310
Legouis, Emile, 1368
Lehmann, John, 2720
Le Mire, Eugene D., 2441
Lemonnier, Pierre, 222
Leo, Brother, 1148
Leonard, John, 2721
Leonov, Valerij P., 2882
Lerner, Max, 1965
Levidova, B.M., 2392
Levidova, I.M., 2392
Levine, Hyman, 922
Levine, Suzanne, 2936
Levy, H., 1370, 1652
Lewin, Ronald, 1823
Lewis, Barbara, 2726, 2883
Lewis, C.S., 2301, 2437, 2442,
    2644, 2669, 2709, 2767
Lewis, Sinclair, 1928, 1999, 2259,
    2281, 2311
Lewyckyj, P., 2265
Ley, Willy, 2443
Leyland, V.B., 2497
Libby, F.E., 2091
Lid, R.W., 2324
Lie, Nils, 2345
Light, Martin, 2281

422

Index

Index

West, Geoffrey, 1516, 1625-26, 1668, 1737, 2172
West, Rebecca [pseudonym of Cicely Fairfield]
Weygandt, Cornelius, 1266
Wheatley, Dennis, 2827, 2861, 2900
Whelpley, James Davenport, 689
Whipple, Leon, 1403, 1706, 1738
Whiteford, Robert Naylor, 898
Whitman, Alden, 2618
Whitman, Walt, 647
Whittemore, Read, 2316
Whitten, Wilfred, 402, 745, 979
Wilcockson, W.H., 955
Wilde, Oscar, 2473
Wiley, Paul L., 2294
Williams, Basil, 51, 87, 121
Williams, Harold, 950
Williams, J.E. Hodder, 143, 157, 178
Williams, Raymond, 2580-81
Williamson, Claude C.H., 991
Williamson, Jack, 2421, 2527, 2619, 2650, 2862, 2998
Williamson, John Stewart. See Jack Williamson
Wills, Garry, 2268
Wilson, Colin, 2150, 2295, 2528, 2625, 2651
Wilson, Edmond, 1518, 2908
Wilson, Harold, 2115
Wilson, Harris, 2236, 2529, 2575, 2582
Wilson, John T., 2583
Wilson, P.W., 1627, 1739
Wimsatt, W.K., 2218
Windle, Bertram C.A., 1071
Winsten, Stephen, 2062, 2175
Wodehouse, P.G., 1475
Wolfe, G. Joseph, 2928
Wolfe, Gary K., 2901, 2953
Wollheim, Donald A., 2362, 2584, 2620
Wolseley, R.E., 1669
Wood, Clement, 844, 899
Wood, Herbert G., 845, 1664
Wood, James Playsted, 2530
Wood, Max, 1874

Woodcock, George, 2024, 2151-52, 2422, 2652
Woodlock, Thomas F., 746
Woodring, Carl, 2423
Woodward, E.L., 1963
Woolf, Leonard, 1267, 1277, 1566
Woolf, Virginia, 900, 951, 1170, 1507, 2049, 2086, 2107, 2121, 2272, 2344, 2483, 2500, 2533, 2566, 2587, 2720, 2758, 2813-14, 2999
Woolsey, Dorothy Bacon, 1221
Wordsworth, William, 2538
Worsley, F.W., 846
Worsley, T.C., 1964
Wren-Lewis, John, 2424
Wright, Cuthbert, 1842
Wright, Dorothea M., 1575
Wright, Harold Bell, 1403
Wright, Walter F., 2585
Wyatt, J.A., 1404
Wyckoff, Elizabeth Porter, 691
Wykes, Alan, 2828

X., 364

Y., F., 1171
Y., T.M., 305
Y., X., 1664
Y., Y., 365
Yarr, P., 2315
Yarrow, Victor S., 847
Yeats, William Butler, 2261
Y[eats]-B[rown], F[rancis], 1405, 1456
Yorke, Gabriel, 1072
Young, Arthur C., 2269, 2446
Young, Filson, 366, 1171, 1222
Young, Kenneth, 2153, 2700

Zalica, Henry, 2263, 2509
Zamyatin, Evgenii (Yevgeny), 1126, 2374, 2437, 2569, 2642, 2932, 2963, 2974
Zangwell, Israel, 25, 53
Zgórzelski, A., 2466
Zolotow, Sam, 2425
Zwerdling, Alex, 2701